The Greek Penal Code

Law 4619/2019

The Greek Penal Code

Law 4619/2019

John A. O'Shea & Daniel A. Webber
LEX GRAECA

LEX GRAECA

The Greek Penal Code
Law 4619/2019

1 3 5 7 9 10 8 6 4 2

First edition published 2025

Lex Graeca
London

ISBN: 978-1-8384106-5-0

Note to Readers – Disclaimer

This publication is designed to provide an accurate and authoritative translation of the legislation covered. Appropriate diligence has been shown in preparing the translation and the translated legal provisions are as they stand on the date of publication.

It is sold on the understanding that the publisher is not engaged in providing legal or advisory/consultancy or other such professional services in general and in relation to the matters translated in particular. If legal advice or other expert assistance is required, the services of a competent professional person in the jurisdiction concerned should be sought.

Readers should also be aware more recent developments and amendments to the original Greek legislation may have occurred since the time of publication and primary sources in Greek should always be consulted in cooperation with your legal advisors to ensure that they are basing decisions on the most recent version of the legislation.

No responsibility for loss caused to any individual or organization acting on or refraining from action as a result of the translated material in this publication can be accepted by Lex Graeca or the authors.

Acknowledgments

This work spanned many years and would have been impossible without the generous contributions of many individuals, to whom the authors owe a tremendous debt of gratitude and who, at the very least, must be named and thanked individually: Alexandros Koliopoulos, John Ieropoulos, Dimitrios Koros, and Chara Katsarelia.

We must also thank Lecturer Thomas Samios for his insightful introduction, thoughtful feedback and selfless assistance in answering our numerous queries through his truly encyclopaedic knowledge of the Penal Code and its history, as well as considerately steering us towards a more thorough approach to our work.

We hope this book proves to be a useful, practical resource for readers and another step on the long road towards producing authoritative translations of the main codes of the Greek legal system. Any errors remain our own, and we welcome any comments and feedback regarding our work (info@lexgraeca.com).

Acknowledgments

Table of Contents

List of Articles of the Greek Penal Code

Πρόλογος

Η μετάφραση του ελληνικού Ποινικού Κώδικα στην αγγλική γλώσσα εντάσσεται στο πλαίσιο της προσπάθειας που έχει αναλάβει ο εκδοτικός οίκος Lex Graeca για να φέρει τους μη ελληνόφωνους αναγνώστες σε επαφή με τους τέσσερεις βασικότερους κώδικες της ελληνικής νομοθεσίας: τον Αστικό Κώδικα, τον Ποινικό Κώδικα, τον Κώδικα Πολιτικής Δικονομίας και τον Κώδικα Ποινικής Δικονομίας.

Από αυτούς, οι ποινικοί κώδικες είναι οι δύο νεότεροι. Ο Ποινικός Κώδικας, ο οποίος ετέθη σε εφαρμογή (όπως και ο Κώδικας Ποινικής Δικονομίας) την 1η Ιουλίου 2019, αποτέλεσε προϊόν μακράς και εργώδους νομοπαρασκευαστικής εργασίας. Κεντρικοί στόχοι του, όπως περιγράφονται στην Αιτιολογική Έκθεση στο σχέδιο του κυρωτικού του Ποινικού Κώδικα νόμου (Ν. 4619/2019), ήταν «κατ' αρχήν ο εξορθολογισμός και εκσυγχρονισμός του συστήματος ποινικών κυρώσεων, η "ανακαίνιση" διατάξεων του Ειδικού Μέρους που με την πάροδο του χρόνου έχουν χάσει τη σημασία και τη ρυθμιστική τους εμβέλεια και η αντιμετώπιση ζητημάτων που επηρεάζονται από την αληθώς επαναστατική τεχνολογική πρόοδο και τις κοινωνικές, πολιτικές και οικονομικές αλλαγές σε εθνικό και οικουμενικό επίπεδο».

Η ανά χείρας μετάφραση του Ποινικού Κώδικα συμπίπτει με την συμπλήρωση έξι ετών από την θέση του σε ισχύ. Στο χρονικό αυτό διάστημα το κείμενό του, το οποίο υπέστη αλλεπάλληλες νομοθετικές μεταβολές, δεν ήταν προσπελάσιμο σε μη ελληνόφωνους αναγνώστες: άτομα που δραστηριοποιούνται στον χώρο των νομικών επαγγελμάτων, διερμηνείς, φοιτητές, ερευνητές και ακαδημαϊκούς δασκάλους, επιχειρηματίες, επενδυτές, ακόμη και σε απλώς φιλομαθείς αλλοδαπούς πολίτες που δεν μετέχουν του οικείου γνωστικού αντικειμένου, οι οποίοι δεν κατανοούν την ελληνική γλώσσα.

Η έκδοση είναι προσανατολισμένη στο να καλύψει τις ανάγκες όλων των παραπάνω προσώπων. Παράλληλα, πέραν όσων αναφέρονται ως προς την στοχοθεσία του έργου στον πρόλογο των μεταφραστών, η παρούσα έκδοση βάζει τέλος στην αμηχανία των διδασκόντων στις ελληνικές Νομικές Σχολές που είναι επιφορτισμένοι με την διδασκαλία των μαθημάτων του Ποινικού Δικαίου τα οποία προσφέρονται στο πρόγραμμα Erasmus+. Η αμηχανία αυτή εκδηλώνεται κάθε φορά που, κατά το εναρκτήριο μάθημα, πρέπει να καταστεί σαφές στους αλλοδαπούς φοιτητές ότι οι ίδιοι δεν έχουν καν την δυνατότητα να μελετήσουν (στο σύνολό του) το κείμενο του ισχύοντος ελληνικού Ποινικού Κώδικα στην αγγλική γλώσσα. Εξάλλου, η προσπάθεια των μεταφραστών συμβάλλει καθοριστικά, ώστε το ελληνικό ποινικό δίκαιο να αποσπάσει την προσοχή που του αναλογεί κατά την εκπόνηση δικαιοσυγκριτικών μελετών από αλλοδαπούς ερευνητές, και κάποιες διατάξεις του να αποτελέσουν ρυθμιστικό πρότυπο για νομοθετικά κείμενα της αλλοδαπής.

Εν γένει, η μετάφραση του Ποινικού Κώδικα στα Αγγλικά εξασφαλίζει διαφάνεια αναφορικά με το ισχύον βασικό corpus του ελληνικού Ποινικού Δικαίου. Η διαφάνεια συμβάλλει στην άρση όχι μόνο τυχόν αθεμελίωτης καχυποψίας, αλλά και κάθε καλόπιστης αμφισβήτησης, εκ μέρους αλλοδαπών, ως προς την ύπαρξη σαφούς κανονιστικού πλαισίου που διέπει το πεδίο του Ποινικού Δικαίου στην Ελλάδα· αυτή η τελευταία (η καλόπιστη αμφισβήτηση) δεν μπορεί να αποκλειστεί, δεδομένων των εκθέσεων διεθνών οργανισμών, στο πρόσφατο παρελθόν, για την κατάσταση της νομοθέτησης στην χώρα μας.

Η συγκεκριμένη, όμως, μετάφραση του Ποινικού Κώδικα αποκτά επιπρόσθετη αξία για έναν ακόμη λόγο: Το κείμενο της μετάφρασης είναι διατυπωμένο σε ρέουσα, καθομιλουμένη αγγλική γλώσσα, στην μορφή που χρησιμοποιείται (και, άρα, γίνεται κατανοητή) καθημερινά από την πλειονότητα των ομιλητών· και τούτο χωρίς σε κανένα σημείο να θυσιάζεται η πιστότητα της μετάφρασης. Με τον τρόπο αυτό, το περιεχόμενο των σχετικών διατάξεων μπορεί να γίνεται κατανοητό ακόμη και από μη νομικούς, κάτι που είναι κρίσιμο στον χώρο του Ποινικού Δικαίου.

Introduction

The translation of the Greece's Penal Code into English is part of the effort undertaken by the Lex Graeca publishing house to introduce non-Greek speakers to the four key Codes of the Greek legal system: the Civil Code, the Penal Code, the Code of Civil Procedure, and the Code of Criminal Procedure.

Of these, the Penal Code and the Code of Criminal Procedure are the most recent ones. The Greek Penal Code, which entered into force on 1 July 2019 (just like the Code of Criminal Procedure), was the product of a long and laborious legislative drafting process. Its central objectives, as outlined in the Explanatory Memorandum of the draft law ratifying the Penal Code (Law 4619/2019), were "in principle, rationalising and modernising the system imposing criminal punishments, 'overhauling' certain provisions of the Special Part which, over time, lost their significance and regulatory impact, and addressing issues affected by the truly revolutionary technological progress achieved and the societal, political and economic changes effected at both national and global level".

This translation of the Penal Code coincides with the sixth anniversary of its entry into force. Over this period of time the text, which has undergone successive legislative amendments, remained inaccessible to non-Greek speakers ranging from persons active in the legal professions, interpreters, students, researchers and academics, businesspeople, investors, even curious foreign citizens who are not familiar with the discipline and do not speak Greek.

This publication is intended to meet the needs of all such persons. In addition, apart from the objectives set out in the translators' Foreword, this publication puts an end to the awkwardness facing instructors at Greek Law Schools charged with teaching criminal law courses offered as part of the Erasmus+ programme. This awkwardness manifests itself every time when, during the first lesson of the course, it must be made clear to foreign students that they will be unable to study the text of the current Greek Penal Code (in its entirety) in English. Moreover, the translators' effort makes a decisive contribution to Greek criminal law itself, drawing to it the attention it deserves in comparative law studies prepared by foreign researchers, and allowing certain provisions of the Code to serve as a regulatory model for foreign legislative texts.

Broadly speaking, having a translation of the Penal Code in English ensures transparency in relation to the basic corpus of Greek criminal law currently in force. Such transparency helps allay not only any unfounded suspicions, but also any bona fides doubts among foreigners concerning the existence of a clear regulatory framework governing the domain of criminal law in Greece. We cannot discount these bona fides doubts given the reports issued in recent years by international organisations about the state of law-making in Greece.

Besides, this translation of the Penal Code brings added value for one more reason: the text of the translation is worded in flowing, vernacular English in a form used (and therefore understood) daily by most English-speakers, without sacrificing the fidelity of the translation to any extent. In this way, the content of the relevant provisions can be understood even by laypersons, which is of crucial importance in criminal law.

Όπως χαρακτηριστικά ανέφερε ο αείμνηστος καθηγητής *Νικόλαος Ανδρουλάκης* (Ποινικό Δίκαιο, Γενικό Μέρος, Ι: Θεωρία για το Έγκλημα, Π.Ν. Σάκκουλας 2006, σ. 110). «[τ]ο νόημα του κανόνα πρέπει να προσδιορίζεται με βάση την γλώσσα της καθημερινής ζωής, το κοινό λεκτικό αισθητήριο στο οποίο ακριβώς αποτείνεται το ποινικό δίκαιο, και όχι με βάση όσα νοούνται φέρ' ειπείν στην επιστημονική γλώσσα με τις οικείες λέξεις. Αποδοχή του αντιθέτου θα θύμιζε, όπως ήδη παρατηρούσε ο *Hegel,* την μέθοδο του τυράννου Διονυσίου των Συρακουσών, ο οποίος ανήρτησε τους νόμους που εισήγαγε σε τόσο ψηλό σημείο, ώστε κανείς από τους πολίτες να μην μπορεί να τους διαβάσει».

Η (αγγλική) γλώσσα, στην οποία έχει γίνει η μετάφραση που περιέχεται στον τόμο αυτό, δεν σχετίζεται επ' ουδενί με την ιστορική καταγωγή του ελληνικού Ποινικού Κώδικα. Είναι γνωστό ότι οι καταβολές του συστήματος του ελληνικού Ποινικού Δικαίου ανάγονται (κυρίως) στον βαυαρικό Ποινικό Κώδικα του *Paul Johann Anselm v. Feuerbach* του έτους 1813. Η αγγλική γλώσσα, αντιθέτως, διαισθητικά ωθεί τον αναγνώστη σε μια δικαιοταξία που, παραδοσιακά, δεν συνδέεται με την δημιουργία και την εξέλιξη της ελληνικής ποινικής νομοθεσίας.

Αυτός, όμως, είναι ίσως και ο σημαντικότερος λόγος για τον οποίο, κατά την γνώμη μου, η ανά χείρας μετάφραση δεν θα πρέπει να θεωρηθεί ότι απευθύνεται μόνο σε μη ελληνόφωνους αναγνώστες, αλλά και σε εμάς τους ίδιους τους Έλληνες.

Η μελέτη του τρόπου με τον οποίο ο ποινικός νομοθέτης αντιλαμβάνεται π.χ. τον ανήλικο δράστη αλλά και το ανήλικο θύμα, την γυναίκα, την οικογένεια και την συμβίωση, τον αδύναμο και τον ανυπεράσπιστο, τον συνάνθρωπο που κινδυνεύει, την σχέση ανάμεσα στον έχοντα δημόσια εξουσία και τον διοικούμενο, την ιδιοκτησία και την περιουσία, την προσωπική ελευθερία σε όλες τις εκφάνσεις της, είναι μερικοί μόνο από τους τομείς κοινωνικής ύλης η ρύθμιση των οποίων φανερώνει το επίπεδο ανάπτυξης των κοινωνικών σχέσεων στην σύγχρονη Ελλάδα.

Η "ενεργητική" ανάγνωση του μεταφρασμένου κειμένου του ελληνικού Ποινικού Κώδικα στην αγγλική γλώσσα είναι πρόσφορη σε μεγάλο βαθμό να ωθήσει και εμάς τους ίδιους, τους Έλληνες πολίτες και ερευνητές, στο να κατανοήσουμε καλύτερα τον νομικό πολιτισμό μας και εν τέλει να αποκτήσουμε συνείδηση της εν γένει πολιτισμικής μας ταυτότητας. Η μελέτη της συγκεκριμένης μετάφρασης του Ποινικού Κώδικα αποτελεί πρωτίστως μια συναρπαστική διαδικασία συνειδητοποίησης του εαυτού μας· και η συνειδητοποίηση αυτή διέρχεται μέσα από την κατανόηση του τρόπου με τον οποίο ένας μεταφραστής, η μητρική γλώσσα του οποίου δεν είναι η ελληνική, αντιλαμβάνεται την γλώσσα μας, τις ιδιαιτερότητές μας, τις σταθμίσεις μας και τις επιλογές μας, και μέσω αυτών φωτίζει το ιστορικό στίγμα που αφήνει στην Ευρώπη και στον κόσμο ο ελληνικός νομικός πολιτισμός, καθώς συμπληρώνονται δύο αιώνες από τότε που ο τόπος μας –η άλλοτε μικρή και απομονωμένη νοτιοανατολική γωνιά της Ευρώπης– συγκροτήθηκε σε Κράτος.

Για όλους τους παραπάνω λόγους χαιρετίζω την σημαντική πρωτοβουλία που ανέλαβε ο εκδοτικός οίκος Lex Graeca για μετάφραση του κειμένου του ελληνικού Ποινικού Κώδικα στην αγγλική γλώσσα. Οι εγγενείς δυσκολίες που συνοδεύουν το εγχείρημα αυτό ξεπεράστηκαν χάρη στην εξαιρετική επιμέλεια των μεταφραστών *John O'Shea* και *Daniel Webber,* την προσήλωσή τους στην λεπτομέρεια, κυρίως όμως στην εγνωσμένη εμπειρία τους στο πεδίο της μετάφρασης νομικών κειμένων.

Εύχομαι η έκδοση αυτή να βρει την απήχηση που της αξίζει και να αποτελέσει εφαλτήριο για ανάλογη προσπάθεια στο πεδίο των σημαντικότερων ειδικών ποινικών νόμων, ώστε όσοι δεν κατανοούν την ελληνική γλώσσα να μπορούν να αποκτήσουν μια αντιπροσωπευτική εικόνα της ελληνικής ποινικής νομοθεσίας και αναφορικά με αδικήματα που δεν τυποποιούνται στο κείμενο του Ποινικού Κώδικα.

Θωμάς Σάμιος
Λέκτορας Νομικής Σχολής ΔΠΘ

As the late professor Nikolaos Androulakis aptly pointed out (Criminal Law, General Part, I: Theory of Crime, P.N. Sakkoulas Publications, 2006, p. 110), "[t]he meaning of a rule must be determined on the basis of the language of everyday life, which is the common linguistic sensibility that criminal law precisely addresses, and not on the basis of what is meant in specialised discourse, for example, by the words in question. Accepting the contrary reminds one of Hegel's reference to the method employed by the tyrant Dionysius of Syracuse, who hung the laws he introduced so high that no citizen could read them".

The language into which the translation contained in this book has been written, i.e. English, bears no relation whatsoever to the historical origins of the Greek Penal Code, whose roots, as is well known, lie primarily in the Bavarian Penal Code drafted by Paul Johann Anselm v. Feuerbach in 1813, ranking the Greek legal system among the family of civil law countries. The English language, on the contrary, impels readers towards a legal order which, traditionally speaking, is unrelated to the creation and development of Greek criminal law, being firmly rooted in the tradition of the common law system.

However, this is perhaps the most important reason why, in my opinion, this translation should not be considered as relevant only to non-Greek speakers, but to us Greeks as well.

Examining how the criminal legislator perceives, for example, juvenile offenders and juvenile victims, women, the family and cohabitation arrangements, the weak and defenceless, a fellow person in peril, the relationship between those wielding public power and those governed by it, ownership and assets, personal liberty in all its manifestations, are just some of the aspects of social life whose regulation reveals the level of development of societal relations in modern Greece.

An 'active' reading of the translated text of the Greek Penal Code in English is, to a large degree, one suitable way of prompting us, Greek citizens and researchers, to better understand our own legal culture and, ultimately, become more generally aware of our own cultural identity. Reading the specific translation of the Greek Penal Code is above all a fascinating process of realising who we are; that realisation comes through understanding how a translator, whose mother tongue is not Greek, understands our language, our particularities, our value judgments and our choices, shedding light on the historical mark that Greek legal culture has left on Europe and the world, at the bicentennial of when our land, once a small, isolated, south-eastern corner of Europe, became a state.

For all above reasons, I applaud the important initiative undertaken by the Lex Graeca publishing house in translating the text of the Greek Penal Code into English. The difficulties inherent in such an endeavour were overcome thanks to the exceptional diligence of the translators, John O'Shea and Daniel Webber, their attention to detail, but, above all, to their proven experience in the field of legal translation.

I hope that this publication will achieve the reach and impact it deserves and serve as a springboard for similar efforts in the field of Greece's most important special criminal laws, so that those who do not speak Greek can acquire a truly representative picture of what Greek criminal law has to say about offences not addressed in the text of the Penal Code.

Thomas Samios
Lecturer
Democritus University of Thrace / School of Law
Division of Criminal Law and Criminology

Foreword

John A. O'Shea & Daniel A. Webber

The *Quadricodex*

This book is the third instalment in the *Quadricodex*, a series of translations of the four major codes underpinning the Greek legal system, namely the Civil Code, the Penal Code, the Code of Civil Procedure and the Code of Criminal Procedure. We have taken the liberty of naming our series after the *Tetravivlos* or *Tetrakodikas*, the popular title in Greek given to the compendium of the aforesaid codes. It is our sincere hope that, following the unprecedented translation and publication of the two Codes of Procedure (Civil and Criminal), we will publish the translation of the remaining Code, i.e. the Civil Code, in the near future.

Purpose

As is the case with other *Lex Graeca* publications, the translation of Law 4619/2019 (including all subsequent amendments in the interim —including the major overhaul in 2024— up to a cut-off date of March 2025, the Greek Penal Code (hereinafter GPC), aims to serve a dual purpose: to satisfy a clear and present need for English-language versions of Greek codes and legislation, on the one hand, and to set a standard in terms of language, quality, accuracy and up-to-dateness for such translations, on the other. It is our intention that all further instalments in the *Lex Graeca* series continue to adhere to this standard.

The overarching aim of *Lex Graeca* publications is to clarify Greek law for an international audience. That audience is diverse, consisting of:

- legal practitioners, who might be engaged to provide legal advice to their foreign clients or explain sections of statutes;
- legal translators, who might be called upon to translate sections of the Code or need a reference text for terminology and style purposes;
- academics, particularly comparatists, who thus far have had little access to information in English about the Greek legal system;
- and the general public, who might be interested in reading about the way Greek laws are structured and the topics touched upon.

The more specific aim of the *Quadricodex* series is to make available for the first time a thoroughly researched English-language translation of the four major statutory texts governing almost every aspect of the Greek legal reality, exhaustively researched and consistent in the terminology used across all four instalments.

A more specific goal of our translation of the GPC is to aid both legal practitioners advising clients who find themselves involved in litigation in Greece and any such persons themselves, where they do not speak Greek and/or are unfamiliar with the stages of Greek legal proceedings, so that they stand aware of their rights and obligations. This potential audience is quite considerable in number; statistics from 2024 show that there are currently over 7,600 non-Greek speakers being held in Greek prisons, accounting for 52% of the total population of detainees[1]. While English may not be their mother tongue, English is often used as the means of communication given its status as an international lingua franca.

Background

In historical terms, the GPC has been the most translated of all major Greek statutes. In chronological order, the first was a translation by Nicholas Lolis (number 18 in the American Series of Foreign Penal Codes), published in 1973, when Greece remained under the military junta of the Colonels. The next was the translation by Vasiliki Chalkiadaki and Emmanouil Billis, published in 2017 (G 124 in the research series of the Max Planck Institute for Foreign and International Criminal Law: Collection of Foreign Criminal Laws in Translation)[2].

While both are eminently readable and feature excellent introductions to the Greek criminal justice system (the former by Dr Giorgos Mangakis, the latter by Dr Emmanuouil Billis), they are both only in English and, more importantly, completely out of date, especially given the overhaul of the Penal Code by Law 4619/2019 and the subsequent major overhaul in 2024 by Law 5090. By way of example, Lolis' translation makes reference to the monarchy and capital punishment, neither of which has existed in Greece since the 1970s. Therefore, we consider both incredibly useful and interesting from a historical perspective, but ultimately obsolete.

Our translation began in early 2024 and the first draft was completed within the same year. A painstaking editing process ensued, lasting over a year in total and consisting of countless hours of back-and-forth between the translators and consulting sessions with Greek law professors and practising attorneys, including translation of the latest amendments to the Code, passed in just March 2025 as part of Law 5187/2025, and another round of consulting so as to be completely up to date when going to press.

Compared to our other publications, our translation of the GPC was an arduous task, for two major reasons: firstly, the fact that, while enacted just six years ago in 2019, the Penal Code has undergone almost 300 amendments, given the propensity of the Greek legislature to regularly amend laws[3]; secondly, the fact that, despite being an overhaul, the 2019 version of the GPC (and all subsequent amendments thereto) took into account the historical context within which the Penal Code evolved over the decades (if not centuries). As a result, and as will be explained in the Issues section of this foreword, a tremendous amount of legal knowledge is implicit and considered a "given" and, therefore, the legal fiction that the original text is addressed to the layperson is indeed confirmed as a fiction, since vast amounts of legal knowledge (past versions of the Code, case-law, etc.) are required to fully grasp all the information being conveyed, whether explicit or tacit.

It goes without saying that, should further changes be made to the GPC, we will be prepared to translate them and publish a second edition of this book.

1 Data available online at https://www.sofron.gov.gr/sofronistika-katastimata/statistika-stoixeia-kratoumenon/

2 Now available online at https://pure.mpg.de/rest/items/item_2498942_17/component/file_3529081/content

3 Sotiropoulos, D. A. & Christopoulos, L., *Polynomia*, *Kakonomia* and Bureaucracy in Greece, An Analysis of Past Failures and Proposals for Improvement, 2017, (in Greek) available at https://www.dianeosis.org/wp-content/uploads/2017/12/Polynomia_Main_UPD_41217.pdf

Methodology

The translation and editing were carried out to the highest professional standards and in accordance with current standard practices, so as to ensure consistency and quality throughout the text. The translation process consisted of four stages (**Research and Compilation, Preparation of Source Text, Translation, Review**) which are outlined below:

i) Research and Compilation

The preliminary stage of our process involved three steps:

- Familiarising ourselves with the actuality of legal proceedings in Greece.
- Identifying the texts (historical and recent) on which sections of the GPC were based, consisting mainly of relevant EU Directives and, where appropriate, foreign Penal Codes, and tracking down reliable English-language versions of such Codes.
- Consulting the explanatory memoranda of the various laws that amended the Code over the years, the most recent being in just 2025.

Having identified the relevant texts, we compiled them and leveraged their terminology in order to:

a) identify such sections and, where appropriate, reproduce or at least adhere to the official English-language text, especially in cases of transposition of EU Directives and Regulations;
b) ensure consistency in both the style applied and the terminology used throughout the translation;
c) identify problematic terms in the target text (TT) not only to be discussed and resolved in the context of this publication, but also to be highlighted for research purposes; and
d) identify issues with the source text (ST), examples of which will be discussed below.

It is self-evident that translations of foreign Codes are just that – translations rather than authoritative, authentic versions of the texts, despite the scholarship involved in their production. We therefore consulted them with a view towards background research and generic illumination of key terms and concepts rather than as a source to be mined for material to use.

As intimated below, the source text presented a host of translational issues to be overcome, primarily given the polysemic nature of Greek legal terminology, so the reference texts were of tertiary importance. The main secondary text we consulted was the Greek Code of Criminal Procedure (GCCP) and the numerous analyses of both the GCCP and the GPC published over the decades by eminent Greek jurists[4]. These works are, inevitably in large part, in Greek and served to illuminate issues concerning procedural reality in the Greek courts rather than point out candidate terms in English, given the paucity of English-language scholarship on modern Greek law, a situation which is gradually improving. Additionally, the terminology used in the scant English language works we consulted was both vertically and horizontally inconsistent, i.e. inconsistent both within a single work and across multiple works.

4 For example, The New Criminal Procedure Code (ed. Margaritis, L., Zachariadis, A.) 2024, 2nd ed. Nomiki Vivliothiki Press (in Greek); Sevastidis, C., Code of Criminal Procedure, Law 4620/2019, Vol. 1, 2nd ed. 2023 Sakkoulas Press (in Greek); Penal Code - Interpretation - Application (ed. Margaritis, M., Margariti, A.), 2024 (5th ed.) P.N Sakkoulas Press (in Greek); The New Penal Code - Article by Article Interpretation (Haralambakis, A.) 2024, 2nd ed. Nomiki Vivliothiki Press (in Greek)

ii) Preparation of Source Text

The second stage of our work, particularly with a view to facilitating the bilingual two-page layout of the book, consisted of identifying the proper version of the source text (i.e. compiling a version that included the very latest amendments to the GPC) to use and then editing it for our purposes. This editing was a two-step process:

a) Pagination

This step concerned achieving a logical layout of the book while adhering to an environmentally friendly, space-saving approach. Given the much shorter word count of the GPC when compared to the other much more voluminous Codes making up the Quadricodex, we opted to insert a page break at the end of almost every Chapter of the Code.

b) Editing of original text for readability purposes

Where the original text included a list within an article, we opted to insert a line break in the original so as to have the items on the list one under the other rather than as parts of long, uninterrupted paragraphs, the sole purpose being to enhance readability and ease of reference[5]. An example can be found in Article 50 of the Code:

Original:

> ***"Άρθρο 50***
> ***Είδη ποινών***
>
> *Κύριες ποινές είναι: α) οι στερητικές της ελευθερίας, β) η χρηματική ποινή και γ) η προσφορά κοινωφελούς εργασίας."*

Translation:

> **"Article 50**
> **Types of punishments**
>
> The main punishments are:
> a) custodial sentences;
> b) monetary penalties; and
> c) community service."

A final minor step was addressing typographical errors in the source text, drawing the reader's attention through the use of explicitation brackets and a corrected version in the target texts. One example can be found in Article 13(c), which will be discussed in the Issues section below.

5 Kimble, J. 'The mighty vertical list', The Clarity Journal 90/2025, pp.18-21; Mika, K., Lists in Legal Drafting: How Brain Science Can Help Student Drafters Produce Documents That Are Easier to Read and Comprehend, 21 Scribes J. Legal Writing 75 (2023–2024), available at https://www.scribes.org/wp-content/uploads/2024/08/Scribes_vol21_09_Lists_in_Legal_Drafting.pdf

iii) Translation

The translation process was carried out according to the exacting requirements and specifications of modern-day professional translation in terms of style and terminology. This was a particularly arduous task, compounded by the frequent amendments to the Code and, as noted above, took over a year, given our day-to-day work as legal translators.

Moreover, we made use of the following standard translation strategies:

a) Explicitation

A major issue in the field of legal translation is explicitation, i.e. the introduction of additional information to convey meaning inherent in a source-text word or phrase. At first glance, this might seem an obvious strategy when called upon to translate a text. However, the demands of legal translation in terms of conciseness, accuracy and, where possible, one-for-one equivalence, particularly in the case of a comparatist approach[6], might make explicitation a less likely candidate. Other objections to its use concern the choice of what needs to be explicitated and what does not, as well as the fact that each instance of explicitation might be too specific or, conversely, too vague an interpretation of the source-text concept. Nevertheless, we believe that all translation is, in essence, an unavoidable interpretation of the source text and have opted to employ explicitation where we felt it necessary, signifying such instances with the use of square brackets in order to provide the additional information we believed necessary for a fuller understanding of the law, particularly by laypeople having to grasp the intricacies of a legal system and language that are foreign to them.

Examples include:

The heading of Article 5:

> *Εγκλήματα που τελέστηκαν στην **ημεδαπή***[7]

Our translation:

> Crimes committed in **[Greece]**

Article 323B:

> *"Όποιος υποκινεί ή καθοδηγεί άλλον σε επαιτεία ή τη διοργανώνει ή τη διευκολύνει, ιδίως υποδεικνύοντας τη μέθοδο και τον τόπο της επαιτείας ή παρέχοντας μέσο μεταφοράς προς αυτόν, τιμωρείται με φυλάκιση έως τριών (3) ετών και χρηματική ποινή, αν η πράξη δεν τιμωρείται βαρύτερα από άλλη διάταξη. Αν **πρόκειται** για άτομο με αναπηρία, συντρέχει ιδιαίτερα επιβαρυντική περίσταση."*

6 Glanert, S., and Legrand, P., 'Foreign Law in Translation: If Truth Be Told…', in Freeman, M. & Smith, F. (eds), *Law and Language: Current Legal Issues Volume 15*, Current Legal Issues (Oxford, 2013; online edn, Oxford Academic, 23 May 2013); Legrand, P., Munday, R., eds. *Comparative Legal Studies: Traditions and Transitions*. Cambridge University Press; 2003; Husa, J. (2023). *Introduction to Comparative Law*. (2 ed.) Hart publishing.

7 In all examples in this Foreword we highlight the terms of interest with bold and underlining for purposes of emphasis.

Our translation:

> "Any person who solicits or instructs another to beg, or organises or facilitates such begging, particularly by indicating the method and place of begging or by providing means of transportation to such place, shall be punished with imprisonment of up to three years and a monetary penalty, unless the act carries a heavier punishment under a different provision. There are particularly aggravating circumstances when the **[person begging]** is a person with disabilities."

In all the above examples, explicitation was chosen in order to clarify a term in the source text but in a way that would not drastically alter the form and content of the original provision. The additional text was inserted either on the basis of common sense and our grasp of the Greek language and syntax, where a term or wording could cause confusion to a reader if translated literally, or having consulted jurists in cases of a term with implicit information to be teased out, so as to ensure that the information added in each case was indeed necessary for readers to fully grasp the intended meaning of the ST phrase we considered problematic or lacking in a certain respect.

Conversely to the above examples, we also sparingly used the translational strategy of implicitation, where we removed information which appears in the ST and which would be superfluous, in our opinion, in the TT. One example can be found in page 123, in the heading of the second section of Chapter II of Book II. The ST reads:

> *"ΠΡΟΣΒΟΛΕΣ ΤΗΣ ΔΙΕΘΝΟΥΣ ΕΙΡΗΝΗΣ ΤΗΣ ΧΩΡΑΣ"*

A literal translation would read "Offences [of/against] the international peace of the country" or even "Affronts to the international peace of the country". Indeed, in the 2017 Billis & Chalkiadaki translation of the GPC, prior to the aforementioned radical overhaul of the Code in 2019, the phrase appeared in the heading of Article 139 and had been rendered as "Offence against the international peace of the country". The 1973 Lolis translation similarly translates the heading of Article 139 as "Attacks Upon the International Peace of the State". However, given the text of the Articles under that section and the criminal offences being described, we consider the information in question superfluous (this is, after all, the Greek Penal Code), and opted to omit it from the translation, as its wording, already problematic in Greek, would lead to a problematic rendering in English if translated literally. We have therefore rendered the phrase in question as "Offences Against International Peace".

It should also be noted that, as is the case with the Civil Code, the Penal Code often provides definitions of concepts within parentheses after an explanation of the concept in question. This approach is not the normal practice in English where a definition would normally be worded as 'x means y'. However, we opted to preserve the Greek formulation of definitions in our translation, as an 'x means y' approach would mean drastically reformulating the text and departing more than considerably from the original. With that in mind, readers should remain alert to words in brackets perhaps functioning as definitions. Examples of definitions found in the GPC include the following:

- Article 31(2)

  "Η πράξη όμως δεν καταλογίζεται σε εκείνον που την τελεί αν αυτός δεν είχε συνείδηση του άδικου χαρακτήρα της λόγω πλάνης που δεν μπορούσε να αποφύγει, μολονότι κατέβαλε την οφειλόμενη από τις περιστάσεις και δυνατή γι' αυτόν επιμέλεια **(συγγνωστή νομική πλάνη)**."

  Our translation:

  "However, the act shall not be imputed to the perpetrator if they were not aware of its wrongful nature due to an unavoidable mistake, despite having shown the greatest diligence they could have shown and which was required under the circumstances **(excusable mistake of law)**."

- Article 167(1)

  "Όποιος με βία ή απειλή βίας επιχειρεί να εξαναγκάσει κάποια αρχή ή υπάλληλο να ενεργήσει πράξη που ανάγεται στα καθήκοντά του ή να παραλείψει νόμιμη πράξη, καθώς και όποιος βιαιοπραγεί εναντίον του ή κατά προσώπου που έχει προσληφθεί ή άλλου υπαλλήλου που έχει προστρέξει για να τον υποστηρίξει κατά τη διάρκεια της νόμιμης ενέργειάς του **(αντίσταση)**, *τιμωρείται με φυλάκιση έως τρία έτη ή χρηματική ποινή."*

  Our translation:

  "Any person who, through use or threat of violence, attempts to force an authority or employee to carry out or omit a lawful act that is part of their duties, and any person who assaults the such employee or a person engaged [to perform duties] or another employee who has come to their aid while carrying out lawful steps **(resistance)** shall be punished with imprisonment of up to three years or a monetary penalty."

This should not be confused with explicitation on our part, for which we use square brackets, as seen in the example from Article 167(1) provided above.

b) Gender-neutral language

Where the Greek text opted for the masculine as the default, we opted for several strategies widely utilised[8] by translation professionals to render sex and gender irrelevant as a consideration without changing the core meaning of the source text[9]:

- Repeating or replacing a singular noun with a plural pronoun, e.g., Article 346(3)(c)

  *γ) σε βάρος νυν ή πρώην συζύγου ή συντρόφου του υπαιτίου ή σε βάρος προσώπου που συνοικεί **με αυτόν** ή έχει **μαζί του** σχέση εργασίας ή υπηρεσίας ή βρίσκεται υπό την επιμέλεια ή την προστασία **του** ή δεν μπορεί να υπερασπίσει **τον εαυτό του**,*

  c) against the spouse or former spouse or partner of the culpable person, or a person who lives with **the perpetrator**, or is **in their** employ or service, or who is under **the perpetrator's** custody or protection, or who cannot defend **themselves**; [or]

- Using a plural noun where the meaning in the ST is intentionally abstract and is not referring to a single specific individual, e.g., Article 69(1)(c):

  *γ) η απέλαση **αλλοδαπού***

  c) deportation of **foreign nationals**.

c) Easified language

This aspect of the task we set ourselves was one of the hardest and most time-consuming to address during both the translation and the editing of the Code. Our objective was to publish a comprehensively researched text that offers, to the greatest extent possible, equivalence of terms used in the Greek legal system —belonging to the civil law family— and terms established in the English-speaking legal world —mostly belonging to the common law family— while still accurately describing the Greek system. As noted by Thomas Samios in his Introduction, the conundrum facing any translator working in this pair of languages (and legal systems) is immediately apparent.

Nevertheless, in our approach towards using easified language, we opted to minimise the use of Latin legal terms, employing them only where we deemed it necessary, and to use terms more immediately accessible and understandable to a layperson rather than a jurist.

The conventions we followed to achieve an easified-language result by and large adhered to common sense, as we understand it, and to the rules prescribed by the European Commission[10], with a view not to simplify or radically reformulate the ST, but to ensure that the TT is clear and comprehensible, reflecting the actual wording and intention of the ST and also being able to be read as a standalone text free from any of the hallmarks of mediocre translations (stunted syntax, excessive adherence to the structure of the original sentence, etc., all of which are by-and-large hallmarks of the translations of the Greek codes to date).

In more concrete terms, the choices we made concerned:

8 https://www.europarl.europa.eu/cmsdata/151780/GNL_Guidelines_EN.pdf

9 Xanthaki, H. (2020). Gender inclusive legislative drafting in English: A drafter's response to Emily Grabham, feminists@law, Vol 10, No 2 (2020), available at: https://journals.kent.ac.uk/index.php/feministsatlaw/article/view/952/1842

10 How to Write Clearly, https://op.europa.eu/en/publication-detail/-/publication/c2dab20c-0414-408d-87b5-dd3c6e5dd9a5

<u>Syntax:</u>

- Changing word order to reflect what is normal in English-language texts, i.e. Subject-Verb-Object syntax where possible, e.g., Article 263A(2):

  > *"Την αναστολή της δίωξης μπορεί να διατάξει και το δικαστήριο, εφόσον τα στοιχεία εισφέρονται μέχρι την έκδοση απόφασης σε δεύτερο βαθμό."*

  Our translation:

  > "The court too may order that prosecution be stayed where such information is provided before a judgment is handed down at second instance."

- Joining sentences where a full stop or a semicolon would not make sense, e.g., Article 783:

  > *"Αρμόδιο κατά το νόμο να κηρύξει και να άρει την αφάνεια, καθώς και να μεταβάλει το χρόνο της έναρξής της είναι το δικαστήριο της τελευταίας κατοικίας που είχε στην Ελλάδα εκείνος που εξαφανίστηκε και, αν δεν υπάρχει κατοικία, της τελευταίας διαμονής του στην Ελλάδα. Αν δεν υπάρχει ούτε διαμονή, το δικαστήριο της πρωτεύουσας του κράτους."*

  Our translation:

  > "The court competent in law to issue and reverse a declaration of a person as absent and to change the time such absence commenced is the court of the last place of domicile of the person who disappeared in Greece and, where there is no such place of domicile, their last place of residence in Greece and, where there is no such place of residence, the court of the capital."

We understand and acknowledge that this may cause citation issues, given the manner in which Greek statutes are cited, but this was an editorial choice made on our part (and used quite sparingly), our primary concern being readability and ease of use of the target text. As always, readers are encouraged to seek professional advice from a Greek attorney and should consider this translation of the GPC as a starting point for understanding the Code and not as a definitive authentic instrument.

- Using semi-colons to better punctuate sentences where we considered this served the purpose of clarity, e.g., in Article 168(4):

> *"Όποιος εισέρχεται σε δομές παροχής υπηρεσιών υγείας, συμπεριλαμβανομένων των κινητών μονάδων παροχής υπηρεσιών υγείας ή προσεγγίζει κινητές μονάδες παροχής υγειονομικών υπηρεσιών άμεσης βοήθειας και με οποιονδήποτε τρόπο, ιδίως με φωνασκίες, θόρυβο, ύβρεις ή απειλές κατά του ιατρικού και νοσηλευτικού προσωπικού, εργαζομένων, υπαλλήλων ή ασθενών διαταράσσει τη λειτουργία τους, τιμωρείται με ποινή φυλάκισης τουλάχιστον ενός (1) έτους και χρηματική ποινή και αν η πράξη συνδέεται με πρόκληση βιαιοπραγίας, με ποινή φυλάκισης τουλάχιστον δύο (2) ετών και χρηματική ποινή."*

Our translation:

> "Any person who enters healthcare facilities, including mobile healthcare units, or who approaches mobile emergency healthcare units, and disrupts their operation in any manner and, in particular, by shouting, making noise, using insults or threats against the medical and nursing staff, workers, employees or patients, shall be punished with imprisonment of at least one year and a monetary penalty; if the act also involves assault, they shall be punished with imprisonment of at least two years and a monetary penalty."

- Changing passive-voice syntax to active-voice where advisable, e.g., in Article 265A(2):

> *"Η έκταση της δήμευσης αποφασίζεται από το δικαστήριο, [...]"*

Our translation:

> "The court shall decide on the extent of confiscation [...]"

Vocabulary:

When in doubt and presented with a multitude of terminological choices, we opted for the most readily understandable term. An indicative —and by no means exhaustive— list is presented below, and should be understood as conventions on our part for the sake of consistency across all relevant texts, with a view to easified language and clarity:

- "*Δόλος*" has been rendered as *"dolus"*, one of the very few cases of legal Latin terms used in our translations. While both the 1973 Lolis and 2017 Billis & Chalkiadaki translations use the terms "intentionally" and "with intent", respectively, we consider that the term, given its further elaboration into three types (*dolus directus*, 1st and 2nd grade, and *dolus eventualis*, as discussed in Article 27 of the GPC), is best rendered as *dolus* rather than intent.
- "*Κατηγορούμενος*" has been rendered as "accused person or defendant" when it is unclear which the stage of criminal proceedings is, e.g., Article 239(a) or Article 381(2), and just "defendant" when it is clear that the person in question has been committed to trial, e.g., Article 2 or Article 465(4).
- "*Φυλάκιση*" has been rendered as "imprisonment", whereas "*κάθειρξη*" has been rendered as "incarceration", as discussed later in this Foreword. Correspondingly, as per Article 18, any crime carrying a sentence of incarceration, whether for life or for a fixed term, is by definition a "felony" ("*κακούργημα*"), while any crime carrying a sentence of imprisonment, confinement in a reformative institution or just a monetary penalty or community service is a "misdemeanour" ("*πλημμέλημα*").
- "*Παράνομη κατακράτηση*" has been rendered as "unlawful detention" rather than the wording seen in European Arrest Warrants, i.e. "illegally restraining", or in the translation of the Hellenic Constitution, i.e. "illegal detention".
- The term "*απομάκρυνση*" has been rendered as "deportation" rather than "removal", as also discussed in the Euphemism section of this Foreword.
- "*Οικείος*" has been rendered as "related party", but with all the qualifications discussed later in this Foreword.
- "*Κατάσχεση*" has been rendered as "seizure/attachment/arrest" in Article 177, given that it applies even in cases of attachment/arrest under civil law provisions.
- "*Άφαντος*" has been rendered as "absentee", as seen in other translations of European codes and as will be discussed in our forthcoming publication of the translation of the Civil Code.
- A court's decision ("*κρίση*" or "*απόφαση*") on individual matters arising during proceedings is a "ruling", e.g., Article 263A(3), whereas its final decision ("*απόφαση*") on the subject-matter of the case is a "judgment", e.g., Article 9(3).
- When "*εδάφιο*" refers to a sentence within a standalone paragraph, it has been rendered as "sentence" (e.g., Article 7), and when it refers to an entire subparagraph among others of a paragraph, it has been rendered as "subparagraph" (e.g., Article 105B(1)(b)).
- References to the "*ΠΚ*", i.e. the Penal Code, e.g., in Article 263A(3), are rendered as "this Code".

iv) Review

The final (but by no means shortest) step in our process was to review the translation, discuss and resolve any issues that arose and highlight any problems we considered worthy of inclusion in the **Issues** section of this Foreword.

This stage was particularly time-consuming, consisting of several passes of revisions and corrections, and involved reaching out to experts to explicate terms and clarify processes. Considering the effort involved, we are exceptionally satisfied with the final result and are confident in its quality and utility for readers.

Issues

In previous *Lex Graeca* publications, we categorised the issues we identified into broad categories and provided indicative examples of each problem. For that purpose have developed a taxonomy of issues which is constantly being updated as our task of translating Greece's codes into English progresses[11]. It should be noted that the GPC has the fewest issues of the four Codes comprising the Quadricodex. While it is beyond the scope of this Foreword to explore the reasons why such issues arise in the Codes we translate, we note that many of the issues we highlight as source text problems are well-known to the Greek legal community; many were discussed again in latest overhaul to the GPC though not, it would appear, addressed[12]. Given the importance of the GPC, we reproduce a broad selection of all these issues that we faced in our translation efforts, with the hope that they are resolved in future amendments of the Code and drive further research into the Greek text.

The six categories into which we classified each issue are as follows:

a) Citation / Typographic / Capitalisation errors
b) Vague / Obscure language
c) Problematic syntax / Odd word choices
d) Polysemic terms/ambiguous language
e) Acronyms & official translations and names of entities
f) Elegant variation - Euphemisms

11 For an overview of the issues in the Codes so far, see O'Shea, J. and Webber, D., 'Translation as a lens through which to view legislation's effectiveness', in *Language for Legislation and Legislation through Language* (ed. Xanthaki, H., Pennisi G., Drinóczi, T.), Routledge Press, forthcoming 2025, where we describe the taxonomy and changes made, as well as providing data on the number of different types of issues in each Code. Interestingly, the Penal Code appears to have the fewest issues of the four main Codes.

12 Just some of the recent critical commentary on amendments to the GPC can be found at the following links: https://www.dikastiko.gr/eidhsh/polemos-gia-toys-kodikes-voles-kathigiton-kai-melon-tis-nomoparaskeyastikis-toy-2019-kata-toy-nomoschedioy-floridi-quot-anamorfosi-i-paramorfosi-toy-poinikoy-systimatos-quot-vinteo/; https://www.capital.gr/me-apopsi/3756880/to-gaitanaki-ton-tropopoiiseon-tou-poinikou-kodika-sunexizetai/

a) Citation / Typographic / Capitalisation errors

i) Citation errors

Where citation errors were identified in the source text, we decided not to alter the Greek but to use explicitation brackets to correct the error in the translation. One such example can be found in Article 394A(2):

> *"2. Αν το αντικείμενο της πράξης της παρ. 1 του άρθρου 394 προήλθε από την αξιόποινη πράξη της **περ. βα' του άρθρου 374**, ο δράστης τιμωρείται με κάθειρξη έως δέκα (10) έτη."*

Our translation:

> "2. If the object of the act provided for in Article 394(1) resulted from the punishable act provided for in **Article 374[1](ba)**, the perpetrator shall be punished with incarceration of up to 10 years."

Article 374 consists of two paragraphs, 1 and 2, but only the first paragraph contains subparagraphs (a) to (e). We therefore inferred that this must be a citation error and that subparagraph (ba) of paragraph 1 is what is meant.

Another example can be found in Article 369:

> *"1. Αν οι πράξεις των άρθρων 361, **362**, 363 και 365 [...]"*

Our translation:

> "1. If the acts provided for in Articles 361, **[362,]** 363 and 365 [...]"

Upon consulting Article 362, highlighted above, we see that it was recently repealed by virtue of Article 136 of Law 5090/2024. We therefore consider this to be a citation error and have pointed this out in our translation using explicitation brackets.

One more example can be seen in Article 312(1)(c), where the Greek reads:

> *"γ) για την πράξη **του πρώτου εδαφίου** της παρ. 1 του άρθρου 310 [...]"*

The above phrase, translated context-blind, would read

> "for the act provided for **in the first sentence** of Article 310(1)"

However, upon reading Article 310(1), we see that paragraph 1 consists of a single sentence. Therefore, any reference to the "first" (or, obviously, any other) sentence of paragraph 1 is a citation error. More importantly, having consulted experts, we are assured that this is the result of a recent amendment where the legislator did not cite the first sentence of Article 310(2) but rather cited (1).

A similar example appears in Article 120, where the following phrase appears:

> "[...] in accordance with Articles 99 and **100** [...]"

As was the case in the previous examples, Article 100 has been repealed, therefore any reference to that Article is a citation error.

Another example similar to the one above is the use of *"ημερήσιες μονάδες"* ("daily penalty units"), a unit of measurement to establish an equivalence between monetary penalties and custodial sentences. However, the relevant provision (paragraph 1 of Article 57) was repealed by virtue of Article 8 of Law 5090/2024. Therefore, the reference to such "daily penalty units", appearing in Articles 82(4), 216(4), 242(5), 374(2), 375(3), 386(2), 386A(3) and 390(2), is an oversight on the part of the legislator.

ii) Typographic errors

Where typographic errors or conventions that do not carry over in translation were encountered in the original document, we normally highlighted the issue using explicitation brackets in the translation. One characteristic example, as mentioned earlier, can be found in Article 13(c):

Original:

> *"Έγγραφο είναι και κάθε μέσο το οποίο χρησιμοποιείται από υπολογιστή ή περιφερειακή μνήμη υπολογιστή, με ηλεκτρονικό, μαγνητικό ή άλλο τρόπο, για εγγραφή, αποθήκευση, **παραγωγή αναπαραγωγή** στοιχείων που δεν μπορούν να διαβαστούν άμεσα [...]"*

There is a punctuation mark (most likely a comma) or other word missing between the two highlighted nouns, which is why our translation reads as follows:

Translation:

> "'Document' also means any medium used by a computer or peripheral computer memory via electronic, magnetic or other means to record, store, produce **[or]** reproduce data that cannot be directly read [...]"

Another example occurs in the Government Gazette version of Law 5090/2024, which heavily amended the GPC. In Article 54 of the said Law, amending Article 363 of the GPC, the following spelling error occurs:

> *"[...] τα **δυαδικά** μέρη [...]"*

The legislator obviously meant to write *"τα διάδικα μέρη"* ("litigants") rather than *"δυαδικά"* ("binary"), and we have corrected the ST and provided a correct translation in the TT.

A similar example occurs in the Government Gazette version of Law 4619/2019 containing the Penal Code, in Article 174(b):

> *" [...] β) επιτίθενται με έργα κατά **ων** υπαλλήλων της φυλακής [...]"*

The first letter of the highlighted word is clearly missing and should have read *"των"*. We have corrected the error in the ST of our publication and translated it without reference to any error.

Another issue we have classified in this category is the inconsistent use of integers in the ST. A mainstay of Greek legal texts (and all public documents) is the repetition of any number written in full with its corresponding figure in parentheses immediately thereafter to avoid instances of forgery or misunderstanding[13], e.g., in Article 168(1):

> *"1. Όποιος εισέρχεται παράνομα σε χώρο δημόσιας υπηρεσίας ή υπηρεσίας οργανισμού τοπικής αυτοδιοίκησης ή νομικού προσώπου δημοσίου δικαίου ή επιχείρησης κοινής ωφέλειας ή παραμένει στους χώρους αυτούς παρά τη ρητή εναντίωση της υπηρεσίας που τους χρησιμοποιεί, τιμωρείται με φυλάκιση έως **τρία (3) έτη** ή χρηματική ποινή."*

However, we see the exact same phrase appearing without the parentheses in Article 147:

> *"Όποιος τελεί τις πράξεις του προηγούμενου άρθρου από αμέλεια, εφόσον τα απόρρητα ήταν υπηρεσιακώς εμπιστευμένα σε αυτόν ή τού ήταν προσιτά λόγω της δημόσιας υπηρεσίας του ή με εντολή κάποιας αρχής, τιμωρείται με φυλάκιση έως **τρία έτη** ή χρηματική ποινή και σε καιρό πολέμου, με φυλάκιση τουλάχιστον **τριών ετών** και χρηματική ποινή."*

In translational terms, the issue is moot, as we acknowledge the Greek system of repeating the figure for confirmation purposes, but have opted to follow the style guide of the European Commission[14], writing out numbers from one to nine and using figures for numbers from 10 and above and not having both the written form of the number and the numerical form.

Another example concerns the heading of Section VI of Chapter V of Book I. All headings of books, sections and chapters prior were in block capitals, while this one, which reads "*Δικαστική άφεση της ποινής*", which we have translated as "Judicial forgiveness of punishments", appears in lower case. We considered this a typographical error and have corrected it by typing the headings in block capitals in both the ST and the TT for reasons of visual consistency and uniformity.

One more issue identified concerned the headings of Chapter IV and Section I of Book II. In the Government Gazette version of Law 4619/2019, no heading is given for the Chapter, which was not the case with any chapter of the GPC before or after, while two headings are given for the Section. Having consulted analyses of the GPC[15], we are assured that this was a typographical error and the correct headings have been provided in both the ST and the TT for the Chapter and Section in question on pages 108 and 109, respectively.

---

13 Iordanidou, A. (ed.), Guide to the Greek Language, Patakis Publications, 2012, (in Greek) p. 91

14 Available at https://commission.europa.eu/system/files/2023-11/styleguide_english_dgt_en.pdf

15 Sevastidis, C., Penal Code (Law 4619/2019), 2024 Sakkoulas Press (in Greek), p. 187.

A final issue occurs in Article 134 and the use of parentheses in paragraphs 2 and 3:

> "2. *[...]*
>
> **<u>(α)</u>** *[...]*
>
> **<u>(β)</u>** *[...]"*
>
> 3. *[...]*
>
> **<u>α)</u>** *[...]*
>
> **<u>β)</u>** *[...]*
>
> **<u>γ)</u>** *[...]*

As is evident, the letters in the list of paragraph 2 are between two parentheses, whereas in paragraph 3 they are only followed by a closing parenthesis. While this obviously has no bearing of legal importance, we consider it a typographic inconsistency and have opted, rather than use explication brackets, to remove the starting parenthesis from each list item of paragraph 2 in both the ST and the TT in order to achieve uniformity across the text.

<u>iii) Capitalisation errors</u>

Throughout our translation of the GPC, we follow English capitalisation rules and norms, being mindful of the debate concerning the capitalisation of key terms in legal documents, even in English[16]. Greek legal texts, perhaps under the influence of the German language (German legal tradition having exerted a massive influence on the development of Greek law) frequently capitalise the initial letters of certain terms, although this is not done systematically. In the GPC there are several instances of arbitrary capitalisation with no definition provided, although we are happy to report that this occurs to a much lesser extent than the other Codes we have translated to date.

One example is the capitalisation of the term "*Κοινωνικής Υπηρεσίας*" ("social services [unit/department]") in Article 129A(1). The term is broad enough (or, conversely, not specific enough) to merit capitalisation, and we have therefore omitted said capitalisation in our translation.

Similarly, in Article 129(3) we encounter the phrase *"[...] υποβάλλει αίτηση προς το Τριμελές Δικαστήριο Ανηλίκων στο Πλημμελειοδικείο του τόπου όπου εκτίεται ο περιορισμός [...]"*. Once again, this reference to a court is not a specific enough (i.e. there is no specific place mentioned) and we therefore do not consider that this merits capitalisation in the TT, which reads as follows: "[...] submit an application to the three-member juvenile court at the court of misdemeanours at the place of confinement [...]".

---

16 This practice is, of course, not wholly accepted. See for example, on the relevant debate, Cutts, M. 'Capitalizing defined terms: Should consumer contracts use initial capitals for definitions?'. The Clarity Journal 90/2025, pp. 12-17.

Another example is the use of the initialism *"ΠΚ"* (standing for *"Ποινικός Κώδικας"*, i.e. "Penal Code"), appearing seven times in the text, e.g., in Article 85 (*"άρθρο 84 ΠΚ"*), Article 105(3) (*"άρθρου 110 ΠΚ"*), etc. We considered this firstly unnecessary, as it is a given that references within a law to numbered articles without any further qualifier would obviously be referring to articles within that very law —and, in fact, there are countless instances of exactly such references, i.e. to numbered articles, clearly referring to other articles of the GPC— and secondly inconsistent, as there are examples of the entire name of the Penal Code being used, e.g., Article 292(4), (*"άρθρο 134 του Ποινικού Κώδικα"*), or of other Codes being used, e.g., Article 70(3) (*"άρθρου 340 του Κώδικα Ποινικής Δικονομίας"*, referring to the Code of Criminal Procedure).

One final example concerns the heading of Article 381, which reads *"Γενική Διάταξη"* ("General provision"). Greek article headings are not normally capitalised, therefore we consider this another example of such arbitrary capitalisation and have opted not to reproduce it in our translation.

b) Vague / Obscure language

The modern Greek language is rich indeed, with numerous pits into which unseasoned translators may fall. The GPC features numerous examples of vague language and obscure terminology not encountered elsewhere that required extensive discussions with Greek legal practitioners to help us threefold by explaining the term, helping us understand what the actual situation in a court of law would be, and enabling us to identify the best candidate term for translation. A few examples are given below to highlight such issues:

- In Article 80(1), we encountered the term *"οικογενειακές υποχρεώσεις"* in the following context:

  Original text:

  > "1. *Κατά την επιμέτρηση της χρηματικής ποινής, το δικαστήριο λαμβάνει υπόψη του*
  > *α) τη βαρύτητα της πράξης και την ενοχή του υπαιτίου γι' αυτήν,*
  > *β) την προσωπική και οικονομική κατάσταση του υπαιτίου, λαμβάνοντας υπόψη ειδικότερα*
  > *βα) τα καθαρά έσοδα που αποκτά από την εργασία του κατά μέσο όρο κάθε ημέρα,*
  > *ββ) άλλα τυχόν εισοδήματα και εν γένει την περιουσία του, καθώς και*
  > *βγ) τις* ***οικογενειακές του υποχρεώσεις****. Άλλες* ***υποχρεώσεις*** *του μπορούν επίσης να συνυπολογισθούν από το δικαστήριο."*

  Our translation:

  > "1. When determining the monetary penalty, the court shall take into consideration:
  > a) the severity of the act and the guilt of the culpable person;
  > b) the personal and financial situation of the culpable person, having particular regard to:
  > ba) the net [income] earned from their work on average each day;
  > bb) any other income and their assets in general; and
  > bc) their **family obligations.** The court may also take into account other **obligations** of the culpable person."

Given the context of the foregoing subparagraphs (one's financial situation, income, assets, etc.), one might consider that the "obligations" being referred to are financial in nature. However, upon discussing the matter with experts on the Penal Code, we are assured that while these may have a financial aspect, they nevertheless stem from family issues. Thus, we shied away from any translation that would insinuate a financial aspect (e.g., "outgoings", "outlays", etc.), as these are also potential translations of the term *"υποχρεώσεις"*.

- The heading of Article 82A reads *"Έγκλημα με ρατσιστικά χαρακτηριστικά ή σε βάρος ανηλίκου ή αδυνάμου προσώπου"*, which we have rendered as "Crimes with racist motivation or committed against a juvenile or person [unable to defend themselves]". Our explicitation at the end aside, we consider the adjective *"ρατσιστικά"* ("racist") a vague term, given that the term *"ρατσισμός"* ("racism") is used in modern Greek to denote any form of prejudice and not just on the basis of race. This now prevalent usage is evident from the text of the Article in question.

  Original text:

  > *"Εάν έχει τελεστεί έγκλημα κατά παθόντος, η επιλογή του οποίου έγινε λόγω των* ***χαρακτηριστικών φυλής, χρώματος, εθνικής ή εθνοτικής καταγωγής, γενεαλογικών καταβολών, θρησκείας, αναπηρίας, γενετήσιου προσανατολισμού, ταυτότητας ή χαρακτηριστικών φύλου****, [...]"*

  Our translation:

  > "If a crime was committed against a victim who was [targeted] due to **characteristics relating to their race, skin colour, national or ethnic origin, genealogical descent, religion, disability, sexual orientation, gender identity or sex characteristics** [...]"

- The term *"ένσημα"* ("stamps") appears in Article 208C in the context of counterfeiting and abuse of such. However, jurisprudence and theory inform us that these stamps go beyond just postal stamps and also include, for instance, social security stamps[17], which is why we consider this a vague term that should cause even a seasoned translator pause.

- Article 354 on disruption of family status makes reference to the concept of *"υποβολή τέκνου"* in verb form:

  > *"Όποιος νοθεύει ή συγκαλύπτει την οικογενειακή τάξη άλλου και ιδίως όποιος* ***υποβάλλει τέκνο*** *τιμωρείται με φυλάκιση έως δύο έτη ή χρηματική ποινή."*

  Our translation:

  > "Any person who alters or conceals another's family status and, in particular, any person who presents a child **[as having a different family status from the one it actually has]** shall be punished with imprisonment of up to two years or a monetary penalty."

17 https://www.areiospagos.gr/nomologia/apofaseis_DISPLAY.asp?cd=DDTNCORKM5LKCSG151XYJL5SS54FMK

We considered this explicitation necessary, as the term in question is vague for two reasons. Firstly, the Greek verb "*υποβάλλω*" normally means "to submit" or "to subject", e.g., submit an application as an example of the former or subject someone to a situation as an example of the latter. However, in this instance, the rare meaning of the verb as "to substitute" is the one being used. Secondly, reference is being made to "*υποβολή τέκνου*", an undefined concept contained in all versions of the GPC going back to the 19th century. In fact, an explanatory memorandum accompanying a draft of the GPC from the early 20th century goes so far as to say no explanation of the concept is required "*διότι είναι πασίδηλος και αναμφίβολος η έννοια του όρου: υποβολή τέκνου» - «τέκνον υποβολιμαίον»*", i.e. "because the concept of the term '*υποβολή τέκνου*' - '*τέκνον υποβολιμαίον*' is patently obvious and indisputable", an obviously circular argument. Given the several papers[18] on the subject which we consulted, and our belief that most laypeople would not be familiar with the rare usage encountered in the GPC, we are content with our translation and believe it is fit for purpose.

c) Problematic syntax / Odd word choices

The GPC is no exception to the odd and esoteric language often found in statutes and legal texts in general, often dubbed legalese. Certain examples which we had to discuss both among ourselves and with legal practitioners in order to resolve are presented below as an illustration of our methodology when such issues arose[19], which was quite often:

- Article 72(4)(a):

    > *"[...] Μετά την παρέλευση του χρόνου αυτού και εφόσον η απέλαση δεν έχει πραγματοποιηθεί, με διάταξη του εισαγγελέα πλημμελειοδικών του τόπου κράτησης αναστέλλεται υποχρεωτικά η απέλαση του αλλοδαπού, τού επιβάλλονται ιδίως οι όροι που προβλέπονται στην παρ. 2 του άρθρου 106 και ο **κρατούμενος** απολύεται αμέσως."*

    In this instance, we have a single referent and two referring expressions, i.e. "*αλλοδαπός*" (foreign national) and "*κρατούμενος*" (detainee), both of which concern the same person. However, the syntax used could result in confusion, leading readers to believe that there are two persons being discussed here. Bearing this in mind, we chose to render the above problematic phrase as follows:

    > "[...] After such period has elapsed and provided deportation has not taken place, the court of misdemeanours public prosecutor at the place of detention must necessarily issue an order suspending deportation of the foreign national, imposing, in particular, the conditions provided for in Article 106(2) on the foreign national, and immediately **releasing [them] from detention**."

18 Samios, T., 'The "Penal Law" of 1833', in *History of Criminal Law and Criminal Institutions*, Ant. N. Sakkoulas, Komotini, 2007; Livieratos, E,, 'Offences against family status in our Penal Code and offences against paternity in our Civil Code', in *Volume in Memoriam of I. K. Papazachariou*, Vol. I, pp. 389-401.

19 The examples in this section clearly run contrary to the well-established rule on the use of consistent terminology. "This rule may be stated: 'Never change your language unless you wish to change your meaning, and always change your language if you wish to change your meaning'", in Butt, P. and Castle, R., Modern Legal Drafting: A Guide to Using Clearer Language, Cambridge University Press (2006), p. 61; see to Piesse, E., *The Elements of Drafting* (10th ed., Lawbook Co., 2004, ed. Aitken, J. and Butt, P.), p. 95.

- Article 113(2):

  "Ο χρονικός περιορισμός της αναστολής δεν ισχύει όταν η αναβολή ή αναστολή της ποινικής δίωξης, ή η αναβολή της δίκης, λαμβάνει χώρα κατ' εφαρμογή των άρθρων 29, 59 ***και*** *61 του Κώδικα Ποινικής Δικονομίας [...]"*

  This is an issue arising frequently in the GPC and in Greek law in general, where the legislator uses the Greek conjunction "*και*" ("and") instead of "*ή*" ("or") where the meaning is definitively disjunctive. Thus, in the example presented above, the meaning is certainly not that all three Articles of the GCCP apply, but that any of them applies in each of the three situations previously enumerated. We have therefore rendered it as follows using explicitation brackets:

  "The above limitation does not apply when the criminal prosecution has been deferred or suspended or the proceedings have been adjourned pursuant to Articles 29, 59 **[or]** 61 of the Code of Criminal Procedure [...]"

- Article 187(2) and (3):

  "2. Αυτός που διευθύνει την ***εγκληματική οργάνωση*** *τιμωρείται με κάθειρξη.*

  3. Όποιος, εκτός από την περίπτωση της πρώτης παραγράφου, οργανώνεται με άλλον ή άλλους για να διαπράξουν κακούργημα τιμωρείται με φυλάκιση τουλάχιστον έξι μηνών. Με φυλάκιση έως τρία έτη τιμωρείται ο υπαίτιος αν ***η κατά το προηγούμενο εδάφιο ένωση*** *έγινε για τη διάπραξη πλημμελήματος με το οποίο επιδιώκεται οικονομικό ή άλλο υλικό όφελος ή η προσβολή της ζωής, της σωματικής ακεραιότητας, της ανηλικότητας, της προσωπικής ελευθερίας, της ιδιοκτησίας ή της περιουσίας."*

  Paragraph 3 makes reference to the "*κατά το προηγούμενο εδάφιο ένωση*", i.e. "the [joining of forces] referred to in the preceding sentence". While one could argue that the phrase "*οργανώνεται με άλλον ή άλλους*", which we have rendered as "joins forces with another person or persons", could serve as a definition of the concept of "*ένωση*", the actual term "*ένωση*" nevertheless appears nowhere in the preceding sentence, or anywhere else in this Article, which is why we consider this an example of odd word choice (if not also a citation error, based on past wording of this Article) worth highlighting.

- Articles 290A and 291(2):

  "[...] αν δεν προβλέπονται βαρύτερες ***κυρώσεις*** *σε άλλες διατάξεις [...]"*

  The usual wording seen in the GPC when encountering this stereotypical phrase is "*βαρύτερη ποινή*" ("heavier punishment/sentence", depending on context). However, in these two instances the text pivots away from this noun and uses the term "*κυρώσεις*" ("sanctions"). We consider this an odd word choice and have rendered the phrase as follows, given the custodial sentences carried, in both cases:

  "[...] unless different provisions lay down heavier **[sentences]** [...]"

- Article 291(2):

> *"2. Με τις ίδιες ποινές κατά τις διακρίσεις των στοιχείων αα΄ έως δδ΄ της προηγούμενης παραγράφου τιμωρείται, εάν δεν προβλέπονται βαρύτερες κυρώσεις σε άλλες διατάξεις, όποιος οδηγεί όχημα σταθερής τροχιάς ή κυβερνά πλοίο ή* ***<u>αεροπλάνο</u>*** *ή χειρίζεται εξ αποστάσεως σύστημα μη επανδρωμένου αεροσκάφους χωρίς να είναι σε θέση να το πράξει με ασφάλεια εξαιτίας της κατανάλωσης οινοπνεύματος ή χρήσης ναρκωτικών ουσιών ή λόγω σωματικής ή πνευματικής εξάντληση."*

Paragraph 1 of the same article uses the term "*αεροσκάφος*" (in the plural genitive), i.e. "aircraft" in general, denoting any air-based means of transport. However, in paragraph 2, we see the term "*αεροπλάνο*" ("aeroplane") used. In fact, immediately after that, reference is made to unmanned aerial vehicles. We consider this an example of odd word choice, given that the legislator obviously does not omit helicopters, for example, from this provision. Paragraph 2 has therefore been rendered as follows, using explicitation brackets:

> "Any person who [operates] a track-based vehicle or commands a ship or **<u>[aircraft]</u>** or remotely handles an unmanned aerial vehicle while being unable to safely do so due to consumption of alcohol or use of narcotic substances or due to physical or mental exhaustion shall be punished with the same sentences, in accordance with the distinctions laid down in points (aa) to (dd) of the preceding paragraph, unless different provisions lay down heavier [sentences]."

- Article 348A:

> *"Άρθρο 348A*
> ***<u>Πορνογραφία ανηλίκων</u>***
>
> *1. Όποιος με πρόθεση παράγει, διανέμει, δημοσιεύει, επιδεικνύει, εισάγει στην Επικράτεια ή εξάγει από αυτήν, μεταφέρει, προσφέρει, πωλεί ή με άλλον τρόπο διαθέτει, αγοράζει, προμηθεύεται, αποκτά ή κατέχει υλικό* ***<u>παιδικής πορνογραφίας</u>*** *[...]"*

The heading of this Article uses the term "*πορνογραφία ανηλίκων*" ("pornography of juveniles", if translated literally). However, in our translation we opted for the established criminal law term of "child pornography":

> "Article 348A
> **<u>Child pornography</u>**"

Nevertheless, as highlighted above, the actual text of the Article in question pivots away from the terminology used in the heading and uses the term "*παιδική πορνογραφία*" (in the genitive), i.e. "child pornography". Apart from the discrepancy from the heading, we consider the actual term used in the heading an example of odd word choice and in this instance, as noted above, we decided to employ the established term in both cases.

- Article 348B:

    "Προσέλκυση ***<u>παιδιών</u>*** *για γενετήσιους λόγους"*

    The heading of this Article uses the term *"παιδί"* (in the plural genitive), i.e. "child". This is a pivot away from the term *"ανήλικος"* ("juvenile") which dominates both Greek legislation in general and the GPC specifically. We have used the term "children" in our translation, thus adhering to the term used in the ST, but consider this word choice worthy of pointing out, and the TT reads as follows:

    "Solicitation of **<u>children</u>** for sexual purposes".

- Article 236(3):

    "Διευθυντής επιχείρησης ή άλλο πρόσωπο που έχει την εξουσία λήψης αποφάσεων ή ελέγχου σε επιχείρηση τιμωρείται με φυλάκιση έως δύο (2) έτη ή χρηματική ποινή, αν η πράξη ***<u>δεν τιμωρείται βαρύτερα</u>****, αν με παραβίαση συγκεκριμένου καθήκοντος επιμέλειας, δεν απέτρεψε [...]"*

    Article 237(3):

    "Διευθυντής επιχείρησης ή άλλο πρόσωπο που έχει την εξουσία λήψης αποφάσεων ή ελέγχου σε επιχείρηση τιμωρείται με φυλάκιση και χρηματική ποινή, εφόσον η πράξη ***<u>δεν τιμωρείται βαρύτερα από άλλη ποινική διάταξη</u>****, αν με παραβίαση συγκεκριμένου καθήκοντος επιμέλειας, δεν απέτρεψε [...]"*

We consider this an inverse example of odd word choice. In this case, we have the odd absence of a phrase used elsewhere. The text used in both these Articles is virtually the same, but the second example adds a qualifier that is absent from the first one. We have rendered the highlighted phrases in accordance with the Greek text, but considered this worthy of pointing out:

Article 236(3):

"[...] unless the act carries a heavier punishment."

Article 237(3):

"[...] unless the act carries a heavier punishment under a different criminal law provision."

d) Polysemic terms

Perhaps the most egregious problem facing translators from Greek into English is the plethora of polysemic terms to convey often completely unrelated concepts. There are numerous examples we could cite, but for the purpose of saving space and illustrating the issue, we will note but seven:

- *Ποινή*

  This term, most usually translated as "penalty" or "punishment", caused us much trepidation in our translation of the code. Article 50 unequivocally stipulates there are three types of punishments: sentences where one is deprived of one's liberty (custodial sentences), fines (monetary penalties), and community service. Given that the various Articles of the GPC provide for different punishments for different crimes or variations thereof, depending on the circumstances of commission, or even provide for combinations of punishments (i.e. both a custodial sentence and a monetary penalty), we have opted to use the term "punishment" as the hypernym when there is no qualification in the ST and each of the three terms given above ("custodial sentence", "monetary penalty" and "community service"), depending on the wording of the ST.

- *Δικαίωμα*

  Depending on the context, this noun can mean "right", as translated in Article 114, or an "amount payable", as translated in Article 244.

- *Κατάστημα*

  This term most commonly means a shop or store (Article 189(1)). However, depending on context, it may mean a medical facility (Article 343(c)), a reformative institution for juveniles (Article 18) or a custodial institution (Article 99(6)).

- *Κατάσχεση*

  This term is one of the most complicated issues we had to address. In our translation of the Code of Criminal Procedure, it was clear that this concerned "seizure" of things. However, in a civil context, we considered the term "attachment" more appropriate (Article 707 of the Code of Civil Procedure). This comes with two provisos. The first concerns "*κατάσχεση εις χείρας τρίτου*", which has been rendered as "garnishment" and is applicable when the thing to be attached is in the possession of a third party, e.g., money held in a bank account, where the third party is the bank. The second concerns ships and aircraft, where, under the international treaties and conventions signed by Greece, the appropriate term is "arrest" (Article 709 of the Code of Civil Procedure). In the context of the GPC, however, it is used in Article 177 to describe all the aforesaid cases, as violation of either seizure or attachment or arrest constitutes a crime. We have therefore included all three options in our translation.

- *Νόθευση*

This highly polysemic term caused us concern as it is used in Article 139 to denote alteration of evidence, in Articles 158 and 164 to denote falsification of election results, and in Article 209, 242 and 243 to denote alteration of intangible payment instruments, public documents and court documents, respectively. However, it is also used in verb form in Article 207 concerning counterfeiting currency. In this context, we have rendered it once again as “to alter”, but with the clarification that this involves increasing the value of currency, e.g., adding a zero to a bank note to change its value from 10 to 100, or gilding a coin in order to create the impression that it is made of gold and therefore has a higher value[20].

- *Κατοχή*

This term is used in different senses in different Articles of the GPC. In Article 372 concerning theft, it is used in the broadest sense of lawful possession of a thing, where one is deprived of such, whereas in Articles 146 and 187A it refers to unlawful possession, information in the former and weapons in the latter. Additionally, in Article 169A, it refers to possession in the civil-law context as a type of ownership right. Lastly, in Article 143 it refers to the occupation of Greek territory by enemy forces in times of war. Thus, prudence is required in order to identify the correct meaning of the term based on the legal context referred to in the source text and to provide a proper rendering in the target text.

- *Πραγματογνωμοσύνη*

This term denotes both expert evidence presented verbally in court (as used in Article 226), as well as expert evidence reports submitted in writing (as used in Articles 69A(4), 82, 265A(1), etc.)

e) Acronyms, official translations and names of entities

Whenever we encountered acronyms, e.g., “*ΦΕΚ*” (Government Gazette Issue), “*ΠΚ*” (Penal Code), etc., we chose not to use existing or create new acronyms in English, but rather to type out the full translation of the term being abbreviated, both in order to save readers from having to consult a table of abbreviations and acronyms and for reasons of clarity. In any event, it should be noted that the number of acronyms used in the GPC is very low[21]. Additionally, we are happy to report that we found no issues concerning the official translations (such as that of the Hellenic Constitution, other than the one noted on page xxx of this Foreword), as discussed in our translation of the Greek Code of Private Maritime Law[22].

As regards names of entities, one example concerns the name of the Ministry of Justice and its respective Minister. They both appears as “*Υπουργός*” (i.e. Minister) and “*Υπουργείο*” (i.e. Ministry) “*Δικαιοσύνης*” (i.e. of Justice), e.g., in Articles 81(3), 105(2), 122(3), 123(2), but in the First Article of Law 4619/2019 containing the Penal Code, it appears as “*Δικαιοσύνης, Διαφάνειας και Ανθρωπίνων Δικαιωμάτων*” (i.e. of Justice, Transparency and Human Rights), the name of the Ministry at the time. We consider this an example of failing to keep up with the ever-changing name of Greek Ministries and their respective Ministers, a separate problem unto itself, as discussed in our Foreword to the translation of the Greek Code of Private Maritime Law[23].

20 Tsamopoulos, A., ‘The Crimes of Counterfeiting of Currency and Other Payment Instruments after Law 4947/2022’, 2023, (in Greek) available at https://ikee.lib.auth.gr/record/348182/files/GRI-2023-39433.pdf

21 Op. cit. fn 11.

22 Webber, D., O’Shea, J., The Greek Code of Private Maritime Law, 2023, Lex Graeca, p. 23.

23 *Ibid.*, p. 18.

Another example concerns the terms used to describe prisons. The term *"σωφρονιστικό κατάστημα"* ("correctional institution") appears several times throughout the text and was the staple term used in the Correctional Code after it was overhauled pursuant to Law 4985/2022, which changed almost all instances of the previous term used, *"κατάστημα κράτησης"* (which we have chosen to render as "custodial institution"), to the aforesaid term, *"σωφρονιστικό κατάστημα"*. However, the "old" term has not been replaced throughout the GPC, as it appears as such in Articles 71(3) and 105(1). The issue is compounded by the use of the term *"φυλακή"* ("prison") in the GPC, e.g., in Articles 65(2), 110(1), 173(1) and 174(1)(b). Moreover, all three terms appear and are used virtually interchangeably in the Correctional Code, as will be discussed in the Foreword of our forthcoming publication of our translation of the Correctional Code.

f) Elegant variation - Euphemisms

The first part of this category stands in contrast to the previous category. Whereas before we were facing a single term having several possible meanings, we now have to consider the problem of several terms being used interchangeably, often within the same Article of the Code, but with their meaning remaining unaltered. This might well be an example of elegant variation, as defined by the brothers Fowler in the early 20th century, but in legal texts, in particular, one cannot but wonder if employing this strategy could cause more harm than good. There are numerous examples to be found in the GPC. With a view towards producing a readable and easified translation, we have made the following translational choices, depending on context:

- *"άσκηση"* and *"κίνηση"* both mean initiation/institution of proceedings;
- *"διαδικασία"* and *"δίκη"* both mean trial/proceedings;
- *"ανασταλτική δύναμη"* and *"αναστέλλουσα ισχύς"* both mean suspensive effect;
- *"αρμόδιος για την έκτιση της ποινής εισαγγελέας"* and *"εισαγγελέας εκτέλεσης ποινών"* both mean public prosecutor competent for the enforcement of sentences;
- *"δικαστικά έξοδα"* and *"δικαστικές δαπάνες"* both mean "court costs";
- *"πράξη ή παράλειψη"* and *"ενέργεια ή παράλειψη"* both mean "act or omission";
- *"περιουσιακά αγαθά"*, *"περιουσιακά στοιχεία"* and *"στοιχεία περιουσίας"* all mean "assets";
- *"ένδεια"* and *"απορία"* both mean "poverty";
- *"απείθεια"* and *"ανυπακοή"* both mean "disobedience" (in the context of this Code; in the Code of Criminal Procedure the former is best rendered as "contempt" of the court).
- *"εθνικότητα"* and *"ιθαγένεια"* both mean "nationality";
- *"παθών"*, *"θύμα"* and *"ζημιωθείς"* all mean "victim";
- *"διάπραξη"* and *"τέλεση"* both mean "commission" of a crime;
- *"παροχή κοινωφελούς εργασίας"* and *"προσφορά κοινωφελούς εργασίας"* both mean community service;
- *"νοσοκομείο"* and *"νοσοκομειακό ίδρυμα"* both mean "hospital";
- *"θεραπευτικό μέτρο"* and *"μέτρο θεραπείας"* both mean "therapeutic measure";
- *"δράστης"*, *"αυτουργός"* and *"φυσικός αυτουργός"* all mean "perpetrator"

As evident above, our solution was to use a single term when faced with such synonymous usage, so as to streamline both our translation and the glossaries.

The second part of this category concerns the use of euphemism throughout the GPC. Examples include various grammatical forms of the following terms:

- *"απομάκρυνση"* ("removal"): this term appears in Article 72(4)(b) and euphemistically refers to deportation, which, as already noted, is curious, given that the heading of the Article in question indeed reads "Deportation of foreign nationals".
- *"πρόσκληση"* ("invitation", most commonly in Modern Greek): this verb is often used when one is "invited" by an authority to do something, e.g., in Article 169. Depending on context, though, this "invitation" may be a euphemism and the intended meaning is far stricter: this is a command issued that compels one to do something. In the example in question, one is lawfully "requested" to provide a service or assistance required by law to a "state employee" (as defined in Article 13 of the GPC and discussed in this Foreword) or allow them entrance, which is why refusing to do so carries the punishment provided for in Article 169.
- *"ανήθικες ασχολίες"* ("immoral activities"): this phrase, appearing in Article 324(2), concerns juveniles who have been removed from the custody of their legitimate carers and have been involved in such activities. Given the often insalubrious nature of the provisions of the GPC, one is struck by the use of such a generic term, which we consider a euphemism and which refers to activities that could impinge on the morality of a juvenile, ranging from sex work to employment in an illegal gambling club[24].
- *"μεταβολή οικογενειακής τάξης"* (literally: "altering one's family status/order"). This phrase, also appearing in Article 324(2), refers to unlawfully putting a child up for adoption, as noted in Supreme Court case-law[25]. Given the generic wording, we consider this another example of euphemism.

Finally, a further issue that is compounded by the combination of all the above issues (a meta-issue, perhaps) is the fact that consulting or reproducing our translation of the Code without referring to the introduction for a better understanding, if not resolution, of the translational issues we faced, could result in risk.

Implicit Legal Knowledge

Having highlighted the issues above, this section explores what, to a large extent, is a solution to a great many of those issues: successfully identifying (and, if necessary, drawing out) the legal knowledge that lies behind the plain face of the words on the page, ensuring that the meaning of the words can be accurately conveyed. Whereas procedural law provisions tend to map out the steps that need to be followed in a legal process, substantive law provisions are often shorter, terser and more definitive/prescriptive, stating a generally applicable rule. This results in a situation where it is taken as read that many legal concepts are (to be) understood by the reader without any further clarification on the part of the legislator.

Some examples of such implicit legal knowledge (and how it impacts the translation solutions provided) are set out below to facilitate English speakers who might not be familiar with the Greek legal system or Greek reality.

24 Georgiadou, N., 'Child Abduction, Article 324 of the Penal Code', 2012, (in Greek) available at: https://repo.lib.duth.gr/jspui/bitstream/123456789/15585/1/GeorgiadouN_2012.pdf

25 https://www.areiospagos.gr/nomologia/apofaseis_DISPLAY.asp?cd=3CJMXBIBGFILY0JBJ7A9GK7VVWTCRJ

- Article 13 provides definitions for several concepts used throughout the GPC. However, the first two subparagraphs provide for two terms where additional knowledge is both implicit (in the first case) and explicit (in the second).
    - More specifically, the first subparagraph provides a definition for the term *"υπάλληλος"*, which would literally be translated as "employee". Given the text of the subparagraph, though, one might readily consider translating the term as "civil servant", as the term means "any person who has been lawfully entrusted, even temporarily, with performing a public, municipal or community function or a function within a different body governed by public law". Nevertheless, following discussions with eminent jurists, we came to understand that this category includes persons employed even on a seasonal and not permanent basis, e.g., seasonal firefighters, who would not be considered "civil servants", where there is a connotation of permanence of employment. We have thus rendered the term in question "state employee".
    - The second subparagraph provides a definition for the term *"οικείος"*, which, as already noted earlier in the Vocabulary section of the Foreword, has been translated as "related party". This choice was made because, as explicitly stated in the second subparagraph, the Greek concept certainly refers to relatives, but also includes persons not related by blood or affinity to another person, e.g., their tutors or probation officers in cases of juveniles. Furthermore, it also extends to former spouses, who, under Greek law, are considered one's relatives. Additionally, broader interpretations of the term have been encountered, where it included, for example, godparents and godchildren. We considered this translational choice necessary as the term "relative" would usually denote a degree of relation based on an existing relationship by blood or marriage and would be excessively restrictive.
- Article 43(2) refers to impossible attempts to commit a crime due to *"ευήθεια"*, a term normally translated as "foolishness" or "feeble-mindedness", e.g., attempting to kill another through use of pins inserted into a voodoo doll, i.e. a situation where any reasonable person of average experience would understand that such an attempt is impossible. A similar provision can be found in the German PC (Article 23(3) - *"grober Unverstand"*). Having discussed the matter with jurists and consulted the exceptional dissertation by Grekidis[26] on the matter, as well as Supreme Court case-law[27], we have rendered the term in question as "naivety", considering that the term covers all cases where this Article would apply.
- In Article 148(2), we see reference being made to either "incarceration of up to 10 years" or, disjunctively, "incarceration" without any further qualifier. In this instance, we have to refer back to Articles 51 and 52. The former Article provides for the categories of custodial sentences and distinguishes between *"κάθειρξη"* and *"φυλάκιση"* for adults. As already noted, faced with the need to distinguish between the two, we adopted the convention of rendering the former as "incarceration" and the latter as "imprisonment". The latter Article provides for incarceration specifically, explicitly distinguishes between "incarceration for life" and "fixed-term incarceration" in paragraph 1, and lays down time-limits for fixed-term incarceration as no shorter than 5 and no longer than 20 years. Moving back to Article 148(2), and applying this knowledge, we come to understand that in the event of espionage during wartime, the sentence to be imposed is left at the discretion of the judge, since no time qualifier is provided, and, while no maximum limit is set, it is implicit that the minimum duration of the custodial sentence to be imposed will be 5 years.

---

26 Grekidis, K., 'Impossible Attempt: A Critical Approach to Criminalisation of Risk-Free Attempt and Article 43 of the PC', 2016, (in Greek) available at https://ikee.lib.auth.gr/record/286243/files/GRI-2016-17998.pdf

27 https://www.areiospagos.gr/nomologia/apofaseis_DISPLAY.asp?cd=PaTUc6nCjGvAyKfljrx7VBHPvERB5Y

- Article 68(1) concerning confiscation makes reference to mixed/intermixed things, as provided for in Article 1057 to 1060 of the Civil Code. We used both terms, as this will be the convention we will be adhering to in our forthcoming translation of the Civil Code, where the distinction concerns solids and liquids. This is why the relevant words appear inside square brackets.
- Article 68(5) employs the phrase *"οικείες βιοτικές σχέσεις"*, which, translated literally, would read "the relevant life relationships". This could lead to confusion for the reader, implying that there is some sort of relationship between the persons entering into transactions. Following consultation of article-by-article analyses of the PC and discussions with jurists, we have rendered this phrase as "in [the normal course of such transactions]" using explicitation to tease out the implicit meaning.
- Article 110A(3) includes the phrase "If the convicted person works" with no further qualifier. This does not mean that a convict holds a specific job outside of a prison context for which they receive pay, but that they work at the custodial institution where they are being held, e.g., in the library or other facility within the institution.
- Article 191A uses the term *"χώροι φύλαξης νεκρών"*, literally translating to "places for storing/guarding/safekeeping the dead". Given Greek funerary customs, which often include holding a wake at the deceased person's home and/or keeping them in viewing rooms at cemeteries before the religious ceremony takes place, one might wonder whether these spaces are included in the provisions of this Article. Following discussions with jurists, we came to understand that it does not include homes, only facilities objectively intended for safekeeping bodies, such as mortuaries and morgues. We have chosen to render this term simply as "mortuaries" but wanted to draw the attention of readers to the nuances of the concept.
- Chapter X of Book II, encompassing Articles 216 to 223, bears the heading *"Εγκλήματα σχετικά με τα υπομνήματα"*, which, translated literally, would read "Crimes in relation to memoranda". However, the aforementioned Articles concern specific documents such as certificates (217), attestations (220) and medical certificates (221), as well as documents in general (222). Given the broad nature of the term being used, and taking into consideration the definition of *"υπομνήματα"* ("memoranda") as "public documents attesting to a true fact"[28] and the fact that the term overlaps with but is not completely identical to the definition of "document" provided in Article 13[29], we have rendered the term *"υπομνήματα"* as "[documents]" within explicitation brackets.
- Article 229(3) mentions a "special register" which is not referred to anywhere else in the Article in question (or, in fact, anywhere else in the GPC). We must refer to extraneous knowledge to ascertain which register is meant. Having consulted jurists and Supreme Court case-law[30], this must be the special register provided for in Article 473 of the Code of Criminal Procedure.
- Article 288(2) employs the term *"δυστύχημα"*. It is an unofficial rule in modern Greek that the term *"ατύχημα"* is used for a non-fatal accident, whereas *"δυστύχημα"* is used for fatal accidents. Having consulted jurists, we were informed that in legal terms *"δυστύχημα"* does not actually require a death to be involved, but there must be a serious dimension, e.g., life-threatening injuries, disfigurement or maiming. Given this consideration, we have chosen to render the term as "serious accident".

---

28 Apergi, D., 'The Crime of Forgery and Related Problems of Concurrence', 2010, (in Greek) available at https://repo.lib.duth.gr/jspui/bitstream/123456789/15461/1/ApergiD_2010.pdf

29 *Ibid.*

30 https://www.areiospagos.gr/nomologia/apofaseis_DISPLAY.asp?cd=55HANSDNUMXX9QJF3JL83H8503FP6A

- Article 300 on compassionate homicide uses the phrase *"σπουδαία και επίμονη απαίτηση"*, which, translated literally, would read "significant/important and persistent request". The first adjective, *"σπουδαία"*, means "serious", in the sense that the person requesting that their life be taken is so convinced and serious in their intention that they are not just making such a request when in abject pain and facing an inescapable death, but repeating the request even when such pain subsides and they are clear of mind and serious of intent. We therefore decided that "serious" would be the best candidate for rendering this term.
- Article 375 makes reference to the concepts of *"εντολοδόχος"*, *"επίτροπος"* and *"κηδεμόνας"*, translated as "mandatary", "tutor" and "custodian", respectively. All the terms are drawn from the Civil Code, the former covered in Articles 719 to 730 and the latter in Articles 813 et seq. The term *"κηδεμόνας"* is frequently used in everyday and legal Greek to denote a child's legal guardian, but does not appear in the Civil Code or other family law statutes, to the best of our knowledge. The information implicit in this instance is that the term refers to *"κηδεμόνας σχολάζουσας κληρονομίας"*, or "custodian of an unclaimed estate", as provided for in the aforesaid Articles of the Civil Code. Therefore, readers ought to consult our forthcoming translation of the Civil Code or consult a Greek lawyer for a better understanding of these concepts.
- Article 390(1) on breach of trust provides for *"βέβαιη ζημία"*, which, translated literally, would read "assured/certain damage". The adjective used has rightly caused consternation among jurists due to its vagueness and polysemy, and several texts[31] have been published precisely on this very term. Various interpretations are put forward by jurists, particularly on the basis of recent jurisprudence since the new GPC was enacted. We have erred on the side of caution and adopted a rendering ("certain") that is in line with the opinion espoused by experts on the matter.

Final Remarks

We hope this book proves to be a useful, practical resource for readers and another step on the long road towards producing authoritative translations of the main codes of the Greek legal system. Any errors remain our own, and we welcome any comments and feedback regarding our work.

31 See, for instance, Delidimos, N., 'Basic Concepts of Criminal Law under revision. Case-law vis-a-vis the Law?', lecture at the National School of Judges, 2024, (in Greek) available at https://www.esdi.gr/wp-content/uploads/2024/07/delidimos_2024.pdf; Delidimos, N., Crimes Against Assets under the Provisions in Force', lecture at the National School of Judges, 2020, (in Greek) available at https://www.esdi.gr/nex/images/stories/pdf/epimorfosi/2020/delidimos_2020.pdf; Choursoglou, S., '"Certain" Damage in the Crime of Breach of Trust under the New PC', *Nova Criminalia,* Issue 11, 2020, (in Greek) available at https://hcba.gr/novacriminalia/285/

δεῖν δὲ τοὺς ὀρθῶς πολιτευομένους οὐ τὰς στοὰς ἐμπιπλάναι γραμμάτων, ἀλλ᾽ ἐν ταῖς ψυχαῖς ἔχειν τὸ δίκαιον

Isocrates, Areopagiticus, 41

ΝΟΜΟΣ ΥΠ' ΑΡΙΘΜ. 4619 Τεύχος Α' 95/11.06.2019

Κύρωση του Ποινικού Κώδικα.

Ο ΠΡΟΕΔΡΟΣ ΤΗΣ ΕΛΛΗΝΙΚΗΣ ΔΗΜΟΚΡΑΤΙΑΣ

Εκδίδομε τον ακόλουθο νόμο που ψήφισε η Βουλή:

Άρθρο πρώτο

Κυρώνεται σύμφωνα με το άρθρο 76 παρ. 6 του Συντάγματος ο Ποινικός Κώδικας, ο οποίος συντάχθηκε από τη νομοπαρασκευαστική επιτροπή που συγκροτήθηκε κατ' εξουσιοδότηση του άρθρου 74 παρ. 1α του ν. 4139/2013 «Νόμος περί εξαρτησιογόνων ουσιών και άλλες διατάξεις» (Α΄74), με την απόφαση 38882/18.5.2015 (ΦΕΚ τ. ΥΟΔΔ 375/26.5.2015) του Υπουργού Δικαιοσύνης, Διαφάνειας και Ανθρωπίνων Δικαιωμάτων, όπως αυτή τροποποιήθηκε με την απόφαση 80884/Φ.279/8.11.2018 (ΦΕΚ τ.ΥΟΔΔ 676/15.11.2018) και συμπληρώθηκε με διαδοχικές αποφάσεις του ίδιου Υπουργού, και έχει ως εξής:

LAW No 4619, GOVERNMENT GAZETTE, Series I, Issue 95/11.06.2019

Ratification of the Penal Code.

THE PRESIDENT OF THE HELLENIC REPUBLIC

We hereby promulgate the following law passed by Parliament:

First Article

The Penal Code, which was drawn up by the legislative drafting committee established pursuant to Article 74(1a) of Law 4139/2013 concerning addictive substances and other provisions (Government Gazette, Series I, Issue 74), by means of Decision No 38882/18.5.2015 of the Minister of Justice, Transparency and Human Rights (Government Gazette, Special Officials and Management Positions of Public Sector and Wider Public Sector Bodies Bulletin, Issue 375/26.5.2015), as amended by Decision No 80884/Φ.279/8.11.2018 (Government Gazette, Special Officials and Management Positions of Public Sector and Wider Public Sector Bodies Bulletin, Issue 676/15.11.2018) and supplemented by subsequent decisions of that same Minister, is hereby ratified in accordance with Article 76(6) of the Constitution, and reads as follows:

ΠΟΙΝΙΚΟΣ ΚΩΔΙΚΑΣ

ΠΡΩΤΟ ΒΙΒΛΙΟ

ΓΕΝΙΚΟ ΜΕΡΟΣ

ΠΡΩΤΟ ΚΕΦΑΛΑΙΟ

Ο ΠΟΙΝΙΚΟΣ ΝΟΜΟΣ

I

ΒΑΣΙΚΕΣ ΑΡΧΕΣ

Άρθρο 1
Καμία ποινή χωρίς νόμο

Έγκλημα δεν υπάρχει χωρίς νόμο που να ισχύει πριν από την τέλεση της πράξης και να ορίζει τα στοιχεία της καθώς και την επιβλητέα γι' αυτή ποινή.

Άρθρο 2
Αναδρομική ισχύς του ηπιότερου νόμου

1. Αν από την τέλεση της πράξης ως την αμετάκλητη εκδίκασή της ίσχυσαν περισσότερες διατάξεις νόμων, εφαρμόζεται αυτή που στη συγκεκριμένη περίπτωση οδηγεί στην ευμενέστερη μεταχείριση του κατηγορουμένου.
2. Αν μεταγενέστερος νόμος χαρακτήρισε την πράξη μη αξιόποινη (ανέγκλητη), παύει η εκτέλεση της ποινής που επιβλήθηκε καθώς και τα ποινικά επακόλουθά της, όπως και η εκτέλεση των μέτρων ασφαλείας.

Άρθρα 3 - 4

(Καταργούνται)

II

ΤΟΠΙΚΑ ΟΡΙΑ ΙΣΧΥΟΣ ΤΩΝ ΠΟΙΝΙΚΩΝ ΝΟΜΩΝ

Άρθρο 5
Εγκλήματα που τελέστηκαν στην ημεδαπή

1. Οι ελληνικοί ποινικοί νόμοι εφαρμόζονται σε όλες τις πράξεις που τελέστηκαν στο έδαφος της επικράτειας, ακόμη και από αλλοδαπούς. Επίσης εφαρμόζονται και στις πράξεις συμμετοχής που τελέστηκαν στο έδαφος της ελληνικής επικράτειας, αν η κύρια πράξη, για την οποία δεν υπάρχει δικαιοδοσία των ελληνικών ποινικών δικαστηρίων, είναι αξιόποινη και κατά τους ελληνικούς ποινικούς νόμους.
2. Οι ελληνικοί ποινικοί νόμοι εφαρμόζονται σε πράξεις που τελούνται σε πλοία που φέρουν την ελληνική σημαία ή αεροσκάφη που έχουν την ελληνική εθνικότητα ανεξάρτητα από το δίκαιο του τόπου τέλεσης αυτών.

PENAL CODE

BOOK I

GENERAL PART

CHAPTER I

PENAL LAW

I

BASIC PRINCIPLES

Article 1
No punishment without law

There is no crime without a law in force prior to the commission of the act prescribing the constituent elements of the act and the punishment it carries.

Article 2
Retroactive effect of the *lex mitior*

1. If, between the commission of an act and its irrevocable adjudication, several statutory provisions were in force, the law which would result in the defendant being treated more favourably applies.
2. If a subsequent law classified the act as non-punishable, the enforcement of the punishment imposed, its penal consequences and the enforcement of security measures shall be terminated.

Articles 3 - 4

[Repealed]

II

TERRITORIAL LIMITS OF THE FORCE OF PENAL LAWS

Article 5
Crimes committed in [Greece]

1. Greek penal laws apply to all acts committed within the territory [of Greece], even if committed by foreign nationals. They also apply to participatory acts committed within the territory of [Greece] if the main act for which the Greek criminal courts lack jurisdiction is also punishable under Greek penal laws.
2. Greek penal laws apply to acts committed on ships flying the Greek flag or aircraft with Greek nationality, irrespective of the law of the place where such acts were committed.

Άρθρο 6
Εγκλήματα ημεδαπών στην αλλοδαπή

1. Οι ελληνικοί ποινικοί νόμοι εφαρμόζονται και για πράξη που χαρακτηρίζεται από αυτούς ως κακούργημα ή πλημμέλημα και τελέστηκε στην αλλοδαπή από ημεδαπό, αν αυτή, με τα συγκεκριμένα χαρακτηριστικά της, είναι αξιόποινη και κατά τους νόμους της χώρας στην οποία τελέστηκε ή αν διαπράχθηκε σε πολιτειακά ασύντακτη χώρα.
2. Η ποινική δίωξη ασκείται και εναντίον αλλοδαπού, ο οποίος κατά την τέλεση της πράξης ήταν ημεδαπός. Επίσης ασκείται και εναντίον εκείνου που απέκτησε την ελληνική ιθαγένεια μετά την τέλεση της πράξης.
3. Στα πλημμελήματα, ακόμη και όταν διώκονται αυτεπαγγέλτως, οι διατάξεις των προηγούμενων παραγράφων εφαρμόζονται μόνο εφόσον υπάρχει έγκληση του παθόντος ή αίτηση της Κυβέρνησης της χώρας όπου τελέστηκε το πλημμέλημα.

Άρθρο 7
Εγκλήματα αλλοδαπών στην αλλοδαπή

1. Οι ελληνικοί ποινικοί νόμοι εφαρμόζονται και κατά αλλοδαπού για πράξη που τελέστηκε στην αλλοδαπή και χαρακτηρίζεται από αυτούς ως κακούργημα ή πλημμέλημα, αν η πράξη αυτή στρέφεται εναντίον Έλληνα πολίτη και είναι αξιόποινη, με τα συγκεκριμένα χαρακτηριστικά της, και κατά τους νόμους της χώρας όπου τελέστηκε ή αν διαπράχθηκε σε πολιτειακά ασύντακτη χώρα. Ως Έλληνας πολίτης για την εφαρμογή του προηγούμενου εδαφίου λογίζεται και το κυοφορούμενο που θα αποκτήσει με τη γέννησή του την ελληνική ιθαγένεια, καθώς και τα νομικά πρόσωπα που εδρεύουν στην ημεδαπή.
2. Η διάταξη της παρ. 3 του προηγούμενου άρθρου έχει και εδώ εφαρμογή.

Άρθρο 8
Εγκλήματα στην αλλοδαπή που τιμωρούνται πάντοτε κατά τους ελληνικούς νόμους

Οι ελληνικοί ποινικοί νόμοι εφαρμόζονται σε ημεδαπούς και αλλοδαπούς, ανεξάρτητα από τους νόμους του τόπου τέλεσης, για τις εξής πράξεις που τελέστηκαν στην αλλοδαπή:
α) εσχάτη προδοσία ή προσβολές της διεθνούς υπόστασης της Χώρας σε βάρος του ελληνικού κράτους,
β) εγκλήματα που αφορούν τη στρατιωτική υπηρεσία και την υποχρέωση στράτευσης στην Ελλάδα,
γ) αξιόποινη πράξη που τέλεσαν ως υπάλληλοι του ελληνικού κράτους, ή οργάνου ή οργανισμού της Ευρωπαϊκής Ένωσης που έχει την έδρα του στην Ελλάδα,
δ) δα) πράξη που στρέφεται εναντίον υπαλλήλου του ελληνικού κράτους ή Έλληνα υπαλλήλου οργάνου ή οργανισμού της Ευρωπαϊκής Ένωσης ή δημόσιου διεθνούς ή υπερεθνικού οργανισμού ή φορέα ή απευθύνεται προς αυτούς, εφόσον τελείται κατά την άσκηση της υπηρεσίας τους ή σε σχέση με την άσκηση των καθηκόντων τους, δβ) δωροδοκία προσώπου που ασκεί δημόσιο λειτούργημα ή υπηρεσία για ξένη χώρα,
ε) ψευδή κατάθεση σε διαδικασία που εκκρεμεί στις ελληνικές αρχές,
στ) τρομοκρατικές πράξεις,
ζ) πειρατεία,
η) εγκλήματα σχετικά με το νόμισμα και τα μέσα πληρωμής πλην των μετρητών,
θ) παράνομη εμπορία ναρκωτικών,
ι) εμπορία ανθρώπων,
ια) κάθε άλλο έγκλημα, για το οποίο ειδικές διατάξεις ή διεθνείς συμβάσεις υπογραμμένες και επικυρωμένες από το ελληνικό κράτος προβλέπουν την εφαρμογή των ελληνικών ποινικών νόμων.

Article 6
Crimes committed abroad by Greek nationals

1. Greek penal laws also apply to any act which such laws classify as a felony or misdemeanour and which was committed abroad by a Greek national if such act, given its specific characteristics, is also punishable under the laws of the country where it was committed, or if it was committed in a country with no constitution.

2. Criminal prosecution shall also be initiated against any foreigner who, at the time the act was committed, was a Greek national. Criminal prosecution shall also be initiated against any person who acquired Greek nationality after the time the act was committed.

3. The provisions of the preceding paragraphs apply to misdemeanours, even when they are subject to public prosecution, only if the victim has filed a victim-initiated complaint or if requested by the government of the country where the misdemeanour was committed.

Article 7
Crimes committed abroad by foreign nationals

1. Greek penal laws also apply to any foreign national in respect of any act which such laws classify as a felony or misdemeanour and which was committed abroad if such act was committed against a Greek citizen and, given its specific characteristics, is also punishable under the laws of the country where it was committed, or if it was committed in a country with no constitution. For the purposes of applying the preceding sentence, an unborn child who will acquire Greek nationality upon being born and legal persons with registered offices in [Greece] shall also be deemed to be Greek citizens.

2. The provisions of paragraph 3 of the preceding Article shall also apply in such a case.

Article 8
Crimes committed abroad which are always punishable under Greek law

Greek penal laws apply to Greek and foreign nationals with regard to the following acts committed abroad, irrespective of the laws of the place where such acts were committed:

a) high treason or offences against the international status of [Greece] impacting the Greek state;

b) crimes concerning military service and the obligation to join the Greek armed forces;

c) punishable acts committed in the capacity of an employee of the Greek state or an agency or organisation of the European Union seated in Greece;

d) da) acts committed against or directed towards an employee of the Greek state or a Greek employee of an agency or organisation of the European Union or a public international or supranational organisation or body, provided such acts are committed while or in relation to performing their duties; db) active bribery of a person performing a public function or service for a foreign country;

e) false testimony in proceedings pending before the Greek authorities;

f) terrorist acts;

g) piracy;

h) crimes concerning currency and non-cash payment instruments;

i) illegal drug trafficking;

j) human trafficking;

k) any other crime to which Greek penal laws apply under specific provisions or international treaties and conventions signed and ratified by the Greek state.

Άρθρο 9

Ακαταδίωκτο εγκλημάτων που τελέστηκαν στην αλλοδαπή

1. Η ποινική δίωξη για πράξη που τελέστηκε στην αλλοδαπή αποκλείεται:

α) αν ο υπαίτιος δικάστηκε για την πράξη αυτή στην αλλοδαπή και αθωώθηκε ή αν, σε περίπτωση που καταδικάστηκε, έχει εκτίσει ή εκτίει νομίμως την ποινή του,

β) αν, σύμφωνα με τον αλλοδαπό νόμο, η πράξη έχει παραγραφεί ή η ποινή που επιβλήθηκε έχει παραγραφεί ή έχει χαριστεί,

γ) αν, σύμφωνα με τον αλλοδαπό νόμο, χρειάζεται έγκληση για τη δίωξη της πράξης και τέτοια έγκληση είτε δεν υποβλήθηκε είτε ανακλήθηκε.

2. Η προηγούμενη παράγραφος δεν ισχύει για τις πράξεις που ορίζει το άρθρο 8.

3. Η ποινική δίωξη αποκλείεται αν έχει εκδοθεί οριστική απόφαση για την ίδια πράξη από δικαστήριο κράτους μέλους της Ευρωπαϊκής Ένωσης.

Άρθρο 10

Υπολογισμός ποινών που εκτίθηκαν στην αλλοδαπή

Η ποινή που εκτίθηκε ολικά ή μερικά στην αλλοδαπή, αν επακολουθήσει καταδίκη στην ημεδαπή για την ίδια πράξη, αφαιρείται από την ποινή που επέβαλαν τα ελληνικά δικαστήρια.

Άρθρο 11

Αναγνώριση αλλοδαπών ποινικών αποφάσεων

1. Αν Έλληνας καταδικαστεί στην αλλοδαπή για πράξη που, σύμφωνα με τις διατάξεις των ημεδαπών νόμων, συνεπάγεται παρεπόμενες ποινές, το αρμόδιο δικαστήριο των πλημμελειοδικών μπορεί να επιβάλει τις ποινές αυτές.

2. Το αρμόδιο δικαστήριο των πλημμελειοδικών μπορεί επίσης να επιβάλει τα μέτρα ασφάλειας που προβλέπουν οι ελληνικοί νόμοι σε όποιον καταδικάστηκε ή αθωώθηκε στην αλλοδαπή.

3. Οι διατάξεις των προηγούμενων παραγράφων δεν ισχύουν στην περίπτωση του άρθρου 9 παρ. 3.

III

ΣΧΕΣΗ ΤΟΥ ΚΩΔΙΚΑ ΜΕ ΤΟΥΣ ΕΙΔΙΚΟΥΣ ΝΟΜΟΥΣ ΚΑΙ ΕΠΕΞΗΓΗΣΗ ΟΡΩΝ

Άρθρο 12

Ειδικοί ποινικοί νόμοι

Οι διατάξεις του γενικού μέρους του Ποινικού Κώδικα εφαρμόζονται και σε αξιόποινες πράξεις που προβλέπονται σε ειδικούς νόμους, αν οι νόμοι αυτοί δεν ορίζουν διαφορετικά με ρητή διάταξή τους.

Article 9

Non-prosecution of crimes committed abroad

1. Criminal prosecution of an act committed abroad is precluded if:

a) the culpable person was tried abroad for the act in question and was acquitted or, if convicted, is serving or has fully served their sentence;

b) if, according to the foreign law [in question], the act or the punishment imposed has become time-barred or a pardon has been granted;

c) if, according to the foreign law [in question], a victim-initiated complaint is required for the act to be prosecuted, and such a complaint was either not submitted or was withdrawn.

2. The preceding paragraph does not apply to the acts provided for in Article 8.

3. Criminal prosecution is precluded if a court of a European Union Member State has handed down a final judgment regarding the same act.

Article 10

Calculation of sentences served abroad

Any sentence served abroad, whether in whole or in part, if followed by a conviction in [Greece] for the same act, shall be deducted from the sentence imposed by the Greek courts.

Article 11

Recognition of foreign criminal judgments

1. If a Greek national is convicted abroad for an act which, under [Greek] statutory provisions, carries ancillary punishments, the competent court of misdemeanours may impose such punishments.

2. The competent court of misdemeanours may also impose the security measures provided for in Greek law on any person convicted or acquitted abroad.

3. The provisions of the preceding paragraphs do not apply in the case provided for in Article 9(3).

III

RELATIONSHIP OF THE CODE TO SPECIAL LAWS AND EXPLANATION OF TERMS

Article 12

Specific penal laws

The provisions of the General Part of the Penal Code also apply to punishable acts provided for in special laws, provided such laws do not expressly provide otherwise.

Άρθρο 13
Έννοια όρων του Κώδικα

Στον Κώδικα οι ακόλουθοι όροι χρησιμοποιούνται με την εξής σημασία:

α) Υπάλληλος είναι εκείνος στον οποίο νόμιμα έχει ανατεθεί, έστω και προσωρινά, η άσκηση υπηρεσίας δημόσιας, δημοτικής ή κοινοτικής ή άλλου νομικού προσώπου δημοσίου δικαίου.

β) Οικείοι είναι όσοι συνδέονται με δεσμό νόμιμης συγγένειας σε ευθεία γραμμή, οι θετοί γονείς και τα θετά τέκνα, οι ανάδοχοι γονείς και τα ανάδοχα τέκνα, οι επίτροποι ή επιμελητές του υπαίτιου και όσοι βρίσκονται υπό την επιτροπεία ή επιμέλεια του υπαιτίου, οι σύζυγοι, οι συμβιούντες με σταθερή συμβίωση ή με σύμφωνο συμβίωσης, οι μνηστευμένοι, οι αδερφοί και οι σύζυγοί τους ή οι συμβιούντες ως ανωτέρω με αυτούς και οι μνηστήρες των αδερφών, ακόμη κι αν ο γάμος, η συμβίωση ή η μνηστεία έχουν λυθεί.

γ) Έγγραφο είναι κάθε γραπτό που προορίζεται ή είναι πρόσφορο να αποδείξει γεγονός που έχει έννομη σημασία όπως και κάθε σημείο που προορίζεται να αποδείξει ένα τέτοιο γεγονός. Έγγραφο είναι και κάθε μέσο το οποίο χρησιμοποιείται από υπολογιστή ή περιφερειακή μνήμη υπολογιστή, με ηλεκτρονικό, μαγνητικό ή άλλο τρόπο, για εγγραφή, αποθήκευση, παραγωγή αναπαραγωγή στοιχείων που δεν μπορούν να διαβαστούν άμεσα, όπως επίσης και κάθε μαγνητικό, ηλεκτρονικό ή άλλο υλικό στο οποίο εγγράφεται οποιαδήποτε πληροφορία, εικόνα, σύμβολο ή ήχος, αυτοτελώς ή σε συνδυασμό, εφόσον τα μέσα και τα υλικά αυτά προορίζονται ή είναι πρόσφορα να αποδείξουν γεγονότα που έχουν έννομη σημασία.

δ) Σωματική βία συνιστά και η περιαγωγή άλλου σε κατάσταση αναισθησίας ή ανικανότητας για αντίσταση με υπνωτικά ή ναρκωτικά ή άλλα ανάλογα μέσα.

ε) Κατ' επάγγελμα τέλεση του εγκλήματος συντρέχει, όταν από την επανειλημμένη τέλεση της πράξης ή από την υποδομή που έχει διαμορφώσει ο υπαίτιος με πρόθεση επανειλημμένης τέλεσης της πράξης προκύπτει σκοπός του υπαιτίου για πορισμό εισοδήματος.

στ) Πληροφοριακό σύστημα είναι συσκευή ή ομάδα διασυνδεδεμένων ή σχετικών μεταξύ τους συσκευών, εκ των οποίων μία ή περισσότερες εκτελούν, σύμφωνα με ένα πρόγραμμα, αυτόματη επεξεργασία ψηφιακών δεδομένων, καθώς και τα ψηφιακά δεδομένα που αποθηκεύονται, αποτελούν αντικείμενο επεξεργασίας, ανακτώνται ή διαβιβάζονται από την εν λόγω συσκευή ή την ομάδα συσκευών με σκοπό τη λειτουργία, τη χρήση, την προστασία και τη συντήρηση των συσκευών αυτών.

ζ) Ψηφιακά δεδομένα είναι η παρουσίαση γεγονότων, πληροφοριών ή εννοιών σε μορφή κατάλληλη προς επεξεργασία από πληροφοριακό σύστημα, συμπεριλαμβανομένου προγράμματος που παρέχει τη δυνατότητα στο πληροφοριακό σύστημα να εκτελέσει μια λειτουργία.

η) Μέσο πληρωμής πλην των μετρητών είναι άυλος ή υλικός προστατευμένος μηχανισμός, αντικείμενο ή αρχείο ή συνδυασμός τους, εκτός από το νόμιμο νόμισμα, ο οποίος επιτρέπει, μόνος του ή σε συνδυασμό με διαδικασία ή σειρά διαδικασιών, στον κάτοχο ή στον χρήστη του να μεταφέρει χρήματα ή νομισματική αξία, μεταξύ άλλων, μέσω ψηφιακών μέσων συναλλαγής. Ως «προστατευμένος μηχανισμός, αντικείμενο ή αρχείο» νοείται μηχανισμός, αντικείμενο ή αρχείο που προστατεύεται από την απομίμηση ή δόλια χρήση, για παράδειγμα μέσω σχεδιασμού, κωδικοποίησης ή υπογραφής.

Article 13

Meaning of terms [used in] the Code

The terms below are used in the Code with the following meaning:

a) “state employee” means any person who has been lawfully entrusted, even temporarily, with performing a public, municipal or community function or a function within a different body governed by public law;

b) “related parties” mean persons lawfully related in the direct line, adoptive parents and adopted children, foster parents and foster children, tutors or juvenile probation officers of the culpable person and persons under the tutorship or the custody of the culpable person, the culpable person's spouse, [person living together in a steady relationship] or civil partner, the person engaged to the culpable person, the culpable person’s siblings and the spouses or partners of such siblings and persons engaged to such siblings, even if the marriage, the relationship or the engagement has been dissolved;

c) “document” means any written text intended or suitable for proving facts of legal importance and any mark [made] with the intention to prove such facts. “Document” also means any medium used by a computer or peripheral computer memory via electronic, magnetic or other means to record, store, produce [or] reproduce data that cannot be directly read, as well as any magnetic, electronic or other material on which any information, image, symbol or sound is recorded, whether independently or in combined form, where such media and materials are intended or suitable for proving facts of legal importance;

d) physical violence also includes rendering another person unconscious or incapable of resisting through use of soporifics or narcotics or other such similar means;

e) commission of a crime [for monetary gain] occurs when it becomes clear, from the repeated commission of the act or from the infrastructure developed by the culpable person with the intention of repeatedly committing the act, that the purpose of the culpable person is to generate income;

f) “information system” means a device or group of interconnected or related devices, one or more of which, on the basis of a [software] program, automatically processes computer data, as well as digital data stored, processed, retrieved or transmitted by that device or group of devices for the purposes of the operation, use, protection and maintenance of such device or devices;

g) “digital data” means a representation of facts, information or concepts in a form suitable for processing in an information system, including a program suitable for causing an information system to perform a function;

h) “non-cash payment instrument” means a non-corporeal or corporeal protected device, object or record, or a combination thereof, other than legal tender, and which, alone or in conjunction with a procedure or a set of procedures, enables the holder or user to transfer money or monetary value, including through digital means of exchange. “Protected device, object or record” means a device, object or record safeguarded against imitation or fraudulent use, for example through design, coding or signature.

ΔΕΥΤΕΡΟ ΚΕΦΑΛΑΙΟ

ΤΟ ΕΓΚΛΗΜΑ

I

Η ΠΡΑΞΗ

Άρθρο 14
Έννοια της αξιόποινης πράξης

1. Έγκλημα είναι πράξη άδικη και καταλογιστή σε εκείνον που την τέλεσε, η οποία τιμωρείται από τον νόμο.
2. Στις διατάξεις των ποινικών νόμων ο όρος «πράξη» περιλαμβάνει και τις παραλείψεις.

Άρθρο 15
Έγκλημα που τελείται με παράλειψη

1. Όπου ο νόμος για την ύπαρξη αξιόποινης πράξης απαιτεί να έχει επέλθει ορισμένο αποτέλεσμα, η μη αποτροπή του τιμωρείται όπως η πρόκλησή του με ενέργεια, αν ο υπαίτιος της παράλειψης είχε ιδιαίτερη νομική υποχρέωση να προβεί σε ενέργεια για την αποτροπή του αποτελέσματος. Η ιδιαίτερη νομική υποχρέωση πηγάζει από νόμο, σύμβαση ή προηγούμενη επικίνδυνη ενέργεια του υπαιτίου.
2. Στις περιπτώσεις των εγκλημάτων με παράλειψη ο δικαστής μπορεί να επιβάλει μειωμένη ποινή (άρθρο 83).

Άρθρο 16
Τόπος τέλεσης της πράξης

Τόπος τέλεσης της πράξης θεωρείται ο τόπος όπου ο υπαίτιος διέπραξε ολικά ή μερικά την αξιόποινη ενέργεια ή παράλειψη, καθώς και ο τόπος όπου επήλθε ή, σε περίπτωση απόπειρας, έπρεπε να επέλθει σύμφωνα με την πρόθεσή του το αποτέλεσμα.

Άρθρο 17
Χρόνος τέλεσης της πράξης

Χρόνος τέλεσης της πράξης θεωρείται ο χρόνος κατά τον οποίο ο υπαίτιος ενέργησε ή όφειλε να ενεργήσει. Ο χρόνος κατά τον οποίο επήλθε το αποτέλεσμα είναι αδιάφορος.

Άρθρο 18
Κατηγορίες αξιοποίνων πράξεων

Οι αξιόποινες πράξεις διακρίνονται σε κακουργήματα και πλημμελήματα. Κάθε πράξη που τιμωρείται με κάθειρξη ισόβια ή πρόσκαιρη είναι κακούργημα. Κάθε πράξη που τιμωρείται με φυλάκιση ή περιορισμό σε ειδικό κατάστημα κράτησης νέων ή μόνο με χρηματική ποινή ή παροχή κοινωφελούς εργασίας είναι πλημμέλημα.

Άρθρο 19
Ποινικός χαρακτήρας πράξεων που έχουν εκδικαστεί

Αν μια πράξη που εκδικάστηκε είναι κακούργημα ή πλημμέλημα, κρίνεται με βάση τη βαρύτερη ποινή που καθορίζεται από τον νόμο γι' αυτή και όχι με βάση την τυχόν ελαφρότερη ποινή που επέβαλε ο δικαστής λόγω ελαφρυντικών περιστάσεων (άρθρο 84) ή για οποιονδήποτε άλλο λόγο μείωσης της ποινής σύμφωνα με το άρθρο 83.

CHAPTER II

CRIME

I

THE ACT

Article 14
Meaning of punishable act

1. A crime is an act which is wrongful, imputable to its perpetrator, and punishable by law.
2. In the provisions of penal laws, the term "act" also includes omissions.

Article 15
Crime committed by omission

1. Where the law requires a certain result to have occurred in order for a punishable act to be constituted, failure to prevent such result is punished in the same way as actively causing such result if the person responsible for the omission was under a particular legal duty to act in order to prevent the result [from occurring]. Such particular legal duty arises from the law, a contract or prior dangerous action of the culpable person.
2. Where a crime was committed by omission, the judge may order a reduced punishment ([see] Article 83).

Article 16
Place of commission of the act

The place where the act was committed is deemed to be the place where the culpable person carried out the punishable action or omission, whether in whole or in part, as well as the place where the result occurred, or, in the case of attempt, where the punishable result should have occurred according to the intention of the culpable person.

Article 17
Time of commission of the act

The time of commission of the act is deemed to be the time when the culpable person acted or ought to have acted. The time when the result occurred is irrelevant.

Article 18
Classification of punishable acts

Punishable acts are distinguished into felonies and misdemeanours. Any act carrying a sentence of incarceration for life or for a fixed term is a felony. Any act carrying a sentence of imprisonment or confinement to a reformative institution or only a monetary penalty or community service is a misdemeanour.

Article 19
Criminal nature of acts [being] adjudicated

Whether an act [being] adjudicated constitutes a felony or a misdemeanour shall be determined on the basis of a more severe punishment prescribed in law for that act, and not on the basis of a more lenient punishment which may have been ordered by the judge due to mitigating circumstances ([see] Article 84) or on any other grounds leading to a reduced punishment in accordance with Article 83.

II

Ο ΑΔΙΚΟΣ ΧΑΡΑΚΤΗΡΑΣ ΤΗΣ ΠΡΑΞΗΣ

Άρθρο 20
Λόγοι άρσης του αδίκου

Εκτός από τις περιπτώσεις των άρθρων 21, 22, 25, 304 παρ. 4, 308 παρ. 3, 367 και 371 παρ. 4, ο άδικος χαρακτήρας της πράξης αίρεται και όταν αυτή αποτελεί ενάσκηση δικαιώματος ή εκπλήρωση καθήκοντος που προβλέπεται στο νόμο.

Άρθρο 21
Προσταγή

1. Δεν είναι άδικη η πράξη την οποία κάποιος επιχειρεί για να εκτελέσει προσταγή που του έδωσε, σύμφωνα με τους νόμιμους τύπους, η αρμόδια αρχή, αν ο νόμος δεν επιτρέπει στον αποδέκτη της προσταγής να εξετάσει αν είναι νόμιμη ή όχι. Στην περίπτωση αυτή ως αυτουργός τιμωρείται εκείνος που έδωσε την προσταγή.

2. Η διάταξη δεν εφαρμόζεται αν η προσταγή είναι προδήλως αντισυνταγματική ή παράνομη.

Άρθρο 22
Άμυνα

1. Δεν είναι άδικη η πράξη που τελείται σε κατάσταση άμυνας.

2. Άμυνα είναι η αναγκαία προσβολή του επιτιθεμένου στην οποία προβαίνει το άτομο προς υπεράσπιση του εαυτού του ή άλλου από παρούσα και άδικη επίθεση που στρέφεται εναντίον τους.

3. Το αναγκαίο μέτρο της άμυνας κρίνεται από τον βαθμό επικινδυνότητας της επίθεσης, από το είδος της προσβολής που απειλείται, από τον τρόπο και την ένταση της επίθεσης και από τις υπόλοιπες περιστάσεις.

Άρθρο 23
Υπέρβαση άμυνας

Όποιος υπερβαίνει τα όρια της άμυνας τιμωρείται, αν η υπέρβαση έγινε με πρόθεση, με ποινή ελαττωμένη, και αν έγινε από αμέλεια, σύμφωνα με τις σχετικές με αυτήν διατάξεις. Μένει ατιμώρητος και δεν του καταλογίζεται η υπέρβαση, αν ενέργησε με αυτόν τον τρόπο εξαιτίας του φόβου ή της ταραχής που του προκάλεσε η επίθεση.

Άρθρο 24
Υπαίτια κατάσταση άμυνας

Δεν απαλλάσσεται από την ποινή που ορίζει ο νόμος όποιος με πρόθεση προκάλεσε την επίθεση άλλου για να διαπράξει εναντίον του αξιόποινη πράξη με το πρόσχημα της άμυνας.

Άρθρο 25
Κατάσταση ανάγκης που αίρει το άδικο

1. Δεν είναι άδικη η πράξη που τελεί κάποιος προς αποτροπή παρόντος και αναπότρεπτου με άλλα μέσα κινδύνου, ο οποίος απειλεί το πρόσωπο ή την περιουσία του ίδιου ή κάποιου άλλου χωρίς δική του υπαιτιότητα, αν η προσβολή που προκλήθηκε στον άλλο είναι σημαντικά κατώτερη κατά το είδος και τη σπουδαιότητα από την προσβολή που απειλήθηκε.

2. Η προηγούμενη διάταξη δεν εφαρμόζεται σε όποιον έχει καθήκον να εκτεθεί στον απειλούμενο κίνδυνο.

3. Η διάταξη του άρθρου 23 έχει αντίστοιχη εφαρμογή και στην περίπτωση αυτού του άρθρου.

II

THE WRONGFULNESS OF THE ACT

Article 20
Grounds for precluding wrongfulness

In addition to the cases provided for in Articles 21, 22, 25, 304(4), 308(3), 367 and 371(4), the wrongfulness of the act is also precluded when such act involves exercise of a right or fulfilment of a duty provided for in law.

Article 21
Order

1. An act is not wrongful if carried out in performance of an order issued by the competent authority in accordance with legal form, where the law does not allow the recipient of such order to examine its lawfulness. In such cases, the person punished as perpetrator is the one who issued the order.
2. This provision does not apply if the order is manifestly unconstitutional or unlawful.

Article 22
Defence

1. An act committed in a defensive state is not wrongful.
2. "Defence" means the necessary force used against an attacker by a person in order to defend themselves or another from a present and wrongful attack against them.
3. The necessity of the defence shall be determined by the danger posed by the attack, the type of harm threatened, the manner and intensity of the attack, and all other circumstances.

Article 23
Excessive defence

Any person who exceeds the limits of defence shall be punished, if the exceedance was intentional, with a reduced punishment, and if such exceedance was done negligently, in accordance with the provisions on negligence. They shall not be punished and the exceedance shall not be imputed to them if they acted in such way due to the fear or distress caused by the attack.

Article 24
Culpable [provocation of] defence

Any person who intentionally provoked another to attack in order to commit a punishable act against them under the pretext of defence is not exempt from the punishment provided for in law.

Article 25
Emergency precluding wrongfulness

1. An act is not wrongful if committed in order to avert a danger which is present and unavoidable by any other means and which, through no fault of a person, threatens them or their assets or another person or their assets, where the harm caused to any other person is significantly less in terms of kind and importance than the harm threatened [by the danger].
2. The preceding provision does not apply to any person with a duty to expose themselves to the potential danger.
3. The provisions of Article 23 also apply *mutatis mutandis* to the case provided for in this Article.

III

Η ΥΠΑΙΤΙΟΤΗΤΑ

Άρθρο 26

Υπαιτιότητα στα κακουργήματα και πλημμελήματα

Τα κακουργήματα και πλημμελήματα τιμωρούνται μόνο όταν τελούνται με δόλο. Κατ' εξαίρεση, στις περιπτώσεις που ορίζει ειδικά ο νόμος, τα πλημμελήματα τιμωρούνται και όταν τελούνται από αμέλεια.

Άρθρο 27

Δόλος

1. Με δόλο (με πρόθεση) πράττει όποιος θέλει την παραγωγή των περιστατικών που κατά τον νόμο απαρτίζουν την έννοια της αξιόποινης πράξης, καθώς και όποιος γνωρίζει ότι από την πράξη του ενδέχεται να παραχθούν αυτά τα περιστατικά και το αποδέχεται.

2. Όπου ο νόμος απαιτεί να έχει τελεστεί η πράξη εν γνώσει ορισμένου περιστατικού, δεν αρκεί ο ενδεχόμενος δόλος. Και όπου ο νόμος απαιτεί η πράξη να έχει τελεστεί με σκοπό την πρόκληση ορισμένου αποτελέσματος απαιτείται ο δράστης να έχει επιδιώξει να προκαλέσει αυτό το αποτέλεσμα.

Άρθρο 28

Αμέλεια

Από αμέλεια πράττει όποιος από έλλειψη της προσοχής την οποία όφειλε κατά τις περιστάσεις και μπορούσε να καταβάλει είτε δεν πρόβλεψε το αξιόποινο αποτέλεσμα που προκάλεσε η πράξη του, είτε το πρόβλεψε ως δυνατό, πίστεψε όμως ότι δεν θα επερχόταν.

Άρθρο 29

Ευθύνη από το αποτέλεσμα

Στις περιπτώσεις που ο νόμος ορίζει ότι κάποια πράξη τιμωρείται με βαρύτερη ποινή όταν έχει ορισμένο αποτέλεσμα, η πρόκληση του οποίου τυποποιείται ως αυτοτελές έγκλημα αμέλειας, η ποινή αυτή επιβάλλεται στον αυτουργό ή στο συμμέτοχο μόνο αν το αποτέλεσμα μπορεί να αποδοθεί τουλάχιστον σε αμέλειά τους, εφόσον η πράξη δεν τιμωρείται βαρύτερα κατ' άλλη διάταξη.

Άρθρο 30

Πραγματική πλάνη

1. Δεν πράττει με δόλο όποιος κατά το χρόνο τέλεσης της αξιόποινης πράξης αγνοεί τα περιστατικά που τη συνιστούν. Αν όμως η άγνοια αυτών των περιστατικών μπορεί να αποδοθεί σε αμέλεια του υπαιτίου, η πράξη του καταλογίζεται ως έγκλημα αμέλειας.

2. Δεν καταλογίζονται στο δράστη περιστατικά που κατά το νόμο επαυξάνουν το αξιόποινο της πράξης του, αν τα αγνοούσε.

III

CULPABILITY

Article 26

Culpability in felonies and misdemeanours

Felonies and misdemeanours are punishable only if committed with *dolus*. By way of exception, where specifically provided for in law, misdemeanours are also punishable when committed through negligence.

Article 27

Dolus

1. A person acts with *dolus* (intent) when they wish to bring about the circumstances which, in law, meet the test for the punishable act, as does [a person] who is aware and accepts that their act may bring about such circumstances.

2. Where the law requires that the act be committed knowing [that] a particular circumstance [will be brought about], *dolus eventualis* does not suffice. Furthermore, where the law requires that the act be committed for the purpose of bringing about a specific result, the perpetrator must have aimed to bring about that result.

Article 28

Negligence

A person acts negligently when, due to lack of the care they could and ought to have shown in the circumstances, they either did not foresee the punishable result that their act brought about, or did foresee it as a possibility but believed it would not occur.

Article 29

[Results-based culpability]

Where the law provides that an act carries a more severe punishment when it brings about a specific result and bringing about such result is classified as a standalone crime of negligence, that punishment shall be imposed on the perpetrator or accessory only if the result in question can be attributed at least to negligence on their part, provided the act does not carry a more severe punishment under a different provision.

Article 30

Mistake of fact

1. A person does not act with *dolus* when, at the time the punishable act is committed, they are not aware that [the constituent elements of their actions] constituted a punishable act. However, where ignorance of such [constituent elements] can be attributed to negligence on the part of the culpable person, the act shall be imputed to them as a crime of negligence.

2. Circumstances which, in law, augment the punishability of the act shall not be imputed to the perpetrator if they were ignorant of such [constituent elements].

IV

ΛΟΓΟΙ ΑΡΣΗΣ ΤΟΥ ΚΑΤΑΛΟΓΙΣΜΟΥ

Άρθρο 31
Νομική πλάνη

1. *Μόνη η άγνοια του αξιοποίνου δεν αρκεί για να αποκλείσει τον καταλογισμό.*

2. *Η πράξη όμως δεν καταλογίζεται σε εκείνον που την τελεί αν αυτός δεν είχε συνείδηση του άδικου χαρακτήρα της λόγω πλάνης που δεν μπορούσε να αποφύγει, μολονότι κατέβαλε την οφειλόμενη από τις περιστάσεις και δυνατή γι' αυτόν επιμέλεια (συγγνωστή νομική πλάνη). Αν ο υπαίτιος μπορούσε να αποφύγει την πλάνη, η πράξη καταλογίζεται σε αυτόν, αλλά το δικαστήριο μπορεί να του επιβάλει μειωμένη ποινή (άρθρο 83).*

Άρθρο 32
Κατάσταση ανάγκης που αίρει τον καταλογισμό

1. *Η πράξη δεν καταλογίζεται σε εκείνον που την τελεί για να αποτρέψει παρόντα και αναπότρεπτο με άλλα μέσα κίνδυνο, ο οποίος απειλεί χωρίς δική του υπαιτιότητα το πρόσωπο ή την περιουσία του ίδιου ή οικείου του, αν η προσβολή που προκλήθηκε στον άλλο από την πράξη είναι κατά το είδος και τη σπουδαιότητα ανάλογη με την προσβολή που απειλήθηκε.*

2. *Οι διατάξεις των παραγράφων 2 και 3 του άρθρου 25 εφαρμόζονται και εδώ.*

Άρθρο 33
Αδυναμία αποφυγής του αδίκου

Η πράξη δεν καταλογίζεται σε εκείνον που την τέλεσε, αν κατά την τέλεσή της αδυνατούσε να συμμορφωθεί προς το δίκαιο λόγω ανυπέρβλητου για τον ίδιο διλήμματος εξαιτίας σύγκρουσης καθηκόντων και η προσβολή που προκλήθηκε από την πράξη είναι κατά το είδος και τη σπουδαιότητα ανάλογη με την προσβολή που απειλήθηκε.

Άρθρο 34
Ανικανότητα προς καταλογισμό

Η πράξη δεν καταλογίζεται στον δράστη αν λόγω ψυχικής ή διανοητικής διαταραχής ή διατάραξης της συνείδησης κατά τον χρόνο τέλεσής της, δεν είχε την ικανότητα να αντιληφθεί το άδικο της πράξης του ή να ενεργήσει σύμφωνα με την αντίληψή του για το άδικο αυτό.

Άρθρο 35
Υπαίτια πρόκληση ανικανότητας

1. *Πράξη που κάποιος αποφάσισε σε κανονική ψυχική κατάσταση, αλλά που για την τέλεσή της έφερε τον εαυτό του σε κατάσταση διαταραγμένης συνείδησης ή σε κατάσταση πλήρους αδυναμίας να ενεργήσει ή να παραλείψει, του καταλογίζεται ως πράξη που τελέστηκε με δόλο.*

2. *Αν η πράξη που τέλεσε σε τέτοια κατάσταση είναι άλλη από εκείνη που είχε αποφασίσει, ο υπαίτιος τιμωρείται με ποινή ελαττωμένη (άρθρο 83).*

3. *Πράξη που κάποιος πρόβλεψε ή μπορούσε να προβλέψει ότι ενδέχεται να τελέσει αν οδηγηθεί σε κατάσταση διαταραγμένης συνείδησης ή σε κατάσταση πλήρους αδυναμίας να ενεργήσει ή να παραλείψει, του καταλογίζεται ως πράξη που τελέστηκε από αμέλεια.*

IV

GROUNDS FOR PRECLUDING IMPUTABILITY

Article 31
Mistake of law

1. Ignorance of punishability alone does not suffice to preclude imputability.
2. However, the act shall not be imputed to the perpetrator if they were not aware of its wrongful nature due to an unavoidable mistake, despite having shown the greatest diligence they could have shown and which was required under the circumstances (excusable mistake of law). If the culpable person could have avoided the mistake, the act shall be imputed to them, but the court may order a reduced punishment ([see] Article 83).

Article 32
Emergency precluding imputability

1. An act shall not be imputed to the perpetrator if committed in order to avert a danger which is present and unavoidable by any other means and which, through no fault of their own, threatens them or their assets or a related party or their assets, where the harm caused to any other person by that act is proportionate in terms of kind and importance to the harm threatened [by the danger].
2. The provisions of Article 25(2) and (3) also apply in such a case.

Article 33
Impossibility of avoiding [the commission of] an unlawful act

An act shall not be imputed to the perpetrator if, when committing the act, they could not comply with the law due to an insurmountable dilemma caused by a conflict of duties and the harm caused by said act is proportionate in terms of kind and importance to the harm threatened.

Article 34
Impossibility of imputability

An act shall not be imputed to the perpetrator if, due to a mental or emotional disorder or loss of faculties when committing the act, they were not able to comprehend that their act was wrongful or to act in accordance with their understanding of such wrongfulness.

Article 35
Culpable incapacitation

1. Any act decided upon by a person who is in command of their faculties but who, in order to commit such act, brought themselves into a state of loss of faculties or state of complete inability to perform an act or omission shall be imputed to them as an act committed with *dolus*.
2. If the culpable person committed a [wrongful] act different from the one they had decided on, a reduced punishment shall be imposed on them ([see] Article 83).
3. Any act which [the perpetrator] foresaw or could have foreseen that they would commit in a state of loss of faculties or a state of complete inability to perform an act or omission shall be imputed to them as an act committed negligently.

V
ΜΕΙΩΜΕΝΟΣ ΚΑΤΑΛΟΓΙΣΜΟΣ

Άρθρο 36
Μειωμένη ικανότητα καταλογισμού

1. Αν εξαιτίας κάποιας από τις καταστάσεις που αναφέρονται στο άρθρο 34, δεν έχει εκλείψει εντελώς, μειώθηκε όμως σημαντικά η ικανότητα για καταλογισμό, επιβάλλεται μειωμένη ποινή (άρθρο 83).

2. Η διάταξη αυτή δεν εφαρμόζεται σε περίπτωση υπαίτιας κατά την έννοια του άρθρου 35 πρόκλησης της μειωμένης ικανότητας.

Άρθρα 37 - 41

(Καταργούνται)

V

REDUCED IMPUTABILITY

Article 36
Reduced imputability

1. If, due to any of the states referred to in Article 34, imputability was not completely extinguished but was significantly reduced, a reduced punishment shall be imposed ([see] Article 83).
2. This provision does not apply in cases of culpable incapacitation within the meaning of Article 35.

Articles 37 - 41

[Repealed]

ΤΡΙΤΟ ΚΕΦΑΛΑΙΟ

ΑΠΟΠΕΙΡΑ ΚΑΙ ΣΥΜΜΕΤΟΧΗ

I

ΑΠΟΠΕΙΡΑ

Άρθρο 42
Έννοια και ποινή της απόπειρας

1. Όποιος, έχοντας αποφασίσει να τελέσει έγκλημα, αρχίζει να εκτελεί την περιγραφόμενη στο νόμο αξιόποινη πράξη, τιμωρείται, αν το έγκλημα δεν ολοκληρώθηκε, με μειωμένη ποινή (άρθρο 83).
2. Το δικαστήριο μπορεί να κρίνει ατιμώρητη την απόπειρα πλημμελήματος για το οποίο ο νόμος προβλέπει ποινή φυλάκισης όχι ανώτερη από ένα έτος ή μόνο χρηματική ποινή ή παροχή κοινωφελούς εργασίας, εκτιμώντας όλες τις περιστάσεις τέλεσης του εγκλήματος.
3. Αν ο υπαίτιος απόπειρας ενός εγκλήματος που τιμωρείται βαρύτερα όταν έχει ορισμένο αποτέλεσμα (άρθρο 29), προκαλέσει με υπαιτιότητά του το αποτέλεσμα αυτό, τιμωρείται με την ποινή του εκ του αποτελέσματος διακρινόμενου εγκλήματος μειωμένη στο μέτρο του άρθρου 83, εφόσον η πράξη δεν τιμωρείται βαρύτερα κατ' άλλη διάταξη.

Άρθρο 43
Απρόσφορη απόπειρα

1. Όποιος επιχείρησε να εκτελέσει έγκλημα με μέσο ή κατά αντικειμένου τέτοιας φύσης ώστε να αποβαίνει απολύτως αδύνατη η τέλεση του εγκλήματος αυτού τιμωρείται με την ποινή του άρθρου 83 μειωμένη στο μισό.
2. Όποιος επιχείρησε τέτοια απρόσφορη απόπειρα από ευήθεια παραμένει ατιμώρητος.

Άρθρο 44
Υπαναχώρηση

1. Η απόπειρα μένει ατιμώρητη αν ο δράστης, αφού άρχισε την εκτέλεση της αξιόποινης πράξης, δεν την ολοκλήρωσε με τη θέλησή του και όχι από εξωτερικά εμπόδια.
2. Αν ο δράστης αποτυχημένου εγκλήματος δεν επαναλάβει άμεσα την πράξη του, με δική του θέληση και όχι από εξωτερικά εμπόδια, τιμωρείται με την ποινή της απόπειρας μειωμένη στο μισό.
3. Με την ποινή της προηγούμενης παραγράφου τιμωρείται και ο δράστης που ολοκλήρωσε την πράξη του, παρεμπόδισε όμως με τη θέλησή του την επέλευση του αξιόποινου αποτελέσματος. Το δικαστήριο μπορεί να κρίνει την απόπειρα ατιμώρητη. Τα ίδια ισχύουν και αν το αποτέλεσμα δεν επήλθε από άλλη αιτία και ο δράστης κατέβαλε πάντως σοβαρή προσπάθεια για να το αποτρέψει. Οι πράξεις των εδαφίων α΄ και γ΄ μένουν ατιμώρητες, αν πρόκειται για έγκλημα το αξιόποινο του οποίου εξαλείφεται με έμπρακτη μετάνοια.
4. Οι προηγούμενες παράγραφοι εφαρμόζονται και για τον συμμέτοχο που με τη θέλησή του εμπόδισε την ολοκλήρωση της πράξης ή την επέλευση του αποτελέσματος.

CHAPTER III

ATTEMPT AND PARTICIPATION

I

ATTEMPT

Article 42
Meaning and punishment of attempt

1. A reduced punishment ([see] Article 83) shall be imposed on any person who, having decided to commit a crime, begins committing the act prescribed in law as punishable, if they do not complete the crime.
2. The court, weighing up all the circumstances under which the crime was [attempted], may decide not to punish an attempted misdemeanour which, in law, carries a sentence of imprisonment of no more than one year, or only a monetary penalty, or community service.
3. If a person who attempted to commit a crime which carries a more severe punishment when a specific result is brought about ([see] Article 29) culpably brings about such result, they shall be punished with the punishment carried by the results-based crime, reduced in accordance with Article 83, unless the act carries a more severe punishment under a different provision.

Article 43
[Impossible] attempt

1. Where any person attempted to commit a crime using means of such a nature or against a thing of such a nature that commission of the crime in question proves absolutely impossible, the punishment provided for in Article 83, reduced by half, shall be imposed on them.
2. Any person who made such an [impossible] attempt due to naivety shall not be punished.

Article 44
Reconsideration

1. An attempt[ed crime] shall not be punished if the perpetrator, having begun to commit the punishable act, did not complete it of their own volition and not due to external obstacles.
2. If the perpetrator of a failed crime does not immediately repeat their act of their own volition and not due to external obstacles, the punishment for attempt reduced by half shall be imposed on them.
3. The punishment provided for in the preceding paragraph shall also be imposed on any perpetrator who completed their act but impeded the occurrence of the punishable result of their own volition. The court may decide not to punish the attempt. This shall also apply if the result did not occur for some other reason and the perpetrator nevertheless made a serious effort to prevent it [from occurring]. The acts provided for in the first and third sentences [of this paragraph] shall not be punished where the wrongfulness of a crime is expunged due to practical repentance.
4. The preceding paragraphs also apply to any accessory who, of their own volition, impeded the act from being completed or the result from occurring.

II

ΣΥΜΜΕΤΟΧΗ

Άρθρο 45

Συναυτουργοί

Αν δύο ή περισσότεροι πραγμάτωσαν από κοινού, εν όλω ή εν μέρει, τα στοιχεία της περιγραφόμενης στον νόμο αξιόποινης πράξης, καθένας τους τιμωρείται ως αυτουργός.

Άρθρο 46

Ηθικός αυτουργός και προβοκάτορας

1. Με την ποινή του αυτουργού τιμωρείται όποιος με πρόθεση προκάλεσε σε άλλον την απόφαση να εκτελέσει την άδικη πράξη που διέπραξε.

2. Όποιος με πρόθεση προκάλεσε σε άλλον την απόφαση να τελέσει κάποιο έγκλημα, με σκοπό να τον καταλάβει ενώ αποπειράται να τελέσει το έγκλημα ή ενώ επιχειρεί αξιόποινη προπαρασκευαστική του πράξη και με τη θέληση να τον ανακόψει από την αποπεράτωση του εγκλήματος, τιμωρείται με την ποινή του αυτουργού μειωμένη στο μισό.

Άρθρο 47

Άμεσος και απλός συνεργός

Όποιος, εκτός από την περίπτωση της παρ. 1 του άρθρου 46, με πρόθεση παρέχει άμεση συνδρομή στον δράστη κατά τη διάρκεια αυτής της πράξης και στην εκτέλεση της κύριας πράξης τιμωρείται με την ποινή του αυτουργού. Αν, εκτός της περίπτωσης του πρώτου εδαφίου, παρέχει με πρόθεση σε άλλον οποιαδήποτε συνδρομή πριν από την τέλεση ή κατά την τέλεση της άδικης πράξης που διέπραξε, τιμωρείται ως συνεργός με ποινή ελαττωμένη (άρθρο 83).

Άρθρο 48

Γενική διάταξη

Το αξιόποινο των συμμετόχων κατά τα άρθρα 46 και 47 είναι ανεξάρτητο από το αξιόποινο εκείνου που τέλεσε την πράξη.

Άρθρο 49

Ιδιαίτερες ιδιότητες ή σχέσεις

1. Όπου ο νόμος, για να είναι μια πράξη αξιόποινη, απαιτεί ιδιαίτερες ιδιότητες ή σχέσεις, αν αυτές υπάρχουν μόνο στον δράστη, τότε οι συμμέτοχοι κατά το άρθρο 46 παρ. 1 και 47 τιμωρούνται με μειωμένη ποινή (άρθρο 83). Αν όμως υπάρχουν μόνο στο πρόσωπο των συμμετόχων, οι τελευταίοι τιμωρούνται ως αυτουργοί και ο δράστης ως συνεργός.

2. Οι ιδιαίτερες ιδιότητες ή σχέσεις ή άλλες περιστάσεις που επιτείνουν, μειώνουν ή αποκλείουν την ποινή λαμβάνονται υπόψη μόνο για εκείνο τον συμμέτοχο στον οποίο υπάρχουν.

II

PARTICIPATION

Article 45
Co-perpetrators

If two or more persons jointly took the steps, whether in whole or in part, required in law for an act to be punishable, each person shall be punished as the perpetrator.

Article 46
Instigators and provocateurs

1. The punishment [to be] imposed on the perpetrator [of a wrongful act] shall be imposed on any person who intentionally induced another to decide to commit such wrongful act.
2. The punishment [to be] imposed on the perpetrator reduced by half shall be imposed on any person who intentionally induced another to decide to commit a crime for the purpose of apprehending them while attempting to commit such crime or while taking a preparatory step and with the intention to prevent them from completing such crime.

Article 47
Direct and simple accomplice

Except in the case referred to in Article 46(1), the [same] punishment imposed on the perpetrator shall be imposed on any person who intentionally provides direct aid to the perpetrator while the act is being committed and in the execution of the main act. Except in the case referred to in the preceding sentence, a reduced punishment ([see] Article 83) shall be imposed on any person [(accomplice)] who intentionally provides any aid to another prior to or during the commission of their wrongful act.

Article 48
General provision

The punishability of accessories under Articles 46 and 47 is independent of the punishability of the person who committed the act.

Article 49
Special capacities or relationships

1. Where the law requires special capacities or relationships in order for an act to be punishable and these relate only the perpetrator, then a reduced punishment ([see] Article 83) shall be imposed on accessories under Articles 46(1) and 47. However, if [such capacities or relationships] relate only to the accessories, they shall be punished as the perpetrators and the actual perpetrator [shall be punished] as an accomplice.
2. Special capacities or relationships or other circumstances which aggravate, mitigate or preclude the punishment shall be taken into consideration only with respect to the accessory to whom they relate.

ΤΕΤΑΡΤΟ ΚΕΦΑΛΑΙΟ

ΠΟΙΝΕΣ ΚΑΙ ΜΕΤΡΑ ΑΣΦΑΛΕΙΑΣ

I

ΚΥΡΙΕΣ ΠΟΙΝΕΣ

Άρθρο 50
Είδη ποινών

Κύριες ποινές είναι:

α) οι στερητικές της ελευθερίας,

β) η χρηματική ποινή και

γ) η προσφορά κοινωφελούς εργασίας.

Άρθρο 51
Ποινές στερητικές της ελευθερίας

1. *Ποινές στερητικές της ελευθερίας είναι η κάθειρξη, η φυλάκιση και ο περιορισμός σε ειδικό κατάστημα κράτησης νέων.*

2. *Για τις πρόσκαιρες στερητικές της ελευθερίας ποινές, η ημέρα υπολογίζεται σε είκοσι τέσσερις ώρες, η εβδομάδα σε επτά ημέρες, ο μήνας και το έτος σύμφωνα με το ημερολόγιο που ισχύει.*

3. *Ο χρόνος της ποινής επιμετράται πάντοτε σε πλήρεις ημέρες, εβδομάδες, μήνες και έτη.*

Άρθρο 52
Κάθειρξη

1. *Η κάθειρξη είναι πρόσκαιρη και κατ' εξαίρεση, εφόσον ο νόμος το ορίζει ρητά, ισόβια.*

2. *Η διάρκεια της πρόσκαιρης κάθειρξης δεν υπερβαίνει τα είκοσι (20) έτη ούτε είναι κατώτερη των πέντε (5) ετών.*

Άρθρο 53
Φυλάκιση

Η διάρκεια της φυλάκισης δεν υπερβαίνει τα πέντε έτη ούτε είναι κατώτερη των δέκα ημερών.

Άρθρο 54
Περιορισμός σε ειδικό κατάστημα κράτησης νέων

Η διάρκεια του περιορισμού σε ειδικό κατάστημα κράτησης νέων δεν υπερβαίνει τα πέντε (5) έτη ούτε είναι κατώτερη των έξι (6) μηνών, αν για την πράξη που τελέστηκε ο νόμος απειλεί κάθειρξη ως δέκα (10) έτη. Αν η απειλούμενη κάθειρξη είναι ισόβια ή πρόσκαιρη ανώτερη από αυτήν του προηγούμενου εδαφίου, η διάρκεια του περιορισμού σε ειδικό κατάστημα κράτησης δεν υπερβαίνει τα δέκα (10) έτη ούτε είναι κατώτερη από δύο (2).

CHAPTER IV

PUNISHMENTS AND SECURITY MEASURES

I

MAIN PUNISHMENTS

Article 50

Types of punishments

The main punishments are [distinguished into]:

a) custodial sentences;

b) monetary penalties; and

c) community service.

Article 51

Custodial sentences

1. Custodial sentences are [distinguished into] incarceration, imprisonment and confinement to a reformative institution.

2. With regard to fixed-term custodial sentences, a day is calculated as [consisting of] 24 hours, a week as [consisting of] seven days, and a month and a year based on the current calendar.

3. The duration of a sentence shall always be measured in full days, weeks, months, and years.

Article 52

Incarceration

1. Incarceration is [distinguished into] fixed-term incarceration and, by way of exception and where expressly provided for in law, incarceration for life.

2. Fixed-term incarceration shall not be longer than 20 years and not shorter than 5 years in duration.

Article 53

Imprisonment

Imprisonment shall not be longer than 5 years and not shorter than 10 days in duration.

Article 54

Confinement to a reformative institution

Confinement to a reformative institution shall not be longer than 5 years and not shorter than 6 months in duration if the act committed carries, in law, a sentence of incarceration of no more than 10 years. If the [act carries a] sentence of incarceration for life or fixed-term incarceration longer than the one referred to in the preceding sentence, confinement to a reformative institution shall not be longer than 10 years and not shorter than 2 [years] in duration.

Άρθρο 55
Παροχή κοινωφελούς εργασίας

Η παροχή κοινωφελούς εργασίας δεν μπορεί να έχει διάρκεια ανώτερη των επτακοσίων είκοσι ωρών ούτε να είναι κατώτερη των εκατό ωρών, εκτός αν ορίζεται διαφορετικά.

Άρθρο 56

(Καταργείται)

Άρθρο 57
Χρηματική ποινή

1. (Καταργείται)

2. Αν δεν ορίζεται διαφορετικά σε ειδικές διατάξεις, η χρηματική ποινή δεν μπορεί να είναι:

α) κατώτερη από τριακόσια (300) ευρώ και ανώτερη από σαράντα χιλιάδες (40.000) ευρώ για πλημμελήματα,

β) κατώτερη από πέντε χιλιάδες (5.000) ευρώ και ανώτερη από εκατόν είκοσι χιλιάδες (120.000) ευρώ για κακουργήματα.

3. (Καταργείται)

4. Με τον θάνατο του καταδικασθέντος διαγράφεται η χρηματική ποινή. Σε καμία περίπτωση δεν εκτελείται εναντίον των κληρονόμων του.

Άρθρο 58

(Καταργείται)

II

ΠΑΡΕΠΟΜΕΝΕΣ ΠΟΙΝΕΣ

Άρθρο 59
Γενική διάταξη

Παρεπόμενες ποινές είναι:

α) η αποστέρηση θέσεων και αξιωμάτων,

β) η απαγόρευση άσκησης επαγγέλματος,

γ) η αφαίρεση άδειας οδήγησης ή εκμετάλλευσης μεταφορικού μέσου,

δ) η δημοσίευση καταδικαστικής απόφασης και

ε) η δήμευση.

Άρθρο 60
Αποστέρηση θέσεων και αξιωμάτων

1. Αν ο υπαίτιος καταδικάστηκε σε ποινή κάθειρξης, το δικαστήριο μπορεί να επιβάλει αποστέρηση της δημόσιας θέσης ή του δημόσιου ή αυτοδιοικητικού αξιώματος που κατέχει, εφόσον η πράξη του συνιστά βαριά παράβαση των καθηκόντων του.

2. Η αποστέρηση επέρχεται μόλις η απόφαση γίνει αμετάκλητη.

Άρθρα 61 - 64

(Καταργούνται)

Article 55
Community service

Unless otherwise provided for, community service shall not be longer than 720 hours and not shorter than 100 hours in duration.

Article 56

[Repealed]

Article 57
Monetary penalty

1. [Repealed]
2. Unless otherwise specifically provided for, a monetary penalty may not be:
a) less than 300 euros and more than 40,000 euros for misdemeanours;
b) less than 5,000 euros and more than 120,000 euros for felonies.
3. [Repealed]
4. Where a convicted person dies, the monetary penalty shall be cancelled. Under no circumstances may [the monetary penalty] be enforced against the heirs [of the convicted person].

Article 58

[Repealed]

II

ANCILLARY PUNISHMENTS

Article 59
General provision

Ancillary punishments are [distinguished into]:
a) forfeiture of posts and offices;
b) prohibition on carrying on an occupation;
c) removal of the driving licence or licence to operate a means of transport;
d) publication of a judgment of conviction; and
e) confiscation.

Article 60
Forfeiture of posts and offices

1. If a culpable person was sentenced to incarceration and their act constitutes a gross breach of duty, the court may order that they forfeit their public post or public or local government office.
2. Forfeiture shall take place once the judgment becomes irrevocable.

Articles 61 - 64

[Repealed]

Άρθρο 65
Απαγόρευση άσκησης επαγγέλματος

1. Αν ο υπαίτιος διέπραξε έγκλημα με βαριά παράβαση των καθηκόντων του επαγγέλματός του, για την άσκηση του οποίου απαιτείται ειδική άδεια της αρχής, και εφόσον του επιβλήθηκε ποινή στερητική της ελευθερίας τουλάχιστον δύο ετών, το δικαστήριο μπορεί να απαγορεύσει την άσκηση του επαγγέλματος αυτού για χρονικό διάστημα από ένα μήνα έως δύο έτη.

2. Η απαγόρευση άσκησης επαγγέλματος αρχίζει μόλις η απόφαση γίνει αμετάκλητη και η διάρκειά της, εφόσον ο δράστης κρατείται, υπολογίζεται από την επομένη της ημέρας κατά την οποία απολύεται από τη φυλακή.

Άρθρο 66
Αφαίρεση άδειας οδήγησης ή εκμετάλλευσης μεταφορικού μέσου

1. Αν ο υπαίτιος διέπραξε έγκλημα που έχει άμεση σχέση με την οδήγηση ή την εκμετάλλευση μεταφορικού μέσου και εφόσον του επιβλήθηκε ποινή στερητική της ελευθερίας τουλάχιστον έξι μηνών, το δικαστήριο μπορεί να διατάξει την αφαίρεση της άδειας οδήγησης που κατέχει, για όλα ή ορισμένου τύπου μεταφορικά μέσα, ή της άδειας εκμετάλλευσης αντιστοίχως για χρονικό διάστημα από ένα μήνα ως ένα έτος.

2. Η διάταξη της παραγράφου 2 του προηγούμενου άρθρου έχει και στην περίπτωση αυτή ανάλογη εφαρμογή.

Άρθρο 67
Δημοσίευση καταδικαστικής απόφασης

1. Το δικαστήριο μπορεί να διατάξει τη δημοσίευση της καταδικαστικής απόφασής του, αν το επιβάλλει το δημόσιο συμφέρον.

2. Η δημοσίευση διατάσσεται στις περιπτώσεις που ορίζει ο νόμος, ύστερα από αίτηση του παθόντος.

3. Στην ίδια απόφαση ορίζεται ο τρόπος της δημοσίευσης και η υποχρέωση καταβολής της δαπάνης γι' αυτήν.

4. Η απόφαση δημοσιεύεται όταν καταστεί αμετάκλητη.

Άρθρο 68
Δήμευση

1. Αντικείμενα ή περιουσιακά στοιχεία που είναι προϊόντα κακουργήματος ή πλημμελήματος το οποίο πηγάζει από δόλο, καθώς και το τίμημά τους, και όσα αποκτήθηκαν με αυτά αμέσως ή εμμέσως, επίσης και αντικείμενα ή περιουσιακά στοιχεία που χρησίμευσαν ή προορίζονταν για την εκτέλεση τέτοιας πράξης μπορούν να δημευθούν αν αυτά ανήκουν στον αυτουργό ή σε κάποιον από τους συμμετόχους. Αν τα παραπάνω αντικείμενα ή περιουσιακά στοιχεία έχουν αναμειχθεί με περιουσία που αποκτήθηκε από νόμιμες πηγές, η σχετική περιουσία υπόκειται σε δήμευση μέχρι την καθορισμένη αξία των αναμειχθέντων αντικειμένων.

2. Δήμευση δεν επιβάλλεται, όταν το δικαστήριο, αυτεπαγγέλτως ή μετά από αίτημα διαδίκου ή τρίτου, κρίνει ότι αυτή είναι στη συγκεκριμένη περίπτωση δυσανάλογη, όπως όταν υπάρχει κίνδυνος να αποστερήσει τον καταδικασθέντα ή τρίτο, ιδίως την οικογένειά τους, από πράγμα που εξυπηρετεί τον αναγκαίο βιοπορισμό τους ή να προκαλέσει σε αυτούς υπέρμετρη και ανεπανόρθωτη βλάβη. Στις περιπτώσεις του προηγούμενου εδαφίου, το δικαστήριο μπορεί να επιβάλει ανάλογα περιορισμένη δήμευση ή να επιβάλει χρηματική ποινή, σύμφωνα με την παράγραφο 4.

Article 65
Prohibition on carrying on an occupation

1. If a culpable person committed a crime [also] involving gross breach of their occupational duties whose exercise requires a special permit from the authorities and a custodial sentence of at least two years was imposed on them, the court may prohibit them from carrying on the occupation in question for a period ranging from one month to two years.
2. The prohibition on carrying on an occupation shall commence once the judgment becomes irrevocable and its duration, if the perpetrator is detained, shall be calculated from the day following the date they were released from prison.

Article 66
Removal of driving licence or licence to operate a means of transport

1. If a culpable person committed a crime directly related to driving or operating a means of transport and a custodial sentence of at least six months was imposed on them, the court may order that the driving licence they hold for all or specific types of means of transport or their licence to operate such means of transport be removed for a period ranging from one month to one year.
2. The provisions of paragraph 2 of the preceding Article also apply *mutatis mutandis* in such a case.

Article 67
Publication of judgments of conviction

1. The court may, where required by the public interest, order that its judgment of conviction be published.
2. Following an application filed by the victim, publication shall be ordered in the cases expressly provided for in law.
3. The method of publication and obligation to pay for such publication shall be specified in the same judgment.
4. The judgment shall be published once it becomes irrevocable.

Article 68
Confiscation

1. Objects or assets which constitute proceeds of a felony or of a misdemeanour committed with *dolus*, as well as their value [after having been sold] and anything directly or indirectly acquired using such objects or assets, as well as objects or assets used or intended to commit such an act may be confiscated if they belong to the perpetrator or any of the accessories. If the aforesaid things or assets have been mixed/ intermixed with assets acquired lawfully, the assets in question shall be subject to confiscation up to the determined value of the mixed/intermixed things.
2. Confiscation shall not be ordered when the court, whether *ex officio* or following a request by a party in the proceedings or a third party, rules that it would be disproportionate in the case in question, such as when there is a risk of depriving the convicted person or a third party and, in particular, their families from a thing which is essential for their livelihood or of causing them excessive and irreparable damage. In the cases referred to in the preceding sentence, the court may, as appropriate, order limited confiscation or a monetary penalty in accordance with paragraph 4.

3. Αν τα αντικείμενα ή τα περιουσιακά στοιχεία της παραγράφου 1 δεν υπάρχουν πλέον ή δεν έχουν βρεθεί, το δικαστήριο μπορεί να επιβάλει δήμευση (αναπληρωματική δήμευση) σε ίσης, κατά το χρόνο έκδοσης της καταδικαστικής απόφασης, αξίας περιουσιακά στοιχεία του δράστη.
4. Αν το δικαστήριο δεν μπορεί να επιβάλει δήμευση στα αντικείμενα ή περιουσιακά στοιχεία των προηγούμενων παραγράφων, επειδή αυτά δεν υπάρχουν ή δεν επαρκούν ή ανήκουν εν όλω ή εν μέρει σε τρίτο, στον οποίο δεν μπορεί να επιβληθεί δήμευση, μπορεί να επιβάλει στον δράστη χρηματική ποινή μέχρι του ποσού που αντιστοιχεί στην αξία των αντικειμένων αυτών.
5. Η δήμευση επιβάλλεται σε τρίτο αν τα αντικείμενα ή περιουσιακά στοιχεία μεταβιβάσθηκαν, άμεσα ή έμμεσα, από τον δράστη σε αυτόν ή αν αποκτήθηκαν από αυτόν ή περιήλθαν με άλλο τρόπο σε αυτόν, εφόσον κατά το χρόνο κτήσης των περιουσιακών στοιχείων γνώριζε ότι ενδέχεται να προέρχονται από κακούργημα ή πλημμέλημα εκ δόλου και ότι σκοπός της μεταβίβασής τους ήταν να αποφευχθεί η δήμευση. Η γνώση, σύμφωνα με το προηγούμενο εδάφιο, πρέπει να προκύπτει από το συνδυασμό περισσότερων ειδικά αναφερόμενων στην απόφαση του δικαστηρίου περιστατικών, όπως ιδίως ότι η μεταβίβαση ή η απόκτηση του περιουσιακού στοιχείου πραγματοποιήθηκε χωρίς αντάλλαγμα ή με αντάλλαγμα σημαντικά κατώτερο από την αγοραία αξία ή από εκείνο που θα προέκυπτε, με βάση τη συνήθη πρακτική, στις οικείες βιοτικές σχέσεις. Η δήμευση επιβάλλεται στον τρίτο μόνο εφόσον δεν μπορεί να επιβληθεί σε βάρος του δράστη δήμευση του ανταλλάγματος που έλαβε για τη μεταβίβαση ή αναπληρωματική δήμευση. Όταν ο τρίτος είναι νομικό πρόσωπο, εξετάζεται αν υπήρχε η προβλεπόμενη γνώση σχετικά με την προέλευση των περιουσιακών στοιχείων, σε όποιον έχει εξουσία εκπροσώπησής του ή είναι εξουσιοδοτημένος για τη λήψη αποφάσεων ή για την άσκηση ελέγχου, στο πλαίσιο του νομικού προσώπου ή της επιχείρησης ή σε όποιον ασκεί εν τοις πράγμασι τα καθήκοντα αυτά.
6. Σε κάθε περίπτωση δήμευσης, το δικαστήριο αποφασίζει αν αυτά που δημεύθηκαν, επιβάλλεται να καταστραφούν ή αν μπορούν να χρησιμοποιηθούν για το δημόσιο συμφέρον ή για κοινωνικούς σκοπούς ή για την ικανοποίηση του θύματος.

III

ΜΕΤΡΑ ΑΣΦΑΛΕΙΑΣ

Άρθρο 69
Γενική διάταξη

1. Μέτρα ασφαλείας, εκτός από τα προβλεπόμενα στα άρθρα 122 και 123, είναι:
α) τα μέτρα θεραπείας ατόμων με ψυχική ή διανοητική διαταραχή,
β) η δήμευση κατά το άρθρο 76 και
γ) η απέλαση αλλοδαπού.
2. Τα μέτρα ασφαλείας δεν μπορούν να επιβληθούν όταν η επιβολή τους παραβιάζει την αρχή της αναλογικότητας ενόψει της βαρύτητας της πράξης που έχει τελεστεί, της πράξης που υπάρχει κίνδυνος να τελεστεί, καθώς και της έντασης αυτού του κινδύνου. Για την αξιολόγηση των όρων αυτών απαιτείται ειδική αιτιολογία.

Άρθρο 69Α
Μέτρα θεραπείας ατόμων που απαλλάσσονται από την ποινή λόγω ψυχικής ή διανοητικής διαταραχής

1. Αν κάποιος που τέλεσε αξιόποινη πράξη, η οποία απειλείται με ποινή στερητική της ελευθερίας τουλάχιστον ενός έτους, απαλλάχθηκε από την ποινή λόγω ψυχικής ή διανοητικής διαταραχής (άρθρο 34), το δικαστήριο διατάσσει κατάλληλο για τη θεραπεία του μέτρο, εφόσον κρίνει ότι, εξαιτίας της κατάστασής του, υπάρχει κατά το χρόνο έκδοσης της απόφασης κίνδυνος, αν αφεθεί ελεύθερος, να τελέσει και άλλα τουλάχιστον ανάλογης βαρύτητας εγκλήματα. Η διάταξη της απόφασης που αφορά στο θεραπευτικό μέτρο εκτελείται με φροντίδα της εισαγγελικής αρχής.

3. If the objects or assets referred to in paragraph 1 no longer exist or have not been found, the court may order confiscation of assets of an equal value at the time the judgment of conviction was handed down which belong to the perpetrator (substitute confiscation).

4. If the court cannot order confiscation of the objects or assets referred to in the preceding paragraphs because they do not exist, or are not sufficient, or belong in whole or in part to a third party in respect of whom confiscation cannot be ordered, it may order the perpetrator to pay a monetary penalty up to the amount corresponding to the value of such things.

5. Confiscation shall be ordered against a third party if the objects or assets were directly or indirectly transferred by the perpetrator to such third party, or were acquired by such third party, or otherwise came into the possession of such third party, provided, at the time the assets were acquired, such third party knew that such objects or assets could have originated from a felony or misdemeanour committed with *dolus* and that the purpose of their transfer was to avoid confiscation. The knowledge referred to in the preceding sentence must arise from a combination of several facts specifically indicated in the court judgment, such as, in particular, the fact that the asset was transferred or acquired without consideration or for consideration considerably lower than the market value [of the asset] or the consideration that would have been achieved, on the basis of ordinary practice, in [the normal course of such transactions]. Confiscation shall be ordered against the third party only if confiscation cannot be ordered against the perpetrator for the consideration they received for the transfer or substitute confiscation. Where the third party is a legal person, [the court] shall examine whether the person with the power to represent the legal person or authorised to make decisions or exercise control within the legal person or the enterprise, or the person who actually performs such duties knew of the provenance of the assets, as provided for [above].

6. In all cases of confiscation, the court shall decide whether whatever was confiscated must be destroyed or can be used in the public interest or for societal purposes or to provide satisfaction to the victim.

III

SECURITY MEASURES

Article 69
General provision

1. Security measures, other than those provided for in Articles 122 and 123, are [distinguished into]:

a) therapeutic measures for persons suffering from a mental or emotional disorder;

b) confiscation in accordance with Article 76; and

c) deportation of foreign nationals.

2. Security measures may not be ordered when this would infringe the principle of proportionality, taking into consideration the severity of the act committed, the act at risk of being committed, and the intensity of such risk. Specific reasoning must be provided concerning the assessment of these conditions.

Article 69A
Therapeutic measures concerning persons exempt from punishment due to mental or emotional disorder

1. If any person who committed a punishable act carrying a custodial sentence of at least one year was exempted from said sentence due to mental or emotional disorder ([see] Article 34), the court shall order an appropriate therapeutic measure where it rules that, due to their condition, there is a risk, at the time the judgment is handed down, if they were to be released, they would commit further crimes of similar severity. The order contained in the judgment concerning the therapeutic measure shall be enforced by the public prosecutor's office.

2. Η προηγούμενη παράγραφος ισχύει για όλα τα εγκλήματα κατά της ζωής ή της σωματικής ακεραιότητας που απειλούνται με ποινή στερητική της ελευθερίας τουλάχιστον τριών μηνών. Δεν ισχύει για τα εγκλήματα κατά της ιδιοκτησίας και της περιουσίας που δεν εμπεριέχουν χρήση βίας ή απειλή βίας.

3. Κατάλληλα θεραπευτικά μέτρα είναι:

(α) η νοσηλεία σε ειδικό τμήμα δημόσιου ψυχιατρικού ή γενικού νοσοκομείου,

(β) η νοσηλεία σε ψυχιατρικό τμήμα δημόσιου ψυχιατρικού ή γενικού νοσοκομείου και

(γ) η υποχρεωτική θεραπεία και ψυχιατρική παρακολούθηση κατά τακτά χρονικά διαστήματα σε κατάλληλη εξωνοσοκομειακή Μονάδα Ψυχικής Υγείας ή εξωτερικά ιατρεία δημόσιου ψυχιατρικού ή γενικού νοσοκομείου.

4. Οι προϋποθέσεις επιβολής του μέτρου βεβαιώνονται με μία τουλάχιστον πραγματογνωμοσύνη που διενεργείται αμέσως μετά τη σύλληψη και με άλλη μία τουλάχιστον πραγματογνωμοσύνη που διενεργείται όσο το δυνατό πλησιέστερα προς τη δικάσιμο, με μέριμνα του εισαγγελέα του δικαστηρίου στο οποίο εισάγεται προς εκδίκαση η υπόθεση. Οι πραγματογνωμοσύνες διενεργούνται από πραγματογνώμονα που επιλέγεται, κατά προτίμηση, από τον κατάλογο που τηρείται στο οικείο Πρωτοδικείο. Στις πραγματογνωμοσύνες προτείνεται και το τυχόν κατάλληλο μέτρο θεραπείας.

Άρθρο 70
Διάρκεια του θεραπευτικού μέτρου

1. Στην απόφαση που διατάσσει το θεραπευτικό μέτρο ορίζεται ο μέγιστος χρόνος της διάρκειάς του, ο οποίος δεν μπορεί να υπερβαίνει τα δύο έτη για τα πλημμελήματα και τα πέντε έτη για τα κακουργήματα. Ένα μήνα τουλάχιστον πριν τη συμπλήρωση του χρόνου αυτού, το Τριμελές Πλημμελειοδικείο στην περιφέρεια του οποίου εκτελείται το θεραπευτικό μέτρο, μπορεί, με ειδικά αιτιολογημένη απόφαση, να διατάξει την παράταση του μέτρου ή την αντικατάστασή του με άλλο για τον ίδιο κατά ανώτατο όριο χρόνο, εφόσον τούτο επιβάλλεται για τις ανάγκες της θεραπείας και εξακολουθούν να υπάρχουν οι προϋποθέσεις της παραγράφου 1 του προηγούμενου άρθρου. Πριν από την έκδοση της απόφασης, το δικαστήριο καλεί τον θεραπευόμενο και το συνήγορό του, καθώς και τη διεύθυνση της μονάδας, όπου εκτελείται το μέτρο, να διατυπώσουν τις απόψεις τους. Κατ' εξαίρεση είναι δυνατή η παράταση του χρόνου διάρκειας του θεραπευτικού μέτρου πέραν των ανωτάτων χρονικών ορίων, με τη διαδικασία και για τους λόγους που προβλέπονται στο δεύτερο και τρίτο εδάφιο, εφόσον για την ύπαρξη των λόγων αυτών και την ανάγκη παράτασης του χρόνου διάρκειας του μέτρου υφίσταται η σύμφωνη γνώμη του θεράποντος ψυχιάτρου του θεραπευομένου και του επιστημονικού διευθυντή της μονάδας θεραπείας. Ο συνολικός χρόνος διάρκειας του θεραπευτικού μέτρου δεν μπορεί να υπερβαίνει τη χρονική διάρκεια του ανώτατου ορίου της ποινής που προβλέπεται στο νόμο για την πράξη που τέλεσε ο θεραπευόμενος.

2. Το ίδιο δικαστήριο, κάθε έτος, τηρώντας την ίδια διαδικασία, αποφασίζει αν το θεραπευτικό μέτρο που έχει επιβληθεί πρέπει να εξακολουθήσει ή να αντικατασταθεί με άλλο. Μπορεί όμως και οποτεδήποτε, με αίτηση του εισαγγελέα, του θεραπευομένου ή της διεύθυνσης της μονάδας όπου εκτελείται το μέτρο, μετά από εισήγηση του θεράποντος ιατρού, να διατάξει την άρση ή αντικατάστασή του. Σε περίπτωση απόρριψης της αίτησης, στην απόφαση απαιτείται να υπάρχει ειδική αιτιολογία ως προς την ανάγκη διατήρησης του θεραπευτικού μέτρου. Νέα αίτηση μπορεί να υποβληθεί μετά την πάροδο τεσσάρων μηνών από την απόρριψη της προηγούμενης.

3. Στη διαδικασία ενώπιον του Τριμελούς Πλημμελειοδικείου κατά τις διατάξεις των παραγράφων 1, εδάφιο β΄ και 2 του άρθρου αυτού, καθώς και του Εφετείου σε περίπτωση άσκησης έφεσης, εάν ο θεραπευόμενος δεν έχει συνήγορο, διορίζεται συνήγορος αυτεπαγγέλτως, κατά τις διατάξεις του άρθρου 340 του Κώδικα Ποινικής Δικονομίας.

2. The preceding paragraph [also] applies to all crimes against life or physical integrity carrying a custodial sentence of at least three months. It does not apply to crimes against property and assets which did not involve the use or threat of violence.
3. Appropriate therapeutic measures are [distinguished into]:
(a) hospitalisation in a special section of a state psychiatric or general hospital;
(b) hospitalisation in a psychiatric section of a state psychiatric or general hospital; and
(c) mandatory treatment and regular psychiatric observation at a suitable outpatient mental health facility or outpatient department of a state psychiatric or general hospital.
4. The conditions for ordering the measure shall be confirmed by at least one expert evidence [report] prepared immediately after the arrest, and by at least one further expert evidence [report] prepared as near as possible to the hearing date [ordered] by the public prosecutor at the court before which the case is brought for adjudication. Expert evidence [reports] shall be prepared by experts preferably chosen from among those included in the list kept [by] the competent court of first instance. Any appropriate therapeutic measure may also be proposed in such expert evidence [report].

Article 70
Duration of therapeutic measures

1. The judgment ordering the therapeutic measure shall set its maximum duration, which may not exceed two years for misdemeanours and five years for felonies. At least one month before this period elapses, the three-member court of misdemeanours in whose district the therapeutic measure is being enforced may issue a specifically reasoned judgment ordering that the measure be extended or replaced by a different measure with up to the same maximum duration, where this is required for the needs of the treatment and provided the conditions laid down in paragraph 1 of the preceding Article continue to be met. Before handing down its judgment, the court shall summon the person being treated and their counsel, as well as the management team of the facility where the measure is being enforced, to present their views. By way of exception, the duration of the therapeutic measure may be extended beyond the maximum time limits, under the procedure and on the grounds provided for in the second and third sentences, where the attending psychiatrist of the person being treated and the scientific director of the medical facility agree that these grounds apply and there is a need to extend the duration of such measure. The total duration of the therapeutic measure may not exceed the maximum duration of the sentence provided for in law for the act committed by the person being treated.
2. Each year, the court, following the same procedure, shall decide whether the therapeutic measure ordered must continue or be replaced by a different measure. However, following an application filed by the public prosecutor, the person being treated or the management team of the facility where the measure is being enforced and a recommendation from the attending physician, the court may order that the measure be terminated or replaced. If the application is dismissed, the judgment must contain specific reasoning as to the need for the therapeutic measure to remain in place. A new application may be filed after four months have elapsed from the date the previous application was dismissed.
3. If the person being treated is not represented by counsel during the proceedings before the three-member court of misdemeanours under the provisions of [the second sentence] of paragraph 1 and paragraph 2 of this Article, and before the court of appeal, where an appeal has been filed, counsel shall be appointed *ex officio* in accordance with the provisions of Article 340 of the Code of Criminal Procedure.

Άρθρο 71
Μέτρα θεραπείας ατόμων μειωμένου καταλογισμού λόγω ψυχικής ή διανοητικής διαταραχής

1. Αν κάποιος τέλεσε αξιόποινη πράξη λόγω ψυχικής ή διανοητικής διαταραχής που μειώνει σημαντικά τον καταλογισμό του (άρθρο 36 παρ. 1) και η πράξη του απειλείται με ποινή στερητική της ελευθερίας τουλάχιστον ενός έτους, το δικαστήριο, εκτός από την επιβολή της μειωμένης ποινής, διατάσσει την εισαγωγή του σε ψυχιατρικό παράρτημα καταστήματος κράτησης ή, σε περίπτωση αναστολής εκτέλεσης της ποινής του, τα θεραπευτικά μέτρα του άρθρου 69Α παρ. 3, εφόσον κρίνει ότι συντρέχει ο περιγραφόμενος στο άρθρο 69Α παρ. 1 κίνδυνος. Οι παράγραφοι 2 και 4 του άρθρου 69Α έχουν και στην περίπτωση αυτή εφαρμογή.

2. Η εκτέλεση του μέτρου γίνεται αμέσως μετά την έκδοση της απόφασης, με φροντίδα της εισαγγελικής αρχής.

3. Το άρθρο 70 έχει και εδώ ανάλογη εφαρμογή. Μετά την ολοκλήρωση του θεραπευτικού μέτρου, ο καταδικασθείς εκτίει την ποινή του, εφόσον δεν έχει ανασταλεί η εκτέλεσή της. Από την ποινή αφαιρείται ο χρόνος νοσηλείας στο ψυχιατρικό παράρτημα καταστήματος κράτησης ή στις μονάδες του άρθρου 69Α παρ. 3, στοιχεία α΄ και β΄. Το Τριμελές Πλημμελειοδικείο του τόπου εκτέλεσης του μέτρου μπορεί όμως να διατάξει τη μη έκτιση της ποινής, αν το έγκλημα για το οποίο επιβλήθηκε είναι πλημμέλημα και η έκτιση δεν θεωρείται πλέον αναγκαία.

Άρθρο 72
Απέλαση αλλοδαπού

1. Με την επιφύλαξη των σχετικών διατάξεων που περιλαμβάνονται σε διεθνείς συμβάσεις που έχουν κυρωθεί από τη χώρα, το δικαστήριο, ανεξάρτητα από τυχόν συντρέχουσα διοικητική διαδικασία σύμφωνα με τις ισχύουσες διατάξεις της νομοθεσίας περί αλλοδαπών, μπορεί να διατάξει την απέλαση κάθε αλλοδαπού (πολίτη τρίτης χώρας ή κράτους μέλους της Ε.Ε.) που καταδικάσθηκε σε κάθειρξη, εάν κρίνει ότι η παραμονή του στη χώρα δεν συμβιβάζεται προς τους όρους της κοινωνικής συμβίωσης, λαμβάνοντας υπόψη ιδίως το είδος του εγκλήματος για το οποίο καταδικάστηκε, τον βαθμό της υπαιτιότητάς του, τις ειδικές συνθήκες τέλεσης της πράξης, τις συνέπειες αυτής, τον χρόνο παραμονής του στο ελληνικό έδαφος, τη νομιμότητα ή μη της παραμονής του, την εν γένει συμπεριφορά, τον επαγγελματικό προσανατολισμό, την ύπαρξη οικογένειας και γενικότερα τον βαθμό ένταξης αυτού στην ελληνική κοινωνία, καθώς και τον βαθμό επικινδυνότητας για τη δημόσια ασφάλεια.

Ειδικά για τους πολίτες κράτους μέλους της Ε.Ε. που έχουν αποδεδειγμένα μόνιμη διαμονή στην ελληνική επικράτεια τουλάχιστον για πέντε (5) έτη, πριν από την τέλεση της πράξης, απέλαση μπορεί να επιβληθεί αν καταδικάστηκαν σε ποινή κάθειρξης τουλάχιστον έξι (6) ετών για τις αξιόποινες πράξεις του δεύτερου εδαφίου της παρ. 6 του άρθρου 105Β ή για τη διακεκριμένη κλοπή του άρθρου 374 και μόνο όταν συντρέχουν και αιτιολογούνται ειδικώς στην απόφαση σοβαροί και επιτακτικοί λόγοι δημοσίας ασφάλειας. Η απέλαση εκτελείται αμέσως μετά την έκτιση της ποινής ή την απόλυση από τις φυλακές.

2. Το δικαστήριο μπορεί, επίσης, να διατάξει την απέλαση από τη χώρα κάθε αλλοδαπού στον οποίο επιβλήθηκε μέτρο ασφάλειας των άρθρων 69Α, 70 και 71. Σε αυτήν την περίπτωση, η απέλαση μπορεί να διαταχθεί σε αντικατάσταση αυτών των μέτρων.

3. Το δικαστήριο που αποφασίζει την απέλαση του αλλοδαπού δράστη, επιβάλλει σε αυτόν απαγόρευση επανεισόδου του στη χώρα για χρονικό διάστημα τουλάχιστον δέκα (10) ετών αν είναι πολίτης τρίτης χώρας και τουλάχιστον πέντε (5) ετών αν είναι πολίτης κράτους μέλους της Ε.Ε..

Το συμβούλιο πλημμελειοδικών του τόπου του δικαστηρίου που επέβαλε την απέλαση, για εξαιρετικούς λόγους που αιτιολογούνται ειδικά και ύστερα από γνώμη της αρμόδιας αστυνομικής αρχής, μπορεί να επιτρέψει, για συγκεκριμένη διάρκεια ή επ' αόριστον, την επιστροφή του αλλοδαπού στη χώρα και πριν από την παρέλευση των ανωτέρω χρονικών διαστημάτων. Νέα αίτηση του αλλοδαπού για επιστροφή μπορεί να υποβληθεί μόνο μετά την πάροδο ενός (1) έτους από την απόρριψη της προηγούμενης.

Article 71
Therapeutic measures for persons with reduced imputability due to mental or emotional disorder

1. If a person committed a punishable act due to a mental or emotional disorder which significantly reduces their imputability ([see] Article 36(1)) and their act carries a custodial sentence of at least one year, the court, in addition to ordering a reduced sentence, shall order that they be committed to a psychiatric facility at a custodial institution or, where enforcement of their sentence is stayed, shall order the therapeutic measures provided for in Article 69A(3), where it rules that the risk described in Article 69A(1) exists. Article 69A(2) and (4) also apply in such a case.
2. The measure shall be enforced by the public prosecutor's office immediately after the judgment is handed down.
3. Article 70 also applies *mutatis mutandis* in such a case. After the therapeutic measure has been completed, the convicted person shall serve their sentence, provided its enforcement has not been stayed. The duration of hospitalisation at a psychiatric facility at a custodial institution or at the facilities referred to in Article 69A(3)(a) and (b) shall be deducted from the sentence. However, the three-member court of misdemeanours at the place where the measure is being enforced may order that the sentence not be served if the crime for which it was ordered is a misdemeanour and serving such sentence is no longer considered necessary.

Article 72
Deportation of foreign nationals

1. Without prejudice to the relevant provisions contained in international treaties and conventions ratified by [Greece], the court, irrespective of any concurrent administrative proceedings taking place in accordance with the applicable provisions of the legislation on foreign nationals, may order the deportation of any foreign national (citizen of a third country or EU Member State) who was sentenced to incarceration if the court considers that such person remaining in [Greece] is not compatible with the [established rules governing] social co-existence, taking into account, in particular: the type of crime of which they were convicted; their degree of culpability; the specific conditions under which the act was committed; the consequences of such act; the length of time they were resident within the territory of Greece; whether or not such residence was lawful; their general conduct; what they [intend to] do for a living; whether or not they have family; and, generally, the extent to which they have integrated into Greek society, as well as the degree of risk [they pose] to public security.
With specific regard to citizens of an EU Member State who are proven to have been permanently resident in the territory of Greece for at least five years before the act was committed, deportation may be ordered if they were sentenced to incarceration of at least six years for [any of] the punishable acts provided for in the second sentence of Article 105B(6) or for aggravated theft under Article 374 and only when serious and overriding reasons of public security exist and are specifically reasoned in the judgment. Deportation shall be enforced immediately after [the person in question] has served their sentence or been released from prison.
2. The court may shall also order deportation of any foreign national on whom a security measure provided for in Articles 69A, 70 [or] 71 has been imposed. In this case, deportation may be ordered to replace such measures.
3. The court ordering deportation of a foreign perpetrator shall ban them from re-entering [Greece] for a period of at least 10 years if they are a citizen of a third country and at least 5 years if they are a citizen of an EU Member State.
Where there are exceptional grounds which are specifically reasoned and following an opinion issued by the competent police authorities, the judicial council of the court of misdemeanours which ordered deportation may allow the foreign national to return to [Greece] for a specific length of time or indefinitely even before the above time periods have elapsed. The foreign national may file a new application to return only after one year has elapsed from the date the previous application was dismissed.

4. α. Η απέλαση εκτελείται με ενέργειες των αρμόδιων αστυνομικών αρχών, σύμφωνα με την οικεία νομοθεσία περί αλλοδαπών, καθώς και τους κανόνες του διεθνούς και του ενωσιακού δικαίου. Πέντε (5) μήνες πριν από τη συμπλήρωση του χρόνου για την υφ' όρον απόλυση του κρατούμενου, ο διευθυντής του καταστήματος κράτησης υποχρεούται να ενημερώσει σχετικά τον εισαγγελέα πλημμελειοδικών του τόπου κράτησης, ώστε ο τελευταίος να παραγγείλει αμέσως στην αρμόδια αστυνομική αρχή τη διερεύνηση του εφικτού της απέλασης και την προετοιμασία για την υλοποίησή της. Τουλάχιστον έναν (1) μήνα πριν από τη συμπλήρωση του χρόνου για την υφ' όρον απόλυση, η αρμόδια αστυνομική αρχή αναφέρει, με αιτιολογημένη έκθεσή της, στον εισαγγελέα του τόπου κράτησης εάν η απέλαση είναι εφικτή. Αν η απέλαση είναι εφικτή, εκτελείται αμέσως μετά την υφ' όρον απόλυση ή την έκτιση της ποινής του κρατουμένου. Με αιτιολογημένη διάταξη του εισαγγελέα πλημμελειοδικών του τόπου κράτησης, η κράτηση μπορεί να παραταθεί για έναν (1) μήνα μόνο από τον χρόνο της υφ' όρον απόλυσης ή έκτισης της ποινής, εφόσον η διαδικασία απέλασης έχει ξεκινήσει και πρόκειται να εκτελεστεί μέσα σε αυτό το χρονικό διάστημα. Μετά την παρέλευση του χρόνου αυτού και εφόσον η απέλαση δεν έχει πραγματοποιηθεί, με διάταξη του εισαγγελέα πλημμελειοδικών του τόπου κράτησης αναστέλλεται υποχρεωτικά η απέλαση του αλλοδαπού, τού επιβάλλονται ιδίως οι όροι που προβλέπονται στην παρ. 2 του άρθρου 106 και ο κρατούμενος απολύεται αμέσως.

β. Αν ο αλλοδαπός παρεμποδίζει την προετοιμασία της απομάκρυνσής του αρνούμενος να συνεργαστεί με τις αρχές και να αποκαλύψει τα πραγματικά του στοιχεία, ο εισαγγελέας πλημμελειοδικών του τόπου κράτησης μπορεί να παρατείνει την κράτησή του μέχρι και τρεις (3) μήνες από τον χρόνο της υφ' όρον απόλυσης ή έκτισης της ποινής. Στην περίπτωση αυτή, όπως και στην περ. α', ο αλλοδαπός παραμένει μέχρι την εκτέλεση της απέλασής του σε ειδικό χώρο του καταστήματος κράτησης ή του θεραπευτικού καταστήματος ή σε ειδικό χώρο των αστυνομικών αρχών που δημιουργούνται για τον σκοπό αυτόν, με εντολή του εισαγγελέα πλημμελειοδικών του τόπου κράτησης. Κατά της εισαγγελικής διάταξης που παρατείνει την κράτηση, ο κρατούμενος μπορεί να υποβάλει προσφυγή, για την οποία αποφαίνεται αμετάκλητα ο αρμόδιος εισαγγελέας εφετών μέσα σε προθεσμία δεκαπέντε (15) ημερών. Μετά από την παρέλευση του τριμήνου, με διάταξη του εισαγγελέα πλημμελειοδικών του τόπου κράτησης αναστέλλεται υποχρεωτικά η απέλαση του αλλοδαπού, τού επιβάλλονται ιδίως οι όροι που προβλέπονται στην παρ. 2 του άρθρου 106 και ο κρατούμενος απολύεται αμέσως.

γ. Όταν η απέλαση καταστεί εφικτή κατά την αιτιολογημένη γνώμη της αστυνομικής αρχής, η απόφαση της αναστολής αυτής ανακαλείται με την ίδια διαδικασία που εκδόθηκε και διατάσσεται η κράτηση του αλλοδαπού για την πραγματοποίηση της απέλασης για χρονικό διάστημα το πολύ δεκαπέντε (15) ημερών.

5. Εάν, σύμφωνα με την αιτιολογημένη έκθεση της αστυνομικής αρχής κατά την περ. α' της παρ. 4, η απέλαση δεν είναι εφικτή για οποιονδήποτε λόγο και ιδίως επειδή:

α) ο αλλοδαπός είναι ανιθαγενής ή ζητεί διεθνή προστασία ή απολαμβάνει διεθνή προστασία, ή

β) δεν λειτουργεί ή δεν συνεργάζεται η προξενική αρχή της χώρας καταγωγής του ή

γ) η χώρα του δεν συνιστά ασφαλή προορισμό ή τυχόν επιστροφή συνιστά παραβίαση του άρθρου 3 της Ευρωπαϊκής Σύμβασης των Δικαιωμάτων του Ανθρώπου ή

δ) δεν τον δέχεται η χώρα καταγωγής του,

τότε, μετά την υφ' όρον απόλυση ή την έκτιση ποινής, ο εισαγγελέας πλημμελειοδικών του τόπου κράτησης αναστέλλει υποχρεωτικά με διάταξή του την απέλαση, επιβάλλει ιδίως τους όρους που προβλέπονται στην παρ. 2 του άρθρου 106 ή ορισμένους από αυτούς και ο κρατούμενος απολύεται αμέσως. Όταν η απέλαση καταστεί εφικτή, εφαρμόζεται αναλόγως η περ. γ' της παρ. 4.

6. Αυτός που παραβιάζει τον όρο ή τους όρους που του έχουν επιβληθεί από τον εισαγγελέα πλημμελειοδικών κατά την αναστολή της απέλασης, τιμωρείται με την ποινή της παρ. 1 του άρθρου 182.

4. a. The competent police authorities shall take steps to enforce deportation in accordance with the relevant legislation on foreign nationals and the rules of international and EU law. Five months before the date on which the detainee is to be conditionally released, the governor of the custodial institution is obligated to inform the court of misdemeanours public prosecutor at the place of detention of this fact so that the latter can immediately order the competent police authorities to inquire into whether deportation is feasible and to take preparatory steps. At least one month before the date on which the detainee is to be conditionally released, the competent police authorities shall submit a reasoned report to the public prosecutor at the place of detention on whether deportation is feasible. If deportation is feasible, it shall be enforced immediately after the detainee has been conditionally released or served their sentence. By means of a reasoned order issued by the court of misdemeanours public prosecutor at the place of detention, detention may be extended by one month only from the date the detainee was conditionally released or finished serving their sentence, provided that the deportation procedure has commenced and is to be enforced within such period. After such period has elapsed and provided deportation has not taken place, the court of misdemeanours public prosecutor at the place of detention must necessarily issue an order suspending deportation of the foreign national, imposing, in particular, the conditions provided for in Article 106(2) on the foreign national, and and they shall be immediately released from detention.
b. If the foreign national obstructs the preparatory steps for their [deportation] by refusing to cooperate with the authorities and to disclose their true identity, the court of misdemeanours public prosecutor at the place of detention may extend such detention for up to three months from the date on which the detainee is to be conditionally released or finishes serving their sentence. In both this case [and in the case provided for] in subparagraph (a) above, following an order from the court of misdemeanours public prosecutor at the place of detention, the foreign national shall, until deportation is enforced, remain in a special area of the custodial institution or therapeutic institution or a special area of police [facilities] created for such purpose. The detainee may seek recourse against the [court of misdemeanours] public prosecutor's order extending the detention on which the competent court of appeal public prosecutor shall decide within a deadline of 15 days. After three months have elapsed, the court of misdemeanours public prosecutor at the place of detention must necessarily issue an order suspending deportation of the foreign national, imposing in particular the conditions provided for in Article 106(2) on the foreign national, and immediately releasing the detainee.
c. Once, in the reasonable opinion of the police authorities, deportation becomes feasible, such suspension decision shall be revoked using the same procedure under which it was issued, and detention of the foreign national for no more than 15 days shall be ordered for the purpose of deportation.

5. If, in accordance with the reasoned report of the police authorities provided for in paragraph 4(a), deportation is not feasible for any reason and, in particular, because:
a) the foreign national is stateless, or claims international protection, or enjoys international protection; or
b) there is no consular authority of their country of origin or [such authority refuses] to collaborate; or
c) their country is not a safe destination, or any return would violate Article 3 of the European Convention on Human Rights; or
d) their country of origin [refuses] to accept them,
then, after the foreign national has been conditionally released or served their sentence, the court of misdemeanours public prosecutor at the place of detention must necessarily issue an order suspending deportation of the foreign national, imposing in particular the conditions provided for in Article 106(2) or certain of these conditions on the foreign national, and immediately releasing the detainee. Paragraph 4(c) applies *mutatis mutandis* once deportation becomes feasible.

6. The punishment provided for in Article 182(1) shall be imposed on any person who violates the condition(s) imposed on them by the court of misdemeanours public prosecutor in the context of suspending their deportation.

Άρθρα 73 – 74

(Καταργούνται)

Άρθρο 75

Παραγραφή μέτρου ασφαλείας

1. Αν από τότε που έγινε αμετάκλητη η απόφαση με την οποία επιβλήθηκε το μέτρο ασφαλείας του άρθρου 69Α περάσει τριετία χωρίς να έχει αρχίσει η εκτέλεσή του, αυτό δεν μπορεί πια να εκτελεστεί, εκτός αν το δικαστήριο που το επέβαλε διατάξει διαφορετικά και δεν έχουν περάσει δέκα έτη από την επιβολή του.

2. Το δικαστήριο μπορεί να διατάξει την εκτέλεση του μέτρου κατά την προηγούμενη παράγραφο μόνο αν ο σκοπός του μέτρου επιβάλλει ακόμα και τότε την εφαρμογή του.

Άρθρο 76

Δήμευση

1. Η δήμευση των αντικειμένων της παραγράφου 1 του άρθρου 68 επιβάλλεται υποχρεωτικά σε βάρος του κατόχου τους, έστω και χωρίς την καταδίκη ορισμένου προσώπου για την τελεσθείσα πράξη, αν από τη φύση τους προκύπτει κίνδυνος της δημόσιας τάξης. Η δήμευση εκτελείται και κατά των κληρονόμων, αν η απόφαση έγινε αμετάκλητη ενόσω ζούσε εκείνος κατά του οποίου απαγγέλθηκε η δήμευση. Αν δεν προηγήθηκε καταδίκη ορισμένου προσώπου ή δεν μπορούσε να γίνει δίωξη, τη δήμευση διατάσσει είτε το δικαστήριο που δίκασε την υπόθεση είτε το αρμόδιο δικαστικό συμβούλιο.

2. Το δικαστήριο ή το δικαστικό συμβούλιο αποφασίζει αν αυτά που δημεύθηκαν, επιβάλλεται να καταστραφούν ή αν μπορούν να χρησιμοποιηθούν για το δημόσιο συμφέρον ή για κοινωνικούς σκοπούς ή για την ικανοποίηση του θύματος.

Άρθρα 77 - 78

(Καταργούνται)

Articles 73 – 74

[Repealed]

Article 75

Time-barring of security measures

1. If three years have elapsed from the date the judgment ordering the security measure referred to in Article 69A became irrevocable and the enforcement of such measure has not commenced, the measure may no longer be enforced, unless the court which ordered [the measure] orders otherwise and provided 10 years have not elapsed since the date [the measure] was ordered.

2. The court may order that the measure be enforced in accordance with the preceding paragraph only if a reason for implementing such measure still exists at that time.

Article 76

Confiscation

1. If the objects referred to in Article 68(1) pose a risk to public order, they shall necessarily be confiscated from their possessor, even if no specific person has been convicted of the act committed. Confiscation shall also be enforced against the heirs [of the possessor] if the judgment became irrevocable while the person against whom confiscation was pronounced is alive. If no specific person was previously convicted or could not be prosecuted, confiscation shall be ordered either by the trial court or by the competent judicial council.

2. The court or judicial council shall decide whether the objects confiscated must be destroyed, or can be used in the public interest, or for societal purposes, or to provide satisfaction to the victim.

Articles 77 - 78

[Repealed]

ΠΕΜΠΤΟ ΚΕΦΑΛΑΙΟ

ΕΠΙΜΕΤΡΗΣΗ ΠΟΙΝΗΣ

I

ΓΕΝΙΚΟΙ ΚΑΝΟΝΕΣ

Άρθρο 79
Δικαστική επιμέτρηση της ποινής

1. Με την επιμέτρηση της ποινής καθορίζεται η ανάλογη και δίκαιη τιμωρία του εγκλήματος με βάση τη βαρύτητα της πράξης και το βαθμό ενοχής του υπαιτίου γι' αυτή. Το δικαστήριο σταθμίζει τα στοιχεία που λειτουργούν υπέρ και σε βάρος του υπαιτίου και συνεκτιμά τις συνέπειες της ποινής για τον ίδιο και τους οικείους του.

2. Για την εκτίμηση της βαρύτητας της πράξης το δικαστήριο λαμβάνει υπόψη του:

α) τη βλάβη που αυτή προξένησε ή τον κίνδυνο που προκάλεσε,

β) τη φύση, το είδος και το αντικείμενο της πράξης, καθώς επίσης όλες τις περιστάσεις χρόνου, τόπου, μέσων και τρόπου που συνόδευσαν την προπαρασκευή ή την εκτέλεσή της.

3. Για την εκτίμηση του βαθμού ενοχής του υπαιτίου, το δικαστήριο εξετάζει:

α) την ένταση του δόλου ή το βαθμό της αμέλειάς του,

β) τα αίτια που τον ώθησαν στην εκτέλεση του εγκλήματος, την αφορμή που του δόθηκε και τον σκοπό που επιδίωξε,

γ) τον χαρακτήρα του και τον βαθμό της ανάπτυξής του που επηρέασαν την πράξη,

δ) τις ατομικές και κοινωνικές περιστάσεις και την προηγούμενη ζωή του στο μέτρο που σχετίζονται με την πράξη,

ε) τον βαθμό της δυνατότητας και της ικανότητάς του να πράξει διαφορετικά,

στ) τη διαγωγή του κατά τη διάρκεια της πράξης και μετά την πράξη και ιδίως τη μετάνοια που επέδειξε και την προθυμία του να επανορθώσει τις συνέπειες της πράξης του.

4. Στοιχεία που λειτουργούν υπέρ του υπαιτίου θεωρούνται ιδίως:

α) το ότι αυτός διαδραμάτισε έναν σαφώς υποδεέστερο ρόλο σε πράξη που τελέστηκε από πολλούς,

β) το ότι τέλεσε την πράξη σε δικαιολογημένη συναισθηματική φόρτιση,

γ) το ότι έθεσε τον εαυτό του στη διάθεση των αρχών χωρίς σημαντική καθυστέρηση, ενώ μπορούσε να διαφύγει,

δ) το ότι διευκόλυνε ουσιωδώς την εξιχνίαση του εγκλήματος.

5. Στοιχεία που λειτουργούν σε βάρος του υπαιτίου θεωρούνται ιδίως:

α) η κατ' επάγγελμα τέλεση της πράξης,

β) η ιδιαίτερη σκληρότητα,

γ) η εκμετάλλευση της εμπιστοσύνης του θύματος,

δ) το γεγονός ότι το θύμα δεν μπορούσε να προστατεύσει τον εαυτό του,

ε) το ότι ο υπαίτιος διαδραμάτισε ιθύνοντα ρόλο σε πράξη που τελέστηκε με συμμετοχή πολλών.

6. Στοιχεία που έχουν αξιολογηθεί από τον νομοθέτη για τον προσδιορισμό της απειλούμενης ποινής δεν λαμβάνονται από το δικαστήριο επιπροσθέτως υπόψη κατά την επιμέτρησή της.

7. Στην απόφαση αναφέρονται ρητά οι λόγοι που δικαιολογούν την κρίση του δικαστηρίου για την επιμέτρηση της ποινής που επέβαλε.

CHAPTER V

DETERMINATION OF THE EXTENT OF THE PUNISHMENT

I

GENERAL RULES

Article 79
Judicial determination of the extent of the punishment

1. Determination of the extent of the punishment [aims at] the appropriate and just punishment of the crime on the basis of the severity of the act and the degree of guilt of the culpable person. The court shall weigh up the circumstances operating to the benefit and detriment of the culpable person, while also taking into consideration the consequences of the punishment for the culpable person and their related parties.

2. When assessing the severity of the act, the court shall take into consideration:

a) the harm or danger caused by the act;

b) the nature, type and object of the act, as well as all circumstances concerning the time, place, means and manner that accompanied the preparation or commission of the act.

3. When assessing the degree of guilt of the culpable person, the court shall examine:

a) the intensity of *dolus* or degree of negligence on their part;

b) the causes which led the culpable person to commit the crime, the opportunity which arose and the objective they sought;

c) their personality and maturity [as factors] which influenced the act;

d) the personal and social circumstances [of the culpable person] and their life prior [to committing the act], insofar as these have any bearing on the act;

e) the degree to which they were able to have and capable of having acted differently; [and]

f) their conduct during and after the act and, in particular, their repentance and willingness to remedy the consequences of their act.

4. The following circumstances, in particular, shall be deemed to operate to the benefit of the culpable person:

a) the fact that they played a clearly minor role in an act committed by several persons;

b) the fact that they committed the act under justified emotional stress;

c) the fact that they surrendered themselves to the authorities without significant delay when they could have absconded instead; [and]

d) the fact that they provided material assistance in solving the crime.

5. The following circumstances, in particular, shall be deemed to operate to the detriment of the culpable person:

a) committing the act [for monetary gain];

b) demonstrating particular cruelty;

c) exploiting the victim's trust;

d) the fact that the victim could not protect themselves; [and]

e) the fact that the culpable person played a major role in an act committed with the participation of several persons.

6. When determining the extent of the punishment [carried by the act], the court shall not additionally take into consideration circumstances which had been taken into consideration by the legislator for determining the punishment carried [by the act].

7. The grounds justifying the court's ruling on the extent of the punishment it imposed shall be expressly set out in the judgment.

Άρθρο 80
Επιμέτρηση και απότιση χρηματικής ποινής

1. Κατά την επιμέτρηση της χρηματικής ποινής, το δικαστήριο λαμβάνει υπόψη του
α) τη βαρύτητα της πράξης και την ενοχή του υπαιτίου γι' αυτήν,
β) την προσωπική και οικονομική κατάσταση του υπαιτίου, λαμβάνοντας υπόψη ειδικότερα
βα) τα καθαρά έσοδα που αποκτά από την εργασία του κατά μέσο όρο κάθε ημέρα,
ββ) άλλα τυχόν εισοδήματα και εν γένει την περιουσία του, καθώς και
βγ) τις οικογενειακές του υποχρεώσεις. Άλλες υποχρεώσεις του μπορούν επίσης να συνυπολογισθούν από το δικαστήριο.
2. [Καταργείται].
3. [Καταργείται].
4. [Καταργείται].
5. [Καταργείται].
6. Σε περίπτωση μη καταβολής της χρηματικής ποινής σύμφωνα με τα παραπάνω αυτή ή το μη καταβληθέν μέρος, βεβαιώνεται κατά το άρθρο 553 ΚΠΔ.

Άρθρο 80Α
Μετατροπή της ποινής φυλάκισης σε χρήμα

1. Κάθε ποινή φυλάκισης μέχρι δύο (2) ετών, αν το δικαστήριο κρίνει ότι δεν υπάγεται στις προϋποθέσεις εφαρμογής των άρθρων 99 και 104 Α, μετατρέπεται σε χρηματική ποινή, υπολογίζοντας κάθε ημέρα σε ποσό από δέκα (10) έως εκατό (100) ευρώ, εκτός αν το δικαστήριο, με την απόφασή του, κρίνει ότι απαιτείται η πραγματική της έκτιση εν όλω ή εν μέρει, για να αποτραπεί ο δράστης από την τέλεση νέων αξιόποινων πράξεων. Η παρ. 1 του άρθρου 80 για το ύψος της μετατροπής εφαρμόζεται αναλόγως.
2. Αν ο καταδικασθείς αδυνατεί να καταβάλει αμέσως το σύνολο της χρηματικής ποινής ή η καταβολή της συνεπάγεται την αδυναμία καταβολής της αποζημίωσης στο θύμα, το δικαστήριο καθορίζει, και αυτεπαγγέλτως, προθεσμία, όχι μεγαλύτερη από τρία (3) έτη, ώστε μέσα σε αυτήν να καταβάλει σε δόσεις ή εφάπαξ την ποινή του.
3. Αν η αδυναμία καταβολής της χρηματικής ποινής ή των δόσεων αυτής οφείλεται σε ουσιώδη αλλαγή των όρων της προσωπικής και οικονομικής κατάστασης του καταδικασθέντος μετά την επιβολή της ποινής, ο καταδικασθείς μπορεί να ζητήσει από το δικαστήριο που εξέδωσε την απόφαση:
α) προθεσμία καταβολής της χρηματικής ποινής ή επέκταση αυτής, η οποία δεν μπορεί να υπερβαίνει συνολικά τα πέντε (5) έτη, ή
β) αντικατάσταση της χρηματικής ποινής από την προσφορά κοινωφελούς εργασίας, στο μέτρο που ορίζει το δικαστήριο σύμφωνα με το άρθρο 104Α.
Κάθε συγκεκριμένο αίτημα μπορεί να υποβληθεί μία (1) μόνο φορά.
4. Σε περίπτωση εφάπαξ καταβολής της χρηματικής ποινής που προέρχεται από μετατροπή ποινής φυλάκισης, χωρίς εφαρμογή των παρ. 2 και 3, δεν εφαρμόζονται οι διατάξεις που προβλέπουν προσαύξησή της.

Άρθρο 81
Επιμέτρηση της ποινής της παροχής κοινωφελούς εργασίας

1. Κατά την επιμέτρηση της ποινής της παροχής κοινωφελούς εργασίας λαμβάνονται υπόψη και η ηλικία, η κατάσταση της υγείας του υπαιτίου, καθώς και οι επαγγελματικές και οικογενειακές του υποχρεώσεις.
2. Στην απόφαση ορίζεται η μέγιστη διάρκεια παροχής της κοινωφελούς εργασίας, που δεν μπορεί να υπερβαίνει τους είκοσι τέσσερις (24) μήνες.

Article 80
Determination and payment of monetary penalties

1. When determining the monetary penalty, the court shall take into consideration:
a) the severity of the act and the guilt of the culpable person;
b) the personal and financial situation of the culpable person, having particular regard to:
ba) the net [income] earned from their work on average each day;
bb) any other income and their assets in general; and
bc) their family obligations. The court may also take into account other obligations of the culpable person.
2. [Repealed]
3. [Repealed]
4. [Repealed]
5. [Repealed]
6. Where the monetary penalty is not paid in accordance with the foregoing, the penalty or the part of the penalty not paid shall be confirmed in accordance with Article 553 of the Code of Criminal Procedure.

Article 80A
Commutation of sentences of imprisonment into monetary penalties

1. Where the court considers that any sentence of imprisonment of up to two years does not meet the conditions for applying Articles 99 and 104A, such sentence shall be commuted to a monetary penalty, calculating each day at between 10 and 100 euros, unless the court, in its judgment, rules that the sentence must actually be served in whole or in part to prevent the perpetrator from committing new punishable acts. Article 80(1) applies *mutatis mutandis* when calculating such commutation.
2. If the convicted person cannot immediately pay the entire monetary penalty or payment results in inability to pay compensation to the victim, the court shall set, even *ex officio*, a deadline no longer than three years within which the convicted person must pay their penalty in instalments or as a lump sum.
3. If the convicted person is unable to pay the monetary penalty or its instalments due to a material change in their personal and financial circumstances which occurred after the penalty was imposed, the convicted person may request that the court which handed down the judgment:
a) set a deadline for payment of the monetary penalty or extend said deadline, which may not exceed five years in total; or
b) replace the monetary penalty with community service, to the extent set by the court in accordance with Article 104A.
Each specific request may be submitted only once.
4. Where a monetary penalty resulting from commutation of a sentence of imprisonment is to be paid as a lump sum and paragraphs 2 and 3 do not apply, the provisions for increasing such penalty do not apply.

Article 81
Determination of the length of community service

1. In determining the length of community service, [the court] shall take into consideration the age, health, professional and family obligations of the culpable person.
2. The maximum length of community service, which may not exceed 24 months, shall be set in the judgment.

3. Η κοινωφελής εργασία πραγματοποιείται προς όφελος του κοινού σε δημόσιες υπηρεσίες, οργανισμούς τοπικής αυτοδιοίκησης ή μη κερδοσκοπικά πρόσωπα ιδιωτικού δικαίου, που ορίζονται με απόφαση του Υπουργού Δικαιοσύνης και των κατά περίπτωση συναρμόδιων Υπουργών.
Μπορεί επίσης να αφορά και σε παροχή υπηρεσιών προς τον παθόντα, αν υπάρχει η σύμφωνη γνώμη του. Με την ίδια απόφαση ορίζονται επίσης η οργάνωση της παροχής κοινωφελούς εργασίας, η διαδικασία επιλογής, ανάθεσης και επίβλεψης της σχετικής εργασίας και κάθε άλλη σχετική λεπτομέρεια.
4. Στην απόφαση καθορίζεται και η χρηματική ποινή που θα πρέπει να αποτίσει ο καταδικασθείς, αν δεν παρέχει με συνέπεια την κοινωφελή εργασία. Τέσσερις (4) ώρες κοινωφελούς εργασίας αντιστοιχούν με εκατό (100) ευρώ χρηματικής ποινής.
5. Αν η εργασία παρέχεται από εκείνον που καταδικάστηκε ελλιπώς ή πλημμελώς με δική του υπαιτιότητα, ο εισαγγελέας εκτέλεσης της ποινής, αφού λάβει υπόψη τη συχνότητα και σοβαρότητα της παραβίασης των υποχρεώσεων από τον καταδικασθέντα, καθώς και τον βαθμό της υπαιτιότητάς του, μπορεί, αφού προβεί σε έγγραφη προειδοποίηση εκείνου που καταδικάστηκε:
α) να παρατείνει την προθεσμία για την εκτέλεση της εργασίας μέχρι ένα (1) επιπλέον έτος,
β) να επιτρέψει την εκτέλεση της χρηματικής ποινής που είχε καθοριστεί σύμφωνα με την προηγούμενη παράγραφο, αφού αφαιρέσει το ποσό που αναλογεί στην ήδη εκτιθείσα ποινή παροχής κοινωφελούς εργασίας, καθορίζοντας για κάθε τέσσερις (4) ώρες εργασίας εκατό (100) ευρώ χρηματικής ποινής.

Άρθρο 82
Υπολογισμός του χρόνου της προσωρινής κράτησης

1. Όταν επιβάλλεται στερητική της ελευθερίας ποινή, αφαιρείται ο χρόνος κράτησης μετά τη σύλληψη, ο χρόνος της προσωρινής κράτησης, καθώς και ο χρόνος παραμονής σε θεραπευτικές μονάδες για διενέργεια πραγματογνωμοσύνης κατά τον Κώδικα Ποινικής Δικονομίας.
2. Στην περίπτωση συρροής εγκλημάτων που συνεκδικάζονται, αφαιρείται από την επιβληθείσα συνολική ποινή ο χρόνος της κράτησης που διατάχθηκε για οποιοδήποτε από αυτά, ακόμη και όταν η απόφαση κήρυξε τον καταδικασθέντα αθώο για το έγκλημα για το οποίο είχε κρατηθεί. Αν ο κρατηθείς αθωωθεί για το έγκλημα για το οποίο είχε κρατηθεί και γι' αυτά που συνεκδικάσθηκαν, ο χρόνος κράτησης αφαιρείται από άλλες ποινές, εφόσον επιβάλλονται για εγκλήματα που διαπράχθηκαν πριν από την κράτηση.
3. Η αρμόδια αρχή για την εκτέλεση των δικαστικών αποφάσεων αφαιρεί από την ποινή τον χρόνο κράτησης που μεσολάβησε από την έκδοση της απόφασης έως τότε που αυτή έγινε αμετάκλητη.
4. Όταν επιβάλλεται μόνο χρηματική ποινή ή ποινή παροχής κοινωφελούς εργασίας για το έγκλημα για το οποίο ο καταδικασθείς είχε κρατηθεί, αφαιρούνται από την ποινή που του επιβλήθηκε οι ημερήσιες μονάδες που αντιστοιχούν στον χρόνο κράτησης.

Άρθρο 82Α
Έγκλημα με ρατσιστικά χαρακτηριστικά ή σε βάρος ανηλίκου ή αδυνάμου προσώπου

Εάν έχει τελεστεί έγκλημα κατά παθόντος, η επιλογή του οποίου έγινε λόγω των χαρακτηριστικών φυλής, χρώματος, εθνικής ή εθνοτικής καταγωγής, γενεαλογικών καταβολών, θρησκείας, αναπηρίας, γενετήσιου προσανατολισμού, ταυτότητας ή χαρακτηριστικών φύλου, το πλαίσιο ποινής διαμορφώνεται ως εξής:
α) Στην περίπτωση πλημμελήματος, που τιμωρείται με φυλάκιση έως ένα (1) έτος, το ελάχιστο όριο της ποινής αυξάνεται κατά έξι (6) μήνες. Στις λοιπές περιπτώσεις πλημμελημάτων, το ελάχιστο όριο αυτής αυξάνεται κατά ένα (1) έτος.
β) Στην περίπτωση κακουργήματος το ελάχιστο όριο ποινής αυξάνεται κατά δύο (2) έτη.
Το παραπάνω πλαίσιο ποινής εφαρμόζεται και όταν τελείται έγκλημα με δόλο σε βάρος ανηλίκου ή προσώπου που δεν μπορεί να υπερασπίσει τον εαυτό του και δεν προβλέπεται βαρύτερο πλαίσιο ποινής από άλλη διάταξη.

3. Community service benefiting the general public shall be performed for public services, local government bodies or non-profit bodies governed by private law, specified in a decision issued by the Minister of Justice and the Ministers jointly competent in each case.
It may also involve the provision of services to the victim, if the latter assents. The same [Ministerial] decision shall also specify how community service is organised, the procedure for selecting, assigning and supervising such community service, and all other relevant details.
4. The judgment shall also set the monetary penalty to be paid by the convicted person if they do not consistently perform their community service. Four hours of community service equate to 100 euros of a monetary penalty.
5. If the convicted person performs the [community] service insufficiently or poorly through fault of their own, the public prosecutor responsible for enforcing the punishment, having taken into consideration the frequency and severity of the convicted person's breach of obligations and degree of culpability, may, after sending written notice to the convicted person:
a) extend the [community] service deadline for up to one additional year; [or]
b) allow enforcement of the monetary penalty set in accordance with the preceding paragraph, after having deducted the amount corresponding to the community service already performed, equating 100 euros of monetary penalty with four hours of community service.

Article 82
Computing the length of temporary detention

1. Where a custodial sentence is imposed, the length of detention after arrest, the length of temporary detention and the length of committal to therapeutic facilities for the preparation of an expert evidence [report] in accordance with the Code of Criminal Procedure shall be deducted [from the custodial sentence].
2. Where the trials of concurrent crimes are joined, the length of detention ordered for any such crime shall be deducted from the overall sentence imposed, even if the convicted person was acquitted of the crime for which they had been detained. If the detained person is acquitted of the crime for which they had been detained and any crimes whose trials were joined, the length of detention shall be deducted from other sentences, provided such sentences are imposed for crimes committed prior to detention.
3. The authority competent for enforcing judgments shall deduct from the sentence the length of detention between the date the judgment was handed down and the moment it become irrevocable.
4. Where only a monetary penalty or community service is imposed for the crime for which the convicted person had been detained, the daily penalty units corresponding to the length of detention shall be deducted from the punishment imposed.

Article 82A
Crimes with racist motivation or committed against a juvenile or person [unable to defend themselves]

If a crime was committed against a victim who was [targeted] due to characteristics relating to their race, skin colour, national or ethnic origin, genealogical descent, religion, disability, sexual orientation, gender identity or sex characteristics, the penalty range shall be as follows:
a) in the case of a misdemeanour carrying a sentence of imprisonment of up to one year, the minimum limit of the sentence shall be increased by six months. In all other cases of misdemeanours, the minimum limit of the sentence shall be increased by one year;
b) in the case of a felony, the minimum limit of the sentence shall be increased by two years.
This penalty range also applies when a crime is committed with *dolus* against a juvenile or a person unable to defend themselves and a more severe penalty range is not laid down in other provisions.

II

ΜΕΙΩΣΗ ΤΗΣ ΑΠΕΙΛΟΥΜΕΝΗΣ ΠΟΙΝΗΣ

Άρθρο 83
Μειωμένη ποινή

Όπου στον νόμο προβλέπεται μειωμένη ποινή χωρίς άλλον προσδιορισμό, το πλαίσιό της καθορίζεται ως εξής:
α) αντί για την ποινή της ισόβιας κάθειρξης, επιβάλλεται κάθειρξη,
β) αντί για την ποινή της κάθειρξης τουλάχιστον δέκα (10) ετών, επιβάλλεται φυλάκιση τουλάχιστον τριών (3) ετών ή κάθειρξη έως δεκατέσσερα (14) έτη,
γ) αντί για την ποινή της κάθειρξης, επιβάλλεται φυλάκιση τουλάχιστον δύο (2) ετών ή κάθειρξη έως δώδεκα (12) έτη,
δ) αντί για την ποινή της κάθειρξης έως δέκα (10) έτη, επιβάλλεται φυλάκιση τουλάχιστον δύο (2) ετών ή κάθειρξη έως έξι (6) έτη,
ε) σε κάθε άλλη περίπτωση, ο δικαστής μειώνει την ποινή ελεύθερα έως το ελάχιστο όριό της. Αν ο νόμος προβλέπει σωρευτικά ποινή φυλάκισης και χρηματική ποινή, μπορεί να επιβληθεί και μόνο η τελευταία.

Άρθρο 84
Ελαφρυντικές περιστάσεις

1. Η ποινή μειώνεται επίσης κατά το μέτρο που προβλέπει το προηγούμενο άρθρο και στις περιπτώσεις που συντρέχουν ελαφρυντικές περιστάσεις.
2. Ελαφρυντικές περιστάσεις θεωρούνται ιδίως:
α) το ότι ο υπαίτιος έζησε ως τον χρόνο που έγινε το έγκλημα έντιμη, ατομική, οικογενειακή, επαγγελματική και γενικά κοινωνική ζωή,
β) το ότι στην πράξη του ωθήθηκε από μη ταπεινά αίτια ή από μεγάλη ένδεια ή υπό την επίδραση σοβαρής απειλής ή υπό την επιβολή προσώπου στο οποίο αυτός οφείλει υπακοή ή με το οποίο βρίσκεται σε σχέση εξάρτησης,
γ) το ότι στην πράξη του ωθήθηκε από ανάρμοστη συμπεριφορά του παθόντος ή παρασύρθηκε από οργή ή βίαιη θλίψη που του προκάλεσε άδικη εναντίον του πράξη,
δ) το ότι επέδειξε ειλικρινή μετάνοια και επιδίωξε να άρει ή να μειώσει τις συνέπειες της πράξης του,
ε) το ότι συμπεριφέρθηκε καλά για σχετικά μεγάλο διάστημα μετά την πράξη του, ακόμα και κατά την κράτησή του.
3. Ως ελαφρυντική περίπτωση λογίζεται και η μη εύλογη διάρκεια της ποινικής διαδικασίας που δεν οφείλεται σε υπαιτιότητα του κατηγορουμένου.

Άρθρο 85
Συρροή λόγων μείωσης της ποινής

Όταν συντρέχουν περισσότεροι από ένας λόγοι για τη μείωση της ποινής κατά το άρθρο 83 ή όταν συντρέχουν ένας ή περισσότεροι τέτοιοι λόγοι μαζί με ελαφρυντικές περιστάσεις (άρθρο 84 ΠΚ), εφαρμόζεται μόνο μία (1) φορά η μείωση της ποινής, σύμφωνα με το μέτρο που προβλέπει το άρθρο 83. Στην επιμέτρηση της ποινής λαμβάνονται υπόψη όλοι οι λόγοι του πρώτου εδαφίου και οι ελαφρυντικές περιστάσεις.

Άρθρα 86 - 93

(Καταργούνται)

II

REDUCTION OF SENTENCES

Article 83
Reduced sentence

Where the law provides for a reduced sentence with no further qualifications, the sentence range shall be as follows:

a) instead of incarceration for life, [fixed-term] incarceration shall be imposed;

b) instead of incarceration of at least 10 years, imprisonment of at least three years or incarceration of up to 14 years shall be imposed;

c) instead of incarceration, imprisonment of at least two years or incarceration of up to 12 years shall be imposed;

d) instead of incarceration up to 10 years, imprisonment of at least two years or incarceration of up to six years shall be imposed;

e) in all other cases, the judge may freely reduce the sentence down to its minimum limit. If the law provides for both imprisonment and a monetary penalty, [the judge] may even impose only the latter.

Article 84
Mitigating circumstances

1. The sentence may also be reduced, to the extent provided for in the preceding Article, where mitigating circumstances apply.

2. Mitigating circumstances are deemed to [include but are not limited to]:

a) the fact that, until the time the crime was committed, the culpable person had lived an honest life in personal, familial, professional and generally social terms;

b) the fact that they were led to commit the act by honest causes, or by extreme poverty, or under the influence of a severe threat, or under compulsion by a person whom they are obligated to obey, or with whom they share a relationship of dependence;

c) the fact that they were led to commit the act by inappropriate conduct on the part of the victim, or were carried away by rage or violent sorrow caused by a wrongful act against them;

d) the fact that they showed honest repentance and sought to eliminate or reduce the consequences of their act;

e) the fact they they behaved well for a relatively long period after their act, even during their detention.

3. Where the unreasonable length of the criminal procedure is not due to the defendant's fault, this shall also be considered to be a mitigating circumstance.

Article 85
Concurrence of grounds for reducing a sentence

Where there are several grounds for reducing a sentence in accordance with Article 83 or when one or more such grounds exist alongside mitigating circumstances ([see] Article 84), the reduction of sentence shall apply only once to the extent provided for in Article 83. All the grounds referred to in the preceding sentence and the mitigating circumstances shall be taken into account when determining the sentence.

Articles 86 - 93

[Repealed]

III

ΣΥΡΡΟΗ ΕΓΚΛΗΜΑΤΩΝ

Άρθρο 94

Συνολική ποινή σε περίπτωση στερητικών της ελευθερίας ποινών

1. Κατά του υπαιτίου δύο (2) ή περισσότερων εγκλημάτων που τελέστηκαν με περισσότερες πράξεις και τιμωρούνται με πρόσκαιρες στερητικές της ελευθερίας ποινές, επιβάλλεται, μετά την επιμέτρησή τους, συνολική ποινή, η οποία αποτελείται από τη βαρύτερη από τις συντρέχουσες ποινές επαυξημένη. Αν οι συντρέχουσες ποινές είναι του ίδιου είδους και ίσης διάρκειας, η συνολική ποινή σχηματίζεται με την επαύξηση μιας από αυτές. Η επαύξηση της βαρύτερης ποινής για κάθε μία (1) από τις συντρέχουσες ποινές δεν μπορεί να είναι μεγαλύτερη από το ένα δεύτερο (1/2) κάθε συντρέχουσας ποινής, ούτε μπορεί η συνολική ποινή να ξεπεράσει τα είκοσι πέντε (25) έτη, όταν η βαρύτερη ποινή είναι κάθειρξη και τα δέκα (10) έτη όταν πρόκειται για φυλάκιση.

2. Αν τα εγκλήματα που συρρέουν τελέστηκαν με μία πράξη, το δικαστήριο επαυξάνει ελεύθερα τη βαρύτερη από τις συντρέχουσες ποινές, αλλά όχι πέρα από το ανώτατο όριο του είδους της ποινής. Στην περίπτωση του εγκλήματος της ανθρωποκτονίας από αμέλεια κατά συρροή, το δικαστήριο σε εξαιρετικές περιπτώσεις δύναται να επιβάλει συνολική ποινή σύμφωνα με την παρ. 1.

3. Αν χορηγήθηκε αμνηστία, χάρη, αναστολή δίωξης, απόλυση υπό όρο ή επήλθε παραγραφή ή αφέθηκε οπωσδήποτε η ποινή για ένα ή περισσότερα από τα εγκλήματα που συρρέουν και των οποίων οι ποινές προσμετρήθηκαν κατά τις διατάξεις της προηγούμενης παραγράφου, εξακολουθεί η εκτέλεση των υπόλοιπων ποινών και, αν συντρέχει περίπτωση, ο εισαγγελέας προκαλεί νέα προσμέτρηση γι' αυτές, αυτεπαγγέλτως ή με αίτηση του καταδικασθέντος.

4. Ποινές στερητικές της ελευθερίας ανώτερες του ενός έτους που επιβάλλονται για κακούργημα ή πλημμέλημα με δόλο το οποίο τέλεσε κρατούμενος κατά τη διάρκεια της αδείας του εκτίονται ολόκληρες μετά την έκτιση της ποινής που επιβλήθηκε ή θα επιβληθεί για την πράξη για την οποία ήταν κρατούμενος.

Άρθρο 95

Συντρέχουσες παρεπόμενες ποινές και μέτρα ασφαλείας

Οι παρεπόμενες ποινές και τα μέτρα ασφαλείας επιβάλλονται ή μπορούν να επιβληθούν μαζί με τη συνολική ποινή, αν το ορίζει ο νόμος για ένα από τα εγκλήματα που συρρέουν.

Άρθρο 96

Συνολική ποινή σε περίπτωση συρροής χρηματικών ποινών

1. Αν συντρέχουν περισσότερες από μία χρηματικές ποινές, η συνολική ποινή που επιβάλλεται αποτελείται από τη βαρύτερή τους, επαυξημένη ανάλογα με την οικονομική κατάσταση του καταδικασθέντος. Η επαύξηση αυτή όμως δεν μπορεί να ξεπεράσει το ένα δεύτερο του αθροίσματος των υπόλοιπων ποινών που συντρέχουν. Αν οι συντρέχουσες ποινές είναι ισόποσες, η συνολική ποινή σχηματίζεται με την επαύξηση μιας από αυτές.

2. Η διάταξη της παρ. 2 του άρθρου 94 εφαρμόζεται και σε αυτό το άρθρο.

III

CONCURRENCE OF CRIMES

Article 94

Total sentence where [several] custodial sentences are imposed

1. Any person culpable of two or more crimes which were committed through several acts and which carry custodial sentences shall be punished, following the determination of the length of the sentence, with a total sentence consisting of the heavier of the concurrent sentences, which shall also be augmented. If the concurrent sentences are identical in type and length, the total sentence shall be [calculated] by augmenting one of them. The augmented heavier sentence for each of the concurrent sentences cannot be longer than half of each concurrent sentence, nor may the total sentence exceed 25 years when the heavier sentence is incarceration, or 10 years when the heavier sentence is imprisonment.

2. If the concurrent crimes were committed through a single act, the court may freely augment the heavier of the concurrent sentences, but not beyond the maximum limit for this type of sentence. In the case of concurrent negligent homicide, the court may, in exceptional circumstances, impose a total sentence in accordance with paragraph 1.

3. If amnesty, pardon, stay of prosecution or conditional release was granted, or if time-barring occurred, or if the sentence was forgiven in any way with regard to one or more of the concurrent crimes whose sentences were calculated in accordance with the provisions of the preceding paragraph, enforcement of the remaining sentences shall continue, and, if necessary, the public prosecutor shall re-calculate them, whether *ex officio* or following an application filed by the convicted person.

4. Custodial sentences longer than one year imposed for a felony or a misdemeanour committed with *dolus* by a detainee during their furlough shall be served in whole after the sentence that has been or will be imposed for the act for which they had been detained has been served.

Article 95

Concurrent ancillary penalties and security measures

Ancillary penalties and security measures shall or may be imposed together with the total sentence, if [such penalties and measures are] provided for in law for one of the concurrent crimes.

Article 96

Overall penalty where concurrent monetary penalties are imposed

1. Where several monetary penalties are to be imposed, the overall penalty imposed shall consist of the heavier of such penalties, augmented in accordance with the financial situation of the convicted person. However, such augmented penalty may not exceed half the sum of the remaining concurrent penalties. If the concurrent penalties are identical in amount, the overall penalty shall be [calculated] by augmenting one of them.

2. The provisions of Article 94(2) also apply in [the case referred to in] this Article.

Άρθρο 96Α
Συνολική ποινή σε περίπτωση συρροής ποινών παροχής κοινωφελούς εργασίας

1. Κατά του υπαιτίου δύο ή περισσότερων εγκλημάτων που τελέστηκαν με περισσότερες πράξεις και τιμωρούνται με ποινή παροχής κοινωφελούς εργασίας, επιβάλλεται, μετά την επιμέτρηση, συνολική ποινή, η οποία αποτελείται από τη βαρύτερη από τις συντρέχουσες ποινές επαυξημένη. Αν οι συντρέχουσες ποινές είναι ίσης διάρκειας, η συνολική ποινή σχηματίζεται με την επαύξηση μιας από αυτές. Η επαύξηση της βαρύτερης ποινής για κάθε μία από τις συντρέχουσες ποινές δεν μπορεί να είναι μεγαλύτερη από το ένα δεύτερο κάθε συντρέχουσας ποινής, ούτε μπορεί η συνολική ποινή να ξεπεράσει τις οκτακόσιες ώρες κοινωφελούς εργασίας.

2. Αν τα εγκλήματα που συρρέουν τελέστηκαν με μία πράξη, το δικαστήριο επαυξάνει ελεύθερα τη βαρύτερη από τις συντρέχουσες ποινές, αλλά όχι πέρα από το ανώτατο όριο του είδους της ποινής.

3. Η ποινή της παροχής κοινωφελούς εργασίας δεν εκτελείται όταν συντρέχει με στερητική της ελευθερίας ποινή μεγαλύτερη των τριών ετών.

Άρθρο 97
Άλλες περιπτώσεις συνολικής ποινής

Οι διατάξεις των άρθρων 94 παρ. 1, 96 παρ. 1 και 96 Α παρ. 1 εφαρμόζονται και όταν κάποιος, προτού εκτιθεί ολοκληρωτικά ή παραγραφεί ή χαριστεί η ποινή που του επιβλήθηκε για κάποια αξιόποινη πράξη, καταδικαστεί για άλλη αξιόποινη πράξη, οποτεδήποτε και αν τελέστηκε αυτή.

Άρθρο 98
Έγκλημα κατ' εξακολούθηση

1. Αν περισσότερες από μία πράξεις του ίδιου προσώπου συνιστούν εξακολούθηση του ίδιου εγκλήματος, το δικαστήριο μπορεί, αντί να εφαρμόσει τις διατάξεις των άρθρων 94 παρ. 1, 96 παρ. 1 και 96 Α παρ. 1, να επιβάλει μία και μόνο ποινή, για την επιμέτρηση της οποίας λαμβάνει υπόψη το όλο περιεχόμενο των μερικότερων πράξεων.

2. Η αξία του αντικειμένου της πράξης και η περιουσιακή βλάβη ή το περιουσιακό όφελος που προκύπτουν από την κατ' εξακολούθηση τέλεση του εγκλήματος λαμβάνονται συνολικά υπόψη αν ο δράστης απέβλεπε με τις μερικότερες πράξεις του στο αποτέλεσμα αυτό. Στις περιπτώσεις αυτές ο ποινικός χαρακτήρας της πράξης προσδιορίζεται με βάση τη συνολική αξία του αντικειμένου και την συνολική περιουσιακή βλάβη ή το συνολικό περιουσιακό όφελος που ανάλογα με το έγκλημα επήλθε ή σκοπήθηκε.

Article 96A

Total sentence where concurrent community service sentences are imposed

1. Any person culpable of two or more crimes which were committed through several acts and which carry community service sentences shall be punished, following the determination of the length of the sentence, with an overall sentence consisting of the heavier of the concurrent sentences, which shall also be augmented. If the concurrent sentences are equal in length, the overall sentence shall be [calculated] by augmenting one of them. The augmented heavier sentence for each of the concurrent sentences cannot be longer than half of each concurrent sentence, nor may the overall sentence exceed 800 hours of community service.

2. If the concurrent crimes were committed through a single act, the court may freely augment the heavier of the concurrent sentences, but not beyond the maximum limit for this type of punishment.

3. A community service sentence shall not be enforced when it is imposed concurrently with a custodial sentence longer than three years.

Article 97

Overall punishment in other cases

The provisions of Articles 94(1), 96(1) and 96A(1) also apply when a person, before the sentence imposed on them for a different punishable act has been served in full, or before it became time-barred, or before they were pardoned, has been convicted of another punishable act, whenever it may have been committed.

Article 98

Crimes committed repeatedly

1. If several acts by the same person constitute repeated commission of the same crime, the court may, instead of applying the provisions of Articles 94(1), 96(1) and 96A(1), impose a single punishment, taking the overall content of the several acts into consideration when determining its extent.

2. The value of the object of an act and the pecuniary damage [caused] or pecuniary gain [obtained] as a result of the repeated commission of a crime shall be taken into consideration overall if the perpetrator sought, through such several acts, to achieve such outcome. In such cases, the criminal nature of the act shall be determined on the basis of the total value of the object and the total pecuniary damage or total pecuniary gain obtained or intended, depending on the crime.

IV

ΑΝΑΣΤΟΛΗ ΕΚΤΕΛΕΣΗΣ ΤΗΣ ΠΟΙΝΗΣ

Άρθρο 99

Έκτιση και αναστολή εκτέλεσης της ποινής και μέρους της ποινής υπό όρο

1. Το δικαστήριο μετά την επιβολή ποινής εφαρμόζει τα άρθρα 80Α ή 104Α, μετατρέποντας την ποινή σε χρηματική ή σε κοινωφελή εργασία, εκτός αν δεν συντρέχουν οι προϋποθέσεις τους, οπότε διατάσσει την πραγματική έκτιση μέρους της ποινής σύμφωνα με την παρ. 5 ή ολόκληρης της ποινής.

Αν ωστόσο, κάποιος που δεν έχει στο παρελθόν καταδικαστεί αμετάκλητα με μία (1) ή περισσότερες αποφάσεις σε στερητική της ελευθερίας ποινή άνω του ενός (1) έτους, καταδικαστεί σε ποινή που δεν υπερβαίνει το ένα (1) έτος, το δικαστήριο με την απόφασή του μπορεί να διατάσσει την αναστολή εκτέλεσης της ποινής για ορισμένο διάστημα, που δεν μπορεί να είναι κατώτερο από ένα (1) και ανώτερο από τρία (3) έτη, αν κρίνει αιτιολογημένα πως η εκτέλεση της ποινής δεν είναι αναγκαία για να αποτρέψει τον κατάδικο από την τέλεση νέων αξιόποινων πράξεων. Ο χρόνος της αναστολής δεν μπορεί να είναι βραχύτερος από τη διάρκεια της ποινής, και αρχίζει από τότε που η απόφαση η οποία την χορηγεί καθίσταται εκτελεστή.

2. Στην ίδια απόφαση το δικαστήριο μπορεί να προσδιορίσει τους όρους υπό τους οποίους παρέχεται η αναστολή εκτέλεσης της ποινής, οι οποίοι, διαζευκτικά ή σωρευτικά, είναι ιδίως:

α) η αποκατάσταση του συνόλου ή μέρους της ζημίας που προκλήθηκε στο θύμα της αξιόποινης πράξης κατά το μέτρο των δυνατοτήτων του καταδικασθέντος,

β) η αφαίρεση της άδειας οδήγησης για χρονικό διάστημα έως ένα (1) έτος, αν η πράξη συνδέεται με σοβαρή παραβίαση των κανόνων οδήγησης,

γ) η καταβολή ποσού ύψους έως δέκα χιλιάδες (10.000) ευρώ για κοινωφελείς σκοπούς,

δ) η εκπλήρωση υποχρεώσεων του καταδικασθέντος για διατροφή ή επιμέλεια άλλων προσώπων,

ε) η συμμετοχή του καταδικασθέντος, εφόσον συναινεί, σε πρόγραμμα απεξάρτησης ή άλλο θεραπευτικό πρόγραμμα,

στ) η συμμετοχή του καταδικασθέντος σε συνεδρίες με επιμελητή κοινωνικής αρωγής,

ζ) η εμφάνιση στο αστυνομικό τμήμα,

η) η απαγόρευση εξόδου από τη Χώρα.

3. Μετά από αίτηση του εισαγγελέα εκτέλεσης της ποινής ή του καταδικασθέντος, το αρμόδιο δικαστήριο μπορεί να αποφασίσει την άρση ή την τροποποίηση των όρων που έχει επιβάλει. Νέα αίτηση του καταδικασθέντος μπορεί να υποβληθεί μετά πάροδο τριμήνου από την απόρριψη της προηγούμενης.

4. Αν ο καταδικασθείς παραβιάζει τους όρους, ο εισαγγελέας εισάγει την υπόθεση στο δικαστήριο εκτέλεσης της ποινής. Το τελευταίο, με βάση τα πιο πάνω κριτήρια, μπορεί:

α) να διατάξει τη μετατροπή της ποινής σε χρηματική κατά το άρθρο 80Α ή σε παροχή κοινωφελούς εργασίας κατά το άρθρο 104Α,

β) να διατάξει την έκτιση μέρους της ποινής φυλάκισης που επιβλήθηκε σύμφωνα με την παρ. 5 ή την έκτιση ολόκληρης της ποινής.

Ο καταδικασθείς κλητεύεται υποχρεωτικά στη συνεδρίαση τουλάχιστον δέκα (10) ημέρες πριν και μπορεί να παραστεί αυτοπροσώπως ή με συνήγορο.

IV

STAY OF ENFORCEMENT OF PENALTIES

Article 99

Serving of sentences, stay of enforcement of sentences, and conditional stay of enforcement of part of sentences

1. The court, after imposing a sentence, shall apply Articles 80A or 104A and commute the sentence into a monetary penalty or community service, unless the conditions for doing so are not met, in which case it shall order that part of the sentence be actually served in accordance with paragraph 5, or that the entire sentence [be actually served].

However, if the court imposes a custodial sentence not longer than one year on a person who had not been previously convicted, pursuant to an irrevocable judgment or judgments, to serve a custodial sentence longer than one year, the court may hand down a judgment ordering stay of enforcement of the sentence for a specific period of time which may not be shorter than one year or longer than three years if it rules, with reasoning provided in the judgment, that enforcement of the sentence is not necessary in order to deter the convicted person from committing new punishable acts. The length of such stay may not be shorter than the length of the sentence, and shall commence from the time the judgment granting such stay becomes enforceable.

2. In the same judgment, the court may specify the conditions under which stay of enforcement of the sentence is granted which, separately or cumulatively, are, in particular:

a) restitution of all or part of the damage caused to the victim of the punishable act, insofar as the convicted person can do so;

b) removal of the driving licence for a period of up to one year, if the act concerns a serious traffic violation;

c) payment of an amount up to 10,000 euros for public-benefit purposes;

d) performance of the convicted person's obligations concerning maintenance or custody of other persons;

e) participation of the convicted person, with their consent, in a rehabilitation or other therapeutic programme;

f) participation of the convicted person in sessions with a probation officer;

g) reporting to a police department;

h) ban on exiting the country.

3. Following an application filed by the public prosecutor responsible for enforcement of the sentence or by the convicted person, the competent court may decide to remove or amend any conditions it has imposed. The convicted person may submit a new application [only] after three months have elapsed since the previous [application] was dismissed.

4. If the convicted person violates the conditions, the public prosecutor shall bring the case before the sentence enforcement court. This court may, based on the above criteria, order that:

a) the sentence be commuted to a monetary penalty in accordance with Article 80A or community service in accordance with Article 104A;

b) part of the sentence of imprisonment imposed in accordance with paragraph 5 be served or that the entire sentence be served.

The convicted person shall necessarily be summonsed to the sitting at least 10 days beforehand, and may enter an appearance in person or via counsel.

5. Αν κάποιος καταδικαστεί σε φυλάκιση που δεν υπερβαίνει τα τρία (3) έτη, το δικαστήριο, εφόσον η μετατροπή της ποινής σε χρηματική κατά το άρθρο 80 Α ή σε παροχή κοινωφελούς εργασίας κατά το άρθρο 104 Α δεν επιτρέπεται με βάση το ύψος της ποινής ή κρίνει πως δεν είναι επαρκής για να αποτρέψει τον καταδικασθέντα από την τέλεση άλλων αξιόποινων πράξεων και ότι για τον σκοπό αυτόν είναι αναγκαία η έκτιση μέρους της στερητικής της ελευθερίας ποινής, μπορεί να διατάξει την πραγματική εκτέλεση του μέρους αυτού, η διάρκεια του οποίου δεν μπορεί να είναι κατώτερη των τριάντα (30) ημερών ούτε ανώτερη των έξι (6) μηνών και την αναστολή εκτέλεσης του υπολοίπου, πέραν των περιπτώσεων της παρ. 1. Στην περίπτωση αυτή αποκλείεται η εφαρμογή του άρθρου 105Β. Ο χρόνος αναστολής για το αναστελλόμενο μέρος της ποινής αρχίζει μετά από την ολοκλήρωση της έκτισης του μέρους της ποινής που δεν ανεστάλη. Οι παρ. 2 και 3 εφαρμόζονται αναλόγως σε περίπτωση εφαρμογής της παρούσας.
6. Αν κάποιος καταδικαστεί σε φυλάκιση επί πλημμελήματος που υπερβαίνει τα τρία (3) έτη, το δικαστήριο διατάζει την πραγματική έκτιση της ποινής σε σωφρονιστικό κατάστημα.
Αν το δικαστήριο κρίνει αιτιολογημένα πως η έκτιση μέρους της ποινής αρκεί για να τον αποτρέψει από την τέλεση νέων αξιόποινων πράξεων διατάζει
α) την πραγματική έκτιση μέρους της ποινής που δεν είναι κατώτερη του ενός πέμπτου (1/5) ούτε ανώτερη των τριών δεκάτων (3/10) και
β) την αναστολή του υπολοίπου της ποινής, πέραν των περιπτώσεων της παρ. 1.
Στην περίπτωση του δεύτερου εδαφίου εφαρμόζονται αναλογικά το δεύτερο, τρίτο και τέταρτο εδάφιο της παρ. 5.
7. Σε περίπτωση μη τήρησης των όρων μετά από την έκτιση μέρους της ποινής το δικαστήριο εκτέλεσης της ποινής, λαμβάνοντας υπόψη τη σοβαρότητα των παραβιάσεων, μπορεί:
α) να τροποποιήσει τους επιβληθέντες ή να επιβάλει επιπρόσθετους όρους,
β) να διατάξει την πραγματική έκτιση μέρους της ποινής φυλάκισης που επιβλήθηκε, το οποίο δεν μπορεί να υπερβαίνει τους έξι (6) μήνες,
γ) να διατάξει την έκτιση του υπολοίπου της ποινής που ανεστάλη.
Ο καταδικασθείς κλητεύεται υποχρεωτικά στη συνεδρίαση τουλάχιστον δέκα (10) ημέρες πριν και μπορεί να παραστεί αυτοπροσώπως ή με συνήγορο.

Άρθρο 100

(Καταργείται)

Άρθρο 101
Ανάκληση της αναστολής

1. Αν μετά τη χορήγηση της αναστολής, αλλά κατά τη διάρκειά της, αποδειχθεί ότι αυτός που την έλαβε είχε προηγουμένως καταδικαστεί αμετάκλητα σε στερητική της ελευθερίας ποινή για κάποια από τις πράξεις που ορίζει το άρθρο 99, το δικαστήριο με αίτηση του εισαγγελέα ανακαλεί την αναστολή που χορηγήθηκε.
2. Αν κατά τη διάρκεια της αναστολής, καταστεί αμετάκλητη καταδίκη, για έγκλημα που τελέστηκε πριν από τη δημοσίευση της απόφασης για την αναστολή, και η ποινή που επιβλήθηκε με μία (1) ή περισσότερες αποφάσεις υπερβαίνει συνολικά το ένα (1) έτος, η αναστολή θεωρείται ότι δεν χορηγήθηκε ποτέ, εκτός αν το δικαστήριο, απαγγέλλοντας τη νέα καταδίκη, ρητά διατάξει με την ίδια απόφαση να διατηρηθεί η αναστολή, επειδή η εκτέλεση της ποινής, την οποία αφορά η αναστολή, δεν είναι απολύτως αναγκαία.

5. If a person is convicted to imprisonment of no more than three years, the court may, if it considers that commuting the sentence to a monetary penalty in accordance with Article 80A or to community service in accordance with Article 104A is not permitted based on the level of the sentence or that it will not suffice to deter the convicted person from committing other punishable acts and that, for this purpose, it is absolutely necessary that they serve part of the custodial sentence, order that this part [of the sentence] be actually served, with a length not shorter than 30 days nor longer than six months, and that enforcement of the remainder of the sentence, other than in the cases provided for in paragraph 1, be stayed. In this case, application of Article 105B is precluded. The length of the stay for the stayed part of the sentence shall commence after [the convicted person] has completed serving the part of the sentence not stayed. Paragraphs 2 and 3 apply *mutatis mutandis* where this provision applies.

6. If a person is sentenced to imprisonment of more than three years for a misdemeanour, the court shall order that the sentence be actually served at a custodial institution.

If the court rules, with reasoning provided in the judgment, that serving part of the sentence suffices to deter [the convicted person] from committing new punishable acts, it shall order[:]

a) that they actually serve part of the sentence which not less than 1/5 and not more than 3/10 [of the sentence]; and

b) that the rest of the sentence, other than in the cases provided for in paragraph 1, be stayed.

The second, third and fourth sentences of paragraph 5 apply *mutatis mutandis* in the case provided for in the second sentence [of this paragraph].

7. If the conditions were not complied with after part of the sentence had been served, the sentence enforcement court, taking into consideration the severity of the violations, may:

a) amend the conditions imposed or impose additional conditions;

b) order that part of the sentence of imprisonment imposed be actually served, which may not exceed six months; [or]

c) order that the remainder of the sentence stayed be served.

The convicted person shall necessarily be summonsed to the sitting at least 10 days beforehand, and may enter an appearance in person or via counsel.

Article 100

[Repealed]

Article 101
Revocation of stay

1. If it is proven, after the stay has been granted but while it is in effect, that the person who was granted the stay had previously been irrevocably convicted to serve a custodial sentence for any of the acts provided for in Article 99, the court, following an application filed by the public prosecutor, shall revoke the stay granted.

2. If, while the stay is in effect, a conviction for a crime committed before the judgment granting the stay is handed down becomes irrevocable, and the sentence imposed pursuant to one or more judgments exceeds one year in total, the stay shall be deemed never to have been granted, unless the court, when pronouncing the new conviction, expressly orders in the same judgment that the stay be maintained because enforcement of the sentence which the stay concerns is not absolutely necessary.

Άρθρο 102
Άρση της αναστολής

1. Αν κατά τον χρόνο της αναστολής ο καταδικασθείς καταδικαστεί και πάλι σε στερητική της ελευθερίας ποινή για έγκλημα δόλου που τελέστηκε κατά τη διάρκεια της αναστολής, η αναστολή αίρεται μόλις καταστεί αμετάκλητη η νέα καταδίκη. Η ποινή που επιβλήθηκε με τη νέα καταδίκη εκτελείται στη συνέχεια μετά την ποινή που είχε ανασταλεί, εκτός αν το δικαστήριο με την ίδια απόφαση ρητά διατάξει να μην αρθεί η αναστολή, επειδή η εκτέλεση της ποινής, την οποία αφορά η αναστολή, δεν είναι απολύτως αναγκαία.
2. Αν η αναστολή δεν ανακληθεί και δεν αρθεί, η ποινή που είχε ανασταλεί θεωρείται σαν να μην είχε επιβληθεί.

Άρθρο 103
Ενέργεια αλλοδαπής απόφασης

Αν η καταδίκη που ορίζουν τα άρθρα 99, 101, 102 επήλθε με απόφαση αλλοδαπού δικαστηρίου, η ενέργειά της όσον αφορά τη χορήγηση, την ανάκληση και την άρση της αναστολής κρίνεται ελεύθερα από το δικαστήριο, εκτός αν ορίζεται διαφορετικά σε διατάξεις διεθνών ή ευρωπαϊκών κειμένων που δεσμεύουν τη Χώρα. Σε περίπτωση άρσης της αναστολής, αρμόδιο είναι το δικαστήριο που χορήγησε την αναστολή.

Άρθρο 104
Δικαστικές δαπάνες και παρεπόμενες ποινές

1. Η αναστολή της ποινής δεν απαλλάσσει τον καταδικασθέντα από την πληρωμή των δικαστικών εξόδων.
2. Οι παρεπόμενες ποινές αναστέλλονται και εξαλείφονται μαζί με την κύρια ποινή, εκτός αν το δικαστήριο διατάξει τη μη αναστολή.

V

ΜΕΤΑΤΡΟΠΗ ΤΗΣ ΣΤΕΡΗΤΙΚΗΣ ΤΗΣ ΕΛΕΥΘΕΡΙΑΣ ΠΟΙΝΗΣ

Άρθρο 104Α
Μετατροπή της φυλάκισης σε κοινωφελή εργασία.

1. Όταν επιβάλλεται φυλάκιση που δεν υπερβαίνει τα δύο (2) έτη και δεν συντρέχει περίπτωση εφαρμογής του άρθρου 99, η ποινή μετατρέπεται σε παροχή κοινωφελούς εργασίας (άρθρο 81), εκτός αν το δικαστήριο κρίνει, με ειδική αιτιολογία, ότι αυτή δεν είναι αρκετή για να αποτρέψει τον δράστη από την τέλεση άλλων εγκλημάτων. Κάθε ημέρα φυλάκισης δεν μπορεί να αντιστοιχεί σε περισσότερες από δύο (2) ώρες κοινωφελούς εργασίας. Σε κάθε περίπτωση, η διάρκεια της κοινωφελούς εργασίας δεν μπορεί να υπερβαίνει τις χίλιες διακόσιες ώρες (1.200) και σε περίπτωση που έχει καθοριστεί συνολική ποινή, τις τρεις χιλιάδες εξακόσιες ώρες (3.600), ούτε να έχει διάρκεια μεγαλύτερη των τριών (3) ετών.
2. Η μετατροπή δεν είναι εφικτή αν ο καταδικασθείς δεν συναινεί ή δεν είναι παρών. Αν ο καταδικασθείς δεν ήταν παρών, μπορεί να ζητήσει τη μετατροπή της ποινής του σε παροχή κοινωφελούς εργασίας με αυτοτελή αίτησή του.

Article 102

Termination of stay

1. If, while the stay is in effect, the convicted person is once again convicted to serve a custodial sentence for a crime of *dolus* committed during such period, the stay shall be removed as soon as the new conviction becomes irrevocable. The sentence imposed in the new [judgment of] conviction shall subsequently be enforced after the stayed sentence, unless the court expressly orders in the same judgment that the stay not be removed because enforcement of the sentence which the stay concerns is not absolutely necessary.

2. If the stay is not revoked and not removed, the stayed sentence shall be deemed not to have been imposed.

Article 103

Effect of judgments handed down by foreign courts

If a conviction provided for in Articles 99, 101 or 102 was imposed pursuant to a judgment handed down by a foreign court, its effect in terms of granting, revoking or removing the stay [of enforcement] shall be freely determined by the court, unless otherwise provided for in international or European texts that are binding on Greece. Where the stay [of enforcement] was removed, the court which granted the stay shall be competent.

Article 104

Court costs and ancillary penalties

1. Stay of [enforcement of] the penalty shall not release the convicted person from [the obligation] to pay court costs.

2. [The enforcement of] ancillary penalties shall be stayed and such penalties shall be extinguished together with the main penalty, unless the court orders no stay.

V

COMMUTATION OF CUSTODIAL SENTENCES

Article 104A

Commutation of imprisonment to community service

1. Where imprisonment of no more than two years is imposed and Article 99 does not apply, the sentence shall be commuted to community service ([see] Article 81), unless the court determines, providing specific reasoning [in its judgment], that this does not suffice to deter the perpetrator from committing other crimes. Each day of imprisonment cannot correspond to more than two hours of community service. In all events, the length of community service cannot exceed 1,200 hours and, where a total sentence was imposed, 3,600 hours, nor be longer than three years.

2. Commutation is not possible if the convicted person does not consent or is not present [at the hearing]. If the convicted person was not present, they may file a standalone application requesting that their sentence be commuted to community service.

3. Αν επήλθε ουσιώδης αλλαγή των όρων της παρ. 1, ο καταδικασθείς μπορεί να ζητήσει νέο υπολογισμό της παρεχόμενης κοινωφελούς εργασίας με αυτοτελή αίτησή του.

4. Η παρ. 3 του άρθρου 81 ισχύει και στην περίπτωση αυτή. Αν η εργασία παρέχεται από εκείνον που καταδικάστηκε ελλιπώς ή πλημμελώς με δική του υπαιτιότητα, ο εισαγγελέας εκτέλεσης της ποινής, αφού λάβει υπόψη τη συχνότητα και σοβαρότητα της παραβίασης των υποχρεώσεων από τον καταδικασθέντα, τον βαθμό της υπαιτιότητάς του και το τμήμα της ποινής που εκτίθηκε, μπορεί:

α) να προβεί σε προειδοποίηση εκείνου που καταδικάστηκε,

β) να παρατείνει την προθεσμία για την εκτέλεση της εργασίας μέχρι ένα (1) επιπλέον έτος,

γ) να εισαγάγει την υπόθεση στο δικαστήριο εκτέλεσης της ποινής με αναλογική εφαρμογή της παρ. 4 του άρθρου 99, το οποίο μπορεί να διατάξει την έκτιση της στερητικής της ελευθερίας ποινής που είχε επιβληθεί πριν από τη μετατροπή αφού αφαιρέσει την εκτιθείσα ποινή και τον χρόνο παροχής κοινωφελούς εργασίας υπολογίζοντας αυτόν σύμφωνα με την παρ. 1.

VI

ΔΙΚΑΣΤΙΚΗ ΑΦΕΣΗ ΤΗΣ ΠΟΙΝΗΣ

Άρθρο 104Β
Λόγοι δικαστικής άφεσης της ποινής

1. Το δικαστήριο μπορεί να μην επιβάλει ποινή στον υπαίτιο πλημμελήματος αν:

α) η βλάβη ή ο κίνδυνος που προκλήθηκαν από την πράξη του ήταν ιδιαιτέρως μικρής βαρύτητας,

β) ο υπαίτιος έχει αποκαταστήσει στο μέτρο του δυνατού την προσβολή που έχει προκαλέσει στον παθόντα, δείχνοντας ειλικρινή μετάνοια,

γ) ο υπαίτιος έχει πληγεί ιδιαίτερα σοβαρά από το αποτέλεσμα της πράξης του, ή

δ) έχει περάσει ασυνήθιστα μεγάλο χρονικό διάστημα από την τέλεση του εγκλήματος.

Για να κρίνει το δικαστήριο αν δεν θα επιβάλλει ποινή ελέγχει αν αυτή, εξαιτίας μίας των ανωτέρω περιστάσεων, δεν εμφανίζεται πλέον αναγκαία ή εμφανίζεται δυσανάλογα επαχθής.

2. Το δικαστήριο δεν επιβάλλει ποινή στον υπαίτιο πλημμελήματος, αν έχει ολοκληρωθεί επιτυχώς διαδικασία αποκαταστατικής δικαιοσύνης μεταξύ αυτού και του παθόντος.

3. If there was a material change in the conditions laid down in paragraph 1, the convicted person may file a standalone application requesting that the [length of] community service be re-calculated.
4. Article 81(3) also applies in such a case. If the convicted person performs the [community] service insufficiently or poorly through fault of their own, the public prosecutor responsible for enforcement of the sentence, having taken into consideration the frequency and severity of the infringement of obligations by the convicted person, their degree of culpability and the part of the sentence served, may:
a) send a notice to the convicted person;
b) extend the [length of community] service by up to one additional year; [or]
c) bring the case before the sentence enforcement court, Article 99(4) applying *mutatis mutandis*; such court may order that the custodial sentence which had been imposed before commutation be served, having deducted the sentence already served and the length of community service [performed] calculated in accordance with paragraph 1.

VI

JUDICIAL FORGIVENESS OF PUNISHMENTS

Article 104B
Grounds for judicial forgiveness of punishments

1. The court may choose not to impose a punishment on the person culpable of a misdemeanour if:
a) the harm or risk caused by their act was of particularly low severity;
b) the culpable person has rectified the harm caused to the victim to the extent possible, demonstrating sincere repentance;
c) the culpable person was particularly seriously impacted by the results of their act; or
d) an unusually long period of time has elapsed since the crime was committed.
In order to determine whether not to impose a punishment, the court shall examine whether the punishment, due to any of the aforesaid circumstances, appears no longer necessary or disproportionately onerous.
2. The court shall not impose a punishment on the person culpable of a misdemeanour if a restorative justice process between them and the victim has been successfully completed.

ΕΚΤΟ ΚΕΦΑΛΑΙΟ

Η ΕΚΤΙΣΗ ΤΩΝ ΠΟΙΝΩΝ

I

ΑΝΤΙΚΑΤΑΣΤΑΣΗ ΤΗΣ ΣΤΕΡΗΤΙΚΗΣ ΤΗΣ ΕΛΕΥΘΕΡΙΑΣ ΠΟΙΝΗΣ

Άρθρο 105

Έκτιση της ποινής στην κατοικία

1. Όποιος καταδικάστηκε σε πρόσκαιρη στερητική της ελευθερίας ποινή και έχει υπερβεί το εβδομηκοστό (70ό) έτος της ηλικίας εκτίει την ποινή ή το υπόλοιπο της ποινής στην κατοικία του, εκτός αν το δικαστήριο, με ειδική αιτιολογία, κρίνει ότι η έκτιση της ποινής σε κατάστημα κράτησης είναι απολύτως αναγκαία για να αποτραπεί από την τέλεση άλλων αντίστοιχης βαρύτητας εγκλημάτων. Αν το πιο πάνω όριο ηλικίας έχει συμπληρωθεί κατά την εκδίκαση της υπόθεσης, αποφασίζει το δικαστήριο που επιβάλλει την ποινή. Σε κάθε άλλη περίπτωση αποφασίζει το συμβούλιο πλημμελειοδικών της περιοχής που εδρεύει το δικαστήριο αυτό, μετά από αίτηση του καταδικασθέντος. Το βούλευμα που απορρίπτει την αίτηση υπόκειται σε έφεση.
2. Η διάταξη της προηγούμενης παραγράφου ισχύει, ανεξαρτήτως ποινής, και για τις μητέρες που έχουν την επιμέλεια ανήλικων τέκνων, μέχρι τη συμπλήρωση του όγδοου (8ου) έτους της ηλικίας τους και ασκείται άπαξ. Ισχύει επίσης, χωρίς τις προϋποθέσεις της παρ. 1, για εκείνους που νοσούν από σύνδρομο επίκτητης ανοσοποιητικής ανεπάρκειας τελικού σταδίου, από χρόνια νεφρική ανεπάρκεια και υποβάλλονται σε τακτική αιμοκάθαρση, από ανθεκτική φυματίωση ή είναι τετραπληγικοί, από κίρρωση του ήπατος με αναπηρία άνω του εξήντα επτά τοις εκατό (67%), από γεροντική άνοια ή από κακοήθη νεοπλάσματα τελικού σταδίου. Για τη διακρίβωση των προϋποθέσεων του προηγούμενου εδαφίου απαιτείται γνωμάτευση δύο ιατρών δημόσιου νοσοκομείου. Με κοινή απόφαση των Υπουργών Δικαιοσύνης και Υγείας μπορεί, ύστερα από γνώμη του Κεντρικού Συμβουλίου Υγείας (ΚΕ.Σ.Υ.), να προστίθενται και άλλα είδη ασθενειών ανάλογης βαρύτητας.
3. Το δικαστήριο ή το δικαστικό συμβούλιο εάν κατά τις προηγούμενες παραγράφους αντικαταστήσει την στερητική της ελευθερίας ποινή με έκτισή της στην κατοικία, μπορεί να επιβάλει στον καταδικασθέντα κατάλληλους κατά την κρίση του όρους από εκείνους που αναφέρονται στο άρθρο 99 παρ. 2 περιπτώσεις δ΄ έως στ΄, με ανάλογη εφαρμογή της παρ. 4 του ίδιου άρθρου, ή έκτιση με ηλεκτρονική επιτήρηση. Το δικαστικό συμβούλιο μπορεί να ανακαλέσει την έκτιση της ποινής στην κατοικία, αν διαπιστωθεί ότι δεν συντρέχουν οι προϋποθέσεις των παρ. 1 και 2 ή ότι ο καταδικασθείς αδικαιολογήτως δεν εκτίει πραγματικά την ποινή στην κατοικία. Για την ανάκληση εφαρμόζεται ανάλογα η παρ. 3 του άρθρου 110 ΠΚ.
4. Ο αρμόδιος για την έκτιση της ποινής εισαγγελέας δύναται:
α) να χορηγεί άδεια εξόδου από την κατοικία για αποδεδειγμένα σοβαρούς λόγους,
β) να παραγγέλλει το αρμόδιο Αστυνομικό Τμήμα του τόπου κατοικίας του καταδικασθέντος να ελέγχει την πραγματική κατ' οίκον έκτιση της ποινής.

CHAPTER VI

SERVING OF SENTENCES

I

SUBSTITUTION OF CUSTODIAL SENTENCES

Article 105
House arrest

1. Any person over the age of 70 convicted to serve a fixed-term custodial sentence shall serve the sentence or its remainder at their home, unless the court, providing specific reasoning [in its judgment], determines that serving the sentence at a custodial institution is absolutely necessary in order to deter the convicted person from committing other crimes of similar severity. If the above age is attained while the case is being adjudicated, the court imposing the sentence shall rule [on the matter]. In all other cases, the judicial council of the court of misdemeanours of the [district] where the court imposing the sentence is seated shall rule [on the matter], following an application filed by the convicted person. A judicial council decision dismissing the application is subject to appeal.

2. The provisions of the preceding paragraph also apply, irrespective of the sentence [imposed], to mothers with custody of juvenile children until they attain the age of eight, and shall be applied only once. These provisions also apply, without the conditions laid down in paragraph 1, to persons who suffer from: end-stage acquired immune deficiency syndrome; chronic renal failure and undergo regular dialysis; drug-resistant tuberculosis or are quadriplegic; liver cirrhosis and are more than 67% disabled; senile dementia; or end-stage malignant neoplasms. An opinion issued by two public hospital physicians is required in order to ascertain that the conditions laid down in the preceding sentence are met. Other types of illnesses of similar severity may be added [to the above] pursuant to a joint decision of the Minister of Justice and the Minister of Health, following an opinion issued by the Central Board of Health.

3. If the court or judicial council substitutes the custodial sentence for house arrest in accordance with the preceding paragraphs, it may impose on the convicted person conditions which are appropriate, in its view, from among those referred to in Article 99(2)(d) to (f), with Article 99(4) applying *mutatis mutandis*, or that they serve their sentence under electronic surveillance. The judicial council may revoke house arrest if it is determined that the conditions laid down in paragraphs 1 and 2 are not met or that the convicted person is unjustifiably not actually serving their sentence at home. Article 110(3) applies *mutatis mutandis* to such revocation.

4. The public prosecutor responsible for the serving of sentences may:

a) grant permission to leave the home on demonstrably serious grounds;

b) order the competent police department at the convicted person's place of domicile to check that they are actually serving their sentence at home.

5. *Εκτός των περιπτώσεων των παρ. 1 και 2, αν με μία ή περισσότερες αποφάσεις έχει επιβληθεί ποινή φυλάκισης, που δεν υπερβαίνει τα δύο (2) έτη, το δικαστήριο, μπορεί, ύστερα από αίτηση του καταδικασθέντος, να αποφασίσει την κατ' οίκον έκτιση της ποινής με ηλεκτρονική επιτήρηση αν κρίνει αιτιολογημένα ότι είναι πρόσφορη για να τον αποτρέψει από την τέλεση άλλων αδικημάτων χωρίς να είναι αναγκαία η μερική ή ολική έκτιση της ποινής σε σωφρονιστικό κατάστημα. Στην περίπτωση του πρώτου εδαφίου εφαρμόζονται αναλογικά η παρ. 1 του άρθρου 284 και η παρ. 4 του άρθρου 285 του Κώδικα Ποινικής Δικονομίας. Αν καταδικασθείς δεν συμμορφώνεται με τις υποχρεώσεις που του επιβλήθηκαν σχετικά με τον κατ' οίκον περιορισμό με ηλεκτρονική επιτήρηση ή σε περίπτωση τέλεσης από αυτόν του εγκλήματος του άρθρου 173Α του παρόντος, ο εισαγγελέας εκτέλεσης ποινών ανακαλεί την απόφαση με διάταξή του και διατάσσει την πραγματική έκτιση της ποινής σε σωφρονιστικό κατάστημα. Η ποινή που εκτίεται με ηλεκτρονική επιτήρηση, θεωρείται ότι έχει αποτιθεί, με τη συμπλήρωση των χρονικών ορίων της παρ. 1 του άρθρου 105Β.*

Άρθρο 105Α

(Καταργείται)

II
ΑΠΟΛΥΣΗ ΚΑΤΑΔΙΚΟΥ ΥΠΟ ΟΡΟ

Άρθρο 105Β
Απόλυση υπό τον όρο της ανάκλησης

1. *Όσοι καταδικάστηκαν σε στερητική της ελευθερίας ποινής μπορούν να απολυθούν υπό τον όρο της ανάκλησης, σύμφωνα με τις πιο κάτω διατάξεις, εφόσον έχουν εκτίσει:*

α) σε περίπτωση φυλάκισης τα δύο πέμπτα (2/5) αυτής ή πρόσκαιρης κάθειρξης τα τρία πέμπτα (3/5) αυτής,

β) σε περίπτωση πρόσκαιρης κάθειρξης για τα εγκλήματα του δευτέρου εδαφίου της παρ. 6, τα τέσσερα πέμπτα (4/5) αυτής και

γ) σε περίπτωση ισόβιας κάθειρξης τουλάχιστον είκοσι (20) έτη.

2. *Για τη χορήγηση της υπό όρο απόλυσης δεν απαιτείται να έχει καταστεί η καταδίκη αμετάκλητη.*

3. *Στην περίπτωση που συντρέχουν σωρευτικά περισσότερες ποινές, ο καταδικασθείς μπορεί να απολυθεί αν έχει εκτίσει το άθροισμα των τμημάτων των ποινών, που προβλέπεται στην παρ. 1. Σε κάθε περίπτωση ο καταδικασθείς μπορεί να απολυθεί αν έχει εκτίσει είκοσι πέντε (25) έτη και όταν το παραπάνω άθροισμα υπερβαίνει το όριο αυτό.*

4. *Αν ο καταδικασθείς εργάζεται, κάθε ημέρα εργασίας υπολογίζεται σύμφωνα με τις σχετικές διατάξεις της σωφρονιστικής νομοθεσίας. Κάθε ημέρα κράτησης κρατουμένων που έχουν ημιπληγία ή παραπληγία, σκλήρυνση κατά πλάκας ή έχουν υποβληθεί σε επέμβαση μεταμόσχευσης καρδιάς, ήπατος, νεφρού ή μυελού των οστών ή είναι φορείς του συνδρόμου επίκτητης ανοσοποιητικής ανεπάρκειας ή έχουν κακοήθη νεοπλάσματα ή νεφρική ανεπάρκεια για την οποία γίνεται τακτική αιμοκάθαρση ή φυματίωση κατά τη διάρκεια της θεραπείας της, υπολογίζεται ευεργετικά ως δύο (2) ημέρες εκτιόμενης ποινής. Το ίδιο ισχύει και για:*

5. Except for the cases provided for in paragraphs 1 and 2, where one or more judgments have imposed a sentence of imprisonment of no more than two years, the court may, following an application from the convicted person, order house arrest under electronic surveillance if it rules, providing reasoning in its judgment, that this is appropriate to deter them from committing other offences without it being necessary to serve all or part of their sentence at a custodial institution. Articles 284(1) and 285(4) of the Code of Criminal Procedure apply *mutatis mutandis mutandis* in the case provided for in the preceding sentence. Where the convicted person fails to comply with the obligations imposed on them concerning house arrest under electronic surveillance or commits the crime provided for in Article 173A, the public prosecutor competent for the enforcement of sentences shall issue an order revoking the decision and shall order that the sentence be actually served at a custodial institution. A sentence served under electronic surveillance shall be deemed to have been served in full when the time periods provided for in Article 105B(1) end.

Article 105A

[Repealed]

II
CONDITIONAL RELEASE OF CONVICTED PERSONS

Article 105B
Conditional release subject to revocation

1. Any person convicted to serve a custodial sentence may be released under the condition of revocation in accordance with the following provisions, provided they have served:

a) 2/5 of the sentence in the case of imprisonment or 3/5 of the sentence in the case of fixed-term incarceration;

b) 4/5 of the sentence in the case of fixed-term incarceration for the crimes referred to in the second subparagraph of paragraph 6 [of this Article]; and

c) 20 years in the case of incarceration for life.

2. It is not necessary for the conviction to have become irrevocable in order for conditional release to be granted.

3. Where several sentences concur cumulatively, the convicted person may be released if they have served the sum of the parts of the sentences provided for in paragraph 1. In all events, the convicted person may be released if they have served 25 years and when the aforesaid sum exceeds that threshold.

4. If the convicted person works [at the prison], each day of work shall be computed in accordance with the relevant provisions of the correctional legislation. Every day of detention shall be beneficially calculated as two days of time served with respect to prisoners suffering from hemiplegia, paraplegia, multiple sclerosis, those who have undergone a heart, liver, kidney, or bone marrow transplant, are carriers of acquired immune deficiency syndrome, suffer from malignant neoplasms, or renal failure and undergo regular dialysis, or from tuberculosis during its treatment. The same also applies to:

α) κρατουμένους με ποσοστό αναπηρίας πενήντα τοις εκατό (50%) και άνω, που δεν μπορούν να εργαστούν, εφόσον κρίνεται ότι η παραμονή τους στο κατάστημα κράτησης καθίσταται ιδιαίτερα επαχθής λόγω αδυναμίας αυτοεξυπηρέτησης,

β) κρατουμένους με ποσοστό αναπηρίας εξήντα επτά τοις εκατό (67%) και άνω,

γ) κρατούμενους στους οποίους απαγορεύεται ύστερα από γνωμάτευση από Κέντρο Πιστοποίησης Αναπηρίας (ΚΕ.Π.Α.) η ανάληψη εργασίας ή απασχόλησης που μπορεί βάσιμα να προκαλέσει σοβαρή και μόνιμη βλάβη στην υγεία τους,

δ) κρατούμενους οι οποίοι νοσηλεύονται σε θεραπευτικά καταστήματα ή νοσοκομεία εφόσον η νοσηλεία τους έχει διαρκέσει τουλάχιστον τέσσερις (4) μήνες,

ε) κρατούμενες μητέρες για όσο διάστημα έχουν μαζί τους τα ανήλικα τέκνα τους,

στ) κρατούμενους που συμμετέχουν σε θεραπευτικό πρόγραμμα ψυχικής απεξάρτησης από ναρκωτικά εγκεκριμένου, κατά το άρθρο 51 του ν. 4139/2013 οργανισμού και

ζ) κρατούμενους για όσο διάστημα διαρκεί η κράτησή τους σε χώρους αστυνομικών τμημάτων ή αστυνομικών διευθύνσεων. Η διακρίβωση των ασθενειών του δεύτερου εδαφίου, καθώς και της αναπηρίας στις περ. α' και β' γίνεται με τη διαδικασία της παρ. 2 του άρθρου 105.

5. Για τη χορήγηση της υπό όρο απόλυσης, ως ποινή που εκτίθηκε θεωρείται αυτή που υπολογίστηκε ευεργετικά είτε κατά την προηγούμενη παράγραφο είτε κατά τις ειδικές διατάξεις που προβλέπουν αντίστοιχο υπολογισμό.

6. Προκειμένου για ποινές κάθειρξης δεν μπορεί να χορηγηθεί στον καταδικασθέντα απόλυση υπό όρο, αν δεν έχει παραμείνει, δίχως τον ευεργετικό υπολογισμό, στο σωφρονιστικό κατάστημα για χρονικό διάστημα ίσο με τα δύο πέμπτα (2/5) της ποινής που του επιβλήθηκε και, σε περίπτωση ισόβιας κάθειρξης, δεκαέξι (16) έτη. Προκειμένου για ποινές κάθειρξης που επιβλήθηκαν για τα κακουργήματα των άρθρων 22 και 23 του ν. 4139/2013, του άρθρου 30 του Κώδικα Μετανάστευσης και Κοινωνικής Ένταξης (ν. 4251/2014, Α' 80), των άρθρων 134, 187, 187 Α, των περ. γ' και δ' της παρ. 1 του άρθρου 265, της παρ. 1 του άρθρου 299, των άρθρων 323Α, 324, 380, 385, καθώς και γι' αυτά του 19ου Κεφαλαίου του Ειδικού Μέρους του παρόντος Κώδικα, απόλυση υπό όρο δεν μπορεί να χορηγηθεί στον καταδικασθέντα αν αυτός δεν έχει παραμείνει, δίχως τον ευεργετικό υπολογισμό, στο σωφρονιστικό κατάστημα για χρονικό διάστημα ίσο με τα τρία πέμπτα (3/5) της ποινής που του επιβλήθηκε, και σε περίπτωση ισόβιας κάθειρξης δεκαοχτώ (18) ετών. Το παραπάνω κατά περίπτωση χρονικό διάστημα προσαυξάνεται κατά το ένα τρίτο (1/3) των λοιπών ποινών που τυχόν έχουν επιβληθεί, στην περίπτωση που αυτές συντρέχουν σωρευτικά. Σε κάθε περίπτωση, όμως, ο καταδικασθείς μπορεί να απολυθεί αν έχει παραμείνει στο κατάστημα είκοσι (20) έτη και αν εκτίει περισσότερες ποινές ισόβιας κάθειρξης, αν έχει παραμείνει είκοσι πέντε (25) έτη. Στις περιπτώσεις συνολικής ποινής πρόσκαιρης κάθειρξης για τα εγκλήματα του δευτέρου εδαφίου που όπως επιβλήθηκε υπερβαίνει κατά τουλάχιστον δέκα (10) έτη το ανώτατο όριο της συνολικής ποινής κάθειρξης, η υφ' όρον απόλυση δύναται να χορηγείται, εφόσον ο κατάδικος έχει εκτίσει πραγματικά δεκαεπτά (17) έτη.

a) detainees who are more than 50% disabled and cannot work, provided their [detention] at the custodial institution is particularly onerous due to inability to care for themselves;

b) detainees who are more than 67% disabled;

c) detainees who have been prohibited, following an opinion issued by a Disability Certification Centre, from any work or occupation which could arguably cause serious and permanent damage to their health;

d) detainees being treated at therapeutic institutions or hospitals, provided their treatment has lasted at least four months;

e) detainee mothers for as long as their juvenile children remain with them;

f) detainees attending a therapeutic drug rehabilitation programme [implemented] by an organisation authorised under Article 51 of Law 4139/2013; and

g) detainees for the duration of their detention at police departments or police directorates. The illnesses referred to in the second subparagraph and the disability referred to in points (a) and (b) shall be ascertained in accordance with the procedure laid down in Article 105(2).

5. For the purposes of granting conditional release, the sentence computed beneficially either in accordance with the preceding paragraph or in accordance with specific provisions stipulating such computation shall be deemed time served.

6. Where a sentence of incarceration has been imposed, conditional release cannot be granted to the convicted person without beneficial calculation if they have not been [held] at the correctional institution for a period equal to 2/5 of the sentence imposed on them and, in the case of incarceration for life, 16 years. Where a sentence of incarceration has been imposed for the felonies referred to in Articles 22 and 23 of Law 4139/2013, Article 30 of the Migration and Social Integration Code (Law 4251/2014, Government Gazette, Series I, Issue 80), Articles 134, 187, 187A, 265(1)(c) and (d), 299(1), 323A, 324, 380, 385 and Chapter 19 of the Special Part of this Code, conditional release cannot be granted to the convicted person unless they have [been held], without beneficial calculation, at a correctional institution for a period equal to 3/5 of the sentence imposed on them and, in the case of incarceration for life, 18 years. The above period, as applicable, shall be augmented by 1/3 of any other sentences imposed, where they concur cumulatively. However, in all events, the convicted person may be released if they have [been held] at a correctional institution for 20 years and, where they are serving several sentences of incarceration for life, if they have [been held] there for 25 years. Where the total sentence of fixed-term incarceration imposed for the crimes referred to in the second subparagraph exceeds the maximum threshold of the total sentence of incarceration by at least 10 years, conditional release may be granted provided the convicted person has actually served 17 years.

Άρθρο 106
Προϋποθέσεις για τη χορήγηση της απόλυσης

1. Η απόλυση υπό όρο μπορεί να μην χορηγηθεί αν κριθεί ότι η διαγωγή του καταδικασθέντος, κατά την έκτιση της ποινής του, σε συνδυασμό με τη διάγνωση της πιθανότητας επανάληψης του εγκλήματος κατά τον χρόνο δοκιμασίας, όπως προκύπτει από τα χαρακτηριστικά του εγκλήματος, σε σχέση με την εκτίμηση των ατομικών και κοινωνικών περιστάσεων του καταδικασθέντος, καθιστά αναγκαία τη συνέχιση της κράτησής του για να αποτραπεί η τέλεση από αυτόν νέων αξιόποινων πράξεων.

2. Στον απολυόμενο μπορούν να επιβληθούν ορισμένες υποχρεώσεις που θα αφορούν τον τρόπο της ζωής του και ιδίως τον τόπο διαμονής του, με ανάλογη εφαρμογή των περ. δ΄ έως ζ΄ της παρ. 2 του άρθρου 99. Οι υποχρεώσεις αυτές, όπως και αυτές που επιβάλλονται από τον νόμο, μπορούν πάντοτε να ανακληθούν ή να τροποποιηθούν αυτεπάγγελτα ή με αίτηση εκείνου που απολύθηκε.

3. Η εποπτεία για την τήρηση των κατά την προηγούμενη παράγραφο υποχρεώσεων μπορεί να ανατεθεί και σε εταιρεία προστασίας αποφυλακιζομένων.

Άρθρο 107
Ανάκληση της απόλυσης

1. Η απόλυση μπορεί να ανακληθεί, αν εκείνος που απολύθηκε δεν συμμορφωθεί με τις υποχρεώσεις που του επιβλήθηκαν κατά την απόλυση ή εφόσον ασκήθηκε σε βάρος του δίωξη για κακούργημα το οποίο τελέστηκε στο χρονικό διάστημα του άρθρου 109.

2. Στην περίπτωση αυτή ο χρόνος από την απόλυση έως τη νέα σύλληψη δεν υπολογίζεται στη διάρκεια της ποινής, ο κατάδικος όμως δεν εμποδίζεται να ζητήσει εκ νέου την υπό όρο απόλυσή του.

Άρθρο 108
Άρση της απόλυσης

1. Η απόλυση αίρεται αν μέσα στο χρονικό διάστημα που προβλέπει το επόμενο άρθρο, εκείνος που απολύθηκε διαπράξει έγκλημα, για το οποίο του επιβλήθηκε αμετακλήτως οποτεδήποτε ποινή στερητική της ελευθερίας ανώτερη από ένα (1) έτος. Στην περίπτωση αυτή, εκτίει αθροιστικά, από τότε που θα γίνει αμετάκλητη η νέα καταδίκη, και ολόκληρο το υπόλοιπο της προηγούμενης ποινής, το οποίο όφειλε να εκτίσει κατά τον χρόνο της απόλυσης. Σε περίπτωση άρσης της απόλυσης για καταδίκη σε ισόβια κάθειρξη εκτίει δέκα (10) επιπλέον έτη και επί σωρευτικής συνδρομής ισοβίων καθείρξεων δεκαπέντε (15) επιπλέον έτη.

2. Η άρση της απόλυσης δεν εμποδίζει τη χορήγηση νέας υπό όρο απόλυσης.

Άρθρο 109
Συνέπειες της μη ανάκλησης

Αν από την απόλυση περάσει το χρονικό διάστημα της ποινής το οποίο υπολειπόταν για έκτιση, σε όσες περιπτώσεις αυτό είναι ανώτερο από τρία (3) έτη, ή αν περάσουν τρία (3) έτη χωρίς να γίνει ανάκληση, η ποινή θεωρείται ότι εκτίθηκε. Η ισόβια κάθειρξη θεωρείται ότι εκτίθηκε, αν περάσουν δέκα (10) έτη από την απόλυση χωρίς να γίνει ανάκληση της απόλυσης.

Article 106
Prerequisites for granting release

1. Conditional release may not be granted if it is ruled that the convicted person's conduct while serving their sentence, coupled with the established fact that they are likely to re-offend during the probationary period, based on the attributes of the crime, and having assessed the convicted person's individual and social circumstances, necessitates their continued detention in order to deter them from committing new punishable acts.

2. Certain obligations may be imposed on the released person with regard to their lifestyle and, in particular, their place of residence, and Article 99(2)(d) to (g) apply *mutatis mutandis*. Such obligations, as well as those imposed by law, may always be revoked or amended *ex officio* or following an application filed by the released person.

3. Supervision of compliance with the obligations referred to in the preceding paragraph may also be assigned to a society for the protection of released persons.

Article 107
Revocation of release

1. The release may be revoked if the released person fails to comply with the obligations imposed on them upon release or if they were prosecuted for a felony committed during the period laid down in in Article 109.

2. In such a case, the period between the release and any new arrest shall not be calculated as part of the sentence; however, the convicted person shall not be prevented from re-applying for conditional release.

Article 108
Termination of release

1. The release shall be terminated if, within the period provided for in the Article below, the person released commits a crime for which a custodial sentence longer than one year was irrevocably imposed on them at any time. In this case, they shall cumulatively serve, from the time the new conviction becomes irrevocable, the total remainder of the previous sentence which they would have otherwise served while on [conditional] release. Where release is terminated due to conviction to incarceration for life, the convicted person shall serve an additional 10 years, and where there are several sentences of incarceration for life, an additional 15 years.

2. Termination of release does not prevent [the court from] granting conditional release once again.

Article 109
Effects of non-revocation

A sentence shall be deemed to have been served if a period of time [equal to that] of the sentence that remained to be served has elapsed since the release, where this exceeds three years, or if three years have elapsed with no revocation having taken place. [A sentence of] incarceration for life shall be deemed to have been served if 10 years have elapsed since the release without the latter having been revoked.

Άρθρο 110

Διαδικασία για τη χορήγηση και την ανάκληση της απόλυσης

1. Για τη χορήγηση της απόλυσης υπό όρο αποφασίζει το συμβούλιο των πλημμελειοδικών του τόπου έκτισης της ποινής. Ο καταδικασθείς κλητεύεται υποχρεωτικά δέκα (10) τουλάχιστον ημέρες πριν από τη συνεδρίαση, κατά την οποία μπορεί να παραστεί αυτοπροσώπως ή με συνήγορο που διορίζει με απλό έγγραφο θεωρημένο από τον διευθυντή της φυλακής ή τις αρμόδιες αρχές.

Αν η καταδίκη αφορά κακουργήματα των Κεφαλαίων Δέκατου Πέμπτου, περί εγκλημάτων κατά της ζωής και προσβολών του εμβρύου, Δέκατου Έκτου, περί εγκλημάτων κατά της σωματικής ακεραιότητας, Δέκατου Όγδοου, περί εγκλημάτων κατά της προσωπικής ελευθερίας και Δέκατου Ένατου, περί εγκλημάτων κατά της γενετήσιας ελευθερίας και οικονομικής εκμετάλλευσης της γενετήσιας ζωής του Ειδικού Μέρους του Ποινικού Κώδικα ή εγκλήματα του ν. 3500/2006 (Α΄ 232), το πρόσωπο που είχε δηλώσει παράσταση προς υποστήριξη της κατηγορίας και έχει υποβάλει σχετικό αίτημα στον αρμόδιο εισαγγελέα του τόπου έκτισης ποινής όσο αυτή διαρκεί, δικαιούται να καταθέσει γραπτό υπόμνημα ενώπιον της γραμματείας του συμβουλίου, αφού ειδοποιηθεί με κάθε πρόσφορο τρόπο πέντε (5) τουλάχιστον ημέρες πριν από τη συνεδρίαση. Ο ανωτέρω, ανεξαρτήτως αν υπέβαλε αίτημα ή αν κατέθεσε υπόμνημα, ειδοποιείται, με κάθε πρόσφορο τρόπο από τον αρμόδιο εισαγγελέα, σε περίπτωση χορήγησης υπό όρο απόλυσης στον καταδικασθέντα.

2. Η απόλυση υπό όρο χορηγείται με αίτηση της διεύθυνσης του καταστήματος στο οποίο κρατείται ο καταδικασθείς. Η αίτηση υποβάλλεται δύο (2) μήνες πριν από τη συμπλήρωση του χρόνου που προβλέπει το άρθρο 105Β. Αν η διεύθυνση του καταστήματος κρίνει ότι συντρέχουν προϋποθέσεις για τη μη χορήγηση της απόλυσης, υποβάλλει σχετική αναφορά μαζί με έκθεση της κοινωνικής υπηρεσίας του καταστήματος στον εισαγγελέα των πλημμελειοδικών, ο οποίος την εισάγει στο συμβούλιο.

3. Για την ανάκληση αποφασίζει το ίδιο δικαστικό συμβούλιο, ύστερα από πρόταση των αρχών που εποπτεύουν αυτόν που απολύθηκε. Το εδάφιο β΄ της πρώτης παραγράφου εφαρμόζεται και στην περίπτωση αυτή.

4. Σε περίπτωση επείγουσας ανάγκης, για να προληφθεί κίνδυνος της δημόσιας τάξης, ο εισαγγελέας πλημμελειοδικών του τόπου διαμονής εκείνου που απολύθηκε μπορεί να διατάξει την προσωρινή σύλληψή του ύστερα από την οποία προκαλείται αμέσως με τη νόμιμη διαδικασία η απόφαση για την ανάκληση. Αν αποφασιστεί η ανάκληση, θεωρείται ότι αυτή επήλθε την ημέρα της σύλληψης.

5. Κατά του βουλεύματος που κρίνει τη χορήγηση της υπό όρο απόλυσης επιτρέπεται έφεση από τον εισαγγελέα και τον καταδικασθέντα για οποιοδήποτε λόγο με ανάλογη εφαρμογή των άρθρων 473 έως 476 ΚΠΔ.

Article 110

Procedure for granting and revoking release

1. The judicial council of the court of misdemeanours of the place where the sentence is being served shall rule on whether to grant conditional release. The convicted person shall necessarily be summonsed at least 10 days prior to the sitting, and may enter an appearance in person or via counsel appointed by an ordinary document certified by the governor of the prison or by the competent authorities. If the conviction relates to felonies under Chapter XV concerning crimes against life and offences against foetuses, Chapter XVI concerning crimes against physical integrity, Chapter XVIII concerning crimes against personal freedom, [or] Chapter IX concerning crimes against sexual freedom and crimes of economic exploitation of sexual life of the Special Part of the Penal Code or crimes under Law 3500/2006 (Government Gazette, Series I, Issue 232), the person who entered an appearance in support of the charge and who submitted a relevant request to the competent public prosecutor at the place where the sentence is being served may, for the duration of such sentence, file a written memorandum with the secretariat of the judicial council, [provided they have] been notified in any expedient manner at least 5 days prior to the sitting. The above person, irrespective of whether they submitted a request or filed a memorandum, shall be notified by the public prosecutor, in any expedient manner, if the convicted person is granted conditional release.

2. Conditional release shall be granted following an application filed by the management of the institution where the convicted person is being held. Such application shall be submitted two months before the length of time provided for in Article 105B elapses. If the management of the institution determines that the conditions for not granting conditional release are met, it shall submit a relevant report, together with a report from the institution's social services [unit], to the court of misdemeanours public prosecutor, who shall bring it before the [judicial] council.

3. The same judicial council shall decide on whether to revoke the release, following a proposal from the authorities supervising the released person. The second sentence of the first paragraph also applies in such a case.

4. Where there is an urgent need and to prevent a risk to public order, the court of misdemeanours public prosecutor at the released person's place of residence may order they be placed under temporary arrest, immediately after which the revocation decision shall be made in accordance with the procedure laid down in law. If revocation is decided, it shall be deemed to have occurred on the day of the arrest.

5. An appeal may be filed by the public prosecutor and by the convicted person on any grounds against the judicial council decision granting conditional release, and Articles 473 to 476 of the Code of Criminal Procedure apply.

Άρθρο 110Α

Απόλυση υπό τον όρο της κατ' οίκον έκτισης της ποινής με ηλεκτρονική επιτήρηση

1. Όσοι καταδικάσθηκαν σε ποινή στερητική της ελευθερίας μπορούν, με αίτησή τους, σύμφωνα με τα οριζόμενα στο άρθρο 106 παρ. 1, να απολυθούν υπό τον όρο του κατ' οίκον περιορισμού με ηλεκτρονική επιτήρηση, όπως αυτός ορίζεται στο άρθρο 284 Κώδικα Ποινικής Δικονομίας, εφόσον έχουν εκτίσει:

α) προκειμένου για φυλάκιση, το ένα πέμπτο (1/5) αυτής,

β) προκειμένου για πρόσκαιρη κάθειρξη, τα δύο πέμπτα (2/5) αυτής και

γ) προκειμένου για ισόβια κάθειρξη, τουλάχιστον δεκατέσσερα (14) έτη.

2. Στην περίπτωση που συντρέχουν σωρευτικά περισσότερες ποινές, ο καταδικασθείς πρέπει να έχει εκτίσει το άθροισμα των τμημάτων των ποινών που προβλέπονται στην προηγούμενη παράγραφο. Σε κάθε περίπτωση μπορεί να απολυθεί, αν έχει εκτίσει είκοσι δύο (22) έτη, ακόμη και όταν το παραπάνω άθροισμα υπερβαίνει το όριο αυτό.

3. Αν ο καταδικασθείς εργάζεται, κάθε ημέρα εργασίας υπολογίζεται σύμφωνα με τις σχετικές διατάξεις της σωφρονιστικής νομοθεσίας.

4. Για τη χορήγηση της υπό όρο απόλυσης, ως ποινή που εκτίθηκε θεωρείται αυτή που υπολογίστηκε ευεργετικά κατά την προηγούμενη παράγραφο. Προκειμένου για ποινές κάθειρξης δεν μπορεί να χορηγηθεί στον καταδικασθέντα η απόλυση, αν δεν έχει παραμείνει στο σωφρονιστικό κατάστημα για χρονικό διάστημα ίσο με το ένα πέμπτο(1/5) της ποινής που του επιβλήθηκε και, σε περίπτωση ισόβιας κάθειρξης, για δώδεκα (12) έτη. Το χρονικό διάστημα του ενός πέμπτου (1/5) ή, σε περίπτωση ισόβιας κάθειρξης, των δώδεκα (12) ετών, προσαυξάνεται κατά το ένα πέμπτο των λοιπών ποινών που τυχόν έχουν επιβληθεί, στην περίπτωση που αυτές συντρέχουν σωρευτικά. Σε κάθε περίπτωση όμως ο καταδικασθείς μπορεί να απολυθεί αν έχει παραμείνει στο κατάστημα δεκατέσσερα (14) έτη και αν εκτίει περισσότερες ποινές ισόβιας κάθειρξης, αν έχει παραμείνει είκοσι (20) έτη.

5. Για την απόλυση του καταδικασθέντος κατά τις διατάξεις του παρόντος άρθρου δεν απαιτείται να έχει καταστεί η καταδίκη αμετάκλητη.

6. Ο απολυθείς σύμφωνα με τις διατάξεις του παρόντος άρθρου επιτρέπεται να ευρίσκεται προκαθορισμένες ώρες της ημέρας εκτός του τόπου του κατ' οίκον περιορισμού του αποκλειστικά για λόγους εργασίας, εκπαίδευσης ή επαγγελματικής κατάρτισης, συμμετοχής του σε εγκεκριμένο πρόγραμμα συντήρησης ή απεξάρτησης από ναρκωτικές ουσίες ή αλκοόλ ή και εκπλήρωσης των υποχρεώσεων που του έχουν επιβληθεί. Οι ώρες απουσίας του καταδικασθέντος από τον τόπο του κατ' οίκον περιορισμού του και το σύνολο των υποχρεώσεών του καθορίζονται είτε με το βούλευμα που διέταξε την απόλυσή του είτε μετά τη χορηγηθείσα απόλυση, με διάταξη του εισαγγελέα πλημμελειοδικών του τόπου έκτισης της ποινής. Με διάταξή του, ο ίδιος εισαγγελέας είτε κατόπιν αίτησης του καταδικασθέντος είτε αυτεπαγγέλτως, αποφασίζει για την αλλαγή του τόπου του κατ' οίκον περιορισμού, την τροποποίηση του προγράμματος των ωρών απουσίας του καταδικασθέντος από αυτόν και την επιβολή ή τροποποίηση των υποχρεώσεων του τελευταίου. Κατά τα λοιπά ισχύουν τα οριζόμενα στο άρθρο 106 παρ. 2 και 3.

7. Η απόλυση σύμφωνα με τις διατάξεις του παρόντος άρθρου μπορεί να μη χορηγηθεί, με ανάλογη εφαρμογή του άρθρου 106. Το δεύτερο εδάφιο της παρ. 1 του άρθρου 110 εφαρμόζεται αναλόγως.

Article 110A

Release on condition of house arrest under electronic surveillance

1. Any person convicted to serve a custodial sentence may, following an application filed in accordance with the provisions of Article 106(1), be released on condition that they be placed under house arrest under electronic surveillance, as provided for in Article 284 of the Code of Criminal Procedure, provided they have served:

a) 1/5 of the sentence in the case of imprisonment;

b) 2/5 of the sentence in the case of fixed-term incarceration; [or]

c) at least 14 years in the case of incarceration for life.

2. Where several sentences concur cumulatively, the convicted person must have served the sum of the parts of the sentences provided for in the preceding paragraph. In all cases, the convicted person may be released if they have served 22 years, even when the aforesaid sum exceeds that threshold.

3. If the convicted person works [at the prison], each day of work shall be computed in accordance with the relevant provisions of correctional legislation.

4. For the purposes of granting conditional release, the sentence computed beneficially in accordance with the preceding paragraph shall be deemed time served. Where a sentence of incarceration has been imposed, release cannot be granted to the convicted person if they have not been [held] at the correctional institution for a period equal to 1/5 of the sentence imposed on them and, in the case of incarceration for life, 12 years. The time period of 1/5 [of the sentence] or, in the case of incarceration for life, 12 years shall be augmented by 1/5 of any other sentences imposed, where they concur cumulatively. However, in all events, the convicted person may be released if they have [been held] at a correctional institution for 14 years and, if they are serving several sentences of incarceration for life, if they have [been held] there for 20 years.

5. It is not necessary for the conviction to have become irrevocable in order for a convicted person to be released in accordance with the provisions of this Article.

6. Any person released in accordance with the provisions of this Article shall be permitted to leave the place where they are under house arrest during specified hours of the day, exclusively for the purpose of work, education, vocational training, attendance at an approved drug or alcohol dependence or rehabilitation programme, and/or fulfilment of the obligations imposed on them. The hours during which the convicted person may leave the place where they are under house arrest and their overall obligations shall be specified either in the judicial council decision which ordered their release or, after release has been granted, in a decree issued by the court of misdemeanours public prosecutor at the place where the sentence is being served. The same public prosecutor, either following an application filed by the convicted person or *ex officio*, shall decide, in a decree, on whether or not to change the place of house arrest, modify the schedule of hours of absence of the convicted person from that place, and impose or amend the convicted person's obligations. In all other respects, the provisions of Article 106(2) and (3) apply.

7. Release in accordance with the provisions of this Article may not be granted, and Article 106 applies *mutatis mutandis*. The second sentence of Article 110(1) applies *mutatis mutandis*.

8. Η απόλυση μπορεί να ανακληθεί, αν ο καταδικασθείς δεν συμμορφώνεται με τις υποχρεώσεις που του επιβλήθηκαν και πιθανολογείται ότι ενόψει της βαρύτητας της παράβασης των υποχρεώσεών του, του τρόπου και των εν γένει συνθηκών που αυτή συντελέστηκε, δεν παρέχει την προσδοκία ότι θα τηρήσει τις υποχρεώσεις του στο μέλλον. Σε περίπτωση ανάκλησης, ο χρόνος από την απόλυση έως τη νέα σύλληψη δεν υπολογίζεται στην εκτιθείσα ποινή. Ο καταδικασθείς διατηρεί πάντως το δικαίωμα να απολυθεί υπό όρο κατ' άρθρο 105Β. Οι παρ. 3 και 4 του άρθρου 110 εφαρμόζονται αναλόγως.

9. Η απόλυση σύμφωνα με τις διατάξεις του παρόντος άρθρου αίρεται, όταν ο καταδικασθείς, κατά το χρονικό διάστημα που προβλέπεται στην παρ. 10, τελέσει κακούργημα ή πλημμέλημα με δόλο που τιμωρείται με ποινή φυλάκισης τουλάχιστον έξι (6) μηνών, για το οποίο καταδικάστηκε αμετακλήτως. Σε περίπτωση άρσης της απόλυσης, ο χρόνος από την απόλυση έως τη νέα σύλληψη δεν υπολογίζεται στην εκτιθείσα ποινή. Ο καταδικασθείς στην περίπτωση αυτή δικαιούται να απολυθεί υπό όρο κατ' άρθρο 105Β, αφού παραμείνει στο σωφρονιστικό κατάστημα ένα επιπλέον έτος σε σχέση με τα οριζόμενα στο άρθρο 105Β παρ. 1. Το ίδιο ισχύει αν, κατά το χρόνο που κατέστη η καταδίκη αμετάκλητη, είχε ήδη χορηγηθεί απόλυση κατ' άρθρο 105Β, χωρίς όμως να έχει παρέλθει το χρονικό διάστημα που αναφέρεται στο άρθρο 109. Δεν εφαρμόζεται το προηγούμενο εδάφιο, αν, κατά το χρόνο που κατέστη η καταδίκη αμετάκλητη, είχε ήδη χορηγηθεί στον καταδικασθέντα η απόλυση υπό όρο κατ' άρθρο 105Β, χωρίς να έχει ανακληθεί, με αποτέλεσμα η ποινή για την οποία χορηγήθηκε η απόλυση να θεωρείται ότι έχει ήδη εκτιθεί κατά τα οριζόμενα στο άρθρο 109.

10. Η με το παρόν άρθρο χορηγούμενη απόλυση εκτείνεται μέχρι του χρονικού σημείου της χορήγησης στον καταδικασθέντα της απόλυσης υπό όρο κατ' άρθρο 105Β.

11. Στις περιπτώσεις των κακουργημάτων των άρθρων 22 και 23 του ν. 4139/2013, 134, 187, 187Α, των περ. γ΄ και δ΄ της παρ. 1 του άρθρου 265, της παρ. 1 του άρθρου 299, 323Α, 324, 380, 385, καθώς και γι' αυτά του 19ου Κεφαλαίου του Ειδικού Μέρους του παρόντος Κώδικα, δεν επιτρέπεται απόλυση υπό τον όρο της κατ' οίκον έκτισης της ποινής με ηλεκτρονική επιτήρηση.

8. The release may be revoked if the convicted person fails to comply with the obligations imposed on them and it is deemed likely on the balance of probabilities that, in view of the severity of the breach of their obligations, the manner in which and general circumstances under which such breach occurred, they are not expected to comply with their obligations in the future. Where release is revoked, the time period between the release and the new arrest shall not be deemed time served. Nevertheless, the convicted person reserves the right to be conditionally released in accordance with Article 105B. Article 110(3) and (4) apply *mutatis mutandis*.

9. Release under the provisions of this Article shall be terminated [if], during the period laid down in paragraph 10, the convicted person committed and was irrevocably convicted of a felony or misdemeanour with *dolus* carrying a sentence of imprisonment of at least six months. Where release is terminated, the time period between the release and the new arrest shall not be deemed time served. In this case, the convicted person is entitled to conditional release in accordance with Article 105B [only] after having been [held] at a correctional institution for one year more than the period laid down in Article 105B(1). The same applies if, at the time the conviction became irrevocable, release had already been granted in accordance with Article 105B but the time period laid down in Article 109 has not elapsed. The preceding sentence does not apply if, at the time the conviction became irrevocable, the convicted person had already been conditionally released in accordance with Article 105B and said release has not been revoked, resulting in the sentence for which release was granted being deemed to have already been served in accordance with the provisions of Article 109.

10. Release granted in accordance with this Article lasts until the time the convicted person is conditionally released in accordance with Article 105B.

11. Release on the condition of house arrest under electronic surveillance is not permitted in the cases of the felonies provided for in Articles 22 and 23 of Law 4139/2013, Articles 134, 187, 187A, 265(1)(c) and (d), 299(1), 323A, 324, 380, 385, as well as those provided for in Chapter 19 of the Special Part of this Code.

ΕΒΔΟΜΟ ΚΕΦΑΛΑΙΟ

ΛΟΓΟΙ ΠΟΥ ΕΞΑΛΕΙΦΟΥΝ ΤΟ ΑΞΙΟΠΟΙΝΟ – ΠΑΡΑΓΡΑΦΗ ΠΟΙΝΩΝ

I

ΠΑΡΑΓΡΑΦΗ ΕΓΚΛΗΜΑΤΩΝ

Άρθρο 111
Χρόνος παραγραφής

1. Το αξιόποινο εξαλείφεται με την παραγραφή.
2. Τα κακουργήματα παραγράφονται μετά είκοσι έτη αν ο νόμος προβλέπει γι' αυτά την ποινή της ισόβιας κάθειρξης και μετά δέκα πέντε έτη σε κάθε άλλη περίπτωση, εκτός αν ο νόμος προβλέπει διαφορετικά.
3. Τα πλημμελήματα παραγράφονται μετά πέντε έτη.
4. Οι πιο πάνω προθεσμίες υπολογίζονται κατά το ισχύον ημερολόγιο.
5. Αν ο νόμος ορίζει διαζευκτικά περισσότερες από μία ποινές, οι πιο πάνω προθεσμίες υπολογίζονται σύμφωνα με τη βαρύτερη απ' αυτές.

Άρθρο 112
Έναρξη του χρόνου παραγραφής

Η προθεσμία της παραγραφής αρχίζει από την ημέρα που τελέστηκε η αξιόποινη πράξη, εκτός αν ορίζεται διαφορετικά. Σε περίπτωση συμμετοχής η προθεσμία αρχίζει από το χρόνο τέλεσης της πράξης του φυσικού αυτουργού.

Άρθρο 113
Αναστολή της παραγραφής

1. Η προθεσμία της παραγραφής αναστέλλεται για όσο χρόνο, σύμφωνα με διάταξη νόμου, δεν μπορεί να αρχίσει ή να εξακολουθήσει η ποινική δίωξη, καθώς και για όσο χρόνο διαρκεί η κύρια διαδικασία και έως ότου γίνει αμετάκλητη η καταδικαστική απόφαση.
2. Η κατά την προηγούμενη παράγραφο αναστολή δεν μπορεί να διαρκέσει περισσότερο από πέντε (5) έτη για τα κακουργήματα και τρία (3) έτη για τα πλημμελήματα. Ο χρονικός περιορισμός της αναστολής δεν ισχύει όταν η αναβολή ή αναστολή της ποινικής δίωξης, ή η αναβολή της δίκης, λαμβάνει χώρα κατ' εφαρμογή των άρθρων 29, 59 και 61 του Κώδικα Ποινικής Δικονομίας ή της παρ. 4Α του άρθρου 7 του ν. 3226/2004 (Α΄ 24).
3. Αν για την ποινική δίωξη απαιτείται έγκληση, η έλλειψή της δεν αναστέλλει την παραγραφή.
4. Η προθεσμία της παραγραφής των κακουργημάτων που στρέφονται κατά ανηλίκου αρχίζει από την ενηλικίωση του θύματος. Η προθεσμία της παραγραφής των εγκλημάτων που προβλέπονται στα άρθρα 323Α, 324 και στο 19ο Κεφάλαιο του Ειδικού Μέρους του παρόντος Κώδικα, όταν αυτά στρέφονται κατά ανηλίκου, αρχίζει ένα (1) έτος μετά από την ενηλικίωση του θύματος, εφόσον πρόκειται για πλημμέλημα, και τρία (3) έτη μετά την ενηλικίωση, εφόσον πρόκειται για κακούργημα.

CHAPTER VII

GROUNDS EXTINGUISHING PUNISHABILITY - TIME-BARRING OF PUNISHMENTS

I

TIME-BARRING OF CRIMES

Article 111
Time-barring period

1. Punishability is extinguished when the time-barring period ends.
2. Unless otherwise provided for in law, felonies become time-barred after 25 years where, in law, they carry a sentence of incarceration for life, and after 15 years in all other cases.
3. Misdemeanours become time-barred after five years.
4. The above deadlines shall be computed in accordance with the calendar in force.
5. If the law provides for several alternative punishments, the above deadlines shall be computed on the basis of the heavier such punishment.

Article 112
Commencement of the time-barring period

Unless otherwise provided for, the time-barring period commences on the day the punishable act was committed. In cases of participation [in the punishable act], the period commences from the time the perpetrator committed the act.

Article 113
Suspension of the time-barring period

1. The time-barring period shall be suspended for as long as criminal prosecution cannot commence or continue due to a statutory provision and as long as the main proceedings are ongoing and until the judgment of conviction has become irrevocable.
2. The suspension referred to in the preceding paragraph cannot last longer than five years for felonies and three years for misdemeanours. The above limitation does not apply when the criminal prosecution has been deferred or suspended or the proceedings have been adjourned pursuant to Articles 29, 59 [or] 61 of the Code of Criminal Procedure or Article 7(4A) of Law 3226/2004 (Government Gazette, Series I, Issue 24).
3. If a victim-initiated complaint is required to initiate criminal prosecution, lack of such complaint does not result in the time-barring period being suspended.
4. The time-barring period for felonies committed against juveniles commences from the date the victim attains the age of majority. The time-barring period for the crimes provided for in Articles 323A, 324 and in Chapter 19 of the Special Part of this Code, when committed against a juvenile, commences one year after the victim attains the age of majority in the case of a misdemeanour, and three years after the victim attains the age of majority in the case of a felony.

II

ΠΑΡΑΙΤΗΣΗ ΑΠΟ ΤΗΝ ΕΓΚΛΗΣΗ

Άρθρο 114
Μη υποβολή έγκλησης ή δήλωση παραίτησης από το δικαίωμα της έγκλησης - Εγκλήματα σε βάρος του Δημοσίου

1. Όταν ο νόμος απαιτεί έγκληση για την ποινική δίωξη κάποιας αξιόποινης πράξης, το αξιόποινο εξαλείφεται αν ο δικαιούχος δεν υποβάλει την έγκληση μέσα σε τρεις μήνες από την ημέρα που έμαθε για την τέλεση της πράξης και για τον δράστη της ή για έναν από τους συμμετόχους.

2. Το ίδιο αποτέλεσμα συνεπάγεται και η ρητή δήλωση του δικαιούχου της έγκλησης ενώπιον της αρμόδιας αρχής, ότι παραιτείται από το δικαίωμα της έγκλησης.

3. Τα εγκλήματα σε βάρος του νομικού προσώπου του ελληνικού δημοσίου, των νομικών προσώπων δημοσίου δικαίου ή των οργανισμών τοπικής αυτοδιοίκησης διώκονται πάντοτε αυτεπαγγέλτως.

Άρθρο 115
Πρόσωπα που δικαιούνται να υποβάλουν έγκληση

1. Έγκληση δικαιούται να υποβάλει ο αμέσως παθών από την αξιόποινη πράξη, εκτός αν ο νόμος ορίζει διαφορετικά.

2. Αν ο παθών δεν έχει συμπληρώσει το δέκατο τρίτο έτος της ηλικίας του ή τελεί υπό δικαστική συμπαράσταση, το δικαίωμα της έγκλησης έχει ο νόμιμος αντιπρόσωπός του. Αν ο παθών έχει συμπληρώσει το δέκατο τρίτο έτος της ηλικίας του, το δικαίωμα της έγκλησης έχουν τόσο ο παθών όσο και ο νόμιμος αντιπρόσωπός του, και μετά τη συμπλήρωση του δέκατου όγδοου έτους της ηλικίας του το δικαίωμα αυτό το έχει μόνο ο παθών.

3. Αν δύο ή περισσότεροι έχουν δικαίωμα έγκλησης, το δικαίωμα του καθενός είναι αυτοτελές.

4. Μετά τον θάνατο του παθόντος το δικαίωμα της έγκλησης μεταβιβάζεται στον επιζώντα σύζυγο ή σε αυτόν που συμβίωνε με τον θανόντα έως τον θάνατό του καθώς και στα τέκνα του, και αν αυτοί δεν υπάρχουν ή είναι δράστες του εγκλήματος, στους γονείς του.

Άρθρο 116
Αδιαίρετο της έγκλησης

Η ποινική δίωξη ασκείται εναντίον όλων των συμμετόχων του εγκλήματος ακόμη και αν η έγκληση που υποβλήθηκε στρέφεται εναντίον ενός από αυτούς.

Άρθρο 117
Ανάκληση της έγκλησης

1. Αυτός που υπέβαλε την έγκληση μπορεί να την ανακαλέσει με τους όρους που ορίζει ο Κώδικας Ποινικής Δικονομίας. Αν η έγκληση έχει υποβληθεί από τον νόμιμο εκπρόσωπο του παθόντος, αυτός διατηρεί το δικαίωμα της ανάκλησης μόνο όσο διαρκεί η νόμιμη εκπροσώπηση. Μετά τη λήξη της, δικαίωμα ανάκλησης έχει ο παθών ή ο νέος νόμιμος εκπρόσωπός του.

2. Μετά την ανάκληση της έγκλησης που υποβλήθηκε δεν μπορεί να υποβληθεί νέα.

3. Η ανάκληση που έγινε για έναν από τους συμμετόχους της πράξης έχει ως συνέπεια την παύση της ποινικής δίωξης και των υπολοίπων, εφόσον και αυτοί διώκονται με έγκληση.

4. Η ανάκληση δεν έχει κανένα αποτέλεσμα για τον κατηγορούμενο που δηλώνει προς την αρχή ότι δεν την αποδέχεται.

II

DISCONTINUATION OF VICTIM-INITIATED COMPLAINT

Article 114
Non-filing of a victim-initiated complaint or filing of a declaration of waiver of the right to [file] a victim-initiated complaint - Crimes against the Greek State

1. When the law requires that a victim-initiated complaint be filed to criminally prosecute a punishable act, punishability is extinguished if the person entitled to file a victim-initiated complaint fails to do so within three months from the day they learned of the act committed and of its perpetrator or any of the accessories.
2. An express declaration made by the person entitled to file a victim-initiated complaint to the competent authority that they waive the right to file a victim-initiated complaint also generates the same result.
3. Crimes against the legal person of the Greek State, bodies governed by public law or local government authorities are always subject to public prosecution.

Article 115
Persons entitled to file a victim-initiated complaint

1. Unless otherwise provided for in law, the direct victim of the punishable act is entitled to file a victim-initiated complaint.
2. If the victim has not yet attained the age of 13 or is under legal guardianship, the entitlement to [file] a victim-initiated complaint lies with their lawful representative. If the victim has attained the age of 13, the entitlement to [file] a victim-initiated complaint lies with [both] the victim [and] their lawful representative; after the victim has attained the age of 18, such entitlement lies only with the victim.
3. If two or more persons are entitled to [file] a victim-initiated complaint, each person enjoys such entitlement separately.
4. Upon death of the victim, their entitlement to [file] a victim-initiated complaint is transferred to their surviving spouse or partner living with them up to the time of their death, as well as to their children and, where are there no such children or partner or where such children or partner committed the crime, to their parents.

Article 116
Indivisibility of victim-initiated complaints

Criminal prosecution shall be initiated against all accessories to the crime, even if the victim-initiated complaint was filed against [only] one of them.

Article 117
Withdrawal of a victim-initiated complaint

1. Any person who filed a victim-initiated complaint may withdraw it in accordance with the conditions laid down in the Code of Criminal Procedure. If the victim-initiated complaint was filed by the victim's lawful representative, the latter retains the right of withdrawal only for the duration of such lawful representation. After it expires, the victim or their new lawful representative is entitled to withdraw the complaint.
2. Once a victim-initiated complaint that was filed is withdrawn, a new one cannot be filed.
3. Any withdrawal which concerns one of the accessories to the act also results in discontinuation of the criminal prosecution against the others, where they have also been [accused of a crime prosecuted] pursuant to a victim-initiated complaint.
4. Withdrawal generates no effect vis-à-vis accused persons who declare to the authorities that they do not accept such withdrawal.

III

ΠΑΡΑΓΡΑΦΗ ΠΟΙΝΩΝ

Άρθρο 118
Χρόνος παραγραφής των ποινών που επιβλήθηκαν

Οι ποινές που επιβλήθηκαν αμετάκλητα, αν έμειναν ανεκτέλεστες, παραγράφονται:

α) η ισόβια κάθειρξη, μετά τριάντα έτη,

β) η πρόσκαιρη κάθειρξη, μετά είκοσι έτη,

γ) η φυλάκιση, οι χρηματικές ποινές και ο περιορισμός σε ειδικό κατάστημα κράτησης νέων μετά δέκα έτη,

δ) η παροχή κοινωφελούς εργασίας μετά πέντε έτη και

ε) οι παρεπόμενες ποινές μαζί με τις κύριες.

Άρθρο 119
Έναρξη του χρόνου παραγραφής των ποινών

Η παραγραφή των ποινών αρχίζει από την ημέρα που η απόφαση έγινε αμετάκλητη, εκτός αν ο νόμος ορίζει διαφορετικά.

Άρθρο 120
Αναστολή της παραγραφής των ποινών

Η προθεσμία της παραγραφής των ποινών αναστέλλεται:

α) για όσο χρόνο σύμφωνα με το νόμο δεν μπορεί να αρχίσει ή να εξακολουθήσει η εκτέλεση μιας ποινής,

β) για όσο χρόνο σύμφωνα με τα άρθρα 99 και 100 έχει ανασταλεί η εκτέλεση της ποινής ή έχει επιτραπεί η καταβολή με δόσεις της χρηματικής ποινής που επιβλήθηκε.

III

TIME-BARRING OF PUNISHMENTS

Article 118

Time-barring period of punishments imposed

Punishments irrevocably imposed, if unenforced, become time-barred as follows:

a) incarceration for life becomes time-barred after 30 years;

b) fixed-term incarceration becomes time-barred after 20 years;

c) imprisonment, monetary penalties and confinement to a reformative institution become time-barred after 10 years;

d) community service becomes time-barred after five years; and

e) ancillary punishments become time-barred at the same time as main punishments.

Article 119

Commencement of time-barring period of punishments

Unless otherwise provided for in law, the time-barring of punishments commences on the date the judgment became irrevocable.

Article 120

Suspension of time-barring of punishments

The time-barring of punishments shall be suspended for as long as:

a) enforcement of a punishment cannot, in law, commence or continue;

b) in accordance with Articles 99 and 100, enforcement of the penalty has been stayed or payment of the monetary penalty imposed in instalments has been allowed.

ΟΓΔΟΟ ΚΕΦΑΛΑΙΟ

ΕΙΔΙΚΕΣ ΔΙΑΤΑΞΕΙΣ ΓΙΑ ΑΝΗΛΙΚΟΥΣ

Άρθρο 121
Ορισμός

1. Στο κεφάλαιο αυτό με τον όρο ανήλικοι νοούνται αυτοί που κατά τον χρόνο τέλεσης της πράξης έχουν ηλικία μεταξύ του δωδέκατου και του δέκατου όγδοου έτους της ηλικίας τους συμπληρωμένων.
2. Οι ανήλικοι υποβάλλονται σε αναμορφωτικά ή θεραπευτικά μέτρα ή σε περιορισμό σε ειδικό κατάστημα κράτησης νέων σύμφωνα με τις διατάξεις των επόμενων άρθρων.

Άρθρο 122
Αναμορφωτικά μέτρα

1. Αναμορφωτικά μέτρα είναι:
α) η επίπληξη του ανηλίκου,
β) η ανάθεση της υπεύθυνης επιμέλειας του ανηλίκου στους γονείς ή στους επιτρόπους του,
γ) η ανάθεση της υπεύθυνης επιμέλειας του ανηλίκου σε ανάδοχη οικογένεια,
δ) η ανάθεση της επιμέλειας του ανηλίκου σε προστατευτικές εταιρείες ή σε ιδρύματα ανηλίκων ή σε επιμελητές ανηλίκων,
ε) η συνδιαλλαγή μεταξύ ανήλικου δράστη και θύματος για έκφραση συγγνώμης και εν γένει για εξώδικη διευθέτηση των συνεπειών της πράξης,
στ) η αποζημίωση του θύματος ή η κατ' άλλον τρόπο άρση ή μείωση των συνεπειών της πράξης από τον ανήλικο,
ζ) η παρακολούθηση κοινωνικών και ψυχολογικών προγραμμάτων σε κρατικούς, δημοτικούς, κοινοτικούς ή ιδιωτικούς φορείς,
η) η φοίτηση σε σχολές επαγγελματικής ή άλλης εκπαίδευσης ή κατάρτισης,
θ) η παρακολούθηση ειδικών προγραμμάτων κυκλοφοριακής αγωγής,
θα) η παρακολούθηση ειδικών εκπαιδευτικών, καλλιτεχνικών ή πολιτιστικών προγραμμάτων σε κρατικούς, δημοτικούς ή ιδιωτικούς φορείς,
θβ) η παρακολούθηση προγραμμάτων αθλητισμού και η συμμετοχή σε αθλητικά σωματεία,
ι) η παροχή κοινωφελούς εργασίας,
ια) η ανάθεση της επιμέλειας και επιτήρησης του ανηλίκου σε προστατευτικές εταιρείες ή σε επιμελητές ανηλίκων και
ιβ) η τοποθέτηση σε κατάλληλο κρατικό, δημοτικό, κοινοτικό ή ιδιωτικό ίδρυμα αγωγής.
2. Σε κάθε περίπτωση, το δικαστήριο μπορεί να επιβάλει ως πρόσθετα αναμορφωτικά μέτρα επιπλέον υποχρεώσεις που αφορούν στον τρόπο ζωής του ανηλίκου ή στη διαπαιδαγώγησή του. Σε εξαιρετικές περιπτώσεις μπορεί να επιβάλει δύο ή περισσότερα από τα μέτρα που προβλέπονται στις περ. α' έως και ια' της παρ. 1.
3. Η επιλογή του αναμορφωτικού μέτρου που πρόκειται να επιβληθεί διέπεται από την αρχή της επικουρικότητας, για την εφαρμογή της οποίας τα αναμορφωτικά μέτρα που προβλέπονται στις περ. α' έως θβ' της παρ. 1 προτάσσονται των υπολοίπων. Το περιεχόμενο και η διάρκεια κάθε μέτρου πρέπει να είναι ανάλογα προς τη βαρύτητα της πράξης που έχει τελεστεί, την προσωπικότητα του ανηλίκου και τις βιοτικές του συνθήκες. Με κοινή απόφαση του Υπουργού Δικαιοσύνης και των κατά περίπτωση συναρμόδιων Υπουργών ρυθμίζονται όλα τα θέματα που αφορούν στην επιβολή και εκτέλεση των μέτρων της πρώτης παραγράφου.
4. Στην απόφαση του δικαστηρίου ορίζεται η μέγιστη διάρκεια του αναμορφωτικού μέτρου.

CHAPTER VIII

SPECIAL PROVISIONS CONCERNING JUVENILES

Article 121
Definition

1. In this Chapter, "juveniles" means persons who, at the time the act was committed, were between 12 and 18 years of age.
2. Juveniles shall be subject to reformative or therapeutic measures or confinement to a reformative institution in accordance with the provisions of the Articles below.

Article 122
Reformative measures

1. Reformative measures are [distinguished into] the following:
a) reprimand of the juvenile;
b) release of the juvenile to their parents or tutors [with instructions to exercise custody more diligently];
c) award of custody of the juvenile to a foster family [with instructions to exercise custody more diligently];
d) award of custody of the juvenile to a society for the protection of juveniles, or a juvenile home, or a juvenile probation officer;
e) conciliation between the juvenile perpetrator and the victim in order for the former to apologise and, generally, to achieve an out-of-court settlement concerning the consequences of the act;
f) compensation of the victim or reversal or reduction of the consequences of the act by the juvenile in a different manner;
g) attendance at social and psychological programmes organised by state, municipal, community or private bodies;
h) enrolment in vocational or other educational or training schools;
i) attendance at special [safe driving] courses;
ia) attendance at special educational, artistic or cultural programmes organised by state, municipal or private bodies;
ib) attendance at sports programmes and membership of sports clubs;
j) community service;
k) award of custody and supervision of the juvenile to a society for the protection of juveniles or a juvenile probation officer; and
l) placement at a suitable state, municipal, community or private residential treatment institution.
2. In all events, the court may impose additional obligations concerning the lifestyle or education of the juvenile as additional reformative measures. In exceptional cases, the court may impose two or more of the measures provided for in points (a) to (k) of paragraph 1.
3. The selection of the reformative measure to be imposed shall be governed by the principle of subsidiarity and, in its application, the reformative measures provided for in points (a) to (ib) of paragraph 1 shall be preferred over the others. The content and duration of each measure must be appropriate given the severity of the act committed, the character of the juvenile and their life circumstances. All issues concerning the imposition and enforcement of the measures provided for in paragraph 1 shall be regulated in a joint decision issued by the Minister of Justice and the jointly competent Ministers in each case.
4. The maximum length of any reformative measure shall be specified in the court judgment.

Άρθρο 123
Θεραπευτικά μέτρα

1. Αν η κατάσταση του ανηλίκου απαιτεί ιδιαίτερη μεταχείριση, ιδίως αν αυτός έχει ψυχική ασθένεια ή οργανική νόσο ή βρίσκεται σε κατάσταση που του δημιουργεί σοβαρή σωματική δυσλειτουργία ή του έχει γίνει έξη η χρήση ηλεκτρονικών υπολογιστών, οινοπνευματωδών ποτών ή ναρκωτικών ουσιών και δεν μπορεί να την αποβάλει με τις δικές του δυνάμεις ή εμφανίζει ουσιώδη καθυστέρηση στην πνευματική και ηθική του ανάπτυξη, το δικαστήριο διατάσσει:

α) την ανάθεση της υπεύθυνης επιμέλειας του ανηλίκου στους γονείς, στους επιτρόπους του ή σε ανάδοχη οικογένεια,

β) την ανάθεση της επιμέλειας του ανηλίκου σε προστατευτικές εταιρείες ή σε επιμελητές ανηλίκων,

γ) την παρακολούθηση συμβουλευτικού θεραπευτικού προγράμματος από τον ανήλικο ή

δ) την παραπομπή του ανηλίκου σε θεραπευτικό ή άλλο κατάλληλο κατάστημα.

Σε εξαιρετικές περιπτώσεις μπορεί να επιβληθούν τα μέτρα που προβλέπονται στα στοιχεία α' ή β' σε συνδυασμό με το μέτρο που προβλέπεται στο στοιχείο γ'.

2. Τα θεραπευτικά μέτρα διατάσσονται ύστερα από προηγούμενη διάγνωση και γνωμοδότηση από εξειδικευμένη ομάδα ιατρών, ψυχολόγων και κοινωνικών λειτουργών, οι οποίοι κατά περίπτωση υπάγονται σε Μονάδα του Υπουργείου Δικαιοσύνης ή σε ιατρικά κέντρα υγείας ή κρατικά νοσηλευτικά ιδρύματα.

Άρθρο 124
Μεταβολή ή άρση μέτρων

1. Το δικαστήριο που δίκασε μπορεί οποτεδήποτε να αντικαταστήσει τα αναμορφωτικά μέτρα που επέβαλε με άλλα, αν το κρίνει αναγκαίο. Αν τα μέτρα εκπλήρωσαν το σκοπό τους, τα αίρει.

2. Το ίδιο μπορεί να πράξει και για τα θεραπευτικά μέτρα ύστερα από γνωμοδότηση, σύμφωνα με το άρθρο 123 παρ. 2.

3. Το δικαστήριο αντικαθιστά τα αναμορφωτικά μέτρα με θεραπευτικά ύστερα από γνωμοδότηση, σύμφωνα με το άρθρο 123 παρ. 2.

4. Η συνδρομή των προϋποθέσεων αντικατάστασης ή άρσης των αναμορφωτικών ή θεραπευτικών μέτρων ελέγχεται από το δικαστήριο το αργότερο μετά την πάροδο ενός έτους από την επιβολή τους.

5. Το δικαστήριο που δίκασε μπορεί, αν συντρέχουν οι προϋποθέσεις του άρθρου 127, να αντικαταστήσει τα αναμορφωτικά μέτρα με κατ' οίκον έκτιση ή με παροχή κοινωφελούς εργασίας και σε περίπτωση που τα παραπάνω δεν επαρκούν, με περιορισμό σε ειδικό κατάστημα κράτησης νέων με μέγιστη διάρκεια τα τρία (3) έτη:

α) εφόσον κατά τη διάρκεια ισχύος τους ασκήθηκε ποινική δίωξη για πράξη που, αν την τελούσε ενήλικος, θα ήταν κακούργημα ή

β) αν παραβιάζονται εξακολουθητικά.

Άρθρο 125
Διάρκεια μέτρων

1. Τα αναμορφωτικά μέτρα που επέβαλε το δικαστήριο παύουν αυτοδικαίως, όταν ο ανήλικος συμπληρώσει το δέκατο όγδοο έτος της ηλικίας. Το δικαστήριο μπορεί, με ειδικά αιτιολογημένη απόφασή του, να παρατείνει τα μέτρα έως τη συμπλήρωση του εικοστού πρώτου έτους.

2. Τα θεραπευτικά μέτρα επιτρέπεται να παραταθούν και μετά το δέκατο όγδοο έτος ύστερα από γνωμοδότηση, σύμφωνα με το άρθρο 123 παρ. 2, έως τη συμπλήρωση του εικοστού πρώτου έτους.

Article 123
Therapeutic measures

1. If the juvenile's condition requires special treatment, particularly if they are suffering from a mental or physical illness, or are in a situation causing them severe bodily dysfunction, or have become addicted to computer use, alcoholic beverages or narcotic substances and cannot overcome such addiction on their own, or are exhibiting a major delay in their intellectual and moral development, the court shall order:

a) that the juvenile [be released] to their parents, tutors or a foster family [with instructions to exercise custody more diligently];

b) award of custody of the juvenile to a society for the protection of juveniles or a juvenile probation officer;

c) attendance by the juvenile at a therapeutic counselling programme; or

d) committal of the juvenile to a therapeutic or other appropriate institution.

In exceptional cases, the measures provided for in points (a) or (b) may be imposed together with the measure provided for in point (c).

2. Therapeutic measures shall be ordered following a prior diagnosis and opinion issued by a specialised team of physicians, psychologists and social workers who belong, as each case might require, to a unit of the Ministry of Justice, or a medical facility, or a state hospital.

Article 124
Modification or termination of measures

1. Where deemed necessary, the trial court may at any time replace any reformative measures it imposed. If the measures have fulfilled their purpose, the court shall terminate them.

2. That court may also do the same with regard to therapeutic measures, following an opinion issued in accordance with Article 123(2).

3. That court may replace reformative measures with therapeutic measures following an opinion issued in accordance with Article 123(2).

4. No later than one year after imposing reformative or therapeutic measures, that court shall check whether the conditions for replacing or terminating such measures are met.

5. If the requirements laid down in Article 127 are met, the trial court may replace reformative measures with house arrest or community service, and if this does not suffice, with confinement to a reformative institution for no more than three years:

a) if criminal prosecution was initiated during such house arrest or community service for an act which, if committed by an adult, would be a felony; or

b) if such house arrest or community service is repeatedly violated.

Article 125
Length of measures

1. Any reformative measures imposed by the court automatically end when the juvenile attains the age of 18. The court may issue a specifically reasoned judgment extending such measures until [the juvenile] attains the age of 21.

2. Following an opinion issued in accordance with Article 123(2), the therapeutic measures may be extended after [the juvenile] has attained the age of 18 and until they attain the age of 21.

Άρθρο 126
Ποινική μεταχείριση των ανηλίκων

1. Η αξιόποινη πράξη που τελέστηκε από ανήλικο δώδεκα έως δεκαπέντε ετών δεν καταλογίζεται σε αυτόν. Το δικαστήριο μπορεί να του επιβάλει αναμορφωτικά ή θεραπευτικά μέτρα.
2. Σε ανήλικο που τέλεσε αξιόποινη πράξη και έχει συμπληρώσει το δέκατο πέμπτο έτος της ηλικίας του επιβάλλονται επίσης αναμορφωτικά ή θεραπευτικά μέτρα, εκτός αν κρίνεται αναγκαίο να επιβληθεί περιορισμός σε ειδικό κατάστημα κράτησης νέων κατά το επόμενο άρθρο.

Άρθρο 127
Περιορισμός σε ειδικό κατάστημα κράτησης νέων

1. Περιορισμός σε ειδικό κατάστημα κράτησης νέων επιβάλλεται μόνο σε ανηλίκους που έχουν συμπληρώσει το δέκατο πέμπτο (15ο) έτος της ηλικίας τους, εφόσον η πράξη τους, αν την τελούσε ενήλικος θα ήταν κακούργημα. Η απόφαση πρέπει να περιέχει ειδική και εμπεριστατωμένη αιτιολογία, από την οποία να προκύπτει γιατί τα αναμορφωτικά ή θεραπευτικά μέτρα δεν κρίνονται στη συγκεκριμένη περίπτωση επαρκή ενόψει των ιδιαίτερων συνθηκών τέλεσης της πράξης και της προσωπικότητας του ανηλίκου. Κρίνοντας από τις περιστάσεις, το δικαστήριο μπορεί να αντικαταστήσει εν όλω ή εν μέρει, την έκτιση του περιορισμού σε ειδικό κατάστημα κράτησης νέων σε κατ' οίκον έκτιση ή σε κοινωφελή εργασία, με αναλογική εφαρμογή των άρθρων 104Α και 105.
2. Στην απόφαση ορίζεται επακριβώς ο χρόνος παραμονής του ανηλίκου στο κατάστημα αυτό, σύμφωνα με το άρθρο 54.

Άρθρο 128

(Καταργείται)

Άρθρο 129
Απόλυση υπό όρο

1. Το δικαστήριο απολύει υπό όρο τον ανήλικο μετά τη λήξη του ενός δευτέρου του περιορισμού σε ειδικό κατάστημα κράτησης νέων και ορίζει τον χρόνο της δοκιμασίας, που δεν μπορεί να υπερβαίνει το υπόλοιπο της ποινής. Για τη χορήγηση της υπό όρο απόλυσης, ως περιορισμός που εκτίθηκε θεωρείται και αυτός που υπολογίστηκε ευεργετικά σύμφωνα με τις ισχύουσες διατάξεις.
2. Η απόλυση υπό όρο χορηγείται οπωσδήποτε, εκτός αν κριθεί με ειδική αιτιολογία ότι η διαγωγή του ανηλίκου κατά την έκτιση του περιορισμού καθιστά απολύτως αναγκαία τη συνέχιση της κράτησής του, για να αποτραπεί η τέλεση από αυτόν νέων αξιόποινων πράξεων.
3. Για τη χορήγηση της υπό όρο απόλυσης, η διεύθυνση του καταστήματος στο οποίο κρατείται ο ανήλικος υποβάλλει αίτηση προς το Τριμελές Δικαστήριο Ανηλίκων στο Πλημμελειοδικείο του τόπου όπου εκτίεται ο περιορισμός μαζί με έκθεση της κοινωνικής υπηρεσίας του καταστήματος δύο (2) μήνες πριν συμπληρωθεί η έκτιση του ενός δευτέρου του περιορισμού που επιβλήθηκε. Ο ανήλικος κλητεύεται υποχρεωτικά δέκα (10) τουλάχιστον ημέρες πριν από τη συνεδρίαση του δικαστηρίου, κατά την οποία μπορεί να παραστεί αυτοπροσώπως ή να εκπροσωπηθεί από συνήγορο που διορίζει με απλό έγγραφο θεωρημένο, ως προς το γνήσιο της υπογραφής, από το διευθυντή του καταστήματος κράτησης, από δικηγόρο ή από τις αρμόδιες αρχές. Το δικαστήριο συνεδριάζει υποχρεωτικά μέσα σε δεκαπέντε (15) ημέρες από τη συμπλήρωση της έκτισης του ημίσεος του περιορισμού που επιβλήθηκε. Αν η αίτηση για απόλυση υπό όρο δε γίνει δεκτή, νέα αίτηση μπορεί να υποβληθεί μετά δύο (2) μήνες από την απόρριψη, εκτός αν υπάρξουν νέα στοιχεία.

Article 126
Criminal treatment of juveniles

1. Any punishable act committed by a juvenile between 12 and 15 years of age cannot be imputed to them. The court may impose reformative or therapeutic measures on [such a juvenile].

2. Reformative or therapeutic measures shall also be imposed on any juvenile who has attained the age of 15 and has committed a punishable act, unless it is deemed necessary that they be confined to a reformative institution in accordance with the Article below.

Article 127
Confinement to a reformative institution

1. Confinement to a reformative institution shall be imposed only on juveniles who have attained the age of 15 provided the [crime they committed], if it had been committed by an adult, would be a felony. The judgment must contain specific and comprehensive reasoning as to why reformative or therapeutic measures are not deemed sufficient in the case in question, taking into consideration the circumstances under which the crime was committed and the juvenile's overall character. Having weighed up the circumstances, the court may replace confinement to a reformative institution, whether in whole or in part, with house arrest or community service, applying Articles 104A and 105 *mutatis mutandis*.

2. The judgment shall specify, in accordance with Article 54, the exact length of the juvenile's stay at such institution.

Article 128

[Repealed]

Article 129
Conditional release

1. The court shall [order] conditional release of the juvenile after half the length of their confinement to a reformative institution has elapsed, and shall set a probationary period which cannot exceed the remainder of the sentence. For the purpose of granting conditional release, any confinement computed beneficially in accordance with the provisions in force shall also be deemed time served.

2. Conditional release shall be granted in all cases unless it is ruled, with specific reasoning [provided in the judgment], that the juvenile's conduct while under confinement absolutely necessitates their continued detention in order to deter them from committing new punishable acts.

3. In order for conditional release to be granted, the management of the institution where the juvenile is confined shall, two months before half the length of confinement has been served, submit an application to the three-member juvenile court at the court of misdemeanours at the place of confinement, together with a report prepared by the social services [unit] of the institution. The juvenile shall necessarily be summonsed at least 10 days prior to the sitting of the court, and may enter an appearance in person or be represented by counsel appointed by an ordinary document, with the authenticity of the juvenile's signature certified by the governor of the [institution where the juvenile is held], by a lawyer, or by the competent authorities. The court shall necessarily conduct a sitting within 15 days of the date half the length of confinement is served. If the application for conditional release is not accepted, a new application may be submitted after two months have elapsed from the date of dismissal, unless new evidence arises.

4. Η απόλυση υπό όρο μπορεί να χορηγηθεί και πριν από την έκτιση του ενός δευτέρου (1/2) του περιορισμού που επιβλήθηκε, μόνο για σπουδαίους λόγους και εφόσον έχει εκτιθεί πραγματικά το ένα τρίτο (1/3) αυτού.
5. Στον απολυόμενο μπορεί να επιβληθούν κατά τη διάρκεια του χρόνου δοκιμασίας υποχρεώσεις που αφορούν στον τρόπο ζωής του και ιδίως στον τόπο διαμονής, στη διαπαιδαγώγηση ή την παρακολούθηση εγκεκριμένου από τον νόμο θεραπευτικού προγράμματος απεξάρτησης από ναρκωτικές ή άλλες ουσίες. Αν ο απολυόμενος παραβιάσει τους όρους που του έχουν επιβληθεί, η απόλυση μπορεί να ανακληθεί, όταν πιθανολογείται ότι ενόψει της βαρύτητας της παράβασης των υποχρεώσεων, του τρόπου και των εν γένει συνθηκών που αυτή συντελέσθηκε, δεν παρέχει ο ανήλικος την προσδοκία ότι στο μέλλον θα τηρήσει τις υποχρεώσεις του. Σε περίπτωση ανάκλησης, ο χρόνος από την απόλυση έως τη νέα σύλληψη δεν υπολογίζεται στην εκτιθείσα ποινή.
6. Αν ο απολυθείς κατά τον χρόνο της δοκιμασίας καταδικασθεί για κακούργημα, η απόλυση αίρεται και εφαρμόζεται το άρθρο 132.
7. Αν μετά την απόλυση παρέλθει ο χρόνος δοκιμασίας τον οποίο όρισε η απόφαση χωρίς να γίνει ανάκληση, η ποινή θεωρείται ότι εκτίθηκε.

Άρθρο 129Α
Απόλυση υπό τον όρο του κατ' οίκον περιορισμού με ηλεκτρονική επιτήρηση

1. Ανήλικοι οι οποίοι καταδικάσθηκαν σε ποινή περιορισμού σε ειδικό κατάστημα κράτησης νέων, μπορούν, μετά από αίτησή τους, να απολυθούν υπό τον όρο του κατ' οίκον περιορισμού με ηλεκτρονική επιτήρηση, όπως αυτός ορίζεται στο άρθρο 284 Κώδικα Ποινικής Δικονομίας, εφόσον έχουν εκτίσει το ένα τρίτο (1/3) της ποινής τους. Η αίτηση συνοδεύεται από έκθεση της Κοινωνικής Υπηρεσίας του καταστήματος κράτησης και έκθεση της Υπηρεσίας Επιμελητών Ανηλίκων, όπου γίνεται ειδική μνεία στο ευρύτερο κοινωνικό περιβάλλον του καταδικασθέντος, με ιδιαίτερη αναφορά στις σχέσεις του με τα πρόσωπα με τα οποία ενδέχεται να συνοικήσει εάν του χορηγηθεί η απόλυση. Οι παρ. 2 και 3 εδ. Β΄ και γ΄ του άρθρου 129 εφαρμόζονται και στην περίπτωση αυτή.
2. Ως ποινή που εκτίθηκε θεωρείται αυτή που υπολογίστηκε ευεργετικά κατά τις ισχύουσες διατάξεις. Η απόλυση υπό τον όρο του κατ' οίκον περιορισμού με ηλεκτρονική επιτήρηση δεν μπορεί πάντως να χορηγηθεί, αν ο ανήλικος δεν έχει παραμείνει στο κατάστημα για χρονικό διάστημα ίσο με το ένα πέμπτο (1/5) της ποινής του.
3. Η παρ. 6 του άρθρου 110 Α έχει και στην περίπτωση αυτή εφαρμογή.
4. Το ίδιο ισχύει και για την παρ. 5 του άρθρου 129. Αν η απόλυση υπό τον όρο του κατ' οίκον περιορισμού με ηλεκτρονική επιτήρηση ανακληθεί, ο ανήλικος διατηρεί το δικαίωμα να απολυθεί υπό όρο κατ' άρθρο 129.
5. Η απόλυση υπό τον όρο του κατ' οίκον περιορισμού με ηλεκτρονική επιτήρηση αίρεται, αν ο απολυθείς κατά το χρονικό διάστημα που διαρκεί η εν λόγω απόλυση τέλεσε, ως ενήλικος, πλημμέλημα με δόλο για το οποίο καταδικάστηκε οποτεδήποτε αμετακλήτως σε ποινή φυλάκισης τουλάχιστον ενός (1) έτους. Στην περίπτωση αυτή, ο χρόνος από την απόλυση έως τη νέα σύλληψη δεν υπολογίζεται στην εκτιθείσα ποινή. Ο ανήλικος διατηρεί το δικαίωμα να απολυθεί υπό όρο κατ' άρθρο 129.

4. Conditional release may also be granted before half the length of confinement has been served, but only on serious grounds and provided 1/3 of the length of confinement has actually been served.

5. During the probationary period, [the court] may impose obligations on the released [juvenile] concerning their lifestyle and, in particular, their place of residence, education or attendance at a legally approved programme for therapeutic rehabilitation from narcotic or other substances. If the released [juvenile] violates the conditions imposed on them, such release may be revoked when it is deemed likely on the balance of probabilities that, in view of the severity of the breach of their obligations, the manner in which and general circumstances under which such breach occurred, they are not expected to comply with their obligations in the future. Where release is revoked, the time period between the release and the new arrest shall not be deemed time served.

6. If, during the probationary period, the released [juvenile] is convicted of a felony, their release shall be terminated and Article 132 applies.

7. If, following release, the probationary period set in the judgment elapses without [the release having been] revoked, the sentence shall be deemed to have been served.

Article 129A

Release on condition of house arrest under electronic surveillance

1. Juveniles sentenced to confinement to a reformative institution may, after filing an application, be released on condition of house arrest under electronic surveillance, as provided for in Article 284 of the Code of Criminal Procedure, provided they have served 1/3 of their sentence. The application shall be accompanied by a report from the social services [unit] of the [reformative] institution and a report from the Juvenile Probation Officer Service, with specific reference to the wider social environment of the convicted [juvenile] and particular reference to their relationships with the persons with whom they might reside if released. Paragraph 2 and the second and third sentences of paragraph 3 of Article 129 also apply in such a case.

2. Any sentence computed beneficially in accordance with the provisions in force shall be deemed time served. Nevertheless, release on condition of house arrest under electronic surveillance cannot be granted if the juvenile has not remained at the [reformative] institution for a period equal to 1/5 of their sentence.

3. Article 110A(6) also applies in such a case.

4. The same applies in the case provided for in Article 129(5). If release on condition of house arrest under electronic surveillance is revoked, the juvenile retains the right to be conditionally released in accordance with Article 129.

5. Release on condition of house arrest under electronic surveillance shall be terminated if, during the release period, the released [juvenile], having become an adult, committed a misdemeanour with *dolus* for which they were irrevocably convicted at any time to serve a sentence of imprisonment of at least one year. In this case, the time period between the release and the new arrest shall not be deemed time served. The juvenile retains the right to be conditionally released in accordance with Article 129.

6. Η απόλυση υπό τον όρο του κατ' οίκον περιορισμού με ηλεκτρονική επιτήρηση αίρεται αν ο απολυθείς, όσο διαρκεί η εν λόγω απόλυση, τέλεσε, ως ενήλικος, κακούργημα ή ως ανήλικος, πράξη που αν την τελούσε ενήλικος θα ήταν κακούργημα, για την οποία και καταδικάστηκε οποτεδήποτε αμετακλήτως. Στην περίπτωση αυτή ο χρόνος από την απόλυση έως τη νέα σύλληψη δεν υπολογίζεται στην εκτιθείσα ποινή και ο ανήλικος αποκτά το δικαίωμα να απολυθεί υπό όρο κατ' άρθρο 129, αφού παραμείνει στο ειδικό κατάστημα κράτησης νέων ένα (1) επιπλέον έτος σε σχέση με τα οριζόμενα στο άρθρο 129 παρ. 1 και 4. Το ίδιο ισχύει αν, κατά το χρόνο που κατέστη η καταδίκη αμετάκλητη, είχε ήδη χορηγηθεί η απόλυση υπό όρο κατ' άρθρο 129, χωρίς όμως να έχει παρέλθει το χρονικό διάστημα που αναφέρεται στο άρθρο 129 παρ. 7. Δεν εφαρμόζεται το προηγούμενο εδάφιο, αν κατά τον χρόνο που κατέστη η καταδίκη αμετάκλητη, είχε ήδη χορηγηθεί η απόλυση υπό όρο κατ' άρθρο 129 χωρίς να έχει ανακληθεί, με αποτέλεσμα να θεωρείται η ποινή για την οποία χορηγήθηκε η απόλυση ήδη εκτιθείσα κατά τα οριζόμενα στο άρθρο 129 παρ. 7.

7. Η παρ. 7 του άρθρου 129 ισχύει και στην περίπτωση αυτή.

Άρθρο 130
Εκδίκαση μετά τη συμπλήρωση του δέκατου όγδοου έτους

1. Η παρ. 1 του άρθρου 126 εφαρμόζεται και για ανηλίκους που τέλεσαν αξιόποινη πράξη πριν τη συμπλήρωση του δέκατου πέμπτου έτους και εισάγονται σε δίκη μετά τη συμπλήρωση του δέκατου όγδοου έτους. Στην περίπτωση αυτή τα αναμορφωτικά μέτρα παύουν αυτοδικαίως όταν ο υπαίτιος συμπληρώσει το εικοστό τρίτο έτος της ηλικίας του.

2. Η διάταξη του άρθρου 127 παρ. 1 εφαρμόζεται και για τους ανηλίκους που τέλεσαν αξιόποινη πράξη μετά τη συμπλήρωση του δέκατου πέμπτου έτους της ηλικίας τους και εισάγονται σε δίκη μετά τη συμπλήρωση του δέκατου όγδοου έτους. Το εδ. β΄ της προηγούμενης παραγράφου ισχύει και στην περίπτωση αυτή.

3. Αν το δικαστήριο κρίνει ότι η επιβολή αναμορφωτικών ή θεραπευτικών μέτρων δεν είναι επαρκής και ότι ο περιορισμός σε ειδικό κατάστημα κράτησης νέων, μολονότι αναγκαίος για τον ποινικό σωφρονισμό του καταδικασθέντος, δεν είναι πλέον σκόπιμος λόγω της ηλικίας του, μπορεί να διατάξει την έκτιση της ποινής σε σωφρονιστικό κατάστημα. Στην περίπτωση αυτή ο καταδικασθείς κρατείται χωριστά από τους άλλους ενήλικους καταδίκους.

4. Την απόφαση αυτή μπορεί να λάβει το δικαστήριο του τόπου έκτισης της ποινής και μετά τον εγκλεισμό στο ειδικό κατάστημα κράτησης νέων, ύστερα από αίτηση της διεύθυνσης του καταστήματος ή του αρμόδιου εισαγγελέα, μετά από ακρόαση των ανωτέρω και του καταδικασθέντος. Όταν ο καταδικασθείς συμπληρώνει το 21ο έτος της ηλικίας του, και στη συνέχεια ανά έτος, το ίδιο δικαστήριο εξετάζει και αυτεπαγγέλτως αν συντρέχει περίπτωση έκτισης της ποινής σε σωφρονιστικό κατάστημα.

Άρθρο 131
Έναρξη εκτέλεσης της απόφασης μετά τη συμπλήρωση του δέκατου όγδοου έτους

1. Αν ο καταδικασθείς σε περιορισμό σε ειδικό κατάστημα κράτησης νέων συμπλήρωσε το δέκατο όγδοο έτος της ηλικίας του πριν αρχίσει η εκτέλεση της απόφασης, το δικαστήριο που δίκασε, αν κρίνει ότι ο περιορισμός αυτός δεν είναι πλέον σκόπιμος λόγω της ηλικίας του καταδικασθέντος, μπορεί να διατάξει την έκτιση της ποινής σε σωφρονιστικό κατάστημα.

2. Οι παράγραφοι 3 εδ. β΄ και 4 του προηγούμενου άρθρου ισχύουν και στην περίπτωση αυτή.

6. Release on condition of house arrest under electronic surveillance shall be terminated if, during the release period, the released [juvenile], having become an adult, committed a felony or, while still a juvenile, committed an act which, if it had been committed by an adult, would be a felony, and for which they were irrevocably convicted at any time. In this case, the time period between the release and the new arrest shall not be deemed time served, and the juvenile acquires the right to be conditionally released in accordance with Article 129 after they have [been held] at a reformative institution for one year more than the period provided for in Article 129(1) and (4). The same applies if, at the time the conviction became irrevocable, conditional release had already been granted in accordance with Article 129 but the time period provided for in Article 129(7) had not elapsed. The preceding sentence does not apply if, at the time the conviction became irrevocable, the convicted [juvenile] had already been conditionally released in accordance with Article 129 and such release had not been revoked, resulting in the sentence for which release was granted being considered to have already been served in accordance with the provisions of Article 129(7).
7. Article 129(7) also applies in such a case.

Article 130

Adjudication after [the juvenile has] attained the age of 18

1. The provisions of Article 126(1) also apply to juveniles who committed a punishable act before attaining the age of 15 and who are committed to trial after having attained the age of 18. In this case, reformative measures shall cease automatically when the culpable person attains the age of 23.
2. The provisions of Article 127(1) also apply to juveniles who committed a punishable act after attaining the age of 15 and who are committed to trial after having attained the age of 18. The second sentence of the preceding paragraph also applies in such a case.
3. If the court rules that imposing reformative or therapeutic measures does not suffice and that confinement to a reformative institution, while necessary for the criminal rehabilitation of the convicted person, is no longer appropriate due to their age, it may order that the sentence be served at a custodial institution. In this case, the convicted [juvenile] shall be held separately from other adult convicts.
4. The court at the place where the sentence is being served may issue such a decision even after the [juvenile] has been committed to a reformative institution, following an application filed by the management of the institution or by the competent public prosecutor and after the foregoing persons and the convicted [juvenile] have been heard. When the convicted person attains the age of 21 and from then on once each year, the same court shall examine, even *ex officio*, whether the sentence ought to be served at a custodial institution.

Article 131

Commencement of enforcement of the judgment after [the juvenile has] attained the age of 18

1. If a [juvenile] sentenced to confinement to a reformative institution attained the age of 18 before enforcement of the judgment commenced, the trial court, if it rules that such confinement is no longer appropriate due to the age of the convicted [juvenile], may order that the sentence be served at a custodial institution.
2. The second sentence of paragraph 3 and paragraph 4 of the preceding Article also apply in such a case.

Άρθρο 132
Συρροή

1. Αν ο κρατούμενος σε ειδικό κατάστημα κράτησης νέων διαπράξει αξιόποινη πράξη πριν συμπληρώσει το δέκατο όγδοο έτος της ηλικίας του ή αν συντρέξει άλλη περίπτωση συρροής κατά το άρθρο 97, το δικαστήριο επαυξάνει την ποινή που είχε καθορίσει με την προηγούμενη απόφασή του χωρίς να υπερβεί τα όρια του άρθρου 54.

2. Το ίδιο ισχύει αν ο κρατούμενος σε ειδικό κατάστημα κράτησης νέων διαπράξει αξιόποινη πράξη μετά τη συμπλήρωση του δέκατου όγδοου και πριν από τη συμπλήρωση του εικοστού πέμπτου έτους της ηλικίας του και το δικαστήριο του επιβάλει περιορισμό σε ειδικό κατάστημα κράτησης νέων, κατ' εφαρμογή του άρθρου 133 περίπτ. α' ή ποινή φυλάκισης.

3. Αν ο κρατούμενος σε ειδικό κατάστημα κράτησης νέων διαπράξει κακούργημα μετά τη συμπλήρωση του δέκατου όγδοου και πριν από τη συμπλήρωση του εικοστού πέμπτου έτους της ηλικίας του, για το οποίο του επιβάλλεται ποινή κάθειρξης, κατ' εφαρμογή του άρθρου 133 στοιχείο β΄, το δικαστήριο επιβάλλει συνολική ποινή κάθειρξης επαυξημένη. Η επαύξηση δεν μπορεί να είναι κατώτερη από το ένα δεύτερο της ποινής που είχε καθορίσει η προηγούμενη απόφαση του δικαστηρίου. Κατά τα λοιπά εφαρμόζονται οι διατάξεις του άρθρου 94 παρ. 1.

Άρθρο 133
Νεαροί ενήλικες

Όταν ο δράστης κατά τον χρόνο τέλεσης αξιόποινης πράξης δεν έχει συμπληρώσει το εικοστό πρώτο (21ο) έτος της ηλικίας του, το δικαστήριο μπορεί:

α) να διατάξει τον περιορισμό του σε ειδικό κατάστημα κράτησης νέων (άρθρο 54) εφόσον κρίνει ότι η τέλεση της πράξης οφείλεται στην ελλιπή ανάπτυξη της προσωπικότητάς του, λόγω της νεαρής ηλικίας και ότι ο περιορισμός αυτός θα είναι αρκετός για να αποφευχθεί η τέλεση άλλων εγκλημάτων, ή

β) να επιβάλει μειωμένη ποινή (άρθρο 83). Στην περίπτωση αυτή εφαρμόζεται η διάταξη της παρ. 3 εδ. Β' του άρθρου 130. Ο κρατούμενος μπορεί να παραμείνει στο ειδικό σωφρονιστικό κατάστημα νέων μέχρι την ηλικία των είκοσι πέντε (25) ετών.

Article 132
Concurrence

1. If a [juvenile] held at a reformative institution commits a punishable act before attaining the age of 18 or if another case of concurrence under Article 97 occurs, the court shall augment the sentence set in its previous judgment without exceeding the limits laid down in Article 54.

2. The same also applies if a [juvenile] held at a reformative institution commits a punishable act after attaining the age of 18 and before attaining the age of 25 and the court sentences them to confinement to a reformative institution, pursuant to Article 133(a), or to imprisonment.

3. If a [juvenile] being held at a reformative institution commits a felony after attaining the age of 18 and before attaining the age of 25 and for which they are sentenced to incarceration pursuant to Article 133(b), the court shall impose an augmented overall sentence of incarceration. Such augmented sentence cannot be less than half the sentence set in the court's previous judgment. In all other respects, the provisions of Article 94(1) apply.

Article 133
Young adults

Where the perpetrator had not attained the age of 21 when they committed a punishable act, the court may:

a) order that they be confined to a reformative institution ([see] Article 54), where it rules that the act was committed because of inadequate development of their character, due to their young age, and that such confinement will suffice to prevent other crimes being committed; or

b) impose a reduced sentence ([see] Article 83). In this case, the provisions of the second sentence of Article 130(3) apply. The detainee may [be held] at the reformative institution until the age of 25.

ΔΕΥΤΕΡΟ ΒΙΒΛΙΟ

ΕΙΔΙΚΟ ΜΕΡΟΣ

ΠΡΩΤΟ ΚΕΦΑΛΑΙΟ

ΠΡΟΣΒΟΛΕΣ ΤΟΥ ΔΗΜΟΚΡΑΤΙΚΟΥ ΠΟΛΙΤΕΥΜΑΤΟΣ

Άρθρο 134
Εσχάτη προδοσία

1. Όποιος επιχειρεί με βία ή απειλή βίας να καταλύσει, να μεταβάλει, να αλλοιώσει ή να καταστήσει ανενεργό, διαρκώς ή προσκαίρως, το δημοκρατικό πολίτευμα που στηρίζεται στη λαϊκή κυριαρχία ή θεμελιώδεις αρχές ή θεσμούς του πολιτεύματος αυτού ή να αποστερήσει τον Πρόεδρο της Δημοκρατίας ή αυτόν που ασκεί την προεδρική εξουσία, τον Πρωθυπουργό, την Κυβέρνηση ή τη Βουλή από την εξουσία που έχουν κατά το Σύνταγμα, τιμωρείται με ισόβια κάθειρξη.

2. Με την ίδια ποινή τιμωρείται και:

α) όποιος επιχειρεί να τελέσει την πράξη της προηγούμενης παραγράφου με κατάχρηση της ιδιότητάς του ως οργάνου του κράτους ή με σφετερισμό της ιδιότητας αυτής, καθώς και

β) όποιος ασκεί την εξουσία που ο ίδιος ή άλλος κατέλαβε με τους τρόπους και τα μέσα που προβλέπει το άρθρο αυτό.

3. Θεμελιώδεις αρχές και θεσμοί του πολιτεύματος θεωρούνται στο Κεφάλαιο αυτό:

α) η ανάδειξη του Αρχηγού του Κράτους με εκλογή,

β) το δικαίωμα του λαού να εκλέγει τη Βουλή με γενικές, άμεσες, ελεύθερες, ίσες και μυστικές ψηφοφορίες μέσα στα συνταγματικά χρονικά πλαίσια,

γ) το κοινοβουλευτικό σύστημα διακυβέρνησης,

δ) η αρχή του πολυκομματισμού,

ε) η αρχή της διάκρισης των λειτουργιών, όπως προβλέπεται στο Σύνταγμα,

στ) η αρχή της δέσμευσης του νομοθέτη από το Σύνταγμα και της εκτελεστικής και της δικαστικής λειτουργίας από το Σύνταγμα και τους νόμους,

ζ) η αρχή της ανεξαρτησίας της δικαιοσύνης και

η) η γενική ισχύς και προστασία των ατομικών δικαιωμάτων που προβλέπει το Σύνταγμα.

Άρθρο 135
Προπαρασκευαστικές πράξεις

1. Όποιος δημόσια ή με τη διάδοση εγγράφων, εικόνων ή παραστάσεων ή μέσω του διαδικτύου προκαλεί με πρόθεση ή προσπαθεί να διεγείρει άλλους στο να επιχειρήσουν πράξεις από εκείνες που αναφέρονται στο προηγούμενο άρθρο τιμωρείται με κάθειρξη έως δέκα έτη.

2. Με την ίδια ποινή τιμωρείται και όποιος οργανώνεται με άλλον ή άλλους με σκοπό να εκτελέσουν πράξη από εκείνες που αναφέρονται στο προηγούμενο άρθρο ή σε συνεννόηση με ξένη κυβέρνηση προπαρασκευάζει την εκτέλεση μιας απ' αυτές τις πράξεις.

BOOK II

SPECIAL PART

CHAPTER I

OFFENCES AGAINST THE DEMOCRATIC SYSTEM OF GOVERNMENT

Article 134
High treason

1. Any person who attempts, through use or threat of violence, to overturn, change, undermine or render permanently or temporarily inactive the democratic system of government which is based on popular sovereignty, or fundamental principles or institutions of that system of government, or deprive the President of the Republic or the person exercising presidential powers, the Prime Minister, the Government or Parliament of the powers vested in them in accordance with the Constitution, shall be punished with incarceration for life.

2. The same sentence shall also be imposed on any person who:

a) attempts to commit the act provided for in the preceding paragraph by abusing their capacity as an officer of the state or by usurping such capacity; and

b) exercises the power they or another seized in the manner and using the means provided for in this Article.

3. For the purposes of this Chapter, the fundamental principles and institutions of the system of government are considered to be:

a) election of the head of state;

b) the people's right to elect Parliament by general, direct, free, equal and secret ballot within the constitutionally prescribed time frames;

c) the parliamentary system of governance;

d) the principle of a multi-party system;

e) the principle of separation of powers, as enshrined in the Constitution;

f) the principle of the legislature being bound by the Constitution and of the executive and the judiciary being bound by the Constitution and the laws;

g) the principle of the independence of justice; and

h) the general effect and protection of the civil rights enshrined in the Constitution.

Article 135
Preparatory acts

1. Any person who, publicly or through dissemination of documents, pictures or depictions or via the internet, intentionally induces or attempts to incite others to commit acts provided for in the preceding Article shall be punished with incarceration of up to 10 years.

2. The same sentence shall be imposed on any person who joins with one or more persons for the purpose of committing acts provided for in the preceding Article or, in collusion with a foreign government, prepares the commission of any such act.

Άρθρο 136

Παρεπόμενες ποινές

Στις περιπτώσεις των άρθρων 134 και 135, μαζί με την ποινή της κάθειρξης το δικαστήριο επιβάλλει και αποστέρηση θέσεων και αξιωμάτων.

Άρθρο 137

Έμπρακτη μετάνοια

1. Στις περιπτώσεις των άρθρων 134 και 135, ο δράστης μένει ατιμώρητος αν με δική του θέληση παρεμπόδισε την επέλευση του αποτελέσματος που επιδίωξε με την πράξη του ή συντέλεσε αποφασιστικά στη ματαίωσή του.

2. Αν στις περιπτώσεις του άρθρου 134 ο δράστης συντέλεσε αποφασιστικά στην αποκατάσταση του δημοκρατικού πολιτεύματος, τιμωρείται με ποινή μειωμένη. Το δικαστήριο όμως μπορεί, εκτιμώντας ελεύθερα όλες τις περιστάσεις, να κρίνει την πράξη του ατιμώρητη.

Άρθρο 137Α

Βασανιστήρια

1. Υπάλληλος ή στρατιωτικός, στα καθήκοντα του οποίου ανάγεται η δίωξη, η ανάκριση ή η εξέταση αξιόποινων πράξεων ή πειθαρχικών παραπτωμάτων ή η εκτέλεση ποινών ή η φύλαξη ή η επιμέλεια κρατουμένων, τιμωρείται με κάθειρξη έως δέκα έτη, εάν υποβάλλει σε βασανιστήρια κατά την εκτέλεση αυτών των καθηκόντων πρόσωπο που βρίσκεται στην εξουσία του με σκοπό:

α) να αποσπάσει από αυτό ή από τρίτο πρόσωπο ομολογία, κατάθεση, πληροφορία ή δήλωση ιδίως αποκήρυξης ή αποδοχής πολιτικής ή άλλης ιδεολογίας,

β) να το τιμωρήσει ή

γ) να εκφοβίσει αυτό ή τρίτα πρόσωπα.

Με την ίδια ποινή τιμωρείται υπάλληλος ή στρατιωτικός, που με εντολή των προϊσταμένων του ή αυτοβούλως σφετερίζεται τέτοια καθήκοντα και τελεί τις πράξεις του προηγούμενου εδαφίου.

2. Με την ίδια ποινή τιμωρούνται τα βασανιστήρια τα οποία τελούνται από τα πρόσωπα και υπό τις περιστάσεις που προβλέπει η προηγούμενη παράγραφος ακόμη και χωρίς τον αναφερόμενο σε αυτή σκοπό, εφόσον η επιλογή του παθόντος γίνεται λόγω των χαρακτηριστικών φυλής, χρώματος, εθνικής ή εθνοτικής καταγωγής, γενεαλογικών καταβολών, θρησκείας, αναπηρίας, γενετήσιου προσανατολισμού, ταυτότητας ή χαρακτηριστικών φύλου. Στην περίπτωση αυτή δεν εφαρμόζεται το άρθρο 82 Α.

3. Επιβάλλεται κάθειρξη τουλάχιστον δέκα ετών αν οι πράξεις των προηγούμενων παραγράφων:

α) τελούνται με μέσα ή τρόπους συστηματικού βασανισμού, ιδίως κτυπήματα στα πέλματα του θύματος (φάλαγγα), ηλεκτροσόκ, εικονική εκτέλεση ή παραισθησιογόνες ουσίες ή

β) έχουν ως αποτέλεσμα τη βαριά σωματική βλάβη του θύματος. Η ποινή αυτή επιβάλλεται και όταν ο υπαίτιος, ως προϊστάμενος, έδωσε την εντολή τέλεσής τους.

Article 136
Ancillary punishments

In the cases referred to in Articles 134 and 135, the court shall, in addition to imposing the sentence of incarceration, also impose forfeiture of posts and offices.

Article 137
Practical repentance

1. In the cases referred to in Articles 134 and 135, the perpetrator shall not be punished if, of their own volition, they prevented the result that they sought to achieve through their act from occurring or they decisively contributed to it not going ahead.

2. If, in the cases referred to in Article 134, the perpetrator decisively contributed to restoring the democratic system of government, they shall be punished with a reduced sentence. However, the court, having freely weighed up all the circumstances, may decide not to punish them for their act.

Article 137A
Torture

1. Any state employee or military personnel whose duties include the prosecution, investigation or examination of punishable acts or disciplinary offences or the enforcement of penalties or the guarding or custody of detainees shall be punished with incarceration of up to 10 years if, in the performance of such duties, they subject a person under their authority to torture for the purpose of:

a) extracting an admission, testimony, information or statement, particularly concerning the denouncement or acceptance of a political or other ideology, from that person or a third party;

b) punishing them; or

c) intimidating them or third parties.

The same sentence shall be imposed on any state employee or military personnel who, on the orders of their superiors or on their own initiative, usurps such duties and commits the acts provided for in the preceding subparagraph.

2. The same sentence shall be imposed in the case of torture committed by the [aforesaid] persons under the circumstances provided for in the preceding paragraph, even without the purpose referred to above, if the victim was [targeted] due to characteristics relating to their race, skin colour, national or ethnic origin, genealogical descent, religion, disability, sexual orientation, gender identity or sex characteristics. Article 82A does not apply in such a case.

3. Incarceration of at least 10 years shall be imposed if the acts provided for in the preceding paragraphs:

a) are committed using means or methods of systematic torture and, in particular, flogging of the victim's feet (foot whipping), electric shocks, mock execution or hallucinatory substances; or

b) result in the victim suffering grievous bodily harm. This sentence shall also be imposed when the culpable person, in their capacity as another's superior, ordered that such acts be committed.

4. Σωματική κάκωση, βλάβη της υγείας, άσκηση παράνομης σωματικής ή ψυχολογικής βίας και κάθε άλλη σοβαρή προσβολή της ανθρώπινης αξιοπρέπειας, που τελείται από τα πρόσωπα και υπό τις περιστάσεις που προβλέπουν οι παράγραφοι 1 και 2, εφόσον δεν υπάγεται στην έννοια των βασανιστηρίων, τιμωρείται με φυλάκιση τουλάχιστον τριών ετών και χρηματική ποινή, αν δεν τιμωρείται βαρύτερα με άλλη διάταξη. Επιβάλλεται κάθειρξη έως δέκα έτη αν συντρέχει η περίπτωση β΄ της προηγούμενης παραγράφου. Ως προσβολές της ανθρώπινης αξιοπρέπειας θεωρούνται ιδίως:

α) η χρησιμοποίηση ανιχνευτή αλήθειας,

β) η παρατεταμένη απομόνωση,

γ) η σοβαρή προσβολή της γενετήσιας αξιοπρέπειας.

5. Αν οι πράξεις των προηγούμενων παραγράφων επέφεραν τον θάνατο του παθόντος, επιβάλλεται κάθειρξη ισόβια ή πρόσκαιρη τουλάχιστον δέκα ετών.

6. Βασανιστήρια συνιστούν, κατά το άρθρο αυτό, κάθε εσκεμμένη πρόκληση έντονου σωματικού πόνου ή σωματικής εξάντλησης επικίνδυνης για την υγεία ή ψυχικού πόνου ικανού να επιφέρει σοβαρή ψυχική βλάβη, καθώς και κάθε παράνομη χρησιμοποίηση χημικών, ναρκωτικών ή άλλων φυσικών ή τεχνικών μέσων με σκοπό να κάμψουν τη βούληση του παθόντος. Δεν υπάγονται στην έννοια των βασανιστηρίων πράξεις ή συνέπειες συμφυείς προς τη νόμιμη εκτέλεση ποινής ή άλλου νόμιμου περιορισμού της ελευθερίας ή προς άλλο νόμιμο μέτρο δικονομικού καταναγκασμού.

7. Η καταδίκη για τις πράξεις των παραγράφων 1 έως 5 συνεπάγεται αυτοδίκαιη αποστέρηση αξιωμάτων και θέσεων, που επέρχεται μόλις η καταδικαστική απόφαση γίνεται αμετάκλητη.

8. Σε περίπτωση που οι πράξεις των παραγράφων 1 έως 5 τελούνται υπό καθεστώς σφετερισμού της λαϊκής κυριαρχίας, η προθεσμία της παραγραφής αρχίζει μόλις αποκατασταθεί η νόμιμη εξουσία.

9. Η συνδρομή των όρων των άρθρων 20 έως 25 ουδέποτε αίρει τον άδικο χαρακτήρα των πράξεων αυτού του άρθρου.

10. Ο παθών των πράξεων του άρθρου αυτού δικαιούται να απαιτήσει από τον αμετακλήτως καταδικασθέντα και από το δημόσιο, που ευθύνονται σε ολόκληρο, αποζημίωση για τις ζημίες που υπέστη και χρηματική ικανοποίηση για ψυχική οδύνη ή περιουσιακή βλάβη.

Άρθρα 137Β - 137Δ

(Καταργούνται)

4. Bodily injury, harm to health, exercise of unlawful physical or psychological violence and any other serious violation of human dignity committed by the [aforesaid] persons under the circumstances provided for in paragraphs 1 and 2, where not defined as torture, shall be punished with imprisonment of at least three years and a monetary penalty, unless such acts carry a heavier punishment under a different provision. Incarceration of up to 10 years shall be imposed if point (b) of the preceding paragraph applies. Violations of human dignity are considered to be the following, in particular:

a) use of a polygraph;

b) prolonged isolation;

c) serious violation of sexual dignity.

5. If the acts provided for in the preceding paragraphs resulted in the victim dying, incarceration for life or fixed-term incarceration of at least 10 years shall be imposed.

6. For the purposes of this Article, torture means any intentional act causing intense physical pain or physical exhaustion that is hazardous to the health [of the victim] or psychological pain capable of causing serious mental harm, as well as any unlawful use of chemical, narcotic or other physical or technical means in order to break the will of the victim. Acts or consequences inherent to lawful enforcement of a penalty or other lawful restriction of freedom or to to any other lawful procedural compulsory measure do not fall within the definition of torture.

7. Being convicted of the acts provided for in paragraphs 1 to 5 entails automatic forfeiture of posts and offices, which shall take place when the judgment of conviction becomes irrevocable.

8. Where the acts provided for in paragraphs 1 to 5 are committed in the context of usurpation of popular sovereignty, the time-barring period shall commence as soon as legitimate power is restored.

9. Fulfilment of the conditions laid down in Articles 20 to 25 shall never expunge the unlawful nature of the acts provided for in this Article.

10. The victim of the acts provided for in this Article is entitled to demand compensation for the harm they suffered and payment of compensation for mental anguish or pecuniary damage from the person irrevocably convicted [of such acts] and from the Greek State, both being severally liable.

Articles 137B - 137D

[Repealed]

ΔΕΥΤΕΡΟ ΚΕΦΑΛΑΙΟ

ΠΡΟΣΒΟΛΕΣ ΤΗΣ ΔΙΕΘΝΟΥΣ ΥΠΟΣΤΑΣΗΣ ΤΗΣ ΧΩΡΑΣ

I

ΠΡΟΣΒΟΛΕΣ ΤΗΣ ΕΔΑΦΙΚΗΣ ΑΚΕΡΑΙΟΤΗΤΑΣ ΤΗΣ ΧΩΡΑΣ

Άρθρο 138
Επιβουλή της ακεραιότητας της χώρας

1. Όποιος επιχειρεί με βία ή απειλή βίας να αποσπάσει από το ελληνικό κράτος τμήμα του εδάφους ή του θαλάσσιου χώρου που ανήκει σε αυτό ή να τα συγχωνεύσει σε άλλο κράτος, τιμωρείται με κάθειρξη ισόβια ή πρόσκαιρη τουλάχιστον δέκα ετών. Με την ίδια ποινή τιμωρείται και όποιος επιχειρεί να τελέσει την πράξη με κατάχρηση της ιδιότητάς του ως οργάνου του κράτους ή με σφετερισμό της ιδιότητας αυτής.
2. Οι διατάξεις των άρθρων 135 έως 137 έχουν και εδώ ανάλογη εφαρμογή.

Άρθρο 139
Νόθευση αποδεικτικών

Όποιος νοθεύει, καταστρέφει ή κρύβει έγγραφα ή άλλα αντικείμενα που χρησιμεύουν για την απόδειξη των εδαφικών δικαιωμάτων του ελληνικού κράτους ή την υποστήριξη συμφερόντων του τιμωρείται με κάθειρξη έως δέκα έτη.

II

ΠΡΟΣΒΟΛΕΣ ΤΗΣ ΔΙΕΘΝΟΥΣ ΕΙΡΗΝΗΣ ΤΗΣ ΧΩΡΑΣ

Άρθρο 140
Έκθεση σε κίνδυνο πολέμου

1. Όποιος επιχειρεί με συνομιλίες ή διαπραγματεύσεις με ξένη κυβέρνηση ή οργάνωση που ασκεί στην πράξη κρατική εξουσία σε ορισμένο τόπο να προκαλέσει πόλεμο ή εχθροπραξίες εναντίον του ελληνικού κράτους ή συμμάχου του, τιμωρείται με κάθειρξη έως δέκα έτη.
2. Αν εξαιτίας των ενεργειών του κηρύχθηκε πραγματικά πόλεμος ή άρχισαν εχθροπραξίες, επιβάλλεται κάθειρξη ισόβια ή πρόσκαιρη τουλάχιστον δέκα ετών.
3. Οι ποινές των προηγούμενων παραγράφων επιβάλλονται αν οι πράξεις δεν τιμωρούνται βαρύτερα με άλλες διατάξεις.
4. Ο δράστης της πράξης της πρώτης παραγράφου μένει ατιμώρητος, αν με δική του θέληση παρεμπόδισε την πρόκληση του πολέμου ή των εχθροπραξιών που επιδίωξε με την πράξη του.

Άρθρο 141
Έκθεση σε κίνδυνο αντιποίνων

1. Όποιος, με πράξεις που θέτουν υπό αμφισβήτηση κυριαρχικά δικαιώματα άλλου κράτους ή με άλλες προκλητικές ενέργειες, εκθέτει το ελληνικό κράτος ή σύμμαχό του ή τους κατοίκους τους σε κίνδυνο αντιποίνων ή εκθέτει σε κίνδυνο διατάραξης τις φιλικές σχέσεις της Ελλάδας ή συμμάχου της με ξένο κράτος, τιμωρείται με φυλάκιση έως τρία έτη ή χρηματική ποινή.
2. Αν τα αντίποινα επήλθαν πραγματικά εξαιτίας των ενεργειών του επιβάλλεται φυλάκιση τουλάχιστον τριών ετών.

CHAPTER II

OFFENCES AGAINST THE INTERNATIONAL STATUS OF [GREECE]

I

OFFENCES AGAINST THE TERRITORIAL INTEGRITY OF [GREECE]

Article 138
Violations of the integrity of [Greece]

1. Any person who, through use or threat of violence, attempts to separate from the Greek state a part of its territory or territorial waters or to merge such with [those of] another state shall be punished with incarceration for life or fixed-term incarceration of at least 10 years. The same penalty shall be imposed on any person who attempts to commit the [aforesaid] act by abusing their capacity as an officer of the state or by usurping such capacity.
2. The provisions of Articles 135 and 137 also apply *mutatis mutandis* in such a case.

Article 139
Alteration of evidence

Any person who alters, destroys or conceals documents or other items which can be used for proving the territorial rights of the Greek state or for supporting its interests shall be punished with incarceration of up to 10 years.

II

OFFENCES AGAINST INTERNATIONAL PEACE

Article 140
Exposure to risk of war

1. Any person who attempts, through talks or negotiations with a foreign government or organisation actually exercising state power at a specific place, to cause war or hostilities against the Greek state or an ally of [the Greek state] shall be punished with incarceration of up to 10 years.
2. If, due to their actions, war was actually declared or hostilities commenced, they shall be punished with incarceration for life or fixed-term incarceration of at least 10 years.
3. The sentences laid down in the preceding paragraphs shall be imposed unless the acts carry a heavier sentence under different provisions.
4. The perpetrator of the act provided for in the first paragraph shall not be punished if, of their own volition, they stopped the war or hostilities they sought to achieve through their act from taking place.

Article 141
Exposure to risk of retaliation

1. Any person who, through acts which call into question the sovereign rights of a different state, or through other provocative acts, exposes the Greek state or any of its allies or inhabitants to the risk of retaliation or exposes the amicable relations between Greece or an ally with a foreign state to the risk of disruption, shall be punished with imprisonment of up to three years or a monetary penalty.
2. If retaliation actually occurred due to their acts, such person shall be punished with imprisonment of at least three years.

Άρθρο 142
Έκθεση σε κίνδυνο αντιποίνων από αμέλεια

Αν η πράξη του προηγούμενου άρθρου τελέστηκε από αμέλεια, επιβάλλεται χρηματική ποινή ή παροχή κοινωφελούς εργασίας και, αν εξαιτίας αυτής επήλθαν αντίποινα, φυλάκιση έως ένα έτος ή χρηματική ποινή.

Άρθρο 142Α
Παραβάσεις κανονισμών της Ευρωπαϊκής Ένωσης

Όποιος με πρόθεση παραβιάζει κυρώσεις ή περιοριστικά μέτρα, που έχουν επιβληθεί σε βάρος κρατών ή οντοτήτων ή οργανισμών ή φυσικών ή νομικών προσώπων, με κανονισμούς της Ευρωπαϊκής Ένωσης τιμωρείται με φυλάκιση έως δύο έτη εκτός αν από άλλη διάταξη προβλέπεται βαρύτερη ποινή. Οι διατάξεις του προηγούμενου εδαφίου εφαρμόζονται και όταν οι προβλεπόμενες σε αυτό πράξεις δεν είναι αξιόποινες, κατά τους νόμους της χώρας στην οποία τελέστηκαν.

III

ΠΡΟΣΒΟΛΕΣ ΤΗΣ ΑΜΥΝΤΙΚΗΣ ΙΚΑΝΟΤΗΤΑΣ ΤΗΣ ΧΩΡΑΣ

Άρθρο 143
Υπηρεσία στον εχθρό

1. Έλληνας πολίτης, ο οποίος σε καιρό πολέμου κατά του ελληνικού κράτους υπηρετεί στον στρατό του εχθρού ή παίρνει όπλα κατά της ελληνικής πολιτείας ή των συμμάχων της τιμωρείται με κάθειρξη ισόβια ή πρόσκαιρη τουλάχιστον δέκα ετών.

2. Με την ίδια ποινή τιμωρείται και όποιος σε έδαφος του ελληνικού κράτους που βρίσκεται υπό εχθρική κατοχή, υποστηρίζει τη δύναμη του εχθρού σε αυτό καταδίδοντας άτομα που αντιστέκονται στις δυνάμεις κατοχής ή προσφέροντας τις υπηρεσίες του σε αυτές, με σκοπό τη διατήρηση του κατοχικού καθεστώτος.

Άρθρο 144
Υποστήριξη της πολεμικής δύναμης του εχθρού

1. Όποιος σε πόλεμο που κηρύχθηκε ή που επίκειται κατά της ελληνικής πολιτείας:

α) ενισχύει τις πολεμικές δυνάμεις του εχθρού υπηρετώντας σε αυτές ως στρατιώτης ή προσφέροντας μέσα ή υπηρεσίες ή

β) βλάπτει τις ελληνικές πολεμικές δυνάμεις καταστρέφοντας, αφαιρώντας ή μη παραδίδοντας τα πιο πάνω μέσα ή αρνούμενος τις οφειλόμενες υπηρεσίες,

τιμωρείται με κάθειρξη ισόβια ή πρόσκαιρη τουλάχιστον δέκα ετών.

2. Ο ξένος υπήκοος που παρέχει στον εχθρικό στρατό τα μέσα ή τις υπηρεσίες της προηγούμενης παραγράφου δεν τιμωρείται, εκτός αν, κατά τον χρόνο της πράξης, κατοικούσε στην Ελλάδα ή σε έδαφος κατεχόμενο από την Ελλάδα ή αν όσα έδωσε προέρχονται από αυτά τα εδάφη.

3. Όποιος σε πόλεμο που κηρύχθηκε ή που επίκειται κατά της ελληνικής πολιτείας επιχειρεί να ενισχύσει τις πολεμικές δυνάμεις του εχθρού ισχυριζόμενος ή διαδίδοντας ειδήσεις σχετικά με τις θέσεις, την ισχύ ή τις ενέργειες των ελληνικών ένοπλων δυνάμεων τιμωρείται με κάθειρξη έως δέκα έτη.

Article 142
Negligent exposure to risk of retaliation

If the act provided for in the preceding Article was committed negligently, a monetary penalty or community service shall be imposed, and if retaliation occurred due to such act, imprisonment of up to one year or a monetary penalty shall be imposed.

Article 142A
Infringement of European Union regulations

Any person who intentionally infringes sanctions or restrictive measures imposed on states, entities, organisations, or natural or legal persons pursuant to European Union regulations shall be punished with imprisonment of up to two years, unless the act carries a heavier sentence under a different provision. The provisions of the preceding sentence apply even when the acts referred to above are not punishable under the laws of the country where they were committed.

III

OFFENCES AGAINST THE DEFENCE CAPABILITIES OF [GREECE]

Article 143
Serving [in the army of] an enemy

1. Any Greek citizen who, in times of war against the Greek state, serves in the enemy's army or takes up arms against the Greek state or its allies shall be punished with incarceration for life or fixed-term incarceration of at least 10 years.

2. The same sentence shall be imposed on any person who, on territory belonging to the Greek state but occupied by an enemy, supports the enemy's forces at such place by informing on persons resisting against the occupying forces or by offering their services to the occupying forces for the purpose of maintaining the occupying regime.

Article 144
Supporting the enemy's armed forces

1. Any person who, during war declared or impending against the Greek state:

a) aids the enemy's armed forces by serving in them as military personnel or by offering [supporting] means or services; or

b) harms the Greek armed forces by destroying, removing or failing to hand over the aforesaid [supporting] means or refusing to offer the services required of them,

shall be punished with incarceration for life or fixed-term incarceration of at least 10 years.

2. Any foreign citizen who provides the enemy with the [supporting] means or services referred to in the preceding paragraph shall not be punished, unless, at the time the act was committed, they resided in Greece or territory occupied by Greece or if what they gave [to the enemy] came from such territory.

3. Any person who, during war declared or impending against the Greek state, attempts to aid the enemy's armed forces by asserting or disseminating news concerning the positions, strength or actions of the Greek armed forces shall be punished with incarceration of up to 10 years.

IV

ΠΡΟΣΒΟΛΕΣ ΚΡΑΤΙΚΩΝ ΑΠΟΡΡΗΤΩΝ

Άρθρο 145

(Καταργείται)

Άρθρο 146
Παραβίαση μυστικών της Πολιτείας

1. Όποιος παραδίδει ή αφήνει να περιέλθει στην κατοχή ή τη γνώση άλλου κρατικό απόρρητο τιμωρείται με κάθειρξη έως δέκα έτη.

2. Αν η πράξη τελείται σε καιρό πολέμου, επιβάλλεται κάθειρξη ισόβια ή πρόσκαιρη τουλάχιστον δέκα ετών.

3. Με τις ποινές των προηγούμενων παραγράφων τιμωρείται και όποιος δημόσια με οποιονδήποτε τρόπο ή μέσω του διαδικτύου ανακοινώνει ή διαδίδει κρατικό απόρρητο.

Άρθρο 147
Παραβίαση μυστικών της Πολιτείας από αμέλεια

Όποιος τελεί τις πράξεις του προηγούμενου άρθρου από αμέλεια, εφόσον τα απόρρητα ήταν υπηρεσιακώς εμπιστευμένα σε αυτόν ή τού ήταν προσιτά λόγω της δημόσιας υπηρεσίας του ή με εντολή κάποιας αρχής, τιμωρείται με φυλάκιση έως τρία έτη ή χρηματική ποινή και σε καιρό πολέμου, με φυλάκιση τουλάχιστον τριών ετών και χρηματική ποινή.

Άρθρο 148
Κατασκοπεία

1. Όποιος παράνομα πετυχαίνει να περιέλθει στην κατοχή ή στη γνώση του κρατικό απόρρητο τιμωρείται με φυλάκιση τουλάχιστον ενός έτους και χρηματική ποινή.

2. Αν όμως ο υπαίτιος ενήργησε με σκοπό να χρησιμοποιήσει το κρατικό απόρρητο για να το διαβιβάσει σε άλλον ή να το ανακοινώσει δημόσια, με τρόπο που μπορεί να προκαλέσει κίνδυνο στα συμφέροντα του κράτους, επιβάλλεται κάθειρξη έως δέκα έτη και αν η πράξη έγινε σε καιρό πολέμου, κάθειρξη.

Άρθρο 149
Έννοια κρατικού απορρήτου

Κρατικό απόρρητο κατά την έννοια των άρθρων 146 έως 148 είναι ένα γεγονός, αντικείμενο ή πληροφορία, η πρόσβαση στα οποία είναι δυνατή σε ένα προσδιορισμένο κύκλο προσώπων και που χαρακτηρίζονται ως μυστικά για να αποφευχθεί ο κίνδυνος προσβολής της εδαφικής ακεραιότητας, της αμυντικής ικανότητας, των διεθνών σχέσεων ή των οικονομικών συμφερόντων του ελληνικού κράτους και της διεθνούς ειρήνης.

Άρθρα 150 - 151

(Καταργούνται)

Άρθρο 152
Παρεπόμενες ποινές

Στα εγκλήματα αυτού του Κεφαλαίου, το δικαστήριο, μαζί με την ποινή, επιβάλλει αποστέρηση θέσεων και αξιωμάτων.

IV

OFFENCES AGAINST STATE SECRETS

Article 145

[Repealed]

Article 146
Violation of state secrets

1. Any person who hands over state secrets or allows another to take possession or cognisance of state secrets shall be punished with incarceration of up to 10 years.
2. If the [above] act is committed during wartime, incarceration for life or fixed-term incarceration of at least 10 years shall be imposed.
3. The sentences laid down in the preceding paragraphs shall also be imposed on any person who discloses or disseminates state secrets publicly, using any means or via the internet.

Article 147
Negligent violation of state secrets

Any person who negligently commits the acts provided for in the preceding Article, where the secrets had been entrusted to them due to their post, or such secrets were accessible to them due to their being a civil servant or on the instructions of an authority, shall be punished with imprisonment of up to three years or a monetary penalty and, during wartime, with imprisonment of at least three years and a monetary penalty.

Article 148
Espionage

1. Any person who unlawfully takes possession or cognisance of state secrets shall be punished with imprisonment of at least one year and a monetary penalty.
2. However, if the person acted for the purpose of using [such] state secrets in order to communicate them to another person or to disclose them publicly in a manner which could place the interests of the [Greek] state at risk, they shall be punished with incarceration of up to 10 years and, if the act was committed during wartime, incarceration.

Article 149
Meaning of state secrets

For the purposes of Articles 146 to 148, "state secrets" means a fact, object or item of information which can be accessed by a specific group of persons and which is classified as secret in order to avoid the risk of offences against the territorial integrity, defence capabilities, international relations or economic interests of the Greek state, and international peace.

Articles 150 - 151

[Repealed]

Article 152
Ancillary penalties

The court shall, in addition to the sentence carried by the crimes provided for in this Chapter, also impose forfeiture of posts and offices.

ΤΡΙΤΟ ΚΕΦΑΛΑΙΟ

ΕΓΚΛΗΜΑΤΑ ΚΑΤΑ ΑΛΛΩΝ ΚΡΑΤΩΝ

Άρθρο 153
Προσβολές κατά των εκπροσώπων άλλου κράτους

Όποιος βιαιοπραγεί κατά του αρχηγού ή μέλους της κυβέρνησης άλλου κράτους κατά τη διάρκεια της παραμονής τους στην Ελλάδα, τιμωρείται με φυλάκιση έως τρία έτη, αν η πράξη δεν τιμωρείται βαρύτερα με άλλη διάταξη.

Άρθρο 154
Προσβολή διπλωματικών αντιπροσώπων

Όποιος τελεί την πράξη του προηγούμενου άρθρου εναντίον πρεσβευτή διαπιστευμένου στην ελληνική πολιτεία ή άλλου διπλωματικού αντιπροσώπου κατά τον χρόνο παραμονής του στην Ελλάδα, τιμωρείται με φυλάκιση έως δύο έτη, αν η πράξη δεν τιμωρείται βαρύτερα από άλλη διάταξη.

Άρθρο 155
Προσβολή συμβόλων άλλου κράτους

Όποιος, για να εκδηλώσει μίσος ή περιφρόνηση, αφαιρεί, καταστρέφει, παραμορφώνει ή ρυπαίνει τη σημαία ή έμβλημα της κυριαρχίας άλλου κράτους, που τελεί σε ειρήνη με την Ελλάδα και είναι αναγνωρισμένο από αυτήν ή διακόπτει ή ηχητικά παρεμποδίζει την ανάκρουση του εθνικού του ύμνου, τιμωρείται με χρηματική ποινή ή παροχή κοινωφελούς εργασίας. Η δίωξη ασκείται μόνο ύστερα από αίτηση της αλλοδαπής κυβέρνησης.

Άρθρο 156
Προϋποθέσεις της δίωξης

Τα εγκλήματα αυτού του Κεφαλαίου διώκονται μόνο αν η Ελλάδα διατηρεί διπλωματικές σχέσεις με το αλλοδαπό κράτος και η αμοιβαιότητα είναι εξασφαλισμένη τόσο κατά τον χρόνο τέλεσης της πράξης, όσο και κατά τον χρόνο εκδίκασής της.

CHAPTER III

CRIMES AGAINST OTHER STATES

Article 153

Offences against representatives of other states

Any person who assaults the head of an other state or a member of the government of an other state during their stay in Greece shall be punished with imprisonment of up to three years, unless the act carries a heavier sentence under a different provision.

Article 154

Offences against diplomatic envoys

Any person who commits the act provided for in the preceding Article against an ambassador accredited in the Greek state or any other diplomatic envoy during their stay in Greece shall be punished with imprisonment of up to two years, unless the act carries a heavier sentence under a different provision.

Article 155

Offences against the symbols of other states

Any person who, in order to express hatred or contempt, removes, destroys, disfigures or sullies the flag or emblem of sovereignty of an other state which is at peace with and is recognised by Greece, or who interrupts or uses sound to hinder the playing of its national anthem shall be punished with a monetary penalty or community service. Prosecution shall be initiated only at the request of the foreign government.

Article 156

Prerequisites for prosecution

The crimes provided for in this Chapter shall be prosecuted only if Greece maintains diplomatic relations with the foreign state [in question] and reciprocity is ensured both at the time the act is committed and at the time the act is adjudicated.

ΤΕΤΑΡΤΟ ΚΕΦΑΛΑΙΟ

ΕΓΚΛΗΜΑΤΑ ΚΑΤΑ ΤΩΝ ΠΟΛΙΤΕΙΑΚΩΝ ΚΑΙ ΠΟΛΙΤΙΚΩΝ ΟΡΓΑΝΩΝ

I

- ΕΓΚΛΗΜΑΤΑ ΚΑΤΑ ΤΟΥ ΠΡΟΕΔΡΟΥ ΤΗΣ ΔΗΜΟΚΡΑΤΙΑΣ, ΤΗΣ ΒΟΥΛΗΣ, ΤΗΣ ΚΥΒΕΡΝΗΣΗΣ ΚΑΙ ΟΡΓΑΝΩΝ ΤΟΠΙΚΗΣ ΑΥΤΟΔΙΟΙΚΗΣΗΣ

Άρθρο 157
Προσβολές κατά του Προέδρου της Δημοκρατίας, της Βουλής ή της Κυβέρνησης και οργάνων τοπικής αυτοδιοίκησης

1. Όποιος με βία ή απειλή βίας επιχειρεί να εξαναγκάσει τον Πρόεδρο της Δημοκρατίας ή εκείνον που ασκεί την προεδρική εξουσία, τη Βουλή, την Κυβέρνηση ή μέλος τους σε εκτέλεση, παράλειψη ή ανοχή πράξης που ανάγεται στα καθήκοντά τους, καθώς και όποιος βιαιοπραγεί εναντίον τους κατά την άσκηση των καθηκόντων τους, τιμωρείται με κάθειρξη έως δέκα έτη. Η ίδια ποινή επιβάλλεται αν η πράξη στρέφεται κατά αρχηγού αναγνωρισμένου κατά τον κανονισμό της Βουλής πολιτικού κόμματος.

2. Ο υπαίτιος των πράξεων της παραγράφου 1 εναντίον του περιφερειάρχη, του δημάρχου, του περιφερειακού ή δημοτικού συμβουλίου τοπικής αυτοδιοίκησης ή μέλους του τιμωρείται με φυλάκιση και χρηματική ποινή.

3. Αν τα πρόσωπα κατά των οποίων στράφηκαν οι πράξεις των προηγούμενων παραγράφων διέτρεξαν κίνδυνο ζωής ή βαριάς σωματικής βλάβης, επιβάλλεται κάθειρξη για την πράξη της παραγράφου 1 και φυλάκιση τουλάχιστον τριών ετών για την πράξη της παραγράφου 2.

Άρθρο 158
Νόθευση εκλογής ή ψηφοφορίας

1. Όποιος με οποιονδήποτε τρόπο προκαλεί την παραγωγή μη γνήσιου αποτελέσματος σε εκλογή ή ψηφοφορία που διενεργείται από τη Βουλή ή κάποια επιτροπή της ή νοθεύει το γνήσιο αποτέλεσμα της εκλογής ή ψηφοφορίας τιμωρείται με φυλάκιση έως δύο έτη ή χρηματική ποινή.

2. Ο υπαίτιος των πράξεων της προηγούμενης παραγράφου σε εκλογή ή ψηφοφορία που διενεργείται από περιφερειακό ή δημοτικό συμβούλιο τοπικής αυτοδιοίκησης ή κάποια επιτροπή τους τιμωρείται με φυλάκιση έως ένα έτος ή χρηματική ποινή.

Άρθρο 159
Δωροληψία πολιτικών προσώπων

1. Με κάθειρξη και χρηματική ποινή από διακόσιες χιλιάδες (200.000) έως τέσσερα εκατομμύρια (4.000.000) ευρώ τιμωρείται ο Πρωθυπουργός, τα μέλη της Κυβέρνησης, οι Υφυπουργοί, οι βουλευτές, οι περιφερειάρχες, οι δήμαρχοι ή τα μέλη των κατά το άρθρο 157 παρ. 2 συμβουλίων ή των επιτροπών τους, οι οποίοι ζητούν ή λαμβάνουν άμεσα ή μέσω τρίτου, για τους εαυτούς τους ή άλλους, οποιασδήποτε φύσης ωφελήματα ανεξαρτήτως αξίας, που δεν δικαιούνται ή απαιτούν τέτοια ως αντάλλαγμα για ενέργεια ή παράλειψή τους, μελλοντική ή ήδη τελειωμένη, που ανάγεται στα καθήκοντά τους ή αντίκειται σε αυτά.

CHAPTER IV

CRIMES AGAINST STATE AND POLITICAL BODIES

I

CRIMES AGAINST THE PRESIDENT OF THE REPUBLIC, PARLIAMENT, THE GOVERNMENT AND LOCAL GOVERNMENT AUTHORITIES

Article 157
Offences against the President of the Republic, Parliament or the Government and local government authorities

1. Any person who, through use or threat of violence, attempts to force the President of the Republic or the person exercising presidential powers, Parliament, the Government or a member of Parliament or Government to carry out, refrain from or tolerate an act which is part of their duties, and any person who assaults the foregoing persons while performing their duties, shall be punished with incarceration of up to 10 years. The same sentence shall be imposed if the act is committed against the leader of a political party recognised under the Standing Orders of the Hellenic Parliament.
2. Any person who commits the acts provided for in paragraph 1 against a regional governor, mayor, regional or municipal local government council or member of such council shall be punished with imprisonment and a monetary penalty.
3. If the persons who were the targets of the acts provided for in the preceding paragraphs faced a risk to their lives or risk of grievous bodily harm, incarceration shall be imposed for the act provided for in paragraph 1 and imprisonment of at least three years for the act provided for in paragraph 2.

Article 158
Falsification of election or voting results

1. Any person who in any manner causes a non-genuine result to be produced in an election or vote held by Parliament or any of its committees, or who falsifies the genuine result of an election or vote shall be punished with imprisonment of up to two years or a monetary penalty.
2. Any person who commits the acts provided for in the preceding paragraph during elections or votes held by a regional or municipal local government council or any committee of such council shall be punished with imprisonment of up to one year or a monetary penalty.

Article 159
Passive bribery of political persons

1. Incarceration and a monetary penalty ranging from 200,000 to 4,000,000 euros shall be imposed on the Prime Minister, members of Government, Deputy Ministers, members of Parliament, regional governors, mayors or members of the councils or committees referred to in Article 157(2) if any of the foregoing persons requests or receives, whether directly or through a third party, for themselves or other persons, advantages of any nature, irrespective of value, to which they are not entitled or who demand such advantages in exchange for any act or omission on their part, whether in the future or already completed, which is part of or would breach their duties.

2. Με τις ίδιες ποινές τιμωρείται το μέλος της Βουλής, των συμβουλίων τοπικής αυτοδιοίκησης και των επιτροπών τους που σχετικά με κάποια εκλογή ή ψηφοφορία η οποία διενεργείται από τα ως άνω σώματα ή επιτροπές δέχεται την παροχή ή υπόσχεση οποιασδήποτε φύσης ωφελήματος, για τον εαυτό του ή για άλλον, ή ζητεί τέτοιο ως αντάλλαγμα για να μη λάβει μέρος στην εκλογή ή ψηφοφορία, για να υποστηρίξει ορισμένο θέμα προς ψήφιση ή για να ψηφίσει με ορισμένο τρόπο.
3. Σε περίπτωση καταδίκης για τις πράξεις των προηγούμενων παραγράφων επιβάλλεται και έκπτωση από τη δημόσια θέση που κατέχει ο καταδικασθείς.
4. Οι παρ. 1 και 2 εφαρμόζονται και όταν η πράξη τελείται από:
α) μέλη κοινοβουλευτικών συνελεύσεων διεθνών ή υπερεθνικών οργανισμών στους οποίους η Ελλάδα είναι μέλος,
β) μέλη του Ευρωπαϊκού Κοινοβουλίου ή της Ευρωπαϊκής Επιτροπής.
Στις περιπτώσεις αυτές οι ελληνικοί ποινικοί νόμοι εφαρμόζονται και όταν η πράξη τελέστηκε στην αλλοδαπή από ημεδαπό, ακόμα κι αν δεν είναι αξιόποινη κατά τους νόμους της χώρας όπου τελέστηκε. Οι παρ. 1 και 2 εφαρμόζονται επίσης όταν η πράξη τελείται από τον Πρωθυπουργό, μέλος της Κυβέρνησης ή Υφυπουργό άλλου κράτους, καθώς και από μέλη του κοινοβουλίου ή συμβουλίου τοπικής αυτοδιοίκησης άλλου κράτους.
5. Οι διατάξεις των άρθρων 238 και 263Α παρ. 2 έως 5 έχουν ανάλογη εφαρμογή και στα εγκλήματα των προηγούμενων παραγράφων.

Άρθρο 159Α
Δωροδοκία πολιτικών προσώπων

1. Όποιος υπόσχεται ή παρέχει στον Πρωθυπουργό ή μέλος της Κυβέρνησης ή Υφυπουργό, βουλευτή, τον περιφερειάρχη ή τον δήμαρχο, άμεσα ή μέσω άλλου, οποιαδήποτε ωφελήματα ανεξαρτήτως αξίας, που δεν δικαιούται για τον εαυτό του ή για άλλον, για ενέργεια ή παράλειψή του μελλοντική ή ήδη τελειωμένη, που ανάγεται στα καθήκοντά του ή αντίκειται σε αυτά, τιμωρείται με κάθειρξη έως δέκα (10) έτη και χρηματική ποινή από εκατό χιλιάδες (100.000) έως πεντακόσιες χιλιάδες (500.000) ευρώ.
2. Με την ίδια ποινή τιμωρείται όποιος σχετικά με εκλογή ή ψηφοφορία που διενεργείται από τη Βουλή, ή το κατά το άρθρο 157 παρ. 2 συμβούλιο τοπικής αυτοδιοίκησης ή επιτροπή τους, υπόσχεται ή παρέχει σε μέλος των πιο πάνω σωμάτων ή των επιτροπών τους οποιαδήποτε ωφελήματα που δεν δικαιούται, για τον εαυτό του ή για άλλον, για να μην λάβει μέρος στην εκλογή ή στην ψηφοφορία ή για να ψηφίσει με ορισμένο τρόπο.
3. Διευθυντής επιχείρησης ή άλλο πρόσωπο που έχει την εξουσία λήψης αποφάσεων ή ελέγχου σε επιχείρηση τιμωρείται με φυλάκιση και χρηματική ποινή, αν η πράξη δεν τιμωρείται βαρύτερα από άλλη ποινική διάταξη, αν με παραβίαση συγκεκριμένου καθήκοντος επιμέλειας δεν απέτρεψε από αμέλεια πρόσωπο που τελεί υπό τις εντολές του ή υπόκειται στον έλεγχο του από την τέλεση προς όφελος της επιχείρησης της πράξης των προηγουμένων παραγράφων.
4. Οι παρ. 1 έως 3 εφαρμόζονται και όταν η πράξη τελείται προς:
α) μέλη κοινοβουλευτικών συνελεύσεων διεθνών ή υπερεθνικών οργανισμών στους οποίους η Ελλάδα είναι μέλος,
β) μέλη του Ευρωπαϊκού Κοινοβουλίου ή της Ευρωπαϊκής Επιτροπής,
γ) τον Πρωθυπουργό, μέλος της Κυβέρνησης ή Υφυπουργό άλλου κράτους, καθώς και μέλη του Κοινοβουλίου ή οποιουδήποτε συμβουλίου τοπικής αυτοδιοίκησης άλλου κράτους.
Στις περιπτώσεις αυτές οι ελληνικοί ποινικοί νόμοι εφαρμόζονται και όταν η πράξη τελείται στην αλλοδαπή από ημεδαπό, ακόμα κι αν δεν είναι αξιόποινη κατά τους νόμους της χώρας όπου τελέστηκε.
5. Οι διατάξεις των άρθρων 238 και 263Α έχουν ανάλογη εφαρμογή και στα εγκλήματα των προηγούμενων παραγράφων.

2. The same penalty shall be imposed on [any] member of Parliament, of local government councils [or] of their committees who, with regard to any election or vote held by the aforesaid bodies or committees, accepts an advantage of any nature, provided or promised, whether for themselves or for another person, or who demands such advantage in exchange for not taking part in the election or vote, for supporting a specific item to be voted on, or for voting in a particular manner.
3. If a person is convicted of the acts provided for in the preceding paragraphs, they also forfeit their public post.
4. Paragraphs 1 and 2 also apply when the act is committed by:
a) members of parliamentary assemblies of national or supranational organisations of which Greece is a member;
b) members of the European Parliament or the European Commission.
In such cases, Greek penal laws also apply when the act was committed by a Greek national abroad, even if [the act] is not punishable under the laws of the country where it was committed. Paragraphs 1 and 2 also apply when the act is committed by the Prime Minister, a member of the government or a deputy minister of an other state, or by members of parliament or a local government council of an other state.
5. The provisions of Articles 238 and 263A(2) to (5) also apply *mutatis mutandis* to the crimes provided for in the preceding paragraphs.

Article 159A
Active bribery of political persons

1. Any person who promises or provides the Prime Minister or a member of Government or Deputy Minister, regional governor or mayor, whether directly or through a third party, any advantages, irrespective of value, to which they are not entitled, whether for themselves or for another person, [in exchange] for any act or omission on their part, whether in the future or already completed, which is part of or breaches their duties, shall be punished with incarceration of up to 10 years and a monetary penalty ranging from 100,000 to 500,000 euros.
2. The same punishment shall be imposed on any person who, in relation to an election or vote held by Parliament or a local government council or committee of the aforesaid bodies, as provided for in Article 157(2), promises or provides a member of the aforesaid bodies or committees any advantages to which they are not entitled, whether for themselves or for another person, [in exchange] for not taking part in the election or vote, or for voting in a particular manner.
3. Where any manager of an enterprise or other person with decision-making or control powers at that enterprise, in breach of a specific duty of care, failed to prevent a person under their instructions or subject to their control from committing the act provided for in the preceding paragraphs to the benefit of that enterprise, they shall be punished with imprisonment and a monetary penalty, unless the act carries a heavier punishment under a different criminal law provision.
4. Paragraphs 1 and 3 also apply when the act is committed by:
a) members of parliamentary assemblies of national or supranational organisations of which Greece is a member;
b) members of the European Parliament or the European Commission;
c) the Prime Minister, a member of Government or a Deputy Minister of an other state, as well as members of parliament or any local government council of an other state.
In such cases, Greek penal laws also apply when the act [was] committed by a Greek national abroad, even if [the act] is not punishable under the laws of the country where it was committed.
5. The provisions of Articles 238 and 263A also apply *mutatis mutandis* to the crimes provided for in the preceding paragraphs.

Άρθρο 160
Αντιποίηση

Όποιος αντιποιείται την άσκηση του αξιώματος των προσώπων που αναφέρονται στο άρθρο 157 τιμωρείται με φυλάκιση έως ένα έτος ή χρηματική ποινή.

Άρθρο 160Α
Διατάραξη συνεδριάσεων

1. Όποιος παρεμποδίζει τη διεξαγωγή συνεδρίασης του Υπουργικού Συμβουλίου, της Βουλής ή κάποιας επιτροπής τους ή τη διαταράσσει με οποιονδήποτε τρόπο, τιμωρείται με φυλάκιση τουλάχιστον τριών μηνών.

2. Όποιος παρεμποδίζει ή διαταράσσει συνεδρίαση των κατά το άρθρο 157 παρ. 2 συμβουλίων ή των επιτροπών τους τιμωρείται με φυλάκιση έως τρία έτη ή χρηματική ποινή.

II

ΕΓΚΛΗΜΑΤΑ ΚΑΤΑ ΤΟΥ ΕΚΛΟΓΙΚΟΥ ΣΩΜΑΤΟΣ

Άρθρο 161
Βία κατά εκλογέων

1. Όποιος με βία ή απειλή βίας ή με κατάχρηση μιας εργασιακής ή οικονομικής σχέσης εξάρτησης, παρεμποδίζει εκλογέα να ασκήσει το εκλογικό του δικαίωμα ή επιβάλλει την ενάσκησή του υπέρ ή κατά ορισμένου υποψηφίου σε εκλογές βουλευτών, ευρωβουλευτών ή αυτοδιοικητικών αρχών ή σε δημοψήφισμα κατά το Σύνταγμα, τιμωρείται με φυλάκιση.

2. Αν το πρόσωπο κατά του οποίου στράφηκε η πράξη διέτρεξε σοβαρό προσωπικό κίνδυνο, επιβάλλεται φυλάκιση τουλάχιστον τριών ετών, αν η πράξη δεν τιμωρείται βαρύτερα από άλλη διάταξη.

3. Το δικαστήριο μαζί με την ποινή για τις πράξεις των προηγούμενων παραγράφων επιβάλλει και αποστέρηση θέσεων και αξιωμάτων.

Άρθρο 162
Εξαπάτηση εκλογέων

Όποιος με ψευδείς ειδήσεις ή συκοφαντικές διαδόσεις που ανάγονται στο πρόσωπο κάποιου υποψηφίου ή με άλλο τρόπο εξαπατά εκλογέα, με αποτέλεσμα αυτός να μην ασκήσει το εκλογικό του δικαίωμα, να ψηφίσει άκυρα ή να μεταβάλλει το εκλογικό του φρόνημα σε κάποια από τις εκλογές ή τα δημοψηφίσματα του άρθρου 161, τιμωρείται με φυλάκιση έως δύο έτη ή χρηματική ποινή.

Άρθρο 163
Παραβίαση της μυστικότητας της ψηφοφορίας

Όποιος, σε κάποια από τις εκλογές ή τα δημοψηφίσματα του άρθρου 161 κατορθώνει με οποιονδήποτε τρόπο να μάθει είτε ο ίδιος είτε τρίτος την ψήφο που έδωσε ο εκλογέας, τιμωρείται με φυλάκιση έως ένα έτος ή χρηματική ποινή.

Article 160
Impersonation

Any person who impersonates any of the persons referred to in Article 157 shall be punished with imprisonment of up to one year or a monetary penalty.

Article 160A
Disruption of meetings

1. Any person who obstructs a meeting of the Cabinet, Parliament or a committee of the aforesaid bodies from being held or disrupts such meeting in any manner shall be punished with imprisonment of at least three months.
2. Any person who obstructs or disrupts a meeting of the councils or committees of such councils referred to in Article 157(2) shall be punished with imprisonment of up to three years or a monetary penalty.

II

CRIMES AGAINST THE ELECTORATE

Article 161
Violence against voters

1. Any person who, through use or threat of violence or abuse of employment or a financial relationship of dependence, hinders a voter from exercising their voting rights, or imposes the exercise of such rights in favour of or against a certain candidate in elections for members of Parliament, members of the European Parliament or local government authorities or in a constitutionally held referendum shall be punished with imprisonment.
2. If the person against whom the act was committed was placed in grave personal danger, imprisonment of at least three years shall be imposed, unless the act carries a heavier sentence under a different provision.
3. In addition to imposing the sentence for the acts provided for in the preceding paragraphs, the court shall also impose forfeiture of posts and offices.

Article 162
Deception of voters

Any person who, through [disseminating] false news or defamatory rumours concerning any candidate or otherwise deceiving a voter so that the latter does not exercise their voting rights, or casts an invalid vote, or changes their voting intentions in any of the elections or referenda referred to in Article 161 shall be punished with imprisonment of up to two years or a monetary penalty.

Article 163
Violation of the secrecy of elections

Any person who, during any of the elections or referenda referred to in Article 161, manages to learn or to enable a third party to learn how a voter voted shall be punished with imprisonment of up to one year or a monetary penalty.

Άρθρο 164
Νόθευση εκλογής

1. Όποιος ψηφίζει χωρίς να έχει δικαίωμα σε κάποια από τις εκλογές ή τα δημοψηφίσματα του άρθρου 161 ή ψηφίζει κατ' επανάληψη ή δίνει πολλές ψήφους ή με οποιονδήποτε άλλο τρόπο προκαλεί την παραγωγή μη γνήσιου αποτελέσματος της εκλογής, καθώς και όποιος νοθεύει το γνήσιο αποτέλεσμα αυτής, τιμωρείται με φυλάκιση έως δύο έτη ή χρηματική ποινή.
2. Αν ο υπαίτιος εκτελούσε υπηρεσία κατά την εκλογή ή το δημοψήφισμα, τιμωρείται με φυλάκιση και χρηματική ποινή.
3. Η παράγραφος 3 του άρθρου 161 εφαρμόζεται και σ' αυτή την περίπτωση.

Άρθρο 165
Δωροδοκία εκλογέα

1. Όποιος σχετικά με κάποια από τις εκλογές ή τα δημοψηφίσματα του άρθρου 161, από την προκήρυξή τους και έως το τέλος της ψηφοφορίας υπόσχεται ή παρέχει σε εκλογέα οποιαδήποτε ωφελήματα που δεν δικαιούται για να παραλείψει να ασκήσει το εκλογικό του δικαίωμα ή για να το ασκήσει με ορισμένο τρόπο, τιμωρείται με φυλάκιση έως τρία έτη και με χρηματική ποινή. Η παράγραφος 3 του άρθρου 161 εφαρμόζεται και σ' αυτή την περίπτωση.
2. Με φυλάκιση έως δύο έτη και χρηματική ποινή τιμωρείται ο εκλογέας, ο οποίος, σχετικά με κάποια από τις εκλογές ή τα δημοψηφίσματα του άρθρου 161 και κατά το χρόνο που προβλέπεται στην προηγούμενη παράγραφο, δέχεται παροχή ή υπόσχεση ωφελημάτων που δεν δικαιούται ή απαιτεί τέτοια για να παραλείψει την άσκηση του εκλογικού του δικαιώματος ή για να το ασκήσει με ορισμένο τρόπο.
3. Όποιος από την προκήρυξη κάποιας από τις εκλογές ή τα δημοψηφίσματα του άρθρου 161 και έως το τέλος της ψηφοφορίας υπόσχεται ή κάνει δωρεά για φιλανθρωπικό σκοπό ή για εκτέλεση έργου σε εκλογική περιφέρεια, δήμο, φιλανθρωπικό κατάστημα, κοινωφελές ίδρυμα ή εκκλησία, ως αντάλλαγμα για να υπερψηφιστεί, καταψηφιστεί ή προτιμηθεί συγκεκριμένος υποψήφιος, τιμωρείται με φυλάκιση έως τρία έτη και με χρηματική ποινή.

Άρθρο 166
Διατάραξη εκλογικής διαδικασίας

1. Όποιος με βία ή απειλή παρεμποδίζει τη διεξαγωγή κάποιας από τις εκλογές ή τα δημοψηφίσματα του άρθρου 161 ή τη διαταράσσει με οποιονδήποτε τρόπο, τιμωρείται με φυλάκιση έως ένα έτος ή χρηματική ποινή.
2. Όποιος σχετικά με κάποια από τις εκλογές ή τα δημοψηφίσματα του άρθρου 161, από την αρχή της ψηφοφορίας και έως την ολοκλήρωση της διαλογής καταστρέφει ολικά ή μερικά κάλπη ή με οποιονδήποτε τρόπο εξαφανίζει την κάλπη, το πρωτόκολλο ή τα πρακτικά της ψηφοφορίας ή τα διαβιβαζόμενα στοιχεία στην αρμόδια αρχή, τιμωρείται με φυλάκιση έως τρία έτη.

Article 164
Falsification of election [results]

1. Any person who votes without the right to do so in any of the elections or referenda referred to in Article 161, or votes repeatedly, or casts multiple votes, or otherwise causes a non-genuine election result to be produced, and any person who falsifies the genuine results of an election, shall be punished with imprisonment of up to two years or a monetary penalty.
2. If the culpable person was performing duties during the election or referendum, they shall be punished with imprisonment and a monetary penalty.
3. Article 161(3) also applies in such a case.

Article 165
Active bribery of voters

1. Any person who, in relation to any of the elections or referenda referred to in Article 161, from the date they are announced and until voting has ended, promises or provides a voter with any advantages to which they are not entitled [in exchange] for the latter not exercising their voting rights or exercising such rights in a specific manner shall be punished with imprisonment of up to three years and a monetary penalty. Article 161(3) also applies in such a case.
2. Any voter who, in relation to any of the elections or referenda referred to in Article 161 and during the period laid down in the preceding paragraph, accepts an advantage, provided or promised, to which they are not entitled or demands such [advantage] in exchange for not exercising their voting rights or exercising such rights in a specific manner shall be punished with imprisonment of up to two years and a monetary penalty.
3. Any person who, from the time any of the elections or referenda referred to in Article 161 are announced and until voting has ended, promises to make or makes a donation for a charitable purpose or for the implementation of a project for a constituency, municipality, charitable institution, public-benefit foundation or church, in exchange for voting in favour of or against or for preference to be given to a specific candidate shall be punished with imprisonment of up to three years and a monetary penalty.

Article 166
Disruption of the election process

1. Any person who, through use or threat of violence, obstructs any of the elections or referenda referred to in Article 161 from being held or disrupts such elections [or referenda] in any manner shall be punished with imprisonment of up to one year or a monetary penalty.
2. Any person who, in relation to any of the elections or referenda referred to in Article 161 and until the counting has ended, destroys a ballot box, whether in whole or in part, or causes the disappearance of a ballot box, report or minutes of the vote or information communicated to the competent authority shall be punished with imprisonment of up to three years.

ΠΕΜΠΤΟ ΚΕΦΑΛΑΙΟ
ΠΡΟΣΒΟΛΕΣ ΚΑΤΑ ΤΗΣ ΠΟΛΙΤΕΙΑΚΗΣ ΕΞΟΥΣΙΑΣ

Άρθρο 167
Βία κατά υπαλλήλων και δικαστικών προσώπων

1. Όποιος με βία ή απειλή βίας επιχειρεί να εξαναγκάσει κάποια αρχή ή υπάλληλο να ενεργήσει πράξη που ανάγεται στα καθήκοντά του ή να παραλείψει νόμιμη πράξη, καθώς και όποιος βιαιοπραγεί εναντίον του ή κατά προσώπου που έχει προσληφθεί ή άλλου υπαλλήλου που έχει προστρέξει για να τον υποστηρίξει κατά τη διάρκεια της νόμιμης ενέργειάς του (αντίσταση), τιμωρείται με φυλάκιση έως τρία έτη ή χρηματική ποινή.

2. Αν η πράξη στράφηκε κατά δικαστικού λειτουργού, διαιτητή ή ενόρκου, ή έγινε από περισσοτέρους, επιβάλλεται φυλάκιση τουλάχιστον δύο ετών και χρηματική ποινή.

3. Αν το πρόσωπο κατά του οποίου στράφηκε η πράξη διέτρεξε σοβαρό προσωπικό κίνδυνο ή η πράξη έγινε από πρόσωπο που οπλοφορεί ή φέρει αντικείμενα με τα οποία μπορεί να προκληθεί σωματική βλάβη, επιβάλλεται φυλάκιση τουλάχιστον τριών ετών και χρηματική ποινή, εφόσον η πράξη δεν τιμωρείται βαρύτερα με άλλη διάταξη.

Άρθρο 167Α
Αθέμιτη επιρροή σε δικαστικούς λειτουργούς

Όποιος εκτός από τις περιπτώσεις των άρθρων 167 και 237 επιχειρεί με αθέμιτη επιρροή ή πίεση ή με απειλή να επιβάλει σε δικαστικό λειτουργό, διαιτητή ή ένορκο την ενέργεια πράξης που ανάγεται στα καθήκοντά του ή την παράλειψη νόμιμης πράξης ή την ευνοϊκή ή δυσμενή μεταχείριση ορισμένου διαδίκου τιμωρείται με φυλάκιση τουλάχιστον ενός έτους και χρηματική ποινή.

Άρθρο 168
Διατάραξη της λειτουργίας υπηρεσίας

1. Όποιος εισέρχεται παράνομα σε χώρο δημόσιας υπηρεσίας ή υπηρεσίας οργανισμού τοπικής αυτοδιοίκησης ή νομικού προσώπου δημοσίου δικαίου ή επιχείρησης κοινής ωφέλειας ή παραμένει στους χώρους αυτούς παρά τη ρητή εναντίωση της υπηρεσίας που τους χρησιμοποιεί, τιμωρείται με φυλάκιση έως τρία (3) έτη ή χρηματική ποινή.

2. Όποιος, με οποιονδήποτε τρόπο, προκαλεί διακοπή ή σοβαρή διατάραξη της ομαλής λειτουργίας δημόσιας υπηρεσίας ή υπηρεσίας οργανισμού τοπικής αυτοδιοίκησης ή νομικού προσώπου δημοσίου δικαίου ή επιχείρησης κοινής ωφέλειας τιμωρείται με φυλάκιση και χρηματική ποινή. Με την ίδια ποινή τιμωρείται και όποιος, χωρίς να διαταράξει την κοινή ειρήνη, εμποδίζει αυθαίρετα ή διαταράσσει σοβαρά τη λειτουργία συλλογικού ή μονοπρόσωπου οργάνου των φορέων του προηγούμενου εδαφίου.

3. Όποιος εισέρχεται παράνομα σε χώρο που χρησιμοποιείται από υπάλληλο πλειστηριασμού κατά τη διαδικασία αναγκαστικής εκτέλεσης ή παραμένει στον χώρο αυτό παρά τη θέληση του υπαλλήλου του πλειστηριασμού που τον χρησιμοποιεί, και προκαλεί έτσι διακοπή ή διατάραξη της ομαλής διεξαγωγής του πλειστηριασμού τιμωρείται με φυλάκιση μέχρι ενός (1) έτους ή με χρηματική ποινή. Με φυλάκιση έως έξι (6) μηνών ή χρηματική ποινή τιμωρείται όποιος παράνομα εισέρχεται ή παραμένει στον προαναφερόμενο χώρο κατά τον χρόνο μη διεξαγωγής του πλειστηριασμού με σκοπό την παρακώλυση αυτού.

CHAPTER V

OFFENCES AGAINST STATE AUTHORITY

Article 167

Violence against state employees and court officials

1. Any person who, through use or threat of violence, attempts to force an authority or state employee to carry out or omit a lawful act that is part of their duties, and any person who assaults such state employee or a person engaged [to perform duties] or another state employee who has come to their aid while taking lawful steps (resistance) shall be punished with imprisonment of up to three years or a monetary penalty.
2. If the act was committed against a judicial functionary, arbitrator or juror or was committed by several persons, imprisonment of at least two years and a monetary penalty shall be imposed.
3. If the person against whom the act was committed was placed in grave personal danger or the act was committed by a person armed with a weapon or objects which can cause bodily harm, imprisonment of at least three years and a monetary penalty shall be imposed, unless the act carries a heavier punishment under a different provision.

Article 167A

Undue influence on judicial functionaries

Any person who, except in the cases provided for in Articles 167 and 237, attempts, through undue influence or pressure or threat, to force a judicial functionary, arbitrator or juror to carry out or omit a lawful act that is part of to their duties or to treat a specific party in proceedings favourably or unfavourably shall be punished with imprisonment of at least one year and a monetary penalty.

Article 168

Disruption of operation of a [public] body

1. Any person who unlawfully enters the premises of a governmental body or local government authority or body governed by public law or public utility company or remains at such premises despite the express objections of the body using such premises shall be punished with imprisonment of up to three years or a monetary penalty.
2. Any person who, in any manner, causes the closure of or serious disruption to the problem-free operation of a governmental body or local government authority or body governed by public law or public utility company shall be punished with imprisonment and a monetary penalty. The same punishment shall be imposed on any person who, without breaching the public peace, arbitrarily obstructs or seriously disrupts the operation of a collective body within or single officer of the bodies referred to in the preceding sentence.
3. Any person who unlawfully enters the premises used by an auctioneer during compulsory enforcement or remains at such premises against the wishes of the auctioneer using such premises, thus stopping or disrupting the problem-free holding of the auction, shall be punished with imprisonment of up to one year or a monetary penalty. Any person who unlawfully enters or remains at the aforesaid premises while the auction is not being held, for the purpose of obstructing such auction, shall be punished with imprisonment of up to six months or a monetary penalty.

4. Όποιος εισέρχεται σε δομές παροχής υπηρεσιών υγείας, συμπεριλαμβανομένων των κινητών μονάδων παροχής υπηρεσιών υγείας ή προσεγγίζει κινητές μονάδες παροχής υγειονομικών υπηρεσιών άμεσης βοήθειας και με οποιονδήποτε τρόπο, ιδίως με φωνασκίες, θόρυβο, ύβρεις ή απειλές κατά του ιατρικού και νοσηλευτικού προσωπικού, εργαζομένων, υπαλλήλων ή ασθενών διαταράσσει τη λειτουργία τους, τιμωρείται με ποινή φυλάκισης τουλάχιστον ενός (1) έτους και χρηματική ποινή και αν η πράξη συνδέεται με πρόκληση βιαιοπραγίας, με ποινή φυλάκισης τουλάχιστον δύο (2) ετών και χρηματική ποινή.

5. Με τις ποινές της παρ. 4 τιμωρείται όποιος εισέρχεται σε χώρο πρωτοβάθμιας ή δευτεροβάθμιας εκπαίδευσης και με οποιονδήποτε τρόπο, ιδίως με φωνασκίες, θόρυβο, ύβρεις ή απειλές κατά του εκπαιδευτικού προσωπικού, εργαζομένων, υπαλλήλων ή μαθητών διαταράσσει τη λειτουργία του.

Άρθρο 168Α
Διατάραξη δικαστικών συνεδριάσεων

Όποιος εμποδίζει αυθαίρετα ή διαταράσσει σοβαρά τις συνεδριάσεις δικαστηρίου ή δικαστικού συμβουλίου τιμωρείται με φυλάκιση έως τρία έτη ή χρηματική ποινή.

Άρθρο 169
Απείθεια

Με φυλάκιση έως έξι μήνες ή χρηματική ποινή τιμωρείται όποιος, ύστερα από νόμιμη πρόσκληση, αρνείται σε κάποιον από τους υπαλλήλους του άρθρου άρθρου 13 περίπτ. α', χωρίς αντίσταση την υπηρεσία ή συνδρομή που οφείλεται κατά τον νόμο ή την είσοδο σε οποιοδήποτε μέρος για να επιχειρηθεί κάποια νόμιμη υπηρεσιακή ενέργεια.

Άρθρο 169Α
Παραβίαση δικαστικών αποφάσεων, συμφωνιών που επικυρώθηκαν από συμβολαιογράφο και πρακτικού διαμεσολάβησης

1. Όποιος δεν συμμορφώθηκε σε προσωρινή διαταγή ή διάταξη δικαστικής απόφασης πολιτικού δικαστηρίου ή σε εισαγγελική διάταξη, που αφορούν τη ρύθμιση της νομής ή της κατοχής, την άσκηση της γονικής μέριμνας, την επικοινωνία με το τέκνο και τη ρύθμιση της χρήσης της οικογενειακής στέγης και της κατανομής των κινητών μεταξύ συζύγων ή την απαγόρευση προσέγγισης και επικοινωνίας μεταξύ προσώπων, τιμωρείται με φυλάκιση έως τρία (3) έτη ή χρηματική ποινή. Με την ίδια ποινή τιμωρείται και όποιος δεν συμμορφώθηκε σε συμφωνία που επικυρώθηκε από συμβολαιογράφο κατά το άρθρο 1441 του Αστικού Κώδικα ή παραβιάζει πρακτικό διαμεσολάβησης που αφορούν στην επικοινωνία των ανήλικων τέκνων.

2. (Καταργείται)

3. Όποιος εν γνώσει ματαιώνει την εκτέλεση της ποινής ή του μέτρου ασφαλείας που επιβλήθηκε σε άλλον τιμωρείται με φυλάκιση έως τρία (3) έτη ή χρηματική ποινή. Η πράξη μένει ατιμώρητη αν ο υπαίτιος την τέλεσε υπέρ κάποιου οικείου του.

4. Any person who enters healthcare facilities, including mobile healthcare units, or who approaches mobile emergency healthcare units, and disrupts their operation in any manner and, in particular, by shouting, making noise, insulting or threatening the medical and nursing staff, workers, employees or patients shall be punished with imprisonment of at least one year and a monetary penalty; if the act also involves assault, they shall be punished with imprisonment of at least two years and a monetary penalty.
5. The punishments laid down in paragraph 4 shall be imposed on any person who enters a primary or secondary school and who disrupts its operation in any manner and, in particular, by shouting, making noise, insulting or threatening educational staff, workers, employees or pupils.

Article 168A
Disruption of court sittings

Any person who arbitrarily obstructs or seriously disrupts the sittings of a court or judicial council shall be punished with imprisonment of up to three years or a monetary penalty.

Article 169
Disobedience

Any person who, after being lawfully requested to do so, refuses, without resistance, to provide any of the state employees referred to in Article 13(a) with the service or assistance required by law or refuses entry to any place in order for lawful steps that are part of their duties to be taken shall be punished with imprisonment of up to six months or a monetary penalty.

Article 169A
Infringement of court judgments, notarised agreements and mediation reports

1. Any person who fails to comply with an interim order or the [operative part] of a judgment handed down by a civil court or a decree issued by a public prosecutor regulating possession or detentorship, exercise of parental responsibility, access to a child and regulation of use of the family home and apportionment of movables between spouses or restraining order between persons shall be punished with imprisonment of up to three years or a monetary penalty. The same punishment shall also be imposed on any person who fails to comply with a notarised agreement in accordance with Article 1441 of the Civil Code or who violates a mediation report with regard to access to juvenile children.
2. [Repealed]
3. Any person who knowingly prevents the enforcement of a punishment or security measure imposed on another person shall be punished with imprisonment of up to three years or a monetary penalty. The above act shall not be punished if the culpable person committed it for the benefit of a related party.

Άρθρο 170
Στάση

1. Όποιος με πρόθεση συμμετέχει σε συγκεντρωμένο πλήθος που διαπράττει με ενωμένες δυνάμεις κάποια από τις πράξεις του άρθρου 167 τιμωρείται με φυλάκιση έως τρία έτη ή χρηματική ποινή.
2. Οι υποκινητές της στάσης, καθώς και εκείνοι που μεταχειρίστηκαν βία ή απειλές βίας ή βιαιοπράγησαν, τιμωρούνται με φυλάκιση τουλάχιστον δύο ετών, αν άλλη διάταξη νόμου δεν τιμωρεί την πράξη με βαρύτερη ποινή.

Άρθρο 171

(Καταργείται)

Άρθρο 172
Ελευθέρωση φυλακισμένου

1. Όποιος με πρόθεση ελευθερώνει φυλακισμένο ή άλλον που κρατείται νόμιμα με διαταγή της αρχής τιμωρείται με φυλάκιση έως τρία έτη ή χρηματική ποινή.
2. Αν ο δράστης της πράξης της προηγούμενης παραγράφου είναι υπάλληλος επιφορτισμένος με τη φύλαξη ή άλλο πρόσωπο επιφορτισμένο με την υποχρέωση αυτή τιμωρείται με φυλάκιση τουλάχιστον δύο ετών. Αν η πράξη τελέστηκε από αμέλεια επιβάλλεται φυλάκιση έως έξι μήνες ή χρηματική ποινή, εφόσον ο δράστης ήταν επιφορτισμένος με τη φύλαξη αυτού που απέδρασε.
3. Ο εξ αμελείας υπαίτιος μένει ατιμώρητος αν με δική του προσπάθεια συλληφθεί εντός ενός μηνός εκείνος που απέδρασε.

Άρθρο 173
Απόδραση κρατουμένου

1. Φυλακισμένος που αποδρά τιμωρείται με φυλάκιση έως ένα έτος, που εκτίεται αθροιστικά, εκτός αν οικειοθελώς επιστρέψει στη φυλακή. Αν αποδράσει άλλος που νόμιμα κρατείται με διαταγή αρχής, επιβάλλεται φυλάκιση έως έξι μήνες ή χρηματική ποινή.
2. Η συμμετοχή σε απόδραση φυλακισμένου ή άλλου που νόμιμα κρατείται με διαταγή της αρχής τιμωρείται με φυλάκιση έως τρία έτη. Αν ο δράστης είναι υπάλληλος επιφορτισμένος με τη φύλαξη του πιο πάνω προσώπου ή άλλο πρόσωπο επιφορτισμένο με την υποχρέωση αυτή επιβάλλεται φυλάκιση τουλάχιστον τριών ετών.

Άρθρο 173Α
Παραβίαση περιορισμού κατ' οίκον με ηλεκτρονική επιτήρηση

1. Όποιος, κατά τον χρόνο που τελεί υπό ηλεκτρονική επιτήρηση, με πρόθεση:
α) αφαιρεί, καταστρέφει, φθείρει ή με οποιονδήποτε τρόπο επεμβαίνει στη συσκευή ή στο σύστημα ηλεκτρονικής επιτήρησης ή
β) με οποιονδήποτε τρόπο αλλοιώνει τα συναφή με την επιτήρηση δεδομένα προσωπικού χαρακτήρα,
τιμωρείται με φυλάκιση. Με την ίδια ποινή τιμωρείται όποιος, κατά τον χρόνο που τελεί υπό ηλεκτρονική επιτήρηση, εκμεταλλευόμενος βλάβη ή μη ορθή λειτουργία της συσκευής ή του συστήματος ηλεκτρονικής επιτήρησης, διαφεύγει από την επιτήρηση των αρμοδίων αρχών. Η ποινή των παραπάνω αδικημάτων εκτίεται αθροιστικά με την ποινή για την πράξη για την οποία ο ηλεκτρονικά επιτηρούμενος ήταν κρατούμενος.
2. Οποιοσδήποτε συμμετέχει στις παραπάνω πράξεις τιμωρείται με φυλάκιση τουλάχιστον ενός έτους. Αν ο συμμετέχων έχει την ιδιότητα του σωφρονιστικού ή αστυνομικού υπαλλήλου ή του αρμόδιου για την ηλεκτρονική επιτήρηση υπαλλήλου, επιβάλλεται φυλάκιση τουλάχιστον δύο ετών.

Article 170
Riot

1. Any person who intentionally participates in an assembly of people who, acting in concert, commit any of the acts provided for in Article 167 shall be punished with imprisonment of up to three years or a monetary penalty.
2. Any person who incited the riot and any person who used or threatened to use violence or who committed assault shall be punished with imprisonment of at least two years, unless the act carries a heavier sentence under a different statutory provision.

Article 171

[Repealed]

Article 172
Freeing of prisoners

1. Any person who intentionally frees a prisoner or other person lawfully detained on the orders of an authority shall be punished with imprisonment of up to three years or a monetary penalty.
2. If the perpetrator of the act provided for in the preceding paragraph is a state employee tasked with guarding [prisoners] or is another person tasked with this duty, they shall be punished with imprisonment of at least two years. If the act was committed negligently and the perpetrator was tasked with guarding the person who escaped, imprisonment of up to six months or a monetary penalty shall be imposed.
3. The negligent person shall not be punished if, through their own efforts, the escapee is arrested within one month.

Article 173
Escape of a [prisoner/detainee]

1. Any prisoner who escapes shall be punished with imprisonment of up to one year, to be served in addition to their sentence, unless they voluntarily return to prison. If any other person lawfully detained on the orders of an authority escapes, imprisonment of up to six months or a monetary penalty shall be imposed.
2. Participation in the escape of a prisoner or other person lawfully detained on the orders of an authority shall be punished with imprisonment of up to three years. If the perpetrator is a state employee tasked with guarding the aforesaid [escapee] or is another person tasked with this duty, imprisonment of at least three years shall be imposed.

Article 173A
Violation of house arrest under electronic surveillance

1. Any person who, while under electronic surveillance, intentionally:
a) removes, destroys, damages or interferes with the device or electronic surveillance system in any manner; or
b) alters the surveillance-related personal data in any manner,
shall be punished with imprisonment. The same sentence shall be imposed on any person who, while under electronic surveillance, takes advantage of a malfunction or improper functioning of the device or electronic surveillance system to escape from surveillance by the competent authorities. The sentence for the above offences shall be added to the [initial] sentence imposed for the act for which the person was placed under electronic surveillance.
2. Any person who participates in the above acts shall be punished with imprisonment of at least one year. If the accessory serves as a correctional or police officer or state employee responsible for electronic surveillance, imprisonment of at least two years shall be imposed.

Άρθρο 174
Στάση κρατουμένων

1. Φυλακισμένοι ή άλλοι κρατούμενοι με νόμιμη διαταγή της αρχής που με ενωμένες δυνάμεις:
α) επιχειρούν βίαια να αποδράσουν,
β) επιτίθενται με έργα κατά ων υπαλλήλων της φυλακής ή του κρατητηρίου ή κατά εκείνων στους οποίους έχει ανατεθεί η φύλαξη ή η επίβλεψη,
γ) επιχειρούν με βία ή με απειλή να εξαναγκάσουν κάποιον από αυτούς σε πράξη ή παράλειψη τιμωρούνται με φυλάκιση τουλάχιστον δύο ετών και χρηματική ποινή.

2. Ο υποκινητής των πράξεων της προηγούμενης παραγράφου τιμωρείται με κάθειρξη έως δέκα έτη. Με την ίδια ποινή τιμωρείται ο υπαίτιος των πράξεων της προηγούμενης παραγράφου αν χρησιμοποίησε όπλο, καθώς και αν κάποιος από τα πρόσωπα κατά των οποίων στράφηκε η πράξη διέτρεξε σοβαρό προσωπικό κίνδυνο.

3. Η ποινή για τις πράξεις των προηγούμενων παραγράφων εκτίεται αθροιστικά με την ποινή που επιβλήθηκε ή που θα επιβληθεί για την πράξη για την οποία ήταν κρατούμενος ο υπαίτιος.

Άρθρο 175
Αντιποίηση

1. Όποιος με πρόθεση αντιποιείται την άσκηση κάποιας δημόσιας, δημοτικής ή κοινοτικής υπηρεσίας τιμωρείται με χρηματική ποινή ή παροχή κοινωφελούς εργασίας.

2. Η διάταξη αυτή εφαρμόζεται και για την αντιποίηση άσκησης υπηρεσίας λειτουργού της Ανατολικής Ορθόδοξης Εκκλησίας του Χριστού ή άλλης θρησκείας γνωστής στην Ελλάδα καθώς και για την αντιποίηση της άσκησης δικηγορίας.

3. Η αντιποίηση δικαστικής ή δικηγορικής ιδιότητας σε σχέση με ένδικη υπόθεση τιμωρείται με φυλάκιση έως ένα έτος ή χρηματική ποινή.

Άρθρο 176

(Καταργείται)

Άρθρο 177
Παραβίαση κατάσχεσης

Όποιος με πρόθεση καταστρέφει, βλάπτει ή υφαιρεί κατασχεμένο πράγμα τιμωρείται με φυλάκιση έως δύο έτη ή χρηματική ποινή.

Άρθρο 178
Παραβίαση σφραγίδων που έθεσε η αρχή

Όποιος με πρόθεση και αυθαίρετα θραύει ή βλάπτει σφραγίδα που έθεσε η αρχή για την κατάσχεση ή για τη φύλαξη κλεισμένων πραγμάτων ή εγγράφων ή για τη βεβαίωση της ταυτότητάς τους ή ματαιώνει με οποιονδήποτε τρόπο μια τέτοια σφράγιση τιμωρείται με φυλάκιση έως ένα έτος ή χρηματική ποινή.

Άρθρο 179
Παραβίαση φύλαξης της αρχής

Όποιος με πρόθεση καταστρέφει, βλάπτει ή με οποιονδήποτε τρόπο αφαιρεί από την εξουσία της αρχής έγγραφα ή άλλα πράγματα που βρίσκονται στη φύλαξή της ή που αυτή τα παρέδωσε στη φύλαξη άλλου τιμωρείται με φυλάκιση έως ένα έτος ή χρηματική ποινή.

Article 174
Riot by [prisoners/detainees]

1. Prisoners or other persons detained on the lawful orders of an authority who, acting in concert:

a) attempt to escape through use of violence;

b) physically assault prison or detention facility employees or those tasked with guarding or surveillance [of such persons];

c) attempt, through use of violence or threat, to force any of the aforesaid persons to carry out an act or omission,

shall be punished with imprisonment of at least two years and a monetary penalty.

2. Any person who incited the acts provided for in the preceding paragraph shall be punished with incarceration of up to 10 years. The same sentence shall be imposed on any person who committed the acts provided for in the preceding paragraph if they used a weapon and if any of the persons against whom the act was committed was placed in grave personal danger.

3. The sentence for the acts provided for in the preceding paragraphs shall be added to the [initial] sentence imposed [on a prisoner] or to be imposed [on a detainee].

Article 175
Impersonation

1. Any person who intentionally impersonates being a public, municipal, or community official shall be punished with a monetary penalty or community service.

2. This provision also applies to any person who impersonates being a minister of the Eastern Orthodox Church or any other religion known in Greece, as well as any person who impersonates being a lawyer.

3. [Any person] who impersonates being a judicial functionary or lawyer in relation to legal proceedings shall be punished with imprisonment of up to one year or a monetary penalty.

Article 176

[Repealed]

Article 177
Violation of seizure/attachment/arrest

Any person who intentionally destroys, damages or [deceptively conceals] a seized/attached/arrested thing shall be punished with imprisonment of up to two years or a monetary penalty.

Article 178
Tampering with seals affixed by an authority

Any person who intentionally and arbitrarily breaks or damages a seal affixed by an authority for the purpose of seizing or safekeeping sealed things or documents, or for verifying their identity, or bypasses such seal in any manner shall be punished with imprisonment of up to one year or a monetary penalty.

Article 179
Violation of an authority's custody

Any person who intentionally destroys, damages or in any manner removes from the control of an authority documents or other things which are in its custody or were delivered by said authority to the custody of another person shall be punished with imprisonment of up to one year or a monetary penalty.

Άρθρο 180

Βλάβη επίσημων κοινοποιήσεων

Όποιος με πρόθεση και αυθαίρετα αφαιρεί, βλάπτει ή παραμορφώνει τις επίσημες κοινοποιήσεις που η αρμόδια αρχή έχει δημόσια τοιχοκολλήσει ή εκθέσει, τιμωρείται με φυλάκιση έως ένα έτος ή με χρηματική ποινή.

Άρθρο 181

Μη ανακοίνωση ανεύρεσης νεκρού κ.λπ.

Όποιος δεν ανακοινώνει αμέσως στις αρχές την ανεύρεση νεκρού ή χωρίς την απαιτούμενη άδεια της αρχής ενταφιάζει ή με οποιονδήποτε τρόπο εξαφανίζει ή ανατέμνει νεκρό, καθώς και όποιος παραβαίνει τις διατάξεις που εκδίδει η αρμόδια αρχή για να αποτρέψει την πρόωρη ταφή, την εξαφάνιση ή την ανατομή νεκρού, τιμωρείται με φυλάκιση έως ένα έτος ή χρηματική ποινή.

Άρθρο 182

Παραβίαση περιορισμών διαμονής

1. Με φυλάκιση έως τριών (3) ετών τιμωρείται όποιος παραβιάζει τους περιορισμούς που του έχουν επιβληθεί νόμιμα στην ελευθερία της διαμονής και τις σχετικές υποχρεώσεις του.

2. Αλλοδαπός ο οποίος απελάθηκε σε εκτέλεση απόφασης δικαστηρίου, σύμφωνα με το άρθρο 72, αν παραβιάσει την απαγόρευση επιστροφής του στη χώρα, τιμωρείται με φυλάκιση τουλάχιστον δύο (2) ετών, η οποία εκτελείται αμέσως, δεν αναστέλλεται, ούτε μετατρέπεται σε καμία περίπτωση, τυχόν δε ασκηθείσα έφεση δεν έχει αναστέλλουσα δύναμη.

Άρθρο 182Α

(Καταργείται)

Article 180
Damage to official notices

Any person who intentionally and arbitrarily removes, damages or defaces official notices publicly posted or displayed by a competent authority shall be punished with imprisonment of up to one year or a monetary penalty.

Article 181
Failure to report the discovery of a dead body etc.

Any person who fails to immediately report the discovery of a dead body to the authorities or who, without the required permission from the [competent] authority, buries a dead body or causes such body to disappear in any manner or dissects such body, and any person who violates the orders issued by the competent authority to prevent premature burial, disappearance or dissection of a dead body shall be punished with imprisonment of up to one year or a monetary penalty.

Article 182
Violation of restrictions on residence

1. Any person who violates the restrictions lawfully imposed on their freedom [to choose their place of] residence and the relevant obligations [these entail] shall be punished with imprisonment of up to three years.

2. If any foreigner who was deported pursuant to a court judgment in accordance with Article 72 violates the ban on them returning to Greece, they shall be punished with imprisonment of at least two years, which shall be enforced immediately, shall not be subject to suspension or commutation under any circumstances, and any appeal filed shall not have a suspensive effect.

Article 182A

[Repealed]

ΕΚΤΟ ΚΕΦΑΛΑΙΟ

ΕΓΚΛΗΜΑΤΑ ΚΑΤΑ ΤΗΣ ΔΗΜΟΣΙΑΣ ΤΑΞΗΣ

Άρθρο 183
Διέγερση σε ανυπακοή

Όποιος δημόσια με οποιονδήποτε τρόπο ή μέσω του διαδικτύου προκαλεί ή διεγείρει σε απείθεια κατά των νόμων ή των διαταγμάτων ή εναντίον άλλων νόμιμων διαταγών της αρχής, τιμωρείται με φυλάκιση έως ένα έτος ή με χρηματική ποινή.

Άρθρο 184
Διέγερση σε διάπραξη εγκλημάτων, βιαιοπραγίες ή διχόνοια

1. Όποιος δημόσια με οποιονδήποτε τρόπο ή μέσω του διαδικτύου προκαλεί ή διεγείρει σε διάπραξη πλημμελήματος ή κακουργήματος και έτσι εκθέτει σε κίνδυνο τη δημόσια τάξη τιμωρείται με φυλάκιση έως ένα έτος ή με χρηματική ποινή.

2. Με φυλάκιση έως τρία έτη ή χρηματική ποινή τιμωρείται η πράξη της προηγούμενης παραγράφου αν με αυτήν επιχειρείται η τέλεση βιαιοπραγιών κατά ομάδας ή προσώπου που προσδιορίζεται με βάση τα χαρακτηριστικά της φυλής, το χρώμα, την εθνική ή εθνοτική καταγωγή, τις γενεαλογικές καταβολές, τη θρησκεία, την αναπηρία, το γενετήσιο προσανατολισμό, την ταυτότητα ή τα χαρακτηριστικά φύλου. Στην περίπτωση αυτή δεν εφαρμόζεται το άρθρο 82Α.

2Α. Όποιος με τη χρήση της τεχνολογίας των πληροφοριών και επικοινωνιών διαθέτει στο κοινό υλικό που περιέχει δεδομένα προσωπικού χαρακτήρα άλλου προσώπου, χωρίς τη συγκατάθεσή του, με σκοπό την υποκίνηση άλλων ατόμων να του προκαλέσουν σωματική ή ψυχολογική βλάβη τιμωρείται με ποινή φυλάκισης έως τριών (3) ετών, αν η πράξη δεν τιμωρείται βαρύτερα από άλλη διάταξη.

3. Με φυλάκιση τιμωρείται η πράξη των προηγούμενων παραγράφων αν είχε ως άμεσο επακόλουθο την τέλεση εγκλημάτων.

4. Με την ποινή της προηγούμενης παραγράφου τιμωρείται και όποιος δημόσια με οποιονδήποτε τρόπο ή μέσω του διαδικτύου προκαλεί ή διεγείρει τους πολίτες σε βιαιοπραγίες μεταξύ τους ή σε αμοιβαία διχόνοια με αποτέλεσμα να προκληθεί διατάραξη της κοινής ειρήνης κατά το άρθρο 189.

Άρθρο 185

(Καταργείται)

Άρθρο 186
Πρόκληση και προσφορά για την τέλεση εγκλήματος

1. Όποιος δίνει ή υπόσχεται αμοιβή σε άλλον για να τελέσει ορισμένο κακούργημα, καθώς και όποιος αποδέχεται αυτήν την προσφορά και αναλαμβάνει την τέλεσή του, τιμωρείται με φυλάκιση έως τρία (3) έτη και χρηματική ποινή, αν η πράξη δεν τιμωρείται βαρύτερα με άλλη διάταξη.

2. Όποιος δίνει ή υπόσχεται αμοιβή σε άλλον για να τελέσει ορισμένο πλημμέλημα, καθώς και όποιος αποδέχεται αυτήν την προσφορά και αναλαμβάνει την τέλεσή του, τιμωρείται με φυλάκιση έως δύο (2) έτη ή χρηματική ποινή, αν η πράξη δεν τιμωρείται βαρύτερα με άλλη διάταξη.

3. Οι πράξεις των παρ. 1 και 2 μπορεί να μείνουν ατιμώρητες αν ο υπαίτιος ανακάλεσε με δική του θέληση την προσφορά ή την αποδοχή της πριν από την έναρξη τέλεσης του εγκλήματος.

CHAPTER VI

CRIMES AGAINST PUBLIC ORDER

Article 183
Incitement to disobedience

Any person who publicly, in any manner or via the internet, causes or incites [others to] disobey the laws or decrees or other lawful orders issued by the authorities shall be punished with imprisonment of up to one year or a monetary penalty.

Article 184
Incitement to commit crimes or violence - Sowing of discord

1. Any person who publicly, in any manner or via the internet, causes or incites [others to] commit a misdemeanour or felony, thus placing public order at risk, shall be punished with imprisonment of up to one year or a monetary penalty.

2. The act provided for in the preceding paragraph shall be punished with imprisonment of up to three years or a monetary penalty if it aims at violence being perpetrated against a group or person on the basis of characteristics relating to their race, skin colour, national or ethnic origin, genealogical descent, religion, disability, sexual orientation, gender identity or sex characteristics. Article 82A does not apply in such a case.

2A. Any person who, through the use of information and communication technology, makes accessible to the public any material containing another's personal data without their consent for the purpose of inciting other persons to cause them physical or psychological harm shall be punished with imprisonment of up to three years, unless the act carries a heavier sentence under a different provision.

3. The act provided for in the preceding paragraphs shall be punished with imprisonment if it directly led to crimes being committed.

4. The sentence laid down in the preceding paragraph shall also be imposed on any person who publicly, in any manner or via the internet, causes or incites citizens to perpetrate violence against each other or sows discord between them leading to a breach of the public peace in accordance with Article 189.

Article 185

[Repealed]

Article 186
Inducement and offer to commit a crime

1. Any person who gives or promises a reward to another in exchange for committing a specific felony, and any person who accepts such offer and undertakes to commit [such felony] shall be punished with imprisonment of up to three years or a monetary penalty, unless the act carries a heavier punishment under a different provision.

2. Any person who gives or promises a reward to another in exchange for committing a specific misdemeanour, and any person who accepts such offer and undertakes to commit [such misdemeanour] shall be punished with imprisonment of up to two years or a monetary penalty, unless the act carries a heavier punishment under a different provision.

3. The [court may opt not to punish the] acts provided for in paragraphs 1 and 2 if the culpable person retracted the offer or acceptance of their own volition before the perpetrator began committing the crime.

4. Όταν οι πράξεις των παρ. 1 και 2 έχουν ως αποδέκτη ανήλικο, τιμωρούνται με ποινή φυλάκισης τουλάχιστον ενός (1) έτους και χρηματική ποινή στην περίπτωση κακουργήματος και με ποινή φυλάκισης και χρηματική ποινή στην περίπτωση πλημμελήματος, ανεξαρτήτως της παροχής ή υπόσχεσης αμοιβής.

Άρθρο 187
Εγκληματική οργάνωση

1. Όποιος συγκροτεί ή εντάσσεται ως μέλος σε επιχειρησιακά δομημένη και με διαρκή εγκληματική δράση οργάνωση τριών ή περισσότερων προσώπων, που επιδιώκει την τέλεση περισσότερων κακουργημάτων τιμωρείται με κάθειρξη έως δέκα έτη και χρηματική ποινή.

2. Αυτός που διευθύνει την εγκληματική οργάνωση τιμωρείται με κάθειρξη.

3. Όποιος, εκτός από την περίπτωση της πρώτης παραγράφου, οργανώνεται με άλλον ή άλλους για να διαπράξουν κακούργημα τιμωρείται με φυλάκιση τουλάχιστον έξι μηνών. Με φυλάκιση έως τρία έτη τιμωρείται ο υπαίτιος αν η κατά το προηγούμενο εδάφιο ένωση έγινε για τη διάπραξη πλημμελήματος με το οποίο επιδιώκεται οικονομικό ή άλλο υλικό όφελος ή η προσβολή της ζωής, της σωματικής ακεραιότητας, της ανηλικότητας, της προσωπικής ελευθερίας, της ιδιοκτησίας ή της περιουσίας.

4. Με φυλάκιση τουλάχιστον τριών ετών και χρηματική ποινή τιμωρείται όποιος με οποιονδήποτε τρόπο παρέχει σε άλλον κάθε είδους περιουσιακά στοιχεία, υλικά ή άυλα, κινητά ή ακίνητα ή κάθε είδους χρηματοοικονομικά μέσα ή οδηγίες, πληροφορίες ή κατευθύνσεις ή στρατολογεί νέα μέλη, γνωρίζοντας ότι με τον τρόπο αυτό διευκολύνει ή υποβοηθά την τέλεση των εγκληματικών δραστηριοτήτων της οργάνωσης της παραγράφου 1.

5.Οι διατάξεις των παραγράφων 1, 2 και 4 του παρόντος άρθρου εφαρμόζονται και όταν οι προβλεπόμενες σε αυτό αξιόποινες πράξεις τελέσθηκαν στην αλλοδαπή από ημεδαπό ή στρέφονταν κατά Έλληνα πολίτη ή κατά νομικού προσώπου που εδρεύει στην ημεδαπή ή κατά του Ελληνικού Κράτους, ακόμη και αν αυτές δεν είναι αξιόποινες κατά τους νόμους της χώρας στην οποία τελέσθηκαν.

6. Στις περιπτώσεις καταδίκης για αξιόποινες πράξεις του παρόντος άρθρου, καθώς και για τα συναφή αδικήματα που συνεκδικάστηκαν με την ίδια απόφαση, η ποινή δεν αναστέλλεται ούτε μετατρέπεται με κανέναν τρόπο, τυχόν ασκηθείσα έφεση δεν έχει ανασταλτική ισχύ, εκτός αν το δικαστήριο, σε περίπτωση καταδίκης για το πλημμέλημα της παρ. 3 και τα συναφή πλημμελήματα ή κακουργήματα τα οποία επισύρουν πρόσκαιρες στερητικές της ελευθερίας ποινές, κρίνει με ειδική αιτιολογία ότι πρέπει να χορηγηθεί η ανασταλτική δύναμη της έφεσης. Στην τελευταία περίπτωση επιβάλλονται υποχρεωτικά οι κατάλληλοι περιοριστικοί όροι.

Άρθρο 187Α
Τρομοκρατικές πράξεις – Τρομοκρατική οργάνωση

1. Όποιος τελεί κακούργημα ή οποιοδήποτε έγκλημα γενικής διακινδύνευσης ή έγκλημα κατά της δημόσιας τάξης υπό συνθήκες ή με τέτοιον τρόπο ή σε τέτοια έκταση που να προκαλεί σοβαρό κίνδυνο για τη χώρα ή για διεθνή οργανισμό και με σκοπό να εκφοβίσει σοβαρά έναν πληθυσμό ή να εξαναγκάσει παρανόμως δημόσια αρχή ή διεθνή οργανισμό να εκτελέσει οποιαδήποτε πράξη ή να απόσχει από αυτή ή να βλάψει σοβαρά ή να καταστρέψει τις θεμελιώδεις συνταγματικές, πολιτικές ή οικονομικές δομές μιας χώρας ή ενός διεθνούς οργανισμού τιμωρείται με την ποινή που προβλέπεται για το τελούμενο έγκλημα αυξημένη ως εξής:

4. Where the [reward] provided for in paragraph 1 and 2 [was given or promised to] a juvenile, they shall be punished with imprisonment of at least one year and a monetary penalty if they committed a felony, and imprisonment and a monetary penalty if they committed a misdemeanour, irrespective of whether the reward was given or promised.

Article 187
Criminal organisation

1. Any person who sets up or joins an operationally structured organisation consisting of three or more persons, engaging in continuous criminal activity and intending to commit further felonies, shall be punished with incarceration of up to 10 years and a monetary penalty.

2. The person directing the criminal organisation shall be punished with incarceration.

3. Except for the case referred to in paragraph 1 [of this Article], any person who joins forces with another person or persons in order to commit a felony shall be punished with imprisonment of at least six months. The culpable person shall be punished with imprisonment of up to three years if the [joining of forces] referred to in the preceding sentence took place in order to commit a misdemeanour aiming at financial or other material gain or an offence against life, physical integrity, juveniles, personal freedom, ownership or property.

4. Any person who, in any manner, provides another with any kind of assets, whether tangible or intangible, movable or immovable, or any kind of financial instruments, or instructions, information or guidance, or who recruits new members knowing that this facilitates or aids the commission of the criminal activities of the organisation provided for in paragraph 1 shall be punished with imprisonment of at least three years and a monetary penalty.

5.The provisions of paragraphs 1, 2 and 4 of this Article also apply where the punishable acts provided for above were committed abroad by or against a Greek citizen, or against a legal person seated in Greece, or against the Greek state, even if such acts are not punishable under the laws of the country where they were committed.

6. In cases of conviction of the punishable acts provided for in this Article and related offences [whose cases were] joined in the same judgment, the punishment shall neither be suspended nor commuted in any manner, and any appeal filed shall not have suspensive effect, unless the court, in the case of conviction for the misdemeanour provided for in paragraph 3 and related misdemeanours or felonies which carry fixed-term custodial sentences, rules, providing specific reasoning [in its judgment], that the appeal must be granted suspensive effect. In the latter case, suitable restrictive measures must necessarily be imposed.

Article 187A
Terrorist acts - Terrorist organisation

1. Any person who commits a felony or any crime of general endangerment, or a crime against public order, under conditions or in such a manner or to such an extent that could place Greece or an international organisation at serious risk, for the purpose of seriously intimidating a population, or unlawfully forcing a public authority or international organisation to carry out or refrain from carrying out any act, or seriously harming or destroying the fundamental constitutional, political or economic structures of a country or an international organisation, shall be punished with the punishment provided for the crime committed, augmented as follows:

α) Αν πρόκειται για ποινή ισόβιας κάθειρξης, προβλεπόμενης διαζευκτικά με ποινή κάθειρξης τουλάχιστον δέκα ετών, επιβάλλεται κάθειρξη ισόβια ή πρόσκαιρη τουλάχιστον δώδεκα ετών.

β) Αν πρόκειται για ποινή κάθειρξης τουλάχιστον δέκα ετών, επιβάλλεται κάθειρξη τουλάχιστον δώδεκα ετών.

γ) Αν πρόκειται για ποινή κάθειρξης, επιβάλλεται κάθειρξη τουλάχιστον επτά ετών.

δ) Αν πρόκειται για ποινή φυλάκισης, το κατώτατο όριο επαυξάνεται κατά ένα έτος.

2. Με κάθειρξη έως δέκα έτη τιμωρείται όποιος συγκροτεί ή εντάσσεται ως μέλος σε δομημένη και με διαρκή δράση ομάδα από τρία ή περισσότερα πρόσωπα που δρουν από κοινού και επιδιώκουν την τέλεση του εγκλήματος της παραγράφου 1 (τρομοκρατική οργάνωση). Με φυλάκιση τουλάχιστον ενός έτους τιμωρείται η πράξη του προηγούμενου εδαφίου, όταν η τρομοκρατική οργάνωση έχει συσταθεί για την τέλεση πλημμελημάτων της παραγράφου 1. Η κατασκευή, προμήθεια ή κατοχή όπλων, εκρηκτικών υλών και χημικών ή βιολογικών υλικών ή υλικών που εκπέμπουν επιβλαβείς για τον άνθρωπο ακτινοβολίες προς εξυπηρέτηση των σκοπών της τρομοκρατικής οργάνωσης συνιστά επιβαρυντική περίσταση. Η μη διάπραξη από την τρομοκρατική οργάνωση οποιουδήποτε από τα σχεδιαζόμενα εγκλήματα συνιστά ελαφρυντική περίσταση.

3. Αυτός που διευθύνει την τρομοκρατική οργάνωση του πρώτου εδαφίου της προηγούμενης παραγράφου τιμωρείται με κάθειρξη. Με την ποινή του προηγούμενου εδαφίου μειωμένη (άρθρο 83) τιμωρείται αυτός που διευθύνει την τρομοκρατική οργάνωση του δεύτερου εδαφίου της προηγούμενης παραγράφου.

4. Όποιος υποκινεί άλλον σε τέλεση ή συμβολή στην τέλεση ορισμένης τρομοκρατικής πράξης, ή σε συμμετοχή σε συγκεκριμένη τρομοκρατική οργάνωση, παρέχοντας σε αυτόν οδηγίες, πληροφορίες ή κατευθύνσεις (στρατολόγηση), τιμωρείται με φυλάκιση τουλάχιστον έξι (6) μηνών αν η προς εκτέλεση πράξη συνιστά κακούργημα και με φυλάκιση έως δύο (2) έτη, αν πρόκειται για πλημμέλημα.

5. Με τις ποινές της προηγούμενης παραγράφου τιμωρείται και όποιος, με οποιονδήποτε τρόπο, εκπαιδεύει άλλον στην κατασκευή ή χρήση εκρηκτικών, πυροβόλων ή άλλων όπλων, επιβλαβών ή επικίνδυνων ουσιών ή άλλων ειδικών μεθόδων ή τεχνικών, με σκοπό την τέλεση ή τη συμβολή στην τέλεση ενός από τα εγκλήματα της παραγράφου 1 και με επίγνωση του γεγονότος ότι η παρασχεθείσα τεχνογνωσία πρόκειται να χρησιμοποιηθεί για τον σκοπό αυτόν. Με την ίδια ποινή τιμωρείται και όποιος με τον ίδιο σκοπό λαμβάνει την εκπαίδευση, αν δεν τιμωρείται βαρύτερα με άλλη διάταξη.

6. Όποιος με οποιονδήποτε τρόπον ή μέσω του διαδικτύου απειλεί με τέλεση τρομοκρατικής πράξης ή προκαλεί ή διεγείρει σε διάπραξή της και έτσι εκθέτει σε κίνδυνο τη δημόσια τάξη τιμωρείται με φυλάκιση.

7. Με την ποινή της προηγούμενης παραγράφου τιμωρείται και όποιος με σκοπό να τελέσει ή να συμβάλει στην τέλεση τρομοκρατικού εγκλήματος, να συμμετάσχει στις δραστηριότητες τρομοκρατικής ομάδας, με επίγνωση του γεγονότος ότι η εν λόγω συμμετοχή θα συμβάλει στις εγκληματικές δραστηριότητες αυτής της ομάδας ή με σκοπό να προσφέρει ή να παρακολουθήσει εκπαίδευση για τέλεση τρομοκρατικών πράξεων, πραγματοποιεί ταξίδι το οποίο διευκολύνει την πραγμάτωση του σκοπού του.

a) incarceration for life or fixed-term incarceration of at least 12 years shall be imposed [where the act carries a sentence] of incarceration for life and there is a provision for an alternative sentence of incarceration of at least 10 years;
b) incarceration of at least 12 years shall be imposed [where the act carries a sentence] of incarceration of at least 10 years;
c) incarceration of at least seven years shall be imposed [where the act carries a sentence] of incarceration; [and]
d) the minimum limit shall be augmented by one year [where the act carries a sentence] of imprisonment.

2. Any person who sets up or joins a structured organisation consisting of three or more persons acting in concert, engaging in continuous activity and intending to commit the crime provided for in paragraph 1 (terrorist organisation) shall be punished with incarceration of up to 10 years. Where the terrorist organisation has been formed in order to commit a misdemeanour provided for in paragraph 1, the act provided for in the preceding sentence shall be punished with imprisonment of at least one year. The manufacture, supply or possession of weapons, explosives and chemical or biological agents or materials emitting radiation harmful to humans to serve the purposes of the terrorist organisation constitute aggravating circumstances. The fact that the terrorist organisation did not commit any of the crimes it had planned constitutes a mitigating circumstance.

3. The person directing the terrorist organisation provided for in the first sentence of the preceding paragraph shall be punished with incarceration. The person directing the terrorist organisation provided for in the second sentence of the preceding paragraph shall be punished with the punishment laid down in the preceding sentence but reduced ([see] Article 83).

4. Any person who solicits another to commit or contribute to committing a specific terrorist act, or to participate in a specific terrorist organisation and provides them with instructions, information or guidance (recruitment) shall be punished with imprisonment of at least six months if the act to be committed is classified as a felony, and imprisonment of up to two years if [the act to be committed is classified as] a misdemeanour.

5. The sentences provided for in the preceding paragraph shall also be imposed on any person who, in any manner, trains another in the making or use of explosives, firearms or other weapons or noxious or hazardous substances, or in other specific methods or techniques, for the purpose of committing one of the crimes provided for in paragraph 1, knowing that the skills provided are intended to be used for this purpose. The same sentence shall also be imposed on any person who receives such training for the same purpose, unless [receiving such training] carries a heavier sentence under a different provision.

6. Any person who, in any manner or via the internet, threatens to commit a terrorist act or induces or incites the commission of such act, thus placing public order at risk, shall be punished with imprisonment.

7. The sentence laid down in the preceding paragraph shall also be imposed on any person who, for the purpose of committing or contributing to committing a terrorist crime, participating in the activities of a terrorist group while knowing that such participation will contribute to the criminal activities of such group, or for the purpose of offering or participating in training to commit terrorist acts, carries out a journey which facilitates the achievement of such purpose.

Άρθρο 187Β

Αξιόποινη υποστήριξη

1. Όποιος παρέχει κάθε είδους περιουσιακά στοιχεία, υλικά ή άυλα, κινητά ή ακίνητα ή κάθε είδους χρηματοοικονομικά μέσα, ανεξάρτητα από τον τρόπο κτήσης τους, σε τρομοκρατική οργάνωση ή σε μεμονωμένο τρομοκράτη ή για τη συγκρότηση τρομοκρατικής οργάνωσης ή για να καταστεί κάποιος τρομοκράτης ή τα εισπράττει, συλλέγει ή διαχειρίζεται χάριν των ανωτέρω, ανεξάρτητα από τη διάπραξη οποιουδήποτε εγκλήματος, τιμωρείται με κάθειρξη έως δέκα (10) έτη. Με φυλάκιση τουλάχιστον ενός έτους τιμωρείται η πράξη του προηγούμενου εδαφίου, όταν η τρομοκρατική οργάνωση έχει συσταθεί ή σκοπείται να συσταθεί μόνο για την τέλεση πλημμελημάτων. Το ίδιο ισχύει όταν ο μεμονωμένος τρομοκράτης τελεί ή σκοπεί να τελέσει μόνο πλημμελήματα.

2. Με φυλάκιση τουλάχιστον έξι (6) μηνών τιμωρείται και όποιος, εν γνώσει της μελλοντικής αξιοποίησής τους, παρέχει ουσιώδεις πληροφορίες για να διευκολύνει ή να υποβοηθήσει την τέλεση από τρομοκρατική οργάνωση ή από μεμονωμένο τρομοκράτη οποιουδήποτε κακουργήματος.

3. Με κάθειρξη ως δέκα (10) έτη τιμωρείται όποιος, με απειλή ή χρήση βίας κατά δικαστικών λειτουργών, ενόρκων, ανακριτικών ή δικαστικών υπαλλήλων, μαρτύρων, πραγματογνωμόνων ή διερμηνέων, ή με δωροδοκία των ίδιων προσώπων, ματαιώνει την αποκάλυψη, τη δίωξη ή την τιμωρία των εγκλημάτων των άρθρων 187 παρ. 1 και 187Α, καθώς και των κακουργημάτων που τελέστηκαν από εγκληματικές ή τρομοκρατικές οργανώσεις, εφόσον η πράξη δεν τιμωρείται βαρύτερα κατ' άλλη διάταξη.

4. Κατά την επιμέτρηση της ποινής των εγκλημάτων της παρ. 1 λαμβάνονται υπόψη ως επιβαρυντικές περιστάσεις οι αμετάκλητες καταδικαστικές αποφάσεις που εκδίδουν δικαστήρια άλλων κρατών μερών της Σύμβασης της Βαρσοβίας της 16ης Μαΐου 2005 του Συμβουλίου της Ευρώπης για τη νομιμοποίηση, ανίχνευση, κατάσχεση και δήμευση εσόδων από εγκληματικές δραστηριότητες και για τη χρηματοδότηση της τρομοκρατίας.

Άρθρο 187Γ

Ευνοϊκά μέτρα

1. Αν κάποιος από τους υπαιτίους των πράξεων των παρ. 1 έως 3 του άρθρου 187 ή των παραγράφων 2 έως 4 του άρθρου 187Α καταστήσει δυνατή με αναγγελία στην αρχή την πρόληψη της διάπραξης ενός από τα σχεδιαζόμενα εγκλήματα, ή με τον ίδιο τρόπο συμβάλλει ουσιωδώς στην εξάρθρωση της οργάνωσης ή στην πλήρη εξιχνίαση εγκλήματος της οργάνωσης που τελέστηκε από άλλον, απαλλάσσεται από την ποινή για τις πράξεις αυτές. Αν δεν έχει ακόμη ασκηθεί ποινική δίωξη, ο εισαγγελέας πλημμελειοδικών με αιτιολογημένη διάταξή του απέχει από την άσκησή της και υποβάλλει τη δικογραφία στον εισαγγελέα εφετών, ο οποίος ενεργεί σύμφωνα με το δεύτερο εδάφιο της παρ. 4 του άρθρου 43 του Κώδικα Ποινικής Δικονομίας. Η ως άνω διάταξη μαζί με τη σύμφωνη γνώμη κοινοποιείται στον Εισαγγελέα, που εποπτεύει τη Διεύθυνση Αντιμετώπισης Οργανωμένου Εγκλήματος και τη Διεύθυνση Αντιμετώπισης Ειδικών Εγκλημάτων Βίας της Ελληνικής Αστυνομίας, για την ενημέρωσή του.

Article 187B
Punishable [forms of] support

1. Any person who provides any kind of assets, whether tangible or intangible, movable or immovable, or any kind of financial means, irrespective of how such were acquired, to a terrorist organisation or an individual terrorist, or for the purpose of setting up a terrorist organisation, or in order for another to become a terrorist, or who [takes receipt of, collects and organises] or manages [such] on behalf of the foregoing persons, irrespective of whether or not any crime was committed, shall be punished with incarceration of up to 10 years. Where a terrorist organisation has been or is intended to be formed only in order to commit misdemeanours, the act provided for in the preceding subparagraph shall be punished with imprisonment of at least one year. The same applies where an individual terrorist commits or intends to commit only misdemeanours.

2. Any person who provides material information in order to facilitate or aid the commission of any felony by a terrorist organisation or an individual terrorist and knowing that [such information] will be used in the future shall also be punished with imprisonment of at least six months.

3. Any person who, through threat or use of violence against judicial functionaries, jurors, investigating or judicial officers, witnesses, experts or interpreters, or through active bribery of the aforesaid persons, [prevents] the uncovering, prosecution or punishment of the crimes provided for in Articles 187(1) and 187A, as well as felonies committed by criminal or terrorist organisations, shall be punished with incarceration of up to 10 years, unless the act carries a heavier sentence under a different provision.

4. In determining the length of the sentence for the crimes provided for in paragraph 1, [any] irrevocable judgments of conviction handed down by courts of other States Parties to the Council of Europe Convention on Laundering, Search, Seizure and Confiscation of the Proceeds from Crime and on the Financing of Terrorism of 16 May 2005 (Warsaw Convention) shall be taken into consideration as aggravating circumstances.

Article 187C
Measures of [leniency]

1. If any of the persons who committed the acts provided for in Article 187(1) to (3) or Article 187A(2) to (4) notifies the authorities and enables them to prevent any of the crimes planned from being committed, or materially contributes in the same manner to dismantling the organisation or fully solving a crime of such organisation committed by another shall be exempt from the punishment for such acts. If criminal prosecution has not yet been initiated, the court of misdemeanours public prosecutor shall issue a reasoned decree not to prosecute, and shall submit the case-file to the court of appeal public prosecutor, who shall take the steps set out in the second sentence of Article 43(4) of the Code of Criminal Procedure. The aforesaid decree, together with the assent [of the court of appeal public prosecutor], shall be notified to the public prosecutor supervising the Organised Crime Directorate and the Special Violent Crime Squad of the Hellenic Police for briefing purposes.

2. Αν στην περίπτωση της παρ. 1 ο υπαίτιος έχει τελέσει κάποιο από τα επιδιωκόμενα εγκλήματα ή έχει τελέσει κάποιο από τα εγκλήματα της παρ. 1 του άρθρου 187Α, το δικαστήριο του επιβάλλει μειωμένη ποινή (άρθρο 83). Το δικαστήριο μπορεί να διατάξει την αναστολή αυτής της ποινής, εκτιμώντας ιδίως την έκταση της συμμετοχής του υπαιτίου στην οργάνωση και τον βαθμό της συμβολής του στην εξάρθρωσή της ή την πλήρη εξιχνίαση του ιδίου ή άλλου εγκλήματός της.

3. Για όποιον καταγγέλλει αξιόποινες πράξεις που τελέστηκαν σε βάρος του από εγκληματική οργάνωση, ο εισαγγελέας πλημμελειοδικών μπορεί, εφόσον η καταγγελία πιθανολογείται βάσιμη, ύστερα από έγκριση του εισαγγελέα εφετών, να απόσχει προσωρινά από την ποινική δίωξη για παραβάσεις του νόμου περί αλλοδαπών και περί εκδιδομένων με αμοιβή προσώπων, ώσπου να εκδοθεί αμετάκλητη απόφαση για τις πράξεις που καταγγέλθηκαν. Αν η κατηγορία αποδειχθεί βάσιμη, η αποχή από την ποινική δίωξη γίνεται οριστική.

4. Η απέλαση αλλοδαπών που βρίσκονται παράνομα στη χώρα και καταγγέλλουν αξιόποινες πράξεις που τελέσθηκαν από εγκληματική ή τρομοκρατική οργάνωση αναστέλλεται μέχρι να εκδοθεί αμετάκλητη απόφαση για τις πράξεις που καταγγέλθηκαν. Όσο χρόνο διαρκεί η αναστολή της απέλασης χορηγείται στους αλλοδαπούς άδεια παραμονής κατά παρέκκλιση από την ισχύουσα νομοθεσία περί αλλοδαπών.

5. Με την επιφύλαξη ειδικότερων διατάξεων, αν ο υπαίτιος πλημμελήματος ή κακουργήματος που τιμωρείται με ποινή πρόσκαιρης κάθειρξης πλην εκείνων που προβλέπονται στις διατάξεις του 19ου Κεφαλαίου του Ειδικού Μέρους του Ποινικού Κώδικα, πριν από την αμετάκλητη καταδίκη του και με δική του πρωτοβουλία συντελέσει ουσιωδώς, με την παροχή πληροφοριών, στην εξάρθρωση εγκληματικής ή τρομοκρατικής οργάνωσης ή την πλήρη εξιχνίαση κακουργήματος των άρθρων 187 και 187Α του Ποινικού Κώδικα, ή την πλήρη εξιχνίαση εγκλήματός της ή οποιουδήποτε άλλου κακουργήματος, ή την ανακάλυψη και σύλληψη δράστη τους, το δικαστήριο του επιβάλλει μειωμένη ποινή (άρθρο 83) εφόσον η βαρύτητα της πράξης του και ο βαθμός ενοχής του είναι προδήλως υποδεέστερα σε σύγκριση με τη βαρύτητα των πράξεων και τον βαθμό ενοχής των δραστών, που αφορούσαν οι πληροφορίες. Σε εξαιρετικές περιπτώσεις και αν η πράξη του υπαιτίου αφορά πλημμέλημα, το δικαστήριο μπορεί να τον απαλλάξει από τη ποινή. Επιπλέον, μπορεί να διατάξει τη μερική ή την πλήρη αναστολή της ποινής φυλάκισης, που του επιβλήθηκε, ή την έκτισή της στην κατοικία του ή τη μετατροπή της σε χρηματική ή σε κοινωφελή εργασία, ανεξάρτητα από τη συνδρομή των όρων που προβλέπονται στα άρθρα 82Α, 99, 104Α και 105. Αν οι ανωτέρω όροι συντρέξουν μετά την αμετάκλητη καταδίκη του υπαιτίου, το αρμόδιο συμβούλιο μπορεί να διατάξει την απόλυσή του από τις φυλακές υπό όρο, ανεξάρτητα από τη συνδρομή των προϋποθέσεων που προβλέπονται στο άρθρο 105Β.

6. Αν για την εξάρθρωση εγκληματικής ή τρομοκρατικής οργάνωσης ή την πλήρη εξιχνίαση κακουργήματος των άρθρων 187 και 187Α του Ποινικού Κώδικα, ή την πλήρη εξιχνίαση εγκλήματός της ή οιουδήποτε άλλου κακουργήματος, ή την ανακάλυψη και σύλληψη δράστη τους, είναι αναγκαία η προσωρινή αποφυλάκιση του ανωτέρω υπαιτίου, το αρμόδιο Συμβούλιο μπορεί, ύστερα από κατά περίπτωση αίτηση της Διεύθυνσης Αντιμετώπισης Οργανωμένου Εγκλήματος ή της Διεύθυνσης Αντιμετώπισης Ειδικών Εγκλημάτων Βίας της Ελληνικής Αστυνομίας και πρόταση του οικείου Εισαγγελέα, να διατάξει την προσωρινή, για ορισμένο χρόνο απόλυσή του από τη φυλακή, εφόσον τούτη κρίνεται αναγκαία για την επαλήθευση της πληροφορίας. Μετά την πάροδο του ορισθέντος χρόνου συνεχίζεται η φυλάκιση του υπαιτίου.

2. Where, in the case of paragraph 1, the culpable person has committed any of the intended crimes or has committed any of the crimes provided for in Article 187A(1), the court may impose on them a reduced sentence ([in accordance with] Article 83). The court may order that such sentence be suspended, taking into consideration, in particular, the extent of the culpable person's participation in the organisation and the extent to which they contributed to dismantling it or to fully solving the same or another crime of such organisation.
3. With regard to any person who reports punishable acts committed against them by a criminal organisation, the court of misdemeanours public prosecutor may, if the report is considered likely on the balance of probabilities and following approval from the court of appeal public prosecutor, temporarily refrain from initiating criminal prosecution for violation of the law concerning foreign nationals and sex work until an irrevocable judgment has been handed down on the reported acts. If the report proves to be well-founded, the decision to refrain from prosecution shall become final.
4. Deportation of foreign nationals who are in Greece unlawfully and who report punishable acts committed by a criminal or terrorist organisation shall be suspended until an irrevocable judgment has been handed down on the reported acts. While such deportation is suspended, the foreign nationals [in question] shall be issued a residence permit by way of derogation from the applicable legislation on foreign nationals.
5. Without prejudice to any more specific provisions, where the person culpable of a misdemeanour or felony punishable by fixed-term incarceration, except for those provided for in the provisions of Chapter XIX of the Special Part of the Penal Code, materially contributes, prior to their irrevocable conviction and on their own initiative, by providing information, to dismantling a criminal or terrorist organisation or to fully solving a felony provided for in Articles 187 and 187A of the Penal Code, or to fully solving a crime of such organisation or any other felony, or to the discovery and arrest of the perpetrator of such crimes, the court shall impose on them a reduced sentence ([in accordance with] Article 83) provided the seriousness of their act and their degree of guilt is clearly lesser compared to the seriousness of the acts and the degree of guilt of the perpetrators whom the information concerned. In exceptional cases, if the culpable person›s act [is] a misdemeanour, the court may opt not to punish them. In addition, [the court] may order partial or full suspension of the sentence of imprisonment imposed on them, or order that they serve their sentence at home, or that it be converted to a monetary penalty or community service, irrespective of whether the conditions laid down in Articles 82A, 99, 104A and 105 are met. Where those conditions are met after the culpable person has been irrevocably convicted, the competent [judicial] council may order their conditional release from prison, irrespective of whether the conditions laid down in Article 105B are met.
6. If, in order to dismantle a criminal or terrorist organisation, or to fully solve a felony provided for in Articles 187 and 187A of the Penal Code, or to fully solve a crime of such organisation, or any other felony, or to discover and arrest the perpetrator of such crimes, temporary release of the said culpable person is necessary, the competent [judicial] council may, following a request from the Organised Crime Directorate or the Special Violent Crime Squad of the Hellenic Police, as appropriate, and a proposal from the competent public prosecutor, order their temporary release from prison for a specific period of time, where that is considered necessary for the information to be verified. After the specific period of time has elapsed, the culpable person›s imprisonment shall continue.

7. Για την αναγγελία που προβλέπεται στις παραγράφους 1 και 2 και την παροχή πληροφοριών που ορίζεται στην παρ. 5 του άρθρου 187Γ, συντάσσεται έκθεση από ανακριτικούς υπαλλήλους της Διεύθυνσης Αντιμετώπισης Οργανωμένου Εγκλήματος ή της Διεύθυνσης Αντιμετώπισης Ειδικών Εγκλημάτων Βίας της Ελληνικής Αστυνομίας, κατά περίπτωση, η οποία υπογράφεται από τον δηλούντα και υποβάλλεται στον Εισαγγελέα που εποπτεύει την εν λόγω διεύθυνση, ο οποίος την τηρεί σε ειδικό, απόρρητο αρχείο και αναθέτει στην αρμόδια διεύθυνση τη διακρίβωση της βασιμότητας των ισχυρισμών του. Η αναφορά της διεύθυνσης με τα αποτελέσματα της έρευνας συσχετίζεται με την έκθεση και υποβάλλονται μαζί στο Δικαστήριο, που δικάζει το κακούργημα ή το πλημμέλημα εκείνου που παρείχε τις πληροφορίες, κατόπιν αιτήσεώς του. Το δικάζον Δικαστήριο λαμβάνει γνώση των ανωτέρω εγγράφων και συνεδριάζει σε Συμβούλιο προκειμένου να αποφανθεί για τη χορήγηση ή μη των ανωτέρω ευεργετημάτων. Στην αιτιολογία της απόφασης γίνεται μνεία μόνο του διαβιβαστικού εγγράφου του ως άνω Εισαγγελέα και της νομικής βάσης της χορήγησης ή μη του ευεργετήματος χωρίς αναφορά σε συγκεκριμένα πραγματικά περιστατικά.

Άρθρο 188

(Καταργείται)

Άρθρο 189
Διατάραξη της κοινής ειρήνης

1. Όποιος συμμετέχει σε συγκεντρωμένο πλήθος που με ενωμένες δυνάμεις διαπράττει βιαιοπραγίες εναντίον προσώπων ή πραγμάτων ή εισβάλλει παράνομα σε ξένα σπίτια, καταστήματα ή άλλα ακίνητα κτήματα, τιμωρείται με φυλάκιση έως τρία έτη ή χρηματική ποινή.

2. Αν οι πιο πάνω πράξεις, καθώς και πράξεις φθοράς ξένης ιδιοκτησίας, γίνονται με σκοπό να παρεμποδίσουν την έκδοση και την ελεύθερη κυκλοφορία εφημερίδων, περιοδικών ή βιβλίων, επιβάλλεται φυλάκιση τουλάχιστον τριών μηνών.

3. Οι υποκινητές της διατάραξης που έχουν καθοδηγητικό ρόλο μέσα στο πλήθος τιμωρούνται με φυλάκιση τουλάχιστον τριών μηνών. Με την ίδια ποινή τιμωρούνται και εκείνοι που τέλεσαν βιαιοπραγίες κατά τη διατάραξη.

4. Όποιος, χωρίς να διαταράσσει την κοινή ειρήνη, εμποδίζει αυθαίρετα ή διαταράσσει σοβαρά μια νόμιμη συλλογική εκδήλωση με σκοπό τη ματαίωσή της, τιμωρείται με φυλάκιση έως δύο έτη ή χρηματική ποινή.

Άρθρο 190
Απειλή διάπραξης εγκλημάτων

Όποιος δημόσια με οποιονδήποτε τρόπο ή μέσω του διαδικτύου απειλεί ότι θα διαπραχθούν εγκλήματα και δημιουργεί έτσι φόβο σε αόριστο αριθμό ανθρώπων ή σε ορισμένο κύκλο ή κατηγορία προσώπων, τιμωρείται με φυλάκιση έως δύο έτη ή με χρηματική ποινή.

7. As regards the notification provided for in paragraphs 1 and 2 and the provision of information provided for in Article 187C(5), a report shall be prepared by the investigating officers from the Organised Crime Directorate or the Special Violent Crime Squad of the Hellenic Police, as appropriate, which shall be signed by the [informant] and submitted to the public prosecutor supervising the Directorate/Squad, who shall keep such report in a special, confidential file and task the competent Directorate/Square with ascertaining whether their assertions are well-founded. The document prepared by the Directorate/ Squad containing the results of the inquiries shall be compared to the report, and they shall be submitted together to the court trying the felony or misdemeanour committed by the [informant], at their request. The trial court shall take cognisance of the said documents and shall meet in council to rule on whether or not to grant the said benefits. The reasoning of the judgment shall make reference only to the cover letter from said public prosecutor and the legal basis on which the benefit was or was not granted, without making reference to specific actual facts.

Article 188

[Repealed]

Article 189

Breach of the public peace

1. Any person who participates in an assembly of people who, acting in concert, perpetrate violence against persons or things or unlawfully intrude into the residences, shops or other immovable properties of others shall be punished with imprisonment of up to three years or a monetary penalty.

2. If the above acts, as well as acts of damage to another's property, take place for the purpose of obstructing the publication and free circulation of newspapers, periodicals or books, imprisonment of at least three months shall be imposed.

3. Any person who incited such breach [of the public peace] and played a leading part in the assembly shall be punished with imprisonment of at least three months. The same sentence shall also be imposed on those who perpetrated violence during such breach [of the public peace].

4. Any person who, without breaching the public peace, arbitrarily obstructs or seriously disrupts a lawful assembly for the purpose of preventing it from going ahead shall be punished with imprisonment of up to two years or a monetary penalty.

Article 190

Threat to commit crimes

Any person who publicly, in any manner or via the internet, threatens that crimes will be committed and thus provokes fear in an indeterminate number of persons or a specific group or category of persons shall be punished with imprisonment of up to two years or a monetary penalty.

Άρθρο 191

Διασπορά ψευδών ειδήσεων

Όποιος δημόσια ή μέσω του διαδικτύου διαδίδει ή διασπείρει με οποιονδήποτε τρόπο ψευδείς ειδήσεις με αποτέλεσμα να προκαλέσει φόβο σε αόριστο αριθμό ανθρώπων ή σε ορισμένο κύκλο ή κατηγορία προσώπων που αναγκάζονται έτσι να προβούν σε μη προγραμματισμένες πράξεις ή σε ματαίωσή τους, με κίνδυνο να προκληθεί ζημία στην οικονομία, στην αμυντική ικανότητα της χώρας ή στη δημόσια υγεία τιμωρείται με φυλάκιση έως τρία (3) έτη ή με χρηματική ποινή. Με την ίδια ποινή τιμωρείται και ο πραγματικός ιδιοκτήτης ή εκδότης του μέσου με το οποίο τελέστηκαν οι πράξεις του παρόντος.

Άρθρο 191Α

Προσβολή συμβόλων ή τόπων ιδιαίτερης εθνικής ή θρησκευτικής σημασίας

1. Όποιος δημόσια αφαιρεί, καταστρέφει, παραμορφώνει ή ρυπαίνει την επίσημη σημαία του κράτους ή έμβλημα της κυριαρχίας του ή ηχητικά παρεμποδίζει τη δημόσια ανάκρουση του εθνικού ύμνου, και έτσι εκθέτει σε κίνδυνο τη δημόσια τάξη, τιμωρείται με φυλάκιση έως δύο έτη ή χρηματική ποινή.

2. Με την ίδια ποινή τιμωρείται όποιος τελεί πράξεις ρύπανσης ή φθοράς σε τόπους ιδιαίτερης εθνικής ή θρησκευτικής σημασίας καθώς και σε χώρους φύλαξης νεκρών ή νεκροταφεία και προκαλεί έτσι φόβο ή ανησυχία σε αόριστο αριθμό ανθρώπων, εφόσον η πράξη δεν τιμωρείται βαρύτερα με άλλη διάταξη.

Άρθρα 192 - 197

(Καταργούνται)

ΕΒΔΟΜΟ ΚΕΦΑΛΑΙΟ

ΕΠΙΒΟΥΛΗ ΤΗΣ ΘΡΗΣΚΕΥΤΙΚΗΣ ΕΙΡΗΝΗΣ

Άρθρα 198 - 199

(Καταργούνται)

Άρθρο 200

Διατάραξη θρησκευτικών συναθροίσεων

1. Όποιος κακόβουλα προσπαθεί να εμποδίσει ή με πρόθεση διαταράσσει μια ανεκτή κατά το πολίτευμα θρησκευτική συνάθροιση για λατρεία ή τελετή, τιμωρείται με φυλάκιση έως δύο έτη.

2. Με την ίδια ποινή τιμωρείται όποιος μέσα σε εκκλησία ή σε τόπο ορισμένο για θρησκευτική συνάθροιση ανεκτή κατά το πολίτευμα ενεργεί υβριστικά ανάρμοστες πράξεις.

Άρθρο 201

(Καταργείται)

ΟΓΔΟΟ ΚΕΦΑΛΑΙΟ

Άρθρα 202 - 206

(Καταργούνται)

Article 191
Spreading of false news

Any person who publicly or via the internet spreads or disseminates false news in any manner and, as a result, provokes fear in an indeterminate number of persons or a specific group or category of persons who are thus forced to take unscheduled steps or cancel [scheduled] steps, with a risk of damaging the economy, the defence capabilities of Greece or public health shall be punished with imprisonment of up to three years or a monetary penalty. The same punishment shall be imposed on the actual owner or publisher of the means used to commit the acts provided for in this [Article].

Article 191A
Desecration of symbols or sites of particular national or religious importance

1. Any person who publicly removes, destroys, disfigures or sullies the official flag of [Greece] or an emblem of its sovereignty or uses sound to hinder the playing of the [Greek] national anthem, thus placing public order at risk, shall be punished with imprisonment of up to two years or a monetary penalty.
2. The same penalty shall be imposed on any person who commits sullying or damaging acts at places of particular national or religious importance and [places intended for the safekeeping of deceased persons] or cemeteries, thus provoking fear or discomfort in an indeterminate number of persons, provided the act does not carry a heavier punishment under a different provision.

Articles 192 - 197

[Repealed]

CHAPTER VII

VIOLATION OF THE RELIGIOUS PEACE

Articles 198 - 199

[Repealed]

Article 200
Disruption of religious gatherings

1. Any person who maliciously attempts to obstruct or intentionally disrupts a religious gathering [of a religion which is accepted by the system of government] being held for the purpose of worship or ceremony shall be punished with imprisonment of up to two years.
2. The same sentence shall be imposed on any person who commits inappropriate acts in an insulting manner in a church or place intended for religious gatherings.

Article 201

[Repealed]

CHAPTER VIII

Articles 202 - 206

[Repealed]

ΕΝΑΤΟ ΚΕΦΑΛΑΙΟ

ΕΓΚΛΗΜΑΤΑ ΣΧΕΤΙΚΑ ΜΕ ΤΟ ΝΟΜΙΣΜΑ, ΑΛΛΑ ΜΕΣΑ ΠΛΗΡΩΜΗΣ ΚΑΙ ΕΝΣΗΜΑ

Άρθρο 207

Παραχάραξη νομίσματος και άλλων υλικών μέσων πληρωμής

1. Όποιος παραποιεί ή νοθεύει νόμισμα οποιουδήποτε κράτους ή εκδοτικής αρχής, είτε κατά είτε πριν από το χρόνο νόμιμης κυκλοφορίας του είτε κατά το διάστημα κατά το οποίο γίνεται δεκτό προς ανταλλαγή από τους αρμόδιους φορείς, με σκοπό να το θέσει σε κυκλοφορία σαν γνήσιο, ή κατέχει πλαστό νόμισμα με τον ίδιο σκοπό, τιμωρείται με κάθειρξη έως δέκα (10) έτη και χρηματική ποινή.

2. Με την ίδια ποινή τιμωρείται και όποιος, με τον ίδιο σκοπό, παραποιεί ή νοθεύει κάθε άλλο υλικό μέσο πληρωμής, εκτός από το νόμισμα, όπως πιστωτικές κάρτες, χρεωστικές κάρτες και λοιπές κάρτες που εκδίδονται από χρηματοπιστωτικά ιδρύματα, ταξιδιωτικές επιταγές, λοιπές επιταγές και συναλλαγματικές.

2Α. Με ποινή φυλάκισης και χρηματική ποινή τιμωρείται όποιος, με τον ίδιο σκοπό, προμηθεύεται ή κατέχει το παραποιημένο ή νοθευμένο υλικό μέσο της παρ. 2.

3. Σε ιδιαίτερα ελαφρές περιπτώσεις μικρού αριθμού πλαστών ή μικρής φερόμενης αξίας τους, οι πράξεις των παρ. 1 και 2 τιμωρούνται με φυλάκιση έως τρία (3) έτη και οι πράξεις της παρ. 2Α με ποινή φυλάκισης έως ένα (1) έτος.

Άρθρο 208

1. Όποιος, εν γνώσει της πλαστότητας, θέτει σε κυκλοφορία σαν γνήσιο πλαστό νόμισμα οποιουδήποτε κράτους ή εκδοτικής αρχής, είτε κατά είτε πριν από τον χρόνο νόμιμης κυκλοφορίας του είτε κατά το διάστημα κατά το οποίο γίνεται δεκτό προς ανταλλαγή από τους αρμόδιους φορείς ή άλλο μέσο πληρωμής, τιμωρείται με κάθειρξη έως δέκα (10) έτη και χρηματική ποινή. Σε ιδιαίτερα ελαφρές περιπτώσεις μικρού αριθμού πλαστών ή μικρής φερόμενης αξίας τους επιβάλλεται φυλάκιση έως δύο (2) έτη.

2. Αν ο υπαίτιος ή αντιπρόσωπός του είχε δεχτεί το πλαστό νόμισμα ή άλλο μέσο πληρωμής σαν γνήσιο, επιβάλλεται φυλάκιση έως έξι (6) μήνες ή χρηματική ποινή. Η ίδια ποινή επιβάλλεται, αν ο υπαίτιος ενήργησε εκτελώντας εντολή εκείνου στον οποίο δόθηκε το νόμισμα ή άλλο μέσο πληρωμής σαν γνήσιο, όταν βρίσκεται σε σχέση εξάρτησης με τον εντολέα ή ζει μαζί του στην ίδια κατοικία.

Άρθρο 208Α

Καθ' υπέρβαση κατασκευή νομίσματος

Με τις ποινές της παραγράφου 1 εδάφια α΄ και β΄ του προηγούμενου άρθρου τιμωρείται και όποιος με πρόθεση κατασκευάζει, προμηθεύεται, κατέχει ή θέτει σε κυκλοφορία νόμισμα είτε κατά είτε πριν από το χρόνο νόμιμης κυκλοφορίας του είτε κατά το διάστημα κατά το οποίο γίνεται δεκτό προς ανταλλαγή από τους αρμόδιους φορείς και για την κατασκευή του οποίου έχουν χρησιμοποιηθεί νόμιμες εγκαταστάσεις και υλικά, χωρίς όμως την άδεια της αρμόδιας αρχής ή καθ' υπέρβαση του σχετικού δικαιώματος.

CHAPTER IX

CRIMES CONCERNING CURRENCY, OTHER PAYMENT INSTRUMENTS AND STAMPS

Article 207

Counterfeiting currency and other tangible payment instruments

1. Any person who forges or alters the currency of any state or issuing authority, whether after or before such currency is placed in lawful circulation or at the time it is accepted for exchange by the competent institutions, for the purpose of placing it in circulation as genuine, or who possesses counterfeit currency for the same purpose, shall be punished with incarceration of up to 10 years and a monetary penalty.

2. The same punishment shall be imposed on any person who, for the same purpose, forges or alters any other tangible payment instrument other than currency, such as credit cards, debit cards and other cards issued by financial institutions, traveller's cheques, other cheques and bills of exchange.

2A. Any person who, for the same purpose, procures or possesses the forged or altered tangible payment instruments referred to in paragraph 2 shall be punished with imprisonment and a monetary penalty.

3. In particularly minor cases involving forgeries low in number or purported value, the acts provided for in paragraphs 1 and 2 shall be punished with imprisonment of up to three years, and the acts provided for in paragraph 2A shall be punished with imprisonment of up to one year.

Article 208

1. Any person who places in circulation forged currency of any state or issuing authority, whether after or before such currency is placed in lawful circulation or at the time it is accepted for exchange by the competent institutions, or other [forged] payment instrument knowing that it was forged shall be punished with incarceration of up to 10 years and a monetary penalty. In particularly minor cases involving forgeries low in number or purported value, imprisonment of up to two years shall be imposed.

2. If the culpable person or their [representative] had accepted the forged currency or other payment instrument as genuine, imprisonment of up to six months or a monetary penalty shall be imposed. The same punishment shall be imposed if the culpable person acted at the instructions of the person to whom the currency or other payment instrument was given as genuine, when they share a relationship of dependence with that person or live with them at the same residence.

Article 208A

Manufacture of currency in excess [of the right to do so]

The penalties laid down in the first and second sentences of paragraph 1 of the preceding Article shall also be imposed on any person who intentionally manufactures, procures, possesses or places into circulation currency, whether after or before such currency is placed in lawful circulation or at the time it is accepted for exchange by the competent institutions, and lawful facilities and materials were used for its manufacture but without the permission of the competent authority or in excess of the right to do.

Άρθρο 208Β

Όποιος παράνομα παράγει, πωλεί, εισάγει, χρησιμοποιεί ή διανέμει για πώληση ή για άλλους εμπορικούς σκοπούς μετάλλια ή μάρκες τα οποία:

α) φέρουν στην όψη τους όρους «ευρώ» ή «λεπτά ευρώ» ή το σύμβολο του ευρώ,

β) έχουν μέγεθος εντός των νόμιμων ορίων αναφοράς, ή

γ) φέρουν στην όψη τους οποιοδήποτε σχέδιο που είναι παρόμοιο με εκείνο των εθνικών εμπρόσθιων όψεων ή των κοινών οπίσθιων όψεων των κερμάτων ευρώ ή είναι πανομοιότυπο ή παρόμοιο με το σχέδιο της στεφάνης των κερμάτων των δύο ευρώ,

τιμωρείται με χρηματική ποινή.

Άρθρο 208Γ

Πλαστογραφία και κατάχρηση ενσήμων

1. Όποιος καταρτίζει πλαστά ή νοθεύει επίσημα ένσημα δηλωτικά αξίας με σκοπό να τα χρησιμοποιήσει σαν γνήσια, εν γνώσει τα χρησιμοποιεί σαν γνήσια ή τα προμηθεύεται γι' αυτόν το σκοπό ή τα προσφέρει στην αγορά ή τα εισάγει σε κυκλοφορία τιμωρείται με φυλάκιση και χρηματική ποινή.

2. Όποιος εν γνώσει ξαναχρησιμοποιεί επίσημα ένσημα δηλωτικά αξίας, που είχαν ήδη χρησιμοποιηθεί, ή τα αποκτά με σκοπό να τα ξαναχρησιμοποιήσει προσφέροντάς τα στην αγορά ή εισάγοντάς τα σε κυκλοφορία τιμωρείται με χρηματική ποινή.

Άρθρο 209

Παραποίηση και νόθευση άυλων μέσων πληρωμής

1. Όποιος παραποιεί ή νοθεύει άυλο μέσο πληρωμής με σκοπό να το θέσει σε κυκλοφορία ως γνήσιο, τιμωρείται με κάθειρξη έως δέκα (10) έτη και χρηματική ποινή.

2. Με ποινή φυλάκισης και χρηματική ποινή τιμωρείται όποιος, με τον ίδιο σκοπό, προμηθεύεται, κατέχει ή διαθέτει το παραποιημένο ή νοθευμένο άυλο μέσο πληρωμής της παρ. 1.

3. Σε ιδιαίτερα ελαφρές περιπτώσεις μικρής αξίας άυλων μέσων πληρωμής, οι πράξεις της παρ. 1 τιμωρούνται με φυλάκιση έως τρία (3) έτη και οι πράξεις της παρ. 2 τιμωρούνται με ποινή φυλάκισης έως ένα (1) έτος.

Άρθρο 210

Παράνομη απόκτηση άυλων μέσων πληρωμής

Με ποινή φυλάκισης τουλάχιστον τριών (3) μηνών και χρηματική ποινή τιμωρείται όποιος αποκτά παρανόμως, ιδίως μέσω παράνομης πρόσβασης σε συστήματα πληροφοριών, παράνομης παρεμβολής σε σύστημα, παράνομης παρεμβολής σε δεδομένα και παράνομης υποκλοπής, άυλα μέσα πληρωμής.

Άρθρο 210Α

Αποδοχή και διάθεση παρανόμως αποκτηθέντων άυλων μέσων πληρωμής

Όποιος προμηθεύεται, κατέχει ή διαθέτει παρανόμως αποκτηθέντα άυλα μέσα πληρωμής τιμωρείται με φυλάκιση έως τρία (3) έτη και χρηματική ποινή.

Article 208B

Any person who unlawfully produces, sells, imports, uses or distributes for sale or other commercial purposes [any] medals and tokens which:

a) bear the terms "euro" or "euro cents" or the euro symbol on their surface;

b) have a size inside the lawful reference band; or

c) bear any design on their surface which is similar to any of the national obverse designs or to the common reverse face of euro coins, or is identical or similar to the edge design of the two-euro coin, shall be punished with a monetary penalty.

Article 208C
Forgery and abuse of stamps

1. Any person who forges or alters official stamps of value for the purpose of using them as genuine, [or] knowingly uses them as genuine, or procures them for this purpose, or markets them, or places them into circulation shall be punished with imprisonment and a monetary penalty.

2. Any person who knowingly re-uses official stamps of value which had already been used, or acquires such for the purpose of re-using them by marketing them or placing them in circulation shall be punished with a monetary penalty.

Article 209
Falsification and alteration of intangible payment instruments

1. Any person who falsifies or alters intangible payment instruments for the purpose of placing such in circulation as genuine shall be punished with incarceration of up to 10 years and a monetary penalty.

2. Any person who, for the same purpose, procures, possesses or makes available the falsified or altered intangible payment instrument referred to in paragraph 1 shall be punished with imprisonment and a monetary penalty.

3. In particularly minor cases involving intangible payment instruments low in value, the acts provided for in paragraph 1 shall be punished with imprisonment of up to three years, and the acts provided for in paragraph 2 shall be punished with imprisonment of up to one year.

Article 210
Unlawful acquisition of intangible payment instruments

Any person who unlawfully acquires intangible payment instruments, particularly by illegally accessing information systems, illegally interfering with a system, illegally interfering with data [or] through illegal interception shall be punished with imprisonment of at least three months and a monetary penalty.

Article 210A
Accepting and making available unlawfully acquired intangible payment instruments

Any person who procures, possesses or makes available unlawfully acquired intangible payment instruments shall be punished with imprisonment of up to three years and a monetary penalty.

Άρθρο 210Β
Διακεκριμένες περιπτώσεις στο πλαίσιο εγκληματικής οργάνωσης

1. Η τέλεση των κακουργημάτων των παρ. 1 και 2 του άρθρου 207, του πρώτου εδαφίου της παρ. 1 του άρθρου 208 και της παρ. 1 του άρθρου 209 στο πλαίσιο εγκληματικής οργάνωσης συνιστά επιβαρυντική περίσταση.
2. Τα πλημμελήματα της παρ. 2 του άρθρου 209, των άρθρων 210 και 210Α, όταν τελούνται στο πλαίσιο εγκληματικής οργάνωσης, τιμωρούνται με ποινή φυλάκισης τουλάχιστον ενός (1) έτους και χρηματική ποινή.

Άρθρο 211
Προπαρασκευαστικές πράξεις

Όποιος, προετοιμάζοντας τη διάπραξη κάποιου από τα εγκλήματα των άρθρων 207, 208, 208Α, 208Β, της παρ. 1 του άρθρου 209 και του άρθρου 210, κατασκευάζει, κατέχει ή διαθέτει εργαλείο, αντικείμενο, μηχανισμό ή ψηφιακά δεδομένα ή άλλα μέσα πρωτίστως σχεδιασμένα ή ειδικά προσαρμοσμένα για τον σκοπό αυτόν, καθώς και ολογραφήματα ή λοιπά συστατικά στοιχεία του νομίσματος ή μέσων πληρωμής πλην των μετρητών, τα οποία χρησιμεύουν για την προστασία από την παραχάραξη του νομίσματος ή την παραποίηση και τη νόθευση των μέσων πληρωμής πλην των μετρητών, τιμωρείται με φυλάκιση έως δύο (2) έτη και χρηματική ποινή.

Άρθρο 212
Έμπρακτη μετάνοια

1. Το αξιόποινο των πράξεων των άρθρων 207, 208, 208Α, 208Β και 209 εξαλείφεται αν ο υπαίτιος με τη θέλησή του και πριν από κάθε κυκλοφορία ακυρώσει ή καταστρέψει τα πλαστά ή καθ' υπέρβαση κατασκευασθέντα πριν εξεταστεί με οποιονδήποτε τρόπο για την πράξη του από τις αρμόδιες αρχές.
2. Εξαλείφεται επίσης το αξιόποινο των πράξεων του άρθρου 211 αν ο υπαίτιος καταστρέψει με τη θέλησή του τα αντικείμενα που αναφέρονται σε αυτό πριν τα χρησιμοποιήσει.

Άρθρο 213
Δήμευση

1. Η δήμευση των πλαστών ή καθ' υπέρβαση κατασκευασθέντων νομισμάτων ή άλλων μέσων πληρωμής, των αντικειμένων του άρθρου 207, 208Α, 208Β και των πλαστών ή επαναχρησιμοποιημένων ενσήμων διατάσσεται και αν ακόμα δεν διωχθεί και καταδικαστεί ορισμένο πρόσωπο και ανεξάρτητα από το αν αυτά ανήκουν ή όχι στον αυτουργό ή τον συμμέτοχο του εγκλήματος.
2. Αν όμως ο κύριος των νομισμάτων ή του υλικού από το οποίο κατασκευάστηκαν είναι αποδεδειγμένα αμέτοχος στην παραχάραξη, τα νομίσματα αχρηστεύονται ως νομίσματα και αποδίδονται ύστερα από αυτό στον κύριο.
3. Τα νομίσματα που κατάσχονται ως ύποπτα προϊόντα παραχάραξης, αποστέλλονται στο αντίστοιχο Εθνικό Κέντρο Ανάλυσης ή Εθνικό Κέντρο Ανάλυσης Κερμάτων Ευρώ για ανάλυση, ανίχνευση και εντοπισμό περαιτέρω προϊόντων παραχάραξης, χωρίς καθυστέρηση και το αργότερο μέχρι να εκδοθεί τελεσίδικη απόφαση κατά την ποινική διαδικασία.

Άρθρα 214 - 215

(Καταργούνται)

Article 210B
Aggravated cases in the context of a criminal organisation

1. Committing the felonies provided for in Article 207(1) and (2), the first sentence of Article 208(1) and Article 209(1) in the context of a criminal organisation constitutes an aggravating circumstance.

2. Where committed in the context of a criminal organisation, the misdemeanours provided for in Articles 209(2), 210 and 210A shall be punished with imprisonment of at least one year and a monetary penalty.

Article 211
Preparatory acts

Any person who, preparing to commit any of the crimes provided for in Articles 207, 208, 208A, 208B, 209(1) and 210, manufactures, possesses or makes available a tool, object, mechanism or digital data or other means primarily designed or specially adapted for this purpose, as well as holograms or other constituent parts of currency or non-cash payment instruments which are used to prevent counterfeiting of currency or falsification and alteration of non-cash payment instruments shall be punished with imprisonment of up to two years and a monetary penalty.

Article 212
Practical repentance

1. The punishability of the acts provided for in Articles 207, 208, 208A, 208B and 209 shall be extinguished if the culpable person, of their own volition and prior to any circulation, invalidates or destroys anything forged or manufactured in excess [of the right to do so] before being [questioned] in any manner by the competent authorities in relation to their act.

2. The punishability of the acts provided for in Article 211 shall also be extinguished if, of their own volition, the culpable person destroys the objects referred to in that Article before using them.

Article 213
Confiscation

1. Confiscation of currency or other payment instruments forged or manufactured in excess [of the right to do so], the objects referred to in Articles 207, 208A and 208B, and forged or re-used stamps shall be ordered even if a specific person has not been prosecuted and convicted and irrespective of whether or not the foregoing belong to the perpetrator of or accessory to the crime.

2. However, if it is proven that the owner of the currency or the material used for its manufacture demonstrably played no part in the counterfeiting, the currency shall be rendered unusable and then returned to the owner.

3. Any currency confiscated as a suspected product of counterfeiting shall be sent to the competent National Analysis Centre or National Euro Coin Analysis Centre for analysis, detection and identification of further products of counterfeiting without delay and no later than the date a *de jure* non-appealable judgment is handed down in the criminal proceedings.

Articles 214 - 215

[Repealed]

ΔΕΚΑΤΟ ΚΕΦΑΛΑΙΟ

ΕΓΚΛΗΜΑΤΑ ΣΧΕΤΙΚΑ ΜΕ ΤΑ ΥΠΟΜΝΗΜΑΤΑ

Άρθρο 216

1. Όποιος καταρτίζει πλαστό ή νοθεύει έγγραφο με σκοπό να παραπλανήσει με τη χρήση του άλλον σχετικά με γεγονός που μπορεί να έχει έννομες συνέπειες τιμωρείται με φυλάκιση και χρηματική ποινή.

2. Με την ίδια ποινή τιμωρείται όποιος για τον παραπάνω σκοπό εν γνώσει χρησιμοποιεί πλαστό ή νοθευμένο έγγραφο.

3. Αν ο υπαίτιος των πράξεων των παρ. 1 και 2 σκόπευε να προσπορίσει στον εαυτό του ή σε άλλον περιουσιακό όφελος βλάπτοντας τρίτον ή σκόπευε να βλάψει άλλον, τιμωρείται:

α) εάν το συνολικό όφελος ή η συνολική ζημία είναι ιδιαίτερα μεγάλη, με φυλάκιση τουλάχιστον τριών (3) μηνών και χρηματική ποινή,

β) εάν το συνολικό όφελος ή η συνολική ζημία υπερβαίνει τις εκατόν είκοσι χιλιάδες (120.000) ευρώ, με κάθειρξη έως δέκα (10) έτη και χρηματική ποινή.

4. Αν οι πράξεις των παρ. 1 και 2 στρέφονται άμεσα κατά του νομικού προσώπου του ελληνικού Δημοσίου, των νομικών προσώπων Δημοσίου Δικαίου ή των οργανισμών τοπικής αυτοδιοίκησης και το συνολικό περιουσιακό όφελος ή η συνολική ζημία υπερβαίνει συνολικά τις εκατόν είκοσι χιλιάδες (120.000) ευρώ, επιβάλλεται κάθειρξη τουλάχιστον δέκα (10) ετών και χρηματική ποινή έως χίλιες (1.000) ημερήσιες μονάδες. Οι πράξεις αυτές παραγράφονται μετά είκοσι (20) έτη.

Άρθρο 217
Πλαστογραφία πιστοποιητικών

1. Όποιος με σκοπό να διευκολύνει την άμεση συντήρηση, την κίνηση ή την κοινωνική πρόοδο αυτού του ίδιου ή άλλου καταρτίζει πλαστό ή νοθεύει πιστοποιητικό ή μαρτυρικό ή άλλο έγγραφο που κατά προορισμό χρησιμεύει για τέτοιους σκοπούς ή εν γνώσει του χρησιμοποιεί τέτοιο πλαστό ή νοθευμένο έγγραφο τιμωρείται με χρηματική ποινή ή παροχή κοινωφελούς εργασίας.

2. Με την ίδια ποινή τιμωρείται όποιος χρησιμοποιεί για τον ίδιο σκοπό τέτοιο έγγραφο, που είναι γνήσιο, είχε εκδοθεί όμως για άλλον.

3. Με φυλάκιση τιμωρείται όποιος καταρτίζει πλαστό ή νοθεύει πτυχίο ή κάθε πιστοποιητικό γνώσεων ή δεξιοτήτων, ή νοθεύει γνήσιο ή κάνει χρήση αυτών, με σκοπό να καταλάβει θέση εργασίας ή να διεκδικήσει βαθμολογική ή μισθολογική προαγωγή στον δημόσιο ή τον ιδιωτικό τομέα.

Άρθρα 218 - 219

(Καταργούνται)

CHAPTER X

CRIMES CONCERNING [DOCUMENTS]

Article 216

1. Any person who forges or alters a document for the purpose of using it to mislead another with regard to a fact which could have legal consequences shall be punished with imprisonment and a monetary penalty.

2. The same punishment shall be imposed on any person who knowingly uses a forged or altered document for the aforesaid purpose.

3. If the person culpable of the acts provided for in paragraphs 1 and 2 sought to obtain pecuniary gain for themselves or another party by harming another or sought to harm another, they shall be punished with:

a) imprisonment of at least three months and a monetary penalty if the total gain or total loss is particularly high; [or]

b) incarceration of up to 10 years and a monetary penalty if the total gain or total loss exceeds 120,000 euros.

4. If the acts provided for in paragraphs 1 and 2 are committed directly against the Greek State as a legal person, any body governed by public law or any local government authority and the total pecuniary gain or total loss exceeds 120,000 euros, incarceration of at least 10 years and a monetary penalty of up to 1,000 daily penalty units shall be imposed. Such acts shall become time-barred after 20 years.

Article 217

Forgery of certificates

1. Any person who, for the purpose of facilitating the direct [earning of a livelihood], mobility or social advancement of themselves or another, prepares a forged certificate or alters a certificate, testimonial or other document intended to be used for such purposes, or who knowingly uses such forged or altered document shall be punished with a monetary penalty or community service.

2. The same punishment shall be imposed on any person who, for the same purpose, uses such a document which is genuine but had been issued for another person.

3. Any person who forges or alters a degree or any other certificate of knowledge or skills, or who alters or uses such a genuine degree or certificate for the purpose of securing employment or seeking a grade or salary promotion in the public or private sector shall be punished with imprisonment.

Articles 218 - 219

[Repealed]

Άρθρο 220

Υφαρπαγή ψευδούς βεβαίωσης

1. Όποιος πετυχαίνει με εξαπάτηση να βεβαιωθεί σε δημόσιο έγγραφο αναληθώς περιστατικό που μπορεί να έχει έννομες συνέπειες, καθώς και όποιος χρησιμοποιεί τέτοια ψευδή βεβαίωση για να εξαπατήσει άλλον σχετικά με το περιστατικό αυτό, τιμωρείται με φυλάκιση έως δύο έτη ή χρηματική ποινή, αν δεν τιμωρείται βαρύτερα κατά τις διατάξεις για την ηθική αυτουργία.

2. Αν όμως υπάρχουν οι όροι του άρθρου 216 παρ. 3 και 4, επιβάλλεται φυλάκιση και χρηματική ποινή.

Άρθρο 221

Ψευδείς ιατρικές πιστοποιήσεις

1. Γιατροί, οδοντίατροι, κτηνίατροι, φαρμακοποιοί, χημικοί και μαίες που εν γνώσει εκδίδουν ψευδείς πιστοποιήσεις, οι οποίες προορίζονται να παρέχουν πίστη σε δημόσια, δημοτική ή κοινοτική αρχή ή νομικό πρόσωπο δημόσιου δικαίου ή σε μια ασφαλιστική επιχείρηση ή που μπορούν να ζημιώσουν άμεσα οικονομικά άλλον τιμωρούνται με φυλάκιση έως δύο έτη ή χρηματική ποινή. Αν οι ψευδείς αυτές πιστοποιήσεις προορίζονται για δικαστική χρήση, αυτοί που τις εκδίδουν τιμωρούνται με φυλάκιση τουλάχιστον έξι μηνών και χρηματική ποινή.

2. Με φυλάκιση έως ένα έτος ή χρηματική ποινή τιμωρείται όποιος χρησιμοποιεί τέτοια ψευδή πιστοποίηση για να εξαπατήσει δημόσια, δημοτική ή κοινοτική αρχή ή νομικό πρόσωπο δημόσιου δικαίου ή ασφαλιστική επιχείρηση. Αν έγινε δικαστική χρήση της ανωτέρω ψευδούς πιστοποίησης, ο διάδικος που έκανε τη χρήση τιμωρείται με φυλάκιση έως δύο έτη ή χρηματική ποινή.

Άρθρο 222

Υπεξαγωγή εγγράφων

Όποιος με σκοπό να βλάψει άλλον αποκρύπτει, βλάπτει ή καταστρέφει έγγραφο του οποίου δεν είναι κύριος ή δεν είναι αποκλειστικά κύριος ή που άλλος έχει δικαίωμα, κατά τις διατάξεις του αστικού δικαίου, να ζητήσει την παράδοση ή την επίδειξή του τιμωρείται με φυλάκιση έως δύο έτη ή χρηματική ποινή.

Άρθρο 223

(Καταργείται)

Article 220

Obtaining an attestation under false pretences

1. Any person who, through deception, succeeds in having a fact which could have legal consequences falsely attested to in a public document, and any person using such an attestation issued under false pretences in order to deceive another in relation to such fact shall be punished with imprisonment of up to two years or a monetary penalty, unless the act carries a heavier punishment under the provisions on instigation.

2. However, if the conditions laid down in Article 216(3) and (4) are met, imprisonment and a monetary penalty shall be imposed.

Article 221

False medical certificates

1. Physicians, dentists, veterinarians, pharmacists, chemists and midwives who knowingly issue false certificates which are intended to provide assurance to a public, municipal or community authority, a body governed by public law or an insurance company or which could cause direct financial losses to another shall be punished with imprisonment of up to two years or a monetary penalty. If such false certificates are intended for use in court, the person issuing them shall be punished with imprisonment of at least six months and a monetary penalty.

2. Any person who uses such false certificates to deceive a public, municipal or community authority or body governed by public law or an insurance company shall be punished with imprisonment of up to one year or a monetary penalty. If the aforesaid false certificate was used in court, the party in the proceedings who used it shall be punished with imprisonment of up to two years or a monetary penalty.

Article 222

Making documents unavailable

Any person who, for the purpose of harming another, hides, damages or destroys a document which they do not own or do not exclusively own or whose handover or presentation another is entitled to request, in accordance with civil law provisions, shall be punished with imprisonment of up to two years or a monetary penalty.

Article 223

[Repealed]

ΕΝΔΕΚΑΤΟ ΚΕΦΑΛΑΙΟ

ΕΓΚΛΗΜΑΤΑ ΣΧΕΤΙΚΑ ΜΕ ΤΗΝ ΑΠΟΝΟΜΗ ΔΙΚΑΙΟΣΥΝΗΣ

Άρθρο 224

Ψευδής κατάθεση

1. Όποιος, ενώ εξετάζεται ως διάδικος ή μάρτυρας σε δικαστήριο ή ενώπιον αρχής αρμόδιας να ενεργεί εξέταση για την κρινόμενη υπόθεση, εν γνώσει του καταθέτει ψευδή στοιχεία σχετικά με την υπόθεση αυτή ή αρνείται ή αποκρύπτει την αλήθεια, τιμωρείται με φυλάκιση τουλάχιστον τριών (3) μηνών έως τρία (3) έτη και χρηματική ποινή.

2. Όποιος εμφανίζεται ως μάρτυρας ενώπιον δικαστηρίου ή άλλης αρχής αρμόδιας να ενεργεί εξέταση και αρνείται να δώσει τη μαρτυρία του τιμωρείται με φυλάκιση έως δύο (2) έτη ή χρηματική ποινή.

3. Αν ο υπαίτιος τέλεσε τις πράξεις των προηγούμενων παραγράφων για να αποφύγει ποινική ευθύνη είτε δική του είτε κάποιου από τους οικείους του, χωρίς να ενοχοποιήσει ψευδώς άλλον, το δικαστήριο μπορεί να τον απαλλάξει από κάθε ποινή.

4. Όποιος, σε κάθε άλλη περίπτωση, όταν εξετάζεται από κάποια αρχή ή από εξουσιοδοτημένο όργανό της ή όταν αναφέρεται σε αυτή, εκθέτει εν γνώσει του ψέματα ή αρνείται ή αποκρύπτει την αλήθεια τιμωρείται με φυλάκιση έως δύο (2) έτη ή χρηματική ποινή.

Άρθρο 225

(Καταργείται)

Άρθρο 226

Ψευδής πραγματογνωμοσύνη ή διερμηνεία

1. Όποιος ως πραγματογνώμονας ή διερμηνέας εν γνώσει εκθέτει ψέματα ή αποκρύπτει την αλήθεια, τιμωρείται με φυλάκιση τουλάχιστον δύο ετών και χρηματική ποινή.

2. Το δικαστήριο επιβάλλει επιπροσθέτως απαγόρευση άσκησης επαγγέλματος για χρονικό διάστημα από ένα έως δύο έτη, η οποία αρχίζει μόλις η απόφαση γίνει αμετάκλητη.

Άρθρο 227

Έμπρακτη μετάνοια

Στις περιπτώσεις του άρθρου 224 η πράξη μένει ατιμώρητη αν ο υπαίτιος με την ελεύθερη θέλησή του ανακάλεσε ενώπιον της ίδιας αρχής την ψευδή κατάθεση με νέα κατάθεση. Η ανάκληση αυτή δεν απαλλάσσει από την ποινή τον υπαίτιο, αν η αρχή έχει ήδη εκδώσει απόφαση ή αν επήλθε σε άλλον κάποια έννομη επιβλαβής συνέπεια.

Άρθρο 228

(Καταργείται)

CHAPTER XI

CRIMES CONCERNING THE ADMINISTRATION OF JUSTICE

Article 224

False testimony

1. Any person who, while being examined as a party in proceedings or as a witness in court or before an authority competent to conduct an examination with regard to the matter in question, knowingly gives false testimony in relation to such matter, or refuses to testify the truth, or conceals the truth shall be punished with imprisonment ranging from three months to three years and a monetary penalty.
2. Any person who appears as a witness before a court or other authority competent to conduct an examination and refuses to give testimony shall be punished with imprisonment of up to two years or a monetary penalty.
3. If the culpable person committed the acts provided for in the preceding paragraphs in order to avoid criminal liability either for themselves or for a related party, without falsely incriminating another, the court may opt not to punish them.
4. In all other cases, any person who, while being examined by an authority or an authorised officer of such authority or reporting to such an authority, knowingly lies or refuses to tell the truth or conceals the truth shall be punished with imprisonment of up to two years or a monetary penalty.

Article 225

[Repealed]

Article 226

False expert evidence or interpretation

1. Any person who, as an expert or an interpreter, knowingly lies or conceals the truth shall be punished with imprisonment of at least two years and a monetary penalty.
2. Additionally, the court shall prohibit them from carrying on their occupation for a period of one to two years, starting on the date the judgment becomes irrevocable.

Article 227

Practical repentance

In the cases provided for in Article 224, the act shall not be punished if the culpable person willingly recanted the false testimony before the same authority and gave new testimony. Such recantation shall not release the culpable person from the punishment if the authority has already issued a decision or another person suffered an adverse legal consequence.

Article 228

[Repealed]

Άρθρο 229

Ψευδής καταμήνυση

1. Όποιος εν γνώσει καταμηνύει άλλον ψευδώς ή αναφέρει γι' αυτόν ενώπιον της αρχής ότι τέλεσε αξιόποινη πράξη ή πειθαρχική παράβαση, τιμωρείται με φυλάκιση τουλάχιστον δύο ετών και χρηματική ποινή.

2. Με την ίδια ποινή τιμωρείται και όποιος εν γνώσει και ψευδώς καθιστά άλλον ύποπτο στην αρχή υποβάλλοντας, αλλοιώνοντας ή αποκρύπτοντας κάποιο αποδεικτικό μέσο για αξιόποινη πράξη ή πειθαρχική παράβαση.

3. Το δικαστήριο με αίτηση του παθόντος μπορεί να του επιτρέψει να δημοσιεύσει την απόφαση με έξοδα του καταδικασθέντος. Το δικαίωμα αυτό παύει να υπάρχει αν η δημοσίευση δεν γίνει μέσα σε έξι μήνες από την καταχώρηση της τελεσίδικης απόφασης στο ειδικό βιβλίο.

Άρθρο 230

Ψευδής καταγγελία

Όποιος, χωρίς να καθιστά άλλον ύποπτο, παριστάνει εν γνώσει του ψευδώς στην αρχή ότι τελέστηκε κάποιο κακούργημα ή πλημμέλημα, τιμωρείται με φυλάκιση έως ένα έτος ή χρηματική ποινή.

Άρθρο 231

Υπόθαλψη - Παρεμπόδιση δικαιοσύνης

1. Όποιος εν γνώσει ματαιώνει τη δίωξη άλλου για κακούργημα ή πλημμέλημα που διέπραξε τιμωρείται με φυλάκιση έως τρία (3) έτη ή χρηματική ποινή.

2. Η υπόθαλψη μπορεί να μένει ατιμώρητη αν ο υπαίτιος την τέλεσε υπέρ κάποιου οικείου του.

3. Όποιος παρεμποδίζει την απονομή της δικαιοσύνης, ασκώντας αυθαίρετη παρέμβαση, πριν ή κατά τη διάρκεια έρευνας οποιασδήποτε αρχής ή σε οποιοδήποτε στάδιο της ποινικής δίκης, με χρήση σωματικής βίας, απειλής, εκφοβισμού, παραπλάνησης, με κατάχρηση θέσης εξουσίας ή εξάρτησης οποιασδήποτε φύσης ή με υπόσχεση ωφελήματος, έναντι άλλου, προκειμένου αυτός να δώσει ψευδή κατάθεση ή να καθυστερήσει να τη δώσει ή να μεταβάλει την κατάθεσή του ή να αρνηθεί να καταθέσει ή να αποκρύψει, καταστρέψει, αλλοιώσει, αφαιρέσει, αντικαταστήσει αποδεικτικά στοιχεία ή να παρεμποδίσει την πρόσβαση σε αυτά ή τη χρήση τους, εφόσον η πράξη του δεν τιμωρείται βαρύτερα από άλλη διάταξη, τιμωρείται:

α) με φυλάκιση τουλάχιστον ενός (1) έτους και χρηματική ποινή αν η διερευνώμενη πράξη αφορά πλημμέλημα, και

β) με φυλάκιση τουλάχιστον τριών (3) ετών και χρηματική ποινή αν η διερευνώμενη πράξη αφορά κακούργημα.

4. Με τις ποινές της παρ. 3 τιμωρείται και όποιος πριν ή κατά τη διάρκεια έρευνας οποιασδήποτε αρχής ή σε οποιοδήποτε στάδιο της ποινικής δίκης αποκρύπτει, καταστρέφει, αλλοιώνει, αφαιρεί, αντικαθιστά αποδεικτικά στοιχεία ή παρεμποδίζει την πρόσβαση σε αυτά ή τη χρήση τους, εφόσον η πράξη του δεν τιμωρείται βαρύτερα από άλλη διάταξη.

Article 229
False accusation

1. Any person who knowingly falsely accuses another person or submits a report to the authorities that another person committed a punishable act or disciplinary offence shall be punished with imprisonment of at least two years and a monetary penalty.

2. The same punishment shall also be imposed on any person who knowingly and falsely causes the authorities to suspect another person by submitting, altering or concealing evidence of a punishable act or disciplinary offence.

3. Following an application filed by the victim, the court may allow the victim to have the judgment published, and the convicted person shall bear the expense [of such publication]. This right expires if the *de jure* non-appealable judgment is not published within six months from the date it is entered in the special register.

Article 230
False report [of a crime]

Any person who, without causing another person to become a suspect, knowingly and falsely reports to an authority that a felony or a misdemeanour was committed shall be punished with imprisonment of up to one year or a monetary penalty.

Article 231
Harbouring [a criminal] - Obstruction of justice

1. Any person who knowingly prevents the prosecution of another person for a felony or a misdemeanour committed by the latter shall be punished with imprisonment of up to three years or a monetary penalty.

2. [The court may opt not to punish] such harbouring if it was committed by the culpable person for the benefit of a related party.

3. Any person who obstructs the administration of justice by arbitrarily intervening, prior to or during inquiries being conducted by any authority or at any stage of the criminal proceedings, through the use of physical violence, threat, intimidation, deception, abuse of a position of power or dependence of any nature against another or through promise of an advantage to another in order for the latter to give false testimony, or delay giving testimony, or alter their testimony, or refuse to testify, or conceal, destroy, alter, remove or replace evidence, or obstruct access to or use of such evidence, shall, unless the act carries a heavier punishment under a different provision, be punished with:

a) imprisonment of at least one year and a monetary penalty if the act being investigated is a misdemeanour; [or]

b) imprisonment of at least three years and a monetary penalty if the act being investigated is a felony.

4. The punishments laid down in paragraph 3 shall also be imposed on any person who, prior to or during inquiries being conducted by any authority or at any stage of the criminal proceedings conceals, destroys, alters, removes or replaces evidence, or obstructs access to or use of such evidence, unless the act carries a heavier punishment under a different provision.

Άρθρο 232
Παρασιώπηση εγκλημάτων

1. Όποιος, ενώ έμαθε με τρόπο αξιόπιστο ότι μελετάται κακούργημα ή ότι άρχισε ήδη η εκτέλεσή του, και σε χρόνο τέτοιον ώστε να μπορεί ακόμα να προληφθεί η τέλεση ή το αποτέλεσμά του, παραλείπει να το αναγγείλει εγκαίρως στην αρχή, τιμωρείται, αν το κακούργημα τελέστηκε ή έγινε απόπειρά του, με φυλάκιση έως τρία έτη ή χρηματική ποινή.
2. Η παράλειψη αυτή μένει ατιμώρητη αν η αναγγελία στην αρχή θα αφορούσε πρόσωπο οικείο εκείνου που την παρέλειψε.

Άρθρο 233
Απιστία δικηγόρων

1. Δικηγόρος που βλάπτει εν γνώσει τα συμφέροντα εκείνου του οποίου έχει αναλάβει τη νομική προστασία, ή που στην ίδια ένδικη υπόθεση βοηθά με συμβουλές ή με παροχή υπηρεσίας και τους δύο διαδίκους, είτε ταυτόχρονα είτε διαδοχικά, τιμωρείται με φυλάκιση έως τρία έτη ή χρηματική ποινή.
2. Αν όμως ενήργησε αφού συνεννοήθηκε με αυτούς που έχουν αντίθετα συμφέροντα ή επιδιώκοντας κέρδος, τιμωρείται με φυλάκιση τουλάχιστον ενός έτους και χρηματική ποινή.

Άρθρο 234
Παραβίαση της μυστικότητας δικαστικών συνεδριάσεων

Με φυλάκιση έως τρία έτη ή χρηματική ποινή τιμωρείται όποιος με οποιονδήποτε τρόπο δημοσιεύει έκθεση για κάποια δικαστική συνεδρίαση που έχει διεξαχθεί κεκλεισμένων των θυρών ή οποιοδήποτε έγγραφο τέτοιας δίκης, εκτός αν το δικαστήριο στο οποίο διεξάγεται η δίκη επιτρέψει τη δημοσίευση.

Article 232
Concealment of crimes

1. Any person who, despite having credibly learned that [commission of] a felony is being planned or its commission has already begun and at a time when its commission or result could still be prevented, fails to notify the authorities in good time shall, if the felony was committed or attempted, be punished with imprisonment of up to three years or a monetary penalty.

2. Such failure shall not be punished if the report to the authorities concerns a related party of the culpable person.

Article 233
Breach of fiduciary duty by lawyers

1. Any lawyer who knowingly prejudices the interests of the person whose legal protection they have undertaken, or assists both parties in the proceedings by providing advice or [legal] services, whether simultaneously or consecutively, in the same case at issue shall be punished with imprisonment of up to three years or a monetary penalty.

2. However, if such lawyer acted having consulted the persons with conflicting interests or in the pursuit of monetary gain, they shall be punished with imprisonment of at least one year and a monetary penalty.

Article 234
Breach of the secrecy of court sittings

Any person who in any way publishes a report on a court sitting held *in camera* or any document of such proceedings shall be punished with imprisonment of up to three years or a monetary penalty, unless the court trying the case permits such publication.

ΔΩΔΕΚΑΤΟ ΚΕΦΑΛΑΙΟ

ΕΓΚΛΗΜΑΤΑ ΣΧΕΤΙΚΑ ΜΕ ΤΗΝ ΥΠΗΡΕΣΙΑ

I

ΧΡΗΣΗ ΤΗΣ ΥΠΗΡΕΣΙΑΣ ΓΙΑ ΙΔΙΩΤΙΚΟ ΟΦΕΛΟΣ

Άρθρο 235
Δωροληψία υπαλλήλου

1. Υπάλληλος ο οποίος ζητεί ή λαμβάνει, άμεσα ή μέσω τρίτου, για τον εαυτό του ή για άλλον, οποιασδήποτε φύσης αθέμιτο ωφέλημα ανεξαρτήτως αξίας ή αποδέχεται την υπόσχεση παροχής τέτοιου ωφελήματος, για ενέργεια ή παράλειψή του σε σχέση με την άσκηση των καθηκόντων του, μελλοντική ή ήδη τελειωμένη, τιμωρείται με φυλάκιση τουλάχιστον ενός (1) έτους και χρηματική ποινή από πέντε χιλιάδες (5.000) έως πενήντα χιλιάδες (50.000) ευρώ. Αν ο υπαίτιος τελεί την πράξη του προηγούμενου εδαφίου κατ' επάγγελμα, τιμωρείται με φυλάκιση τουλάχιστον τριών (3) ετών και χρηματική ποινή από δέκα χιλιάδες (10.000) έως εκατό χιλιάδες (100.000) ευρώ.

2. Αν η ως άνω ενέργεια ή παράλειψη του υπαιτίου αντίκειται στα καθήκοντα του, τιμωρείται με κάθειρξη έως δέκα (10) έτη και χρηματική ποινή από πενήντα χιλιάδες (50.000) έως τριακόσιες χιλιάδες (300.000) ευρώ. Αν ο υπαίτιος τελεί την πράξη του προηγούμενου εδαφίου κατ' επάγγελμα τιμωρείται με κάθειρξη και χρηματική ποινή από εκατό χιλιάδες (100.000) έως δύο εκατομμύρια (2.000.000) ευρώ.

3. Υπάλληλος ο οποίος ζητεί ή λαμβάνει, για τον εαυτό του ή για άλλον, αθέμιτη παροχή περιουσιακής φύσης, επωφελούμενος από την ιδιότητά του, τιμωρείται με φυλάκιση, αν η πράξη δεν τιμωρείται βαρύτερα από άλλη ποινική διάταξη.

4. Προϊστάμενοι υπηρεσιών ή επιθεωρητές ή πρόσωπα που έχουν την εξουσία λήψης αποφάσεων ή ελέγχου σε υπηρεσίες του Δημοσίου, των οργανισμών τοπικής αυτοδιοίκησης και των νομικών προσώπων δημοσίου δικαίου τιμωρούνται με φυλάκιση έως τρία (3) έτη ή χρηματική ποινή, εφόσον η πράξη δεν τιμωρείται βαρύτερα από άλλη ποινική διάταξη, αν με παράβαση συγκεκριμένου υπηρεσιακού καθήκοντος δεν απέτρεψαν από αμέλεια πρόσωπο που τελεί υπό τις εντολές τους ή υπόκειται στον έλεγχό τους από την τέλεση πράξης των προηγούμενων παραγράφων.

5. Οι παρ. 1 και 2 εφαρμόζονται και όταν οι πράξεις τελούνται από λειτουργούς ή άλλους υπαλλήλους που απασχολούνται με οποιαδήποτε συμβατική σχέση σε:

α) όργανο ή οργανισμό της Ευρωπαϊκής Ένωσης,

β) κάθε δημόσιο διεθνή ή υπερεθνικό οργανισμό ή φορέα, ανεξαρτήτως αν εδρεύει στην Ελλάδα ή η Ελλάδα είναι μέλος αυτού, καθώς και από κάθε πρόσωπο, αποσπασμένο ή όχι, που εκτελεί καθήκοντα τα οποία αντιστοιχούν σε αυτά που εκτελούν οι λειτουργοί ή άλλοι υπάλληλοι, ακόμα κι αν οι πράξεις των περ. α' και β' δεν είναι αξιόποινες κατά τους νόμους της χώρας όπου τελέστηκαν. Οι παρ. 1 και 2 εφαρμόζονται και όταν οι πράξεις τελούνται από υπάλληλο ξένης χώρας.

CHAPTER XII

CRIMES CONCERNING [PUBLIC] SERVICE

I

USE OF [PUBLIC] SERVICE FOR PERSONAL GAIN

Article 235

Passive bribery by a state employee

1. Any state employee who requests or receives, whether directly or through a third party, for themselves or for another person, any kind of undue advantage, irrespective of value, or accepts the promise of such an advantage, [in exchange] for any act or omission on their part, whether in the future or already completed, which is part of their duties shall be punished with imprisonment of at least one year and a monetary penalty ranging from 5,000 to 50,000 euros. If the culpable person commits the act provided for in the preceding sentence [for monetary gain], they shall be punished with imprisonment of at least three years and a monetary penalty ranging from 10,000 to 100,000 euros.

2. If the aforesaid act or omission by the culpable person is in breach of their duties, they shall be punished with incarceration of up to 10 years and a monetary penalty ranging from 50,000 to 300,000 euros. If the culpable person commits the act provided for in the preceding sentence [for monetary gain], they shall be punished with incarceration and a monetary penalty ranging from 100,000 to 2,000,000 euros.

3. Any state employee who requests or receives, whether for themselves or for another person, an undue pecuniary gain, benefitting from their capacity, shall be punished with imprisonment, unless the act carries a heavier sentence under a different criminal law provision.

4. Heads of department, or inspectors, or persons with decision-making or control powers at government bodies, local government authorities and bodies governed by public law shall be punished with imprisonment of up to three years or a monetary penalty, unless the act carries a heavier punishment under a different criminal law provision, if they failed, through negligence and by breaching a specific [public] service duty, to prevent a person subordinate to them or subject to their control from committing any of the acts provided for in the preceding paragraphs.

5. Paragraphs 1 and 2 also apply when the acts are committed by functionaries or other state employees engaged under any contractual relationship by:

a) an institution or body of the European Union;

b) any public international or supranational organisation or agency, irrespective of whether it is seated in Greece or whether Greece is a member of such, as well as any person, whether or not seconded, performing duties corresponding to those performed by functionaries or other state employees, even when the acts provided for in points (a) and (b) are not punishable under the laws of the country where they were committed. Paragraphs 1 and 2 also apply when such acts are committed by an employee of a foreign country.

Άρθρο 236
Δωροδοκία υπαλλήλου

1. Όποιος προσφέρει, υπόσχεται ή παρέχει σε υπάλληλο, άμεσα ή μέσω τρίτου, οποιασδήποτε φύσης αθέμιτο ωφέλημα ανεξαρτήτως αξίας, για τον εαυτό του ή για άλλον, για ενέργεια ή παράλειψη του υπαλλήλου σε σχέση με την άσκηση των καθηκόντων του, μελλοντική ή ήδη τελειωμένη, τιμωρείται με φυλάκιση τουλάχιστον ενός έτους και χρηματική ποινή από τρεις χιλιάδες (3.000) έως πενήντα χιλιάδες (50.000) ευρώ.

2. Αν η ως άνω ενέργεια ή παράλειψη αντίκειται στα καθήκοντα του υπαλλήλου, ο υπαίτιος τιμωρείται με κάθειρξη έως οκτώ (8) έτη και χρηματική ποινή από είκοσι χιλιάδες (20.000) έως διακόσιες χιλιάδες (200.000) ευρώ.

3. Διευθυντής επιχείρησης ή άλλο πρόσωπο που έχει την εξουσία λήψης αποφάσεων ή ελέγχου σε επιχείρηση τιμωρείται με φυλάκιση έως δύο (2) έτη ή χρηματική ποινή, αν η πράξη δεν τιμωρείται βαρύτερα, αν με παραβίαση συγκεκριμένου καθήκοντος επιμέλειας, δεν απέτρεψε από αμέλεια πρόσωπο που τελεί υπό τις εντολές του ή υπόκειται στον έλεγχό του από την τέλεση προς όφελος της επιχείρησης πράξης των προηγούμενων παραγράφων.

4. Οι διατάξεις των παρ. 1, 2 και 3 εφαρμόζονται και όταν οι πράξεις τελούνται προς:
α) λειτουργούς ή άλλους υπαλλήλους με οποιαδήποτε συμβατική σχέση οργάνου ή οργανισμού της Ευρωπαϊκής Ένωσης και κάθε δημόσιου διεθνούς ή υπερεθνικού οργανισμού ή φορέα ανεξαρτήτως αν εδρεύει στην Ελλάδα ή αν η Ελλάδα είναι μέλος αυτού, καθώς και προς κάθε πρόσωπο, αποσπασμένο ή όχι, που εκτελεί καθήκοντα τα οποία αντιστοιχούν σε αυτά που εκτελούν οι λειτουργοί ή άλλοι υπάλληλοι ή
β) οποιοδήποτε πρόσωπο που ασκεί δημόσιο λειτούργημα ή υπηρεσία για ξένη χώρα.
Στις περιπτώσεις αυτές οι ελληνικοί ποινικοί νόμοι εφαρμόζονται και όταν η πράξη τελείται στην αλλοδαπή από ημεδαπό, ακόμα κι αν δεν είναι αξιόποινη κατά τους νόμους της χώρας όπου τελέστηκε και για τη δίωξη του πλημμελήματος της παρ. 1 δεν απαιτείται η κατά το άρθρο 6 παρ. 3 έγκληση ή αίτηση.

Άρθρο 237
Δωροληψία και δωροδοκία δικαστικών λειτουργών

1. Όποιος καλείται κατά τον νόμον να εκτελέσει δικαστικά καθήκοντα ή ο διαιτητής, αν ζητήσει ή λάβει, άμεσα ή μέσω τρίτου, για τον εαυτό του ή για άλλον, οποιασδήποτε φύσης αθέμιτο ωφέλημα, ή αποδεχθεί την υπόσχεση παροχής τέτοιου ωφελήματος, για ενέργεια του ή παράλειψη, μελλοντική ή ήδη τελειωμένη, που ανάγεται στην εκτέλεση των καθηκόντων του κατά την απονομή της δικαιοσύνης ή την επίλυση διαφοράς, τιμωρείται με κάθειρξη και χρηματική ποινή από εκατό χιλιάδες (100.000) έως δύο εκατομμύρια (2.000.000) ευρώ.

2. Με κάθειρξη έως δέκα (10) έτη και χρηματική ποινή από τριάντα χιλιάδες (30.000) έως διακόσιες πενήντα χιλιάδες (250.000) ευρώ τιμωρείται όποιος για τον πιο πάνω σκοπό υπόσχεται ή παρέχει τέτοια ωφελήματα, άμεσα ή μέσω τρίτου, στα πρόσωπα της προηγούμενης παραγράφου, για τους εαυτούς τους ή για άλλον.

3. Διευθυντής επιχείρησης ή άλλο πρόσωπο που έχει την εξουσία λήψης αποφάσεων ή ελέγχου σε επιχείρηση τιμωρείται με φυλάκιση και χρηματική ποινή, εφόσον η πράξη δεν τιμωρείται βαρύτερα από άλλη ποινική διάταξη, αν με παραβίαση συγκεκριμένου καθήκοντος επιμέλειας δεν απέτρεψε από αμέλεια πρόσωπο που τελεί υπό τις εντολές του ή υπόκειται στον έλεγχο του από την τέλεση προς όφελος της επιχείρησης της πράξης της προηγούμενης παραγράφου.

Article 236
Active bribery of a state employee

1. Any person who offers, promises or provides a state employee, whether directly or through a third party, any kind of undue advantage, irrespective of value, whether for themselves or other persons, [in exchange] for any act or omission by that employee, whether in the future or already completed, which [is part] of their duties shall be punished with imprisonment of at least one year and a monetary penalty ranging from 3,000 to 50,000 euros.

2. If the aforesaid act or omission conflicts with the state employee's duties, the culpable person shall be punished with incarceration of up to eight years and a monetary penalty ranging from 20,000 to 200,000 euros.

3. Where any manager of an enterprise or other person with decision-making or control powers at that enterprise, in breach of a specific duty of care, fails to prevent a person under their instructions or subject to their control from committing the act provided for in the preceding paragraphs to the benefit of that enterprise, they shall be punished with imprisonment of up to two years or a monetary penalty, unless the act carries a heavier punishment.

4. The provisions of paragraphs 1, 2 and 3 also apply when the acts are committed in relation to:

a) functionaries or other state employees engaged under any contractual relationship by an institution or body of the European Union and any public international or supranational organisation or agency, irrespective of whether it is seated in Greece or whether Greece is a member of such, as well as in relation to any person, whether or not seconded, performing duties corresponding to those performed by functionaries or other state employees; or

b) any person performing a public function or service for a foreign country.

In such cases, Greek penal laws also apply when the act [was] committed by a Greek national abroad, even if [the act] is not punishable under the laws of the country where it was committed and a victim-initiated complaint or application referred to in Article 6(3) is not required to prosecute the misdemeanour provided for in paragraph 1.

Article 237
Active and passive bribery of judicial functionaries

1. If any person appointed by law to perform judicial duties or a mediator requests or receives, whether directly or through a third party, for themselves or for another person, any kind of undue advantage, or accepts a promise of such advantage, in exchange for any act or omission on their part, whether in the future or already completed, which [forms part] of their duties in the administration of justice or resolution of a dispute shall be punished with incarceration and a monetary penalty ranging from 100,000 to 2,000,000 euros.

2. Any person who, for the same purpose, promises or provides such advantages, whether directly or through a third party, to the persons referred to in the preceding paragraph, whether for themselves or for another, shall be punished with incarceration of up to 10 years and a monetary penalty ranging from 30,000 to 250,000 euros.

3. Where any manager of an enterprise or other person with decision-making or control powers at that enterprise, in breach of a specific duty of care, fails to prevent a person under their instructions or subject to their control from committing the act provided for in the preceding paragraph to the benefit of that enterprise, they shall be punished with imprisonment and a monetary penalty, unless the act carries a heavier punishment under a different criminal law provision.

4. Οι διατάξεις των προηγούμενων παραγράφων εφαρμόζονται και όταν οι πράξεις τελούνται:
α) από ή προς μέλη του Δικαστηρίου ή του Ελεγκτικού Συνεδρίου της Ευρωπαϊκής Ένωσης,
β) από ή προς όσους ασκούν δικαστικά καθήκοντα ή καθήκοντα διαιτητή σε διεθνή δικαστήρια των οποίων η δικαιοδοσία είναι αποδεκτή από την Ελλάδα,
γ) προς δικαστές, ενόρκους ή διαιτητές άλλων κρατών σχετικά με την άσκηση των δικαστικών τους καθηκόντων ή
δ) από ή προς δικαστές που είναι αποσπασμένοι σε ενωσιακούς ή διεθνείς οργανισμούς ή όργανα, ανεξαρτήτως του εάν αυτοί ασκούν δικαστικά καθήκοντα. Στις περιπτώσεις αυτές οι ελληνικοί ποινικοί νόμοι εφαρμόζονται και όταν η πράξη τελείται στην αλλοδαπή από ή προς ημεδαπό, ακόμα κι αν δεν είναι αξιόποινη κατά τους νόμους της χώρας όπου τελέστηκε.

Άρθρο 237Α
Εμπορία επιρροής – Μεσάζοντες

1. Όποιος ζητεί ή λαμβάνει, άμεσα ή μέσω τρίτου, οποιασδήποτε φύσης ωφέλημα, για τον εαυτό του ή για άλλον, ή αποδέχεται την υπόσχεση παροχής τέτοιου ωφελήματος ως αντάλλαγμα για αθέμιτη επιρροή την οποία ισχυρίζεται ή επιβεβαιώνει, ψευδώς ή αληθώς, ότι μπορεί να ασκήσει σε κάποιο από τα πρόσωπα που αναφέρονται στα άρθρα 159Α, 235 παρ. 1 και 237 παρ. 1, ώστε αυτά να προβούν σε πράξη ή παράλειψη που ανάγεται στην άσκηση των καθηκόντων τους, τιμωρείται με φυλάκιση και χρηματική ποινή.
2. Με φυλάκιση έως τρία έτη ή χρηματική ποινή τιμωρείται όποιος προσφέρει, υπόσχεται ή παρέχει, άμεσα ή μέσω τρίτου, οποιασδήποτε φύσης ωφέλημα, για τον εαυτό του ή για άλλον, σε πρόσωπο που ισχυρίζεται ή επιβεβαιώνει, ψευδώς ή αληθώς, ότι μπορεί να ασκήσει αθέμιτη επιρροή σε κάποιο από τα πρόσωπα που απαριθμούνται στα άρθρα 159Α, 235 παρ. 1 και 237 παρ. 1, ώστε αυτά να προβούν σε πράξη ή παράλειψη που ανάγεται στην άσκηση των καθηκόντων τους.

Άρθρο 237Β

Για την εφαρμογή των άρθρων 235 και 236, υπάλληλοι θεωρούνται και όσοι υπηρετούν μόνιμα ή μη και με οποιαδήποτε ιδιότητα ή σχέση σε οργανισμούς ή επιχειρήσεις οποιασδήποτε νομικής μορφής που ανήκουν εξ ολοκλήρου ή κατά την πλειοψηφία των μετοχών τους στο Κράτος, σε οργανισμούς τοπικής αυτοδιοίκησης ή σε νομικά πρόσωπα δημοσίου δικαίου ή των οποίων τη διοίκηση διορίζει εξ ολοκλήρου ή κατά πλειοψηφία το Κράτος ή οι οργανισμοί τοπικής αυτοδιοίκησης ή τα νομικά πρόσωπα δημοσίου δικαίου.

Άρθρο 238
Δήμευση

Στις περιπτώσεις των άρθρων 235 έως και 237Α το δικαστήριο επιβάλλει στον καταδικασθέντα και την παρεπόμενη ποινή της δήμευσης (άρθρο 68).

4. The provisions of the preceding paragraphs also apply when the acts are committed:

a) by or in relation to members of the Court of Justice of the European Union or the European Court of Auditors;

b) by or in relation to any person performing judicial duties or arbitrator duties at international courts whose jurisdiction is accepted by Greece;

c) in relation to judges, jurors or arbitrators of other states in regard to the performance of their judicial duties; or

d) by or in relation to judges seconded to EU or international bodies/organisations or institutions, irrespective of whether they perform judicial duties. In such cases, Greek penal laws also apply when the act [was] committed by or in relation to a Greek national abroad, even if [the act] is not punishable under the laws of the country where it was committed.

Article 237A

Trading in influence - Intermediaries

1. Any person who requests or receives, whether directly or through a third party, any kind of advantage, whether for themselves or for another person, or who accepts the promise of such an advantage in exchange for undue influence which they assert or confirm, whether falsely or truly, that they can exert over any of the persons referred to in Articles 159A, 235(1) and 237(1) in order for the latter to carry out an act or omission [which is part] of their duties shall be punished with imprisonment and a monetary penalty.

2. Any person who offers, promises or provides, whether directly or through a third party, any kind of advantage, whether for themselves or for another person, to a person who asserts or confirms, whether falsely or truly, that they can exert undue influence over any of the persons referred to in Articles 159A, 235(1) and 237(1) in order for the latter to carry out an act or omission [which is part] of their duties shall be punished with imprisonment of up to three years or a monetary penalty.

Article 237B

For [the purposes of] applying Articles 235 and 236, “state employees” also means any persons serving, whether or not full-time and in any capacity or relationship, at organisations or enterprises of any legal form which are wholly owned or majority owned by the Greek State, local government authorities or bodies governed by public law, or whose management is wholly or majority appointed by the Greek State or local government authorities or bodies governed by public law.

Article 238

Confiscation

In the cases provided for in Articles 235 to 237A, the court shall also impose the ancillary penalty of confiscation ([see] Article 68) on the convicted person.

II

ΚΑΤΑΧΡΗΣΗ ΥΠΑΛΛΗΛΙΚΗΣ ΙΔΙΟΤΗΤΑΣ

Άρθρο 239
Κατάχρηση εξουσίας

Υπάλληλος στα καθήκοντα του οποίου ανάγεται η δίωξη ή η ανάκριση αξιόποινων πράξεων:

α) αν μεταχειρίστηκε παρανόμως εκβιαστικά μέσα για να πετύχει οποιαδήποτε έγγραφη ή προφορική κατάθεση κατηγορουμένου, μάρτυρα ή πραγματογνώμονα τιμωρείται με φυλάκιση τουλάχιστον δύο ετών και χρηματική ποινή, εφόσον η πράξη δεν τιμωρείται βαρύτερα κατά το άρθρο 137 Α,

β) αν εν γνώσει του εξέθεσε σε δίωξη ή τιμωρία κάποιον αθώο ή παρέλειψε να διώξει κάποιον υπαίτιο, τιμωρείται με κάθειρξη έως δέκα έτη και χρηματική ποινή, αν πρόκειται για κακούργημα και με φυλάκιση τουλάχιστον τριών ετών και χρηματική ποινή, αν πρόκειται για πλημμέλημα.

Άρθρο 240
Παραβάσεις στην εκτέλεση των ποινών

1. Υπάλληλος στα καθήκοντα του οποίου ανάγεται η εκτέλεση των ποινών τιμωρείται με φυλάκιση τουλάχιστον τριών ετών και χρηματική ποινή αν εν γνώσει του εκτέλεσε παράνομα ποινή ή μέτρο ασφαλείας ή παρέλειψε την εκτέλεση.

2. Με τις ποινές της προηγούμενης παραγράφου τιμωρείται και ο αρμόδιος για την εκτέλεση εντάλματος σύλληψης υπάλληλος, που δεν το εκτελεί.

3. Αν οι παραβάσεις των προηγούμενων παραγράφων οφείλονται σε αμέλεια, επιβάλλεται φυλάκιση έως ένα έτος ή χρηματική ποινή.

Άρθρο 241
Παραβίαση οικιακού ασύλου

Υπάλληλος που, χρησιμοποιώντας την υπαλληλική του ιδιότητα εισέρχεται στην κατοικία άλλου χωρίς ο άλλος να το θέλει, εκτός από τις περιπτώσεις που το προβλέπει ο νόμος και χωρίς τις νόμιμες διατυπώσεις, τιμωρείται με φυλάκιση έως τρία έτη ή χρηματική ποινή.

Άρθρο 242
Ψευδής βεβαίωση, νόθευση κ.λπ.

1. Υπάλληλος που στα καθήκοντά του ανάγεται η έκδοση ή σύνταξη ορισμένων δημοσίων εγγράφων, αν σε τέτοια έγγραφα βεβαιώνει με πρόθεση ψευδώς περιστατικό που μπορεί να έχει έννομες συνέπειες, τιμωρείται με φυλάκιση τουλάχιστον ενός έτους και χρηματική ποινή.

2. Με την ίδια ποινή τιμωρείται ο υπάλληλος ο οποίος με πρόθεση νοθεύει, καταστρέφει, βλάπτει ή υπεξάγει έγγραφο που του εμπιστεύθηκαν ή του είναι προσιτό λόγω της υπηρεσίας του.

3. Αν όμως ο υπαίτιος κάποιας από τις πράξεις των παραγράφων 1 και 2 είχε σκοπό να προσπορίσει στον εαυτό του ή σε άλλον αθέμιτο όφελος ή να βλάψει παράνομα άλλον, επιβάλλεται κάθειρξη έως δέκα έτη και χρηματική ποινή εάν το συνολικό όφελος ή η συνολική βλάβη υπερβαίνουν το ποσό των 120.000 ευρώ.

II

ABUSE OF STATE EMPLOYEE STATUS

Article 239
Abuse of power

If any state employee whose duties involve the prosecution or investigation of punishable acts:
a) unlawfully used extortionary measures to obtain any written or verbal testimony from an accused person or defendant, witness or expert shall be punished with imprisonment of at least two years and a monetary penalty, unless the act carries a heavier punishment under Article 137A;
b) knowingly exposed an innocent person to prosecution or punishment or failed to prosecute a culpable person shall be punished with incarceration of up to 10 years and a monetary penalty, in the case of a felony, and with imprisonment of at least three years and a monetary penalty, in the case of a misdemeanour.

Article 240
Violations regarding the enforcement of punishments

1. If any state employee whose duties involve the enforcement of punishments knowingly enforced a punishment or security measure unlawfully or failed to enforce [such punishment or security measure] shall be punished with imprisonment of at least three years and a monetary penalty.
2. The punishments laid down in the preceding paragraph shall also be imposed on any state employee who is competent to enforce an arrest warrant and fails to do so.
3. If the violations provided for in the preceding paragraphs are due to negligence, imprisonment of up to one year or a monetary penalty shall be imposed.

Article 241
Violation of the [right to respect for the home]

Any state employee who, using their capacity as such, enters the home of another person against the wishes of such person, save where provided for in law, and without [following the] legal formalities shall be punished with imprisonment of up to three years or a monetary penalty.

Article 242
False attestation, alteration, etc.

1. If any state employee whose duties involve issuing or preparing specific public documents falsely and intentionally attests, in such documents, to a fact which could have legal consequences, they shall be punished with imprisonment of at least one year and a monetary penalty.
2. The same penalty shall be imposed on any state employee who intentionally alters, destroys, damages or makes unavailable a document which was entrusted to them or which they can access due to their employment.
3. However, if the person culpable of the acts provided for in paragraphs 1 and 2 sought to obtain an undue gain for themselves or another or to unlawfully prejudice another, they shall be punished with incarceration of up to 10 years and a monetary penalty if the total gain or total loss exceeds 120,000 euros.

4. Με την ποινή της παρ. 1 τιμωρείται όποιος εν γνώσει του χρησιμοποιεί το έγγραφο που είναι πλαστό ή νοθευμένο ή έχει υπεξαχθεί. Αν όμως είχε σκοπό να προσπορίσει στον εαυτό του ή σε άλλον αθέμιτο όφελος ή να βλάψει παράνομα άλλον και το συνολικό όφελος ή η συνολική βλάβη υπερβαίνουν το ποσό των 120.000 ευρώ, επιβάλλεται η ποινή της παραγράφου 3.
5. Αν οι πράξεις των προηγούμενων παραγράφων στρέφονται άμεσα κατά του νομικού προσώπου του ελληνικού Δημοσίου, των νομικών προσώπων Δημοσίου Δικαίου ή των οργανισμών τοπικής αυτοδιοίκησης και το συνολικό όφελος ή η συνολική βλάβη υπερβαίνουν το ποσό των 120.000 ευρώ, επιβάλλεται κάθειρξη τουλάχιστον δέκα ετών και χρηματική ποινή έως χίλιες ημερήσιες μονάδες. Οι πράξεις αυτές παραγράφονται μετά είκοσι έτη.

Άρθρο 243
Νόθευση δικαστικού εγγράφου

1. Όποιος κατά την εκτέλεση των δικαστικών ή διαιτητικών του καθηκόντων εν γνώσει αλλοιώνει το διατακτικό απόφασης δικαστηρίου ή δικαστικού συμβουλίου ή διαιτητικής απόφασης, ή το αποτέλεσμα ψηφοφορίας για την έκδοσή της, τιμωρείται με φυλάκιση τουλάχιστον τριών ετών και χρηματική ποινή. Η ίδια ποινή επιβάλλεται όταν η πράξη αφορά τα πρακτικά συνεδριάσεων δικαστηρίου ή δικαστικού συμβουλίου.
2. Αν ο υπαίτιος της πράξης της προηγούμενης παραγράφου σκόπευε να προσπορίσει στον εαυτό του ή σε άλλον παράνομο περιουσιακό όφελος βλάπτοντας τρίτο ή σκόπευε να βλάψει άλλον, τιμωρείται με κάθειρξη έως δέκα έτη και χρηματική ποινή εάν το συνολικό περιουσιακό όφελος ή η συνολική ζημία υπερβαίνουν το ποσό των 120.000 ευρώ.
3. Με φυλάκιση τουλάχιστον έξι μηνών και χρηματική ποινή τιμωρείται και όποιος άλλος, κατά την εκτέλεση των υπηρεσιακών του καθηκόντων, γίνεται υπαίτιος του εγκλήματος της πρώτης παραγράφου, καθώς και όποιος εν γνώσει κάνει χρήση των πιο πάνω αποφάσεων. Αν συντρέχει η επιβαρυντική περίσταση της παραγράφου 2 επιβάλλεται φυλάκιση τουλάχιστον τριών ετών και χρηματική ποινή.

Άρθρο 244
Παράνομη βεβαίωση ή είσπραξη δικαιωμάτων του Δημοσίου

Υπάλληλος που εν γνώσει βεβαιώνει ή εισπράττει φόρους, δασμούς, τέλη ή άλλα φορολογήματα, δικαστικά έξοδα ή οποιαδήποτε άλλα δικαιώματα του Δημοσίου που δεν οφείλονται τιμωρείται με φυλάκιση έως τρία έτη ή χρηματική ποινή.

Άρθρα 245 - 250

(Καταργούνται)

Άρθρο 251
Παραβίαση δικαστικού απορρήτου

1. Όποιος καλείται κατά νόμο να ασκήσει δικαστικά καθήκοντα ή ο διαιτητής, αν με οποιονδήποτε τρόπο γνωστοποιεί σε άλλον, αφήνει να περιέλθει στην κατοχή ή γνώση άλλου, ανακοινώνει ή διαδίδει δικαστικό απόρρητο, τιμωρείται με φυλάκιση και χρηματική ποινή. Αν με την πράξη σκόπευε να προσπορίσει στον εαυτό του ή σε άλλον οποιοδήποτε όφελος ή να βλάψει άλλον, επιβάλλεται φυλάκιση τουλάχιστον τριών ετών και χρηματική ποινή. Η παράβαση αυτή τιμωρείται και αν τελέστηκε μετά την αποχώρηση από την υπηρεσία.
2. Με την ίδια ποινή τιμωρείται και εκείνος στον οποίο το δικαστικό απόρρητο ήταν προσιτό λόγω της υπηρεσίας του ή της συμμετοχής του στη διαδικασία ως δικηγόρου ή διαδίκου.

4. The punishment laid down in paragraph 1 shall be imposed on any person who knowingly uses a document which was forged or altered or made unavailable. However, if they sought to obtain an undue gain for themselves or another or to unlawfully harm another and the total gain or total loss exceeds 120,000 euros, the punishment laid down in paragraph 3 shall be imposed.

5. If the acts provided for in the preceding paragraphs are committed directly against the Greek State as a legal person, any body governed by public law or any local government authority and the total gain or total loss exceeds 120,000 euros, incarceration of at least 10 years and a monetary penalty of up to 1,000 daily penalty units shall be imposed. Such acts shall become time-barred after 20 years.

Article 243
Alteration of a court document

1. Any person who, in performing their judicial or arbitration duties, knowingly alters the operative part of a court judgment or judicial council decision or arbitration award or the results of a vote for the issuance of the foregoing shall be punished with imprisonment of at least three years and a monetary penalty. The same punishment shall be imposed if the act concerns the transcript of a court or judicial council sitting.

2. If the person culpable of the act provided for in the preceding paragraph sought to obtain an unlawful pecuniary gain for themselves or another by harming a third party or sought to harm another, they shall be punished with incarceration of up to 10 years and a monetary penalty if the total pecuniary gain or total loss exceeds 120,000 euros.

3. Any other person who, in performing their duties, commits the crime provided for in the first paragraph and any person who knowingly uses the above judgments, decisions or awards shall be punished with imprisonment of at least six months and a monetary penalty. If the aggravating circumstances provided for in paragraph 2 apply, imprisonment of at least three years and a monetary penalty shall be imposed.

Article 244
Unlawful attestation or collection of amounts payable to the Greek State

Any state employee who knowingly attests or collects taxes, duties, fees or other levies, court costs, or any other amounts payable to the Greek State which are not owed shall be punished with imprisonment of up to three years or a monetary penalty.

Articles 245 - 250

[Repealed]

Article 251
Breach of judicial secrecy

1. Any person appointed by law to perform judicial duties or any arbitrator who, in any manner, discloses to another, allows another to take possession or cognisance of, announces or disseminates judicial secrets, shall be published with imprisonment and a monetary penalty. If they sought, through such act, to obtain any gain for themselves or another or sought to harm another, imprisonment of at least three years and a monetary penalty shall be imposed. Such breach shall be punished even if committed after [the culpable person] had left service.

2. The same punishment shall also be imposed on any person who could access the judicial secret due to their employment or participation in proceedings as a lawyer or party in the proceedings.

3. Το δικαστικό απόρρητο κατά το άρθρο αυτό αφορά γεγονότα, έγγραφα ή πληροφορίες όταν αυτά σχετίζονται με:
α) συνεδρίαση δικαστικού συμβουλίου,
β) διάσκεψη ή μυστική ψηφοφορία,
γ) πράξεις που διενεργούνται στη διάρκεια της ανάκρισης,
δ) συνεδρίαση δικαστηρίου που έχει διεξαχθεί κεκλεισμένων των θυρών, όταν από τη δημοσιοποίηση των στοιχείων της προκαλείται κίνδυνος προσβολής άλλου ή
ε) στοιχεία που σχετίζονται με διαιτησία ή διαμεσολάβηση, όταν η δημοσιοποίησή τους δημιουργεί κίνδυνο προσβολής του ενός μέρους.

Άρθρο 252
Παραβίαση υπηρεσιακού απορρήτου

1. Υπάλληλος που κατά παράβαση των καθηκόντων του γνωστοποιεί σε άλλον απόρρητα που του εμπιστεύτηκαν ή γνωρίζει λόγω της υπηρεσίας του, τιμωρείται με φυλάκιση και χρηματική ποινή. Η παράβαση αυτή τιμωρείται και αν τελέστηκε μετά την αποχώρηση του υπαλλήλου από την υπηρεσία.
2. Με την ίδια ποινή τιμωρείται και εκείνος που χρησιμοποιεί το υπηρεσιακό απόρρητο εν γνώσει της προέλευσής του, με σκοπό να βλάψει το κράτος ή άλλον.
3. Το υπηρεσιακό απόρρητο κατά το άρθρο αυτό αφορά έγγραφα ή πληροφορίες που με νόμο ή απόφαση της αρμόδιας αρχής έχουν χαρακτηριστεί εμπιστευτικά.

Άρθρο 253

(Καταργείται)

Άρθρο 254
Αποσιώπηση λόγου εξαίρεσης

Υπάλληλος για τον οποίο υπάρχει νόμιμος λόγος να εξαιρεθεί σε κάποια υπόθεση και που εν γνώσει του αποσιωπά το περιστατικό αυτό και ενεργεί σ' αυτήν την υπόθεση, τιμωρείται με φυλάκιση έως τρία έτη ή χρηματική ποινή, αν η αποσιώπηση έγινε με σκοπό την αθέμιτη ωφέλεια του ίδιου ή άλλου ή τη βλάβη άλλου. Επιβάλλεται φυλάκιση ή χρηματική ποινή, όταν η πράξη τελείται από δικαστικό λειτουργό ή διαιτητή.

Άρθρο 255
Αθέμιτη συμμετοχή

Υπάλληλος που, άμεσα ή έμμεσα και ιδίως χρησιμοποιώντας άλλο πρόσωπο ή με πράξεις συγκαλυμμένες, πήρε μέρος σε πλειστηριασμό, μίσθωση, δημοπρασία ή σε οποιαδήποτε άλλη πράξη στην οποία ασκεί τα υπηρεσιακά του καθήκοντα, τιμωρείται με φυλάκιση μέχρι δύο ετών και με χρηματική ποινή.

Άρθρα 256 - 258

(Καταργούνται)

Άρθρο 259
Παράβαση καθήκοντος

Υπάλληλος που με πρόθεση παραβαίνει τα καθήκοντα της υπηρεσίας του με σκοπό να προσπορίσει στον εαυτό του ή σε άλλον παράνομο όφελος ή να βλάψει το κράτος ή κάποιον άλλο τιμωρείται με φυλάκιση έως δύο έτη ή χρηματική ποινή, αν η πράξη αυτή δεν τιμωρείται με άλλη ποινική διάταξη.

3. For the purposes of this Article, judicial secrecy concerns facts, documents or information related to:
a) the sitting of a judicial council;
b) deliberations or votes by secret ballot;
c) steps taken during an investigation;
d) a court sitting held *in camera*, when disclosure of its details places another at risk of harm; or
e) information relating to arbitration or mediation, when its disclosure places a party [in such arbitration or mediation] at risk of harm.

Article 252
Breach of official secrecy

1. Any state employee who, in breach of their duties, discloses to another secrets which were entrusted to them or of which they are aware due to their employment shall be punished with imprisonment and a monetary penalty. Such breach shall be punished even if committed after the employee in question had left service.
2. The same punishment shall be imposed on any person who uses an official secret, whilst being aware of its provenance, for the purpose of harming the Greek State or another person.
3. For the purposes of this Article, official secrecy concerns documents or information which, by law or by decision of a competent authority, have been classified as confidential.

Article 253

[Repealed]

Article 254
Concealment of grounds for exemption

Where there are legitimate grounds for exempting any state employee from a case and they knowingly conceal this fact and take steps in the case in question, they shall be punished with imprisonment of up to three years or a monetary penalty, if the concealment took place for the purpose of obtaining an undue advantage for themselves or another or for the purpose of harming another. Where the act is committed by a judicial functionary or arbitrator, imprisonment or a monetary penalty shall be imposed.

Article 255
Undue participation

Any state employee who, whether directly or indirectly, and, in particular, by using another person or through concealed actions, took part in a public auction, leasing, or sale or any other act in which they perform their official duties shall be punished with imprisonment of up to two years and a monetary penalty.

Articles 256 - 258

[Repealed]

Article 259
Breach of duty

Any state employee who intentionally breaches their official duties for the purpose of obtaining an unlawful gain for themselves or another or for the purpose of harming the Greek State or another person shall be punished with imprisonment of at least two years or a monetary penalty, unless this act carries a heavier punishment under a different criminal law provision.

Άρθρο 260
Ανυποταξία σε πολιτική αρχή

Στρατιωτικός διοικητής, αξιωματικός ή υπαξιωματικός ή αστυνομικός υπάλληλος ο οποίος παραλείπει να συγκεντρώσει και να χρησιμοποιήσει την ένοπλη ή αστυνομική δύναμη που έχει στις διαταγές του, αν και η αρμόδια πολιτική αρχή τον κάλεσε νόμιμα να το πράξει, τιμωρείται με φυλάκιση έως τρία έτη ή χρηματική ποινή.

Άρθρα 261 - 262

(Καταργούνται)

Άρθρο 263
Παρεπόμενες ποινές

1. Στις περιπτώσεις των άρθρων 235, 237, 239, 242, 243, η αμετάκλητη καταδίκη του υπαιτίου συνεπάγεται αυτοδικαίως έκπτωση από τη δημόσια θέση και τα αξιώματα που κατέχει.
2. Η διάταξη του άρθρου 238 εφαρμόζεται αναλόγως σε όλα τα εγκλήματα των άρθρων 239 έως 260, καθώς και του άρθρου 396, εφόσον έχουν προσπορίσει στους υπαιτίους περιουσιακά οφέλη.

Άρθρο 263Α
Ευνοϊκά μέτρα

1. (Καταργείται)
2. Αν ο υπαίτιος των πράξεων των άρθρων 236 παρ. 1, 2 και 3 και 237 παρ. 2 και 3 ή ο συμμέτοχος στις πράξεις των άρθρων 235 παρ. 1, 2 και 3, 237 παρ. 1 και 239 έως 260, καθώς και του άρθρου 390, όταν τελείται από υπάλληλο, συμβάλει ουσιωδώς, με αναγγελία στην αρχή, στην αποκάλυψη της συμμετοχής υπαλλήλου στις πράξεις αυτές, τιμωρείται με ποινή μειωμένη στο μέτρο του άρθρου 44 παρ. 2. Το δικαστήριο μπορεί να διατάξει την αναστολή εκτέλεσης της ποινής αυτής, ανεξάρτητα αν συντρέχουν οι όροι του άρθρου 99. Το Συμβούλιο Πλημμελειοδικών με βούλευμα που εκδίδεται ύστερα από πρόταση του αρμοδίου εισαγγελέα, διατάσσει την αναστολή της ασκηθείσας ποινικής δίωξης κατά του υπαιτίου για ορισμένο χρονικό διάστημα, προκειμένου να επιβεβαιωθεί η αλήθεια των εισφερόμενων στοιχείων. Την αναστολή της δίωξης μπορεί να διατάξει και το δικαστήριο, εφόσον τα στοιχεία εισφέρονται μέχρι την έκδοση απόφασης σε δεύτερο βαθμό. Με το ίδιο βούλευμα ή απόφαση μπορεί να διαταχθεί και η άρση ή η αντικατάσταση των μέτρων δικονομικού καταναγκασμού που έχουν επιβληθεί. Αν μετά την αναστολή της ποινικής δίωξης προκύψει ότι τα εισφερθέντα από τον υπαίτιο στοιχεία δεν ήσαν επαρκή για την άσκηση ποινικής δίωξης κατά του υπαλλήλου, το σχετικό βούλευμα ή απόφαση ανακαλείται και συνεχίζεται κατά του υπαιτίου η ανασταλείσα ποινική δίωξη.
3. Υπάλληλος, υπαίτιος ή συμμέτοχος για την τέλεση των πράξεων των άρθρων 235 έως 260, καθώς και του άρθρου 390, ο οποίος συμβάλλει ουσιωδώς, με αναγγελία στην αρχή, στην αποκάλυψη της συμμετοχής στις πράξεις αυτές άλλων υπαλλήλων που κατέχουν θέση ανώτερη της δικής του, ή συμμέτοχος μη υπάλληλος στις πράξεις αυτές, εξαιρουμένης της τελέσεως από αυτόν της πράξης του άρθρου 236 ΠΚ, τιμωρείται σύμφωνα με τα οριζόμενα στην παρ. 2, εφόσον ο ίδιος έχει μεταβιβάσει στο Δημόσιο όλα τα περιουσιακά στοιχεία που έχει αποκτήσει, αμέσως ή εμμέσως, από την τέλεση ή τη συμμετοχή στην τέλεση των παραπάνω εγκλημάτων. Αν κατ' εξαίρεση η μεταβίβαση αυτή δεν έχει ολοκληρωθεί μέχρι το στάδιο της επιμέτρησης της ποινής, το δικαστήριο μπορεί να επιφυλαχθεί ως προς την επί ποινής κρίση του, διακόπτοντας προς τούτο τη διαδικασία για ορισμένη ημερομηνία και χωρίς το χρονικό περιορισμό του άρθρου 352 παρ. 1 του Κώδικα Ποινικής Δικονομίας. Στην περίπτωση αυτή ορίζει και τις συγκεκριμένες μεταβιβάσεις ή άλλες ενέργειες στις οποίες πρέπει να προβεί ο δράστης για να τύχει του σχετικού ευεργετήματος. Με την απόφαση περί διακοπής της δίκης το δικαστήριο μπορεί να διατάξει και την άρση ή την αντικατάσταση των μέτρων δικονομικού καταναγκασμού που έχουν επιβληθεί.

Article 260
Insubordination to a civil authority

If any military commander, officer, non-commissioned officer or police officer fails to muster and deploy the armed or police forces under their command, despite having been lawfully called to do so by the competent civil authority, they shall be punished with imprisonment of up to three years or a monetary penalty.

Articles 261 - 262

[Repealed]

Article 263
Ancillary penalties

1. In the cases provided for in Articles 235, 237, 239, 242, 243, the irrevocable conviction of the culpable person entails automatic forfeiture of their public post and offices.
2. The provisions of Article 238 apply *mutatis mutandis* to all the crimes provided for in Articles 239 to 260, as well as Article 396, where the culpable person obtained a pecuniary gain.

Article 263A
Measures of [leniency]

1. [Repealed]
2. If a person who committed the acts provided for in Articles 236(1), (2) and (3) and 237(2) and (3) or an accessory to the acts provided for in Articles 235(1), (2) and (3), 237(1) and 239 to 260, as well as Article 390, where committed by a state employee, materially contributes, by notifying the authorities, to uncovering the participation of a state employee in such acts, they shall be punished with a punishment reduced in accordance with Article 44(2). The court may order that enforcement of such punishment be stayed, irrespective of whether the conditions laid down in Article 99 are met. The judicial council of the court of misdemeanours, by means of a judicial council decision issued on a proposal from the competent public prosecutor, shall order that criminal prosecution instituted against the culpable person be stayed for a specific period of time, until the veracity of the information provided can be verified. The court too may order that prosecution be stayed where such information is provided before a judgment is handed down at second instance. Such judicial council decision or judgment may also order that any procedural compulsory measures imposed be terminated or replaced. If it becomes clear, after criminal prosecution was stayed, that the information provided by the culpable person does not suffice to institute criminal prosecution against the state employee, the relevant judicial council decision or judgment shall be revoked and the criminal prosecution of the culpable person which had been stayed shall resume.
3. Any state employee who has committed or was an accessory to the acts provided for in Articles 235 to 260, as well as Article 390 and who materially contributes, by notifying the authorities, to uncovering the participation in such acts of other state employees holding a post superior to their own, or an accessory to such acts who is not a state employee, except where that person commits the act provided for in Article 235 of this Code, shall be punished in accordance with the provisions of paragraph 2, provided they have transferred to the Greek State all assets acquired, whether directly or indirectly, from committing or participating in the commission of the above crimes. By way of exception, if this transfer has not been completed before the extent of the punishment has been determined, the court may reserve judgment on the punishment, staying the proceedings to this end until a specific date and without applying the time limit laid down in Article 352(1) of the Code of Criminal Procedure. In this case, [the court] shall also indicate the specific transfers to be carried out or other steps to be taken by the perpetrator in order to be granted the relevant benefit. In its ruling ordering that proceedings be stayed, the court may also order the termination or replacement of any procedural compulsory measures imposed.

4. α) Αν κάποιος από τους υπαιτίους των εγκλημάτων των άρθρων 235 έως 260, 390 και 396 ή πράξεων νομιμοποίησης εσόδων που προέρχονται άμεσα από τις συγκεκριμένες εγκληματικές δραστηριότητες, εισφέρει αποδεικτικά στοιχεία για τη συμμετοχή στις πράξεις αυτές προσώπων που διατελούν ή διατέλεσαν μέλη της Κυβέρνησης ή Υφυπουργοί, το δικαστικό συμβούλιο, με βούλευμα που εκδίδεται ύστερα από πρόταση του εισαγγελέα, διατάσσει την αναστολή της ασκηθείσας σε βάρος του ποινικής δίωξης και την αμελλητί παραπομπή της δικογραφίας στη Βουλή. Την παραπάνω αναστολή μπορεί να διατάξει το δικαστήριο και όταν τα στοιχεία εισφέρονται μέχρι την έκδοση απόφασης σε δεύτερο βαθμό. Με το ίδιο βούλευμα ή απόφαση μπορεί να διαταχθεί και η άρση ή η αντικατάσταση των μέτρων δικονομικού καταναγκασμού που έχουν ταχθεί.

β) Αν η Βουλή κρίνει, σύμφωνα με τη διάταξη της παρ. 3 του άρθρου 86 του Συντάγματος, ότι τα στοιχεία δεν είναι επαρκή για την άσκηση ποινικής δίωξης σε βάρος Υπουργού ή Υφυπουργού, το βούλευμα ή η απόφαση ανακαλείται και η ανασταλείσα ποινική δίωξη συνεχίζεται. Αν η Βουλή αποφασίσει την άσκηση ποινικής δίωξης σε βάρος Υπουργού ή Υφυπουργού κατά το άρθρο 86 του Συντάγματος, σε περίπτωση καταδίκης από το Ειδικό Δικαστήριο, ο κατά το προηγούμενο εδάφιο συμμέτοχος που εισέφερε τα αποδεικτικά στοιχεία τιμωρείται με ποινή μειωμένη στο μέτρο του άρθρου 44 παρ. 2. Το δικαστήριο μπορεί να διατάξει την αναστολή εκτέλεσης της ποινής αυτής κατά τα οριζόμενα στην παρ. 2.

5. Αν η κίνηση της ποινικής διαδικασίας δεν είναι δυνατή λόγω εξάλειψης του αξιόποινου, σύμφωνα με τα οριζόμενα στο άρθρο 86 παρ. 3 εδ. Β΄ του Συντάγματος, στον κατηγορούμενο επιβάλλεται ποινή μειωμένη στο μέτρο του άρθρου 44 παρ. 2. Το δικαστήριο μπορεί να διατάξει και την αναστολή εκτέλεσης της ποινής αυτής, κατά τα οριζόμενα στην παρ. 2.

4. a) If any person who committed the crimes provided for in Articles 235 to 260, 390 and 396 or the crime of laundering money originating directly from those specific criminal activities contributes evidence that persons who are or were members of Government or Deputy Ministers participated in such acts, the judicial council shall, by means of a judicial council decision issued on a proposal from the public prosecutor, order that criminal prosecution instituted against them be stayed and that the case-file be remitted to Parliament without delay. The court may also order the above where such information is provided before a judgment is handed down at second instance. Such judicial council decision or judgment may also order that any procedural compulsory measures imposed be terminated or replaced.
b) If, in accordance with the provisions of Article 86(3) of the Constitution, Parliament considers that the evidence does not suffice to institute criminal prosecution against a Minister or Deputy Minister, the judicial council decision or ruling shall be revoked and the criminal prosecution which had been stayed shall resume. If Parliament decides that criminal prosecution should be instituted against a Minister or Deputy Minister in accordance with Article 86 of the Constitution and [said Minister or Deputy Minister] is convicted by the Special Court, the accessory referred to in the preceding paragraph who contributed the evidence shall receive a punishment reduced in accordance with Article 44(2). The court may order that enforcement of such punishment be stayed in accordance with the provisions of paragraph 2.
5. If criminal proceedings cannot be instituted due to expungement of punishability, in accordance with the provisions of the second sentence of Article 86(3) of the Constitution, a punishment reduced in accordance with Article 44(2) shall be imposed on the defendant. The court may also order that enforcement of such punishment be stayed, in accordance with the provisions of paragraph 2.

ΔΕΚΑΤΟ ΤΡΙΤΟ ΚΕΦΑΛΑΙΟ

ΚΟΙΝΩΣ ΕΠΙΚΙΝΔΥΝΑ ΕΓΚΛΗΜΑΤΑ

Άρθρο 264
Εμπρησμός

1. Όποιος προξενεί πυρκαγιά, τιμωρείται:

α) με φυλάκιση και χρηματική ποινή, αν από την πράξη μπορεί να προκύψει κοινός κίνδυνος για ξένα πράγματα,

β) με κάθειρξη έως δέκα (10) έτη και χρηματική ποινή, αν από την πράξη μπορεί να προκύψει κίνδυνος για άνθρωπο,

γ) με κάθειρξη και χρηματική ποινή, αν στην περίπτωση των περ. α' ή β' η πράξη προκάλεσε σημαντική βλάβη σε εγκαταστάσεις κοινής ωφέλειας ή είχε ως αποτέλεσμα τη βαριά σωματική βλάβη ανθρώπου,

δ) με ισόβια κάθειρξη, αν στην περίπτωση της περ. β' η πράξη είχε ως αποτέλεσμα τον θάνατο άλλου.

2. Όποιος προκαλεί από αμέλεια την πυρκαγιά από την οποία μπορεί να προκύψει κοινός κίνδυνος για ξένα πράγματα ή κίνδυνος για άνθρωπο, τιμωρείται με φυλάκιση έως τρία (3) έτη στις περ. α' και β' της παρ. 1 και με ποινή φυλάκισης και χρηματική ποινή στις περ. γ' και δ' της ίδιας παραγράφου.

Άρθρο 265
Εμπρησμός σε δάση - Προπαρασκευαστικές πράξεις - Παραβίαση προληπτικών μέτρων

1. Όποιος προξενεί πυρκαγιά σε δάσος ή δασική έκταση κατά την έννοια του νόμου ή σε έκταση που έχει νόμιμα κηρυχθεί δασωτέα ή αναδασωτέα, τιμωρείται:

α) με κάθειρξη έως δέκα (10) έτη και χρηματική ποινή, αν δε ο δράστης σκόπευε να προσπορίσει στον εαυτό του ή σε άλλον παράνομο περιουσιακό όφελος συνιστά επιβαρυντική περίσταση,

β) με κάθειρξη έως δέκα (10) έτη και χρηματική ποινή αν από την πράξη μπορεί να προκύψει κίνδυνος για άνθρωπο,

γ) με κάθειρξη τουλάχιστον δέκα (10) έτη και χρηματική ποινή αν στην περίπτωση των περ. α' ή β' η πράξη προκάλεσε σημαντική βλάβη σε εγκαταστάσεις κοινής ωφέλειας ή είχε ως αποτέλεσμα τη βαριά σωματική βλάβη ανθρώπου ή η φωτιά εξαπλώθηκε σε μεγάλη έκταση ή είχε ως επακόλουθο σοβαρή ή ευρεία ρύπανση ή υποβάθμιση ή σοβαρή ή ευρεία οικολογική και περιβαλλοντική διατάραξη ή καταστροφή,

δ) με ισόβια κάθειρξη αν στην περ. β' η πράξη είχε ως αποτέλεσμα τον θάνατο άλλου.

2. Όποιος στις περιπτώσεις της παρ. 1 προκαλεί από αμέλεια την πυρκαγιά σε δάσος ή δασική έκταση κατά την έννοια του νόμου ή σε έκταση που έχει κηρυχθεί δασωτέα ή αναδασωτέα τιμωρείται με φυλάκιση τουλάχιστον τριών (3) μηνών και χρηματική ποινή, και αν από την πράξη μπορεί να προκύψει κίνδυνος για άνθρωπο, ή η φωτιά εξαπλώθηκε σε μεγάλη έκταση ή είχε ως επακόλουθο σοβαρή ή ευρεία ρύπανση ή υποβάθμιση ή σοβαρή ή ευρεία οικολογική και περιβαλλοντική διατάραξη ή καταστροφή, τιμωρείται με φυλάκιση τουλάχιστον τριών (3) ετών και χρηματική ποινή.

CHAPTER XIII

CRIMES ENDANGERING THE GENERAL PUBLIC

Article 264

Arson

1. Any person who causes a fire shall be punished with:

a) imprisonment and a monetary penalty if the act could result in common danger to things owned by others;

b) incarceration of up to 10 years and a monetary penalty if the act could result in danger to a human being;

c) incarceration and a monetary penalty if, in the cases of points (a) and (b), the act caused serious damage to public utility facilities or resulted in grievous bodily harm of a person; [or]

d) incarceration for life if, in the case of point (b), the act resulted in the death of another person.

2. Any person who negligently causes a fire which could result in common danger to things owned by others or danger to a human being shall be punished with imprisonment of up to three years in the cases of points (a) and (b) of paragraph 1, and with imprisonment and a monetary penalty in the cases of points (c) and (d) of the same paragraph.

Article 265

Forest arson - Preparatory acts - Violation of preventive measures

1. Any person who causes a fire in a forest or forested area within the meaning of the law or an area lawfully declared afforestable or reforestable shall be punished with:

a) incarceration of up to 10 years and a monetary penalty; there are aggravating circumstances when the perpetrator sought to obtain an unlawful pecuniary gain for themselves or another;

b) incarceration of up to 10 years and a monetary penalty if the act could result in danger to a human being;

c) incarceration of at least 10 years and a monetary penalty if, in the cases of points (a) and (b), the act caused serious damage to public utility facilities, or resulted in grievous bodily harm of a person, or the fire spread to a large area, or resulted in serious or widespread pollution or degradation or serious or widespread ecological and environmental disruption or destruction; [or]

d) incarceration for life if, in the case of point (b), the act resulted in the death of another person.

2. Any person who, in the cases provided for in paragraph 1, negligently causes a fire in a forest or forested area, within the meaning of the law, or an area declared afforestable or reforestable, shall be punished with imprisonment of at least three months and a monetary penalty, and if the act could result in danger to a human being, or the fire spreading to a large area, or resulted in serious or widespread pollution or degradation or serious or widespread ecological and environmental disruption or destruction, they shall be punished with imprisonment of at least three years and a monetary penalty.

3. Όποιος ανάβει ή διατηρεί φωτιά για οποιοδήποτε σκοπό ή εκτελεί θερμές εργασίες ή κάνει χρήση συσκευών που προκαλούν σπινθήρα ή ειδών πυροτεχνίας ή βεγγαλικών σε δάση, δασικές εκτάσεις, κηρυγμένες δασωτέες ή αναδασωτέες εκτάσεις, ιδιωτικά δάση, περιοχές «Natura», εκτάσεις περιαστικού πρασίνου εντός των πόλεων και των οικιστικών περιοχών, όπως πάρκα και άλση, χορτολιβαδικές και αγροτικές εκτάσεις ή σε οποιονδήποτε χώρο σε ακτίνα έως τριακοσίων (300) μέτρων από αυτές, σε ημέρες που ο δείκτης επικινδυνότητας, σύμφωνα με τον Ημερήσιο Χάρτη πρόβλεψης κινδύνου πυρκαγιάς που εκδίδεται από τη Γενική Γραμματεία Πολιτικής Προστασίας είναι 4 (πολύ υψηλή) ή 5 (κατάσταση συναγερμού), τιμωρείται με φυλάκιση τουλάχιστον ενός (1) έτους και χρηματική ποινή αν η πράξη του δεν τιμωρείται βαρύτερα από άλλη ποινική διάταξη. Αν η ανωτέρω πράξη είχε ως επακόλουθο την πρόκληση πυρκαγιάς, η οποία επέφερε σοβαρή ή ευρεία οικολογική και περιβαλλοντική διατάραξη ή καταστροφή ή είχε ως αποτέλεσμα τη βαριά σωματική βλάβη ανθρώπου, τιμωρείται με κάθειρξη και χρηματική ποινή και αν επήλθε θάνατος με κάθειρξη τουλάχιστον δέκα (10) ετών και χρηματική ποινή.

4. Όποιος, προετοιμάζοντας τη διάπραξη του εγκλήματος της παρ. 1, κατασκευάζει, προμηθεύεται ή κατέχει εμπρηστικές ύλες ή άλλα αντικείμενα, πρόσφορα για την πρόκληση και την εξάπλωση δασικής πυρκαγιάς τιμωρείται με ποινή φυλάκισης τουλάχιστον τριών (3) ετών και χρηματική ποινή, αν δε τελεί την ανωτέρω πράξη εντός δάσους ή δασικής έκτασης και σε ακτίνα έως τριακοσίων (300) μέτρων από αυτά, σε ημέρες που ο δείκτης επικινδυνότητας, σύμφωνα με τον Ημερήσιο Χάρτη πρόβλεψης κινδύνου πυρκαγιάς που εκδίδεται από τη Γενική Γραμματεία Πολιτικής Προστασίας είναι 4 (πολύ υψηλή) ή 5 (κατάσταση συναγερμού) σε ποινή κάθειρξης έως οκτώ (8) ετών και χρηματική ποινή.

5. Όποιος αποθηκεύει, τοποθετεί ή εγκαταλείπει εύφλεκτες ύλες εντός δασών ή δασικών εκτάσεων, τιμωρείται με ποινή φυλάκισης και χρηματική ποινή, αν η πράξη αυτή δεν τιμωρείται βαρύτερα από άλλη ποινική διάταξη. Αν η πράξη του συνέβαλε στην εξάπλωση δασικής πυρκαγιάς, τιμωρείται με ποινή φυλάκισης τουλάχιστον τριών (3) ετών και χρηματική ποινή.

6. Στις περιπτώσεις καταδίκης για αξιόποινες πράξεις του παρόντος, η ποινή δεν αναστέλλεται ούτε μετατρέπεται με κανέναν τρόπο, και η έφεση που ασκείται δεν έχει ανασταλλουσα ισχύ, εκτός αν, στην περίπτωση της παρ. 2, του πρώτου εδαφίου της παρ. 3 και της παρ. 5, το δικαστήριο με ειδική αιτιολογία κρίνει εξαιρετικώς υπέρ της μετατροπής της ποινής.

7. Το ύψος της χρηματικής ποινής για τα αδικήματα του παρόντος δεν μπορεί να είναι κατώτερο από δέκα χιλιάδες (10.000) ούτε ανώτερο από διακόσιες χιλιάδες (200.000) ευρώ.

Άρθρο 265Α
Δήμευση σε περίπτωση εμπρησμού σε δάση

1. Στο έγκλημα εμπρησμού σε δάση από πρόθεση, τετελεσμένο και σε απόπειρα (παρ. 1 άρθρου 265), καθώς και στις περιπτώσεις εμπρησμού σε δάση από αμέλεια από τις οποίες προκλήθηκε πυρκαγιά που είχε ως αποτέλεσμα θάνατο ή βαριά σωματική βλάβη ή εξαπλώθηκε σε μεγάλη έκταση ή είχε ως επακόλουθο σοβαρή ή ευρεία ρύπανση ή υποβάθμιση ή σοβαρή ή ευρεία οικολογική και περιβαλλοντική διατάραξη ή καταστροφή (παρ. 2 άρθρου 265), μπορεί να δημευτεί κατά την κρίση του δικαστηρίου με την καταδικαστική απόφαση τμήμα περιουσίας, του αυτουργού και των συμμετόχων στο έγκλημα, μη συμπεριλαμβανομένων πάντως στη δήμευση των περιουσιακών στοιχείων που εξυπηρετούν τις βασικές ανάγκες διαβίωσης του καταδικασθέντος και της οικογένειάς του. Για τον υπολογισμό του ύψους της ζημίας, διατάσσεται πραγματογνωμοσύνη σύμφωνα με τα άρθρα 183 έως 208 του Κώδικα Ποινικής Δικονομίας.

2. Η έκταση της δήμευσης αποφασίζεται από το δικαστήριο, το οποίο την προσδιορίζει με βάση τη βλάβη που προκλήθηκε αφού σταθμίσει για τον υπολογισμό της και τα στοιχεία του άρθρου 79.

3. Το άρθρο 261 του Κώδικα Ποινικής Δικονομίας περί δυνατότητας δέσμευσης περιουσιακών στοιχείων αντίστοιχης αξίας με τη βλάβη που επήλθε, εφαρμόζεται αναλόγως.

3. Any person who lights or keeps a fire lit for any purpose or carries out hot works or uses devices that produce sparks, or pyrotechnic items or fireworks in forests, forested areas, areas declared afforestable or reforestable, private forests, 'Natura' areas, peri-urban green areas within cities and residential districts, such as parks and woods, pasture and farmland or in any area within a 300-metre radius of such on days when the risk index, according to the daily fire risk prediction map issued by the General Secretariat for Civil Protection, is 4 (very high) or 5 (state of alert), shall be punished with imprisonment of at least one year and a monetary penalty, unless the act carries a heavier punishment under a different criminal law provision. If the above act resulted in a fire which caused serious or widespread ecological and environmental disruption or destruction, or resulted in grievous bodily harm to a person, they shall be punished with incarceration and a monetary penalty, and if a person died, with incarceration of at least 10 years and a monetary penalty.

4. Any person who, in preparing to commit the crime provided for in paragraph 1, manufactures, procures, or possesses incendiary materials or other items which could cause [or] spread a forest fire, shall be punished with imprisonment of at least three years and a monetary penalty, and if they commit such crime within a forest or forested area and within a 300-metre radius of such on days when the risk index, according to the daily fire risk prediction map issued by the General Secretariat for Civil Protection, is 4 (very high) or 5 (state of alert), they shall be punished with incarceration of up to eight years and a monetary penalty.

5. Any person who stores, places or leaves flammable materials within forests or forested areas shall be punished with imprisonment and a monetary penalty, unless this act carries a heavier punishment under a different criminal law provision. If such act contributed to the spread of a forest fire, they shall be punished with imprisonment of at least three years and a monetary penalty.

6. In cases of conviction of the punishable acts provided for in this Article, the punishment shall neither be suspended nor commuted in any manner, and any appeal filed shall not have suspensive effect, unless the court, in the case provided for in paragraph 2, the first sentence of paragraph 3 [or] paragraph 5, providing specific reasoning [in its judgment], rules on exceptional grounds that the punishment must be commuted.

7. The monetary penalty for the crimes provided for in this Article may not be less than 10,000 nor more than 200,000 euros.

Article 265A
Confiscation in cases of forest arson

1. In cases of the crime of intentional forest arson, whether committed or attempted (as provided for in Article 265(1)) and in cases of negligent forest arson, which caused a fire that resulted in death or grievous bodily harm, or spread to a large area, or resulted in serious or widespread pollution or degradation or serious or widespread ecological and environmental disruption or destruction (as provided for in Article 265(2)), the court, in its judgment of conviction, may order that part of the assets of the perpetrator and accessories to the crime be confiscated, but not including the assets necessary for the basic subsistence needs of the convicted person and their family. In order to calculate the level of damage, preparation of an expert evidence report shall be ordered in accordance with Articles 183 to 208 of the Code of Criminal Procedure.

2. The court shall decide on the extent of confiscation, determining such extent based on the damage caused, having weighed up the information referred to in Article 79 for the purpose of such calculation.

3. Article 261 of the Code of Criminal Procedure on the possibility of freezing assets with a value equivalent to the damage caused applies *mutatis mutandis*.

Άρθρα 266 - 267

(Καταργούνται)

Άρθρο 268
Πλημμύρα

1. Όποιος προξενεί πλημμύρα τιμωρείται:
α) με φυλάκιση αν από την πράξη μπορεί να προκύψει κοινός κίνδυνος για ξένα πράγματα,
β) με κάθειρξη έως δέκα (10) έτη αν από την πράξη μπορεί να προκύψει κίνδυνος για άνθρωπο,
γ) με κάθειρξη αν στην περίπτωση των στοιχείων α΄ ή β΄ η πράξη προκάλεσε σημαντική βλάβη σε εγκαταστάσεις κοινής ωφέλειας ή είχε ως αποτέλεσμα τη βαριά σωματική βλάβη ανθρώπου,
δ) με κάθειρξη τουλάχιστον δέκα (10) ετών αν στην περίπτωση του στοιχείου β΄ η πράξη είχε ως αποτέλεσμα το θάνατο άλλου. Αν προκλήθηκε ο θάνατος μεγάλου αριθμού ανθρώπων, το δικαστήριο μπορεί να επιβάλει ισόβια κάθειρξη.
2. Όποιος στις περιπτώσεις της προηγούμενης παραγράφου προκαλεί από αμέλεια την πλημμύρα από την οποία μπορεί να προκύψει κοινός κίνδυνος για ξένα πράγματα ή κίνδυνος για άνθρωπο, τιμωρείται με φυλάκιση έως τρία (3) έτη.

Άρθρο 269

(Καταργείται)

Άρθρο 270
Έκρηξη

1. Όποιος προξενεί έκρηξη με οποιοδήποτε τρόπο, και ιδίως με την χρήση εκρηκτικών υλών, τιμωρείται:
α) με φυλάκιση αν από την πράξη μπορεί να προκύψει κοινός κίνδυνος για ξένα πράγματα,
β) με κάθειρξη έως δέκα (10) έτη αν από την πράξη μπορεί να προκύψει κίνδυνος για άνθρωπο,
γ) με κάθειρξη αν στην περίπτωση των στοιχείων α΄ ή β΄ η πράξη προκάλεσε σημαντική βλάβη σε εγκαταστάσεις κοινής ωφέλειας ή είχε ως αποτέλεσμα τη βαριά σωματική βλάβη ανθρώπου,
δ) με κάθειρξη τουλάχιστον δέκα (10) ετών αν στην περίπτωση του στοιχείου β΄ η πράξη είχε ως αποτέλεσμα το θάνατο άλλου. Αν προκλήθηκε ο θάνατος μεγάλου αριθμού ανθρώπων, το δικαστήριο μπορεί να επιβάλει ισόβια κάθειρξη.
2. Όποιος στις περιπτώσεις της προηγούμενης παραγράφου προκαλεί από αμέλεια την έκρηξη από την οποία μπορεί να προκύψει κοινός κίνδυνος για ξένα πράγματα ή κίνδυνος για άνθρωπο τιμωρείται με φυλάκιση έως τρία (3) έτη.

Άρθρο 271

(Καταργείται)

Άρθρο 272
Κατασκευή και κατοχή εκρηκτικών και εμπρηστικών υλών

1. Όποιος κατασκευάζει, προμηθεύεται ή κατέχει εκρηκτικές ή εμπρηστικές ύλες, βόμβες ή μηχανισμούς, από τα οποία μπορεί να προκληθεί κίνδυνος για άνθρωπο τιμωρείται με φυλάκιση τουλάχιστον τριών (3) ετών.
2. Η πράξη της προηγούμενης παραγράφου τιμωρείται με κάθειρξη έως δέκα (10) έτη αν ο υπαίτιος την τελεί ενώ συμμετέχει σε δημόσια συνάθροιση πλήθους ή αφορά μεγάλη ποσότητα των ανωτέρω υλικών ή αντικειμένων.
3. Ο δράστης δεν τιμωρείται αν πριν εξεταστεί από τις αρχές παρέδωσε με τη θέλησή του σε αυτές τα πιο πάνω υλικά ή αντικείμενα ή κατέστησε γι' αυτές δυνατό να τα αποκτήσουν στην κατοχή τους ή απέτρεψε με άλλον τρόπο τον κίνδυνο να γίνει χρήση αυτών.

Articles 266 - 267

[Repealed]

Article 268
[Causing] flooding

1. Any person who causes flooding shall be punished with:
a) imprisonment if the act could result in common danger to things owned by others;
b) incarceration of up to 10 years if the act could result in danger to a human being;
c) incarceration if, in the cases of points (a) and (b), the act caused serious harm to public utility facilities or resulted in grievous bodily harm of a person; [or]
d) incarceration of at least ten years if, in the case of point (b), the act resulted in the death of another person. If [the act] caused the death of a large number of persons, the court may impose incarceration for life.
2. Any person who, in the cases provided for in the preceding paragraph, negligently causes flooding which could result in common danger to things owned by others or danger to a human being shall be punished with imprisonment of up to three years.

Article 269

[Repealed]

Article 270
[Causing an] explosion

1. Any person who causes an explosion by any means and, in particular, by using explosives shall be punished with:
a) imprisonment if the act could result in common danger to things owned by others;
b) incarceration of up to 10 years if the act could result in danger to a human being;
c) incarceration if, in the cases of points (a) and (b), the act caused serious harm to public utility facilities or resulted in grievous bodily harm of a person; [or]
d) incarceration of at least ten years if, in the case of point (b), the act resulted in the death of another person. If [the act] caused the death of a large number of persons, the court may impose incarceration for life.
2. Any person who, in the cases provided for in the preceding paragraph, negligently causes an explosion which could result in common danger to things owned by others or danger to a human being shall be punished with imprisonment of up to three years.

Article 271

[Repealed]

Article 272
Manufacture and possession of explosive and incendiary materials

1. Any person who manufactures, procures or possesses explosive or incendiary materials, bombs or mechanisms which can cause danger to a human being shall be punished with imprisonment of at least three years.
2. The act provided for in the preceding paragraph shall be punished with incarceration of up to 10 years if the culpable person commits it while attending a public assembly or [the act] involves a large quantity of the aforesaid materials or items.
3. The perpetrator shall not be punished if, prior to being examined by the authorities, they handed over the aforesaid materials or items of their own volition, or enabled [the authorities] to take possession of them, or otherwise averted the risk of [the aforesaid materials or items] being used.

Άρθρο 273
Κοινώς επικίνδυνη βλάβη

1. Όποιος καταστρέφει ή προξενεί βλάβη σε πράγμα δικό του ή ξένο, κινητό ή ακίνητο, όπως ηλεκτρικές εγκαταστάσεις, οικοδομικά ή άλλα έργα για την προστασία από φυσικές και άλλες καταστροφές, τιμωρείται:
α) με φυλάκιση έως τρία (3) έτη αν από την πράξη μπορεί να προκύψει κοινός κίνδυνος για ξένα πράγματα,
β) με φυλάκιση τουλάχιστον ενός (1) έτους αν από την πράξη μπορεί να προκύψει κίνδυνος για άνθρωπο,
γ) με κάθειρξη έως δέκα (10) έτη αν στην περίπτωση του στοιχείου β΄ η πράξη είχε ως αποτέλεσμα τη βαριά σωματική βλάβη, ή τον θάνατο άλλου. Αν προκλήθηκε ο θάνατος μεγάλου αριθμού ανθρώπων, το δικαστήριο μπορεί να επιβάλει κάθειρξη τουλάχιστον δέκα (10) ετών.
2. Όποιος στις περιπτώσεις της προηγούμενης παραγράφου προκαλεί από αμέλεια την καταστροφή ή τη βλάβη από την οποία μπορεί να προκύψει κοινός κίνδυνος για ξένα πράγματα ή κίνδυνος για άνθρωπο τιμωρείται με φυλάκιση έως δύο (2) έτη ή χρηματική ποινή.

Άρθρο 274

(Καταργείται)

Άρθρο 275
Άρση ασφαλιστικών εγκαταστάσεων

1. Όποιος σε μεταλλεία, σε εργοστάσια ή σε άλλες εργασίες που η λειτουργία τους είναι επικίνδυνη για τη ζωή των εργαζομένων, καταστρέφει ή με οποιονδήποτε τρόπο αχρηστεύει εγκαταστάσεις που ασφαλίζουν από αυτόν τον κίνδυνο ή διακόπτει τη λειτουργία τους, τιμωρείται:
α) με φυλάκιση τουλάχιστον ενός έτους (1) και χρηματική ποινή αν από την πράξη μπορεί να προκύψει κίνδυνος για άνθρωπο,
β) με κάθειρξη αν στην περίπτωση του στοιχείου α΄ η πράξη είχε ως αποτέλεσμα τη βαριά σωματική βλάβη,
γ) με κάθειρξη τουλάχιστον δέκα (10) ετών αν στην περίπτωση του στοιχείου α΄ η πράξη είχε ως αποτέλεσμα τον θάνατο άλλου. Αν προκλήθηκε ο θάνατος μεγάλου αριθμού ανθρώπων, το δικαστήριο μπορεί να επιβάλει ισόβια κάθειρξη.
2. Όποιος στις περιπτώσεις της προηγούμενης παραγράφου προκαλεί από αμέλεια την καταστροφή, την αχρήστευση ή τη διακοπή λειτουργίας ασφαλιστικής εγκατάστασης από την οποία μπορεί να προκύψει κίνδυνος για άνθρωπο, τιμωρείται με φυλάκιση έως τρία (3) έτη.

Άρθρο 276

(Καταργείται)

Άρθρο 277
Πρόκληση ναυαγίου

1. Όποιος προκαλεί τη βύθιση ή την προσάραξη πλοίου τιμωρείται:
α) με φυλάκιση αν από την πράξη μπορεί να προκύψει κοινός κίνδυνος για ξένα πράγματα,
β) με κάθειρξη έως δέκα (10) έτη αν από την πράξη μπορεί να προκύψει κίνδυνος για άνθρωπο,
γ) με κάθειρξη αν στην περίπτωση των στοιχείων α΄ ή β΄ η πράξη προκάλεσε σημαντική βλάβη σε εγκαταστάσεις κοινής ωφέλειας ή είχε ως αποτέλεσμα τη βαριά σωματική βλάβη ανθρώπου,
δ) με κάθειρξη τουλάχιστον δέκα (10) ετών αν στην περίπτωση του στοιχείου β΄ η πράξη είχε ως αποτέλεσμα το θάνατο άλλου. Αν προκλήθηκε ο θάνατος μεγάλου αριθμού ανθρώπων, το δικαστήριο μπορεί να επιβάλει ισόβια κάθειρξη.
2. Όποιος στις περιπτώσεις της προηγούμενης παραγράφου προκαλεί από αμέλεια τη βύθιση ή την προσάραξη πλοίου από την οποία μπορεί να προκύψει κοινός κίνδυνος για ξένα πράγματα ή κίνδυνος για άνθρωπο, τιμωρείται με φυλάκιση έως τρία (3) έτη.

Article 273
Damage endangering the general public

1. Any person who destroys or causes damage to a thing, whether belonging to them or another person, whether movable or immovable, such as electrical installations, construction or other projects for protection against natural and other disasters, shall be punished with:
a) imprisonment of up to three years if the act could result in common danger to things owned by others;
b) imprisonment of at least one year if the act could result in danger to a human being;
c) incarceration of at least 10 years if, in the case of point (b), the act resulted in grievous bodily harm or the death of another person. If [the act] caused the death of a large number of persons, the court may impose incarceration of at least 10 years.
2. Any person who, in the cases provided for in the preceding paragraph, negligently causes destruction or damage which could result in common danger to things owned by others or danger to a human being shall be punished with imprisonment of up to two years or a monetary penalty.

Article 274

[Repealed]

Article 275
Disabling safety apparatus

1. Any person who, at a mine, factory or other worksite where operations dangerous for the life of workers take place, destroys or otherwise renders useless apparatus protecting against such danger or interrupts the operation of such apparatus shall be punished with:
a) imprisonment of at least one year and a monetary penalty if the act could result in danger to a human being;
b) incarceration if, in the case of point (a), the act resulted in grievous bodily harm;
c) incarceration of at least 10 years if, in the case of point (a), the act resulted in the death of another person. If [the act] caused the death of a large number of persons, the court may impose incarceration for life.
2. Any person who, in the cases provided for in the preceding paragraph, negligently destroys, renders useless or interrupts the operation of safety apparatus which could result in danger to a human being shall be punished with imprisonment of up to three years.

Article 276

[Repealed]

Article 277
Causing a shipwreck

1. Any person who causes the sinking or grounding of a ship shall be punished with:
a) imprisonment if the act could result in common danger to things owned by others;
b) incarceration of up to 10 years if the act could result in danger to a human being;
c) incarceration if, in the cases of points (a) and b), the act caused serious harm to public utility facilities or resulted in grievous bodily harm of a person; [or]
d) incarceration of at least ten years if, in the case of point (b), the act resulted in the death of another person. If [the act] caused the death of a large number of persons, the court may impose incarceration for life.
2. Any person who, in the cases provided for in the preceding paragraph, negligently causes the sinking or grounding of a ship which could result in common danger to things owned by others or danger to a human being shall be punished with imprisonment of up to three years.

Άρθρο 278

(Καταργείται)

Άρθρο 279
Δηλητηρίαση πραγμάτων προορισμένων για χρήση από το κοινό

1. Όποιος δηλητηριάζει:

α) πηγές, πηγάδια, βρύσες ή άλλες διοχετεύσεις ή δεξαμενές νερού,

β) τρόφιμα, ποτά ή άλλα πράγματα που είναι προορισμένα για πώληση ή για χρήση από το κοινό των οποίων η χρήση μπορεί να προκαλέσει κίνδυνο για άνθρωπο,

τιμωρείται με κάθειρξη έως δέκα (10) έτη και χρηματική ποινή.

Με την ίδια ποινή τιμωρείται και όποιος εισάγει σε κάποιο από αυτά άλλες ύλες που μπορούν να προκαλέσουν το ίδιο αποτέλεσμα. Με την ίδια ποινή τιμωρείται επίσης όποιος κατέχει προς πώληση, πωλεί ή θέτει με οποιοδήποτε τρόπο σε κυκλοφορία τα υπό στοιχείο β΄ πράγματα.

2. Οι πράξεις της παρ. 1 τιμωρούνται:

α) με κάθειρξη αν είχαν ως αποτέλεσμα τη βαριά σωματική βλάβη,

β) με κάθειρξη τουλάχιστον δέκα (10) ετών αν είχαν ως αποτέλεσμα το θάνατο άλλου.

Αν προκλήθηκε ο θάνατος μεγάλου αριθμού ανθρώπων, το δικαστήριο μπορεί να επιβάλει ισόβια κάθειρξη.

3. Αν στις περιπτώσεις της παρ. 1 η πράξη τελείται από αμέλεια και από αυτήν μπορεί να προκύψει κίνδυνος για άνθρωπο, επιβάλλεται φυλάκιση έως τρία (3) έτη.

Άρθρο 280

(Καταργείται)

Άρθρο 281
Επιβλαβή φάρμακα

1. Όποιος, χωρίς την απαιτούμενη άδεια, παρασκευάζει ή επεξεργάζεται ή θέτει σε κυκλοφορία φάρμακα, που η χρήση τους μπορεί να προκαλέσει βλάβη στην υγεία ή κίνδυνο για τη ζωή ανθρώπου, τιμωρείται με φυλάκιση τουλάχιστον ενός (1) έτους.

2. Αν κάποια από τις προαναφερόμενες πράξεις τελέστηκε από αμέλεια, επιβάλλεται φυλάκιση μέχρι ενός (1) έτους ή χρηματική ποινή, εκτός αν η εν λόγω πράξη τιμωρείται, σύμφωνα με άλλη, ειδικότερη διάταξη, με αυστηρότερη ποινή.

Άρθρα 282 - 284

(Καταργούνται)

Άρθρο 285
Παραβίαση μέτρων για την πρόληψη ασθενειών

1. Όποιος παραβιάζει τα μέτρα που έχει διατάξει ο νόμος ή η αρμόδια αρχή για να αποτραπεί η εισβολή ή η διάδοση μιας μεταδοτικής ασθένειας τιμωρείται:

α) με φυλάκιση έως τρία (3) έτη ή χρηματική ποινή αν από την πράξη μπορεί να προκύψει κοινός κίνδυνος για ζώα,

β) με φυλάκιση και χρηματική ποινή αν από την πράξη μπορεί να προκύψει κίνδυνος μετάδοσης της ασθένειας σε αόριστο αριθμό ανθρώπων.

Article 278

[Repealed]

Article 279
Poisoning of things intended for public use

1. Any person who poisons:
a) springs, wells, drinking fountains or other water channels or reservoirs;
b) food, beverages or other things intended for sale to or use by the public and whose use could result in danger to a human being,
shall be punished with incarceration of up to 10 years and a monetary penalty.
The same punishment shall also be imposed on any person who introduces other substances into the above which could cause the same result. The same punishment shall also be imposed on any person who possesses the things referred to in point (b) for the purpose of sale, sells them or places them into circulation in any manner.
2. The acts provided for in paragraph 1 shall be punished with:
a) incarceration if they resulted in grievous bodily harm;
b) incarceration of at least 10 years if they resulted in the death of another person.
If [the act] caused the death of a large number of persons, the court may impose incarceration for life.
3. If, in the cases provided for in paragraph 1, the act is committed negligently and could result in danger to human [life], imprisonment of up to three years shall be imposed.

Article 280

[Repealed]

Article 281
Hazardous medicines

1. Any person who, without the authorisation required, prepares or processes or places into circulation medicines whose use could harm the health of a human or endanger human life shall be punished with imprisonment of at least one year.
2. If any of the aforesaid acts was committed negligently, imprisonment of up to one year or a monetary penalty shall be imposed, unless the act in question carries a heavier punishment under a different provision.

Articles 282 - 284

[Repealed]

Article 285
Violation of disease prevention measures

1. Any person who violates the measures ordered by law or by a competent authority to prevent the incursion or spread of a contagious disease shall be punished with:
a) imprisonment of up to three years or a monetary penalty if the act could result in common danger to animals;
b) imprisonment and a monetary penalty if the act could result in the risk of the disease being transmitted to an indeterminate number of persons.

2. Αν η παραβίαση είχε ως αποτέλεσμα μεταδοθεί η ασθένεια σε ζώα, επιβάλλεται φυλάκιση τουλάχιστον τριών (3) ετών και χρηματική ποινή, και αν είχε ως αποτέλεσμα να μεταδοθεί σε άνθρωπο, επιβάλλεται κάθειρξη έως δέκα (10) έτη.
3. Αν η παραβίαση είχε ως αποτέλεσμα το θάνατο άλλου επιβάλλεται κάθειρξη τουλάχιστον δέκα (10) ετών και αν προκλήθηκε ο θάνατος, μεγάλου αριθμού ανθρώπων, το δικαστήριο μπορεί να επιβάλλει ισόβια κάθειρξη.
4. Όποιος στις περιπτώσεις της παρ. 1 από αμέλεια παραβιάζει τα μέτρα και από την παραβίαση μπορεί να προκύψει:
α) κοινός κίνδυνος για ζώα, τιμωρείται με χρηματική ποινή ή παροχή κοινωφελούς εργασίας, και
β) κίνδυνος μετάδοσης της ασθένειας σε αόριστο αριθμό ανθρώπων,
τιμωρείται με φυλάκιση έως δύο (2) έτη ή χρηματική ποινή.

Άρθρο 286
Παραβίαση κανόνων οικοδομικής

1. Όποιος κατά την εκπόνηση μελέτης ή τη διεύθυνση ή την εκτέλεση οικοδομικού ή άλλου ανάλογου έργου ή κατεδάφισης ενεργεί παρά τους κοινώς αναγνωρισμένους τεχνικούς κανόνες, τιμωρείται:
α) με φυλάκιση τουλάχιστον ενός (1) έτους και χρηματική ποινή αν από την πράξη μπορεί να προκύψει κίνδυνος για άνθρωπο,
β) με κάθειρξη αν στην περίπτωση του στοιχείου α΄ η πράξη είχε ως αποτέλεσμα τη βαριά σωματική βλάβη,
γ) με κάθειρξη τουλάχιστον δέκα (10) ετών αν στην περίπτωση του στοιχείου α΄ η πράξη είχε ως αποτέλεσμα το θάνατο άλλου. Αν προκλήθηκε ο θάνατος μεγάλου αριθμού ανθρώπων, το δικαστήριο μπορεί να επιβάλει ισόβια κάθειρξη.
2. Όποιος στις περιπτώσεις της προηγούμενης παραγράφου παραβιάζει από αμέλεια τους κοινώς αναγνωρισμένους τεχνικούς κανόνες και από την παραβίαση μπορεί να προκύψει κίνδυνος για άνθρωπο τιμωρείται με φυλάκιση έως δύο (2) έτη ή χρηματική ποινή.
3. Η παραγραφή των εγκλημάτων της παραγράφου 1 στοιχεία β΄ και γ΄ αρχίζει από την επέλευση του θανάτου ή της βαριάς σωματικής βλάβης και πάντως δεν μπορεί να υπερβεί τα τριάντα (30) έτη από την παραβίαση των κανόνων.

Άρθρο 287

(Καταργείται)

Άρθρο 288
Παρεμπόδιση αποτροπής κοινού κινδύνου και παράλειψη οφειλόμενης βοήθειας

1. Όποιος ματαιώνει ή δυσχεραίνει την ενέργεια που είναι αναγκαία για να αποτραπεί ή να κατασταλεί ένας κοινός κίνδυνος που υπάρχει ή που επίκειται για τη ζωή ή την υγεία ανθρώπου ή για ξένες ιδιοκτησίες τιμωρείται με φυλάκιση έως τρία έτη ή χρηματική ποινή.
2. Όποιος σε περίπτωση δυστυχήματος ή κοινού κινδύνου ή κοινής ανάγκης δεν προσφέρει τη βοήθεια που του ζητήθηκε και που μπορούσε να προσφέρει, χωρίς ο ίδιος να διατρέξει ουσιώδη κίνδυνο, τιμωρείται με χρηματική ποινή ή παροχή κοινωφελούς εργασίας.

Άρθρο 289
Έμπρακτη μετάνοια και δικαστική άφεση της ποινής

1. Στις περιπτώσεις της παρ. 2 των άρθρων 264, 268, 270, 273, 275, 277 και 286, της παρ. 3 του άρθρου 279, και της παρ. 4 του άρθρου 285 ο υπαίτιος δεν τιμωρείται, αν με τη θέλησή του αποτρέψει τον κίνδυνο ή με τη γρήγορη αναγγελία του προς τις αρχές δώσει αφορμή για την αποτροπή του.
2. Στις περιπτώσεις των εγκλημάτων του παρόντος κεφαλαίου το δικαστήριο μπορεί να κρίνει την πράξη ατιμώρητη αν ο υπαίτιος με τη θέλησή του αποτρέψει την εξέλιξη του κινδύνου ή με τη γρήγορη αναγγελία του προς τις αρχές δώσει αφορμή για την αποτροπή της.

2. If the violation resulted in the disease being transmitted to animals, imprisonment of at least three years and a monetary penalty shall be imposed, and if it resulted in [the disease] being transmitted to a human being, incarceration of up to 10 years shall be imposed.
3. If the violation resulted in the death of another person, incarceration of at least ten (10) years shall be imposed, and if it caused the death of a large number of persons, the court may impose incarceration for life.
4. Any person who, in the cases provided for in paragraph 1, negligently violates the measures and such violation could result in:
a) common danger to animals, shall be punished with a monetary penalty or community service; and
b) the risk of the illness being transmitted to an indeterminate number of persons,
shall be punished with imprisonment of up to two years or a monetary penalty.

Article 286
Violation of construction rules

1. Any person who, when designing or directing or executing construction or other relevant works or demolitions, acts contrary to generally recognised technical rules shall be punished with:
a) imprisonment of at least one year and a monetary penalty if the act could result in danger to a human being;
b) incarceration if, in the case of point (a), the act resulted in grievous bodily harm;
c) incarceration of at least 10 years if, in the case of point (a), the act resulted in the death of another person. If [the act] caused the death of a large number of persons, the court may impose incarceration for life.
2. Any person who, in the cases provided for in the preceding paragraph, negligently violates generally recognised technical rules and such violation could result in danger to a human being shall be punished with imprisonment of up to two years or a monetary penalty.
3. The time-barring period for the crimes provided for in paragraph 1(b) and (c) shall commence from the date on which the death or grievous bodily harm [in question] occurred and, in all cases, cannot exceed 30 years from the date the rules were violated.

Article 287

[Repealed]

Article 288
Obstructing the aversion of a common danger and failure to offer assistance requested

1. Any person who prevents or impedes an action necessary to avert or contain an existing or impending danger to human life or health or another's property shall be punished with imprisonment of up to three years or a monetary penalty.
2. Any person who, in the case of a serious accident or of a common danger or common emergency, fails to offer the assistance requested and which they could have offered without placing themselves in substantial danger shall be punished with a monetary penalty or community service.

Article 289
Practical repentance and judicial forgiveness of punishments

1. In the cases provided for in Articles 264(2), 265, 268, 270, 273, 275, 277 and 286, 279(3) and 285(4), the culpable person shall not be punished if they prevented the danger of their own volition, or helped avert it by promptly reporting it to the authorities.
2. In the cases of the crimes provided for in this Chapter, the court may decide not to punish the culpable person for the act if, of their own volition, they prevented the danger from progressing or helped avert it by promptly reporting it to the authorities.

ΔΕΚΑΤΟ ΤΕΤΑΡΤΟ ΚΕΦΑΛΑΙΟ

ΕΓΚΛΗΜΑΤΑ ΚΑΤΑ ΣΥΓΚΟΙΝΩΝΙΩΝ, ΤΗΛΕΠΙΚΟΙΝΩΝΙΩΝ ΚΑΙ ΑΛΛΩΝ ΚΟΙΝΩΦΕΛΩΝ ΕΓΚΑΤΑΣΤΑΣΕΩΝ

I

ΕΓΚΛΗΜΑΤΑ ΚΑΤΑ ΤΩΝ ΣΥΓΚΟΙΝΩΝΙΩΝ

Άρθρο 290
Επικίνδυνες παρεμβάσεις στην οδική συγκοινωνία

1. Όποιος διαταράσσει την ασφάλεια της συγκοινωνίας στους δρόμους:
α) με καταστροφή, βλάβη ή μετακίνηση εγκαταστάσεων ή οχημάτων,
β) με τοποθέτηση ή διατήρηση εμποδίων,
γ) με αλλοίωση σημείων ή σημάτων ή με τοποθέτηση ή διατήρηση εσφαλμένων σημείων ή σημάτων ή
δ) με άλλες, εξίσου επικίνδυνες για την ασφάλεια της συγκοινωνίας πράξεις,
τιμωρείται:
αα) με φυλάκιση έως τρία (3) έτη αν από την πράξη μπορεί να προκύψει κοινός κίνδυνος για ξένα πράγματα,
ββ) με φυλάκιση τουλάχιστον ενός (1) έτους αν από την πράξη μπορεί να προκύψει κίνδυνος για άνθρωπο,
γγ) με κάθειρξη έως δέκα (10) έτη αν η πράξη είχε ως αποτέλεσμα τη βαριά σωματική βλάβη άλλου ή προκάλεσε σημαντική βλάβη σε κοινωφελείς εγκαταστάσεις,
δδ) με κάθειρξη τουλάχιστον δέκα (10) ετών αν η πράξη είχε ως αποτέλεσμα τον θάνατο άλλου.
Αν προκλήθηκε ο θάνατος μεγάλου αριθμού ανθρώπων, το δικαστήριο μπορεί να επιβάλει ισόβια κάθειρξη.
2. Όποιος στις περιπτώσεις της προηγούμενης παραγράφου προκαλεί από αμέλεια τη διατάραξη της ασφάλειας της συγκοινωνίας από την οποία μπορεί να προκύψει κοινός κίνδυνος για ξένα πράγματα ή κίνδυνος για άνθρωπο, τιμωρείται με φυλάκιση έως δύο (2) έτη ή χρηματική ποινή.

Άρθρο 290Α
Επικίνδυνη οδήγηση

1. Όποιος κατά τη συγκοινωνία στους δρόμους ή στις πλατείες:
α) οδηγεί όχημα, μολονότι δεν είναι σε θέση να το πράξει με ασφάλεια εξαιτίας της κατανάλωσης οινοπνεύματος ή χρήσης ναρκωτικών ουσιών ή λόγω σωματικής ή πνευματικής εξάντλησης ή
β) οδηγεί όχημα σε εθνικές ή περιφερειακές οδούς αντίστροφα στο ρεύμα της εκάστοτε κατεύθυνσης ή σε πεζοδρόμους, πεζοδρόμια ή πλατείες, ή οδηγεί όχημα που είναι τεχνικά ανασφαλές ή με ανασφαλή τρόπο φορτωμένο ή προβαίνει κατά την οδήγηση σε επικίνδυνους ελιγμούς ή μετέχει σε αυτοσχέδιους αγώνες, ή
γ) οδηγεί όχημα i) σε αυτοκινητόδρομο ή σε οδό ταχείας κυκλοφορίας με ταχύτητα που υπερβαίνει το επιτρεπόμενο όριο ταχύτητας κατά τουλάχιστον εξήντα (60) χλμ. ανά ώρα και αν πρόκειται για λεωφορείο ή φορτηγό αυτοκίνητο, κατά τουλάχιστον τριάντα (30) χλμ. ανά ώρα, ii) εντός κατοικημένης περιοχής ή σε άλλο οδικό δίκτυο με ταχύτητα που υπερβαίνει το επιτρεπόμενο όριο ταχύτητας κατά τουλάχιστον σαράντα (40) χλμ. ανά ώρα και αν πρόκειται για λεωφορείο ή φορτηγό αυτοκίνητο, κατά τουλάχιστον είκοσι (20) χλμ. ανά ώρα, ή
δ) οδηγεί όχημα στη λωρίδα έκτακτης ανάγκης (Λ.Ε.Α.) εκτός των περιπτώσεων αποκλειστικού προορισμού της, ή
ε) παραβιάζει ερυθρό σηματοδότη,
τιμωρείται, αν δεν προβλέπονται βαρύτερες κυρώσεις σε άλλες διατάξεις:
αα) με φυλάκιση έως τρία (3) έτη, αν από την πράξη μπορεί να προκύψει κοινός κίνδυνος σε ξένα πράγματα,
ββ) με φυλάκιση τουλάχιστον ενός (1) έτους, αν από την πράξη μπορεί να προκύψει κίνδυνος για άνθρωπο,
γγ) με κάθειρξη έως δέκα (10) έτη, αν η πράξη είχε ως αποτέλεσμα τη βαριά σωματική βλάβη ή προκάλεσε σημαντική βλάβη σε κοινωφελείς εγκαταστάσεις,
δδ) με κάθειρξη τουλάχιστον δέκα (10) ετών, αν η πράξη είχε ως αποτέλεσμα τον θάνατο άλλου.
Αν προκλήθηκε ο θάνατος μεγάλου αριθμού ανθρώπων, το δικαστήριο μπορεί να επιβάλει ισόβια κάθειρξη.

CHAPTER XIV

CRIMES AGAINST TRANSPORTATION SYSTEMS, TELECOMMUNICATIONS AND OTHER PUBLIC UTILITY FACILITIES

I

CRIMES AGAINST TRANSPORTATION SYSTEMS

Article 290
Hazardous interference with road transportation

1. Any person who disrupts the safety of road transportation:
a) by destroying, damaging or moving installations or vehicles;
b) by placing or maintaining obstacles;
c) by altering notices or signs or by placing or maintaining incorrect notices or signs; or
d) through other acts equally hazardous to transportation safety,
shall be punished with:
aa) imprisonment of up to three years if the act could result in common danger to things owned by others;
bb) imprisonment of at least one year if the act could result in danger to a human being;
cc) incarceration of up to 10 years if the act resulted in grievous bodily harm of another or major damage to public utility facilities;
dd) incarceration of at least ten years if the act resulted in the death of another person.
If [the act] caused the death of a large number of persons, the court may impose incarceration for life.
2. Any person who, in the cases provided for in the preceding paragraph, negligently causes a disruption of transportation safety which could result in common danger to things owned by others or danger to a human being shall be punished with imprisonment of up to two years or a monetary penalty.

Article 290A
Dangerous driving

1. Any person who, in the context of transportation on roads or squares:
a) drives a vehicle while being unable to safely do so due to consumption of alcohol, or use of narcotic substances, or due to physical or mental exhaustion; or
b) drives a vehicle on motorways or ring-roads in oncoming traffic or on a pedestrianised street, pavements or squares, or drives a technically unsafe vehicle, or unsafely drives a loaded vehicle, or manoeuvres dangerously while driving, or participates in street racing; or
c) drives a vehicle
i) on a national road or express road at a speed exceeding the maximum speed limit by at least 60 km/h and, in the case of a bus or lorry, by at least 30 km/h;
ii) within a residential area or other road network at a speed exceeding the maximum speed limit by at least 40 km/h and, in the case of a bus or lorry, by at least 20 km/h; or
d) drives a vehicle in the emergency lane, except exclusively for its intended purpose; or
e) fails to stop for a red traffic light,
shall, unless different provisions lay down heavier [sentences], be punished with:
aa) imprisonment of up to three years if the act could result in common danger to things owned by others;
bb) imprisonment of at least one year if the act could result in danger to a human being;
cc) incarceration of up to 10 years if the act resulted in grievous bodily harm or major damage to public utility facilities; [or]
dd) incarceration of at least 10 years if the act resulted in the death of another person.
If [the act] caused the death of a large number of persons, the court may impose incarceration for life.

2. Όποιος στις περιπτώσεις της προηγούμενης παραγράφου οδηγεί επικίνδυνα από αμέλεια και από την πράξη του αυτή μπορεί να προκύψει κοινός κίνδυνος για ξένα πράγματα ή κίνδυνος για άνθρωπο, τιμωρείται με φυλάκιση έως δύο (2) έτη ή χρηματική ποινή.

Άρθρο 291

Επικίνδυνες παρεμβάσεις στη συγκοινωνία μέσων σταθερής τροχιάς, πλοίων και αεροσκαφών

1. Όποιος διαταράσσει την ασφάλεια της συγκοινωνίας μέσων σταθερής τροχιάς, πλοίων ή αεροσκαφών:
α) με καταστροφή, βλάβη, μετακίνηση ή αφαίρεση εξοπλισμού λειτουργίας, κίνησης, ηλεκτροδότησης ή ασφάλειας, εγκαταστάσεων ή συγκοινωνιακών μέσων,
β) με τοποθέτηση ή διατήρηση εμποδίων,
γ) με αλλοίωση σημείων ή σημάτων ή με τοποθέτηση ή διατήρηση εσφαλμένων σημείων ή σημάτων,
δ) με παραβίαση των κανόνων τεχνικού ελέγχου ή ασφαλούς φόρτωσης των συγκοινωνιακών μέσων,
ε) με παραβίαση των κανόνων λειτουργίας συστημάτων μη επανδρωμένων αεροσκαφών,
στ) με άλλες, εξίσου επικίνδυνες, για την ασφάλεια της συγκοινωνίας πράξεις
τιμωρείται:
αα) με φυλάκιση αν από την πράξη μπορεί να προκύψει κοινός κίνδυνος για ξένα πράγματα,
ββ) με κάθειρξη έως δέκα (10) έτη αν από την πράξη μπορεί να προκύψει κίνδυνος για άνθρωπο,
γγ) με κάθειρξη αν η πράξη είχε ως αποτέλεσμα τη βαριά σωματική βλάβη ή προκάλεσε σημαντική βλάβη σε εγκαταστάσεις κοινής ωφέλειας,
δδ) με ισόβια κάθειρξη αν η πράξη είχε ως αποτέλεσμα τον θάνατο άλλου.

2. Με τις ίδιες ποινές κατά τις διακρίσεις των στοιχείων αα΄ έως δδ΄ της προηγούμενης παραγράφου τιμωρείται, εάν δεν προβλέπονται βαρύτερες κυρώσεις σε άλλες διατάξεις, όποιος οδηγεί όχημα σταθερής τροχιάς ή κυβερνά πλοίο ή αεροπλάνο ή χειρίζεται εξ αποστάσεως σύστημα μη επανδρωμένου αεροσκάφους χωρίς να είναι σε θέση να το πράξει με ασφάλεια εξαιτίας της κατανάλωσης οινοπνεύματος ή χρήσης ναρκωτικών ουσιών ή λόγω σωματικής ή πνευματικής εξάντλησης.

3. Όποιος στις περιπτώσεις των προηγούμενων παραγράφων από αμέλεια προκαλεί τη διατάραξη της ασφάλειας της συγκοινωνίας ή οδηγεί επικίνδυνα και από την πράξη του αυτή μπορεί να προκύψει κοινός κίνδυνος για ξένα πράγματα ή κίνδυνος για άνθρωπο, τιμωρείται με φυλάκιση έως τρία (3) έτη.

Άρθρο 292

Παρακώλυση συγκοινωνιών

1. Όποιος παρεμποδίζει ή διαταράσσει σε μεγάλη έκταση ή για μεγάλο χρονικό διάστημα τη λειτουργία των κοινόχρηστων συγκοινωνιακών μέσων, και ιδίως μέσων σταθερής τροχιάς, πλοίου, αεροπλάνου ή λεωφορείου, τιμωρείται με φυλάκιση.

2. Αν η πράξη τελέστηκε από αμέλεια, επιβάλλεται χρηματική ποινή ή παροχή κοινωφελούς εργασίας.

2. Any person who, acting negligently, in the cases provided for in the preceding paragraph, drives dangerously and this act could result in common danger to things owned by others or danger to a human being shall be punished with imprisonment of up to two years or a monetary penalty.

Article 291
Hazardous interference with track-based, ship and aircraft transportation

1. Any person who disrupts the safety of track-based, ship or aircraft transportation:
a) by destroying, damaging, moving or removing equipment for the operation, movement, power supply or safety of facilities or means of transport;
b) by placing or maintaining obstacles;
c) by altering notices or signs or by placing or maintaining incorrect notices or signs;
d) by violating rules concerning technical inspection or safe loading of means of transport;
e) by violating the operating rules for unmanned aircraft systems; [or]
f) through other acts equally hazardous to transportation safety,
shall be punished with:
aa) imprisonment if the act could result in common danger to things owned by others;
bb) incarceration of up to 10 years if the act could result in danger to a human being;
cc) incarceration if the act resulted in grievous bodily harm or major damage to public utility facilities; [or]
dd) incarceration for life if the act resulted in the death of another person.

2. Any person who [operates] a track-based vehicle or commands a ship or [aircraft] or remotely handles an unmanned aerial vehicle while being unable to safely do so due to consumption of alcohol or use of narcotic substances or due to physical or mental exhaustion shall be punished with the same sentences, in accordance with the distinctions laid down in points (aa) to (dd) of the preceding paragraph, unless different provisions lay down heavier [sentences].

3. Any person who, in the cases provided for in the preceding paragraphs, negligently causes a disruption of transportation safety or [operates the vehicle in question] dangerously and this act could result in common danger to things owned by others or danger to a human being shall be punished with imprisonment of up to three years.

Article 292
Obstructing transportation systems

1. Any person who impedes or causes widespread or long-term disruption to the operation of public transportation systems and, in particular, track-based vehicles, ships, aircraft or buses shall be punished with imprisonment.

2. If the act was committed negligently, a monetary penalty or community service shall be imposed.

II

ΕΓΚΛΗΜΑΤΑ ΚΑΤΑ ΤΩΝ ΤΗΛΕΠΙΚΟΙΝΩΝΙΩΝ ΚΑΙ ΑΛΛΩΝ ΚΟΙΝΩΦΕΛΩΝ ΕΓΚΑΤΑΣΤΑΣΕΩΝ

Άρθρο 292Α
Εγκλήματα κατά της ασφάλειας των τηλεφωνικών επικοινωνιών

1. Όποιος χωρίς δικαίωμα αποκτά πρόσβαση σε σύνδεση ή σε δίκτυο παροχής υπηρεσιών τηλεφωνίας ή σε σύστημα υλικού ή λογισμικού, που χρησιμοποιείται για την παροχή τέτοιων υπηρεσιών, και με τον τρόπο αυτόν θέτει σε κίνδυνο την ασφάλεια των τηλεφωνικών επικοινωνιών, τιμωρείται με φυλάκιση τουλάχιστον ενός (1) έτους και χρηματική ποινή. Αν ο υπαίτιος της πράξης του προηγούμενου εδαφίου είναι ο εργαζόμενος ή συνεργάτης του παρόχου υπηρεσιών τηλεφωνίας, τιμωρείται με φυλάκιση τουλάχιστον δύο (2) ετών και χρηματική ποινή. Με την ποινή του προηγουμένου εδαφίου τιμωρείται και ο πάροχος υπηρεσιών τηλεφωνίας ή ο νόμιμος εκπρόσωπός του ο οποίος αθέμιτα θέτει σε κίνδυνο την ασφάλεια των τηλεφωνικών επικοινωνιών.

2. Ο πάροχος υπηρεσιών τηλεφωνίας ή ο νόμιμος εκπρόσωπος αυτού, ο οποίος παραβιάζει διάταξη κανονισμού της Αρχής Διασφάλισης του Απορρήτου των Επικοινωνιών (ΑΔΑΕ) ή όρο της Γενικής Άδειας ή του δικαιώματος χρήσης ραδιοσυχνότητας ή του δικαιώματος χρήσης αριθμού, που αναφέρονται στην ασφάλεια των ηλεκτρονικών επικοινωνιών, τιμωρείται με φυλάκιση τουλάχιστον δύο (2) ετών και χρηματική ποινή.

3. Ο πάροχος υπηρεσιών τηλεφωνίας ή ο νόμιμος εκπρόσωπος αυτού ή ο κατά τον νόμο υπεύθυνος για τη διασφάλιση του απορρήτου των επικοινωνιών, που παραλείπει να λάβει τα αναγκαία μέτρα για την αποτροπή πράξης της παρ. 1, τιμωρείται με φυλάκιση τουλάχιστον δύο (2) ετών και χρηματική ποινή, εφόσον η πράξη τελέστηκε ή έγινε απόπειρα τέλεσής της, ανεξάρτητα αν θα τιμωρηθεί ο υπαίτιος.

4. Αν ο υπαίτιος των πράξεων των προηγούμενων παραγράφων είχε σκοπό να προσπορίσει στον εαυτό του ή σε άλλον παράνομο περιουσιακό όφελος ή να προκαλέσει περιουσιακή ζημία σε άλλον, τιμωρείται με φυλάκιση τουλάχιστον τριών (3) ετών και χρηματική ποινή. Εφόσον το συνολικό όφελος ή η συνολική ζημία υπερβαίνουν το ποσό των εκατόν είκοσι χιλιάδων (120.000) ευρώ, ο υπαίτιος τιμωρείται με κάθειρξη έως δέκα (10) έτη και χρηματική ποινή. Αν από τις πράξεις των προηγούμενων παραγράφων μπορεί να τεθούν σε κίνδυνο θεμελιώδεις αρχές και θεσμοί του Πολιτεύματος, όπως μνημονεύονται στο άρθρο 134 του Ποινικού Κώδικα ή απόρρητο που αναφέρεται στην ασφάλεια του κράτους ή στην ασφάλεια εγκαταστάσεων κοινής ωφέλειας, επιβάλλεται κάθειρξη.

5. Όποιος αθέμιτα διαθέτει στο εμπόριο ή με άλλον τρόπο προσφέρει προς εγκατάσταση ειδικά τεχνικά μέσα για την τέλεση των πράξεων της παρ. 1 ή δημόσια διαφημίζει ή προσφέρει τις υπηρεσίες του για την τέλεσή τους τιμωρείται με φυλάκιση έως δύο (2) έτη ή χρηματική ποινή.

Άρθρο 292Β
Παρακώλυση λειτουργίας πληροφοριακών συστημάτων

1. Όποιος χωρίς δικαίωμα παρεμποδίζει σοβαρά ή διακόπτει τη λειτουργία συστήματος πληροφοριών με την εισαγωγή, διαβίβαση, διαγραφή, καταστροφή, αλλοίωση ψηφιακών δεδομένων ή με αποκλεισμό της πρόσβασης στα δεδομένα αυτά, τιμωρείται με φυλάκιση και χρηματική ποινή.

II

CRIMES AGAINST TELECOMMUNICATIONS AND OTHER PUBLIC UTILITY FACILITIES

Article 292A
Crimes against the security of telephone communications

1. Any person who obtains unauthorised access to a connection, or a telephony service provision network, or a hardware or software system used to provide such services, and thus endangers the security of telephone communications shall be punished with imprisonment of at least one year and a monetary penalty. If the person who committed the act provided for in the preceding sentence is a worker or associate of a telephony service provider, they shall be punished with imprisonment of at least two years and a monetary penalty. Any telephony service provider or its lawful representative who unlawfully endangers the safety of telephone communications shall also be punished with the punishment laid down in the preceding sentence.

2. Any telephony service provider or its lawful representative who violates any provision of the regulations issued by the Hellenic Authority for Communication Security and Privacy or any term contained in the General Authorisation [granted by the Hellenic Telecommunications & Post Commission] or the rights to use a radio frequency, or rights to use a [telephone] number, which concern the security of electronic communications shall be punished with imprisonment of at least two years and a monetary penalty.

3. Any telephony service provider of its lawful representative or the person responsible in law for ensuring the confidentiality of communications who fails to take the measures necessary to prevent the act provided for in paragraph 1 shall be punished with imprisonment of at least two years and a monetary penalty, provided the act was committed or attempted, irrespective of whether the person who committed such act is punished.

4. If the person who committed [any of] the acts provided for in the preceding paragraphs sought to obtain an unlawful pecuniary gain for themselves or another, or sought to cause pecuniary damage to another, they shall be punished with imprisonment of at least three years and a monetary penalty. If the total gain or total loss exceeds the amount of 120,000 euros, the culpable person shall be punished with incarceration of up to 10 years and a monetary penalty. If the acts provided for in the preceding paragraphs could place fundamental principles and institutions of the system of government at risk, as set out in Article 134 of this Code, or place confidentiality concerning state security or the security of public utility facilities at risk, incarceration shall be imposed.

5. Any person who unlawfully markets or otherwise offers for installation special technical means for committing the acts provided for in paragraph 1 or who publicly advertises or offers their services in order to commit such acts shall be punished with imprisonment of up to two years or a monetary penalty.

Article 292B
Obstructing the operation of information systems

1. Any person who, without the right to do so, seriously hinders or interrupts the functioning of an information system by inputting, transmitting, deleting, destroying or altering digital data or by precluding access to such data shall be punished with imprisonment and a monetary penalty.

2. Η πράξη της πρώτης παραγράφου τιμωρείται:
α) με φυλάκιση τουλάχιστον ενός έτους και χρηματική ποινή, αν τελέστηκε με τη χρήση εργαλείου που έχει σχεδιαστεί κατά κύριο λόγο για πραγματοποίηση επιθέσεων που επηρεάζουν μεγάλο αριθμό συστημάτων πληροφοριών ή επιθέσεων που προκαλούν σοβαρές ζημίες και ιδίως επιθέσεων που προκαλούν μεγάλης έκτασης ή για μεγάλο χρονικό διάστημα διατάραξη των υπηρεσιών των συστημάτων πληροφοριών, οικονομική ζημιά ιδιαίτερα μεγάλης αξίας ή σημαντική απώλεια δεδομένων,
β) με φυλάκιση τουλάχιστον δύο ετών και χρηματική ποινή, αν προκάλεσε σοβαρές ζημίες και ιδίως μεγάλης έκτασης ή για μεγάλο χρονικό διάστημα διατάραξη των υπηρεσιών των συστημάτων πληροφοριών, οικονομική ζημία ιδιαίτερα μεγάλης αξίας ή σημαντική απώλεια δεδομένων και
γ) με φυλάκιση τουλάχιστον τριών ετών και χρηματική ποινή, αν τελέστηκε κατά συστημάτων πληροφοριών που αποτελούν μέρος υποδομής για την προμήθεια του πληθυσμού με ζωτικής σημασίας αγαθά ή υπηρεσίες. Ως ζωτικής σημασίας αγαθά ή υπηρεσίες νοούνται ιδίως η εθνική άμυνα, η υγεία, οι συγκοινωνίες, οι μεταφορές και η ενέργεια.

Άρθρο 292Γ

Με φυλάκιση έως δύο έτη ή χρηματική ποινή τιμωρείται όποιος χωρίς δικαίωμα και με σκοπό τη διάπραξη των εγκλημάτων του άρθρου 292Β παράγει, πωλεί, προμηθεύεται προς χρήση, εισάγει, κατέχει, διανέμει ή με άλλο τρόπο διακινεί:
α) συσκευές ή προγράμματα υπολογιστή, σχεδιασμένα ή προσαρμοσμένα κυρίως για το σκοπό της διάπραξης των εγκλημάτων του άρθρου 292Β,
β) συνθηματικά ή κωδικούς πρόσβασης ή άλλα παρεμφερή δεδομένα με τη χρήση των οποίων είναι δυνατόν να αποκτηθεί πρόσβαση στο σύνολο ή μέρος ενός πληροφοριακού συστήματος.

Άρθρο 292Δ
Προσβολές του απορρήτου των τηλεπικοινωνιών του κοινού

1. Όποιος χωρίς δικαίωμα αποκτά πρόσβαση σε σύνδεση ή σε δίκτυο παροχής στο κοινό υπηρεσιών τηλεφωνίας ή ηλεκτρονικής επικοινωνίας ή σε σύστημα υλικού ή λογισμικού που χρησιμοποιείται για την παροχή τέτοιων υπηρεσιών, εάν από την πράξη μπορεί να προκύψει κοινός κίνδυνος για το απόρρητο του περιεχομένου τηλεφωνικών ή ηλεκτρονικών επικοινωνιών ή των στοιχείων της θέσης ή κίνησης αυτών, τιμωρείται με φυλάκιση τουλάχιστον δύο ετών και χρηματική ποινή.
2. Αν ο δράστης της πράξης της προηγούμενης παραγράφου είναι πάροχος υπηρεσιών τηλεφωνίας ή ηλεκτρονικής επικοινωνίας ή νόμιμος εκπρόσωπος αυτού ή μέλος της διοίκησης ή υπεύθυνος της διασφάλισης του απορρήτου ή εργαζόμενος ή συνεργάτης του παρόχου ή αποβλέπει να προσπορίσει στον εαυτό του ή σε άλλον παράνομο περιουσιακό όφελος επιβάλλεται φυλάκιση τουλάχιστον τριών ετών και χρηματική ποινή.

Άρθρο 292Ε
Παρακώλυση των τηλεπικοινωνιών

1. Όποιος παρεμποδίζει ή διαταράσσει σε μεγάλη έκταση ή για μεγάλο χρονικό διάστημα τη λειτουργία εγκατάστασης παροχής στο κοινό υπηρεσιών τηλεφωνίας ή ηλεκτρονικών επικοινωνιών και ιδίως του διαδικτύου με αθέμιτη παρέμβαση σε πράγμα ή σε σύστημα πληροφοριών ή σε ηλεκτρονικά δεδομένα που εξυπηρετούν τη λειτουργία αυτής, τιμωρείται με φυλάκιση τουλάχιστον ενός έτους και χρηματική ποινή.
2. Η παράγραφος 2 του προηγούμενου άρθρου εφαρμόζεται και για την πράξη της παραγράφου 1.
3. Αν η πράξη τελέστηκε από αμέλεια, επιβάλλεται χρηματική ποινή ή παροχή κοινωφελούς εργασίας.

2. The act provided for in the first paragraph shall be punished with:
a) imprisonment of at least one year and a monetary penalty if committed using a tool predominantly designed to carry out attacks affecting a large number of information systems or attacks causing serious damage and, in particular, attacks causing widespread or long-term disruption of information system services, economic damage of particularly high value or significant loss of data;
b) imprisonment of at least two years and a monetary penalty if it caused serious damage and particularly widespread or long-term disruption of information system services, economic damage of particularly high value or significant loss of data; [or]
c) imprisonment of at least three years and a monetary penalty if committed against information systems forming part of infrastructure for providing the population with vital goods or services. "Vital goods or services" means, in particular, national defence, health, the public transportation sector, the transport sector and the energy sector.

Article 292C

Imprisonment of up to two years or a monetary penalty shall be imposed on any person who, without the right to do so and for the purpose of committing the crimes provided for in Article 292B, produces, sells, procures for use, imports, possesses, distributes or otherwise [makes available]:
a) computer hardware or software programs designed or adapted primarily for the purpose of committing [any of] the crimes provided for in Article 292B; [or]
b) passwords or access codes or similar data by which the whole or any part of an information system can be accessed.

Article 292D
Offences against the confidentiality of public communications

1. Any person who obtains unauthorised access to a connection, or a public telephony or electronic communications service provision network, or a hardware or software system used to provide such services, and this act could result in common danger to the confidentiality of the content of telephone or electronic communications or location or traffic data concerning such communications shall be punished with imprisonment of at least two years and a monetary penalty.
2. If the perpetrator of the act provided for in the preceding paragraph is a telephony or electronic communications service provider, or its lawful representative, or a member of its management team, or the person responsible for ensuring confidentiality, or an employee or associate of the provider, or sought to obtain an unlawful pecuniary gain for themselves or another, they shall be punished with imprisonment of at least three years and a monetary penalty.

Article 292E
Obstructing telecommunications

1. Any person who hinders or causes widespread or long-term disruption of the operation of a facility providing telephony or electronic communications services to the public and, in particular, the internet by unlawfully interfering with a thing or information system or electronic data enabling such facility to function shall be punished with imprisonment of at least one year and a monetary penalty.
2. Paragraph 2 of the preceding Article also applies to the act provided for in paragraph 1.
3. If the act was committed negligently, a monetary penalty or community service shall be imposed.

Άρθρο 293
Παρακώλυση της λειτουργίας άλλων κοινωφελών εγκαταστάσεων

1. Όποιος αθέμιτα με οποιοδήποτε τρόπο παρεμποδίζει ή διαταράσσει σε μεγάλη έκταση ή για μεγάλο χρονικό διάστημα τη λειτουργία εγκατάστασης που εξυπηρετεί την παροχή στο κοινό:

α) ταχυδρομικών υπηρεσιών,

β) νερού, φωτισμού, φυσικού αερίου, θερμότητας ή κινητήριας δύναμης,

τιμωρείται με φυλάκιση τουλάχιστον ενός (1) έτους και χρηματική ποινή.

2. Η παρ. 2 του άρθρου 292Β εφαρμόζεται και για την πράξη της παρ. 1.

3. Αν από την πράξη προκλήθηκε κατάσταση κοινής ανάγκης, επιβάλλεται κάθειρξη έως δέκα (10) έτη.

4. Αν η πράξη τελέστηκε από αμέλεια, επιβάλλεται φυλάκιση έως έξι (6) μήνες ή χρηματική ποινή.

Άρθρα 294 - 297

(Καταργούνται)

Άρθρο 298
Έμπρακτη μετάνοια και δικαστική άφεση της ποινής

1. Η διάταξη του άρθρου 289 παρ. 1 έχει ανάλογη εφαρμογή και στις περιπτώσεις των παραγράφων 2 των άρθρων 290, 290Α και 292 και της παρ. 3 του άρθρου 291.

2. Η διάταξη του άρθρου 289 παρ. 2 έχει ανάλογη εφαρμογή και στα εγκλήματα αυτού του κεφαλαίου.

Article 293

Obstructing the operation of other public utility facilities

1. Any person who unlawfully hinders or causes widespread or long-term disruption to the operation of a facility providing the public with:

a) postal services;

b) water, lighting, natural gas, heat or motive force,

shall be punished with imprisonment of at least one year and a monetary penalty.

2. Article 292B(2) also applies to the act provided for in paragraph 1.

3. If the act caused an emergency, incarceration of up to 10 years shall be imposed.

4. If the act was committed negligently, imprisonment of up to six months or a monetary penalty shall be imposed.

Articles 294 - 297

[Repealed]

Article 298

Practical repentance and judicial forgiveness of punishments

1. Article 289(1) also applies *mutatis mutandis* to the cases provided for in Articles 290(2), 290A, 292 and 291(3).

2. The provisions of Article 289(2) also apply *mutatis mutandis* to the crimes provided for in this Chapter.

ΔΕΚΑΤΟ ΠΕΜΠΤΟ ΚΕΦΑΛΑΙΟ

ΕΓΚΛΗΜΑΤΑ ΚΑΤΑ ΤΗΣ ΖΩΗΣ ΚΑΙ ΠΡΟΣΒΟΛΕΣ ΤΟΥ ΕΜΒΡΥΟΥ

I

ΕΓΚΛΗΜΑΤΑ ΒΛΑΒΗΣ ΤΗΣ ΖΩΗΣ ΤΟΥ ΑΝΘΡΩΠΟΥ

Άρθρο 299

Ανθρωποκτονία με δόλο

1. Όποιος σκότωσε άλλον τιμωρείται με ισόβια κάθειρξη.

2. Αν η πράξη αποφασίστηκε και εκτελέστηκε σε βρασμό ψυχικής ορμής, επιβάλλεται κάθειρξη.

Άρθρο 300

Ανθρωποκτονία κατ' απαίτηση

Όποιος αποφάσισε και εκτέλεσε ανθρωποκτονία ύστερα από σπουδαία και επίμονη απαίτηση του θύματος και από οίκτο γι' αυτόν που έπασχε από ανίατη ασθένεια τιμωρείται με φυλάκιση.

Άρθρο 301

Συμμετοχή σε αυτοκτονία

Όποιος κατέπεισε άλλον να αυτοκτονήσει, αν τελέστηκε η αυτοκτονία ή έγινε απόπειρά της, καθώς και όποιος έδωσε βοήθεια κατά την τέλεσή της, η οποία διαφορετικά δεν θα ήταν εφικτή, τιμωρείται με φυλάκιση.

Άρθρο 302

Ανθρωποκτονία από αμέλεια

1. Όποιος από αμέλεια σκότωσε άλλον, τιμωρείται με φυλάκιση τουλάχιστον δύο (2) ετών.

2. Αν το θύμα της πράξης της παρ. 1 είναι οικείος του υπαιτίου, το δικαστήριο μπορεί να απαλλάξει τον υπαίτιο από κάθε ποινή, αν πεισθεί ότι λόγω της ψυχικής οδύνης που υπέστη από τις συνέπειες της πράξης του δεν χρειάζεται να υποβληθεί σε ποινή.

Άρθρο 303

Παιδοκτονία

Μητέρα που με πρόθεση σκότωσε το παιδί της κατά ή μετά τον τοκετό, αλλά ενώ εξακολουθούσε ακόμη η διατάραξη του οργανισμού της από αυτόν, τιμωρείται με κάθειρξη έως δέκα έτη.

CHAPTER XV

CRIMES AGAINST LIFE AND OFFENCES AGAINST FOETUSES

I

CRIMES [AGAINST] HUMAN LIFE

Article 299

Homicide with *dolus*

1. Any person who killed another shall be punished with incarceration for life.

2. If the act had been decided upon and was carried out in a fit of rage, incarceration shall be imposed.

Article 300

Compassionate homicide

Any person who decided upon and committed homicide following the serious and persistent request of the victim and out of compassion for the person suffering from an incurable disease shall be punished with imprisonment.

Article 301

Participation in suicide

Any person who persuades another to commit suicide, where the suicide was committed or attempted, and any person who aided in its commission, which would have otherwise not been feasible, shall be punished with imprisonment.

Article 302

Negligent homicide

1. Any person who negligently killed another shall be punished with imprisonment of at least two years.

2. If the victim of the act provided for in paragraph 1 was a related party of the culpable person, the court may opt not to punish the latter if the court is convinced that, due to mental anguish they suffered from the consequences of committing such act, it is not necessary to impose a sentence on them.

Article 303

Infanticide

Any mother who intentionally kills her child during, or after childbirth but while the disturbance to her body due to childbirth persists, shall be punished with incarceration of up to ten years.

II
ΠΡΟΣΒΟΛΕΣ ΤΟΥ ΕΜΒΡΥΟΥ

Άρθρο 304
Διακοπή της κύησης

1. Όποιος χωρίς τη συναίνεση της εγκύου διακόπτει την κύησή της τιμωρείται με κάθειρξη έως δέκα έτη.
2. Όποιος με τη συναίνεση της εγκύου ή των προσώπων που έχουν τη γονική μέριμνα ή επιμέλειά της αν αυτή είναι ανίκανη να συναινέσει, διακόπτει την εγκυμοσύνη της, τιμωρείται με φυλάκιση έως τρία έτη ή χρηματική ποινή και αν ενεργεί κατ' επάγγελμα, με φυλάκιση τουλάχιστον δύο ετών και χρηματική ποινή. Με την ίδια ποινή, μειωμένη κατά το μέτρο του άρθρου 83, τιμωρείται και όποιος προμηθεύει σε έγκυο τα μέσα για τη διακοπή της εγκυμοσύνης της, εφόσον έγινε τουλάχιστον απόπειρα αυτής.
3. Έγκυος που μετά την εικοστή τέταρτη εβδομάδα της κύησης διακόπτει την εγκυμοσύνη της ή επιτρέπει σε άλλον να την διακόψει τιμωρείται με φυλάκιση έως έξι μήνες ή χρηματική ποινή.
4. Δεν είναι άδικη πράξη η τεχνητή διακοπή της εγκυμοσύνης που ενεργείται από την έγκυο ή με τη συναίνεση των προσώπων που αναφέρονται στην παράγραφο 2 από γιατρό μαιευτήρα γυναικολόγο με τη συμμετοχή αναισθησιολόγου, σε οργανωμένη νοσηλευτική μονάδα, αν συντρέχει μία από τις ακόλουθες περιπτώσεις:
α) Δεν έχουν συμπληρωθεί δώδεκα εβδομάδες εγκυμοσύνης.
β) Η εγκυμοσύνη είναι αποτέλεσμα βιασμού, αποπλάνησης ανήλικης, αιμομιξίας ή κατάχρησης γυναίκας ανίκανης να αντισταθεί και δεν έχουν συμπληρωθεί δεκαεννέα εβδομάδες εγκυμοσύνης.
γ) Έχουν διαπιστωθεί, με τα μέσα προγεννητικής διάγνωσης, ενδείξεις σοβαρής ανωμαλίας του εμβρύου που επάγονται τη γέννηση παθολογικού νεογνού ή υπάρχει αναπότρεπτος κίνδυνος για τη ζωή της εγκύου ή κίνδυνος σοβαρής και διαρκούς βλάβης της σωματικής ή ψυχικής υγείας της. Στην περίπτωση αυτή απαιτείται σχετική βεβαίωση και του κατά περίπτωση αρμόδιου γιατρού.
5. Με φυλάκιση έως τρία έτη ή χρηματική ποινή τιμωρείται όποιος κατά την πραγματοποίηση προγεννητικού ελέγχου μετά την εικοστή εβδομάδα της κύησης ή κατά τη διάρκεια του τοκετού και πριν από την εμφάνιση του παιδιού στον εξωτερικό κόσμο, προκαλεί με αμέλεια διακοπή της κύησης ή βαριά βλάβη στο έμβρυο, που έχει ως αποτέλεσμα τον θάνατο του νεογνού.

Άρθρο 304Α
Σωματική βλάβη εμβρύου ή νεογνού

1. Όποιος βιαιοπραγεί σε βάρος εγκύου ή της χορηγεί φάρμακα ή άλλες ουσίες, με αποτέλεσμα να προκληθεί βαριά βλάβη στο έμβρυο ή να εμφανίσει το νεογνό βαριά πάθηση του σώματος ή της διάνοιάς του, τιμωρείται με φυλάκιση τουλάχιστον ενός έτους. Επιβάλλεται φυλάκιση έως ένα έτος ή χρηματική ποινή αν ο υπαίτιος έχει αμέλεια ως προς το αποτέλεσμα αυτό της πράξης του.
2. Με φυλάκιση έως δύο έτη ή χρηματική ποινή τιμωρείται όποιος κατά την πραγματοποίηση προγεννητικού ελέγχου μετά την εικοστή εβδομάδα της κύησης ή κατά τη διάρκεια του τοκετού και πριν από την εμφάνιση του παιδιού στον εξωτερικό κόσμο προκαλεί από αμέλειά του βαριά βλάβη στο έμβρυο ή γίνεται υπαίτιος στο να εμφανίσει το νεογνό βαριά πάθηση του σώματος ή της διάνοιάς του.

Άρθρο 305

(Καταργείται)

II

OFFENCES AGAINST FOETUSES

Article 304
Termination of pregnancy

1. Any person who terminates a pregnancy without the pregnant woman's consent shall be punished with incarceration of up to 10 years.

2. Any person who terminates a pregnancy with the consent of the pregnant woman or of those charged with her custody, where she lacks competence to give consent, shall be punished with imprisonment of up to three years or a monetary penalty, and if they do so [for monetary gain], with imprisonment of at least two years and a monetary penalty. The same punishment, reduced in accordance with Article 83, shall also be imposed on any person who supplies the pregnant woman with the means to terminate her pregnancy, provided such termination was at least attempted.

3. Any pregnant woman who, after the 24th week of the pregnancy, terminates her pregnancy or allows another to terminate it shall be punished with imprisonment of up to six months or a monetary penalty.

4. Artificial termination of a pregnancy, when [initiated] by the pregnant woman or with the consent of the person referred to in paragraph 2 and performed by an obstetrician-gynaecologist with the assistance of an anaesthesiologist at an organised hospital is not a wrongful act, provided any one of the following circumstances applies:

a) [the first] 12 weeks of pregnancy have not elapsed;

b) the pregnancy is the result of rape, enticement of a juvenile, incest or abuse of a woman lacking capacity to resist and [the first] 19 weeks of pregnancy have not elapsed;

c) indications of a serious anomaly of the foetus entailing birth of a pathologically ill newborn have been detected using means of prenatal diagnosis, or there is an unavoidable danger to the life of the pregnant woman or of serious and permanent harm to her physical or mental health. In this case, a relevant certificate issued by the physician competent in each case is required.

5. Any person who, during a prenatal screening performed after the 20th week of pregnancy or during labour and before the child is born, negligently causes termination of the pregnancy or severe harm to the foetus resulting in its death shall be punished with imprisonment of up to three years or a monetary penalty.

Article 304A
Bodily harm to a foetus or a newborn

1. Any person who assaults a pregnant woman or administers medicines or other substances to her causing the foetus to suffer severe harm or the newborn to develop a severe physical or mental condition shall be punished with imprisonment of at least one year. If the culpable person was negligent as regards the results of their act, imprisonment of up to one year or a monetary penalty shall be imposed.

2. Any person who, during a prenatal screening performed after the 20th week of pregnancy or during labour and before the child is born, negligently causes the foetus to suffer severe harm or is responsible for the newborn developing a severe physical or mental condition shall be punished with imprisonment of up to two years or a monetary penalty.

Article 305

[Repealed]

III

ΕΓΚΛΗΜΑΤΑ ΔΙΑΚΙΝΔΥΝΕΥΣΗΣ ΤΗΣ ΖΩΗΣ

Άρθρο 306

Έκθεση

1. Όποιος εκθέτει άλλον και έτσι τον καθιστά αβοήθητο, καθώς και όποιος αφήνει αβοήθητο ένα πρόσωπο που το έχει στην προστασία του ή που έχει υποχρέωση να το διατρέφει και να το περιθάλπει ή να το μεταφέρει, ή ένα πρόσωπο που ο ίδιος υπαίτια τραυμάτισε, τιμωρείται με φυλάκιση τουλάχιστον έξι μηνών.

2. Αν η πράξη προκάλεσε στον παθόντα:

α) βαριά σωματική βλάβη, επιβάλλεται φυλάκιση τουλάχιστον τριών ετών,

β) θάνατο, επιβάλλεται κάθειρξη έως δέκα έτη.

Άρθρο 307

Παράλειψη προσφοράς βοήθειας

Όποιος παραλείπει να σώσει άλλον από κίνδυνο ζωής, αν και μπορεί να το πράξει χωρίς κίνδυνο της δικής του ζωής ή υγείας, τιμωρείται με φυλάκιση έως ένα έτος ή χρηματική ποινή.

III

CRIMES INVOLVING ENDANGERMENT OF LIFE

Article 306
Exposure [to danger]

1. Any person who exposes another person [to danger] and thus renders them helpless, and any person who leaves helpless another person who is under their protection or whom they are obligated to maintain and care for or transport, or whom they culpably injured shall be punished with imprisonment of at least six months.

2. If the act caused:

a) grievous bodily harm to the victim, imprisonment of at least three years shall be imposed;

b) death of the victim, incarceration of up to 10 years shall be imposed.

Article 307
Failure to offer assistance

Any person who fails to save another person from a danger to their life, despite being able to do so without risk to their own life or health, shall be punished with imprisonment of up to one year or a monetary penalty.

ΔΕΚΑΤΟ ΕΚΤΟ ΚΕΦΑΛΑΙΟ

ΕΓΚΛΗΜΑΤΑ ΚΑΤΑ ΤΗΣ ΣΩΜΑΤΙΚΗΣ ΑΚΕΡΑΙΟΤΗΤΑΣ

Άρθρο 308
Σωματική βλάβη

1. Όποιος προξενεί σε άλλον σωματική κάκωση ή βλάβη της υγείας του τιμωρείται με φυλάκιση έως δύο (2) έτη ή χρηματική ποινή. Αν η κάκωση ή βλάβη της υγείας που του προξένησε είναι εντελώς ελαφρά, τιμωρείται με χρηματική ποινή ή παροχή κοινωφελούς εργασίας.

2. Για τη δίωξη της πράξης της προηγούμενης παραγράφου απαιτείται έγκληση, εκτός αν ο παθών είναι υπάλληλος και η πράξη τελέσθηκε κατά την εκτέλεση της υπηρεσίας του ή για λόγους σχετικούς με την εκτέλεσή της ή υπάλληλος του πλειστηριασμού κατά τη διαδικασία της αναγκαστικής εκτέλεσης και η πράξη τελέσθηκε με αφορμή τον πλειστηριασμό, οπότε η δίωξη είναι αυτεπάγγελτη.

3. Η σωματική βλάβη της παρ. 1 δεν είναι άδικη, όταν επιχειρείται με τη συναίνεση του παθόντος και δεν προσκρούει στα χρηστά ήθη.

4. Ο υπαίτιος της πράξης της παρ. 1 είναι δυνατό να απαλλαγεί από κάθε ποινή αν παρασύρθηκε στην πράξη από δικαιολογημένη αγανάκτηση, εξαιτίας μιας αμέσως προηγούμενης πράξης που τέλεσε ο παθών εναντίον του ή ενώπιόν του και που ήταν ιδιαίτερα σκληρή ή βάναυση.

Άρθρο 309
Επικίνδυνη σωματική βλάβη

Αν η πράξη του προηγούμενου άρθρου τελέστηκε με τρόπο που μπορούσε να προκαλέσει στον παθόντα κίνδυνο ζωής ή βαριά σωματική βλάβη, επιβάλλεται φυλάκιση έως τρία (3) έτη.

Άρθρο 310
Βαριά σωματική βλάβη

1. Αν η πράξη του άρθρου 308 είχε ως επακόλουθο τη βαριά σωματική βλάβη επιβάλλεται φυλάκιση τουλάχιστον ενός (1) έτους.

2. Όποιος προκαλεί σε άλλον βαριά σωματική βλάβη τιμωρείται με φυλάκιση τουλάχιστον δύο (2) ετών. Αν επιδίωκε την πρόκληση της βαριάς σωματικής βλάβης, τιμωρείται με κάθειρξη.

3. Βαριά σωματική βλάβη υπάρχει ιδίως αν η πράξη προξένησε στον παθόντα κίνδυνο ζωής ή βαριά και μακροχρόνια αρρώστια ή σοβαρό ακρωτηριασμό ή αναπηρία ή μόνιμη παραμόρφωση ή αν τον εμπόδισε σημαντικά και για πολύ χρόνο να χρησιμοποιεί το σώμα ή τη διάνοιά του.

Άρθρο 311
Θανατηφόρα σωματική βλάβη

Αν η σωματική βλάβη είχε επακόλουθο το θάνατο του παθόντος, επιβάλλεται κάθειρξη έως δέκα έτη. Αν ο υπαίτιος επιδίωκε τη βαριά σωματική βλάβη του παθόντος επιβάλλεται κάθειρξη.

CHAPTER XVI

CRIMES AGAINST PHYSICAL INTEGRITY

Article 308
Bodily harm

1. Any person who causes bodily injury to or harms the health of another person shall be punished with imprisonment of up to two years or a monetary penalty. If the injury or harm to the health caused is completely minor, [the perpetrator] shall be punished with a monetary penalty or community service.
2. A victim-initiated complaint is required to institute [criminal] prosecution of the act provided for in the preceding paragraph, unless the victim is a state employee and the act was committed in the performance of their duties or on grounds related to such performance, or an auctioneer during compulsory enforcement and the act was committed in relation to the auction, in which case the act is subject to public prosecution.
3. The bodily harm provided for in paragraph 1 is not wrongful if it is committed with the consent of the harmed person and it is not contrary to morality.
4. The [court may opt] not to impose any punishment on the person culpable of the act provided for in paragraph 1 if they [committed] the act having been compelled by justifiable rage due to an immediately preceding and particularly cruel or brutal act committed by the victim against or in the presence of the culpable person.

Article 309
Dangerous bodily harm

If the act provided for in the preceding Article was committed in a manner which could endanger the life of or cause grievous bodily harm to the victim, imprisonment of up to three years shall be imposed.

Article 310
Grievous bodily harm

1. If the act provided for in Article 308 resulted in grievous bodily harm, imprisonment of at least one year shall be imposed.
2. Any person who causes grievous bodily harm to another shall be punished with imprisonment of at least two years. If they intended to cause grievous bodily harm, they shall be punished with incarceration.
3. There is grievous bodily harm, in particular, if the act endangered the life of the victim, or caused them to develop a severe and long-term illness, or led to serious amputation or disability or permanent disfigurement, or significantly hindered them for a long time from using their body or intellect.

Article 311
Fatal bodily harm

If the bodily harm resulted in the victim's death, incarceration of up to 10 years shall be imposed. If the culpable person intended to cause grievous bodily harm, incarceration shall be imposed.

Άρθρο 312

Σωματική βλάβη αδυνάμων ατόμων

1. Με την επιφύλαξη διατάξεων ειδικών ποινικών νόμων, όποιος προκαλεί σωματική κάκωση ή βλάβη της υγείας σε ανήλικο ή σε πρόσωπο που δεν μπορεί να υπερασπίσει τον εαυτό του, τιμωρείται:

α) για την πράξη του πρώτου εδαφίου της παρ. 1 του άρθρου 308, με φυλάκιση τουλάχιστον ενός (1) έτους,

β) για την πράξη του άρθρου 309, με φυλάκιση τουλάχιστον δύο (2) ετών,

γ) για την πράξη του πρώτου εδαφίου της παρ. 1 του άρθρου 310, με φυλάκιση τουλάχιστον τριών (3) ετών και αν επεδίωκε την πρόκληση βαριάς σωματικής βλάβης, με κάθειρξη και

δ) για την πράξη του άρθρου 311, με κάθειρξη.

2. Με την πρόκληση σωματικής βλάβης κατά την περ. γ' της παρ. 1 εξομοιώνεται και η μεθοδευμένη πρόκληση έντονου σωματικού πόνου ή σωματικής εξάντλησης επικίνδυνης για την υγεία, ή ψυχικού πόνου ικανού να επιφέρει σοβαρή ψυχική βλάβη, ιδίως με την παρατεταμένη απομόνωση σε βάρος των προσώπων της παρ. 1.

3. (Καταργείται)

4. (Καταργείται)

Άρθρο 313

Συμπλοκή

Αν εξαιτίας συμπλοκής ή επίθεσης που έγινε από πολλούς επήλθε επικίνδυνη σωματική βλάβη ανθρώπου, καθένας από εκείνους που πήραν μέρος στη συμπλοκή ή στην επίθεση τιμωρείται για μόνη τη συμμετοχή του σε αυτή με φυλάκιση έως τρία (3) έτη και αν το θύμα είναι ανήλικο ή επήλθε θάνατος ή βαριά σωματική βλάβη ανθρώπου, με φυλάκιση τουλάχιστον ενός (1) έτους. Αν συμμετείχαν πρόσωπα τα οποία έκαναν χρήση όπλου και επήλθε θάνατος ή βαριά σωματική βλάβη ανθρώπου, η πράξη του πρώτου εδαφίου τιμωρείται με κάθειρξη έως οκτώ (8) έτη.

Άρθρο 314

Σωματική βλάβη από αμέλεια

1. Όποιος από αμέλεια προκαλεί σωματική κάκωση ή βλάβη της υγείας άλλου τιμωρείται με φυλάκιση έως δύο (2) έτη ή χρηματική ποινή ή παροχή κοινωφελούς εργασίας. Αν η σωματική βλάβη που προκλήθηκε είναι βαριά, τιμωρείται με φυλάκιση έως τρία (3) έτη, και αν αυτή είναι εντελώς ελαφρά, επιβάλλεται χρηματική ποινή ή παροχή κοινωφελούς εργασίας.

2. Για την ποινική δίωξη της πράξης της προηγούμενης παραγράφου απαιτείται έγκληση. Η δίωξη είναι αυτεπάγγελτη αν ο υπαίτιος ήταν οδηγός οχήματος ή υπόχρεος λόγω της υπηρεσίας ή του επαγγέλματός του να καταβάλει ιδιαίτερη επιμέλεια ή προσοχή. Όταν ο υπαίτιος οδηγός οχήματος δεν μεταφέρει επιβάτες ή πράγματα με σκοπό βιοπορισμού, η ποινική δίωξη ασκείται αυτεπαγγέλτως, ο εισαγγελέας όμως με διάταξή του απέχει από την ποινική δίωξη αν ο παθών δηλώσει ότι δεν επιθυμεί την ποινική δίωξη του δράστη. Αν η δήλωση υποβληθεί μετά την άσκηση ποινικής δίωξης, το δικαστήριο παύει οριστικά αυτήν.

Article 312

Bodily harm to persons [unable to defend themselves]

1. Without prejudice to the provisions of specific penal laws, any person who causes bodily injury to or harms the health of a juvenile or a person unable to defend themselves shall be punished with:

a) imprisonment of at least one year for the act provided for in the first sentence of Article 308(1);

b) imprisonment of at least two years for the act provided for in Article 309;

c) imprisonment of at least three years for the act provided for in Article 310(1), and incarceration if they intended to cause grievous bodily harm; [or]

d) incarceration for the act provided for in Article 311.

2. Methodically causing intense physical pain or physical exhaustion that is dangerous to the health [of the victim], or mental [anguish] which could cause serious mental harm, particularly by placing the persons provided for in paragraph 1 in prolonged isolation, shall be treated as equivalent to causing bodily harm, [carrying the sentence] provided for in paragraph 1(c).

3. [Repealed]

4. [Repealed]

Article 313

Brawl

If, due to a brawl or attack involving several persons, a person suffered dangerous bodily harm, each person participating in the brawl or attack shall be punished only for their participation in the brawl or attack with imprisonment of up to three years, and if the victim is a juvenile or if death of or grievous bodily harm to a person occurred, with imprisonment of at least one year. If participants used a weapon [in the brawl or attack] and this resulted in death of or grievous bodily harm to another person, the act provided for in the preceding sentence shall be punished with incarceration of up to 8 years.

Article 314

Negligent bodily harm

1. Any person who negligently causes bodily injury to or harms the health of another person shall be punished with imprisonment of up to two years or a monetary penalty or community service. If the bodily harm caused is grievous, they shall be punished with imprisonment of up to three years, and if it is completely minor, with a monetary penalty or community service.

2. A victim-initiated complaint is required to [institute] criminal prosecution of the act provided for in the preceding paragraph. The act is subject to public prosecution if the culpable person was driving a vehicle or was obligated, while on duty or due to the duties assigned to them, to be particularly diligent or attentive. When the culpable vehicle driver does not carry passengers or things for a living, the act shall be subject to public prosecution, but the public prosecutor may issue an order abstaining from prosecution if the victim declares that they do not wish the perpetrator to be prosecuted. If such declaration is made after criminal prosecution has been instituted, the court shall definitively terminate prosecution.

Άρθρο 315
Ακρωτηριασμός γυναικείων γεννητικών οργάνων

1. Όποιος με τη χρήση κάθε μορφής βίας ή απειλής βίας ή άλλων εξαναγκαστικών μέσων ή με επιβολή ή κατάχρηση εξουσίας ή αποσπώντας τη συναίνεση με τη χρήση απατηλών μέσων ή παρασύροντάς την, εκμεταλλευόμενος την ευάλωτη θέση στην οποία βρίσκεται, εξαναγκάζει γυναίκα να υποβληθεί σε εκτομή, αγκτηριασμό ή οποιονδήποτε άλλον ακρωτηριασμό στο σύνολο ή σε μέρος των μεγάλων χειλέων του αιδοίου, των μικρών χειλέων του αιδοίου ή της κλειτορίδας, τιμωρείται με ποινή φυλάκισης τουλάχιστον δύο (2) ετών και χρηματική ποινή αν δεν συντρέχει περίπτωση να τιμωρηθεί αυστηρότερα με άλλη διάταξη. Αν η πράξη διαπράχθηκε από μέλος της οικογένειας ή από πρόσωπο που συνοικούσε με το θύμα ή από δύο ή περισσότερα πρόσωπα ή με χρήση όπλου ή απειλή χρήσης όπλου ή σε βάρος ανήλικης γυναίκας ή από λόγους εκδίκησης, συντρέχει ιδιαίτερα επιβαρυντική περίσταση.

2. Αν κάποια από τις πράξεις της παρ. 1 στις οποίες εξαναγκάστηκε το θύμα, είχε ως επακόλουθο τον θάνατο ή προξένησε βαριά σωματική βλάβη, επιβάλλεται κάθειρξη.

3. Με τις ποινές των παρ. 1 και 2 τιμωρείται και όποιος, για λόγους μη ιατρικούς και υπό τις περιστάσεις της παρ. 1, διενεργεί εκτομή, αγκτηριασμό ή οποιονδήποτε άλλον ακρωτηριασμό στο σύνολο ή σε μέρος των μεγάλων χειλέων του αιδοίου, των μικρών χειλέων του αιδοίου ή της κλειτορίδας σε βάρος των προσώπων της παρ. 1.

Άρθρο 315Α
Εγκλήματα κατά της σωματικής ακεραιότητας υπαλλήλου - Ιδιαίτερα επιβαρυντική περίσταση

Η τέλεση των εγκλημάτων των άρθρων 308 έως 311 εναντίον υπαλλήλου κατά την εκτέλεση της υπηρεσίας του ή για λόγους σχετικούς με την εκτέλεσή της συνιστά ιδιαίτερα επιβαρυντική περίσταση.

ΔΕΚΑΤΟ ΕΒΔΟΜΟ ΚΕΦΑΛΑΙΟ

Άρθρα 316 - 321

(Καταργούνται)

Article 315

Female genital mutilation

1. Any person who, through use of any form of violence or threat of violence or other means of coercion, or through imposition or abuse of power, or by obtaining a woman's consent using fraudulent means, or by inveigling her by exploiting the vulnerable situation in which she finds herself, forces a woman to undergo excision, infibulation or any other mutilation to the whole or any part of the labia majora, labia minora or clitoris, shall be punished with imprisonment of at least two years and a monetary penalty, unless the act carries a heavier punishment under a different provision. There are particularly aggravating circumstances when the act is committed by a family member or a person living with the victim, or by two or more persons, or with the use of a weapon or the threat of using a weapon, or against a juvenile.

2. If any of the acts provided for in paragraph 1 which the victim was forced to undergo resulted in death or grievous bodily harm, incarceration shall be imposed.

3. The punishments laid down in paragraphs 1 and 2 shall also be imposed on any person who, for non-medical reasons and under the circumstances provided for in paragraph 1, excises, infibulates or performs any other mutilation to the whole or any part of the labia majora, labia minora or clitoris on the persons provided for in paragraph 1.

Article 315A

Crimes against the physical integrity of a state employee - Particularly aggravating circumstances

There are particularly aggravating circumstances when the crimes provided for in Articles 308 to 311 are committed against a state employee performing their duties or for reasons related to such performance.

CHAPTER XVII

Articles 316 - 321

[Repealed]

ΔΕΚΑΤΟ ΟΓΔΟΟ ΚΕΦΑΛΑΙΟ

ΕΓΚΛΗΜΑΤΑ ΚΑΤΑ ΤΗΣ ΠΡΟΣΩΠΙΚΗΣ ΕΛΕΥΘΕΡΙΑΣ

Άρθρο 322

Αρπαγή

1. Όποιος με εξαπάτηση, βία ή απειλή βίας συλλαμβάνει, απάγει ή παράνομα κατακρατεί άλλον, έτσι ώστε να τον αποστερεί από την προστασία της πολιτείας και ιδίως όποιος περιάγει άλλον σε ομηρία ή σε άλλη παρόμοια κατάσταση στέρησης της ελευθερίας, τιμωρείται με κάθειρξη έως δέκα έτη. Αν η πράξη έγινε με σκοπό να εξαναγκαστεί ο παθών ή κάποιος άλλος σε πράξη, παράλειψη ή ανοχή για την οποία δεν υπάρχει υποχρέωσή του, επιβάλλεται κάθειρξη, εφόσον η πράξη δεν τιμωρείται βαρύτερα με βάση τους κανόνες της συρροής.

2. Με κάθειρξη τιμωρείται η πράξη της παραγράφου 1 εδ. α΄, ακόμα κι όταν έγινε χωρίς τη χρήση των μέσων που αναφέρονται σε αυτή, όταν τελείται από υπάλληλο ή από πρόσωπα ή ομάδες προσώπων που ενεργούν με την άδεια, υποστήριξη ή συναίνεση κρατικής αρχής, εφόσον ακολουθείται από άρνηση παραδοχής της στέρησης της ελευθερίας ή από απόκρυψη της τύχης ή του τόπου όπου βρίσκεται το θύμα (βίαιη εξαφάνιση). Αποτελεί επιβαρυντική περίσταση η τέλεση της πράξης σε βάρος εγκύου, ανηλίκου ή ατόμου που δεν μπορεί να υπερασπίσει τον εαυτό του.

3. Τιμωρείται με κάθειρξη τουλάχιστον δέκα ετών, όποιος, ως προϊστάμενος, έδωσε εντολή για την τέλεση της πράξης της προηγούμενης παραγράφου, εφόσον αυτή τελέστηκε ή έγινε απόπειρά της.

4. Όποιος ως προϊστάμενος δεν έλαβε όλα τα αναγκαία και εύλογα μέτρα, εντός της εξουσίας του, για την πρόληψη ή την καταστολή της τέλεσης μιας πράξης βίαιης εξαφάνισης ή για την παραπομπή της πράξης αυτής στις αρμόδιες αρχές προς έρευνα και ποινική δίωξη τιμωρείται με φυλάκιση τουλάχιστον τριών ετών, εάν η πράξη του δεν τιμωρείται βαρύτερα κατά τις διατάξεις περί συμμετοχής.

5. Η επίκληση των άρθρων 20 έως 25 δεν μπορεί να άρει τον άδικο χαρακτήρα των πράξεων των παραγράφων 2 και 3.

6. Η καταδίκη υπαλλήλου για τις πράξεις των παραγράφων 2, 3 και 4 επισύρει αυτοδικαίως αποστέρηση της θέσης που κατέχει. Εάν οι πράξεις αυτές τελούνται υπό καθεστώς σφετερισμού του δημοκρατικού πολιτεύματος, η προθεσμία της παραγραφής αρχίζει μόλις αποκατασταθεί η νόμιμη εξουσία.

Άρθρα 322Α - 323

(Καταργούνται)

CHAPTER XVIII

CRIMES AGAINST PERSONAL FREEDOM

Article 322

[Unlawfully depriving another of their freedom]

1. Any person who, through deception, use or threat of violence, abducts or unlawfully detains a person, thus depriving them of the protection of the state, and, in particular, any person who takes another hostage or similarly deprives them of their freedom shall be punished with incarceration of up to 10 years. If the act was committed for the purpose of forcing the victim or another person to take, refrain from taking, or tolerate an action when they are not obligated to do so, incarceration shall be imposed, unless the act carries a heavier sentence under the rules on concurrence.

2. The act provided for in the first sentence of paragraph 1 shall be punished with incarceration, even if committed without using the means referred to above, when committed by a state employee or persons or groups of persons acting with the authorisation, support or acquiescence of a state authority, provided it is followed by a refusal to acknowledge the deprivation of freedom or by concealment of the fate or whereabouts of the victim (enforced disappearance). There are aggravating circumstances when the act is committed against a pregnant woman, a juvenile or a person unable to defend themselves.

3. Any person who, as another's superior, ordered the commission of the act provided for in the preceding paragraph shall be punished with incarceration of at least 10 years, provided the act was committed or attempted.

4. Any person who, as another's superior, failed to take all necessary and reasonable measures, within their remit to prevent or suppress the commission of an act of enforced disappearance or to report such act to the competent authorities for the purpose of inquiries and criminal prosecution shall be punished with imprisonment of at least three years, unless the act carries a heavier sentence under the provisions on participation.

5. Invoking Articles 20 to 25 cannot preclude the unlawful nature of the acts provided for in paragraphs 2 and 3.

6. Any state employee convicted of the acts provided in paragraphs 2, 3 and 4 automatically forfeits their post. Where these acts are committed in the context of usurpation of the democratic system of government, the time-barring period shall begin to run as soon as legitimate power is restored.

Articles 322A - 323

[Repealed]

Άρθρο 323Α
Εμπορία ανθρώπων

1. Όποιος με τη χρήση βίας, απειλής βίας ή άλλων εξαναγκαστικών μέσων ή με επιβολή ή κατάχρηση εξουσίας, στρατολογεί, απάγει, μεταφέρει, κατακρατεί παράνομα, υποθάλπει, παραδίδει ή παραλαμβάνει άλλον με σκοπό την εκμετάλλευσή του, τιμωρείται με κάθειρξη και χρηματική ποινή.

2. Με την ίδια ποινή τιμωρείται ο υπαίτιος και αν, για να επιτύχει τον ίδιο σκοπό, τελεί τις πράξεις της προηγούμενης παραγράφου αποσπώντας τη συναίνεση άλλου με τη χρήση απατηλών μέσων ή παρασύροντάς τον εκμεταλλευόμενος την ευάλωτη θέση στην οποία βρίσκεται.

3. Με κάθειρξη τουλάχιστον δέκα (10) ετών και χρηματική ποινή τιμωρείται η πράξη των προηγούμενων παραγράφων όταν:

α) τελείται κατ' επάγγελμα,

β) τελείται από υπάλληλο ο οποίος κατά την άσκηση της υπηρεσίας του ή επωφελούμενος από την ιδιότητά του αυτή διαπράττει ή συμμετέχει με οποιονδήποτε τρόπο στην πράξη,

γ) συνδέεται με την παράνομη είσοδο, παραμονή ή έξοδο του παθόντος από τη χώρα ή

δ) είχε ως αποτέλεσμα τη βαριά σωματική βλάβη του παθόντος. Επιβάλλεται ισόβια κάθειρξη, αν η πράξη είχε ως αποτέλεσμα το θάνατο.

4. Με τις ποινές της προηγούμενης παραγράφου τιμωρείται η πράξη των παρ. 1 και 2 όταν στρέφεται κατά ανηλίκου, ακόμα κι όταν τελείται χωρίς τη χρήση των μέσων που αναφέρονται σε αυτές. Με τις ίδιες ποινές τιμωρείται και όποιος, με τα μέσα των παρ. 1 και 2 στρατολογεί ανήλικο με σκοπό τη χρησιμοποίησή του σε ένοπλες επιχειρήσεις.

5. Η έννοια της εκμετάλλευσης στις προηγούμενες παραγράφους περιλαμβάνει τον πορισμό παράνομου περιουσιακού οφέλους από:

α) την υπαγωγή του σε καθεστώς δουλείας ή σε παρεμφερείς προς τη δουλεία πρακτικές,

β) την υπαγωγή του σε καθεστώς ειλωτείας,

γ) την εργασία ή την επαιτεία του θύματος (εργασιακή εκμετάλλευση),

δ) την τέλεση εγκληματικών πράξεων από αυτό,

ε) την αφαίρεση κυττάρων, ιστών ή οργάνων του σώματός του,

στ) την τέλεση από αυτό γενετήσιων πράξεων, πραγματικών ή προσποιητών, ή την παροχή εργασίας ή υπηρεσιών που έχουν ως αποκλειστικό σκοπό τη γενετήσια διέγερση (γενετήσια εκμετάλλευση) ή

ζ) τον εξαναγκασμό του σε τέλεση γάμου.

6. Με φυλάκιση τουλάχιστον τριών (3) ετών και χρηματική ποινή τιμωρείται όποιος εν γνώσει, χωρίς να χρησιμοποιεί τα μέσα των παρ. 1 και 2, προσλαμβάνει στην εργασία του πρόσωπο που είναι θύμα εμπορίας, δέχεται τις υπηρεσίες του προσώπου αυτού, τελεί μαζί του γενετήσια πράξη ή δέχεται τα έσοδα από την εκμετάλλευσή του.

7. Τιμωρείται με φυλάκιση και χρηματική ποινή όποιος, χωρίς να χρησιμοποιεί τα μέσα των παρ. 1 και 2, εξωθεί σε επαιτεία ανηλίκους, με σκοπό την εκμετάλλευση των εσόδων τους.

8. Για όποιον καταγγέλλει αξιόποινες πράξεις που τελέστηκαν σε βάρος του από υπαιτίους των πράξεων των προηγούμενων παραγράφων, ο εισαγγελέας πλημμελειοδικών μπορεί, εφόσον η καταγγελία πιθανολογείται βάσιμη, ύστερα από έγκριση του εισαγγελέα εφετών, να απόσχει προσωρινά από την ποινική δίωξη για παραβάσεις του νόμου περί αλλοδαπών και περί εκδιδομένων με αμοιβή προσώπων, καθώς και για παραβάσεις λόγω συμμετοχής τους σε εγκληματικές δραστηριότητες, εφόσον η συμμετοχή αυτή ήταν άμεση συνέπεια του γεγονότος ότι ήταν παθόντες των αδικημάτων των προηγούμενων παραγράφων, ώσπου να εκδοθεί αμετάκλητη απόφαση για τις πράξεις που καταγγέλθηκαν. Αν η καταγγελία αποδειχθεί βάσιμη, η αποχή από την ποινική δίωξη γίνεται οριστική.

Article 323A
Human trafficking

1. Any person who, through threat or use of violence or other means of coercion or through imposition or abuse of power, enlists, transports, unlawfully detains, harbours, hands over or takes receipt of another person for the purpose of exploiting them shall be punished with incarceration and a monetary penalty.
2. The same punishment shall be imposed on the culpable person even if, in order to achieve the same purpose, they commit the acts provided for in the preceding paragraph by obtaining the other person's consent using fraudulent means or inveigles them by exploiting their vulnerable situation.
3. The act provided for in the preceding paragraphs shall be punished with incarceration of at least ten years and a monetary penalty when:
a) committed [for monetary gain];
b) committed by a state employee who commits or participates in any manner in the act while performing their duties or benefiting from their status;
c) associated with the victim's unlawful entry into, stay in or exit from [Greece]; or
d) it resulted in grievous bodily harm to the victim. Incarceration for life shall be imposed if the act resulted in death.
4. The punishments laid down in the preceding paragraph shall be imposed if the act provided for in paragraphs 1 and 2 is committed against a juvenile, even if committed without using the means referred to in those paragraphs. The same punishments shall also be imposed on any person who, using the means referred to in paragraphs 1 and 2, enlists a juvenile for the purpose of using them in combat operations.
5. The concept of exploitation in the preceding paragraphs includes the acquisition of an unlawful pecuniary gain from:
a) subjecting [the victim] to slavery or similar practices;
b) subjecting [the victim] to servitude;
c) forcing the victim to work or beg (labour exploitation);
d) crimes committed by [the victim];
e) removal of cells, tissue or organs from [the victim's] body;
f) commission of sexual acts, whether real or simulated, by the victim, or provision of labour or services [by the victim] for the exclusive purpose of sexual arousal (sexual exploitation); or
g) forcing [the victim] to marry.
6. Any person who, without using the means referred to in paragraphs 1 and 2, knowingly hires a person who is the victim of trafficking, accepts services from such a person, engages in a sexual act with them, or accepts the proceeds from their exploitation shall be punished with imprisonment of at least three years and a monetary penalty.
7. Any person who, without using the means referred to in paragraphs 1 and 2, forces juveniles to beg for the purpose of exploiting their proceeds shall be punished with imprisonment and a monetary penalty.
8. With regard to any person who reports punishable acts committed against them by persons culpable of the acts provided for in the preceding paragraphs, the court of misdemeanours public prosecutor may, if the report is considered likely on the balance of probabilities and following approval from the court of appeal public prosecutor, temporarily refrain from initiating criminal prosecution for violation of the law concerning foreign nationals and sex work, as well as for violations due to their participation in criminal activities, provided such participation was the direct result of the fact that they were the victims of the offences provided for in the preceding paragraphs, until an irrevocable judgment has been handed down on the reported acts. If the report proves to be well-founded, the decision to refrain from prosecution shall become final.

Άρθρο 323Β

Διευκόλυνση επαιτείας

Όποιος υποκινεί ή καθοδηγεί άλλον σε επαιτεία ή τη διοργανώνει ή τη διευκολύνει, ιδίως υποδεικνύοντας τη μέθοδο και τον τόπο της επαιτείας ή παρέχοντας μέσο μεταφοράς προς αυτόν, τιμωρείται με φυλάκιση έως τριών (3) ετών και χρηματική ποινή, αν η πράξη δεν τιμωρείται βαρύτερα από άλλη διάταξη. Αν πρόκειται για άτομο με αναπηρία, συντρέχει ιδιαίτερα επιβαρυντική περίσταση.

Άρθρο 324

Αρπαγή ανηλίκων

1. Όποιος αφαιρεί ανήλικο από τους γονείς, τους επιτρόπους ή από οποιονδήποτε δικαιούται να μεριμνήσει για το πρόσωπό του ή όποιος υποστηρίζει την εκούσια διαφυγή του ανηλίκου από την εξουσία των παραπάνω προσώπων τιμωρείται με φυλάκιση. Αν ο ανήλικος από τη στέρηση της επιμέλειας διέτρεξε σοβαρό κίνδυνο ζωής ή βαριάς βλάβης της υγείας του, ο δράστης τιμωρείται με φυλάκιση τουλάχιστον ενός έτους.

2. Αν ο ανήλικος δεν έχει συμπληρώσει τα δεκατέσσερα έτη, επιβάλλεται κάθειρξη έως δέκα έτη, εκτός εάν η πράξη τελέστηκε από ανιόντα, οπότε εφαρμόζεται η προηγούμενη παράγραφος. Σε κάθε περίπτωση, αν ο υπαίτιος τέλεσε την πράξη από κερδοσκοπία ή με σκοπό να μεταχειριστεί τον ανήλικο σε ανήθικες ασχολίες ή να επιτύχει τη μεταβολή της οικογενειακής τάξης του ανηλίκου επιβάλλεται κάθειρξη έως δέκα έτη.

3. Αν ο υπαίτιος των πράξεων των προηγουμένων παραγράφων είχε σκοπό να εισπράξει λύτρα ή να εξαναγκάσει άλλον σε πράξη ή παράλειψη, επιβάλλεται κάθειρξη. Στην περίπτωση που ο δράστης με τη θέλησή του και προτού εκπληρωθεί οποιοσδήποτε όρος ή αξίωσή του απελευθέρωσε και απέδωσε υγιή και σώο τον ανήλικο επιβάλλεται φυλάκιση.

Άρθρο 325

Παράνομη κατακράτηση

Όποιος, εκτός από τις περιπτώσεις των άρθρων 322 και 323Α, απάγει ή κατακρατεί άλλον χωρίς τη θέλησή του ή του στερεί με άλλον τρόπο την ελευθερία της κίνησής του τιμωρείται με φυλάκιση ή χρηματική ποινή και αν η κατακράτηση διήρκεσε επί μακρό χρονικό διάστημα ή τελέστηκε κατά παράβαση των διατάξεων του άρθρου 6 του Συντάγματος, με φυλάκιση τουλάχιστον δυο ετών και χρηματική ποινή.

Άρθρα 326 - 329

(Καταργούνται)

Article 323B
Facilitation of begging

Any person who solicits or instructs another to beg, or organises or facilitates such begging, particularly by indicating the method and place of begging or by providing means of transportation to such place shall be punished with imprisonment of up to three years and a monetary penalty, unless the act carries a heavier punishment under a different provision. There are particularly aggravating circumstances when the [person begging] is a person with disabilities.

Article 324
Child abduction

1. Any person who removes a juvenile from their parents, tutors or any person entitled to care for the juvenile, or any person who supports the voluntary escape of a juvenile from the authority of the aforesaid persons shall be punished with imprisonment. If, due to deprivation of care, the juvenile was exposed to serious danger to their life or severe harm to their health, the perpetrator shall be punished with imprisonment of at least one year.

2. If the juvenile has not attained the age of 14, incarceration of up to 10 years shall be imposed [on the perpetrator], unless the act was committed by a relative in the ascending line, in which case the preceding paragraph applies. In all cases, if the culpable person committed the act for the purpose of profiteering, or for the purpose of involving the juvenile in immoral activities, or for the purpose of altering the family status of the juvenile, they shall be punished with incarceration of up to 10 years.

3. If the person who committed the acts provided for in the preceding paragraphs intended to collect a ransom or force another person to take or refrain from an act, incarceration shall be imposed. If the perpetrator, willingly and before any of their conditions or demands were met, freed the juvenile and surrendered them safe and sound, imprisonment shall be imposed.

Article 325
Unlawful detention

Except in the cases provided for in Articles 322 and 323A, any person who abducts or detains another against their wishes or otherwise deprives them of their freedom of movement shall be punished with imprisonment or a monetary penalty, and if the detention lasted a long time or was committed in violation of the provisions of Article 6 of the Constitution, with imprisonment of at least two years and a monetary penalty.

Articles 326 - 329

[Repealed]

Άρθρο 330
Παράνομη βία

1. Όποιος με σωματική βία ή απειλή σωματικής βίας ή άλλης παράνομης πράξης ή παράλειψης εξαναγκάζει άλλον σε πράξη, παράλειψη ή ανοχή για τις οποίες ο παθών δεν έχει υποχρέωση, τιμωρείται με φυλάκιση έως δύο έτη ή χρηματική ποινή, ανεξάρτητα αν το απειλούμενο κακό στρέφεται εναντίον εκείνου που απειλείται ή κάποιου από τους οικείους του.

2. Με την επιφύλαξη διατάξεων ειδικών ποινικών νόμων, αν η πράξη της παρ. 1 τελείται σε βάρος ανηλίκου ή προσώπου που δεν μπορεί να υπερασπίσει τον εαυτό του, επιβάλλεται φυλάκιση τουλάχιστον έξι (6) μηνών.

3. Όποιος με τη χρήση οποιασδήποτε μορφής βίας ή απειλής βίας ή άλλων εξαναγκαστικών μέσων ή με επιβολή ή κατάχρηση εξουσίας, ή αποσπώντας τη συναίνεση με τη χρήση απατηλών μέσων ή παρασύροντάς τον, εκμεταλλευόμενος την ευάλωτη θέση στην οποία βρίσκεται, εξαναγκάζει ή δελεάζει άλλον να συνάψει γάμο ή σύμφωνο συμβίωσης, τιμωρείται με ποινή φυλάκισης τουλάχιστον δύο (2) ετών και χρηματική ποινή. Αν η πράξη αφορά στη σύναψη γάμου ή συμφώνου συμβίωσης στο έδαφος κράτους άλλου από εκείνο στο οποίο διαμένει ο εξαναγκαζόμενος ή αν η πράξη διαπράχθηκε από μέλος της οικογένειας ή από πρόσωπο που συνοικούσε με το θύμα ή από δύο ή περισσότερα πρόσωπα ή με τη χρήση όπλου ή απειλή χρήσης όπλου, συντρέχει ιδιαίτερα επιβαρυντική περίσταση.

Άρθρο 331
Αυτοδικία

Όποιος ασκεί αυθαίρετα αξίωση σχετική με δικαίωμα που ή το έχει πραγματικά ή από πεποίθηση το οικειοποιείται τιμωρείται με χρηματική ποινή ή παροχή κοινωφελούς εργασίας. Για την ποινική δίωξη απαιτείται έγκληση.

Άρθρο 332

(Καταργείται)

Άρθρο 333
Απειλή

1. Όποιος προκαλεί σε άλλον τρόμο ή ανησυχία, απειλώντας αυτόν με βία ή άλλη παράνομη πράξη ή παράλειψη, τιμωρείται με φυλάκιση έως ένα (1) έτος ή χρηματική ποινή. Όποιος προκαλεί σε άλλον τρόμο ή ανησυχία με συνεχή συμπεριφορά του πρώτου εδαφίου ή με την επίμονη καταδίωξη ή παρακολούθηση των κινήσεων και των δραστηριοτήτων του, όπως ιδίως με επανειλημμένες επισκέψεις στο οικογενειακό, κοινωνικό ή εργασιακό περιβάλλον αυτού, παρά την εκφρασμένη αντίθετη βούλησή του τιμωρείται με ποινή φυλάκισης έως δύο (2) έτη.

Article 330
Unlawful violence

1. Any person who, through use or threat of physical violence or other unlawful act or omission, forces another to take, refrain from taking, or tolerate an act when they are not obligated to do so shall be punished with imprisonment of up to two years or a monetary penalty, regardless of whether or not the threat of harm was directed against the person being threatened or any of their related parties.
2. Without prejudice to the provisions of special penal laws, if the act provided for in paragraph 1 is committed against a juvenile or a person unable to defend themselves, imprisonment of at least six months shall be imposed.
3. Any person who, through use of any form of violence or threat of violence or other means of coercion, or through imposition or abuse of power, or obtaining another's consent using fraudulent means, or inveigling them by exploiting the vulnerable situation in which they find themselves, forces or lures another to enter into marriage or a civil partnership shall be punished with imprisonment of at least two years and a monetary penalty. There are particularly aggravating circumstances when the act concerns marriage or civil partnership entered into within the territory of a state other than the one where the victim resides, or when the act is committed by a family member or a person living with the victim, or by two or more persons, or with the use of a weapon or the threat of using a weapon.

Article 331
Self-redress

Any person who arbitrarily enforces a claim concerning a right which they actually have or are [convinced] they have shall be punished with a monetary penalty or community service. A victim-initiated complaint is required to institute criminal prosecution.

Article 332

[Repealed]

Article 333
Threat

1. Any person who causes another person terror or apprehension by threatening them with violence or any other unlawful act or omission shall be punished with imprisonment of up to one year or a monetary penalty. Any person who causes another person terror or apprehension thorough continuously engaging in the conduct described in the preceding sentence or by persistently pursuing or surveilling their movements and activities, such as, in particular, by repeatedly visiting their family, social or work environment despite the other person's expressed wishes to the contrary shall be punished with imprisonment of up to two years.

1Α. Όποιος θέτει άλλον υπό παρακολούθηση, συνεχή ή κατ' επανάληψη, με τη χρήση της τεχνολογίας των πληροφοριών και επικοινωνιών, με σκοπό την ιχνηλάτηση ή την επιτήρηση των κινήσεων και των δραστηριοτήτων του, προκαλώντας σε αυτόν τρόμο ή ανησυχία, τιμωρείται με ποινή φυλάκισης έως δύο (2) έτη.

2. Με την επιφύλαξη διατάξεων ειδικών ποινικών νόμων, αν οι πράξεις των παρ. 1 και 1Α τελούνται σε βάρος ανηλίκου ή προσώπου που δεν μπορεί να υπερασπίσει τον εαυτό του επιβάλλεται φυλάκιση έως τρία (3) έτη.

3. Για την ποινική δίωξη των πράξεων των παρ. 1 και 1Α απαιτείται έγκληση.

Άρθρο 334
Διατάραξη οικιακής ειρήνης

1. Όποιος εισέρχεται παράνομα ή παραμένει παρά τη θέληση του δικαιούχου στην κατοικία άλλου ή στο χώρο που αυτός χρησιμοποιεί για την εργασία του ή σε χώρο περικλεισμένο που αυτός κατέχει τιμωρείται με φυλάκιση έως δύο έτη ή χρηματική ποινή.

2. Οι πιο πάνω πράξεις ή πράξεις βίας εναντίον προσώπων ή πραγμάτων, καθώς και πράξεις φθοράς ξένης ιδιοκτησίας, που γίνονται με σκοπό να παρεμποδίσουν την έκδοση και την ελεύθερη κυκλοφορία εφημερίδων ή περιοδικών, καθώς και την ελεύθερη κυκλοφορία βιβλίων, τιμωρούνται με φυλάκιση έως τρία έτη ή χρηματική ποινή.

3. Για την ποινική δίωξη της πράξης της παραγράφου 1 απαιτείται έγκληση.

Άρθρο 335

(Καταργείται)

1A. Any person who continuously or repeatedly surveils another using information and communication technology for the purpose of tracking or monitoring their movements and activities, [thereby] causing them terror or apprehension, shall be punished with imprisonment of up to two years.

2. Without prejudice to the provisions of specific penal laws, if the acts provided for in paragraphs 1 and 1A are committed against a juvenile or a person unable to defend themselves, imprisonment of up to three years shall be imposed.

3. A victim-initiated complaint is required to institute criminal prosecution for the acts provided for in paragraphs 1 and 1A.

Article 334
Breach of domestic peace

1. Any person who unlawfully enters or remains within the residence of another person or the place they use for their work or an enclosed area they possess against the wishes of such other person shall be punished with imprisonment of up to two years or a monetary penalty.

2. If the aforesaid acts, or acts of violence against persons or things, or acts of damage to the property of another are committed for the purpose of obstructing the publication and free circulation of newspapers or magazines, as well as the free circulation of books, the perpetrator shall be punished with imprisonment of up to three years or a monetary penalty.

3. A victim-initiated complaint is required to institute criminal prosecution for the act provided for in paragraph 1.

Article 335

[Repealed]

ΔΕΚΑΤΟ ΕΝΑΤΟ ΚΕΦΑΛΑΙΟ

ΕΓΚΛΗΜΑΤΑ ΚΑΤΑ ΤΗΣ ΓΕΝΕΤΗΣΙΑΣ ΕΛΕΥΘΕΡΙΑΣ ΚΑΙ ΕΓΚΛΗΜΑΤΑ ΟΙΚΟΝΟΜΙΚΗΣ ΕΚΜΕΤΑΛΛΕΥΣΗΣ ΤΗΣ ΓΕΝΕΤΗΣΙΑΣ ΖΩΗΣ

Άρθρο 336

Βιασμός

1. *Όποιος με σωματική βία ή με απειλή σοβαρού και άμεσου κινδύνου ζωής ή σωματικής ακεραιότητας εξαναγκάζει άλλον σε επιχείρηση ή ανοχή γενετήσιας πράξης τιμωρείται με κάθειρξη τουλάχιστον δέκα (10) ετών.*

2. *Γενετήσια πράξη είναι η συνουσία και οι ίσης βαρύτητας με αυτήν πράξεις.*

3. *Αν η πράξη της παρ. 1 έγινε από δύο ή περισσότερους δράστες που ενεργούσαν από κοινού ή είχε ως συνέπεια τον θάνατο του παθόντος ή αν ο παθών είναι ανήλικος, επιβάλλεται ισόβια κάθειρξη.*

4. *Όποιος, εκτός από την περίπτωση της παρ. 1, τελεί γενετήσια πράξη χωρίς τη συναίνεση του παθόντος, τιμωρείται με κάθειρξη έως δέκα (10) έτη.*

Άρθρο 337

Προσβολή της γενετήσιας αξιοπρέπειας

1. *Όποιος με χειρονομίες γενετήσιου χαρακτήρα, με προτάσεις που αφορούν γενετήσιες πράξεις, με γενετήσιες πράξεις που τελούνται ενώπιον άλλου ή με επίδειξη των γεννητικών του οργάνων, προσβάλλει βάναυσα την τιμή άλλου, τιμωρείται με φυλάκιση έως ένα (1) έτος ή χρηματική ποινή. Για την ποινική δίωξη απαιτείται έγκληση, εκτός αν ο παθών είναι ανήλικος.*

2. *Με φυλάκιση έως δύο (2) έτη ή χρηματική ποινή τιμωρείται η πράξη της προηγουμένης παραγράφου, αν ο παθών είναι νεότερος των δώδεκα (12) ετών.*

3. *Ενήλικος, ο οποίος μέσω διαδικτύου ή άλλων μέσων ή τεχνολογιών πληροφορικής αποκτά επαφή με πρόσωπο που δεν συμπλήρωσε τα δεκαπέντε (15) έτη και με χειρονομίες ή προτάσεις, προσβάλλει την τιμή του ανηλίκου στο πεδίο της γενετήσιας ζωής του, τιμωρείται με φυλάκιση τουλάχιστον δύο (2) ετών. Αν επακολούθησε συνάντηση ο ενήλικος τιμωρείται με φυλάκιση τουλάχιστον τριών (3) ετών.*

4. *Όποιος προβαίνει σε χειρονομίες γενετήσιου χαρακτήρα ή διατυπώνει προτάσεις για τέλεση γενετήσιων πράξεων σε πρόσωπο που εξαρτάται εργασιακά από αυτόν ή εκμεταλλευόμενος τη θέση προσώπου που έχει ενταχθεί σε διαδικασία αναζήτησης θέσης εργασίας, τιμωρείται με φυλάκιση έως τρία (3) έτη.*

5. *Όποιος κοινοποιεί ή αποστέλλει σε άλλον, χωρίς τη συναίνεσή του, με οποιονδήποτε τρόπο ή με τη χρήση της τεχνολογίας των πληροφοριών και επικοινωνιών, πραγματική ή σχεδιασμένη εικόνα ή οπτικό ή οπτικοακουστικό υλικό αποτυπωμένο σε ηλεκτρονικό ή άλλο υλικό φορέα, που απεικονίζει γεννητικά όργανα, κατά τρόπο που δύναται να προκαλέσει φόβο, ανησυχία ή σοβαρή ψυχολογική βλάβη στο πρόσωπο που λαμβάνει το υλικό αυτό, τιμωρείται με φυλάκιση έως τρία (3) έτη. Αν το αδίκημα του προηγούμενου εδαφίου διαπράχθηκε κατά ανηλίκου ή προσώπου που φέρει την ιδιότητα δημόσιου εκπροσώπου, δημοσιογράφου ή υπερασπιστή των ανθρωπίνων δικαιωμάτων ή ο δράστης τελεί σε ιεραρχική σχέση ή σχέση εξάρτησης με το θύμα, συντρέχει ιδιαίτερα επιβαρυντική περίσταση.*

CHAPTER XIX

CRIMES AGAINST SEXUAL FREEDOM AND CRIMES OF ECONOMIC EXPLOITATION OF SEXUAL LIFE

Article 336
Rape

1. Any person who, using physical violence or threatening grievous and imminent danger to the life or physical integrity of another person, forces them to engage in or tolerate a sexual act shall be punished with incarceration of at least 10 years.
2. "Sexual act" means intercourse and acts of the same gravity.
3. If the act provided for in the preceding paragraph is committed by two or more perpetrators acting in unison, or resulted in the death of the victim, or if the victim is juvenile, incarceration for life shall be imposed.
4. In addition to the case provided for in paragraph 1, any person who engages in a sexual act without the victim's consent shall be punished with incarceration of up to 10 years.

Article 337
Offences against sexual dignity

1. Any person who, using sexual gestures, making proposals concerning sexual acts, engaging in sexual acts in the presence of another or exposing their genitals, flagrantly offends the honour of another shall be punished with imprisonment of up to one year or a monetary penalty. A victim-initiated complaint is required to institute criminal prosecution, unless the victim is a juvenile.
2. The act provided for in the preceding paragraph shall be punished with imprisonment of up to two years or a monetary penalty if the victim is under 12 years of age.
3. Any adult who, using the internet or any other computer means or technologies, established contact with a person who has not attained the age of 15 and, using gestures or making proposals, offends the sexual honour of the juvenile shall be punished with imprisonment of at least two years. If a meeting ensued, the adult shall be punished with imprisonment of at least three years.
4. Any person who makes sexual gestures or proposals to engage in sexual acts to a person in their employ or while exploiting the latter's status as a job-seeker shall be punished with imprisonment of up to three years.
5. Any person who shares with or sends to another person, without their consent, in any manner or using information and communication technology, a real or drawn image or visual or audiovisual material recorded on an electronic or other physical storage medium depicting genitals in a manner that can cause fear, apprehension or serious psychological harm to the recipient shall be punished with imprisonment of up to three years. There are particularly aggravating circumstances when the offence provided for in the preceding sentence is committed against a juvenile or a person who is a public representative, a journalist or a human rights defender, or when the perpetrator is in a hierarchical relationship or relationship of dependence with the victim.

Άρθρο 338
Κατάχρηση ανικάνου προς αντίσταση σε γενετήσια πράξη

1. Όποιος με κατάχρηση της διανοητικής ή σωματικής αναπηρίας άλλου ή της από οποιαδήποτε αιτία ανικανότητάς του να αντισταθεί ενεργεί με αυτόν γενετήσια πράξη τιμωρείται με κάθειρξη.

2. Αν η πράξη της προηγούμενης παραγράφου έγινε από δύο ή περισσότερους που ενεργούσαν από κοινού, επιβάλλεται κάθειρξη τουλάχιστον δέκα (10) ετών.

Άρθρο 339
Γενετήσιες πράξεις με ανηλίκους ή ενώπιόν τους

1. Όποιος ενεργεί γενετήσια πράξη με πρόσωπο νεότερο των δεκαπέντε ετών ή το παραπλανά με αποτέλεσμα να ενεργήσει ή να υποστεί τέτοια πράξη τιμωρείται, αν δεν υπάρχει περίπτωση να τιμωρηθεί βαρύτερα με τα άρθρα 342 και 351Α, ως εξής:

α) αν ο παθών δεν συμπλήρωσε τα δώδεκα (12) έτη, με κάθειρξη τουλάχιστον δέκα (10) ετών,

β) αν ο παθών συμπλήρωσε τα δώδεκα (12) έτη, με κάθειρξη.

2. Οι γενετήσιες πράξεις μεταξύ ανηλίκων κάτω των δεκαπέντε (15) ετών δεν τιμωρούνται, εκτός αν η μεταξύ τους διαφορά ηλικίας είναι μεγαλύτερη των τριών (3) ετών, οπότε μπορούν να επιβληθούν μόνο αναμορφωτικά ή θεραπευτικά μέτρα.

3. Όποιος εξωθεί ή παρασύρει ανήλικο, που δεν συμπλήρωσε τα δεκαπέντε (15) έτη, να παρακολουθεί μέσω χρήσης της τεχνολογίας των πληροφοριών και επικοινωνιών ή να παρίσταται σε γενετήσια πράξη μεταξύ άλλων, χωρίς να συμμετέχει σε αυτήν, τιμωρείται με φυλάκιση τουλάχιστον δύο (2) ετών και χρηματική ποινή αν ο ανήλικος είναι μικρότερος των δεκατεσσάρων (14) ετών και με φυλάκιση έως τρία (3) έτη ή χρηματική ποινή αν έχει συμπληρώσει το δέκατο τέταρτο (14ο) έτος της ηλικίας του.

Άρθρο 340
Γενική διάταξη

Αν κάποια από τις πράξεις των άρθρων 338 και 339 είχε ως συνέπεια τον θάνατο του παθόντος επιβάλλεται ισόβια κάθειρξη.

Άρθρο 341

(Καταργείται)

Άρθρο 342
Κατάχρηση ανηλίκων

1. Ο ενήλικος ο οποίος ενεργεί γενετήσιες πράξεις με ανήλικο, τον οποίον του έχουν εμπιστευθεί για να τον επιβλέπει ή να τον φυλάσσει, έστω και προσωρινά, τιμωρείται ως εξής:

α) αν ο παθών δεν συμπλήρωσε τα δεκατέσσερα (14) έτη, με κάθειρξη τουλάχιστον δέκα (10) ετών και χρηματική ποινή,

β) αν ο παθών συμπλήρωσε τα δεκατέσσερα (14) έτη, με κάθειρξη και χρηματική ποινή.

Συνιστά επιβαρυντική περίσταση η τέλεση της πράξης της παρ. 1:

Article 338

Sexual abuse of a person unable to resist

1. Any person who abuses the mental or physical disability of another or their inability, due to any reason, to resist in order to engage in a sexual act with them shall be punished with incarceration.

2. If the act referred to in the preceding paragraph is committed by two or more perpetrators acting in unison, incarceration of at least 10 years shall be imposed.

Article 339

Sexual acts with or in the presence of juveniles

1. Any person who engages in a sexual act with a person under 15 years of age or who entices them into engaging in or undergoing such an act shall be punished, unless the act carries a heavier sentence under Articles 342 and 351A, with:

a) incarceration of at least 10 years if the victim has not attained the age of 12;

b) incarceration if the victim has attained the age of 12.

2. Sexual acts between juveniles under 15 years of age shall not be punished, unless their age difference is greater than three years, in which case only reformative or therapeutic measures may be imposed.

3. Any person who forces or inveigles a juvenile who has not attained the age of 15 to watch, using information and communication technology, or be present during a sexual act between others, without participating in such act, shall be punished with imprisonment of at least two years and a monetary penalty if the juvenile is under 14 years of age, and imprisonment of up to three years and a monetary penalty if the juvenile has attained the age of 14.

Article 340

General provision

If any of the acts provided for in Articles 338 and 339 resulted in the death of the victim, incarceration for life shall be imposed.

Article 341

[Repealed]

Article 342

Child sexual abuse

1. Any adult who engages in sexual acts with a juvenile whose supervision or care was entrusted to them, even temporarily, shall be punished with:

a) incarceration of at least 10 years and a monetary penalty if the victim has not attained the age of 14;

b) incarceration and a monetary penalty if the victim has attained the age of 14.

There are aggravating circumstances when the act provided for in paragraph 1 is committed by:

α) από οικείο,

β) από πρόσωπο που συνοικεί με τον ανήλικο ή διατηρεί φιλικές σχέσεις με τους οικείους του,

γ) από εκπαιδευτικό, παιδαγωγό, γυμναστή ή άλλο πρόσωπο που παραδίδει μαθήματα στον ανήλικο,

δ) από πρόσωπο που δέχεται τις υπηρεσίες του ανηλίκου,

ε) από κληρικό με τον οποίο ο ανήλικος διατηρεί πνευματική σχέση,

στ) από ψυχολόγο, ιατρό, νοσοκόμο ή από ειδικό επιστήμονα που παρέχει τις υπηρεσίες του στον ανήλικο,

ζ) από πρόσωπο που καταχράται τη διανοητική ή σωματική αναπηρία του ανηλίκου.

2. Ο ενήλικος ο οποίος απευθύνει χειρονομίες, προτάσεις ή εξιστορεί ή απεικονίζει ή παρουσιάζει πράξεις γενετήσιου χαρακτήρα σε ανήλικο, τον οποίον του έχουν εμπιστευθεί για να τον επιβλέπει ή να τον φυλάσσει, έστω και προσωρινά, τιμωρείται με φυλάκιση τουλάχιστον έξι (6) μηνών.

Άρθρο 343
Κατάχρηση σε γενετήσια πράξη

Με φυλάκιση τουλάχιστον δύο (2) ετών και χρηματική ποινή τιμωρούνται:

α) όποιος υποχρεώνει άλλον σε επιχείρηση ή ανοχή γενετήσιας πράξης, με κατάχρηση σχέσης εργασιακής εξάρτησης οποιασδήποτε φύσης,

β) όποιος υποχρεώνει άλλον σε επιχείρηση ή ανοχή γενετήσιας πράξης, εκμεταλλευόμενος την θέση του παθόντος, ως προσώπου, το οποίο αναζητά εργασία,

γ) οι διορισμένοι ή οπωσδήποτε εργαζόμενοι σε φυλακές ή άλλα κρατητήρια, σε αστυνομικές υπηρεσίες, σε σχολές, παιδαγωγικά ιδρύματα, νοσοκομεία, κλινικές ή κάθε είδους θεραπευτικά καταστήματα ή σε άλλα ιδρύματα προορισμένα να περιθάλπουν πρόσωπα που έχουν ανάγκη από βοήθεια αν, με κατάχρηση της θέσης τους, υποχρεώσουν σε γενετήσια πράξη πρόσωπο που έχει εισαχθεί σε αυτά τα ιδρύματα.

Άρθρο 344
Έγκληση

Στην περίπτωση του άρθρου 336 η ποινική δίωξη ασκείται αυτεπαγγέλτως, αλλά αν ο παθών δηλώσει ότι δεν επιθυμεί την ποινική δίωξη, ο εισαγγελέας μπορεί να απόσχει οριστικά από την ποινική δίωξη ή, αν αυτή έχει ασκηθεί, να εισαγάγει την υπόθεση στο αρμόδιο δικαστικό συμβούλιο, το οποίο μπορεί να παύσει οριστικά την ποινική δίωξη εκτιμώντας τη δήλωση του θύματος ότι η δημοσιότητα από την ποινική δίωξη θα έχει συνέπεια τον σοβαρό ψυχικό τραυματισμό του.

Άρθρο 345
Γενετήσια πράξη μεταξύ συγγενών

1. Η γενετήσια πράξη μεταξύ συγγενών εξ αίματος ή από υιοθεσία, ανιούσας και κατιούσας γραμμής και μεταξύ αμφιθαλών ή ετεροθαλών αδελφών τιμωρείται:

α) ως προς τους ανιόντες με κάθειρξη έως δέκα (10) ετών,

β) ως προς τους κατιόντες με φυλάκιση και

γ) μεταξύ αδελφών με φυλάκιση έως δύο (2) έτη.

2. Συγγενείς κατιούσας γραμμής ή αδελφοί μπορούν να απαλλαγούν από κάθε ποινή, αν κατά τον χρόνο της πράξης δεν είχαν συμπληρώσει το δέκατο όγδοο (18ο) έτος.

a) a related party;
b) a person who resides with the juvenile or is friends with their related parties;
c) a teacher, instructor, trainer or other person giving lessons to the juvenile;
d) a person accepting services from the juvenile;
e) a member of the clergy with whom the juvenile has a spiritual relationship;
f) a psychologist, physician, nurse or specialist providing their services to the juvenile;
g) a person abusing the juvenile's mental or physical disability.

2. Any adult who makes gestures or proposals or who recounts or depicts or presents sexual acts to a juvenile whose supervision or care was entrusted to them, even temporarily, shall be punished with imprisonment of at least six months.

Article 343
Sexual abuse

Imprisonment of at least two years and a monetary penalty shall be imposed on:
a) any person who forces another to engage in or tolerate a sexual act by abusing an employment relationship of any type;
b) any person who forces another to engage in or tolerate a sexual act by exploiting the victim's status as a job-seeker;
c) any person appointed at or, in all cases, working at prisons or other detention facilities, police facilities, schools, educational establishments, hospitals, clinics or any manner of therapeutic institution or other foundations intended to treat persons in need of assistance, or any person who, by abusing their position, forces a person committed to such foundations to [engage in] a sexual act.

Article 344
Victim-initiated complaint

In the case provided for in Article 336, criminal prosecution shall be instituted *ex officio*, but if the victim declares that they do not wish the perpetrator to be prosecuted, the public prosecutor may definitively refrain from criminal prosecution or, if it has been instituted, bring the case before the competent judicial council, which may definitively discontinue criminal prosecution, taking into consideration the victim's declaration that the publicity generated by the criminal prosecution will cause them severe psychological trauma.

Article 345
Sexual acts between relatives

1. Sexual acts between persons related by blood or adoption, in the ascending and descending line and between full siblings or half-siblings, shall be punished with:
a) incarceration of up to 10 years as regards relatives in the ascending line;
b) imprisonment as regards descendants; and
c) imprisonment of up to two years between siblings.

2. [The court may opt not to punish] relatives in the descending line or siblings if they had not attained the age of 18 at the time of the act.

Άρθρο 346

Εκδικητική πορνογραφία

1. Όποιος χωρίς δικαίωμα κοινολογεί σε τρίτο πρόσωπο ή αναρτά σε κοινή θέα, πραγματική, αλλοιωμένη ή σχεδιασμένη εικόνα ή κάθε είδους οπτικό ή οπτικοακουστικό υλικό, στο οποίο αποτυπώνεται μη δημόσια πράξη άλλου που αφορά στη γενετήσια ζωή του, τιμωρείται με φυλάκιση τουλάχιστον τριών (3) ετών και χρηματική ποινή.

2. Όποιος απειλεί άλλον ότι θα τελέσει τις πράξεις της παρ. 1 τιμωρείται με ποινή φυλάκισης τουλάχιστον ενός (1) έτους. Αν ο υπαίτιος της πράξης του προηγούμενου εδαφίου εξαναγκάζει άλλον σε πράξη ή παράλειψη ή ανοχή για την οποία αυτός δεν έχει υποχρέωση, τιμωρείται με ποινή φυλάκισης τουλάχιστον δύο (2) ετών.

3. Με κάθειρξη έως οκτώ (8) έτη και χρηματική ποινή τιμωρείται η πράξη της παρ. 1 αν τελείται:

α) με ανάρτηση στο διαδίκτυο ή σε μέσο κοινωνικής δικτύωσης με αόριστο αριθμό αποδεκτών,

β) από ενήλικο και αφορά σε ανήλικο,

γ) σε βάρος νυν ή πρώην συζύγου ή συντρόφου του υπαιτίου ή σε βάρος προσώπου που συνοικεί με αυτόν ή έχει μαζί του σχέση εργασίας ή υπηρεσίας ή βρίσκεται υπό την επιμέλεια ή την προστασία του ή δεν μπορεί να υπερασπίσει τον εαυτό του,

δ) με σκοπό να προσπορίσει ο υπαίτιος στον εαυτό του ή σε άλλον περιουσιακό όφελος.

4. Αν κάποια από τις πράξεις των προηγούμενων παραγράφων οδήγησε το θύμα σε απόπειρα αυτοκτονίας επιβάλλεται κάθειρξη και χρηματική ποινή. Αν η πράξη του προηγούμενου εδαφίου οδήγησε στο θάνατο επιβάλλεται κάθειρξη τουλάχιστον δέκα (10) ετών και χρηματική ποινή.

Άρθρο 347

(Καταργείται)

Άρθρο 348

Διευκόλυνση προσβολών της ανηλικότητας

1. Όποιος κατ' επάγγελμα ή από κερδοσκοπία επιχειρεί να διευκολύνει, έστω και συγκαλυμμένα, με τη δημοσίευση αγγελίας ή εικόνας ή αριθμού τηλεφωνικής σύνδεσης ή με τη μετάδοση ηλεκτρονικών μηνυμάτων ή με οποιονδήποτε άλλο τρόπο τη γενετήσια πράξη με ανήλικο τιμωρείται με φυλάκιση τουλάχιστον τριών ετών και χρηματική ποινή.

2. Όποιος οργανώνει, χρηματοδοτεί, κατευθύνει, εποπτεύει, διαφημίζει ή μεσολαβεί με οποιονδήποτε τρόπο ή μέσο σε διενέργεια ταξιδιών με σκοπό από τους μετέχοντες σε αυτά την τέλεση γενετήσιων πράξεων σε βάρος ανηλίκου, τιμωρείται με κάθειρξη έως δέκα έτη. Όποιος με τον παραπάνω σκοπό μετέχει σε ταξίδια του προηγούμενου εδαφίου τιμωρείται με φυλάκιση τουλάχιστον ενός έτους, ανεξάρτητα από την ευθύνη του για την τέλεση άλλων αξιόποινων πράξεων.

Article 346

Revenge pornography

1. Any person who, without the right to do so, communicates to a third party or exposes in public view an actual, altered or drawn picture or any type of visual or audiovisual material depicting a non-public sexual act involving another person shall be punished with imprisonment of at least three years and a monetary penalty.

2. Any person who threatens another with committing the acts provided for in paragraph 1 shall be punished with imprisonment of at least one year. If the person who committed the act provided for in the preceding sentence forces another to take, refrain from taking, or tolerate an act when they are not obligated to do so shall be punished with imprisonment of at least two years.

3. The act provided for in paragraph 1 shall be punished with incarceration of up to eight years and a monetary penalty if committed:

a) through an upload to the internet or social media with an indeterminate number of recipients;

b) by an adult in relation to [another] adult;

c) against the spouse or former spouse or partner of the culpable person, or a person who lives with the perpetrator, or is in their employ or service, or who is under the perpetrator's custody or protection, or who cannot defend themselves; [or]

d) for the purpose of the perpetrator or another party obtaining a pecuniary gain.

4. If any of the acts provided for in the preceding paragraphs led the victim to attempt suicide, incarceration and a monetary penalty shall be imposed. If the act provided for in the preceding sentence led to the death [of the victim], incarceration of at least 10 years and a monetary penalty shall be imposed.

Article 347

[Repealed]

Article 348

Facilitating offences against juveniles

1. Any person who, [for monetary gain] or profit, attempts to facilitate sexual acts with a juvenile, even covertly, by publishing an advertisement or picture or telephone number or by sending electronic messages or in any other manner shall be punished with imprisonment of at least three years and a monetary penalty.

2. Any person who, in any manner or using any means, organises, funds, directs, supervises, advertises or arranges travel for the purpose of travellers engaging in sexual acts involving a juvenile shall be punished with incarceration of up to 10 years. Any person who, for the aforesaid purpose, participates in the travels referred to in the preceding sentence shall be punished with imprisonment of at least one year, irrespective of whether or not they committed other punishable acts.

Άρθρο 348Α
Πορνογραφία ανηλίκων

1. Όποιος με πρόθεση παράγει, διανέμει, δημοσιεύει, επιδεικνύει, εισάγει στην Επικράτεια ή εξάγει από αυτήν, μεταφέρει, προσφέρει, πωλεί ή με άλλον τρόπο διαθέτει, αγοράζει, προμηθεύεται, αποκτά ή κατέχει υλικό παιδικής πορνογραφίας ή διαδίδει ή μεταδίδει πληροφορίες σχετικά με την τέλεση των παραπάνω πράξεων, τιμωρείται με φυλάκιση τουλάχιστον ενός (1) έτους και χρηματική ποινή.

2. Όποιος με πρόθεση παράγει, προσφέρει, πωλεί ή με οποιονδήποτε τρόπο διαθέτει, διανέμει, διαβιβάζει, αγοράζει, προμηθεύεται ή κατέχει υλικό παιδικής πορνογραφίας ή διαδίδει πληροφορίες σχετικά με την τέλεση των παραπάνω πράξεων, μέσω πληροφοριακών συστημάτων, τιμωρείται με φυλάκιση τουλάχιστον δύο (2) ετών και χρηματική ποινή.

3. Υλικό παιδικής πορνογραφίας, κατά την έννοια των παρ. 1 και 2 συνιστά η αναπαράσταση ή η πραγματική ή η εικονική αποτύπωση σε ηλεκτρονικό ή άλλο υλικό φορέα των γεννητικών οργάνων ή του σώματος εν γένει του ανηλίκου ή προσώπου που εμφανίζεται ως ανήλικο, κατά τρόπο που προδήλως προκαλεί γενετήσια διέγερση, καθώς και της πραγματικής ή εικονικής γενετήσιας πράξης που διενεργείται από ή με ανήλικο ή πρόσωπο που εμφανίζεται ως ανήλικο.

4. Οι πράξεις των παρ. 1 και 2 τιμωρούνται με κάθειρξη και χρηματική ποινή:

α. αν τελέσθηκαν κατ' επάγγελμα,

β. αν η παραγωγή του υλικού της παιδικής πορνογραφίας συνδέεται με την εκμετάλλευση της ανάγκης, της ψυχικής ή της διανοητικής ασθένειας ή της σωματικής δυσλειτουργίας, λόγω οργανικής νόσου ανηλίκου ή με την άσκηση ή απειλή χρήσης βίας ανηλίκου ή με τη χρησιμοποίηση ανηλίκου που δεν έχει συμπληρώσει το δέκατο πέμπτο έτος ή αν η παραγωγή του υλικού της παιδικής πορνογραφίας εξέθεσε τη ζωή του ανηλίκου σε σοβαρό κίνδυνο και

γ. αν δράστης της παραγωγής του υλικού παιδικής πορνογραφίας είναι πρόσωπο στο οποίο έχουν εμπιστευθεί ανήλικο για να τον επιβλέπει ή να τον φυλάσσει, έστω και προσωρινά.

5. Αν η παραγωγή του υλικού της παιδικής πορνογραφίας συνδέεται με τη χρησιμοποίηση ανηλίκου που δεν έχει συμπληρώσει το δωδέκατο έτος της ηλικίας του, επιβάλλεται κάθειρξη τουλάχιστον δέκα (10) ετών και χρηματική ποινή. Η ίδια ποινή επιβάλλεται αν η πράξη των περ. β΄ και γ΄ της προηγούμενης παραγράφου είχε ως αποτέλεσμα τη βαριά σωματική βλάβη του παθόντος, αν δε αυτή είχε ως αποτέλεσμα το θάνατο, επιβάλλεται ισόβια κάθειρξη.

6. Όποιος εν γνώσει αποκτά πρόσβαση σε υλικό παιδικής πορνογραφίας μέσω πληροφοριακών συστημάτων, τιμωρείται με φυλάκιση έως τρία (3) έτη ή χρηματική ποινή.

Άρθρο 348Β
Προσέλκυση παιδιών για γενετήσιους λόγους

Όποιος με πρόθεση, μέσω πληροφοριακών συστημάτων, προτείνει σε ανήλικο που δεν συμπλήρωσε τα δεκαπέντε έτη, να συναντήσει τον ίδιο ή τρίτο, με σκοπό τη διάπραξη σε βάρος του ανηλίκου των αδικημάτων των άρθρων 339 παρ. 1 και 2 ή 348Α, όταν η πρόταση αυτή ακολουθείται από περαιτέρω πράξεις που οδηγούν σε μία τέτοια συνάντηση, τιμωρείται με φυλάκιση τουλάχιστον δύο ετών και χρηματική ποινή.

Article 348A
Child pornography

1. Any person who intentionally produces, distributes, publishes, exhibits, imports into or exports out of Greece, transports, offers, sells or otherwise makes available, purchases, procures, acquires, or possesses child pornography material, or who disseminates or transmits information concerning the commission of such acts shall be punished with imprisonment of at least one year and a monetary penalty.
2. Any person who intentionally produces, offers, sells or otherwise makes available, distributes, transmits, purchases, procures or possesses child pornography material, or who disseminates information concerning the commission of such acts through information systems shall be punished with imprisonment of at least two years and a monetary penalty.
3. "Child pornography material", within the meaning of paragraphs 1 and 2, means the representation or actual or simulated depiction on an electronic or other physical storage medium of the genitals or, in general, the body of a juvenile or person appearing to be a juvenile in a way that manifestly causes sexual arousal, or of a real or simulated sexual act performed by or with a juvenile or person appearing to be a juvenile.
4. The acts provided for in paragraphs 1 and 2 shall be punished with incarceration and a monetary penalty if:
a. they were committed [for monetary gain];
b. the production of the child pornography material is connected with the exploitation of need, emotional or mental illness or bodily dysfunction caused by the physical illness of a juvenile, or through use or threat of violence against a juvenile, or the use of a juvenile who has not attained the age of 15, or if the production of the child pornography material placed the life of the juvenile in serious danger; [or]
c. the perpetrator of the production of child pornography material is one of the persons entrusted with the juvenile's supervision and care, even temporarily.
5. If the production of the child pornography material [involves] a juvenile who has not attained the age of 12, incarceration of at least 10 years and a monetary penalty shall be imposed. The same penalty shall be imposed if the act provided for in cases (b) and (c) of the preceding paragraph led to grievous bodily harm to the victim; if it resulted in death [of the victim], incarceration for life shall be imposed.
6. Any person who knowingly obtains access to child pornography material through information systems shall be punished with imprisonment of up to three years or a monetary penalty.

Article 348B
Solicitation of children for sexual purposes

Any person who intentionally and using information systems proposes to a juvenile who has not attained the age of 15 a meeting with them or with a third person for the purpose of committing the offences provided for in Articles 339(1) and (2) or 348A against the juvenile, or when such proposal is followed by further acts leading to such a meeting, shall be punished with imprisonment of at least two years and a monetary penalty.

Άρθρο 348Γ
Πορνογραφικές παραστάσεις ανηλίκων

1. Όποιος εξωθεί ή παρασύρει ανήλικο προκειμένου να συμμετάσχει σε πορνογραφικές παραστάσεις ή διοργανώνει αυτές, τιμωρείται ως εξής:

α) αν ο παθών δεν συμπλήρωσε τα δώδεκα (12) έτη, με κάθειρξη,

β) αν ο παθών συμπλήρωσε τα δώδεκα (12) αλλά όχι τα δεκατέσσερα (14) έτη, με κάθειρξη έως δέκα (10) έτη,

γ) αν ο παθών συμπλήρωσε τα δεκατέσσερα (14) έτη, με φυλάκιση τουλάχιστον δύο (2) ετών.

Όποιος εν γνώσει του, παρακολουθεί πορνογραφική παράσταση στην οποία συμμετέχουν ανήλικοι τιμωρείται στις περ. α' και β' του πρώτου εδαφίου με φυλάκιση τουλάχιστον δύο (2) ετών και στην περ. γ' με φυλάκιση τουλάχιστον ενός (1) έτους.

2. Εφόσον οι πράξεις της προηγούμενης παραγράφου τελέστηκαν με τη χρήση βίας ή απειλής, προκειμένου να συμμετάσχει ανήλικος σε πορνογραφικές παραστάσεις ή με σκοπό την επιδίωξη οικονομικού οφέλους από αυτές, επιβάλλεται:

α) στην περίπτωση α΄ της προηγούμενης παραγράφου κάθειρξη τουλάχιστον δέκα ετών,

β) στην περίπτωση β΄ κάθειρξη,

γ) στην περίπτωση γ΄ κάθειρξη έως δέκα έτη.

3. Πορνογραφική παράσταση, κατά την έννοια των προηγουμένων παραγράφων, συνιστά η οργανωμένη απευθείας έκθεση, που προορίζεται για θέαση ή ακρόαση, μεταξύ άλλων και με χρήση της τεχνολογίας των πληροφοριών και επικοινωνιών:

α) ανηλίκου που επιδίδεται σε πραγματική ή εικονική πράξη γενετήσιου χαρακτήρα ή

β) των γεννητικών οργάνων ή του σώματος εν γένει του ανηλίκου κατά τρόπο που προδήλως προκαλεί γενετήσια διέγερση.

Άρθρο 348Δ
Γενική διάταξη

Οι διατάξεις των άρθρων 339, 342, 348, 348Α, 348Β, 348Γ, 349 και 351Α εφαρμόζονται και για πράξεις που τέλεσε ημεδαπός στην αλλοδαπή, ανεξάρτητα αν ήταν αξιόποινες και κατά τους νόμους της χώρας που τελέστηκαν.

Άρθρο 349
Μαστροπεία

1. Όποιος, για να εξυπηρετήσει την ακολασία άλλων, προάγει ή εξωθεί στην πορνεία ανήλικο ή υποθάλπει ή εξαναγκάζει ή διευκολύνει ή συμμετέχει στην πορνεία ανηλίκων, τιμωρείται με κάθειρξη έως δέκα (10) έτη και χρηματική ποινή.

2. Με κάθειρξη και χρηματική ποινή τιμωρείται ο υπαίτιος αν το έγκλημα τελέστηκε:

α) εναντίον προσώπου νεότερου των δεκαπέντε (15) ετών,

β) με απατηλά μέσα,

γ) από τον ανιόντα συγγενή εξ αίματος ή εξ αγχιστείας ή από θετό γονέα, σύζυγο, επίτροπο ή από άλλον στον οποίο έχουν εμπιστευθεί τον ανήλικο για ανατροφή, διδασκαλία επίβλεψη ή φύλαξη, έστω και προσωρινή,

δ) από υπάλληλο ο οποίος κατά την άσκηση της υπηρεσίας του ή επωφελούμενος από την ιδιότητά του αυτή διαπράττει ή συμμετέχει με οποιονδήποτε τρόπο στην πράξη,

ε) με τη χρήση ηλεκτρονικών μέσων επικοινωνίας,

στ) με προσφορά ή υπόσχεση πληρωμής χρημάτων ή οποιουδήποτε άλλου ανταλλάγματος.

Article 348C
Pornographic performance involving a juvenile

1. Any person who forces or lures a juvenile into participating in pornographic performances or who organises such performances shall be punished with:
a) incarceration if the victim has not attained the age of 12;
b) incarceration of up to 10 years if the victim has attained the age of 12 but not the age of 14;
c) imprisonment of at least two years if the victim has attained the age of 14.
Any person who knowingly attends a pornographic performance involving the participation of juveniles shall be punished, in cases (a) and (b) of the preceding sentence, with imprisonment of at least two years and, in case (c), with imprisonment of at least one year.
2. If the acts provided for in the preceding paragraph were committed through use or threat of violence in order for the juvenile to participate in pornographic performances or for the purpose of obtaining monetary gain from such performances, [the following sentences] shall be imposed:
a) incarceration of at least 10 years in case (a) of the preceding paragraph;
b) incarceration in case (b);
c) incarceration of up to 10 years in case (c).
3. "Pornographic performance", within the meaning of the preceding paragraphs, means an organised live exhibition, intended to be seen or heard, including, *inter alia*, by means of information and communication technology, of:
a) a juvenile engaged in a real or simulated sexual act; or
b) the genitals or, in general, the body of a juvenile in a way that manifestly causes sexual arousal.

Article 348D
General provision

The provisions of Articles 339, 342, 348, 348A, 348B, 348C, 349 and 351A also apply to acts committed by a Greek national abroad, irrespective of whether or not such acts were also punishable under the laws of the country where they were committed.

Article 349
Procuring

1. Any person who, in order to serve the debauchery of others, introduces or procures a juvenile to engage in prostitution, or who fosters [the conditions for], compels, facilitates or participates in child prostitution shall be punished with incarceration of up to 10 years and a monetary penalty.
2. The culpable person shall be punished with incarceration and a monetary penalty if the crime was committed:
a) against a person under 15 years of age;
b) using fraudulent means;
c) by a relative by blood or marriage in the ascending line, or an adoptive parent, spouse, tutor or other person entrusted, even temporarily, with the juvenile's upbringing, teaching, supervision or care;
d) by a state employee who commits or participates in any manner in the act while performing their duties or benefiting from their status;
e) using electronic means of communication; [or]
f) offering or promising to pay money or any other consideration.

3. Εκτός των περιπτώσεων του άρθρου 323Α, όποιος κατ' επάγγελμα ή από κερδοσκοπία προάγει ή εξωθεί ή εξαναγκάζει άλλον στην πορνεία ή εκμεταλλεύεται τα έσοδα από την πορνεία άλλου τιμωρείται με φυλάκιση τουλάχιστον δεκαοκτώ (18) μηνών και με χρηματική ποινή. Η τέλεση της πράξης από υπάλληλο, ο οποίος κατά την άσκηση της υπηρεσίας του ή επωφελούμενος από την ιδιότητά του αυτή διαπράττει ή συμμετέχει με οποιονδήποτε τρόπο στην πράξη, συνιστά επιβαρυντική περίσταση.

Άρθρο 350

(Καταργείται)

Άρθρο 350Α
Ειδικά ευνοϊκά μέτρα

Στις περιπτώσεις των άρθρων 348Α, 348Β, 348Γ, 349 εφαρμόζεται αναλογικά η πρόβλεψη της παραγράφου 8 του άρθρου 323Α.

Άρθρο 351

(Καταργείται)

Άρθρο 351Α
Γενετήσια πράξη με ανήλικο έναντι αμοιβής

1. Η γενετήσια πράξη με ανήλικο που τελείται από ενήλικο με αμοιβή ή με άλλα υλικά ανταλλάγματα ή η γενετήσια πράξη μεταξύ ανηλίκων που προκαλείται από ενήλικο με τον ίδιο τρόπο και τελείται ενώπιον αυτού ή άλλου ενηλίκου τιμωρείται:

α) αν ο παθών δεν συμπλήρωσε τα δώδεκα (12) έτη, με κάθειρξη τουλάχιστον δέκα (10) ετών και χρηματική ποινή,

β) αν ο παθών συμπλήρωσε τα δώδεκα (12), όχι όμως και τα δεκαπέντε (15) έτη, με κάθειρξη και χρηματική ποινή και

γ) αν συμπλήρωσε τα δεκαπέντε (15) έτη, με φυλάκιση τουλάχιστον τριών (3) ετών και χρηματική ποινή.

2. Αν η πράξη της πρώτης παραγράφου είχε ως αποτέλεσμα τον θάνατο του παθόντος επιβάλλεται ισόβια κάθειρξη.

Άρθρο 352

(Καταργείται)

Άρθρο 352Α
Ψυχοδιαγνωστική εξέταση και θεραπεία του δράστη και του θύματος εγκλημάτων κατά της γενετήσιας ελευθερίας και της οικονομικής εκμετάλλευσης της γενετήσιας ζωής

1. Όταν το θύμα είναι ανήλικο, ο ύποπτος ή κατηγορούμενος για εγκλήματα κατά της γενετήσιας ελευθερίας και εγκλήματα οικονομικής εκμετάλλευσης της γενετήσιας ζωής, υποβάλλεται σε διαγνωστική εξέταση της ψυχογενετήσιας κατάστασής του. Η εξέταση αυτή διατάσσεται μόνο εφόσον συναινεί ο καθ' ου αφορά αυτή κατά την προδικασία από τον αρμόδιο εισαγγελέα ή, αν διενεργείται τακτική ανάκριση, από τον αρμόδιο ανακριτή και κατά την κύρια διαδικασία από το δικαστήριο.

2. Αν κάποιος καταδικασθεί για έγκλημα που αναφέρεται στην προηγούμενη παράγραφο, το δικαστήριο υπό την προϋπόθεση της παραγράφου 1 μπορεί να διατάξει και την παρακολούθηση προγράμματος ψυχογενετήσιας θεραπείας του, η οποία εκτελείται κατά τον χρόνο έκτισης της ποινής ή ανεξάρτητα από αυτήν. Στα προγράμματα αυτά συμμετέχουν και οι διωκόμενοι ή οι υπόδικοι, εφόσον συναινούν, χωρίς η συμμετοχή τους αυτή να επηρεάζει το δικαίωμα της υπεράσπισης και το τεκμήριο της αθωότητας.

3. Except in the cases referred to in Article 323A, any person who, [for monetary gain] or profit, persuades or forces or compels another to engage in prostitution or exploits the proceeds from another's prostitution shall be punished with imprisonment of at least 18 months and a monetary penalty. There are aggravating circumstances when the act is perpetrated by a state employee who commits or participates in any manner in the act while performing their duties or benefiting from their status.

Article 350

[Repealed]

Article 350A
Special favourable measures

The provisions of Article 323A(8) apply *mutatis mutandis* to the cases referred to in Articles 348A, 348B, 348C [and] 349.

Article 351

[Repealed]

Article 351A
Sexual acts involving a juvenile for pay

1. Any sexual act involving a juvenile, committed by an adult for pay or other material consideration, or any sexual act between juveniles procured by an adult in the same manner and committed in the presence of that adult or a different adult carries a sentence of:
a) incarceration of at least 10 years and a monetary penalty if the victim has not attained the age of 12;
b) incarceration and a monetary penalty if the victim has attained the age of 12 but not the age of 15;
c) imprisonment of at least three years and a monetary penalty if the victim has attained the age of 15.
2. If the act provided for in the first paragraph resulted in the death of the victim, incarceration for life shall be imposed.

Article 352

[Repealed]

Article 352A
Psychodiagnostic examination of and therapy for the perpetrator and victim of crimes against sexual freedom and exploitation of sexual life

1. Where the victim is a juvenile, the person who is suspected or stands accused of crimes against sexual freedom and exploitation of sexual life shall undergo a diagnostic examination of their psychosexual state. This examination shall be ordered only with the consent of the person in question by the competent public prosecutor during the preliminary procedure, by the competent investigating magistrate if an ordinary investigation is being conducted, or by the court during the main proceedings.
2. If a person is convicted of a crime provided for in the preceding paragraph, the court, under the conditions laid down in paragraph 1, may also order that they attend a psychosexual therapy programme, to take place while they serve their sentence or [irrespective of such sentence]. Such programmes shall also be attended by persons under prosecution or on remand, provided they consent, without such participation on their part prejudicing their right of defence and the presumption of innocence.

3. Σε ειδική εξέταση της ψυχικής και σωματικής κατάστασής του υποβάλλεται και το ανήλικο θύμα των πράξεων της παραγράφου 1, προκειμένου να κριθεί αν έχει ανάγκη θεραπείας. Η θεραπεία του ανήλικου θύματος διατάσσεται κατά την προδικασία από τον αρμόδιο εισαγγελέα ή, αν διενεργείται τακτική ανάκριση, από τον αρμόδιο ανακριτή και κατά την κύρια διαδικασία από το δικαστήριο.

4. Αν κριθεί αναγκαίο για την προστασία του ανήλικου θύματος, ο εισαγγελέας, ο ανακριτής ή το δικαστήριο διατάσσει την απομάκρυνση του υπαιτίου από το περιβάλλον του θύματος ή την απομάκρυνση του θύματος και την προσωρινή διαμονή του σε προστατευμένο περιβάλλον, καθώς και την απαγόρευση της μεταξύ υπαιτίου και θύματος επικοινωνίας.

Άρθρο 352Β
Προστασία της ιδιωτικής ζωής του ανήλικου θύματος

Όποιος, από την καταγγελία πράξης που υπάγεται στα εγκλήματα κατά της γενετήσιας ελευθερίας και οικονομικής εκμετάλλευσης της γενετήσιας ζωής έως την έκδοση αμετάκλητης απόφασης, δημοσιοποιεί με οποιονδήποτε τρόπο περιστατικά που θα μπορούσαν να οδηγήσουν στην αποκάλυψη της ταυτότητας του ανήλικου θύματος, τιμωρείται με φυλάκιση έως δύο έτη.

Άρθρο 353
Προσβολή γενετήσιας ευπρέπειας

1. Όποιος εν γνώσει προσβάλλει βάναυσα τη γενετήσια ευπρέπεια άλλου με πράξη γενετήσιου χαρακτήρα που ενεργείται ενώπιόν του τιμωρείται με χρηματική ποινή ή παροχή κοινωφελούς εργασίας. Αν η πράξη του προηγούμενου εδαφίου ενεργείται ενώπιον προσώπου νεότερου των δεκαπέντε (15) ετών τιμωρείται με φυλάκιση έως τρία (3) έτη ή χρηματική ποινή.

2. Για την ποινική δίωξη της πράξης του πρώτου εδαφίου της παρ. 1 απαιτείται έγκληση.

3. The juvenile victim of the act provided for in paragraph 1 shall also undergo a special examination of their emotional state and physical condition in order to determine whether they require therapy. Such therapy shall be ordered by the competent public prosecutor during the preliminary procedure, by the competent investigating magistrate if an ordinary investigation is being conducted, or by the court during the main proceedings.

4. If deemed necessary to protect the juvenile victim, the public prosecutor, the investigating magistrate or the court shall order that the perpetrator be removed from the victim's environment or that the victim be removed and temporarily placed in a protected environment, as well as prohibit communication between the culpable person and the victim.

Article 352B
Protection of the juvenile victim's privacy

Any person who discloses in any manner facts from the report of an act classified as a crime against sexual freedom and exploitation of sexual life before an irrevocable judgment is handed down and this could lead to the disclosure of the juvenile victim's identity shall be punished with imprisonment of up to two years.

Article 353
Offences against sexual decency

1. Any person who knowingly and flagrantly violates the sexual decency of another through a sexual act performed in the presence of the latter shall be punished with a monetary penalty or community service. If the act referred to in the preceding paragraph is committed in the presence of a person under 15 years of age, [the perpetrator] shall be punished with imprisonment of up to three years or a monetary penalty.

2. A victim-initiated complaint is required to institute criminal prosecution for the act provided for in paragraph 1.

ΕΙΚΟΣΤΟ ΚΕΦΑΛΑΙΟ

ΕΓΚΛΗΜΑΤΑ ΣΧΕΤΙΚΑ ΜΕ ΤΗΝ ΟΙΚΟΓΕΝΕΙΑ

Άρθρο 354
Διατάραξη της οικογενειακής τάξης

Όποιος νοθεύει ή συγκαλύπτει την οικογενειακή τάξη άλλου και ιδίως όποιος υποβάλλει τέκνο τιμωρείται με φυλάκιση έως δύο έτη ή χρηματική ποινή.

Άρθρο 355

(Καταργείται)

Άρθρο 356
Διγαμία

Ο σύζυγος ή αυτός που έχει συνάψει σύμφωνο συμβίωσης αν τελέσει νέο γάμο ή συνάψει νέο σύμφωνο συμβίωσης πριν αμετακλήτως διαλυθεί ή ακυρωθεί ο προηγούμενος γάμος ή το προηγούμενο σύμφωνο συμβίωσης, καθώς επίσης και εκείνος που συνάπτει μαζί του νέο γάμο ή νέο σύμφωνο συμβίωσης εν γνώσει ότι υπάρχει γάμος ή σύμφωνο συμβίωσης που δεν λύθηκε ή δεν ακυρώθηκε, τιμωρείται με φυλάκιση έως δύο έτη ή χρηματική ποινή.

Άρθρο 357

(Καταργείται)

Άρθρο 358
Παραβίαση της υποχρέωσης διατροφής

Όποιος κακόβουλα παραβιάζει την υποχρέωση διατροφής που την επιβάλει σε αυτόν ο νόμος και έχει αναγνωριστεί, έστω προσωρινά, με εκτελεστό τίτλο, με τρόπο τέτοιο ώστε ο δικαιούχος να υποστεί στερήσεις ή να αναγκαστεί να δεχτεί την βοήθεια άλλων, τιμωρείται με φυλάκιση έως ένα (1) έτος ή χρηματική ποινή.

Άρθρο 359
Εγκατάλειψη εγκύου

Όποιος εγκαταλείπει σε απορία γυναίκα που έμεινε απ' αυτόν έγκυος και που λόγω της εγκυμοσύνης ή του τοκετού της δεν μπορεί να φροντίσει τον εαυτό της τιμωρείται με φυλάκιση έως δύο έτη ή χρηματική ποινή. Για την ποινική δίωξη απαιτείται έγκληση.

CHAPTER XX

DOMESTIC CRIMES

Article 354
Disruption of family status

Any person who alters or conceals another's family status and, in particular, any person who presents a child [as having a different family status from the one it actually has] shall be punished with imprisonment of up to two years or a monetary penalty.

Article 355

[Repealed]

Article 356
Bigamy

Any spouse or civil partner who enters into marriage or a civil partnership anew before the previous marriage or civil partnership was irrevocably dissolved or annulled, and the person entering into marriage or civil partnership anew with them while being aware that the marriage or civil partnership has not been dissolved or annulled shall be punished with imprisonment of up to two years or a monetary penalty.

Article 357

[Repealed]

Article 358
Violation of the obligation to pay maintenance

Any person who, acting maliciously, violates the obligation to pay maintenance imposed on them by law and recognised, even temporarily, by an enforceable title in such a manner that the beneficiary suffers hardship or is forced to accept help from other persons shall be punished with imprisonment of up to one year or a monetary penalty.

Article 359
Abandonment of a pregnant woman

Any person who abandons a woman they impregnated, leaving her in poverty and unable to care for herself due to her pregnancy or childbirth, shall be punished with imprisonment of up to two years or a monetary penalty. A victim-initiated complaint is required to institute criminal prosecution.

Άρθρο 360

Παραμέληση της εποπτείας ανηλίκου - συμπαραστατούμενου

1. Όποιος, ενώ έχει υποχρέωση εποπτείας ανηλίκου παραλείπει να τον παρεμποδίσει από την τέλεση αξιόποινης πράξης, τιμωρείται με φυλάκιση έως ένα (1) έτος, αν δεν συντρέχει περίπτωση να τιμωρηθεί αυστηρότερα με άλλη διάταξη.

2. Αν ο υπαίτιος της παράλειψης είναι πρόσωπο που έχει την επιμέλεια του ανηλίκου και ιδίως γονέας, επιβάλλεται φυλάκιση έως τρία (3) έτη και χρηματική ποινή και σε περίπτωση που η πράξη ενέχει στοιχεία βίας και στρέφεται κατά ανηλίκου θύματος ή είναι πράξη που αν την τελούσε ενήλικος θα ήταν κακούργημα, επιβάλλεται φυλάκιση τουλάχιστον ενός (1) έτους και χρηματική ποινή τουλάχιστον δέκα χιλιάδες (10.000) ευρώ. Η τέλεση της ανωτέρω παράλειψης από πρόσωπα, υπό την επιμέλεια των οποίων έχει τεθεί ο ανήλικος σύμφωνα με τα άρθρα 122 και 123, συνιστά επιβαρυντική περίσταση.

3. Με την ποινή της παρ. 1 τιμωρείται και όποιος του έχει ανατεθεί με προσωρινή διαταγή ή οριστική δικαστική απόφαση η δικαστική συμπαράσταση προσώπου που κηρύχθηκε ανίκανο για όλες τις δικαιοπραξίες (πλήρης στερητική δικαστική συμπαράσταση), όταν παραλείπει να τον παρεμποδίσει από την τέλεση αξιόποινης πράξης.

Άρθρο 360Α

Παραβάσεις σχετικά με την υιοθεσία ανηλίκου

1. Όποιος υιοθετεί ανήλικο με σκοπό να τον απασχολήσει σε δραστηριότητες επικίνδυνες για την υγεία του και τον απασχολεί σε αυτές, τιμωρείται, εφόσον δεν συντρέχει άλλη αξιόποινη πράξη που τιμωρείται βαρύτερα, με φυλάκιση τουλάχιστον ενός (1) έτους και χρηματική ποινή.

2. Με φυλάκιση και χρηματική ποινή τιμωρείται εκείνος που δίνει σε υιοθεσία το παιδί του, εκείνος που υιοθετεί, καθώς και εκείνος που μεσολαβεί στην υιοθεσία αποκομίζοντας ο ίδιος ή προσπορίζοντας σε άλλον αθέμιτο όφελος.

3. Εκείνος που τελεί κατ' επάγγελμα τις αξιόποινες πράξεις των προηγούμενων παραγράφων τιμωρείται με κάθειρξη έως δέκα (10) έτη και χρηματική ποινή.

Article 360

[Failure] to supervise a juvenile - person under guardianship

1. Any person under the obligation to supervise a juvenile who fails to hinder the juvenile from committing a punishable act shall be punished with imprisonment of up to one year, unless the act carries a heavier sentence under a different provision.

2. If the person responsible for such failure has custody of the juvenile and, in particular, is the parent [of the juvenile], imprisonment of up to three years and a monetary penalty shall be imposed; where the act involves violence and is committed against a juvenile victim or is an act which, if committed by an adult, would be a felony, imprisonment of at least one year and a monetary penalty of at least 10,000 euros shall be imposed. There are aggravating circumstances when the above failure is committed by persons in whose custody the juvenile was placed in accordance with Articles 122 and 123.

3. The punishment laid down in paragraph 1 shall also be imposed on any person who is assigned, by interim order or final court judgment, guardianship of a person declared as lacking capacity to enter into all legal transactions (full privative legal guardianship) and who fails to hinder [such person under guardianship] from committing a punishable act.

Article 360A

Violations concerning adoption of a juvenile

1. Any person who adopts a juvenile for the purpose of involving them in activities hazardous to their health and who does so shall be punished with imprisonment of at least one year and a monetary penalty, unless there is another concurrent punishable act carrying a heavier punishment.

2. Any person who gives up their child for adoption, the person adopting the child and the person mediating the adoption for the purpose of obtaining an undue gain for themselves or another shall be punished with imprisonment and a monetary penalty.

3. Any person who commits the punishable acts referred to in the preceding paragraphs [for monetary gain] shall be punished with incarceration of up to 10 years and a monetary penalty.

ΕΙΚΟΣΤΟ ΠΡΩΤΟ ΚΕΦΑΛΑΙΟ

ΕΓΚΛΗΜΑΤΑ ΚΑΤΑ ΤΗΣ ΤΙΜΗΣ

Άρθρο 361
Εξύβριση

1. Όποιος, εκτός από τις περιπτώσεις της συκοφαντικής δυσφήμησης (άρθρο 363) προσβάλλει την τιμή άλλου με λόγο ή με έργο ή με οποιονδήποτε άλλον τρόπο, έχοντας τέτοιον σκοπό, τιμωρείται με φυλάκιση έως έξι (6) μήνες ή χρηματική ποινή. Αν τελεί την ανωτέρω πράξη δημόσια με οποιονδήποτε τρόπο ή μέσω διαδικτύου, επιβάλλεται φυλάκιση έως ένα (1) έτος ή χρηματική ποινή και αν η προσβολή ανάγεται σε σχέσεις του ιδιωτικού ή του οικογενειακού βίου, επιβάλλεται φυλάκιση έως δύο (2) έτη ή χρηματική ποινή.

2. Η παρ. 4 του άρθρου 308 εφαρμόζεται και στην περίπτωση του πρώτου εδαφίου της παρ. 1.

Άρθρα 361Α - 362

(Καταργούνται)

Άρθρο 363
Συκοφαντική δυσφήμηση

Όποιος με οποιονδήποτε τρόπο ενώπιον τρίτου ισχυρίζεται ή διαδίδει για κάποιον άλλον εν γνώσει του ψευδές γεγονός που μπορεί να βλάψει την τιμή ή την υπόληψη του άλλου τιμωρείται με φυλάκιση τουλάχιστον τριών (3) μηνών και χρηματική ποινή και αν τελεί την πράξη δημόσια με οποιονδήποτε τρόπο ή μέσω του διαδικτύου, με φυλάκιση τουλάχιστον έξι (6) μηνών και χρηματική ποινή. Στην έννοια του τρίτου δεν περιλαμβάνονται δημόσιοι λειτουργοί ή υπάλληλοι που λαμβάνουν γνώση των ισχυρισμών για τα διάδικα μέρη, κατά την ενάσκηση καθήκοντος στο πλαίσιο πολιτικής, ποινικής ή διοικητικής δίκης.

Άρθρο 364

(Καταργείται)

Άρθρο 365
Προσβολή μνήμης νεκρού

Όποιος με τις πράξεις των άρθρων 361 και 363 προσβάλλει τη μνήμη νεκρού ή την τιμή προσώπου που έχει κηρυχθεί άφαντο, τιμωρείται, με χρηματική ποινή ή παροχή κοινωφελούς εργασίας.

Άρθρο 366
Γενικές διατάξεις

1. (Καταργείται)

2. Αν στις περιπτώσεις των άρθρων 363 και 365 το γεγονός που ισχυρίστηκε ή διέδωσε ο υπαίτιος είναι πράξη αξιόποινη για την οποία ασκήθηκε ποινική δίωξη, αναστέλλεται η δίκη για τη δυσφήμηση έως το τέλος της ποινικής δίωξης. Θεωρείται αποδεδειγμένο ότι το γεγονός είναι αληθινό αν η απόφαση είναι καταδικαστική.

3. (Καταργείται)

CHAPTER XXI

CRIMES AGAINST HONOUR

Article 361
Insult

1. Any person who, except in cases of aggravated defamation ([see] Article 363), insults the honour of another person through their words or deeds or in any other manner shall be punished with imprisonment of up to six months or a monetary penalty. If the above act was committed publicly in any manner or via the internet, imprisonment of up to one year or a monetary penalty shall be imposed, and if the insult concerns the private or family life [of the victim], imprisonment of up to two years or a monetary penalty shall be imposed.
2. Article 308(4) also applies in the cases provided for in the first sentence of paragraph 1.

Articles 361A - 362

[Repealed]

Article 363
Defamation

Any person who, in any manner and in the presence of a third party, asserts or disseminates a fact they know is false concerning another person which could harm their honour or reputation shall be punished with imprisonment of at least three months and a monetary penalty, and if the act is committed publicly in any manner or via the internet, imprisonment of at least six months and a monetary penalty shall be imposed. The concept of third party does not include public functionaries or state employees who become aware of assertions concerning litigants when performing their duties in the context of civil, criminal or administrative proceedings.

Article 364

[Repealed]

Article 365
Disparaging the memory of a deceased person

Any person who, through the acts provided for in Articles 361 and 363, disparages the memory of a deceased person or the honour of an absentee, shall be punished with a monetary penalty or community service.

Article 366
General provisions

1. [Repealed]
2. If, in the cases provided for in Articles 363 and 365, the fact asserted or disseminated by the culpable person concerns a punishable act for which criminal prosecution was instituted, the defamation proceedings shall be stayed until such criminal prosecution has ended. The veracity of the fact shall be deemed proven if a judgment of conviction is handed down.
3. [Repealed]

Άρθρο 367

(Καταργείται)

Άρθρο 368

Έγκληση

1. Για την ποινική δίωξη των πράξεων των άρθρων 361, 363 και 365 απαιτείται έγκληση.

2. Στην περίπτωση του άρθρου 365 δικαίωμα να υποβάλλουν έγκληση έχουν ο σύζυγος που επέζησε και τα παιδιά του νεκρού ή του άφαντου, και αν αυτοί δεν υπάρχουν, οι γονείς και οι αδελφοί του.

Άρθρο 369

Δημοσίευση καταδικαστικής απόφασης

1. Αν οι πράξεις των άρθρων 361, 362, 363 και 365 τελέστηκαν δημόσια με οποιονδήποτε τρόπο ή μέσω του διαδικτύου, το δικαστήριο μπορεί, με αίτηση εκείνου που υπέβαλε την έγκληση, να διατάξει τη δημοσίευση της καταδικαστικής απόφασης. Στην απόφαση ορίζεται ο τρόπος δημοσίευσης και η προθεσμία εντός της οποίας πρέπει να πραγματοποιηθεί.

2. Αν η πράξη τελέστηκε με δημοσίευμα στον τύπο ή μέσω του διαδικτύου, η δημοσίευση πρέπει να γίνει με την καταχώρηση στα ίδια μέσα, στην ίδια θέση και με τα ίδια στοιχεία, όπως καταχωρίστηκε και το υβριστικό δημοσίευμα και πρέπει να περιλαμβάνει τουλάχιστον τα ουσιώδη στοιχεία του σκεπτικού και το διατακτικού της απόφασης. Αν ο υπόχρεος σε δημοσίευση δεν τηρήσει την υποχρέωσή του τιμωρείται με φυλάκιση έως ένα έτος ή με χρηματική ποινή.

Article 367

[Repealed]

Article 368
Victim-initiated complaint

1. A victim-initiated complaint is required to institute criminal prosecution for the acts provided for in Articles 361, 363 and 365.

2. In the case provided for in Article 365, the surviving spouse and children of the deceased person or absentee and, if there are no such persons, the parents and siblings of the deceased person or absentee, have the right to file a victim-initiated complaint.

Article 369
Publication of judgments of conviction

1. If the acts provided for in Articles 361, [362,] 363 and 365 were committed publicly in any manner or via the internet, the court may, at the request of the person who filed the victim-initiated complaint, order that the judgment of conviction be published. The judgment shall specify the manner of publication and the deadline within which it must take place.

2. If the act was committed by means of a publication in the press or via the internet, the publication [ordered by the court] must take place using the same medium, at the same location and using the same [typography] as the insulting publication, and must include, as a minimum, the essential elements of the reasoning and operative part of the judgment. If the person obligated to make such publication fails to do so, they shall be punished with imprisonment of up to one year or a monetary penalty.

ΕΙΚΟΣΤΟ ΔΕΥΤΕΡΟ ΚΕΦΑΛΑΙΟ

ΠΡΟΣΒΟΛΕΣ ΑΤΟΜΙΚΟΥ ΑΠΟΡΡΗΤΟΥ ΚΑΙ ΕΠΙΚΟΙΝΩΝΙΑΣ

Άρθρο 370
Παραβίαση απορρήτου εγγράφων

1. Όποιος αθέμιτα και με σκοπό να λάβει γνώση του περιεχομένου τους ανοίγει ξένη κλειστή επιστολή ή άλλο κλειστό έγγραφο ή παραβιάζει κλειστό χώρο, στον οποίο είναι αυτά φυλαγμένα, ή με οποιονδήποτε τρόπο εισχωρεί σε ξένα απόρρητα διαβάζοντας ή αντιγράφοντας ή αποτυπώνοντας με άλλο τρόπο επιστολή ή άλλο έγγραφο τιμωρείται με φυλάκιση έως δύο έτη ή χρηματική ποινή.

2. Με την ποινή της προηγούμενης παραγράφου τιμωρείται και όποιος αθέμιτα αποκτά πρόσβαση σε ηλεκτρονικό μήνυμα ή ηλεκτρονική αλληλογραφία άλλου.

3. Αν ο δράστης των πράξεων των προηγούμενων παραγράφων είναι υπάλληλος οργανισμού ή επιχείρησης παροχής ταχυδρομικών, τηλεγραφικών ή ηλεκτρονικών υπηρεσιών τιμωρείται με φυλάκιση τουλάχιστον ενός έτους έως τρία έτη ή χρηματική ποινή.

4. Για την ποινική δίωξη των πράξεων των παραγράφων 1 και 2 απαιτείται έγκληση.

Άρθρο 370Α
Παραβίαση του απορρήτου τηλεφωνικής επικοινωνίας και προφορικής συνομιλίας

1. Όποιος αθέμιτα παγιδεύει ή με οποιονδήποτε άλλον τρόπο παρεμβαίνει σε συσκευή, σύνδεση ή δίκτυο παροχής υπηρεσιών σταθερής ή κινητής τηλεφωνίας ή σε σύστημα υλικού ή λογισμικού, που χρησιμοποιείται για την παροχή τέτοιων υπηρεσιών, με σκοπό ο ίδιος ή άλλος να πληροφορηθεί ή να αποτυπώσει σε υλικό φορέα το περιεχόμενο τηλεφωνικής συνδιάλεξης μεταξύ τρίτων ή δεδομένα επικοινωνίας (κίνησης και θέσης) τιμωρείται με κάθειρξη μέχρι δέκα (10) ετών. Με την ίδια ποινή τιμωρείται η πράξη του προηγούμενου εδαφίου και όταν ο δράστης αποτυπώσει σε υλικό φορέα το περιεχόμενο της τηλεφωνικής επικοινωνίας του με άλλον, χωρίς τη ρητή συναίνεση του τελευταίου.

2. Όποιος αθέμιτα παρακολουθεί με ειδικά τεχνικά μέσα ή αποτυπώνει σε υλικό φορέα προφορική συνομιλία μεταξύ τρίτων που δεν διεξάγεται δημόσια ή αποτυπώνει σε υλικό φορέα μη δημόσια πράξη άλλου, τιμωρείται με κάθειρξη μέχρι δέκα (10) ετών. Με την ίδια ποινή τιμωρείται η πράξη του προηγούμενου εδαφίου και όταν ο δράστης αποτυπώσει σε υλικό φορέα το περιεχόμενο της συνομιλίας του με άλλον χωρίς τη ρητή συναίνεση του τελευταίου.

3. Όποιος κάνει χρήση της πληροφορίας ή του υλικού φορέα επί του οποίου αυτή έχει αποτυπωθεί με τους τρόπους που προβλέπονται στις παραγράφους 1 και 2, τιμωρείται με κάθειρξη μέχρι δέκα (10) ετών.

4. Αν ο δράστης των πράξεων των παραγράφων 1, 2 και 3 είναι πάροχος υπηρεσιών τηλεφωνίας ή νόμιμος εκπρόσωπος αυτού ή μέλος της διοίκησης ή υπεύθυνος διασφάλισης του απορρήτου ή εργαζόμενος ή συνεργάτης του παρόχου ή ενεργεί ιδιωτικές έρευνες ή τελεί τις πράξεις αυτές κατ' επάγγελμα ή απέβλεπε στην είσπραξη αμοιβής, επιβάλλεται κάθειρξη μέχρι δέκα (10) ετών και χρηματική ποινή.

5. Αν οι πράξεις των παραγράφων 1 και 3 συνιστούν παραβίαση στρατιωτικού ή διπλωματικού απορρήτου ή αφορούν απόρρητο που αναφέρεται στην ασφάλεια του κράτους ή την ασφάλεια εγκαταστάσεων κοινής ωφέλειας, επιβάλλεται κάθειρξη.

CHAPTER XXII

OFFENCES AGAINST PERSONAL PRIVACY AND COMMUNICATION

Article 370
Violation of the secrecy of documents

1. Any person who, unduly and for the purpose of taking cognisance of the content of a sealed letter or other sealed document, opens such, breaks into a locked place where such are kept, or in any way violates the [privacy] of others by reading, copying, or otherwise making an imprint of a letter or other document shall be punished with imprisonment of up to two years or a monetary penalty.
2. The punishment laid down in the preceding paragraph shall also be imposed on any person who obtains unauthorised access to an electronic message or e-mail of another person.
3. If the perpetrator of the acts provided for in the preceding paragraphs is an employee of an organisation or enterprise providing postal, telegram or electronic services, they shall be punished with imprisonment of one to three years or a monetary penalty.
4. A victim-initiated complaint is required to institute criminal prosecution for the acts provided for in paragraphs 1 and 2.

Article 370A
Violation of the confidentiality of telephone communications and private conversations

1. Any person who unduly intercepts or otherwise interferes with a device, a connection, or a fixed or mobile telephony service provision network, or a hardware or software system used to provide such services, for the purpose of them or another learning or recording on a physical storage medium the content of a telephone conversation between third parties or communication data (traffic and location) shall be punished with incarceration of up to 10 years. The same sentence shall also be imposed when the perpetrator records the content of their telephone communication with another person on a physical storage medium without that person's express consent.
2. Any person who unduly uses special technical means to monitor or records a private conversation between third parties on a physical storage medium, or records a private act of another person on a physical storage medium shall be punished with incarceration of up to 10 years. The same sentence shall also be imposed when the perpetrator records the content of their conversation with another person on a physical storage medium without that person's express consent.
3. Any person making use of the information or physical storage medium on which such information has been recorded in the manner provided for in paragraphs 1 and 2 shall be punished with incarceration of up to 10 years.
4. If the perpetrator of the acts provided for in paragraphs 1, 2 and 3 is a telephony service provider, or its lawful representative, or a member of its management team, or the person responsible for ensuring confidentiality, or a worker or associate of the provider, or private investigator, or commits such acts [for monetary gain] or sought to collect a fee, they shall be punished with incarceration of up to 10 years and a monetary penalty.
5. If the acts provided for in paragraphs 1 and 3 constitute a violation of military or diplomatic secrecy or concern a secret relating to state security or the security of public utility facilities, incarceration shall be imposed.

Άρθρο 370Β

Παράνομη πρόσβαση σε σύστημα πληροφοριών ή σε δεδομένα

1. Όποιος κατά παράβαση μέτρου προστασίας και χωρίς δικαίωμα αποκτά πρόσβαση σε μέρος ή στο σύνολο συστήματος πληροφοριών ή σε ηλεκτρονικά δεδομένα τιμωρείται με φυλάκιση έως δύο έτη ή χρηματική ποινή. Σε ιδιαίτερα ελαφρές περιπτώσεις η πράξη μένει ατιμώρητη.

2. Αν ο δράστης είναι στην υπηρεσία του νόμιμου κατόχου του συστήματος πληροφοριών ή των δεδομένων, η πράξη της προηγούμενης παραγράφου τιμωρείται μόνο αν απαγορεύεται ρητά από εσωτερικό κανονισμό ή από έγγραφη απόφαση του κατόχου ή αρμόδιου υπαλλήλου του.

3. Αν η πράξη της παραγράφου 1 αναφέρεται σε επιστημονικά ή επαγγελματικά απόρρητα επιχείρησης του δημόσιου ή ιδιωτικού τομέα τιμωρείται με φυλάκιση έως τρία έτη ή χρηματική ποινή.

4. Αν ο δράστης είναι στην υπηρεσία του νόμιμου κατόχου των στοιχείων καθώς και αν το απόρρητο είναι ιδιαίτερα μεγάλης οικονομικής αξίας, επιβάλλεται φυλάκιση και χρηματική ποινή.

5. Για την ποινική δίωξη των πράξεων των παραγράφων 1 και 4 απαιτείται έγκληση.

Άρθρο 370Γ

1. Όποιος αθέμιτα αντιγράφει, αποτυπώνει, χρησιμοποιεί, αποκαλύπτει σε τρίτον ή οπωσδήποτε παραβιάζει στοιχεία ή προγράμματα υπολογιστών, τα οποία συνιστούν κρατικά, επιστημονικά ή επαγγελματικά απόρρητα ή απόρρητα επιχείρησης του δημοσίου ή ιδιωτικού τομέα, τιμωρείται με φυλάκιση τουλάχιστον τριών μηνών. Ως απόρρητα θεωρούνται και εκείνα που ο νόμιμος κάτοχός τους, από δικαιολογημένο ενδιαφέρον τα μεταχειρίζεται ως απόρρητα, ιδίως όταν έχει λάβει μέτρα για να παρεμποδίζονται τρίτοι να λάβουν γνώση τους.

2. Αν ο δράστης είναι στην υπηρεσία του κατόχου των στοιχείων, καθώς και αν το απόρρητο είναι ιδιαίτερα μεγάλης οικονομικής σημασίας, επιβάλλεται φυλάκιση τουλάχιστον ενός έτους.

3. Οι πράξεις που προβλέπονται στο άρθρο αυτό διώκονται με έγκληση.

Άρθρο 370Δ

1. Όποιος χωρίς δικαίωμα αντιγράφει ή χρησιμοποιεί προγράμματα υπολογιστών, τιμωρείται με χρηματική ποινή ή παροχή κοινωφελούς εργασίας.

2. Όποιος χωρίς δικαίωμα αποκτά πρόσβαση στο σύνολο ή τμήμα πληροφοριακού συστήματος ή σε στοιχεία που μεταδίδονται με συστήματα τηλεπικοινωνιών, παραβιάζοντας απαγορεύσεις ή μέτρα ασφαλείας που έχει λάβει ο νόμιμος κάτοχος του, τιμωρείται με φυλάκιση.

3. Αν ο δράστης είναι στην υπηρεσία του νόμιμου κατόχου του πληροφοριακού συστήματος ή των στοιχείων, η πράξη της προηγούμενης παραγράφου τιμωρείται μόνο αν απαγορεύεται ρητά από εσωτερικό κανονισμό ή από έγγραφη απόφαση του κατόχου ή αρμόδιου υπαλλήλου.

Article 370B

Unlawful access to an information system or data

1. Any person who, in breach of protective measures and without the right to do so, obtains access to part or all of an information system or electronic data shall be punished with imprisonment of two years or a monetary penalty. In particularly minor cases, the act shall not be punished.

2. If the perpetrator is in the employ of the lawful possessor of the information system or the data, the act referred to in the preceding paragraph shall only be punished if it is explicitly prohibited under an internal regulation or a written decision of the possessor or of a competent employee of the latter.

3. If the act provided for in paragraph 1 concerns scientific or professional secrets of a public corporation or of a private enterprise, imprisonment of up to three years or a monetary penalty shall be imposed.

4. If the perpetrator is in the employ of the lawful possessor of the data [or] if the secret is of particularly high economic value, imprisonment and a monetary penalty shall be imposed.

5. A victim-initiated complaint is required to institute criminal prosecution for the acts provided for in paragraphs 1 and 4.

Article 370C

1. Any person who unduly copies, records, uses, discloses to a third party or, in any event, violates computer data or programs which constitute state, scientific or professional secrets or secrets of a public corporation or a private enterprise shall be punished with imprisonment of at least three months. Any information which the lawful possessor treats as secret due to a legitimate interest, particularly when they have taken measures to hinder third parties from taking cognisance of such information, shall also be considered secret.

2. If the perpetrator is in the employ of the possessor of the data [or] if the secret carries major economic importance, imprisonment of at least one year shall be imposed.

3. A victim-initiated complaint is required in order to prosecute the acts provided for in this Article.

Article 370D

1. Any person who, without the right to do so, copies or uses computer programs shall be punished with a monetary penalty or community service.

2. Any person who, without the right to do so, obtains access to all or part of an information system or to data transmitted using telecommunication systems by breaching the prohibitions or security measures put in place by their lawful possessor shall be punished with imprisonment.

3. If the perpetrator is in the employ of the lawful possessor of the information system or the data, the act referred to in the preceding paragraph shall only be punished if it is explicitly prohibited under an internal regulation or a written decision of the possessor or of a competent employee of the latter.

Άρθρο 370Ε

1. Όποιος, αθέμιτα, με τη χρήση τεχνικών μέσων, παρακολουθεί ή αποτυπώνει σε υλικό φορέα μη δημόσιες διαβιβάσεις δεδομένων ή ηλεκτρομαγνητικές εκπομπές από, προς ή εντός πληροφοριακού συστήματος ή παρεμβαίνει σε αυτές με σκοπό ο ίδιος ή άλλος να πληροφορηθεί το περιεχόμενό τους, τιμωρείται με κάθειρξη μέχρι δέκα (10) ετών.

2. Με την ποινή της παραγράφου 1 τιμωρείται όποιος κάνει χρήση της πληροφορίας ή του υλικού φορέα επί του οποίου αυτή έχει αποτυπωθεί με τους τρόπους που προβλέπεται στην παράγραφο 1.

3. Αν οι πράξεις των παραγράφων 1 και 2 συνιστούν παραβίαση στρατιωτικού ή διπλωματικού απορρήτου ή αφορούν απόρρητο που αναφέρεται στην ασφάλεια του Κράτους σε καιρό πολέμου, επιβάλλεται κάθειρξη.

Άρθρο 370ΣΤ

Απαγόρευση διακίνησης λογισμικών, συσκευών παρακολούθησης και άλλων δεδομένων

1. Με φυλάκιση τουλάχιστον δύο (2) ετών τιμωρείται όποιος παράγει, πωλεί, προμηθεύεται προς χρήση, εισάγει, εξάγει, κατέχει, διανέμει ή με άλλο τρόπο διακινεί λογισμικά ή συσκευές παρακολούθησης, με δυνατότητα υποκλοπής, καταγραφής και κάθε είδους άντλησης περιεχομένου ή και δεδομένων επικοινωνίας (κίνησης και θέσης), με τα οποία μπορούν να τελεσθούν οι πράξεις του άρθρου 370Α.

2. Με φυλάκιση τουλάχιστον δύο (2) ετών τιμωρείται όποιος, χωρίς δικαίωμα και με σκοπό τη διάπραξη κάποιου από τα εγκλήματα των άρθρων 370Β, 370Γ, των παραγράφων 2 και 3 του άρθρου 370Δ και του άρθρου 370Ε, παράγει, πωλεί, προμηθεύεται προς χρήση, εισάγει, εξάγει, κατέχει, διανέμει ή με άλλο τρόπο διακινεί συνθηματικά ή κωδικούς πρόσβασης ή άλλα παρεμφερή δεδομένα, με τη χρήση των οποίων είναι δυνατόν να αποκτηθεί πρόσβαση στο σύνολο ή μέρος ενός πληροφοριακού συστήματος.

Άρθρο 371

Παραβίαση επαγγελματικής εχεμύθειας

1. Κληρικοί, δικηγόροι και κάθε είδους νομικοί παραστάτες, συμβολαιογράφοι, γιατροί, μαίες, νοσοκόμοι, φαρμακοποιοί και άλλοι λειτουργοί ή επαγγελματίες, στους οποίους κάποιοι εμπιστεύονται συνήθως λόγω του επαγγέλματός τους ή της ιδιότητάς τους ιδιωτικά απόρρητα, καθώς και οι βοηθοί των προσώπων αυτών, οι οποίοι φανερώνουν ιδιωτικά απόρρητα, που τους τα εμπιστεύτηκαν ή που τα έμαθαν λόγω του επαγγέλματός τους ή της ιδιότητάς τους, τιμωρούνται με φυλάκιση έως ένα έτος ή χρηματική ποινή.

2. Με την ίδια ποινή τιμωρείται όποιος, λόγω του θανάτου κάποιου από τα πρόσωπα της πρώτης παραγράφου, γίνεται κάτοχος εγγράφων ή σημειώσεών του σχετικών με την άσκηση του επαγγέλματος ή του λειτουργήματός του και φανερώνει από αυτά ιδιωτικά απόρρητα.

3. Για την ποινική δίωξη απαιτείται έγκληση.

4. Η πράξη δεν είναι άδικη και μένει ατιμώρητη αν ο υπαίτιος απέβλεπε στην εκπλήρωση καθήκοντος ή στη διαφύλαξη δικαιολογημένου ουσιώδους συμφέροντος, δημόσιου ή του ίδιου ή κάποιου άλλου, το οποίο δεν μπορούσε να διαφυλαχθεί διαφορετικά.

Article 370E

1. Any person who, by using technical means, unduly monitors or records on a physical storage medium non-public data transfers or electromagnetic transmissions from, to or within an information system or interferes with such for the purpose of them or another learning their content shall be punished with incarceration of up to 10 years.

2. The sentence laid down in paragraph 1 shall [also] be imposed on any person making use of the information or physical storage medium on which such information has been recorded in the manner provided for in paragraph 1.

3. If the acts provided for in paragraphs 1 and 2 constitute a violation of military or diplomatic secrecy or concern a secret relating to state security during wartime, incarceration shall be imposed.

Article 370F

Prohibition on making available software, surveillance devices and other data

1. Any person who produces, sells, procures for use, imports, exports, possesses, distributes or otherwise makes available surveillance software or devices capable of intercepting, recording and otherwise extracting communication content and/or data (traffic and location) which can be used to commit the acts provided for in Article 370A shall be punished with imprisonment of at least two years.

2. Any person who, without the right to do so and for the purpose of committing any of the crimes provided for in Articles 370B, 370C, 370D(2) and (3) and 370E, produces, sells, procures for use, imports, exports, possesses, distributes or otherwise makes available passwords or access codes or other such data which can be used to access all or part of an information data shall be punished with imprisonment of at least two years.

Article 371

Violation of professional secrecy

1. Any members of the clergy, lawyers and all manner of legal counsel, notaries public, physicians, midwives, nurses, pharmacists and other functionaries or professionals usually entrusted, due to their profession or capacity, with private secrets, as well as the assistants of such persons, who disclose private secrets which were entrusted to them or of which they took cognisance due to their profession or capacity shall be punished with imprisonment of up to one year or a monetary penalty.

2. The same punishment shall [also] be imposed on any person who, due to the death of any of the persons referred to in the first paragraph, acquires possession of their documents or notes concerning the exercise of their profession or function and discloses private secrets contained in such.

3. A victim-initiated complaint is required to institute criminal prosecution.

4. If the culpable person aimed to perform a duty or safeguard a legitimate material interest, whether of the Greek State or of their own or of another person, which could not have been otherwise safeguarded, this act is not wrongful and is not punishable.

ΕΙΚΟΣΤΟ ΤΡΙΤΟ ΚΕΦΑΛΑΙΟ

ΕΓΚΛΗΜΑΤΑ ΚΑΤΑ ΠΕΡΙΟΥΣΙΑΚΩΝ ΑΓΑΘΩΝ

I

ΕΓΚΛΗΜΑΤΑ ΚΑΤΑ ΤΗΣ ΙΔΙΟΚΤΗΣΙΑΣ

Άρθρο 372
Κλοπή

1. Όποιος αφαιρεί ξένο (ολικά ή εν μέρει) κινητό πράγμα από την κατοχή άλλου με σκοπό να το ιδιοποιηθεί παράνομα, τιμωρείται με φυλάκιση και χρηματική ποινή και αν το αντικείμενο της κλοπής είναι ιδιαίτερα μεγάλης αξίας, με φυλάκιση τουλάχιστον ενός (1) έτους και χρηματική ποινή.
2. Κινητό πράγμα θεωρείται κατά τον Κώδικα και η ηλεκτρική και κάθε άλλης μορφής ενέργεια.

Άρθρο 373

(Καταργείται)

Άρθρο 374
Διακεκριμένη κλοπή

1. Η κλοπή τιμωρείται με κάθειρξη έως δέκα έτη και χρηματική ποινή αν:
α) ο υπαίτιος αφαιρεί από τόπο προορισμένο για θρησκευτική λατρεία, πράγμα αφιερωμένο σε αυτή καλλιτεχνικής ή αρχαιολογικής ή ιστορικής σημασίας,
β) ο υπαίτιος αφαιρεί πράγμα επιστημονικής ή καλλιτεχνικής ή αρχαιολογικής ή ιστορικής σημασίας που βρίσκεται σε συλλογή εκτεθειμένη σε κοινή θέα ή σε δημόσιο οίκημα ή σε άλλο δημόσιο τόπο,
βα) ο υπαίτιος αφαιρεί πράγμα προορισμένο από τη θέση του ή από την κατασκευή του για την εξυπηρέτηση της λειτουργίας ή την ασφάλεια της συγκοινωνίας μέσων σταθερής τροχιάς, πλοίων ή αεροσκαφών,
ββ) ο υπαίτιος αφαιρεί πράγμα που αποτελεί τμήμα εξοπλισμού δικτύου μεταφοράς ή διανομής ηλεκτρικής ενέργειας ή δικτύου αποχέτευσης ομβρίων και ακαθάρτων υδάτων,
γ) η συνολική αξία των αφαιρεθέντων αντικειμένων υπερβαίνει το ποσό των εκατόν είκοσι χιλιάδων (120.000) ευρώ,
δ) τελέστηκε από δύο ή περισσότερους που είχαν οργανωθεί με σκοπό την τέλεση κλοπών,
ε) η πράξη τελέστηκε από πρόσωπο που διαπράττει κλοπές κατ' επάγγελμα.
2. Αν η κλοπή στρέφεται άμεσα κατά του νομικού προσώπου του ελληνικού δημοσίου, των νομικών προσώπων δημοσίου δικαίου ή των οργανισμών τοπικής αυτοδιοίκησης και η αξία του αντικειμένου της υπερβαίνει συνολικά το ποσό των 120.000 ευρώ επιβάλλεται κάθειρξη τουλάχιστον δέκα ετών και χρηματική ποινή έως χίλιες ημερήσιες μονάδες. Η πράξη αυτή παραγράφεται μετά είκοσι έτη.

Άρθρο 374Α
Αυθαίρετη χρήση μεταφορικού μέσου

Όποιος χρησιμοποιεί ξένο μηχανοκίνητο μεταφορικό μέσο χωρίς τη συγκατάθεση του ιδιοκτήτη ή κατόχου του, τιμωρείται με φυλάκιση έως δύο έτη ή χρηματική ποινή.

CHAPTER XXIII

CRIMES AGAINST ASSETS

I

CRIMES AGAINST OWNERSHIP

Article 372
Theft

1. Any person who removes a movable thing belonging (in whole or in part) to another person from their possession for the purpose of unlawfully appropriating it shall be punished with imprisonment and a monetary penalty; if the object of the theft is of particularly high value, they shall be punished with imprisonment of at least one year and a monetary penalty.
2. Under this Code, electricity and all other forms of energy are also considered movable things.

Article 373

[Repealed]

Article 374
Aggravated theft

1. Theft shall be punished with incarceration of up to 10 years and a monetary penalty if:
a) the culpable person removes a votive thing of artistic or archaeological or historical value from a place intended for religious worship;
b) the culpable person removes a thing of scientific or artistic or archaeological or historical value which forms part of a collection exhibited in public view, or is located in a public building, or at another public place;
ba) the culpable person removes a thing intended, due to its location or construction, to [ensure] the operation or safety of track-based means of transportation, ships or aircraft;
bb) the culpable person removes a thing which forms part of the equipment of networks for the transmission or distribution of electricity or networks for the drainage of rainwater and wastewater;
c) the total value of the things removed exceeds 120,000 euros;
d) it was committed by two or more persons who had organised themselves for the purpose of committing theft; [or]
e) the act was perpetrated by a person committing theft [for monetary gain].
2. If any theft was committed directly against the Greek State as a legal person, bodies governed by public law or local government authorities and the value of the thing stolen exceeds 120,000 euros in total, incarceration of at least 10 years and a monetary penalty of up to 1,000 daily penalty units shall be imposed. Such acts shall become time-barred after 20 years.

Article 374A
Unauthorised use of a vehicle

Any person who uses another's motor vehicle without the consent of its owner or possessor shall be punished with imprisonment of up to two years or a monetary penalty.

Άρθρο 375
Υπεξαίρεση

1. Όποιος ιδιοποιείται παράνομα ξένο (ολικά ή εν μέρει) κινητό πράγμα που περιήλθε στην κατοχή του με οποιονδήποτε τρόπο τιμωρείται με φυλάκιση έως δύο (2) έτη και αν το αντικείμενο είναι ιδιαίτερα μεγάλης αξίας, με φυλάκιση τουλάχιστον τριών (3) μηνών και χρηματική ποινή. Αν πρόκειται για αντικείμενο που το έχουν εμπιστευθεί στον υπαίτιο λόγω ανάγκης ή λόγω της ιδιότητάς του ως εντολοδόχου, επιτρόπου ή κηδεμόνα του παθόντος ή ως μεσεγγυούχου ή διαχειριστή ξένης περιουσίας, ο υπαίτιος τιμωρείται με φυλάκιση τουλάχιστον ενός (1) έτους και χρηματική ποινή.

2. Αν η αξία του αντικειμένου στην παρ. 1 υπερβαίνει συνολικά το ποσό των εκατόν είκοσι χιλιάδων (120.000) ευρώ ο υπαίτιος τιμωρείται με κάθειρξη έως δέκα (10) έτη και χρηματική ποινή.

3. Αν η υπεξαίρεση στρέφεται άμεσα κατά του νομικού προσώπου του ελληνικού δημοσίου, των νομικών προσώπων δημοσίου δικαίου ή των οργανισμών τοπικής αυτοδιοίκησης και η αξία του αντικειμένου της υπερβαίνει συνολικά το ποσό των εκατόν είκοσι χιλιάδων (120.000) ευρώ, επιβάλλεται κάθειρξη τουλάχιστον δέκα (10) ετών και χρηματική ποινή έως χίλιες (1.000) ημερήσιες μονάδες. Η πράξη αυτή παραγράφεται μετά είκοσι (20) έτη.

4. Με το ξένο πράγμα εξομοιώνεται και:

α) το τίμημα που έλαβε ο υπαίτιος για κινητό πράγμα που του είχαν εμπιστευθεί για να το πουλήσει, καθώς και

β) το κινητό πράγμα που απέκτησε ο υπαίτιος με χρήματα ή με άλλο πράγμα που του είχαν εμπιστευθεί για να αγοράσει ή να ανταλλάξει αντίστοιχα το πράγμα που απέκτησε.

Άρθρο 376

(Καταργείται)

Άρθρο 377
Κλοπή και υπεξαίρεση μικρής αξίας

Αν τα εγκλήματα των άρθρων 372 και 375 παρ. 1 έχουν αντικείμενο πράγμα μικρής αξίας, επιβάλλεται χρηματική ποινή ή παροχή κοινωφελούς εργασίας. Αν, όμως, η πράξη τελέστηκε από ανάγκη για άμεση χρήση ή ανάλωση του αντικειμένου της κλοπής ή υπεξαίρεσης, το δικαστήριο μπορεί να κρίνει την πράξη ατιμώρητη. Το πρώτο εδάφιο δεν εφαρμόζεται σε περίπτωση κλοπής ή υπεξαίρεσης που έχει ως αντικείμενο υλικό μέσο πληρωμής πλην των μετρητών.

Άρθρο 378
Φθορά ξένης ιδιοκτησίας

1. Όποιος καταστρέφει ή βλάπτει ξένο (ολικά ή εν μέρει) πράγμα ή με άλλον τρόπο καθιστά ανέφικτη τη χρήση του τιμωρείται με φυλάκιση έως δύο (2) έτη ή χρηματική ποινή. Αν το πράγμα είναι μικρής αξίας ή η ζημία που προκλήθηκε είναι ελαφρά, ο υπαίτιος τιμωρείται με χρηματική ποινή ή παροχή κοινωφελούς εργασίας. Αν το πράγμα είναι ιδιαίτερα μεγάλης αξίας ή τοποθετημένο σε δημόσιο χώρο ή η πράξη έγινε χωρίς πρόκληση από τον παθόντα, τιμωρείται με φυλάκιση τουλάχιστον ενός έτους και χρηματική ποινή.

2. Με φυλάκιση τουλάχιστον δύο ετών και χρηματική ποινή τιμωρείται ο υπαίτιος αν το αντικείμενο της πράξης που προβλέπεται στο εδάφιο α΄ της προηγούμενης παραγράφου είναι πράγμα που χρησιμεύει για κοινό όφελος ή καλλιτεχνικό ή ιστορικό μνημείο ή αν η φθορά έγινε με φωτιά ή με εκρηκτικές ύλες.

Article 375
Misappropriation

1. Any person who unlawfully appropriates a movable thing which belongs (in whole or in part) to another person and which came into the possession [of the former] by any means shall be punished with imprisonment of up to two years; if the thing is of particularly high value, they shall be punished with imprisonment of at least three months and a monetary penalty. If the thing was entrusted to the culpable person out of necessity or due to their capacity as a mandatary, tutor or custodian of the victim or as sequestrator or manager of another person's assets, the culpable person shall be punished with imprisonment of at least one year and a monetary penalty.
2. If the value of the thing referred to in paragraph 1 exceeds 120,000 euros in total, the culpable person shall be punished with incarceration of up to 10 years and a monetary penalty.
3. If the misappropriation was committed directly against the Greek State as a legal person, bodies governed by public law or local government authorities and the value of the thing exceeds 120,000 euros in total, incarceration of at least 10 years and a monetary penalty of up to 1,000 daily penalty units shall be imposed. Such acts shall become time-barred after 20 years.
4. The following shall also be treated as things belonging to another:
a) the price received by the culpable person for a movable thing entrusted to them for the purpose of selling it; and
b) a movable thing the culpable person acquired using money or a different thing entrusted to them for purchasing or exchanging such with the thing they acquired, respectively.

Article 376

[Repealed]

Article 377
Theft and misappropriation of low-value [things]

If the crimes provided for in Articles 372 and 375(1) concern a low-value thing, a monetary penalty or community service shall be imposed. However, if the act was committed out of necessity for the immediate use or consumption of the thing stolen or misappropriated, the court may decide not to punish [the culpable person]. The first sentence [of this Article] does not apply to cases of theft or misappropriation concerning any tangible non-cash payment instrument.

Article 378
Damage to another's property

1. Any person who destroys or damages a thing belonging to another (in whole or in part) or otherwise renders its use impossible shall be punished with imprisonment of up to two years or a monetary penalty. If the thing is of low value or the damage caused is minor, the culpable person shall be punished with a monetary penalty or community service. However, if the thing is of particularly high value or is installed in a public place, or the act was carried out without provocation by the victim, [the perpetrator] shall be punished with imprisonment of at least one year and a monetary penalty.
2. If the thing [damaged] is used for the public benefit, or is an artistic or historical monument, or if the damage was caused by fire or explosives, the culpable person shall be punished with imprisonment of at least two years and a monetary penalty.

Άρθρο 379
Φθορά ψηφιακών δεδομένων

1. Όποιος, χωρίς δικαίωμα, διαγράφει, καταστρέφει, αλλοιώνει ή αποκρύπτει ψηφιακά δεδομένα ενός συστήματος πληροφοριών, καθιστά ανέφικτη τη χρήση τους ή με οποιονδήποτε τρόπο αποκλείει την πρόσβαση στα δεδομένα αυτά τιμωρείται με φυλάκιση έως δύο (2) έτη και χρηματική ποινή. Αν η ζημία που προκλήθηκε είναι ελαφρά, ο υπαίτιος τιμωρείται με χρηματική ποινή ή παροχή κοινωφελούς εργασίας.

2. Η πράξη της παρ. 1 τιμωρείται:

α) με φυλάκιση έως τρία (3) έτη και χρηματική ποινή, αν επλήγη μεγάλος αριθμός πληροφοριακών συστημάτων και η πράξη τελέστηκε με τη χρήση εργαλείου που έχει σχεδιαστεί κατά κύριο λόγο για τον σκοπό αυτόν,

β) με φυλάκιση τουλάχιστον ενός (1) έτους και χρηματική ποινή, αν προκάλεσε σοβαρές ζημίες και ιδίως μεγάλης έκτασης ή για μεγάλο χρονικό διάστημα διατάραξη των υπηρεσιών των συστημάτων πληροφοριών, οικονομική ζημία ιδιαίτερα μεγάλης αξίας ή σημαντική απώλεια δεδομένων, ή αν τελέστηκε κατά πληροφοριακών συστημάτων που αποτελούν μέρος υποδομής για την προμήθεια του πληθυσμού με ζωτικής σημασίας αγαθά ή υπηρεσίες. Ως ζωτικής σημασίας αγαθά ή υπηρεσίες νοούνται ιδίως η εθνική άμυνα, η υγεία, οι συγκοινωνίες, οι μεταφορές και η ενέργεια.

3. Με φυλάκιση έως δύο (2) έτη και χρηματική ποινή τιμωρείται όποιος χωρίς δικαίωμα και με σκοπό τη διάπραξη του εγκλήματος της παρ. 1 κατασκευάζει, κατέχει, εισάγει ή διαθέτει:

α) συσκευές ή πληροφοριακά συστήματα, πρωτίστως σχεδιασμένα ή ειδικά προσαρμοσμένα για τον σκοπό της διάπραξης του εγκλήματος της παρ. 1 ή

β) συνθηματικά ή κωδικούς πρόσβασης ή άλλα παρεμφερή δεδομένα με τη χρήση των οποίων είναι δυνατόν να αποκτηθεί πρόσβαση στο σύνολο ή μέρος ενός πληροφοριακού συστήματος.

Απαλλάσσεται από κάθε ποινή όποιος καταστρέφει με δική του θέληση τις παραπάνω συσκευές ή προγράμματα υπολογιστή ή δεδομένα πριν τα χρησιμοποιήσει για τη διάπραξη του εγκλήματος του προηγούμενου εδαφίου.

Άρθρο 379Α
Διακεκριμένες περιπτώσεις στο πλαίσιο εγκληματικής οργάνωσης

Τα πλημμελήματα της παρ. 1 του άρθρου 372 και του πρώτου εδαφίου της παρ. 1 του άρθρου 375 που αφορούν σε υλικά μέσα πληρωμής πλην των μετρητών, καθώς και των παρ. 1 και 2 του άρθρου 379, όταν τελούνται στο πλαίσιο εγκληματικής οργάνωσης, τιμωρούνται με ποινή φυλάκισης τουλάχιστον ενός (1) έτους και χρηματική ποινή.

Article 379

Damage to digital data

1. Any person who, without the right to do so, deletes, damages, alters or suppresses digital data on an information system, renders their use impossible or otherwise precludes access to such data shall be punished with imprisonment of up to two years and a monetary penalty. If the damage caused is minor, the culpable person shall be punished with a monetary penalty or community service.

2. The act provided for in paragraph 1 shall be punished with:

a) imprisonment of up to three years and a monetary penalty if a large number of information systems were affected and the act was committed using a tool predominantly designed for this purpose;

b) imprisonment of at least one year and a monetary penalty if it caused serious damage and particularly widespread or long-term disruption of information system services, economic damage of particularly high value or significant loss of data, or was committed against information systems forming part of infrastructure to provide the population with vital goods or services. "Vital goods or services" means, in particular, national defence, health, the public transportation sector, the transport sector and the energy sector.

3. Imprisonment of up to two years and a monetary penalty shall be imposed on any person who, without the right to do so and for the purpose of committing the crime provided for in paragraph 1, manufactures, possesses, imports or makes available:

a) devices or information systems predominantly designed or specially adapted for the purpose of committing the crime provided for in paragraph 1; or

b) passwords or access codes or similar data by which the whole or any part of an information system can be accessed.

Any person who destroys the above devices or computer programs or data of their own volition before using them to commit the crime provided for in the preceding sentence shall not be punished.

Article 379A

Aggravated cases in the context of a criminal organisation

Where the misdemeanours provided for in Article 372(1) and the first sentence of Article 375(1) concerning tangible non-cash payment instruments and the misdemeanours provided for in Article 379(1) and (2) are committed in the context of a criminal organisation, imprisonment of at least one year and a monetary penalty shall be imposed.

Άρθρο 380
Ληστεία

1. Όποιος με σωματική βία εναντίον προσώπου ή με απειλές ενωμένες με επικείμενο κίνδυνο σώματος ή ζωής αφαιρεί από άλλον ξένο (ολικά ή εν μέρει) κινητό πράγμα ή τον εξαναγκάζει να του το παραδώσει για να το ιδιοποιηθεί παράνομα, τιμωρείται με κάθειρξη και χρηματική ποινή.

2. Αν από την πράξη επήλθε ο θάνατος κάποιου προσώπου ή βαριά σωματική βλάβη ή αν η πράξη εκτελέστηκε με ιδιαίτερη σκληρότητα εναντίον προσώπου, επιβάλλεται ισόβια κάθειρξη.

3. Οι ποινές των προηγούμενων παραγράφων επιβάλλονται και σε εκείνον που καταλήφθηκε επ' αυτοφώρω να κλέβει και μεταχειρίζεται σωματική βία εναντίον προσώπου ή απειλές ενωμένες με επικείμενο κίνδυνο σώματος ή ζωής για να διατηρήσει το κλοπιμαίο.

Άρθρο 381
Γενική Διάταξη

1. Για την ποινική δίωξη των εγκλημάτων που προβλέπονται στο άρθρο 374Α, στην παρ. 1 του άρθρου 375, στο άρθρο 377, στο πρώτο και δεύτερο εδάφιο της παρ. 1 του άρθρου 378 και στην παρ. 1 του άρθρου 379 απαιτείται έγκληση.

2. Το αξιόποινο των εγκλημάτων που προβλέπονται στα άρθρα 372 έως 378 εξαλείφεται αν ο υπαίτιος, με δική του θέληση και πριν από την πρώτη εξέτασή του ως υπόπτου ή κατηγορουμένου για την πράξη, αποδώσει το πράγμα ή ικανοποιήσει εντελώς τον ζημιωθέντα χωρίς παράνομη βλάβη τρίτου. Η μερική μόνο απόδοση ή ικανοποίηση εξαλείφει το αξιόποινο κατά το αντίστοιχο μέρος. Στην περίπτωση του άρθρου 374Α, μαζί με την απόδοση του πράγματος απαιτείται και η πλήρης ικανοποίηση του ζημιωθέντος.

3. Εάν ο υπαίτιος των πλημμελημάτων που προβλέπονται στα άρθρα 372 έως 378 μέχρι το τέλος της αποδεικτικής διαδικασίας στο πρωτοβάθμιο δικαστήριο αποδώσει αποδεδειγμένα, ιδίως ενώπιον δημόσιας αρχής ή με τραπεζική κατάθεση ή με μη ανακλητή δημόσια παρακατάθεση, το πράγμα ή ικανοποιήσει εντελώς τον ζημιωθέντα, χωρίς παράνομη βλάβη τρίτου, καταβάλλοντας την αξία του, μπορεί να απαλλάσσεται από κάθε ποινή εφόσον πληρώσει επιπλέον τους τόκους υπερημερίας από την ημέρα τέλεσης του εγκλήματος.

4. Εάν ο υπαίτιος των κακουργημάτων που προβλέπονται στα άρθρα 372 έως 378 μέχρι το τέλος της αποδεικτικής διαδικασίας στο πρωτοβάθμιο δικαστήριο αποδώσει αποδεδειγμένα, ιδίως ενώπιον δημόσιας αρχής ή με τραπεζική κατάθεση ή με μη ανακλητή δημόσια παρακατάθεση, το πράγμα ή ικανοποιήσει πλήρως τον ζημιωθέντα, χωρίς παράνομη βλάβη τρίτου, καταβάλλοντας την αξία του, εφόσον πληρώσει επιπλέον τους τόκους υπερημερίας από την ημέρα τέλεσης του εγκλήματος, τιμωρείται με μειωμένη ποινή κατ' άρθρο 83 και εφόσον κριθεί από τις περιστάσεις, αν η απόδοση ή η πλήρης ικανοποίηση λάβει χώρα μέχρι την αμετάκλητη παραπομπή, μπορεί να απαλλαγεί από κάθε ποινή.

Άρθρα 382 - 384

(Καταργούνται)

Article 380
Robbery

1. Any person who, using physical violence against another person or through threats of imminent danger to the body or life of another, removes a movable thing (whether in whole or in part) from another or forces another to surrender such thing to them for the purpose of unlawfully appropriating it shall be punished with incarceration and a monetary penalty.

2. If the act resulted in the death of or grievous bodily harm to a person or if the act was committed with particular brutality against a person, incarceration for life shall be imposed.

3. The sentences laid down in the preceding paragraphs shall also be imposed on any person caught in the act stealing, using physical violence against a person or making threats of imminent danger to the body or life of another in order to retain the stolen property.

Article 381
General provision

1. A victim-initiated complaint is required to institute criminal prosecution for the crimes provided for in Articles 374A, 375(1), 377, the first and second sentences of Article 378(1), and Article 379(1).

2. The punishability of the crimes provided for in Articles 372 to 378 shall be extinguished if the culpable person, of their own volition and before being first examined in relation to the act as a suspect or accused person or defendant, surrenders the thing or provides just satisfaction to the victim, without unlawful damage to a third party. Partial surrender or satisfaction only expunges punishability up to the corresponding part. In the case provided for in Article 374A, both surrendering the thing and providing just satisfaction to the victim are required.

3. If the person who committed [any] of the misdemeanours provided for in Articles 372 to 378 demonstrably surrenders the thing by the end of the taking of evidence at first instance, particularly in the presence of a public authority or via bank deposit or irrevocable public permanent deposit, or provides just satisfaction to the victim, without unlawful damage to a third party, by paying its value, they may be exempted from all punishment, provided they also pay default interest from the date the crime was committed.

4. If the person who committed [any] of the felonies provided for in Articles 372 to 378 demonstrably surrenders the thing by the end of the taking of evidence at first instance, particularly in the presence of a public authority or via bank deposit or irrevocable public permanent deposit, or provides just satisfaction to the victim, without unlawful damage to a third party, by paying its value, provided they also pay default interest from the date the crime was committed, they shall receive a reduced punishment under Article 83 and, if deemed necessary under the circumstances, where the surrender or just satisfaction occurred before the perpetrator was irrevocably committed to trial, they may be exempted from all punishment.

Articles 382 - 384

[Repealed]

II

ΕΓΚΛΗΜΑΤΑ ΚΑΤΑ ΤΗΣ ΠΕΡΙΟΥΣΙΑΣ

Άρθρο 385

Εκβίαση

1. Όποιος, με σκοπό να αποκομίσει ο ίδιος ή τρίτος παράνομο περιουσιακό όφελος, εξαναγκάζει άλλον με βία ή απειλή σε πράξη, παράλειψη ή ανοχή από την οποία επέρχεται ζημία στην περιουσία του εξαναγκαζομένου ή άλλου τιμωρείται με φυλάκιση τουλάχιστον ενός (1) έτους και χρηματική ποινή.
2. Αν η πράξη της προηγούμενης παραγράφου τελέστηκε με σωματική βία εναντίον προσώπου ή με απειλές ενωμένες με επικείμενο κίνδυνο σώματος ή ζωής τιμωρείται σύμφωνα με όσα ορίζονται στις παρ. 1 και 2 του άρθρου 380 ΠΚ.
3. Η εκβίαση τιμωρείται με φυλάκιση τουλάχιστον τριών (3) ετών και χρηματική ποινή αν ο υπαίτιος μεταχειρίστηκε βία ή απειλή βλάβης της επιχείρησης, του επαγγέλματος, του λειτουργήματος ή άλλης δραστηριότητας που ασκεί ο εξαναγκαζόμενος ή άλλος ή προσφέρθηκε να παρέχει ή παρέχει προστασία για την αποτροπή πρόκλησης τέτοιας βλάβης από τρίτον. Αν την παραπάνω πράξη τέλεσε πρόσωπο που διαπράττει τέτοιες πράξεις κατ' επάγγελμα, επιβάλλεται κάθειρξη έως δέκα έτη και χρηματική ποινή.

Άρθρο 386

Απάτη

1. Όποιος με την εν γνώσει παράσταση ψευδών γεγονότων σαν αληθινών ή την αθέμιτη απόκρυψη ή παρασιώπηση αληθινών γεγονότων βλάπτει ξένη περιουσία πείθοντας κάποιον σε πράξη, παράλειψη ή ανοχή με σκοπό από τη βλάβη αυτής της περιουσίας να αποκομίσει ο ίδιος ή άλλος παράνομο περιουσιακό όφελος τιμωρείται με φυλάκιση, και αν η ζημία που προξενήθηκε είναι ιδιαίτερα μεγάλη, με φυλάκιση τουλάχιστον τριών (3) μηνών και χρηματική ποινή. Αν η ζημία που προκλήθηκε υπερβαίνει συνολικά το ποσό των εκατόν είκοσι χιλιάδων (120.000) ευρώ επιβάλλεται κάθειρξη έως δέκα (10) έτη και χρηματική ποινή.
2. Αν η απάτη στρέφεται άμεσα κατά του νομικού προσώπου του ελληνικού δημοσίου, των νομικών προσώπων δημοσίου δικαίου ή των οργανισμών τοπικής αυτοδιοίκησης και η ζημιά που προκλήθηκε υπερβαίνει συνολικά το ποσό των εκατόν είκοσι χιλιάδων (120.000) ευρώ επιβάλλεται κάθειρξη τουλάχιστον δέκα (10) ετών και χρηματική ποινή έως χίλιες (1.000) ημερήσιες μονάδες. Η πράξη αυτή παραγράφεται μετά είκοσι (20) έτη.

II

CRIMES AGAINST PROPERTY

Article 385

Extortion

1. Any person who, for the purpose of obtaining an unlawful pecuniary gain for themselves or another, uses violence against or threatens another to force them to take, refrain from taking, or tolerate an act resulting in damage to the property of that or another person shall be punished with imprisonment of at least one year and a monetary penalty.

2. If the act provided for in the preceding paragraph was committed using physical violence against a person or threats of imminent danger to the[ir] body or life [of another person] shall be punished in accordance with the provisions of Article 380(1) and (2) of this Code.

3. If the culpable person used violence or threatened to damage the business, occupation, function or other activity of the [victim] or of another person, or offered to provide or does provide protection to prevent such damage being caused by a third party, such extortion shall be punished with imprisonment of at least three years and a monetary penalty. If the above act was perpetrated by a person committing such acts [for monetary gain], incarceration of up to 10 years and a monetary penalty shall be imposed.

Article 386

Fraud

1. Any person who, by knowingly presenting false facts as true or illicitly suppressing or concealing true facts, causes damage to third-party property by persuading another to take, refrain from taking, or tolerate an act for the purpose of obtaining unlawful pecuniary gain for themselves or another through damage to such third-party property shall be punished with imprisonment, and if the damage caused is particularly high, with imprisonment of at least three months and a monetary penalty. If the damage caused exceeds 120,000 euros in total, incarceration of up to 10 years and a monetary penalty shall be imposed.

2. If [any] fraud was committed directly against the Greek State as a legal person, bodies governed by public law or local government authorities and the damage caused exceeds 120,000 euros in total, incarceration of at least 10 years and a monetary penalty of up to 1,000 daily penalty units shall be imposed. Such acts shall become time-barred after 20 years.

Άρθρο 386Α
Απάτη με υπολογιστή

1. Όποιος, με σκοπό να προσπορίσει στον εαυτό του ή σε άλλον παράνομο περιουσιακό όφελος, βλάπτει ξένη περιουσία, επηρεάζοντας το αποτέλεσμα μιας διαδικασίας επεξεργασίας δεδομένων υπολογιστή:

α) με τη μη ορθή διαμόρφωση προγράμματος υπολογιστή,

β) με τη χωρίς δικαίωμα παρέμβαση σε πληροφοριακό σύστημα,

γ) με τη χρησιμοποίηση μη ορθών ή ελλιπών ψηφιακών δεδομένων υπολογιστή, ιδίως δεδομένων αναγνώρισης της ταυτότητας,

δ) με τη χωρίς δικαίωμα εισαγωγή, αλλοίωση, διαγραφή, μετάδοση ή εξάλειψη ορθών ψηφιακών δεδομένων υπολογιστή, ιδίως ψηφιακών δεδομένων αναγνώρισης της ταυτότητας, ή

ε) με τη χωρίς δικαίωμα αξιοποίηση λογισμικού προορισμένου για τη μετακίνηση χρημάτων ή νομισματικής αξίας

τιμωρείται με φυλάκιση, και αν η ζημία που προξενήθηκε είναι ιδιαίτερα μεγάλη, με φυλάκιση τουλάχιστον τριών (3) μηνών και χρηματική ποινή.

Αν η ζημία που προκλήθηκε υπερβαίνει συνολικά το ποσό των εκατόν είκοσι χιλιάδων (120.000) ευρώ, επιβάλλεται κάθειρξη έως δέκα (10) έτη και χρηματική ποινή.

2. Όποιος κατασκευάζει, διαθέτει ή κατέχει πρόγραμμα ή πληροφοριακό σύστημα που προορίζεται για τη διάπραξη του εγκλήματος της παρ. 1 τιμωρείται με φυλάκιση έως δύο (2) έτη και χρηματική ποινή. Απαλλάσσεται από κάθε ποινή όποιος καταστρέφει με δική του θέληση το παραπάνω πρόγραμμα ή πληροφοριακό σύστημα πριν το χρησιμοποιήσει για τη διάπραξη του εγκλήματος της παρ. 1.

3. Αν η απάτη με υπολογιστή στρέφεται άμεσα κατά του νομικού προσώπου του Ελληνικού Δημοσίου, των νομικών προσώπων δημοσίου δικαίου ή των οργανισμών τοπικής αυτοδιοίκησης και η ζημία που προκλήθηκε υπερβαίνει συνολικά το ποσό των εκατόν είκοσι χιλιάδων (120.000) ευρώ, επιβάλλεται κάθειρξη τουλάχιστον δέκα (10) ετών και χρηματική ποινή έως χίλιες (1.000) ημερήσιες μονάδες. Η πράξη αυτή παραγράφεται μετά είκοσι (20) έτη.

Άρθρο 386Β
Απάτη σχετική με τις επιχορηγήσεις

1. Όποιος κατά την υποβολή αιτήματος σε αρχή που είναι αρμόδια για την έγκριση επιχορήγησης εν γνώσει δηλώνει μη ορθά ή ελλιπή στοιχεία ή παραλείπει να γνωστοποιήσει γεγονότα, που προβλέπονται από τον νόμο ή από εκείνον που δίνει την επιχορήγηση βάσει νόμου, εφόσον με τα στοιχεία αυτά εγκρίνεται, παρέχεται ή αποφεύγεται η αξίωση επιστροφής, η επέκταση της παροχής ή η διατήρηση της επιχορήγησης προς τον ίδιο ή τρίτον τιμωρείται, εφόσον το αίτημα ικανοποιήθηκε, με φυλάκιση τουλάχιστον ενός έτους και χρηματική ποινή και αν το ποσό της επιχορήγησης υπερβαίνει συνολικά το ποσό των 120.000 ευρώ επιβάλλεται κάθειρξη έως δέκα έτη και χρηματική ποινή.

2. Όποιος, σε εγκεκριμένη επιχορήγηση, χρησιμοποιεί αντικείμενο ή χρηματική παροχή, των οποίων η χρήση περιορίζεται από νομικές διατάξεις ή από εκείνον που δίνει την επιχορήγηση, κατά παράβαση των περιορισμών αυτών τιμωρείται με φυλάκιση τουλάχιστον ενός έτους και χρηματική ποινή.

Article 386A
Computer fraud

1. Any person who causes damage to third-party property by affecting the results of a computer data processing operation for the purpose of obtaining unlawful pecuniary gain for themselves or another:

a) by improperly configuring a computer program;

b) by interfering, without right, with an information system;

c) by using incorrect or incomplete digital computer data and, in particular, identification data;

d) by, without right, introducing, altering, deleting, transmitting or suppressing correct digital computer data and, in particular, digital identification data; or

e) by, without right, using software intended for the transfer of money or monetary value

shall be punished with imprisonment, and if the damage caused is particularly high, with imprisonment of at least three months and a monetary penalty.

If the damage caused exceeds 120,000 euros in total, incarceration of up to 10 years and a monetary penalty shall be imposed.

2. Any person who manufactures, makes available or possesses a program or information system intended for committing the crime provided for in paragraph 1 shall be punished with imprisonment of up to two years and a monetary penalty. Any person who destroys the aforesaid program or information system of their own volition before using it to commit the crime provided for in paragraph 1 shall not be punished.

3. If [any] computer fraud was committed directly against the Greek State as a legal person, bodies governed by public law or local government authorities and the damage caused exceeds 120,000 euros in total, incarceration of at least 10 years and a monetary penalty of up to 1,000 daily penalty units shall be imposed. Such acts shall become time-barred after 20 years.

Article 386B
Subsidy fraud

1. Any person who, when submitting a request to an authority competent to authorise a subsidy, knowingly declares incorrect or incomplete data or fails to disclose facts required by law or by the person providing the subsidy on the basis of law, provided such data are used to authorise, provide or avoid a recovery claim, the extension of the provision or maintenance of the subsidy to them or a third party shall be punished with imprisonment of at least one year and a monetary penalty if the request was satisfied, and with incarceration of up to 10 years and a monetary penalty if the subsidy amounts exceeds 120,000 euros in total.

2. Any person who, in the context of an authorised subsidy, uses a thing or monetary benefit whose use is restricted under statutory provisions or by the person providing the subsidy in breach of such restrictions shall be punished with imprisonment of at least one year and a monetary penalty.

Άρθρο 387
Απάτη μικρής αξίας

Αν η ζημία που προκλήθηκε από τα εγκλήματα των άρθρων 386 και 386Α είναι μικρής αξίας, εφαρμόζεται η διάταξη του άρθρου 377.

Άρθρο 388

(Καταργείται)

Άρθρο 389
Απατηλή πρόκληση βλάβης

1. Όποιος βλάπτει παράνομα ξένη περιουσία πείθοντας κάποιον με την εν γνώσει παράσταση ψευδών γεγονότων σαν αληθινών ή με αθέμιτη απόκρυψη ή παρασιώπηση των αληθινών σε πράξη, παράλειψη ή ανοχή τιμωρείται με φυλάκιση έως δύο έτη ή χρηματική ποινή.

2. Αν η ζημία που προκλήθηκε είναι μικρής αξίας επιβάλλεται χρηματική ποινή.

Άρθρο 390
Απιστία

1. Όποιος κατά παράβαση των κανόνων επιμελούς διαχείρισης προκαλεί εν γνώσει βέβαιη ζημία στην περιουσία άλλου, της οποίας βάσει νόμου ή δικαιοπραξίας έχει την επιμέλεια ή διαχείριση (ολική ή μερική ή μόνο για ορισμένη πράξη), τιμωρείται με φυλάκιση και αν η ζημία που προξενήθηκε είναι ιδιαίτερα μεγάλη, με φυλάκιση τουλάχιστον τριών (3) μηνών και χρηματική ποινή. Αν η ζημία που προκλήθηκε υπερβαίνει συνολικά το ποσό των εκατόν είκοσι χιλιάδων (120.000) ευρώ επιβάλλεται κάθειρξη έως δέκα (10) έτη και χρηματική ποινή.

2. Αν η απιστία στρέφεται άμεσα κατά του νομικού προσώπου του ελληνικού δημοσίου, των νομικών προσώπων δημοσίου δικαίου ή των οργανισμών τοπικής αυτοδιοίκησης και η ζημία που προκλήθηκε υπερβαίνει συνολικά των ποσό των εκατόν είκοσι χιλιάδων (120.000) ευρώ επιβάλλεται κάθειρξη τουλάχιστον δέκα (10) ετών και χρηματική ποινή έως χίλιες (1.000) ημερήσιες μονάδες. Η πράξη αυτή παραγράφεται μετά είκοσι (20) έτη.

Άρθρα 391 - 393

(Καταργούνται)

Άρθρο 394
Αποδοχή και διάθεση προϊόντων εγκλήματος

1. Όποιος αποκρύπτει, αγοράζει, λαμβάνει ως ενέχυρο ή με άλλον τρόπο δέχεται στην κατοχή του πράγμα που προήλθε από αξιόποινη πράξη ή μεταβιβάζει σε άλλον την κατοχή τέτοιου πράγματος ή συνεργεί σε μεταβίβαση ή με οποιονδήποτε τρόπο ασφαλίζει την κατοχή του σε άλλον, τιμωρείται, ανεξάρτητα αν είναι τιμωρητέος ή όχι ο υπαίτιος του εγκλήματος από το οποίο προέρχεται το πράγμα, με φυλάκιση έως τρία (3) έτη, και αν πρόκειται για πράγμα ιδιαίτερα μεγάλης αξίας με φυλάκιση τουλάχιστον τριών (3) μηνών και χρηματική ποινή.

2. Αν το αντικείμενο της πράξης της προηγούμενης παραγράφου είναι μικρής αξίας, ο δράστης τιμωρείται με χρηματική ποινή.

3. Με τα πράγματα που προέρχονται από αξιόποινη πράξη εξομοιώνεται και το τίμημά τους, καθώς επίσης και τα αντικείμενα που αποκτήθηκαν μέσω αυτών.

4. Όποιος κατέχει κλεμμένο ή παρανόμως ιδιοποιημένο υλικό μέσο πληρωμής πλην των μετρητών, καθώς και όποιος προμηθεύεται ή με οποιονδήποτε άλλον τρόπο ιδιοποιείται κλεμμένο υλικό μέσο πληρωμής πλην των μετρητών, τιμωρείται με φυλάκιση έως τρία (3) έτη και χρηματική ποινή.

Article 387
Fraud [resulting in low-value damage]

If the damage caused by the crimes provided for in Articles 386 and 386A is of low value, the provisions of Article 377 apply.

Article 388

[Repealed]

Article 389
Fraudulently causing damage

1. Any person who, by knowingly presenting false facts as true or unlawfully suppressing or concealing true facts, unlawfully causes damage to third-party property by persuading another to take, refrain from taking, or tolerate an act shall be punished with imprisonment of up to two years or a monetary penalty.
2. If the damage caused is of low value, a monetary penalty shall be imposed.

Article 390
Breach of trust

1. Any person who, in breach of the rules of orderly management, knowingly causes assured damage to another's property in their care or under their management (whether in whole or in part or only for a specific act) on the basis of the law or a legal transaction shall be punished with imprisonment, and if the damage caused is particularly high, with imprisonment of at least three months and a monetary penalty. If the damage caused exceeds 120,000 euros in total, incarceration of up to 10 years and a monetary penalty shall be imposed.
2. If the breach of trust was committed directly against the Greek State as a legal person, bodies governed by public law or local government authorities and the damage caused exceeds 120,000 euros in total, incarceration of at least 10 years and a monetary penalty of up to 1,000 daily penalty units shall be imposed. Such acts shall become time-barred after 20 years.

Articles 391 - 393

[Repealed]

Article 394
Acceptance and making available of proceeds of crime

1. Any person who conceals, purchases, receives as a pledge or otherwise takes into their possession a thing resulting from a punishable act, who transfers possession of such a thing to another person, or who is an accomplice to the transfer [of such a thing], or in any way ensures possession of [that thing] by another person shall be punished, irrespective of whether or not the person who committed the crime in question is to be punished, with imprisonment of up to three years, and if the thing is of particularly high value, with imprisonment of at least three months and a monetary penalty.
2. If the thing the act provided for in the preceding paragraph relates to is of low value, the perpetrator shall be punished with a monetary penalty.
3. The price [achieved by selling] things [obtained as a result of] punishable acts and objects acquired using [such things] shall also be treated as [proceeds of crime].
4. Any person in possession of any stolen or unlawfully appropriated tangible non-cash payment instrument and any person procuring or otherwise appropriating any stolen tangible non-cash payment instrument shall be punished with imprisonment of up to three years and a monetary penalty.

Άρθρο 394Α

Διακεκριμένη αποδοχή και διάθεση προϊόντων εγκλήματος

1. Τα πλημμελήματα των περ. α' έως ε' της παρ. 1 του άρθρου 386Α που αφορούν σε μέσα πληρωμής πλην των μετρητών, καθώς και της παρ. 4 του άρθρου 394, όταν τελούνται στο πλαίσιο εγκληματικής οργάνωσης, τιμωρούνται με ποινή φυλάκισης τουλάχιστον ενός (1) έτους και χρηματική ποινή.

2. Αν το αντικείμενο της πράξης της παρ. 1 του άρθρου 394 προήλθε από την αξιόποινη πράξη της περ. βα' του άρθρου 374, ο δράστης τιμωρείται με κάθειρξη έως δέκα (10) έτη.

Άρθρο 395

Παρακώλυση συναγωνισμού

1. Όποιος σε προκηρύξεις δημοσίων έργων ή προμήθειες του ελληνικού δημοσίου, νομικών προσώπων δημοσίου δικαίου ή οργανισμών τοπικής αυτοδιοίκησης εμποδίζει με εναρμονισμένες πρακτικές ή συμφωνίες μεταξύ επιχειρήσεων, με βία ή απειλές, τον ελεύθερο συναγωνισμό ή απομακρύνει με δώρα ή υποσχέσεις αυτόν που συμμετέχει στη διαδικασία τιμωρείται με φυλάκιση τουλάχιστον τριών ετών και χρηματική ποινή, αν η πράξη δεν τιμωρείται βαρύτερα από άλλη διάταξη.

2. Όποιος σε δημόσιους πλειστηριασμούς εμποδίζει με βία ή με απειλές τον ελεύθερο συναγωνισμό ή απομακρύνει με δώρα ή υποσχέσεις αυτόν που συμμετέχει στη διαδικασία ή έχει την πρόθεση να καταθέσει προσφορά τιμωρείται με φυλάκιση τουλάχιστον ενός έτους και χρηματική ποινή.

Άρθρο 396

Δωροληψία και δωροδοκία στον ιδιωτικό τομέα

1. Με φυλάκιση τουλάχιστον ενός (1) έτους και χρηματική ποινή, τιμωρείται όποιος εργάζεται ή παρέχει υπηρεσίες με οποιαδήποτε ιδιότητα ή σχέση στον ιδιωτικό τομέα και, κατά την άσκηση της επιχειρηματικής δραστηριότητας, ζητεί ή λαμβάνει, άμεσα ή έμμεσα, οποιασδήποτε φύσης αθέμιτο ωφέλημα για τον ίδιο ή για άλλον ή δέχεται υπόσχεση τέτοιου ωφελήματος ως αντάλλαγμα για ενέργεια ή παράλειψή του κατά παράβαση των καθηκόντων του, όπως αυτά διαγράφονται από τον νόμο, ή προκύπτουν από τη φύση της θέσης ή της υπηρεσίας του.

2. Με την ίδια ποινή τιμωρείται και όποιος, κατά την άσκηση επιχειρηματικής δραστηριότητας, υπόσχεται, προσφέρει ή παρέχει, άμεσα ή έμμεσα, οποιασδήποτε φύσης αθέμιτο ωφέλημα σε πρόσωπο που εργάζεται ή παρέχει υπηρεσίες με οποιαδήποτε ιδιότητα στον ιδιωτικό τομέα, για τον ίδιο ή για τρίτον, για ενέργεια ή για παράλειψη κατά παράβαση των ως άνω καθηκόντων του.

2Α. Οι πράξεις των προηγούμενων παραγράφων μένουν ατιμώρητες αν ο υπαίτιος, με δική του θέληση και πριν εξετασθεί ως ύποπτος ή κατηγορούμενος για την πράξη του, την αναγγείλει στον εισαγγελέα πλημμελειοδικών ή σε οποιονδήποτε ανακριτικό υπάλληλο ή άλλη αρμόδια αρχή, εγχειρίζοντας έγγραφη αναφορά ή προφορικά, οπότε συντάσσεται σχετική έκθεση.

3. Η διάταξη του άρθρου 263Α εφαρμόζεται αναλόγως.

Article 394A

Aggravated acceptance and making available of proceeds of crime

1. Where the misdemeanours provided for in Article 386A(1)(a) to (e) concerning non-cash payment instruments and the misdemeanours provided for in Article 394(4) are committed in the context of a criminal organisation, imprisonment of at least one year and a monetary penalty shall be imposed.
2. If the object of the act provided for in Article 394(1) resulted from the punishable act provided for in Article 374[1](ba), the perpetrator shall be punished with incarceration of up to 10 years.

Article 395

Impeding competition

1. Any person who, in the context of public works notices [issued by] or procurement procedures [held] by the Greek State, legal bodies governed by public law or local government authorities, uses concerted practices or agreements between undertakings, violence or threats to impede free competition or uses gifts or promises [to persuade] a tenderer to withdraw from the procedure shall be punished with imprisonment of at least three years and a monetary penalty, unless the act carries a heavier punishment under a different provision.
2. Any person who, in the context of a public auction, uses violence or threats to impede [participants from freely competing with each other] or uses gifts or promises [to persuade] a person participating in the auction or intending to submit a bid to withdraw from the auction shall be punished with imprisonment of at least one year and a monetary penalty.

Article 396

Passive and active bribery in the private sector

1. Any person who works or provides services in any capacity or under any relationship in the private sector and, while carrying on business activities, requests or receives, whether directly or indirectly, any kind of undue advantage for themselves or another or accepts a promise of such advantage in exchange for any act or omission on their part in breach of their duties, as prescribed in law or arising from the nature of their post or service, shall be punished with imprisonment of at least one year and a monetary penalty.
2. The same punishment shall also be imposed on any person who, while carrying on business activities, promises, offers or provides, whether directly or indirectly, any kind of undue advantage to a person working or providing services in any capacity in the private sector for that person or for a third party [in exchange] for any act or omission in breach of such duties.
2A. The acts provided for in the preceding paragraphs shall not be punished if the culpable person, of their own volition and before being examined as a suspect or accused person or defendant in relation to their act, reports it to the court of misdemeanours public prosecutor or any investigating officer or other competent authority by means of a written report or verbally, in which case a report shall be prepared.
3. The provisions of Article 263A apply *mutatis mutandis*.

Άρθρο 397
Καταδολίευση δανειστών

1. Ο οφειλέτης ο οποίος εν γνώσει ματαιώνει ολικά ή εν μέρει την ικανοποίηση του δανειστή του εκποιώντας ή αποκρύπτοντας στοιχεία της περιουσίας του τιμωρείται με φυλάκιση έως δύο έτη ή χρηματική ποινή.

2. Με την ποινή της προηγούμενης παραγράφου τιμωρείται και ο οφειλέτης ο οποίος εν γνώσει ματαιώνει ολικά ή εν μέρει την ικανοποίηση του δανειστή του που έχει σε βάρος του βέβαιη και εκκαθαρισμένη απαίτηση, αν ενόψει της επικείμενης εκπλήρωσης της υποχρέωσής του:

α) βλάπτει, καταστρέφει, καθιστά χωρίς αξία, αποκρύπτει ή απαλλοτριώνει χωρίς ισότιμο και αξιόχρεο αντάλλαγμα οποιοδήποτε περιουσιακό του στοιχείο ή

β) κατασκευάζει ψεύτικα χρέη ή ψεύτικες δικαιοπραξίες.

3. Με φυλάκιση τουλάχιστον δύο ετών και χρηματική ποινή τιμωρούνται οι πράξεις των προηγούμενων παραγράφων αν η περιουσιακή ζημία που προκλήθηκε στον δανειστή είναι ιδιαίτερα μεγάλη.

4. Οι ποινές των προηγούμενων παραγράφων επιβάλλονται και σε εκείνον που επιχειρεί τις πράξεις υπέρ του οφειλέτη.

Άρθρο 398
Αλιεία στην αιγιαλίτιδα ζώνη και τα εσωτερικά ύδατα

Όποιος ασκεί αλιευτική δραστηριότητα με σκάφος ή άλλο πλωτό μέσο που φέρει σημαία τρίτης χώρας, χωρίς την προβλεπόμενη κατά τις οικείες διατάξεις άδεια της αρμόδιας αρχής, εντός της αιγιαλίτιδας ζώνης και των εσωτερικών υδάτων της Ελληνικής Επικράτειας, τιμωρείται με φυλάκιση.

Άρθρα 399 - 403

(Καταργούνται)

Άρθρο 404
Τοκογλυφία

1. Όποιος σε δικαιοπραξία για την παροχή οποιασδήποτε πίστωσης, ανανέωσής της ή παράταση της προθεσμίας πληρωμής εκμεταλλεύεται την οικονομική ανάγκη, την πνευματική αδυναμία, την κουφότητα ή την απειρία εκείνου που παίρνει την πίστωση, συνομολογώντας ή παίρνοντας για τον εαυτό του ή για τρίτον περιουσιακά ωφελήματα, που με βάση τις ειδικές περιστάσεις είναι προφανώς δυσανάλογα προς την παροχή του υπαιτίου ή συνομολογεί ή παίρνει για τον εαυτό του ή για τρίτον περιουσιακά ωφελήματα που υπερβαίνουν το κατά τον νόμο θεμιτό ποσοστό τόκου τιμωρείται με φυλάκιση τουλάχιστον έξι (6) μηνών και χρηματική ποινή. Αν η πράξη έχει τελεστεί με περισσότερους τρόπους αφορά όμως τα ίδια περιουσιακά ωφελήματα, στον υπαίτιο επιβάλλεται μία μόνο ποινή, κατά την επιμέτρηση της οποίας λαμβάνεται υπόψη η συνολική εγκληματική δράση του.

2. Αν ο υπαίτιος επιχειρεί κατ' επάγγελμα τις τοκογλυφικές πράξεις της παρ. 1 τιμωρείται με κάθειρξη έως οκτώ (8) έτη και χρηματική ποινή.

Article 397
Defrauding creditors

1. Any debtor who knowingly prevents, whether in whole or in part, the satisfaction of their creditor['s claim] by selling or concealing assets shall be punished with imprisonment of up to two years or a monetary penalty.

2. The punishment laid down in the preceding paragraph shall also be imposed on any debtor who knowingly prevents, whether in whole or in part, the satisfaction of their creditor's specific claim for a fixed amount if, in view of the impending performance of their obligation, they:

a) prejudice, destroy, render worthless, conceal or alienate any asset without good and valuable consideration; or

b) fabricate false debts or false legal transactions.

3. The acts provided for in the preceding paragraphs shall be punished with imprisonment of at least two years and a monetary penalty if the pecuniary damage caused to the creditor is particularly high.

4. The punishments laid down in the preceding paragraphs shall also be imposed on any person attempting [such] acts to benefit the debtor.

Article 398
Fishing in the territorial sea and inland waters [of Greece]

Any person who, on a vessel or other floating craft flying the flag of a third country, engages in fishing activities without the authorisation of the competent authority, as provided for in the relevant provisions, within the territorial sea and inland waters of the territory of Greece shall be punished with imprisonment.

Articles 399 - 403

[Repealed]

Article 404
Usury

1. Any person who, in the context of a legal transaction to provide or renew any credit or extend its payment deadline, exploits the financial [hardship], intellectual weakness, imprudence or inexperience of the person receiving the credit by stipulating or acquiring, whether for themselves or another, pecuniary gains which, under the specific circumstances, are clearly disproportionate to the [credit provided] by the culpable person, or who stipulates or acquires, whether for themselves or another, pecuniary gains which exceed the interest rate allowed by law shall be punished with imprisonment of at least six months and a monetary penalty. If the act was committed in [various other] ways but concerns the same pecuniary gains, only one punishment shall be imposed on the culpable person, [but] their overall criminal activities shall be taken into consideration when determining the extent of the punishment.

2. If the culpable person commits the usurious acts provided for in paragraph 1 [for monetary gain], they shall be punished with incarceration of up to eight years and a monetary penalty.

Άρθρο 405
Γενική Διάταξη

1. Για την ποινική δίωξη των εγκλημάτων που προβλέπονται στα άρθρα 387 και 389, στο πρώτο εδάφιο της παρ. 1 του άρθρου 390, στο άρθρο 397 και στην παρ. 1 του άρθρου 404 απαιτείται έγκληση.

2. Το αξιόποινο των εγκλημάτων που προβλέπονται στο άρθρο 386, στις παρ. 1 και 3 του άρθρου 386Α και στα άρθρα 386Β, 387, 389, 390, 394, 397 και 404 εξαλείφεται αν ο υπαίτιος, με δική του θέληση και πριν από την πρώτη εξέτασή του ως υπόπτου ή κατηγορουμένου ικανοποιήσει εντελώς τον ζημιωθέντα χωρίς παράνομη βλάβη τρίτου. Η μερική μόνο ικανοποίηση εξαλείφει το αξιόποινο κατά το αντίστοιχο μόνο μέρος.

3. Εάν ο υπαίτιος των πλημμελημάτων της παρ. 2 μέχρι το τέλος της αποδεικτικής διαδικασίας στο πρωτοβάθμιο δικαστήριο ικανοποιήσει εντελώς τον ζημιωθέντα, καταβάλλοντας αποδεδειγμένα, ιδίως ενώπιον δημόσιας αρχής ή με τραπεζική κατάθεση ή με μη ανακλητή δημόσια παρακατάθεση, το κεφάλαιο και τους τόκους υπερημερίας, από την ημέρα τέλεσης του εγκλήματος, μπορεί να απαλλάσσεται από κάθε ποινή.

4. Εάν ο υπαίτιος των κακουργημάτων που προβλέπονται στην παρ. 2, μέχρι το τέλος της αποδεικτικής διαδικασίας στο πρωτοβάθμιο δικαστήριο ικανοποιήσει πλήρως τον ζημιωθέντα, καταβάλλοντας αποδεδειγμένα, ιδίως ενώπιον δημόσιας αρχής ή με τραπεζική κατάθεση ή με μη ανακλητή δημόσια παρακατάθεση, το κεφάλαιο και τους τόκους υπερημερίας, από την ημέρα τέλεσης του εγκλήματος, τιμωρείται με μειωμένη ποινή κατά το άρθρο 83 και εφόσον κριθεί από τις περιστάσεις, αν η πλήρης ικανοποίηση λάβει χώρα μέχρι την αμετάκλητη παραπομπή, μπορεί να απαλλαγεί από κάθε ποινή.

Άρθρα 406 - 459

(Καταργούνται)

Article 405
General provision

1. A victim-initiated complaint is required to institute criminal prosecution against the crimes provided for in Articles 387 and 389, the first sentence of Article 390(1), Article 397 and Article 404(1).

2. The punishability of the crimes provided for in Articles 386, 386A(1) and (3) and 386B, 387, 389, 390, 394, 397 and 404 shall be extinguished if the culpable person, of their own volition and before being first examined as a suspect or accused person or defendant, provides complete satisfaction to the victim, without unlawful damage to a third party. Partial satisfaction only expunges punishability up to the corresponding part.

3. If the person who committed [any] of the misdemeanours provided for in paragraph 2 provides complete satisfaction to the victim by the end of the taking of evidence at first instance by demonstrably paying, particularly in the presence of a public authority or via bank deposit or irrevocable public permanent deposit, the principal and default interest from the date the crime was committed, they may be exempted from all punishment.

4. If the person who committed [any] of the felonies provided for in paragraph 2 provides full satisfaction to the victim by the end of the taking of evidence at first instance by demonstrably paying, particularly in the presence of a public authority or via bank deposit or irrevocable public permanent deposit, the principal and default interest from the date the crime was committed, they shall receive a reduced punishment under Article 83 and, if deemed necessary under the circumstances, where just satisfaction occurred before the perpetrator was irrevocably committed to trial, they may be exempted from all punishment.

Articles 406 - 459

[Repealed]

ΤΡΙΤΟ ΒΙΒΛΙΟ

ΜΕΤΑΒΑΤΙΚΕΣ ΔΙΑΤΑΞΕΙΣ

Άρθρο 460

Ο παρών Ποινικός Κώδικας αρχίζει να ισχύει από την 1η Ιουλίου 2019.

Άρθρο 461

Από την έναρξη ισχύος του παρόντος Ποινικού Κώδικα καταργείται ο Ποινικός Κώδικας που ισχύει από την 1η Ιανουαρίου 1951, καθώς και κάθε διάταξη που τροποποιούσε τον νόμο αυτόν.

Άρθρο 462

Από την έναρξη ισχύος του παρόντος Ποινικού Κώδικα καταργείται ο νόμος 1608/1950 που ισχύει από την 1η Ιανουαρίου 1951, καθώς και κάθε διάταξη που τροποποιούσε το νόμο αυτό.

Άρθρο 463

(Καταργείται)

Άρθρο 464

Εκκρεμείς ποινικές διαδικασίες, που έχουν ανοίξει χωρίς την υποβολή εγκλήσεως με αντικείμενο πράξεις για την δίωξη των οποίων απαιτείται έγκληση στον παρόντα Κώδικα ενώ διώκονταν αυτεπαγγέλτως υπό το προϊσχύσαν δίκαιο, συνεχίζονται, εφόσον ο δικαιούμενος να υποβάλει έγκληση δηλώσει εντός τεσσάρων μηνών από την έναρξη της ισχύος του παρόντος ότι επιθυμεί την πρόοδό τους.

Άρθρο 465

1. Οι διατάξεις του προϊσχύσαντος Ποινικού Κώδικα για τη μετατροπή της ποινής σε χρηματική ποινή, την αναστολή εκτέλεσης της ποινής και την απόλυση υπό όρο εφαρμόζονται για πράξεις που τελέστηκαν μέχρι τη θέση σε ισχύ του παρόντος. Σε περίπτωση αρχικής ή επιγενόμενης συρροής χρηματικής ποινής του άρθρου 80 του προϊσχύοντος Ποινικού Κώδικα με χρηματική ποινή του άρθρου 57 ΠΚ ή ειδικών ποινικών νόμων που εξακολουθούν να ισχύουν, σχηματίζεται συνολική ποινή κατά το άρθρο 96 ΠΚ.

2. Για τους μέχρι την έναρξη ισχύος του νέου Ποινικού Κώδικα [ν. 4619/2019 (Α' 95)] καταδικασθέντες αμετακλήτως σε πρόσκαιρες στερητικές της ελευθερίας ποινές, για τις οποίες καθορίστηκε, σύμφωνα με τις παρ. 1 και 2 του άρθρου 94 ΠΚ, συνολική ποινή υπερβαίνουσα τα είκοσι (20) ή δεκαπέντε (15) έτη πρόσκαιρης κάθειρξης, καθώς και τα οχτώ (8) ή πέντε (5) έτη φυλάκισης αντίστοιχα, ως εκτιτέα ποινή για την απόλυση υπό όρο αυτών λογίζονται τα είκοσι (20), δεκαπέντε (15), οχτώ (8) και πέντε (5) έτη, αντίστοιχα.

3. (Καταργείται)

4. Υποθέσεις, για τις οποίες μέχρι την έναρξη ισχύος του παρόντος έχει γίνει επίδοση κλητήριου θεσπίσματος ή κλήσης στον κατηγορούμενο, εκδικάζονται από το δικαστήριο στο οποίο έχουν εισαχθεί.

BOOK III

TRANSITIONAL PROVISIONS

Article 460

This Code shall enter into force on 1 July 2019.

Article 461

As of the entry of this Code into force, the Penal Code which entered into force on 1 January 1951 and any provision amending the law [ratifying that Code] is repealed.

Article 462

As of the entry of this Code into force, Law 1608/1950 which entered into force on 1 January 1951 and any provision amending that law is repealed.

Article 463

[Repealed]

Article 464

Any pending criminal procedure which was instituted without a victim-initiated complaint in relation to an act whose criminal prosecution requires a victim-initiated complaint under this Code, whereas it was subject to public prosecution under the law previously in force, shall be continued if the person entitled to file a complaint declares, within four months from the date this Code enters into force, that they wish the procedure to continue.

Article 465

1. The provisions of the Penal Code previously in force on commutation of sentences to a monetary penalty, stay of enforcement of penalties and conditional release apply to acts committed before this Code entered into force. In the case of initial or subsequent concurrence of a monetary penalty under Article 80 of the Penal Code previously in force with a monetary penalty under Article 57 of this Code or specific penal laws which remain in force, an overall punishment shall be determined in accordance with Article 96 of this Code.

2. With regard to persons who, before the new Penal Code (Law 4619/2019, Government Gazette, Series I, Issue 95) [entered into force], were irrevocably convicted to custodial sentences for which, in accordance with Article 94(1) and (2), a total sentence of fixed-term incarceration over 20 or 15 years or of imprisonment of 8 or 5 years was set, the sentence to be served in order for them to be granted conditional release is 20, 15, 8 and 5 years, respectively.

3. [Repealed]

4. Cases for which a summons or writ of summons was served on the defendant before the entry of this Code into force shall be tried by the court before which they were brought for trial.

Άρθρο 466

Σε περίπτωση εξάλειψης του αξιοποίνου, λόγω παραγραφής, εγκλημάτων που ο χαρακτήρας τους μεταβλήθηκε από κακούργημα σε πλημμέλημα κατ' εφαρμογήν των διατάξεων του παρόντος Κώδικα, δεν επηρεάζονται οι αστικές αξιώσεις του παθόντος.

Άρθρο 467

Για εκκρεμείς υποθέσεις, στις οποίες συμπληρώνεται ο χρόνος παραγραφής κατ' εφαρμογή των άρθρων 111 επ., την παύση της ποινικής δίωξης μπορεί να διατάσσει, με σύμφωνη γνώμη του εισαγγελέα εφετών, ο αρμόδιος εισαγγελέας πλημμελειοδικών, θέτοντας τη δικογραφία στο αρχείο.

Άρθρο 468

Τα πταίσματα καταργούνται. Εκκρεμείς υποθέσεις τίθενται στο αρχείο με πράξη του κατά τόπον αρμόδιου εισαγγελέα πλημμελειοδικών.

Άρθρο 469

(Καταργείται)

Άρθρο δεύτερο

Ο παρών νόμος αρχίζει να ισχύει από την 1η Ιουλίου 2019.

Παραγγέλλομε τη δημοσίευση του παρόντος στην Εφημερίδα της Κυβερνήσεως και την εκτέλεσή του ως νόμου του Κράτους.

Article 466

Where the punishability of crimes whose classification was changed from a felony to a misdemeanour pursuant to the provisions of this Code is extinguished due to time-barring, the victim's civil claims are not affected.

Article 467

In pending cases where the time-barring period ends pursuant to Articles 111 *et seq.*, the competent court of misdemeanours public prosecutor may, with the assent of the court of appeal public prosecutor, order discontinuation of the criminal prosecution and place the case on file.

Article 468

Petty offences are abolished. Pending cases shall be placed on file pursuant to a [decision] of the locally competent court of misdemeanours public prosecutor.

Article 469

[Repealed]

Second Article

This Law shall enter into force on 1 July 2019.

This Law shall be published in the Government Gazette and enforced as a law of the State.

How to Use the Glossaries

As you can see, our glossaries contain three columns: the first contains the source term, the second the translation, and the third either makes references to other Articles of this Code or other relevant Codes; it may also contain an exhortation to consult the Foreword where we discuss issues that arose in the choice of term and the translation solutions provided. The references to Articles are primarily used when a single source term is rendered in different ways within the Code because the context in each Article mentioned is different. References to Articles in other Codes are used because either the term also appears there, or the content that appears there is relevant as well, or because the term has been rendered differently there because the context is different.

Greek to English Glossary

EL	EN	Notes
Αγγελία	Advertisement	
Αγκτηριασμός	Infibulation	
Αγροτική έκταση	Farmland	
Άδεια	Authorisation	See 2010 Convention on Enforced Disappearance
Άδεια (κρατούμενου)	Furlough	
Άδεια εκμετάλλευσης μεταφορικού μέσου	Licence to operate a means of transport	
Άδεια οδήγησης	Driving licence	
Αδέρφι / Αδερφός / Αδελφός	Sibling	
Άδικος χαρακτήρας (πράξης)	Wrongfulness	
Αδύναμο άτομο/πρόσωπο	Person unable to defend themselves	
Αεροσκάφος	Aircraft	
Αθέμιτη επιρροή	Undue influence	
Αθέμιτο ωφέλημα	Undue advantage	
Αθώωση	Acquittal	
Αιγιαλίτιδα ζώνη	Territorial sea	
Αιμομιξία	Incest	
Αίτημα	Request	
Αίτηση	Application	
Αιτιολόγηση	Reasoning	
Ακάθαρτα ύδατα	Wastewater	
Ακαταδίωκτο	Non-prosecution	
Ακίνητο	Immovable	
Ακολασία	Debauchery	
Ακρωτηριασμός γυναικείων γεννητικών οργάνων	Female genital mutilation	See Article 315
Ακρωτηριασμός	Amputation	See Article 310
Ακτινοβολία	Radiation	

Αλιεία	Fishing	
Αλλοδαπή	Abroad	
Αλλοδαπή απόφαση	Judgment handed down by a foreign court	
Αλλοδαπός	Foreign national	
Αλλοίωση (δεδομένων)	Alteration	
Άλσος	Woods	
Αμέλεια	Negligence	
Άμεσος συνεργός	Direct accomplice	
Αμετάκλητη απόφαση	Irrevocable judgment	
Αμετάκλητος	Irrevocable	
Αμνηστία	Amnesty	
Αμοιβή	Reward	
Άμυνα	Defence	
Αμφιθαλής αδελφός	Full sibling	
Αναβολή (δίκης)	Adjournment	
Αναβολή (ποινικής δίωξης)	Deferral	
Αναγκαστική εκτέλεση	Compulsory enforcement	
Ανάγκες διαβίωσης	Subsistence needs	
Αναγνώριση (απόφασης)	Recognition	
Αναδασωτέα (έκταση)	Reforestable	
Ανάδοχη οικογένεια	Foster family	
Ανάδοχο τέκνο	Foster child	
Ανάδοχος γονέας	Foster parent	
Αναδρομική ισχύς	Retroactive effect	
Αναισθησιολόγος	Anaesthesiologist	
Ανάκληση	Withdrawal Revocation Retraction	See Article 117 See Article 101 See Article 186(3)
Ανάκληση (κατάθεσης)	Recantation	
Ανάκριση	Investigation	
Ανακριτής	Investigating magistrate	
Ανακριτικός υπάλληλος	Investigating officer	
Ανάλωση	Consumption	

Ανάμειξη	Mixture/Intermixture	See Civil Code, Articles 1059-1060 See Foreword
Αναμορφωτικό μέτρο	Reformative measure	
Αναπηρία	Disability	
Αναπληρωματική δήμευση	Substitute confiscation	
Ανάρμοστη πράξη	Inappropriate act	
Ανασταλτική δύναμη	Suspensive effect	See Foreword
Αναστέλλουσα ισχύς	Suspensive effect	See Foreword
Αναστολή (εκτέλεσης ποινής)	Stay (of enforcement)	
Αναστολή (παραγραφής)	Suspension	
Αναστολή (ποινικής δίωξης από Υπουργό)	Suspension	
Ανατέμνω	To dissect	
Ανατομή	Dissection	
Αναφορά	Report	
Ανεπανόρθωτη βλάβη	Irreparable damage	
Ανεύρεση	Discovery	
Ανήλικος	Juvenile	
Ανησυχία	Apprehension	See Article 333
Ανθρώπινη αξιοπρέπεια	Human dignity	
Ανθρωποκτονία	Homicide	
Ανθρωποκτονία από αμέλεια	Negligent homicide	
Ανίατη ασθένεια	Incurable disease	
Ανιθαγενής	Stateless	
Ανικανότητα αντίστασης	Incapacibility of resisting	
Ανικανότητα δικαιοπραξίας	Lack of capacity to enter into legal transactions	
Ανιχνευτής αλήθειας	Polygraph	
Ανοχή	Tolerance	
Αντάλλαγμα	Consideration	
Αντιγραφή	Copying	
Αντικείμενο	Object	
Αντιποίηση	Impersonation	
Αντίποινα	Retaliation	
Αντίσταση	Resistance	
Αντισυνταγματικός	Unconstitutional	

Ανυπακοή	Disobedience	See Article 183 See Foreword
Ανυποταξία	Insubordination	
Αξιόποινο	Punishability	
Αξιόποινος	Punishable	
Αξιοπρέπεια	Dignity	
Αξιωματικός	Officer	
Αξίωση (απαγωγέα)	Demand	
Αξίωση επιστροφής	Recovery claim	
Απαγόρευση	Prohibition	
Απαγόρευση εξόδου από χώρα	Ban on exiting the country	
Απαγόρευση προσέγγισης και επικοινωνίας	Restraining order	
Απαγωγή	Abduction	
Απαίτηση	Claim	
Απαλλαγή (από ποινή)	Exemption	See Article 187C(1)
Απάτη	Fraud	
Απάτη με υπολογιστή	Computer fraud	
Απάτη σχετική με τις επιχορηγήσεις	Subsidy fraud	
Απείθεια	Disobedience	See Article 169 See Foreword
Απειλή	Threat	
Απειλή βίας	Threat of violence	
Απειρία	Inexperience	
Απέλαση	Deportation	
Απιστία	Breach of fiduciary duty	
Απλός συνεργός	Simple accomplice	
Αποδεικτική διαδικασία	Taking of evidence	
Αποδεικτικό μέσο	Evidence	
Απόδοση (πράγματος)	Surrender	
Αποδοχή	Acceptance	
Αποδοχή και διάθεση προϊόντων εγκλήματος	Acceptance and making available of proceeds of a crime	
Αποζημίωση	Compensation	
Αποκατάσταση (ζημίας)	Restitution	
Αποκήρυξη	Denouncement	

Αποκλεισμός πρόσβασης	Preclusion of access	
Απολυόμενος / Αποφυλακιζόμενος	Released person	
Απομίμηση	Imitation	
Απομόνωση	Isolation	
Απονομή δικαιοσύνης	Administration of justice	
Απόπειρα	Attempt	
Αποπλάνηση	Enticement	See Article 304
Απορία	Poverty	See Foreword
Αποσιώπηση	Concealment	See Article 254
Απόσπαση	Secondment	
Αποστέρηση (θέσεων και αξιωμάτων)	Forfeiture of posts and offices	
Αποτροπή	Prevention	
Αποτύπωση	Imprinting	
Αποχέτευση (ομβρίων, ακαθάρτων υδάτων)	Drainage	
Απρόσφορη απόπειρα	Impossible attempt	
Απώλεια δεδομένων	Loss of data	
Άρθρο	Article	
Αρπαγή	Unlawfully depriving another of their freedom	
Αρπαγή ανηλίκου	Child abduction	
Άρση απόλυσης	Termination of release	
Αρχή	Authority	
Αρχή της αναλογικότητας	Principle of proportionality	
Αρχή της επικουρικότητας	Principle of subsidiarity	
Αρχηγός κράτους	Head of state	
Αρχής Διασφάλισης του Απορρήτου των Επικοινωνιών	Hellenic Authority for Communication Security and Privacy	
Ασθένεια	Illness Disease	See Article 105(2) See Article 285
Αστική αξίωση	Civil claim	
Αστυνομικές δυνάμεις	Police forces	
Αστυνομική υπηρεσία	Police facility	
Αστυνομικό τμήμα	Police department	
Αστυνομικός υπάλληλος	Police officer	

Ασφάλεια του κράτους	State security	
Ασφαλής προορισμός	Safe destination	
Ασφαλιστική εγκατάσταση	Safety apparatus	
Ασφαλιστική επιχείρηση	Insurance company	
Ατομικό δικαίωμα	Civil right	
Άυλος	Intangible	
Αυτεπαγγέλτως	*Ex officio*	
Αυτοδικία	Self-redress	
Αυτοδιοίκηση	Local government	
Αυτοκινητόδρομος	Motorway	
Αυτοκτονία	Suicide	
Αυτοσχέδιος αγώνας	Street racing	
Αυτουργός	Perpetrator	See Article 21
Άφαντος	Absentee	See Civil Code, Articles 40-50
Άφεση	Forgiveness	
Βαριά παράβαση (καθήκοντος)	Gross breach of duty	
Βαριά σωματική βλάβη	Grievous bodily harm	
Βαρύτερη ποινή	More severe penalty	
Βαρύτητα	Severity	
Βασανιστήρια	Torture	
Βέβαιη και εκκαθαρισμένη απαίτηση	Specific claim for a fixed amount	
Βεβαίωση	Confirmation	See Article 80; see Code of Criminal Procedure, Article 553
Βεγγαλικά	Fireworks	
Βία	Violence	
Βίαιη εξαφάνιση	Enforced disappearance	
Βιαιοπραγία	Assault	
Βιασμός	Rape	
Βιβλίο	Book	
Βιολογικό υλικό	Biological agent	
Βιοτικές συνθήκες	Life circumstances	
Βοηθός	Assistant	

Βόμβα	Bomb	
Βούλευμα	Judicial council decision	
Βουλή	Parliament	
Βρύση	Drinking fountain	
Βύθιση	Sinking	
Γάμος	Marriage	
Γενεαλογικές καταβολές	Genealogical descent	
Γενετήσια αξιοπρέπεια	Sexual dignity	
Γενετήσια διέγερση	Sexual arousal	
Γενετήσια ελευθερία	Sexual freedom	
Γενετήσια ευπρέπεια	Sexual decency	
Γενετήσια ζωή	Sexual life	
Γενετήσια πράξη	Sexual act	
Γενετήσιος προσανατολισμός	Sexual orientation	
Γενική άδεια	General authorisation	
Γενική Γραμματεία Πολιτικής Προστασίας	General Secretariat for Civil Protection	
Γενικό μέρος (ΠΚ)	General Part	
Γενικό νοσοκομείο	General hospital	
Γέννηση	Birth	
Γεννητικά όργανα	Genitals	
Γνήσιο υπογραφής	Authenticity of signature	
Γνήσιος	Genuine	
Γονέας	Parent	
Γονική μέριμνα	Parental responsibility	
Γυμναστής	Trainer	
Γυναικολόγος	Gynaecologist	
Δανειστής	Creditor	
Δασική έκταση	Forested area	
Δασμός	Duty	See Article 244
Δάσος	Forest	
Δασωτέα (έκταση)	Afforestable	
Δεδομένα	Data	
Δεδομένα αναγνώρισης της ταυτότητας	Identification data	
Δεδομένα προσωπικού χαρακτήρα	Personal data	

Δείκτης επικινδυνότητας	Risk index	
Δεξαμενή νερού	Reservoir	
Δέσμευση (περιουσιακών στοιχείων)	Freezing	
Δηλητηρίαση	Poisoning	
Δήμαρχος	Mayor	
Δήμευση	Confiscation	
Δημοκρατικό πολίτευμα	Democratic system of government	
Δήμος	Municipality	
Δημόσια ασφάλεια	Public security	See Article 72
Δημόσια τάξη	Public order	
Δημοσίευση	Publication	
Δημόσιο έργο	Public works	
Δημόσιο λειτούργημα	Public function	
Δημόσιο οίκημα	Public building	
Δημόσιο συμφέρον	Public interest	
Δημόσιο ψυχιατρείο	State psychiatric hospital	
Δημοσιογράφος	Journalist	
Δημόσιος εκπρόσωπος	Public representative	
Δημόσιος πλειστηριασμός	Public auction	
Δημόσιος τομέας	Public sector	
Δημόσιος τόπος	Public place	
Δημοψήφισμα	Referendum	
Διαβίβαση (δεδομένων)	Transmission	
Διαγραφή (δεδομένων)	Deletion	
Διαγωγή	Conduct	
Διαδικασία αποκαταστατικής δικαιοσύνης	Restorative justice process	
Διάδικος	Party in proceedings / Litigant	
Διαδίκτυο	Internet	
Διάδοση	Dissemination	
Διαιτησία	Arbitration	
Διαιτητής	Arbitrator	
Διαιτητική απόφαση	Arbitration award	
Διακεκριμένη κλοπή	Aggravated theft	
Διακεκριμένη περίπτωση (εγκλήματος)	Aggravated case	

Διακίνηση (αγαθών)	To make (goods) available	See Article 7 of Directive 2013/40/EU
Διακοπή κύησης	Termination of pregnancy	
Διάκριση των λειτουργιών	Separations of powers	
Διακυβέρνηση	Governance	
Διαμεσολάβηση	Mediation	See Article 169
Διαμόρφωση (προγράμματος υπολογιστή)	Configuration	
Διανοητική αναπηρία	Mental disability	
Διανοητική ασθένεια	Mental illness	See Article 348A(4)(b)
Διανοητική διαταραχή	Emotional disorder	
Διάνοια	Intellect	
Διανομή	Distribution	
Διαπίστευση	Accreditation	
Διαπραγμάτευση	Negotiation	
Διάπραξη	Commission	See Foreword
Διάσκεψη (συμβουλίου)	Deliberations	
Διασπορά ψευδών ειδήσεων	Spreading of false news	
Διατακτικό	Operative part of a judgment	
Διάταξη	Provision	
Διαταράξη (οικολογική, περιβαλλοντική)	Disruption	
Διατάραξη της κοινής ειρήνης	Breach of the public peace	
Διατάραξη υπηρεσιών	Disruption of services	
Διατροφή	Maintenance	
Διατύπωση	Formality	
Διαφεύγω	To abscond	
Διαχειριστής ξένης περιουσίας	Manager of another person's assets	See Civil Code, Articles 730-740
Διγαμία	Bigamy	
Διέγερση	Incitement	
Διεθνείς σχέσεις	International relations	
Διεθνής οργανισμός	International organisation	
Διεθνής προστασία	International protection	
Διερμηνέας	Interpreter	
Διερμηνεία	Interpretation	
Διεύθυνση Αντιμετώπισης Ειδικών Εγκλημάτων Βίας	Special Violent Crime Squad	

Διεύθυνση Αντιμετώπισης Οργανωμένου Εγκλήματος	Organised Crime Directorate	
Διευθυντής επιχείρηση	Manager of an enterprise	
Δικαιοδοσία	Jurisdiction	
Δικαιοπραξία	Legal transaction	
Δικαιούχος	Beneficiary	
Δικαίωμα υπεράσπισης	Right of defence	
Δικάσιμος	Hearing date	
Δικαστήριο	Court	
Δικαστήριο ανηλίκων	Juvenile court	
Δικαστήριο εκτέλεσης ποινής/ποινών	Sentence enforcement court	
Δικαστήριο που δικάζει υπόθεση / Δικάζον δικαστήριο	Trial court	
Δικαστήριο της Ευρωπαϊκής Ένωσης	Court of Justice of the European Union	
Δικαστής	Judge	
Δικαστικά έξοδα	Court costs	See Article 244
Δικαστικές δαπάνες	Court costs	See Article 104
Δικαστική απόφαση	Court judgment	
Δικαστική άφεση ποινής	Judicial forgiveness of penalties	
Δικαστική λειτουργία	Judiciary	
Δικαστική συμπαράσταση	Legal guardianship	
Δικαστικό απόρρητο	Judicial secrecy	
Δικαστικό συμβούλιο	Judicial council	See Article 76(1)
Δικαστικός λειτουργός	Judicial functionary	
Δικαστικός υπάλληλος	Court clerk	
Δίκη	Proceedings	
Δικηγόρος	Lawyer	
Διοικητική δίκη	Administrative proceedings	
Διπλωματικό απόρρητο	Diplomatic secrecy	
Διπλωματικός αντιπρόσωπος	Diplomatic envoy	
Διχόνοια	Discord	
Δίωξη	Prosecution	
Δόλια χρήση	Fraudulent use	
Δόλος	*Dolus*	

Δόση	Instalment	
Δουλεία	Slavery	
Δράστης	Perpetrator	See Article 27
Δρόμος	Road	
Δυστύχημα	Serious accident	
Δυσφήμηση	Defamation	
Δωρεά	Donation	
Δώρο	Gift	
Δωροδοκία	Active bribery	
Δωροληψία	Passive bribery	
Δωροληψία και δωροδοκία στον ιδιωτικό τομέα	Passive and active bribery in the private sector	
Έγγραφο	Document	
Έγκλημα	Crime	
Έγκλημα γενικής διακινδύνευσης	Crime of general endangerment	
Έγκλημα διωκώμενο αυτεπάγγελτα	Crime subject to public prosecution	
Έγκλημα κατ' εξακολούθηση	Crime committed repeatedly	
Έγκλημα κατά της γενετήσιας ελευθερίας	Crime against sexual freedom	
Έγκλημα κατά της δημόσιας τάξης	Crime against public order	
Έγκλημα κατά της ζωής	Crime against life	
Έγκλημα κατά της σωματικής ακεραιότητας	Crime against physical integrity	
Έγκλημα με ρατσιστικά χαρακτηριστικά	Crime with racist motivation	
Έγκλημα οικονομικής εκμετάλλευσης της γενετήσιας ζωής	Crime of economic exploitation of sexual life	
Εγκληματική οργάνωση	Criminal organisation	
Έγκληση	Victim-initiated complaint	
Έγκυος	Pregnant woman	
Εδαφικά δικαιώματα	Territorial rights	
Εδάφιο	Sentence	See Foreword
Έδαφος (χώρας)	Territory	See Article 138
Έδρα (νομικού προσώπου)	Registered offices	
Εθνική άμυνα	National defence	
Εθνική καταγωγή	National origin	

Εθνική οδός	National road	
Εθνικός ύμνος	National anthem	
Εθνικότητα	Nationality	See Article 5
Εθνοτική καταγωγή	Ethnic origin	
Είδη πυροτεχνίας	Pyrotechnic items	
Ειδικό βιβλίο	Special register	
Ειδικό Δικαστήριο	Special Court	
Ειδικό κατάστημα κράτησης νέων	Reformative institution	
Ειδικός επιστήμονας	Specialist	
Εικονική εκτέλεση	Mock execution	
Εικονικός	Simulated	See Article 348A(3)
Ειλωτεία	Servitude	
Ειρήνη	Peace	
Εισαγγελέας	Public prosecutor	
Εισαγγελική διάταξη	Decree issued by a public prosecutor	
Εισαγωγή (αγαθών)	Import	
Εισαγωγή (δεδομένων)	Input	
Εισαγωγή (σε ψυχιατρική μονάδα)	Committal	
Εκβίαση	Extortion	
Εκβιαστικά μέσα	Extortionary measures	
Εκδίκαση	Adjudication	
Εκδικητική πορνογραφία	Revenge pornography	
Έκδοση (απόφασης)	Handing down of judgment	
Εκδότης	Publisher	
Έκθεση	Exposure Report	See Article 306 See Article 72(4)(a)
Εκκλησία	Church	
Εκλογέας	Voter	
Εκλογή	Election	
Εκλογική διαδικασία	Election process	
Εκλογική περιφέρεια	Constituency	
Εκλογικό δικαίωμα	Voting right	
Εκλογικό σώμα	Electorate	
Εκμετάλλευση	Exploitation	

Εκπαίδευση	Training	
Εκπαιδευτικό προσωπικό	Educational staff	
Εκπαιδευτικός	Teacher	
Εκρηκτική ύλη	Explosive	
Έκρηξη	Explosion	
Έκταση περιαστικού πράσινου	Peri-urban green area	
Εκτέλεση	Enforcement	
Εκτελεστική λειτουργία	Executive	
Εκτελεστός τίτλος	Enforceable title	
Έκτιση	To serve	
Έκτιση της ποινής στην κατοικία	House arrest	
Εκτομή	Excision	
Εκφοβισμός	Intimidation	
Ελαφριά περίπτωση	Minor case	
Ελαφρότερη ποινή	More lenient penalty	
Ελαφρυντικές περιστάσεις	Mitigating circumstances	
Ελεγκτικό Συνέδριο της Ευρωπαϊκής Ένωσης	European Court of Auditors	
Έλεγχος	Control	
Ελεύθερος συναγωνισμός	Free competition	
Ελληνικό κράτος / Δημόσιο	Greek state	
Έμβρυο	Foetus	
Εμπιστευτικός	Confidential	
Εμπιστοσύνη	Trust	
Εμπορία ανθρώπων	Human trafficking	
Εμπορία επιρροής	Trading in influence	
Εμπορία ναρκωτικών	Drug trafficking	
Έμπρακτη μετάνοια	Practical repentance	
Εμπρησμός	Arson	
Εμπρησμός σε δάση	Forest arson	
Εμπρηστική ύλη	Incendiary material	
Εμπρόσθια όψη (νομίσματος)	Obverse	
Εναρμονισμένες πρακτικές	Concerted practices	
Ένδεια	Poverty	See Foreword
Ενδεχόμενος δόλος	*Dolus eventualis*	
Ενέργεια	Energy	

Ενήλικος	Adult	
Έννομη σημασία	Legal importance	
Ένοπλες δυνάμεις	Armed forces	
Ένοπλες επιχειρήσεις	Combat operations	
Ένορκος	Juror	
Ενοχοποίηση	Incrimination	
Ένσημο	Stamp	See Foreword
Ένταλμα σύλληψης	Arrest warrant	
Ενταφιάζω	To bury	
Εντελής ικανοποίηση	Just satisfaction	
Έντιμη ζωή	Honest life	
Εξαίρεση (υπαλλήλου, δικαστικού λειτουργού)	Exemption	See Article 254
Εξάλειψη	Extinction	
Εξαναγκαστικά μέσα	Means of coercion	
Εξάντληση	Exhaustion	
Εξαπάτηση	Deception	
Εξέταση	Examination	
Έξη	Addiction	
Εξιχνίαση	To solve (a crime)	
Εξουσία λήψης αποφάσεων	Decision-making powers	
Εξύβριση	Insult	See Article 361
Εξώδικη διευθέτηση	Out-of-court settlement	
Εξωτερικό ιατρείο	Outpatient department	
Επ' αυτοφώρω	In the act	
Επάγγελμα	Profession	
Επαγγελματικό απόρρητο	Professional secret	
Επαιτεία	Begging	
Επαύξηση (ποινής)	Augmentation	
Επαχθής	Onerous	
Επιβαρυντικές περιστάσεις	Aggravating circumstances	
Επιβάτης	Passenger	
Επιβλαβής ουσία	Noxious substance	
Επιβολή	Ordering	
Επίδειξη	Presentation	
Επίθεση	Attack	

Επιθεωρητής	Inspector	
Επικίνδυνη οδήγηση	Dangerous driving	
Επικίνδυνη ουσία	Hazardous substance	
Επικίνδυνη παρέμβαση	Hazardous interference	
Επικοινωνία (με τέκνο)	Access	See Article 169A(1)
Επικράτεια	Territory	See Article 5
Επικύρωση	Ratification	
Επιμέλεια	Custody Diligence	See Article 13 See Article 32
Επιμελητής (ανηλίκου)	Juvenile probation officer	
Επιμελητής κοινωνικής αρωγής	Probation officer	
Επιμέτρηση ποινής	Determination of the extent of the penalty	
Επίπληξη	Reprimand	
Επιστημονικό απόρρητο	Scientic secret	
Επιστολή	Letter	
Επιταγή	Cheque	
Επιτιθέμενος	Attacker	
Επιτροπεία	Tutorship	
Επιτροπή	Committee	
Επίτροπος (ανηλίκου)	Tutor	
Επιχειρηματική δραστηριότητα	Business activity	
Επιχείρηση	Business Enterprise	See Article 385(3) See Article 68(5)
Επιχείρηση δημοσίου τομέα	Public corporation	
Επιχείρηση ιδιωτικού τομέα	Private enterprise	
Επιχείρηση κοινής ωφελείας	Public utility company	
Επιχειρησιακά δομημένη οργάνωση	Operationally structured organisation	
Επιχορήγηση	Subsidy	
Εποπτεία	Supervision	
Εργαζόμενος	Worker	
Εργαλείο	Tool	
Εργασιακή εκμετάλλευση	Labour exploitation	
Εργοστάσιο	Factory	
Έρευνα	Inquiries	

Έσοδα (εκμετάλλευσης)	Proceeds	See Article 323A(6)
Εσχάτη προδοσία	High treason	
Εσωτερικά ύδατα	Inland waters	
Ετεροθαλής αδελφός	Half-sibling	
Ευήθεια	Naivety	
Ευθύνη εις ολόκληρον	Several liability	
Ευρώ	Euro	
Ευρωβουλευτής	Member of European Parliament	
Ευρωπαϊκή Ένωση	European Union	
Ευρωπαϊκή Επιτροπή	European Commission	
Ευρωπαϊκή Σύμβαση των Δικαιωμάτων του Ανθρώπου	European Convention on Human Rights	
Εφάπαξ (ποσό)	Lump sum	
Έφεση	Appeal	
Εφετείο	Court of appeal	
Εφημερίδα	Newspaper	
Εχθροπραξία	Hostility	
Εχθρός	Enemy	
Ζημία (πράγματος)	Damage	
Ζημιωθείς	Victim	See Article 381 See Foreword
Ζώο	Animal	
Ζωτικής σημασίας αγαθά ή υπηρεσίες	Vital goods or services	
Ηθική αυτουργία	Instigation	
Ηθικός αυτουργός	Instigator	
Ηλεκτρική εγκατάσταση	Electrical installation	
Ηλεκτρική ενέργεια	Electricity	
Ηλεκτρομαγνητική εκπομπή	Electromagnetic transmission	
Ηλεκτρονικά δεδομένα	Electronic data	
Ηλεκτρονικά μέσα επιτήρησης	Electronic surveillance equipment	
Ηλεκτρονικές επικοινωνίες	Electronic communications	
Ηλεκτρονική αλληλογραφία	E-mail	
Ηλεκτρονική επιτήρηση	Electronic surveillance	
Ηλεκτρονική υπηρεσία	Electronic service	

Ηλεκτρονικό μέσο	Electronic means	
Ηλεκτρονικό μήνυμα	Electronic message	
Ηλεκτρονικός φορέας	Electronic storage medium	
Ηλεκτροσόκ	Electric shocks	
Ημεδαπός	Greek national	
Ημερήσια μονάδα	Daily penalty unit	
Ημερήσιος χάρτης πρόβλεψης κινδύνου πυρκαγιάς	Daily fire risk prediction map	
Ηπιότερος νόμος	*Lex mitior*	
Θαλάσσιος χώρος	Territorial waters	
Θανατηφόρα σωματική βλάβη	Fatal bodily harm	
Θέληση	Volition	
Θεραπεία	Treatment	See Article 69A(3)(c)
Θεραπευόμενος	Person being treated	
Θεραπευτικό κατάστημα	Therapeutic institution	
Θεραπευτικό μέτρο	Therapeutic measure	See Foreword
Θεραπευτικό πρόγραμμα	Therapeutic programme	
Θεράπων ιατρός	Attending physician	
Θερμές εργασίες	Hot works	
Θερμότητα	Heat	
Θετό τέκνο	Adopted child	
Θετός γονέας	Adoptive parent	
Θλίψη	Sorrow	
Θόρυβος	Noise	
Θραύση	Breaking	
Θρησκεία	Religion	
Θρησκευτική συνάθροιση	Religious gathering	
Θύμα	Victim	See Article 79(5)(d) See Foreword
Ιατρικό προσωπικό	Medical staff	
Ιατρός	Physician	
Ιδιοκτησία	Ownership	
Ιδιοκτήτης	Owner	
Ιδιότητα	Capacity	

Ιδιωτική ζωή	Privacy	
Ιδιωτικό απόρρητο	Private secret	
Ιδιωτικός βίος	Private life	
Ιδιωτικός τομέας	Private sector	
Ίδρυμα	Foundation	
Ιεραρχική σχέση	Hierarchical relationship	
Ιθαγένεια	Nationality	See Article 7
Ικανοποίηση (δανειστή)	Satisfaction	
Ισόβια κάθειρξη	Incarceration for life	
Ισότιμο και αξιόχρεο αντάλλαγμα	Good and valuable consideration	
Ιστορικό μνημείο	Historical monument	
Ιστός	Tissue	
Κάθειρξη	Incarceration	
Καθήκον	Duty	See Article 243
Καιρός πολέμου	Wartime	
Κακούργημα	Felony	
Καλλιτεχνικό μνημείο	Artistic monument	
Κάλπη	Ballot box	
Κανονισμός (ΕΕ)	Regulation	
Κανονισμός της Βουλής	Standing Orders of the Hellenic Parliament	
Κατ' επάγγελμα τέλεση εγκλήματος	Commission of a crime for monetary gain	
Καταβολή	Payment	
Καταγγελία	Report	
Καταδικασθείς	Convicted person	
Καταδικαστική απόφαση	Judgment of conviction	
Καταδίκη	Conviction	
Καταδολίευση δανειστών	Defrauding creditors	
Καταδότης	Informant	
Κατάθεση	Testimony	
Καταλογισμός	Imputability	
Κατάλογος	List	

Κατανάλωση οινοπνεύματος	Consumption of alcohol	
Κατασκοπεία	Espionage	
Κατάσταση αναισθησίας	Unconsciousness	
Κατάσταση (κοινής) ανάγκης	Emergency	
Κατάστημα	Shop	
Κατάστημα κράτησης	Custodial institution	See Foreword
Καταστροφή	Destruction	
Κατάσχεση	Seizure	
Κατάχρηση ανηλίκων	Child sexual abuse	
Κατάχρηση εξουσίας	Abuse of power	
Κατάχρηση σε γενετήσια πράξη	Sexual abuse	
Κατεδάφιση	Demolition	
Κατηγορούμενος	Accused person Defendant	See Foreword
Κατοικημένη περιοχή	Residential area	
Κατοχή	Detentorship Occupation Possession	See Article 169A(1) See Article 143(2) See Article 146(1) See Foreword
Κάτοχος	Possessor	See Foreword
Κεκλεισμένων των θυρών	*In camera*	
Κεντρικό Συμβούλιο Υγείας (ΚΕΣΥ)	Central Board of Health	
Κέρμα	Coin	
Κηδεμόνας	Custodian	See Foreword
Κινητήρια δύναμη	Motive force	
Κινητό	Movable	
Κινητό πράγμα	Movable thing	
Κλειστός χώρος	Locked place	
Κληρικός	Member of the clergy	
Κληρονόμος	Heir	
Κλήση	Summon	
Κλήτευση	Summonsing	
Κλητήριο θέσπισμα	Writ of summons	
Κλινική	Clinic	
Κλοπή	Theft	

Κλοπή και υπεξαίρεση μικρής αξίας	Theft and misappropriation of low-value [things]	
Κλοπιμαίο	Stolen property	
Κοινή θέα	Public view	
Κοινοβουλευτική συνέλευση	Parliamentary assembly	
Κοινοποίηση	Notice	See Article 180
Κοινός κίνδυνος	Common danger	
Κοινωνικός λειτουργός	Social worker	
Κοινώς επικίνδυνη βλάβη	Damage endangering the general public	
Κοινώς επικίνδυνο έγκλημα	Crime endangering the general public	
Κοινωφελές ίδρυμα	Public-benefit foundation	
Κοινωφελής σκοπός	Public-benefit purpose	
Κουφότητα	Imprudence	See Civil Code, Article 179
Κρατηθείς	Detainee	
Κρατητήριο	Detention facility	
Κρατική εξουσία	State power	
Κρατικό απόρρητο	State secret	
Κράτος	State	See Article 138(1)
Κράτος μέλος (ΕΕ)	Member State	
Κρίση	Ruling	See Foreword
Κτηνίατρος	Veterinarian	
Κυβέρνηση	Government	
Κύηση / Εγκυμοσύνη	Pregnancy	
Κυκλοφορία (νομίσματος)	Circulation	
Κυοφορούμενο	Unborn child	
Κύρια διαδικασία	Main proceedings	
Κύρια ποινή	Main penalty	
Κυριαρχία	Sovereignty	
Κύρωση	Sanction	
Κύτταρο	Cell	
Κώδικας Ποινικής Δικονομίας	Code of Criminal Procedure	
Κωδικός πρόσβασης	Access code	

Λαϊκή κυριαρχία	Popular sovereignty	
Λατρεία	Worship	
Λειτούργημα	Function	
Λειτουργός	Functionary	
Λεπτό ευρώ	Euro cent	
Λεωφορείο	Bus	
Ληστεία	Robbery	
Λογισμικό	Software	
Λόγος	Ground	
Λύτρα	Ransom	
Λωρίδα έκτακτης ανάγκης (ΛΕΑ)	Emergency lane	
Μαθητής	Pupil	
Μαία	Midwife	
Μαιευτήρας	Obstetrician	
Μάρκα	Token	
Μάρτυρας	Witness	
Μαστροπεία	Procuring	
Μειωμένη ποινή	Reduced punishment	
Μέρος (διαιτησίας, διαμεσολάβησης, κτλ.)	Party	
Μεσάζων	Intermediary	
Μεσεγγυούχος	Sequestrator	See Civil Code, Articles 359 et seq., 831 et seq.
Μέσο	Medium	
Μέσο κοινωνικής δικτύωσης	Social media	
Μέσο πληρωμής	Payment instrument	
Μέσο πληρωμής πλην των μετρητών	Non-cash payment instrument	
Μέσο σταθερής τροχιάς	Track-based means of transportation	
Μεσολάβηση	Mediation	See Article 360A(2)
Μεταλλείο	Mine	
Μετάλλιο	Medal	
Μετάνοια	Repentance	
Μετατροπή (ποινής)	Commutation	

Μεταφορές	Transport (sector)	
Μεταφορικό μέσο	Means of transport	
Μεταχείριση	Treatment	See Article 123(1)
Μετρητά	Cash	
Μέτρο ασφάλειας	Security measure	
Μέτρο δικονομικού καταναγκασμού	Procedural compulsory measure	
Μέτρο θεραπείας	Therapeutic measure	See Foreword
Μη επανδρωμένο αεροσκάφος	Unmanned aircraft system	
Μηχανισμός	Mechanism	
Μηχανοκίνητο μεταφορικό μέσο	Motor vehicle	
Μίσος	Hatred	
Μνημείο	Monument	
Μνηστεία	Engagement	
Μνηστευμένος / Μνηστήρας	Engaged person	
Μονάδα ψυχικής υγείας	Mental health facility	
Μυστική ψηφοφορία	Secret ballot	
Ναρκωτική ουσία	Narcotic substance	
Ναρκωτικό μέσο	Narcotic	
Ναυάγιο	Shipwreck	
Νεαρός ενήλικας	Young adult	
Νεκρός	Dead body Deceased person	See Article 181 See Article 365
Νεογνό	Newborn	
Νερό	Water	
Νόθευση	Alteration	See Foreword
Νομή	Possession	See Foreword
Νομική πλάνη	Mistake of law	
Νομική προστασία	Legal protection	
Νομικό πρόσωπο	Legal person	
Νομικό πρόσωπο δημοσίου δικαίου	Body governed by public law	
Νόμιμο νόμισμα	Legal tender	
Νόμιμος	Lawful	
Νόμιμος αντιπρόσωπος	Legal representative	

Νόμιμος εκπρόσωπος	Lawful representative	
Νόμιμος τύπος	Legal form	
Νόμισμα	Currency	
Νομισματική αξία	Monetary value	
Νομοθέτης	Legislature	
Νόμος	Law	
Νοσηλεία	Hospitalisation Treatment	See Article 69A(3) See Article 105B(4)(d)
Νοσηλευτικό ίδρυμα	Hospital	See Article 123(2)
Νοσηλευτικό προσωπικό	Nursing staff	
Νοσοκομείο	Hospital	See Article 69A(3)
Νοσοκόμος	Nurse	
Ξένη περιουσία	Third-party property	
Οδική συγκοινωνία	Road transportation	
Οδικό δίκτυο	Road network	
Οδοντίατρος	Dentist	
Οδός ταχείας κυκλοφορίας	Express road	
Οικείος	Related party	See Foreword
Οικιστική περιοχή	Residential district	
Οικογενειακή στέγη	Family home	
Οικογενειακή τάξη	Family status	
Οικογενειακός βίος	Family life	
Οικοδομικό έργο	Construction project	
Οικονομική ζημία	Economic damage	
Οινοπνευματώδες ποτό	Alcoholic beverage	
Ολογράφημα	Hologram	
Όμβρια ύδατα	Rainwater	
Όμηρος	Hostage	
Ομολογία	Admission	
Οντότητα	Entity	
Οπίσθια όψη (νομίσματος)	Reverse	
Όπλα	Arms	See Article 143(1)
Όπλο	Weapon	See Article 313
Οπτικό υλικό	Visual material	

Οπτικοακουστικό υλικό	Audiovisual material	
Οργανική νόσος	Physical illness	
Οργανισμός	Organisation	
Οργανισμός τοπικής αυτοδιοίκησης	Local government authority	
Όργανο	Agency	See Article 8
Όργανο (σώματος)	Organ	
Όργανο του κράτους	Officer of the state	
Οργή	Rage	
Οριστική απόφαση	Final judgment	
Όρος	Condition	
Ουσιώδες συμφέρον	Substantial interest	
Όχημα	Vehicle	
Όψη (νομίσματος)	Surface	
Παθών	Victim	See Article 115 See Foreword
Παιδαγωγικό ίδρυμα	Educational establishment	
Παιδαγωγός	Instructor	
Παιδί	Child	See Article 303
Παιδοκτονία	Infanticide	
Παράβαση καθήκοντος	Breach of duty	
Παραβίαση (σφραγίδας)	Tampering	
Παραβίαση κανόνων οδήγησης	Traffic violation	
Παραγραφή	Time-barring	
Παράγραφος	Paragraph	
Παραγωγή	Production	
Παράδοση	Handover	
Παραισθησιογόνος ουσία	Hallucinatory substance	
Παρακώλυση συναγωνισμού	Impeding competition	
Παράλειψη	Omission	
Παράλειψη οφειλόμενης βοήθειας	Failure to offer assistance requested	
Παράλειψη προσφοράς βοήθειας	Failure to offer assistance	
Παραμέληση εποπτείας ανηλίκου	Failure to supervise a juvenile	
Παραμόρφωση	Disfigurement	

Παράνομη βία	Unlawful violence	
Παράνομη βλάβη τρίτου	Unlawful damage to a third party	
Παράνομη κατακράτηση	Unlawful detention	
Παράνομη πρόσβαση σε σύστημα πληροφοριών ή σε δεδομένα	Unlawful access to an information system or data	
Παράνομος	Unlawful	
Παραπλάνηση	Misleading	See Article 216
Παραπλάνηση (ανηλίκου)	Enticement	See Article 339
Παραποίηση (νομίσματος)	Falsification	
Παραπομπή (υπόθεσης)	Remittal	
Παραπομπή στο ακροατήριο	Commital to trial	
Παρασιώπηση	Concealment	See Article 386(1)
Παραχάραξη	Counterfeiting	
Παρεμβολή	Interference	
Παρέμποδιση δικαιοσύνης	Obstruction of justice	
Παρεπόμενη ποινή	Ancillary penalty	
Πάρκο	Park	
Παροχή κοινωφελούς εργασίας	Community service	See Foreword
Πάροχος	Provider	
Πεζοδρόμιο	Pavement	
Πεζόδρομος	Pedestrianised street	
Πειθαρχική παράβαση	Disciplinary offence	
Πειθαρχικό παράπτωμα	Disciplinary conduct	
Πειρατεία	Piracy	
Περιοδικό	Periodical	
Περιορισμός	Confinement	
Περιοριστικό μέτρο	Restrictive measure	
Περιουσία	Property	
Περιουσιακή βλάβη	Property damage	
Περιουσιακή ζημία	Pecuniary damage	
Περιουσιακό αγαθό	Asset	See Foreword
Περιουσιακό όφελος	Pecuniary gain	
Περιουσιακό στοιχείο	Asset	See Foreword

Περιοχή 'Natura'	Natura area	
Περιφέρεια (δικαστηρίου)	District	
Περιφερειακή οδός	Ring-road	
Περιφερειάρχης	Regional governor	
Περιφρόνηση	Contempt	
Πηγάδι	Well	
Πηγή	Spring	
Πιστοποιητικό	Certificate	
Πίστωση	Credit	
Πιστωτική κάρτα	Credit card	
Πλαίσιο ποινής	Penalty range	
Πλαστό νόμισμα	Counterfeit currency	
Πλαστογραφία	Forgery	
Πλατεία	Square	
Πλειστηριασμός	Auction	
Πληθυσμός	Population	
Πλημμελειοδικείο / Δικαστήριο πλημμελειοδικών	Court of misdemeanours	
Πλημμέλημα	Misdemeanour	
Πλήρης στερητική δικαστική συμπαράσταση	Full privative legal guardianship	
Πληροφορία	Information	
Πληροφοριακό σύστημα	Information system	See Article 292B
Πλοίο	Ship	
Πλυμμήρα	Flooding	
Πλωτό μέσο	Floating craft	
Ποινή	Penalty Punishment Sentence	See Foreword
Ποινή στερητική της ελευθερίας	Custodial sentence	
Ποινική δίκη	Criminal proceedings	
Ποινική δίωξη	Criminal prosecution	
Ποινική ευθύνη	Criminal liability	
Ποινικό δικαστήριο	Criminal court	
Ποινικός Κώδικας	Penal Code	

Ποινικός νόμος	Penal law	
Πόλεμος	War	
Πολιτεία	State	See Article 143(1)
Πολιτειακή εξουσία	State authority	
Πολίτης	Citizen	
Πολιτική αρχή	Civil authority	
Πολιτική δίκη	Civil proceedings	
Πολιτικό κόμμα	Political party	
Πολιτικό πρόσωπο	Political person	
Πορισμός εισοδήματος	Generation of income	
Πορνεία	Prostitution	
Πορνεία ανηλίκων	Child prostitution	
Πορνογραφία ανηλίκων	Child pornography	
Πορνογραφική παράσταση	Pornographic performance	
Ποσοστό τόκου	Interest rate	
Ποτό	Beverage	
Πραγματική πλάνη	Mistake of fact	
Πραγματογνώμονας	Expert	
Πραγματογνωμοσύνη	Expert evidence report	See Foreword
Πρακτικά (δικαστηρίου)	Transcript	
Πρακτικό διαμεσολάβησης	Mediation report	
Πράξη	Act	
Πράξη συμμετοχής	Participatory act	
Πρεσβευτής	Ambassador	
Προαγωγή	Promotion	
Προγεννητικός έλεγχος	Prenatal screening	
Πρόγραμμα απεξάρτησης	Rehabilitation programme	
Πρόγραμμα υπολογιστή	Software program	
Προδικασία	Preliminary procedure	
Προεδρική εξουσία	Presidential powers	
Πρόεδρος της Δημοκρατίας	President of the Republic	
Προειδοποίηση	Notice	See Article 81(5)
Προέλευση	Provenance	
Πρόθεση	Intention	
Προθεσμία	Deadline	

Προϊόν (εγκλήματος)	Proceeds	See Article 394
Προϊστάμενος	Superior (of another person)	
Προκαταβολή	Payment in advance	
Προκήρυξη	Notice	See Article 395(1)
Πρόκληση	Inducement	
Πρόκληση (παθόντος)	Provocation	
Προληπτικό μέτρο	Preventive measure	
Προμήθεια	Procurement	
Προξενική αρχή	Consular authority	
Προπαρασκευαστική πράξη	Preparatory act	
Προσάραξη	Grounding	
Πρόσβαση	Access	See Article 231(3)
Προσβολή	Harm Insult	See Article 22(3) See Article 361(1)
Προσβολή (συμβόλων κτλ.)	Desecration	
Προσβολή μνήμης νεκρού	Disparaging the memory of a deceased person	
Προσβολή της ανθρώπινης αξιοπρέπειας	Violation of human dignity	
Προσβολή της διεθνούς υπόστασης της Χώρας	Treason	
Προσέλκυση παιδιών	Solicitation of children	
Πρόσκαιρη κάθειρξη	Fixed-term incarceration	
Προσποιητός	Simulated	See Article 323(5)(f)
Προσταγή	Order	
Προστατευμένος μηχανισμός, αντικείμενο ή αρχείο	Protected device, object or record	
Προστατευτική εταιρεία	Society for the protection of juveniles	
Προσφορά	Offer	
Προσφορά κοινωφελούς εργασίας	Community service	See Foreword
Προσωπική ελευθερία	Personal freedom	
Προσωπικότητα	Character	
Προσωρινή διαταγή (δικαστηρίου)	Interim order	
Προσωρινή κράτηση	Temporary detention	

Προφορική συνομιλία	Private conversation	
Πρωθυπουργός	Prime Minister	
Πρωτοβάθμιο δικαστήριο	First-instance court	
Πρωτοδικείο	Court of first instance	
Πταίσμα	Petty offence	
Πτυχίο	Degree	
Πυρκαγιά	Fire	See Foreword
Πυροβόλο	Firearm	
Πώληση	Sale	
Ραδιοσυχνότητα	Radio frequency	
Ρύπανση	Pollution	
Σήμα (συγκοινωνιών)	Sign	
Σημαία	Flag	
Σημείο	Mark	
Σημείο (συγκοινωνιών)	Notice	See Article 290(1)(c)
Σημειώσεις	Notes	
Σκάφος	Vessel	
Σκεπτικό (απόφασης)	Reasoning	
Σκληρότητα	Cruelty	
Σπινθήρας	Spark	
Στάση	Riot	
Στέφανη (νομίσματος)	Edge	
Στήριξη	Support	
Στοιχεία θέσης	Location data	
Στοιχεία κίνησης	Traffic data	
Στοιχείο περιουσίας	Asset	See Foreword
Στρατιωτική υπηρεσία	Military service	
Στρατιωτικό απόρρητο	Military secrecy	
Στρατιωτικός	Military personnel	
Στρατιωτικός διοικητής	Military commander	
Στρατολόγηση	Recruitment	
Στρατός	Army	
Συγγένεια σε ευθεία γραμμή	Related directly	
Συγγενής	Relative	

Συγγενής ανιούσας γραμμής / Ανιών	Relative in the ascending line	
Συγγενής κατιούσας γραμμής / Κατιών	Relative in the descending line	
Σύγγνωστη νομική πλάνη	Excusable mistake of law	
Συγκατάθεση	Consent	See Article 184(2A)
Συγκοινωνία μέσων σταθερής τροχιάς	Track-based transportation	
Συγκοινωνίες	Transportation systems	
Σύζυγος	Spouse	
Συκοφαντικές διαδόσεις	Defamatory rumours	
Συκοφαντική δυσφήμηση	Aggravated defamation	
Σύλληψη	Arrest	
Συλλογική εκδήλωση	Assembly	
Σύμβαση (διεθνής)	Treaty or convention	
Συμβιών (με σταθερή συμβίωση)	Person living together in a steady relationship	
Συμβιών (με σύμφωνο συμβίωσης)	Civil partner	
Συμβίωση	Relationship/Partnership	
Συμβολαιογράφος	Notary public	
Σύμβολο	Symbol	
Συμβούλιο (δικαστηρίου)	Judicial council	See Article 72(3)
Σύμμαχος	Ally	
Συμμετοχή	Participation	
Συμμέτοχος	Accessory	
Συμπλοκή	Brawl	
Συμφέρον	Interest	
Συμφωνία	Agreement	
Συμφωνίες μεταξύ επιχειρήσεων	Agreements between undertakings	
Σύμφωνο συμβίωσης	Civil partnership	
Συναίνεση	Acquiescence Consent	See Article 322(2) See Article 304(1)
Συναισθηματική φόρτιση	Emotional stress	
Συναλλαγματική	Bill of exchange	
Συναυτουργός	Co-perpetrator	
Σύνδεση	Connection	
Συνδιαλλαγή	Conciliation	

Συνεδρία (δικαστηρίου)	Sitting	
Συνεδρία (με επιμελητή)	Session	
Συνεδρίαση	Meeting	
Συνείδηση	Faculties	See Foreword
Συνεκδίκαση	Joinder	
Συνέπεια	Consequence	
Συνεργάτης	Associate	
Συνεργός	Accomplice	
Συνήγορος	Counsel	
Συνθηματικό	Password	
Συνολική ποινή	Overall penalty Total sentence	See Article 96 See Article 94
Συνουσία	Intercourse	
Σύνταγμα	Constitution	
Συντρέχουσα ποινή	Concurrent penalty Concurrent sentence	See Article 96(1) See Article 94(1)
Σύντροφος	Partner	
Συρροή εγκλημάτων	Concurrence of crimes	
Συσκευή	Device	
Συσκευή	Device	
Συσκευή παρακολούθησης	Surveillance device	
Συσκευή υπολογιστή	Computer hardware	
Συστατικό	Constituent part	
Σύστημα πληροφοριών	Information system	See Article 210
Σύστημα υλικού	Hardware	
Σφετερισμός	Usurpation	
Σφραγίδα	Seal	
Σχέδιο	Design	
Σχέση εργασιακής εξάρτησης	Employment relationship	
Σώμα	Body	
Σωματική ακεραιότητα	Physical integrity	
Σωματική αναπηρία	Physical disability	
Σωματική βία	Physical violence	
Σωματική βλάβη	Bodily harm	
Σωματική βλάβη από αμέλεια	Negligent bodily harm	

Σωματική δυσλειτουργία	Bodily dysfunction	
Σωματική εξάντληση	Physical exhaustion	
Σωματική κάκωση	Bodily injury	
Σωματική κατάσταση	Physical condition	
Σωματικός πόνος	Physical pain	
Σωφρονιστικό κατάστημα	Custodial institution	See Foreword
Σωφρονιστικός υπάλληλος	Correctional officer	
Τακτική ανάκριση	Ordinary investigation	
Ταξιδιωτική επιταγή	Traveller's cheque	
Ταραχή	Distress	
Ταυτότητα	Identity	
Ταυτότητα φύλου	Gender identity	
Ταφή	Burial	
Ταχυδρομικές υπηρεσίες	Postal services	
Τεκμήριο αθωότητας	Presumption of innocence	
Τέκνο	Child	See Article 354
Τέλεση	Commission	See Foreword
Τελεσίδικη απόφαση	*De jure* non-appealable judgment	
Τελετή	Ceremony	
Τέλος	Fee	
Τεχνητή διακοπή κύησης	Artificial termination of pregnancy	
Τεχνικοί κανόνες	Technical rules	
Τεχνογνωσία	Skills	
Τεχνολογία πληροφοριών και επικοινωνιών	Information and communication technology	
Τηλεγραφική υπηρεσία	Telegram service	
Τηλεπικοινωνιακό μέσο	Telecommunications means	
Τηλεπικοινωνίες	Telecommunications	
Τηλεπικοινωνίες του κοινού	Public telecommunications	
Τηλεφωνία	Telephony	
Τηλεφωνικές επικοινωνίες	Telephone communications	
Τηλεφωνική συνδιάλεξη	Telephone conversation	
Τιμή	Honour	
Τίμημα	Value	

Τοκετός	Childbirth	
Τοκογλυφία	Usury	
Τόκος υπερημερίας	Default interest	
Τόπος προορισμένος για θρησκευτική λατρεία	Place intended for religious worship	
Τόπος τέλεσης	Place of commission	
Τριμελές (δικαστήριο)	Three-member (court)	
Τρομοκρατική οργάνωση	Terrorist organisation	
Τρομοκρατική πράξη	Terrorist act	
Τρόμος	Terror	
Τρόφιμο	Food	
Ύβρη	Insult	See Article 168(4)
Υβριστικό δημοσίευμα	Insulting publication	
Υγεία	Health	
Υιοθεσία	Adoption	
Υλικό παιδικής πορνογραφίας	Child pornography material	
Υλικός	Tangible	
Υλικός φορέας	Physical storage medium	
Υπαίτια κατάσταση άμυνας	Culpable provocation of defence	
Υπαίτιος	Culpable person	
Υπαιτιότητα	Culpability	
Υπάλληλος	State employee	See Foreword
Υπάλληλος πλειστηριασμού	Auctioneer	
Υπαξιωματικός	Non-commissioned officer	
Υπεξαγωγή εγγράφων	Making documents unavailable	
Υπεξαίρεση	Misappropriation	
Υπερασπιστής ανθρώπινων δικαιωμάτων	Human rights defender	
Υπέρβαση άμυνας	Excessive defence	
Υπερεθνικός	Supranational	
Υπέρμετρος	Excessive	
Υπηρεσιακό απόρρητο	Official secrecy	
Υπνωτικό μέσο	Soporific	
Υποβάθμιση	Degradation	

Υποβολή τέκνου	Presenting a child as having a different family status from its actual one
Υποδομή	Infrastructure
Υποθάλπω	To harbour
Υπόθαλψη	Harbouring [a criminal]
Υπόθεση	Case
Υποκινώ	To incite
Υποκλοπή	Interception
Υπόληψη	Reputation
Υπολογιστής	Computer
Ύποπτος	Suspect
Υπόσχεση	Promise
Υπουργείο Δικαιοσύνης	Ministry of Justice
Υπουργικό Συμβούλιο	Cabinet
Υπουργός	Minister
Υπουργός Δικαιοσύνης	Minister of Justice
Υπουργός Υγείας	Minister of Health
Υποχρέωση	Obligation
Υποψήφιος	Candidate
Υφ' όρον απόλυση / Απόλυση υπό όρο	Conditional release
Υφαρπαγή ψευδούς βεβαίωσης	Obtaining an attestation under false pretences
Υφυπουργός	Deputy Minister
Φάλαγγα	Foot whipping
Φάρμακο	Medicine
Φαρμακοποιός	Pharmacist
Φθορά ξένης ιδιοκτησίας	Damage to another's property
Φιλανθρωπικό κατάστημα	Charitable institution
Φόβος	Fear
Φορολόγημα	Levy
Φόρος	Tax
Φορτηγό όχημα	Lorry
Φυλακή	Prison
Φυλάκιση	Imprisonment

Φυλακισμένος	Prisoner	
Φύλαξη (πράγματος)	Custody	
Φύλαξη (προσώπου)	Care	See Article 349(2)(c)
Φυσική καταστροφή	Natural disaster	
Φυσικό άεριο	Natural gas	
Φυσικό πρόσωπο	Natural person	
Φυσικός αυτουργός	Perpetrator	See Article 112
Φωνασκία	Shouting	
Φωτιά	Fire	See Foreword
Φωτισμός	Lighting	
Χαρακτηριστικά φυλής	Race	
Χαρακτηριστικά φύλου	Sex characteristics	
Χάρη	Pardon	
Χειρονομία	Gesture	
Χημικό υλικό	Chemical agent	
Χημικός	Chemist	
Χορτολιβαδική έκταση	Pasture	
Χρέος	Debt	
Χρεωστική κάρτα	Debit card	
Χρήμα	Money	
Χρηματική ικανοποίηση	Payment of compensation	
Χρηματική ποινή	Monetary penalty	
Χρηματοοικονομικά μέσα	Financial instruments	
Χρηματοπιστωτικό ίδρυμα	Financial institution	
Χρηστά ήθη	Morality	
Χρόνος δοκιμασίας	Probationary period	
Χρόνος τέλεσης	Time of commission	
Χρόνος/Διάρκεια (ποινής)	Length	
Χρώμα (προσώπου)	Skin colour	
Χώρα καταγωγής	Country of origin	
Ψευδείς ειδήσεις	False information	
Ψευδές γεγονός	False fact	
Ψευδής είδηση	False news	
Ψευδής καταγγελία	False report [of a crime]	

Ψευδής κατάθεση	False testimony	
Ψηφιακά δεδομένα	Digital data	
Ψηφιακό μέσο συναλλαγής	Digital means of exchange	
Ψηφοφορία	Vote	
Ψυχιατρική παρακολούθηση	Psychiatric observation	
Ψυχική ασθένεια	Mental illness	See Article 123(1)
Ψυχική βλάβη	Mental harm	
Ψυχική διαταραχή	Mental disorder	
Ψυχική κατάσταση	Emotional state	
Ψυχική οδύνη	Mental anguish	
Ψυχικός πόνος	Psychological pain	
Ψυχογενετήσια κατάσταση	Psychosexual state	
Ψυχοδιαγνωστική εξέταση	Psychodiagnostic examination	
Ψυχολογική βία	Psychological violence	
Ψυχολόγος	Psychologist	
Ωφέλημα	Advantage	

English to Greek Glossary

EN	EL	Notes
Abduction	Απαγωγή	
Abroad	Αλλοδαπή	
Absentee	Άφαντος	See Civil Code, Articles 40-50
Abuse of power	Κατάχρηση εξουσίας	
Acceptance	Αποδοχή	
Acceptance and making available of proceeds of a crime	Αποδοχή και διάθεση προϊόντων εγκλήματος	
Access	Επικοινωνία (με τέκνο) Πρόσβαση	See Article 169A(1) See Article 231(3)
Access code	Κωδικός πρόσβασης	
Accessory	Συμμέτοχος	
Accomplice	Συνεργός	
Accreditation	Διαπίστευση	
Accused person	Κατηγορούμενος	See Foreword
Acquiescence	Συναίνεση	See Article 322(2)
Acquittal	Αθώωση	
Act	Πράξη	
Active bribery	Δωροδοκία	
Addiction	Έξη	
Adjournment	Αναβολή (δίκης)	
Adjudication	Εκδίκαση	
Administration of justice	Απονομή δικαιοσύνης	
Administrative proceedings	Διοικητική δίκη	
Admission	Ομολογία	
Adopted child	Θετό τέκνο	
Adoption	Υιοθεσία	
Adoptive parent	Θετός γονέας	
Adult	Ενήλικος	
Advantage	Ωφέλημα	
Advertisement	Αγγελία	

Afforestable	Δασωτέα (έκταση)	
Agency	Όργανο	See Article 8
Aggravated case	Διακεκριμένη περίπτωση (εγκλήματος)	
Aggravated defamation	Συκοφαντική δυσφήμηση	
Aggravated theft	Διακεκριμένη κλοπή	
Aggravating circumstances	Επιβαρυντικές περιστάσεις	
Agreement	Συμφωνία	
Agreements between undertakings	Συμφωνίες μεταξύ επιχειρήσεων	
Aircraft	Αεροσκάφος	
Alcoholic beverage	Οινοπνευματώδες ποτό	
Ally	Σύμμαχος	
Alteration	Αλλοίωση (δεδομένων) Νόθευση	See Foreword
Ambassador	Πρεσβευτής	
Amnesty	Αμνηστία	
Amputation	Ακρωτηριασμός	See Article 310
Anaesthesiologist	Αναισθησιολόγος	
Ancillary penalty	Παρεπόμενη ποινή	
Animal	Ζώο	
Appeal	Έφεση	
Application	Αίτηση	
Apprehension	Ανησυχία	See Article 333
Arbitration	Διαιτησία	
Arbitration award	Διαιτητική απόφαση	
Arbitrator	Διαιτητής	
Armed forces	Ένοπλες δυνάμεις	
Arms	Όπλα	See Article 143(1)
Army	Στρατός	
Arrest	Σύλληψη	
Arrest warrant	Ένταλμα σύλληψης	
Arson	Εμπρησμός	
Article	Άρθρο	
Artificial termination of pregnancy	Τεχνητή διακοπή κύησης	
Artistic monument	Καλλιτεχνικό μνημείο	
Assault	Βιαιοπραγία	

Assembly	Συλλογική εκδήλωση	
Asset	Περιουσιακό αγαθό Περιουσιακό στοιχείο Στοιχείο περιουσίας	See Foreword
Assistant	Βοηθός	
Associate	Συνεργάτης	
Attack	Επίθεση	
Attacker	Επιτιθέμενος	
Attempt	Απόπειρα	
Attending physician	Θεράπων ιατρός	
Auction	Πλειστηριασμός	
Auctioneer	Υπάλληλος πλειστηριασμού	
Audiovisual material	Οπτικοακουστικό υλικό	
Augmentation	Επαύξηση (ποινής)	
Authenticity of signature	Γνήσιο υπογραφής	
Authorisation	Άδεια	See 2010 Convention on Enforced Disappearance
Authority	Αρχή	
Ballot box	Κάλπη	
Ban on exiting the country	Απαγόρευση εξόδου από χώρα	
Begging	Επαιτεία	
Beneficiary	Δικαιούχος	
Beverage	Ποτό	
Bigamy	Διγαμία	
Bill of exchange	Συναλλαγματική	
Biological agent	Βιολογικό υλικό	
Birth	Γέννηση	
Bodily dysfunction	Σωματική δυσλειτουργία	
Bodily harm	Σωματική βλάβη	
Bodily injury	Σωματική κάκωση	
Body	Σώμα	
Body governed by public law	Νομικό πρόσωπο δημοσίου δικαίου	
Bomb	Βόμβα	
Book	Βιβλίο	

Brawl	Συμπλοκή	
Breach of duty	Παράβαση καθήκοντος	
Breach of fiduciary duty	Απιστία	
Breach of the public peace	Διατάραξη της κοινής ειρήνης	
Breaking	Θραύση	
Burial	Ταφή	
Bus	Λεωφορείο	
Business	Επιχείρηση	See Article 385(3)
Business activity	Επιχειρηματική δραστηριότητα	
Cabinet	Υπουργικό Συμβούλιο	
Candidate	Υποψήφιος	
Capacity	Ιδιότητα	
Care	Φύλαξη (προσώπου)	See Article 349(2)(c)
Case	Υπόθεση	
Cash	Μετρητά	
Cell	Κύτταρο	
Central Board of Health	Κεντρικό Συμβούλιο Υγείας (ΚΕΣΥ)	
Ceremony	Τελετή	
Certificate	Πιστοποιητικό	
Character	Προσωπικότητα	
Charitable institution	Φιλανθρωπικό κατάστημα	
Chemical agent	Χημικό υλικό	
Chemist	Χημικός	
Cheque	Επιταγή	
Child	Παιδί Τέκνο	See Article 303 See Article 354
Child abduction	Αρπαγή ανηλίκου	
Child pornography	Πορνογραφία ανηλίκων	
Child pornography material	Υλικό παιδικής πορνογραφίας	
Child prostitution	Πορνεία ανηλίκων	
Child sexual abuse	Κατάχρηση ανηλίκων	
Childbirth	Τοκετός	
Church	Εκκλησία	
Circulation	Κυκλοφορία (νομίσματος)	
Citizen	Πολίτης	

Civil authority	Πολιτική αρχή	
Civil claim	Αστική αξίωση	
Civil partner	Συμβιών (με σύμφωνο συμβίωσης)	
Civil partnership	Σύμφωνο συμβίωσης	
Civil proceedings	Πολιτική δίκη	
Civil right	Ατομικό δικαίωμα	
Claim	Απαίτηση	
Clinic	Κλινική	
Code of Criminal Procedure	Κώδικας Ποινικής Δικονομίας	
Coin	Κέρμα	
Combat operations	Ένοπλες επιχειρήσεις	
Commission	Διάπραξη Τέλεση	See Foreword
Commission of a crime for monetary gain	Κατ' επάγγελμα τέλεση εγκλήματος	
Commital to trial	Παραπομπή στο ακροατήριο	
Committal	Εισαγωγή (σε ψυχιατρική μονάδα)	
Committee	Επιτροπή	
Common danger	Κοινός κίνδυνος	
Community service	Παροχή κοινωφελούς εργασίας Προσφορά κοινωφελούς εργασίας	See Foreword
Commutation	Μετατροπή (ποινής)	
Compensation	Αποζημίωση	
Compulsory enforcement	Αναγκαστική εκτέλεση	
Computer	Υπολογιστής	
Computer fraud	Απάτη με υπολογιστή	
Computer hardware	Συσκευή υπολογιστή	
Concealment	Αποσιώπηση Παρασιώπηση	See Article 254 See Article 386(1)
Concerted practices	Εναρμονισμένες πρακτικές	
Conciliation	Συνδιαλλαγή	
Concurrence of crimes	Συρροή εγκλημάτων	
Concurrent penalty	Συντρέχουσα ποινή	See Article 96(1)

Concurrent sentence	Συντρέχουσα ποινή	See Article 94(1)
Condition	Όρος	
Conditional release	Υφ' όρον απόλυση / Απόλυση υπό όρο	
Conduct	Διαγωγή	
Confidential	Εμπιστευτικός	
Configuration	Διαμόρφωση (προγράμματος υπολογιστή)	
Confinement	Περιορισμός	
Confirmation	Βεβαίωση	See Article 80; see Code of Criminal Procedure, Article 553
Confiscation	Δήμευση	
Connection	Σύνδεση	
Consent	Συγκατάθεση Συναίνεση	See Article 184(2A) See Article 304(1)
Consequence	Συνέπεια	
Consideration	Αντάλλαγμα	
Constituency	Εκλογική περιφέρεια	
Constituent part	Συστατικό	
Constitution	Σύνταγμα	
Construction project	Οικοδομικό έργο	
Consular authority	Προξενική αρχή	
Consumption	Ανάλωση	
Consumption of alcohol	Κατανάλωση οινοπνεύματος	
Contempt	Περιφρόνηση	
Control	Έλεγχος	
Convicted person	Καταδικασθείς	
Conviction	Καταδίκη	
Co-perpetrator	Συναυτουργός	
Copying	Αντιγραφή	
Correctional officer	Σωφρονιστικός υπάλληλος	
Counsel	Συνήγορος	
Counterfeit currency	Πλαστό νόμισμα	
Counterfeiting	Παραχάραξη	
Country of origin	Χώρα καταγωγής	

Court	Δικαστήριο	
Court clerk	Δικαστικός υπάλληλος	
Court costs	Δικαστικά έξοδα Δικαστικές δαπάνες	See Foreword
Court judgment	Δικαστική απόφαση	
Court of appeal	Εφετείο	
Court of first instance	Πρωτοδικείο	
Court of Justice of the European Union	Δικαστήριο της Ευρωπαϊκής Ένωσης	
Court of misdemeanours	Πλημμελειοδικείο / Δικαστήριο πλημμελειοδικών	
Credit	Πίστωση	
Credit card	Πιστωτική κάρτα	
Creditor	Δανειστής	
Crime	Έγκλημα	
Crime against life	Έγκλημα κατά της ζωής	
Crime against physical integrity	Έγκλημα κατά της σωματικής ακεραιότητας	
Crime against public order	Έγκλημα κατά της δημόσιας τάξης	
Crime against sexual freedom	Έγκλημα κατά της γενετήσιας ελευθερίας	
Crime committed repeatedly	Έγκλημα κατ' εξακολούθηση	
Crime endangering the general public	Κοινώς επικίνδυνο έγκλημα	
Crime of economic exploitation of sexual life	Έγκλημα οικονομικής εκμετάλλευσης της γενετήσιας ζωής	
Crime of general endangerment	Έγκλημα γενικής διακινδύνευσης	
Crime subject to public prosecution	Έγκλημα διωκώμενο αυτεπάγγελτα	
Crime with racist motivation	Έγκλημα με ρατσιστικά χαρακτηριστικά	
Criminal court	Ποινικό δικαστήριο	
Criminal liability	Ποινική ευθύνη	
Criminal organisation	Εγκληματική οργάνωση	
Criminal proceedings	Ποινική δίκη	
Criminal prosecution	Ποινική δίωξη	

Cruelty	Σκληρότητα	
Culpability	Υπαιτιότητα	
Culpable person	Υπαίτιος	
Culpable provocation of defence	Υπαίτια κατάσταση άμυνας	
Currency	Νόμισμα	
Custodial institution	Κατάστημα κράτησης Σωφρονιστικό κατάστημα	See Foreword
Custodial sentence	Ποινή στερητική της ελευθερίας	
Custodian	Κηδεμόνας	See Foreword
Custody	Επιμέλεια	See Article 13
Custody	Φύλαξη (πράγματος)	
Daily fire risk prediction map	Ημερήσιος χάρτης πρόβλεψης κινδύνου πυρκαγιάς	
Daily penalty unit	Ημερήσια μονάδα	
Damage	Ζημία (πράγματος)	
Damage endangering the general public	Κοινώς επικίνδυνη βλάβη	
Damage to another's property	Φθορά ξένης ιδιοκτησίας	
Dangerous driving	Επικίνδυνη οδήγηση	
Data	Δεδομένα	
De jure non-appealable judgment	Τελεσίδικη απόφαση	
Dead body	Νεκρός	See Article 181
Deadline	Προθεσμία	
Debauchery	Ακολασία	
Debit card	Χρεωστική κάρτα	
Debt	Χρέος	
Deceased person	Νεκρός	See Article 365
Deception	Εξαπάτηση	
Decision-making powers	Εξουσία λήψης αποφάσεων	
Decree issued by a public prosecutor	Εισαγγελική διάταξη	
Defamation	Δυσφήμηση	
Defamatory rumours	Συκοφαντικές διαδόσεις	
Default interest	Τόκος υπερημερίας	
Defence	Άμυνα	
Defendant	Κατηγορούμενος	See Foreword
Deferral	Αναβολή (ποινικής δίωξης)	

Defrauding creditors	Καταδολίευση δανειστών	
Degradation	Υποβάθμιση	
Degree	Πτυχίο	
Deletion	Διαγραφή (δεδομένων)	
Deliberations	Διάσκεψη (συμβουλίου)	
Demand	Αξίωση (απαγωγέα)	
Democratic system of government	Δημοκρατικό πολίτευμα	
Demolition	Κατεδάφιση	
Denouncement	Αποκήρυξη	
Dentist	Οδοντίατρος	
Deportation	Απέλαση	
Deputy Minister	Υφυπουργός	
Desecration	Προσβολή (συμβόλων κτλ.)	
Design	Σχέδιο	
Destruction	Καταστροφή	
Detainee	Κρατηθείς	
Detention facility	Κρατητήριο	
Detentorship	Κατοχή	
Determination of the extent of the penalty	Επιμέτρηση ποινής	
Device	Συσκευή	
Device	Συσκευή	
Digital data	Ψηφιακά δεδομένα	
Digital means of exchange	Ψηφιακό μέσο συναλλαγής	
Dignity	Αξιοπρέπεια	
Diligence	Επιμέλεια	See Article 32
Diplomatic envoy	Διπλωματικός αντιπρόσωπος	
Diplomatic secrecy	Διπλωματικό απόρρητο	
Direct accomplice	Άμεσος συνεργός	
Disability	Αναπηρία	
Disciplinary conduct	Πειθαρχικό παράπτωμα	
Disciplinary offence	Πειθαρχική παράβαση	
Discord	Διχόνοια	
Discovery	Ανεύρεση	
Disease	Ασθένεια	See Article 285
Disfigurement	Παραμόρφωση	

Disobedience	Ανυπακοή Απείθεια	See Article 183 See Article 169 See Foreword
Disparaging the memory of a deceased person	Προσβολή μνήμης νεκρού	
Disruption	Διαταράξη (οικολογική, περιβαλλοντική)	
Disruption of services	Διατάραξη υπηρεσιών	
Dissection	Ανατομή	
Dissemination	Διάδοση	
Distress	Ταραχή	
Distribution	Διανομή	
District	Περιφέρεια (δικαστηρίου)	
Document	Έγγραφο	
Dolus	Δόλος	
Dolus eventualis	Ενδεχόμενος δόλος	
DonationS	Δωρεά	
Drainage	Αποχέτευση (ομβρίων, ακαθάρτων υδάτων)	
Drinking fountain	Βρύση	
Driving licence	Άδεια οδήγησης	
Drug trafficking	Εμπορία ναρκωτικών	
Duty	Δασμός Καθήκον	See Article 244 See Article 243
Economic damage	Οικονομική ζημία	
Edge	Στέφανη (νομίσματος)	
Educational establishment	Παιδαγωγικό ίδρυμα	
Educational staff	Εκπαιδευτικό προσωπικό	
Election	Εκλογή	
Election process	Εκλογική διαδικασία	
Electorate	Εκλογικό σώμα	
Electric shocks	Ηλεκτροσόκ	
Electrical installation	Ηλεκτρική εγκατάσταση	
Electricity	Ηλεκτρική ενέργεια	
Electromagnetic transmission	Ηλεκτρομαγνητική εκπομπή	
Electronic communications	Ηλεκτρονικές επικοινωνίες	

Electronic data	*Ηλεκτρονικά δεδομένα*	
Electronic means	*Ηλεκτρονικό μέσο*	
Electronic message	*Ηλεκτρονικό μήνυμα*	
Electronic service	*Ηλεκτρονική υπηρεσία*	
Electronic storage medium	*Ηλεκτρονικός φορέας*	
Electronic surveillance	*Ηλεκτρονική επιτήρηση*	
Electronic surveillance equipment	*Ηλεκτρονικά μέσα επιτήρησης*	
E-mail	*Ηλεκτρονική αλληλογραφία*	
Emergency	*Κατάσταση (κοινής) ανάγκης*	
Emergency lane	*Λωρίδα έκτακτης ανάγκης (ΛΕΑ)*	
Emotional disorder	*Διανοητική διαταραχή*	
Emotional state	*Ψυχική κατάσταση*	
Emotional stress	*Συναισθηματική φόρτιση*	
Employment relationship	*Σχέση εργασιακής εξάρτησης*	
Enemy	*Εχθρός*	
Energy	*Ενέργεια*	
Enforceable title	*Εκτελεστός τίτλος*	
Enforced disappearance	*Βίαιη εξαφάνιση*	
Enforcement	*Εκτέλεση*	
Engaged person	*Μνηστευμένος / Μνηστήρας*	
Engagement	*Μνηστεία*	
Enterprise	*Επιχείρηση*	See Article 68(5)
Enticement	*Αποπλάνηση* *Παραπλάνηση (ανηλίκου)*	See Article 304 See Article 339
Entity	*Οντότητα*	
Espionage	*Κατασκοπεία*	
Ethnic origin	*Εθνοτική καταγωγή*	
Euro	*Ευρώ*	
Euro cent	*Λεπτό ευρώ*	
European Commission	*Ευρωπαϊκή Επιτροπή*	
European Convention on Human Rights	*Ευρωπαϊκή Σύμβαση των Δικαιωμάτων του Ανθρώπου*	
European Court of Auditors	*Ελεγκτικό Συνέδριο της Ευρωπαϊκής Ένωσης*	
European Union	*Ευρωπαϊκή Ένωση*	

Evidence	Αποδεικτικό μέσο	
Ex officio	Αυτεπαγγέλτως	
Examination	Εξέταση	
Excessive	Υπέρμετρος	
Excessive defence	Υπέρβαση άμυνας	
Excision	Εκτομή	
Excusable mistake of law	Σύγγνωστη νομική πλάνη	
Executive	Εκτελεστική λειτουργία	
Exemption	Απαλλαγή (από ποινή) Εξαίρεση (υπαλλήλου, δικαστικού λειτουργού)	See Article 187C(1) See Article 254
Exhaustion	Εξάντληση	
Expert	Πραγματογνώμονας	
Expert evidence report	Πραγματογνωμοσύνη	See Foreword
Exploitation	Εκμετάλλευση	
Explosion	Έκρηξη	
Explosive	Εκρηκτική ύλη	
Exposure	Έκθεση	See Article 306
Express road	Οδός ταχείας κυκλοφορίας	
Extinction	Εξάλειψη	
Extortion	Εκβίαση	
Extortionary measures	Εκβιαστικά μέσα	
Factory	Εργοστάσιο	
Faculties	Συνείδηση	See Foreword
Failure to offer assistance	Παράλειψη προσφοράς βοήθειας	
Failure to offer assistance requested	Παράλειψη οφειλόμενης βοήθειας	
Failure to supervise a juvenile	Παραμέληση εποπτείας ανηλίκου	
False fact	Ψευδές γεγονός	
False information	Ψευδείς ειδήσεις	
False news	Ψευδής είδηση	
False report [of a crime]	Ψευδής καταγγελία	
False testimony	Ψευδής κατάθεση	
Falsification	Παραποίηση (νομίσματος)	
Family home	Οικογενειακή στέγη	

Family life	Οικογενειακός βίος	
Family status	Οικογενειακή τάξη	
Farmland	Αγροτική έκταση	
Fatal bodily harm	Θανατηφόρα σωματική βλάβη	
Fear	Φόβος	
Fee	Τέλος	
Felony	Κακούργημα	
Female genital mutilation	Ακρωτηριασμός γυναικείων γεννητικών οργάνων	See Article 315
Final judgment	Οριστική απόφαση	
Financial institution	Χρηματοπιστωτικό ίδρυμα	
Financial instruments	Χρηματοοικονομικά μέσα	
Fire	Πυρκαγιά Φωτιά	See Foreword
Firearm	Πυροβόλο	
Fireworks	Βεγγαλικά	
First-instance court	Πρωτοβάθμιο δικαστήριο	
Fishing	Αλιεία	
Fixed-term incarceration	Πρόσκαιρη κάθειρξη	
Flag	Σημαία	
Floating craft	Πλωτό μέσο	
Flooding	Πλυμμήρα	
Foetus	Έμβρυο	
Food	Τρόφιμο	
Foot whipping	Φάλαγγα	
Foreign national	Αλλοδαπός	
Forest	Δάσος	
Forest arson	Εμπρησμός σε δάση	
Forested area	Δασική έκταση	
Forfeiture of posts and offices	Αποστέρηση (θέσεων και αξιωμάτων)	
Forgery	Πλαστογραφία	
Forgiveness	Άφεση	
Formality	Διατύπωση	
Foster child	Ανάδοχο τέκνο	

Foster family	Ανάδοχη οικογένεια
Foster parent	Ανάδοχος γονέας
Foundation	Ίδρυμα
Fraud	Απάτη
Fraudulent use	Δόλια χρήση
Free competition	Ελεύθερος συναγωνισμός
Freezing	Δέσμευση (περιουσιακών στοιχείων)
Full privative legal guardianship	Πλήρης στερητική δικαστική συμπαράσταση
Full sibling	Αμφιθαλής αδελφός
Function	Λειτούργημα
Functionary	Λειτουργός
Furlough	Άδεια (κρατούμενου)
Gender identity	Ταυτότητα φύλου
Genealogical descent	Γενεαλογικές καταβολές
General authorisation	Γενική άδεια
General hospital	Γενικό νοσοκομείο
General Part	Γενικό μέρος (ΠΚ)
General Secretariat for Civil Protection	Γενική Γραμματεία Πολιτικής Προστασίας
Generation of income	Πορισμός εισοδήματος
Genitals	Γεννητικά όργανα
Genuine	Γνήσιος
Gesture	Χειρονομία
Gift	Δώρο
Good and valuable consideration	Ισότιμο και αξιόχρεο αντάλλαγμα
Governance	Διακυβέρνηση
Government	Κυβέρνηση
Greek national	Ημεδαπός
Greek state	Ελληνικό κράτος / Δημόσιο
Grievous bodily harm	Βαριά σωματική βλάβη
Gross breach of duty	Βαριά παράβαση (καθήκοντος)
Ground	Λόγος
Grounding	Προσάραξη

Guardian	Φύλαξη (προσώπου)	
Gynaecologist	Γυναικολόγος	
Half-sibling	Ετεροθαλής αδελφός	
Hallucinatory substance	Παραιθησιογόνος ουσία	
Handing down of judgment	Έκδοση (απόφασης)	
Handover	Παράδοση	
Harbouring [a criminal]	Υπόθαλψη	
Hardware	Σύστημα υλικού	
Harm	Προσβολή	See Article 22(3)
Hatred	Μίσος	
Hazardous interference	Επικίνδυνη παρέμβαση	
Hazardous substance	Επικίνδυνη ουσία	
Head of state	Αρχηγός κράτους	
Health	Υγεία	
Hearing date	Δικάσιμος	
Heat	Θερμότητα	
Heir	Κληρονόμος	
Hellenic Authority for Communication Security and Privacy	Αρχής Διασφάλισης του Απορρήτου των Επικοινωνιών	
Hierarchical relationship	Ιεραρχική σχέση	
High treason	Εσχάτη προδοσία	
Historical monument	Ιστορικό μνημείο	
Hologram	Ολογράφημα	
Homicide	Ανθρωποκτονία	
Honest life	Έντιμη ζωή	
Honour	Τιμή	
Hospital	Νοσηλευτικό ίδρυμα Νοσοκομείο	See Article 123(2) See Article 69A(3)
Hospitalisation	Νοσηλεία	See Article 69A(3)
Hostage	Όμηρος	
Hostility	Εχθροπραξία	
Hot works	Θερμές εργασίες	
House arrest	Έκτιση της ποινής στην κατοικία	
Human dignity	Ανθρώπινη αξιοπρέπεια	
Human rights defender	Υπερασπιστής ανθρώπινων δικαιωμάτων	

Human trafficking	*Εμπορία ανθρώπων*	
Identification data	*Δεδομένα αναγνώρισης της ταυτότητας*	
Identity	*Ταυτότητα*	
Illness	*Ασθένεια*	See Article 105(2)
Imitation	*Απομίμηση*	
Immovable	*Ακίνητο*	
Impeding competition	*Παρακώλυση συναγωνισμού*	
Impersonation	*Αντιποίηση*	
Import	*Εισαγωγή (αγαθών)*	
Impossible attempt	*Απρόσφορη απόπειρα*	
Imprinting	*Αποτύπωση*	
Imprisonment	*Φυλάκιση*	
Imprudence	*Κουφότητα*	See Civil Code, Article 179
Imputability	*Καταλογισμός*	
In camera	*Κεκλεισμένων των θυρών*	
In the act	*Επ' αυτοφώρω*	
Inappropriate act	*Ανάρμοστη πράξη*	
Incapacibility of resisting	*Ανικανότητα αντίστασης*	
Incarceration	*Κάθειρξη*	
Incarceration for life	*Ισόβια κάθειρξη*	
Incendiary material	*Εμπρηστική ύλη*	
Incest	*Αιμομιξία*	
Incitement	*Διέγερση*	
Incrimination	*Ενοχοποίηση*	
Incurable disease	*Ανίατη ασθένεια*	
Inducement	*Πρόκληση*	
Inexperience	*Απειρία*	
Infanticide	*Παιδοκτονία*	
Infibulation	*Αγκτηριασμός*	
Informant	*Καταδότης*	
Information	*Πληροφορία*	
Information and communication technology	*Τεχνολογία πληροφοριών και επικοινωνιών*	

Information system	Πληροφοριακό σύστημα Σύστημα πληροφοριών	See Article 292B See Article 210
Infrastructure	Υποδομή	
Inland waters	Εσωτερικά ύδατα	
Input	Εισαγωγή (δεδομένων)	
Inquiries	Έρευνα	
Inspector	Επιθεωρητής	
Instalment	Δόση	
Instigation	Ηθική αυτουργία	
Instigator	Ηθικός αυτουργός	
Instructor	Παιδαγωγός	
Insubordination	Ανυποταξία	
Insult	Εξύβριση Προσβολή Ύβρη	See Article 361 See Article 361(1) See Article 168(4)
Insulting publication	Υβριστικό δημοσίευμα	
Insurance company	Ασφαλιστική επιχείρηση	
Intangible	Άυλος	
Intellect	Διάνοια	
Intention	Πρόθεση	
Interception	Υποκλοπή	
Intercourse	Συνουσία	
Interest	Συμφέρον	
Interest rate	Ποσοστό τόκου	
Interference	Παρεμβολή	
Interim order	Προσωρινή διαταγή (δικαστηρίου)	
Intermediary	Μεσάζων	
International organisation	Διεθνής οργανισμός	
International protection	Διεθνής προστασία	
International relations	Διεθνείς σχέσεις	
Internet	Διαδίκτυο	
Interpretation	Διερμηνεία	
Interpreter	Διερμηνέας	
Intimidation	Εκφοβισμός	

Investigating officer	Ανακριτικός υπάλληλος	
Investigating magistrate	Ανακριτής	
Investigation	Ανάκριση	
Irreparable damage	Ανεπανόρθωτη βλάβη	
Irrevocable	Αμετάκλητος	
Irrevocable judgment	Αμετάκλητη απόφαση	
Isolation	Απομόνωση	
Joinder	Συνεκδίκαση	
Journalist	Δημοσιογράφος	
Judge	Δικαστής	
Judgment handed down by a foreign court	Αλλοδαπή απόφαση	
Judgment of conviction	Καταδικαστική απόφαση	
Judicial council	Δικαστικό συμβούλιο Συμβούλιο (δικαστηρίου)	See Article 76(1) See Article 72(3)
Judicial council decision	Βούλευμα	
Judicial forgiveness of penalties	Δικαστική άφεση ποινής	
Judicial functionary	Δικαστικός λειτουργός	
Judicial secrecy	Δικαστικό απόρρητο	
Judiciary	Δικαστική λειτουργία	
Jurisdiction	Δικαιοδοσία	
Juror	Ένορκος	
Just satisfaction	Εντελής ικανοποίηση	
Juvenile	Ανήλικος	
Juvenile court	Δικαστήριο ανηλίκων	
Juvenile probation officer	Επιμελητής (ανηλίκου)	
Labour exploitation	Εργασιακή εκμετάλλευση	
Lack of capacity to enter into legal transactions	Ανικανότητα δικαιοπραξίας	
Law	Νόμος	
Lawful	Νόμιμος	
Lawful representative	Νόμιμος εκπρόσωπος	
Lawyer	Δικηγόρος	
Legal form	Νόμιμος τύπος	
Legal guardianship	Δικαστική συμπαράσταση	

Legal importance	*Έννομη σημασία*	
Legal person	*Νομικό πρόσωπο*	
Legal protection	*Νομική προστασία*	
Legal representative	*Νόμιμος αντιπρόσωπος*	
Legal tender	*Νόμιμο νόμισμα*	
Legal transaction	*Δικαιοπραξία*	
Legislature	*Νομοθέτης*	
Length	*Χρόνος/Διάρκεια (ποινής)*	
Letter	*Επιστολή*	
Levy	*Φορολόγημα*	
Lex mitior	*Ηπιότερος νόμος*	
Licence to operate a means of transport	*Άδεια εκμετάλλευσης μεταφορικού μέσου*	
Life circumstances	*Βιοτικές συνθήκες*	
Lighting	*Φωτισμός*	
List	*Κατάλογος*	
Local government	*Αυτοδιοίκηση*	
Local government authority	*Οργανισμός τοπικής αυτοδιοίκησης*	
Location data	*Στοιχεία θέσης*	
Locked place	*Κλειστός χώρος*	
Lorry	*Φορτηγό όχημα*	
Loss of data	*Απώλεια δεδομένων*	
Lump sum	*Εφάπαξ (ποσό)*	
Main penalty	*Κύρια ποινή*	
Main proceedings	*Κύρια διαδικασία*	
Maintenance	*Διατροφή*	
Making documents unavailable	*Υπεξαγωγή εγγράφων*	
Manager of an enterprise	*Διευθυντής επιχείρηση*	
Manager of another person's assets	*Διαχειριστής ξένης περιουσίας*	See Civil Code, Articles 730-740
Mark	*Σημείο*	
Marriage	*Γάμος*	
Mayor	*Δήμαρχος*	
Means of coercion	*Εξαναγκαστικά μέσα*	

Means of transport	Μεταφορικό μέσο	
Mechanism	Μηχανισμός	
Medal	Μετάλλιο	
Mediation	Διαμεσολάβηση Μεσολάβηση	See Article 169 See Article 360A(2)
Mediation report	Πρακτικό διαμεσολάβησης	
Medical staff	Ιατρικό προσωπικό	
Medicine	Φάρμακο	
Medium	Μέσο	
Meeting	Συνεδρίαση	
Member of European Parliament	Ευρωβουλευτής	
Member of the clergy	Κληρικός	
Member State	Κράτος μέλος (ΕΕ)	
Mental anguish	Ψυχική οδύνη	
Mental disability	Διανοητική αναπηρία	
Mental disorder	Ψυχική διαταραχή	
Mental harm	Ψυχική βλάβη	
Mental health facility	Μονάδα ψυχικής υγείας	
Mental illness	Διανοητική ασθένεια Ψυχική ασθένεια	See Article 348A(4)(b) See Article 123(1)
Midwife	Μαία	
Military commander	Στρατιωτικός διοικητής	
Military personnel	Στρατιωτικός	
Military secrecy	Στρατιωτικό απόρρητο	
Military service	Στρατιωτική υπηρεσία	
Mine	Μεταλλείο	
Minister	Υπουργός	
Minister of Health	Υπουργός Υγείας	
Minister of Justice	Υπουργός Δικαιοσύνης	
Ministry of Justice	Υπουργείο Δικαιοσύνης	
Minor case	Ελαφριά περίπτωση	
Misappropriation	Υπεξαίρεση	
Misdemeanour	Πλημμέλημα	
Misleading	Παραπλάνηση	Article 216, intro note
Mistake of fact	Πραγματική πλάνη	

Mistake of law	Νομική πλάνη	
Mitigating circumstances	Ελαφρυντικές περιστάσεις	
Mixture/Intermixture	Ανάμειξη	See Civil Code, Articles 1059-1060 See Foreword
Mock execution	Εικονική εκτέλεση	
Monetary penalty	Χρηματική ποινή	
Monetary value	Νομισματική αξία	
Money	Χρήμα	
Monument	Μνημείο	
Morality	Χρηστά ήθη	
More lenient penalty	Ελαφρότερη ποινή	
More severe penalty	Βαρύτερη ποινή	
Motive force	Κινητήρια δύναμη	
Motor vehicle	Μηχανοκίνητο μεταφορικό μέσο	
Motorway	Αυτοκινητόδρομος	
Movable	Κινητό	
Movable thing	Κινητό πράγμα	
Municipality	Δήμος	
Naivety	Ευήθεια	
Narcotic	Ναρκωτικό μέσο	
Narcotic substance	Ναρκωτική ουσία	
National anthem	Εθνικός ύμνος	
National defence	Εθνική άμυνα	
National origin	Εθνική καταγωγή	
National road	Εθνική οδός	
Nationality	Εθνικότητα Ιθαγένεια	See Article 5 See Article 7
Natura area	Περιοχή 'Natura'	
Natural disaster	Φυσική καταστροφή	
Natural gas	Φυσικό άεριο	
Natural person	Φυσικό πρόσωπο	
Negligence	Αμέλεια	
Negligent bodily harm	Σωματική βλάβη από αμέλεια	
Negligent homicide	Ανθρωποκτονία από αμέλεια	

Negotiation	Διαπραγμάτευση	
Newborn	Νεογνό	
Newspaper	Εφημερίδα	
Noise	Θόρυβος	
Non-cash payment instrument	Μέσο πληρωμής πλην των μετρητών	
Non-commissioned officer	Υπαξιωματικός	
Non-prosecution	Ακαταδίωκτο	
Notary public	Συμβολαιογράφος	
Notes	Σημειώσεις	
Notice	Κοινοποίηση Προειδοποίηση Προκήρυξη Σημείο (συγκοινωνιών)	See Article 180 See Article 81(5) See Article 395(1) See Article 290(1)(c)
Noxious substance	Επιβλαβής ουσία	
Nurse	Νοσοκόμος	
Nursing staff	Νοσηλευτικό προσωπικό	
Object	Αντικείμενο	
Obligation	Υποχρέωση	
Obstetrician	Μαιευτήρας	
Obstruction of justice	Παρέμποδιση δικαιοσύνης	
Obtaining an attestation under false pretences	Υφαρπαγή ψευδούς βεβαίωσης	
Obverse	Εμπρόσθια όψη (νομίσματος)	
Occupation	Κατοχή	
Offer	Προσφορά	
Officer	Αξιωματικός	
Officer of the state	Όργανο του κράτους	
Official secrecy	Υπηρεσιακό απόρρητο	
Omission	Παράλειψη	
Onerous	Επαχθής	
Operationally structured organisation	Επιχειρησιακά δομημένη οργάνωση	
Operative part of a judgment	Διατακτικό	
Order	Προσταγή	
Ordering	Επιβολή	

Ordinary investigation	Τακτική ανάκριση	
Organ	Όργανο (σώματος)	
Organisation	Οργανισμός	
Organised Crime Directorate	Διεύθυνση Αντιμετώπισης Οργανωμένου Εγκλήματος	
Out-of-court settlement	Εξώδικη διευθέτηση	
Outpatient department	Εξωτερικό ιατρείο	
Overall penalty	Συνολική ποινή	See Article 96
Owner	Ιδιοκτήτης	
Ownership	Ιδιοκτησία	
Paragraph	Παράγραφος	
Pardon	Χάρη	
Parent	Γονέας	
Parental responsibility	Γονική μέριμνα	
Park	Πάρκο	
Parliament	Βουλή	
Parliamentary assembly	Κοινοβουλευτική συνέλευση	
Participation	Συμμετοχή	
Participatory act	Πράξη συμμετοχής	
Partner	Σύντροφος	
Party	Μέρος (διαιτησίας, διαμεσολάβησης, κτλ.)	
Party in proceedings / Litigant	Διάδικος	
Passenger	Επιβάτης	
Passive and active bribery in the private sector	Δωροληψία και δωροδοκία στον ιδιωτικό τομέα	
Passive bribery	Δωροληψία	
Password	Συνθηματικό	
Pasture	Χορτολιβαδική έκταση	
Pavement	Πεζοδρόμιο	
Payment	Καταβολή	
Payment in advance	Προκαταβολή	
Payment instrument	Μέσο πληρωμής	
Payment of compensation	Χρηματική ικανοποίηση	
Peace	Ειρήνη	

Pecuniary damage	Περιουσιακή ζημία	
Pecuniary gain	Περιουσιακό όφελος	
Pedestrianised street	Πεζόδρομος	
Penal Code	Ποινικός Κώδικας	
Penal law	Ποινικός νόμος	
Penalty	Ποινή	See Foreword
Penalty range	Πλαίσιο ποινής	
Periodical	Περιοδικό	
Peri-urban green area	Έκταση περιαστικού πράσινου	
Perpetrator	Αυτουργός Δράστης Φυσικός αυτουργός	See Foreword
Person being treated	Θεραπευόμενος	
Person living together in a steady relationship	Συμβιών (με σταθερή συμβίωση)	
Person unable to defend themselves	Αδύναμο άτομο/πρόσωπο	
Personal data	Δεδομένα προσωπικού χαρακτήρα	
Personal freedom	Προσωπική ελευθερία	
Petty offence	Πταίσμα	
Pharmacist	Φαρμακοποιός	
Physical condition	Σωματική κατάσταση	
Physical disability	Σωματική αναπηρία	
Physical exhaustion	Σωματική εξάντληση	
Physical illness	Οργανική νόσος	
Physical integrity	Σωματική ακεραιότητα	
Physical pain	Σωματικός πόνος	
Physical storage medium	Υλικός φορέας	
Physical violence	Σωματική βία	
Physician	Ιατρός	
Piracy	Πειρατεία	
Place intended for religious worship	Τόπος προορισμένος για θρησκευτική λατρεία	
Place of commission	Τόπος τέλεσης	
Poisoning	Δηλητηρίαση	
Police department	Αστυνομικό τμήμα	

Police facility	Αστυνομική υπηρεσία	
Police forces	Αστυνομικές δυνάμεις	
Police officer	Αστυνομικός υπάλληλος	
Political party	Πολιτικό κόμμα	
Political person	Πολιτικό πρόσωπο	
Pollution	Ρύπανση	
Polygraph	Ανιχνευτής αλήθειας	
Popular sovereignty	Λαϊκή κυριαρχία	
Population	Πληθυσμός	
Pornographic performance	Πορνογραφική παράσταση	
Possession	Κατοχή Νομή	See Foreword
Possessor	Κάτοχος	See Foreword
Postal services	Ταχυδρομικές υπηρεσίες	
Poverty	Απορία Ένδεια	See Foreword
Practical repentance	Έμπρακτη μετάνοια	
Preclusion of access	Αποκλεισμός πρόσβασης	
Pregnancy	Κύηση / Εγκυμοσύνη	
Pregnant woman	Έγκυος	
Preliminary procedure	Προδικασία	
Prenatal screening	Προγεννητικός έλεγχος	
Preparatory act	Προπαρασκευαστική πράξη	
Presentation	Επίδειξη	
Presenting a child as having a different family status from its actual one	Υποβολή τέκνου	
President of the Republic	Πρόεδρος της Δημοκρατίας	
Presidential powers	Προεδρική εξουσία	
Presumption of innocence	Τεκμήριο αθωότητας	
Prevention	Αποτροπή	
Preventive measure	Προληπτικό μέτρο	
Prime Minister	Πρωθυπουργός	
Principle of proportionality	Αρχή της αναλογικότητας	
Principle of subsidiarity	Αρχή της επικουρικότητας	
Prison	Φυλακή	

Prisoner	Φυλακισμένος	
Privacy	Ιδιωτική ζωή	
Private conversation	Προφορική συνομιλία	
Private enterprise	Επιχείρηση ιδιωτικού τομέα	
Private life	Ιδιωτικός βίος	
Private secret	Ιδιωτικό απόρρητο	
Private sector	Ιδιωτικός τομέας	
Probation officer	Επιμελητής κοινωνικής αρωγής	
Probationary period	Χρόνος δοκιμασίας	
Procedural compulsory measure	Μέτρο δικονομικού καταναγκασμού	
Proceedings	Δίκη	
Proceeds	Έσοδα (εκμετάλλευσης) Προϊόν (εγκλήματος)	See Article 323A(6) See Article 394
Procurement	Προμήθεια	
Procuring	Μαστροπεία	
Production	Παραγωγή	
Profession	Επάγγελμα	
Professional secret	Επαγγελματικό απόρρητο	
Prohibition	Απαγόρευση	
Promise	Υπόσχεση	
Promotion	Προαγωγή	
Property	Περιουσία	
Property damage	Περιουσιακή βλάβη	
Prosecution	Δίωξη	
Prostitution	Πορνεία	
Protected device, object or record	Προστατευμένος μηχανισμός, αντικείμενο ή αρχείο	
Provenance	Προέλευση	
Provider	Πάροχος	
Provision	Διάταξη	
Provocation	Πρόκληση (παθόντος)	
Psychiatric observation	Ψυχιατρική παρακολούθηση	
Psychodiagnostic examination	Ψυχοδιαγνωστική εξέταση	
Psychological pain	Ψυχικός πόνος	

Psychological violence	*Ψυχολογική βία*	
Psychologist	*Ψυχολόγος*	
Psychosexual state	*Ψυχογενετήσια κατάσταση*	
Public auction	*Δημόσιος πλειστηριασμός*	
Public building	*Δημόσιο οίκημα*	
Public corporation	*Επιχείρηση δημοσίου τομέα*	
Public function	*Δημόσιο λειτούργημα*	
Public interest	*Δημόσιο συμφέρον*	
Public order	*Δημόσια τάξη*	
Public place	*Δημόσιος τόπος*	
Public prosecutor	*Εισαγγελέας*	
Public representative	*Δημόσιος εκπρόσωπος*	
Public sector	*Δημόσιος τομέας*	
Public security	*Δημόσια ασφάλεια*	See Article 72
Public telecommunications	*Τηλεπικοινωνίες του κοινού*	
Public utility company	*Επιχείρηση κοινής ωφελείας*	
Public view	*Κοινή θέα*	
Public works	*Δημόσιο έργο*	
Publication	*Δημοσίευση*	
Public-benefit foundation	*Κοινωφελές ίδρυμα*	
Public-benefit purpose	*Κοινωφελής σκοπός*	
Publisher	*Εκδότης*	
Punishability	*Αξιόποινο*	
Punishable	*Αξιόποινος*	
Punishment	*Ποινή*	See Foreword
Pupil	*Μαθητής*	
Pyrotechnic items	*Είδη πυροτεχνίας*	
Race	*Χαρακτηριστικά φυλής*	
Radiation	*Ακτινοβολία*	
Radio frequency	*Ραδιοσυχνότητα*	
Rage	*Οργή*	
Rainwater	*Όμβρια ύδατα*	
Ransom	*Λύτρα*	
Rape	*Βιασμός*	
Ratification	*Επικύρωση*	

Reasoning	Αιτιολόγηση	
Reasoning	Σκεπτικό (απόφασης)	
Recantation	Ανάκληση (κατάθεσης)	
Recognition	Αναγνώριση (απόφασης)	
Recovery claim	Αξίωση επιστροφής	
Recruitment	Στρατολόγηση	
Reduced punishment	Μειωμένη ποινή	
Referendum	Δημοψήφισμα	
Reforestable	Αναδασωτέα (έκταση)	
Reformative institution	Ειδικό κατάστημα κράτησης νέων	
Reformative measure	Αναμορφωτικό μέτρο	
Regional governor	Περιφερειάρχης	
Registered offices	Έδρα (νομικού προσώπου)	
Regulation	Κανονισμός (ΕΕ)	
Rehabilitation programme	Πρόγραμμα απεξάρτησης	
Related directly	Συγγένεια σε ευθεία γραμμή	
Related party	Οικείος	See Foreword
Relationship/Partnership	Συμβίωση	
Relative	Συγγενής	
Relative in the ascending line	Συγγενής ανιούσας γραμμής / Ανιών	
Relative in the descending line	Συγγενής κατιούσας γραμμής / Κατιών	
Released person	Απολυόμενος / Αποφυλακιζόμενος	
Religion	Θρησκεία	
Religious gathering	Θρησκευτική συνάθροιση	
Remittal	Παραπομπή (υπόθεσης)	
Repentance	Μετάνοια	
Report	Αναφορά Έκθεση Καταγγελία	See Article 110(2) See Article 72(4)(a) See Article 187C(3)
Reprimand	Επίπληξη	
Reputation	Υπόληψη	
Request	Αίτημα	
Reservoir	Δεξαμενή νερού	

Residential area	Κατοικημένη περιοχή	
Residential district	Οικιστική περιοχή	
Resistance	Αντίσταση	
Restitution	Αποκατάσταση (ζημίας)	
Restorative justice process	Διαδικασία αποκαταστατικής δικαιοσύνης	
Restraining order	Απαγόρευση προσέγγισης και επικοινωνίας	
Restrictive measure	Περιοριστικό μέτρο	
Retaliation	Αντίποινα	
Retraction	Ανάκληση	See Article 186(3)
Retroactive effect	Αναδρομική ισχύς	
Revenge pornography	Εκδικητική πορνογραφία	
Reverse	Οπίσθια όψη (νομίσματος)	
Revocation	Ανάκληση	See Article 101
Reward	Αμοιβή	
Right of defence	Δικαίωμα υπεράσπισης	
Ring-road	Περιφερειακή οδός	
Riot	Στάση	
Risk index	Δείκτης επικινδυνότητας	
Road	Δρόμος	
Road network	Οδικό δίκτυο	
Road transportation	Οδική συγκοινωνία	
Robbery	Ληστεία	
Ruling	Κρίση	See Foreword
Safe destination	Ασφαλής προορισμός	
Safety apparatus	Ασφαλιστική εγκατάσταση	
Sale	Πώληση	
Sanction	Κύρωση	
Satisfaction	Ικανοποίηση (δανειστή)	
Scientic secret	Επιστημονικό απόρρητο	
Seal	Σφραγίδα	
Secondment	Απόσπαση	
Secret ballot	Μυστική ψηφοφορία	
Security measure	Μέτρο ασφάλειας	
Seizure	Κατάσχεση	

Self-redress	Αυτοδικία	
Sentence	Εδάφιο Ποινή	See Foreword
Sentence enforcement court	Δικαστήριο εκτέλεσης ποινής/ ποινών	
Separations of powers	Διάκριση των λειτουργιών	
Sequestrator	Μεσεγγυούχος	See Civil Code, Articles 359 et seq., 831 et seq.
Serious accident	Δυστύχημα	
Servitude	Ειλωτεία	
Session	Συνεδρία (με επιμελητή)	
Several liability	Ευθύνη εις ολόκληρον	
Severity	Βαρύτητα	
Sex characteristics	Χαρακτηριστικά φύλου	
Sexual abuse	Κατάχρηση σε γενετήσια πράξη	
Sexual act	Γενετήσια πράξη	
Sexual arousal	Γενετήσια διέγερση	
Sexual decency	Γενετήσια ευπρέπεια	See intro
Sexual dignity	Γενετήσια αξιοπρέπεια	
Sexual freedom	Γενετήσια ελευθερία	
Sexual life	Γενετήσια ζωή	
Sexual orientation	Γενετήσιος προσανατολισμός	
Ship	Πλοίο	
Shipwreck	Ναυάγιο	
Shop	Κατάστημα	
Shouting	Φωνασκία	
Sibling	Αδέρφι / Αδερφός / Αδελφός	
Sign	Σήμα (συγκοινωνιών)	
Simple accomplice	Απλός συνεργός	
Simulated	Εικονικός Προσποιητός	See Article 348A(3) See Article 323(5)(f)
Sinking	Βύθιση	
Sitting	Συνεδρία (δικαστηρίου)	
Skills	Τεχνογνωσία	
Skin colour	Χρώμα (προσώπου)	

Slavery	Δουλεία	
Social media	Μέσο κοινωνικής δικτύωσης	
Social worker	Κοινωνικός λειτουργός	
Society for the protection of juveniles	Προστατευτική εταιρεία	
Software	Λογισμικό	
Software program	Πρόγραμμα υπολογιστή	
Solicitation of children	Προσέλκυση παιδιών	
Soporific	Υπνωτικό μέσο	
Sorrow	Θλίψη	
Sovereignty	Κυριαρχία	
Spark	Σπινθήρας	
Special Court	Ειδικό Δικαστήριο	
Special register	Ειδικό βιβλίο	
Special Violent Crime Squad	Διεύθυνση Αντιμετώπισης Ειδικών Εγκλημάτων Βίας	
Specialist	Ειδικός επιστήμονας	
Specific claim for a fixed amount	Βέβαιη και εκκαθαρισμένη απαίτηση	
Spouse	Σύζυγος	
Spreading of false news	Διασπορά ψευδών ειδήσεων	
Spring	Πηγή	
Square	Πλατεία	
Stamp	Ένσημο	See Foreword
Standing Orders of the Hellenic Parliament	Κανονισμός της Βουλής	
State	Κράτος Πολιτεία	See Article 138(1) See Article 143(1)
State authority	Πολιτειακή εξουσία	
State employee	Υπάλληλος	See Foreword
State power	Κρατική εξουσία	
State psychiatric hospital	Δημόσιο ψυχιατρείο	
State secret	Κρατικό απόρρητο	
State security	Ασφάλεια του κράτους	
Stateless	Ανιθαγενής	
Stay (of enforcement)	Αναστολή (εκτέλεσης ποινής)	
Stolen property	Κλοπιμαίο	

Street racing	Αυτοσχέδιος αγώνας	
Subsidy	Επιχορήγηση	
Subsidy fraud	Απάτη σχετική με τις επιχορηγήσεις	
Subsistence needs	Ανάγκες διαβίωσης	
Substantial interest	Ουσιώδες συμφέρον	
Substitute confiscation	Αναπληρωματική δήμευση	
Suicide	Αυτοκτονία	
Summon	Κλήση	
Summonsing	Κλήτευση	
Superior (of another person)	Προϊστάμενος	
Supervision	Εποπτεία	
Support	Στήριξη	
Supranational	Υπερεθνικός	
Surface	Όψη (νομίσματος)	
Surrender	Απόδοση (πράγματος)	
Surveillance device	Συσκευή παρακολούθησης	
Suspect	Ύποπτος	
Suspension	Αναστολή (παραγραφής)	
Suspension	Αναστολή (ποινικής δίωξης από Υπουργό)	
Suspensive effect	Ανασταλτική δύναμη Αναστέλλουσα ισχύς	See Foreword
Symbol	Σύμβολο	
Taking of evidence	Αποδεικτική διαδικασία	
Tampering	Παραβίαση (σφραγίδας)	
Tangible	Υλικός	
Tax	Φόρος	
Teacher	Εκπαιδευτικός	
Technical rules	Τεχνικοί κανόνες	
Telecommunications	Τηλεπικοινωνίες	
Telecommunications means	Τηλεπικοινωνιακό μέσο	
Telegram service	Τηλεγραφική υπηρεσία	
Telephone communications	Τηλεφωνικές επικοινωνίες	
Telephone conversation	Τηλεφωνική συνδιάλεξη	
Telephony	Τηλεφωνία	

Temporary detention	Προσωρινή κράτηση	
Termination of pregnancy	Διακοπή κύησης	
Termination of release	Άρση απόλυσης	
Territorial rights	Εδαφικά δικαιώματα	
Territorial sea	Αιγιαλίτιδα ζώνη	
Territorial waters	Θαλάσσιος χώρος	
Territory	Έδαφος (χώρας) Επικράτεια	See Article 138 See Article 5
Terror	Τρόμος	
Terrorist act	Τρομοκρατική πράξη	
Terrorist organisation	Τρομοκρατική οργάνωση	
Testimony	Κατάθεση	
Theft	Κλοπή	
Theft and misappropriation of low-value [things]	Κλοπή και υπεξαίρεση μικρής αξίας	
Therapeutic institution	Θεραπευτικό κατάστημα	
Therapeutic measure	Θεραπευτικό μέτρο Μέτρο θεραπείας	See Foreword
Therapeutic programme	Θεραπευτικό πρόγραμμα	
Third-party property	Ξένη περιουσία	
Threat	Απειλή	
Threat of violence	Απειλή βίας	
Three-member (court)	Τριμελές (δικαστήριο)	
Time of commission	Χρόνος τέλεσης	
Time-barring	Παραγραφή	
Tissue	Ιστός	
To abscond	Διαφεύγω	
To bury	Ενταφιάζω	
To dissect	Ανατέμνω	
To harbour	Υποθάλπω	
To incite	Υποκινώ	
To make (goods) available	Διακίνηση (αγαθών)	See Article 7 of Directive 2013/40/EU
To serve	Έκτιση	

To solve (a crime)	Εξιχνίαση	
Token	Μάρκα	
Tolerance	Ανοχή	
Tool	Εργαλείο	
Torture	Βασανιστήρια	
Total sentence	Συνολική ποινή	See Article 94
Track-based means of transportation	Μέσο σταθερής τροχιάς	
Track-based transportation	Συγκοινωνία μέσων σταθερής τροχιάς	
Trading in influence	Εμπορία επιρροής	
Traffic data	Στοιχεία κίνησης	
Traffic violation	Παραβίαση κανόνων οδήγησης	
Trainer	Γυμναστής	
Training	Εκπαίδευση	
Transcript	Πρακτικά (δικαστηρίου)	
Transmission	Διαβίβαση (δεδομένων)	
Transport (sector)	Μεταφορές	
Transportation systems	Συγκοινωνίες	
Traveller's cheque	Ταξιδιωτική επιταγή	
Treason	Προσβολή της διεθνούς υπόστασης της Χώρας	
Treatment	Θεραπεία Μεταχείριση Νοσηλεία	See Article 69A(3)(c) See Article 123(1) See Article 105B(4)(d)
Treaty or convention	Σύμβαση (διεθνής)	
Trial court	Δικαστήριο που δικάζει υπόθεση / Δικάζον δικαστήριο	
Trust	Εμπιστοσύνη	
Tutor	Επίτροπος (ανηλίκου)	
Tutorship	Επιτροπεία	
Unborn child	Κυοφορούμενο	
Unconsciousness	Κατάσταση αναισθησίας	
Unconstitutional	Αντισυνταγματικός	
Undue advantage	Αθέμιτο ωφέλημα	
Undue influence	Αθέμιτη επιρροή	

Unlawful	Παράνομος	
Unlawful access to an information system or data	Παράνομη πρόσβαση σε σύστημα πληροφοριών ή σε δεδομένα	
Unlawful damage to a third party	Παράνομη βλάβη τρίτου	
Unlawful detention	Παράνομη κατακράτηση	
Unlawful violence	Παράνομη βία	
Unlawfully depriving another of their freedom	Αρπαγή	
Unmanned aircraft system	Μη επανδρωμένο αεροσκάφος	
Usurpation	Σφετερισμός	
Usury	Τοκογλυφία	
Value	Τίμημα	
Vehicle	Όχημα	
Vessel	Σκάφος	
Veterinarian	Κτηνίατρος	
Victim	Ζημιωθείς Θύμα Παθών	See Article 381 See Article 79(5)(d) See Article 115 See Foreword
Victim-initiated complaint	Έγκληση	
Violation of human dignity	Προσβολή της ανθρώπινης αξιοπρέπειας	
Violence	Βία	
Visual material	Οπτικό υλικό	
Vital goods or services	Ζωτικής σημασίας αγαθά ή υπηρεσίες	
Volition	Θέληση	
Vote	Ψηφοφορία	
Voter	Εκλογέας	
Voting right	Εκλογικό δικαίωμα	
War	Πόλεμος	
Wartime	Καιρός πολέμου	
Wastewater	Ακάθαρτα ύδατα	
Water	Νερό	
Weapon	Όπλο	See Article 313

Well	Πηγάδι	
Withdrawal	Ανάκληση	See Article 117
Witness	Μάρτυρας	
Woods	Άλσος	
Worker	Εργαζόμενος	
Worship	Λατρεία	
Writ of summons	Κλητήριο θέσπισμα	
Wrongfulness	Άδικος χαρακτήρας (πράξης)	
Young adult	Νεαρός ενήλικας	

www.ingramcontent.com/pod-product-compliance
Lightning Source LLC
LaVergne TN
LVHW081940200926
848484LV00009B/2480